CLEVELAND

A History in Motion

Transportation, Industry & Community in Northeast Ohio

Authors: John J. Grabowski & Diane Ewart Grabowski, Photo Editor: Mark Tebeau

First Edition

Copyright©2000, by Heritage Media Corporation

ISBN: 1-886483-38-8, Library of Congress Card Catalog Number: 99-073076

Authors: John J. Grabowski & Diane Ewart Grabowski

Photo Editor: Mark Tebeau

Project Editor: John Woodward

Coordinating Editors: Renee Kim, Betsy Lelja, Elizabeth Lex,
Sara Rufner, Mary Ann Stabile, Adriane Wessels

Production Staff: Astrit Bushi, Jeff Caton, Dave Hermstead,
Jay Kennedy, Vincent Kornegay, John Leyva, Marianne Mackey,
Gavin Rattmann, Charlie Silvia

Project Manager: Sally Kamman

Project Coordinators: Moira Beale, Clarys Holliday,
Tara Kamman, Anne Violand

Profile Writers: Marcia Meermans Aghajanian, Eileen Beal,
Mary Gannon, Marv Gisser, Patrice Kelly, Lori Lesko,
Meta McMillian, Jay Miller, Michelle Palmer, Eileen Figure Sandlin,
Betty Schall, Connie Sievers, Jane Spear

Human Resources Manager: Ellen Ruby

Administration: Juan Diaz, Debbie Hunter, Azalea Maes,
Majka Penner, Scott Reid, Patrick Rucker, Cory Sottek

Publisher: C.E. Parks

Editor-in-Chief: Lori M. Parks

VP/Sales: Jill DeLeary

VP/Corporate Development: Bart Barica

CFO: Randall Peterson

Production Manager: Deborah Sherwood

Managing Editor: Betsy Baxter Blondin

Art Director: Gina Mancini

Assistant Art Director: Susie Passons

Published by
Heritage Media Corp., Heritage Building
1954 Kellogg Avenue, Carlsbad, California 92008, www.heritagemedia.com
Published in cooperation with the Western Reserve Historical Society, www.wrhs.org
Printed by Heritage Media Corp. in the United States of America

Cleveland: A History in Motion

Convention & Visitors Bureau

for DVT

table of contents

table of contents *continued*

acknowledgments

From the Authors

As authors of this volume, we owe a great deal to the amateur and professional historians whose works provided the foundation for our interpretation of the history of northeastern Ohio. Their interest in and devotion to discovering and writing about the history of everything from automobiles to immigration have made this book possible. Beyond this, we owe a special debt to the late Dr. David D. Van Tassel for his vision and effort in creating *The Encyclopedia of Cleveland History*. The *Encyclopedia* itself and our long involvement with the project have given us both information and insights vital in writing *Cleveland: A History in Motion*.

What we have presented here in words has been considerably enriched by the accompanying images. We thank our photo editor, Dr. Mark Tebeau, for his many hours of work in seeking out appropriate and vibrant illustrations that have helped give additional meaning to the text. Mark's task was one not only of selection, but of coordination and negotiation as well. The images he has chosen and the captions he has written have helped us put Cleveland's history in motion. We join him in thanking the individuals and organizations he acknowledges and with him give a special "thank you" to the planning staff for the new Crawford Museum of Transportation and Industry, whose collective knowledge about Cleveland industry and transportation provided great support for our work on this volume.

From the Photo Editor

A large number of people and institutions helped to identify historical images to accompany the evocative text of John and Diane Grabowski. The following individuals were especially generous with their assistance: Bill Barrow and Bill Becker at the Cleveland Press Collection, Cleveland State University, Amy Dawson at Cleveland Public Library, Fred Lautzenheiser of the archives at The Cleveland Clinic Foundation, Carl LaVigne at the Great Lakes Historical Society in Vermilion, Ohio, Mark Schutte at the Convention and Visitors Bureau of Greater Cleveland, and Marvin Smith at the NASA Glenn Research Center. Photographer Herbert Ascherman Jr. was extraordinary. His great skill shows in the images he created for this book. At the Western Reserve Historical Society, the Crawford Museum of Transportation and Industry Design Task Force provided much assistance. Carol MacKay, Chris Grasso and especially Chris Dawson went above and beyond the call of duty. Also, Barbara Billings, Rich Palmer, Ann Sindelar, Marie Weiss and the staff at the Library of the Western Reserve Historical Society repeatedly and courteously provided helpful guidance. At Heritage Media, Betsy Blondin, Gina Mancini and Cory Sottek kept me on the right track. I owe a special debt to John Grabowski and Diane Grabowski who provided guidance in selecting and captioning these photographs. Final thanks are due to Kristin Mickelson who too often shared her evenings and weekends with this project.

Robert A. Epler

Acknowledgments

foreword

You are about to embark on a journey of discovery. Whether you are a resident of Cleveland or an occasional visitor, as you read through *Cleveland: A History in Motion*, take time to pause over the photographs and reflect on the vitality of a great urban city. See what Cleveland was built on, where it is today, and envision where it is going. After all, is it not the endlessly rich and vibrant social, cultural and historical fabric of cities that draws us to them? I know you will discover a new city — a renaissance city!

Clearly, *A History in Motion* is a fitting title for Cleveland. Not only have our waterways and transportation systems played a prominent historical role in the City's evolution, by every indication, our history remains a story still unfolding. Indeed, one of the discoveries you will make as you read this book is that a new Cleveland is emerging, a city transformed in recent years by the commitment and character of its citizens. I can only marvel at the spirit exuded by our business and civic leaders, our families and our children, and especially by the countless unsung heroes who have quietly dedicated their lives to Cleveland's grand rebirth. Without them, this book might be only a recounting of the past rather than a celebration of Cleveland's present and future.

The cultural, civic and commercial rebirth of Cleveland did not occur overnight. Despite a downturn in the overall fortunes of big cities after World War II, a fundamental belief in the critical role of cities never was extinguished. In Cleveland, the true believers ignored the naysayers, remained committed to our history and traditions, and maintained a vision of what our great city was and still could become. In fact, even as cities lost their luster, the seeds were being planted for a resurgence. By tapping into the character of our American culture, the indomitable will to succeed and thrive, a revived Cleveland emerged from a collective awareness that the good life for all citizens — even those who moved to surrounding locations — remains connected to the health and well-being of a region's urban core. It is this vision that will guide us into the future.

So today, as you will see in this impressive book, Cleveland has made the most of its opportunities to preserve all that is best about its history and traditions. Since the beginning of my tenure, the people have spoken and the message has been resoundingly clear: our City not only survived, but once again became the place where residents can work, play, worship, raise a family, grow old and build lives with solid values. As a steward of these hopes and desires, I bear responsibility for ensuring that we bury the pessimism of the past and nurture the optimism that enriches us as we move into the future. Herein lies yet another discovery — the greater the challenge, the more Greater Clevelanders rise to the occasion. I have seen this phenomenon time and again.

The contributors to this book, each in their own fashion, possess the kind of civic spirit that characterizes our city. Many of them have national and international reputations. Others are young but full of promise. Without question, our private, public and nonprofit institutions comprise the many reasons why Cleveland is now a destination of choice for over 7 million visitors each year.

So, come on board! Discover Cleveland! Uncover its many treasures. You will discover that many Northeast Ohio residents are moving back into Cleveland. New housing is being constructed at a record pace, not seen in decades. And our transportation systems continue to play a key role in our local economy and remain a high priority. Perhaps you already know these things, or perhaps you may need to visit our City to see for yourself. For now, read the stories by the contributors to *Cleveland: A History in Motion*, and you will get a feel for the way in which people and organizations come together to marshal their best ideas and values toward a common objective: A CITY POISED TO THRIVE IN THE 21ST CENTURY.

For some of you, reading this book will be like stepping off of an airplane into a new city — and all the fun and excitement new adventures offer. Enjoy your trip.

Michael R. White
Michael R. White
Mayor, City of Cleveland

preface

Cleveland is a fortunate city in that it has an interesting and diverse history. It is also fortunate in that many writers, both scholarly and popular, have made that history or a portion of it the subject of books and articles. Few American cities can boast of a fuller civic bookshelf than Cleveland.

This was foremost in our minds when we were first asked by Heritage Media to write a history of Cleveland. We questioned whether we could contribute anything new, given the number of general pictorial histories of the city and the existence of comprehensive volumes such as *The Encyclopedia of Cleveland History*. It seemed that enough was, perhaps, enough. However, further thought convinced us that an alternative approach was possible. We decided to look at the city's past through a different lens, one that was not focused on politics, ethnicity or business, nor entirely based on a strict chronology.

What intrigued us was the role that Cleveland's geographic location has played throughout its recorded history, particularly as it has served to anchor and attract transportation connections. From the earliest period of settlement, these connections were local, regional and global, and for many years they also functioned as the city's sole communications network. Until the city was wired for telegraphy in the mid-19th century, a letter, newspaper or messenger could reach Cleveland only as fast as the fastest vehicle could travel by land or water.

The importance of particular forms of transport — wagons, boats, trains, automobiles and aircraft — in Cleveland's past has long been recognized. Dozens of books detail the history of these transportation technologies, and general histories of the city have never failed to give them credit for their role in the city and region's development. However, none of the literature has sought to view the community's history through the lens of transportation or, more precisely, movement.

That is how we have chosen to approach the history of Cleveland and northeastern Ohio: that is, to see it as a history of things and especially of people in motion. It is the story of why and how one particular site on the globe served as a destination or a starting point for countless journeys. It is a story of how particular geographic advantages meshed with the technology of transportation to create a community that has always been globally connected, receiving people and raw materials and giving back products and ideas, both shaping and shaped by transportation. Movement, to and from and within Greater Cleveland, is to our minds the essence of its history, and so forms the theme of this book.

While its subtitle contains the words transportation and industry, it is not meant to be a comprehensive history of these subjects in Cleveland and northeastern Ohio. There are books by experts in these fields that provide a far more detailed picture of the trains, interurbans, steel mills, businesses and related aspects of regional history. Their titles may be found in the bibliography. We, the authors, owe a debt to the writers and scholars who produced these works, for their research has provided the foundation for our more general look at Cleveland's history as a story of motion.

One additional word in the subtitle, community, is central to our view of history. First, it implies that the "Cleveland" of our title is not merely so many square miles of land defined by city limits at a given date. Cleveland in this sense includes the entire area for which the city itself has served as an economic and psychological center. This area has tended to grow over time.

Second, while the city is the framework or the shell, the community is the interaction, the life that goes on within that shell, always moving and changing. Historians may focus on devices, companies or events, but invariably they must look beyond them, to the people whose actions gave them existence. Although geography, transportation and industry have combined to create a community, it is equally true that the millions of individuals within that community have altered geography, used transportation and built industry.

Cleveland's history has been put in motion by people, a few famous, some known to a small cadre of historians, and the majority remembered, if at all, only by their families. All of us who have ever lived here have a story behind us, either of our own arrival in Cleveland, or that of a parent, a grandparent or a more distant ancestor. Most of us have some personal connection, past or present, to the network of transportation and industry that forms the subject of this book. We hope that the various individual stories we have woven into our narrative will serve to remind the reader of the contributions of not only these specific men and women, but also all the others who have journeyed to northeastern Ohio in the past, and those who will continue to do so in the future. ●

introduction *by John and Diane Grabowski*

On January 1, 2000, the Public Broadcasting Service of the United States aired a daylong transmission of the worldwide celebrations of the new millennium's arrival. It was a tour de force of communications technology, and a time-zone-by-time-zone review of the new global culture that many saw as the hallmark of the late 20th century.

Indeed, as that century drew to a close, the issue of globalization received more and more attention. People celebrated the creation of a global village, they worried about the consequences of global competition and either praised or damned what was viewed as an evolving global culture. Whatever their view of the consequences, however, everyone marveled at the new transportation and communications technologies that played such a major role in rapidly shrinking the world.

Yet something was nearly forgotten in the midst of the celebration. That was the fact that globalization is far from a new phenomenon. Over decades and over centuries, whether willingly or no, people have been linked in a network, or rather an interconnected series of networks, spanning oceans and continents.

One person who had not forgotten was Richard Cartwright Austin. The great-grandson of Samuel Austin, the founder of Cleveland's Austin Company, Richard Austin was well aware that global connections had long been in place and that they had helped shape the history of Cleveland, Ohio, the community into which he had been born. In 1872 his great-grandfather had traveled halfway around the world from England to Cleveland, where he established a building firm that would become the foundation of a major American architectural, engineering and construction business. In more recent times, the career of his father, Allan, was witness to the fact that globalization had long resisted barriers created by ideologies and politics.

Allan Austin had helped build one of the world's largest automobile factories in the early 1930s. That factory was located not in Cleveland or Detroit, but in the

Soviet Union, in a city that would be known as Gorky. The factory and an adjacent workers' city was built by the Austin Company as a part of the USSR's First Five-Year Plan, at a time when no formal diplomatic relations existed between the United States and what a future American president would call the "evil empire." Payment for the project would help keep the Cleveland-based company solvent during the Great Depression, while the plant in Gorky would go on to produce the vehicles that helped the Red Army turn back the Nazi onslaught in the following decade.

In 1998 Richard Austin traveled to Gorky — now again known by its pre-Soviet name of Nizhny Novgorod — to rediscover this chapter in his family's past. Warmly greeted by the staff of the GAZ (the Russian-language acronym for Gorky Automobile Factory) plant and its museum, he knew that the historical connection had endured, and that human ties, once established, could reach across geographical and political division and down through time itself. He returned again in 1999, accompanied by staff members of Cleveland's Western Reserve Historical Society. Austin and the WRHS representatives met with GAZ museum staff to plan an exhibit, which would tell the story of this global link between Cleveland and the Soviet Union to a wider audience. In April 2000 the Russian team came to Cleveland to continue planning for the exhibit.

This is just one example of how northeastern Ohio has been interconnected with the rest of the world throughout its recorded history. The region's past is built on these connections and on the transportation technologies that made them possible. Just as jets, diesel trains and superhighways sped Americans and Russians between Cleveland and Nizhny Novgorod, other, less sophisticated means of travel ranging from canoes to steamboats and from footpaths to canals linked the region to the broader world in the years past. In combination, these various forms of transport have served to bring millions of people to this one particular place on the earth's surface and to take their products and ideas to countless other people around the globe.

Transportation has served to build community, both in northeastern Ohio and globally. Here it has gathered a diverse population, which has, with reasonable success, learned to live and work together in harmony. This process has not been without problems, nor is it complete. Now at the beginning of a new millennium, transportation is challenging not only distance but also the national identities that still separate the globe into separate communities, so many of which have provided the base for Greater Cleveland's own multiethnic community.

Nonetheless, barriers between states and empires, whether based on nationality, economics or ideology, do fall over time. We have seen the crumbling of the barriers that divided the world between two superpowers for much of the 20th century. The Cold War is already fading into historical memory. Cleveland, although a young city compared to the urban centers of the Old World, had its beginnings more than 200 years ago. To us, the issues of empire that surrounded the community's birth so far in the past may seem distant and trivial. Certainly they were not to the rival nations — native American, French and British — determined to control territory that already served as the center of a far-flung transportation network and promised to be a prime spot for settlement and trade. ●

A strike by taxi drivers causes more congestion than usual at Euclid and East 3rd Street in 1934.

Cleveland State University, Cleveland Press Collection

Setting Cleveland in Motion

Working, Building, Inventing

Immigrants, entrepreneurs, politicians and professionals set Cleveland and its history in motion. Whether celebrating or struggling, everyday people etched their stories into the city's landscapes — its roads, buildings, bridges and statues. They built the city's infrastructure, developed neighborhoods and produced the goods that drove the region's economy, all the while creating families and communities.

Skilled stonemasons constructed the symbolic pylons of the Lorain-Carnegie Bridge in the 1930s.
The bridge was renamed in honor of entertainer Bob Hope, whose father, a skilled immigrant stonemason,
helped carve the decorative pylons.

Cleveland State University, Cleveland Press Collection

Stonemasons assembled the pylons of the Lorain-Carnegie Bridge (Hope Memorial Bridge) in 1932.

Western Reserve Historical Society

Bridges, such as the Central Viaduct shown here in 1910,
provided crucial transportation links between Cleveland's east and west side.
Western Reserve Historical Society

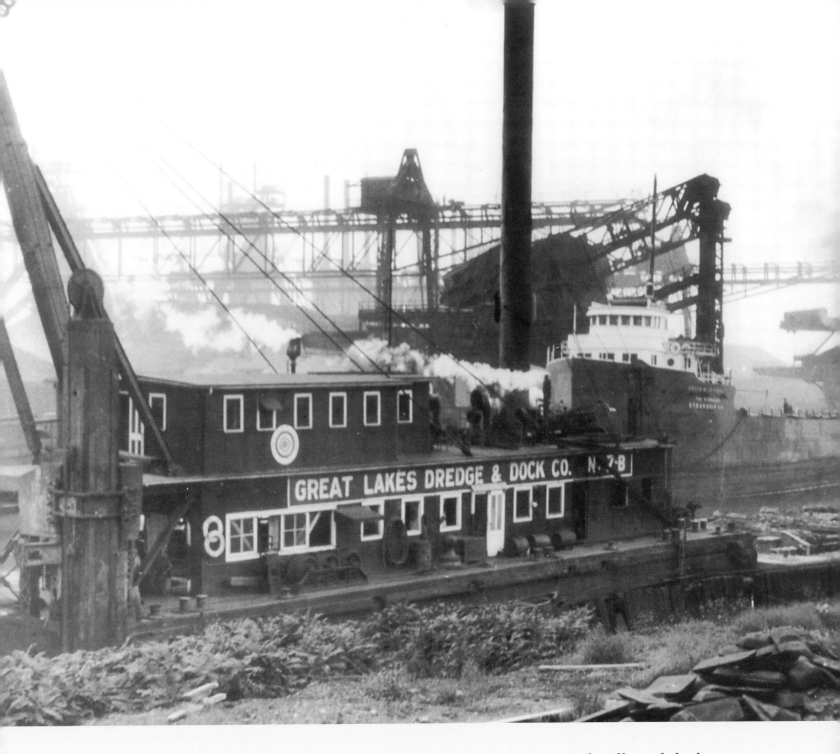

Despite the Depression, The Cuyahoga River and the adjacent steel mills and docks seem abuzz with activity in this 1934 photograph.
Cleveland State University, Cleveland Press Collection

Even before automobiles were common, blizzards could bring cities to a halt. A streetcar makes its way through Cleveland's snowy streets following a snowstorm early in the 20th century.

Western Reserve Historical Society

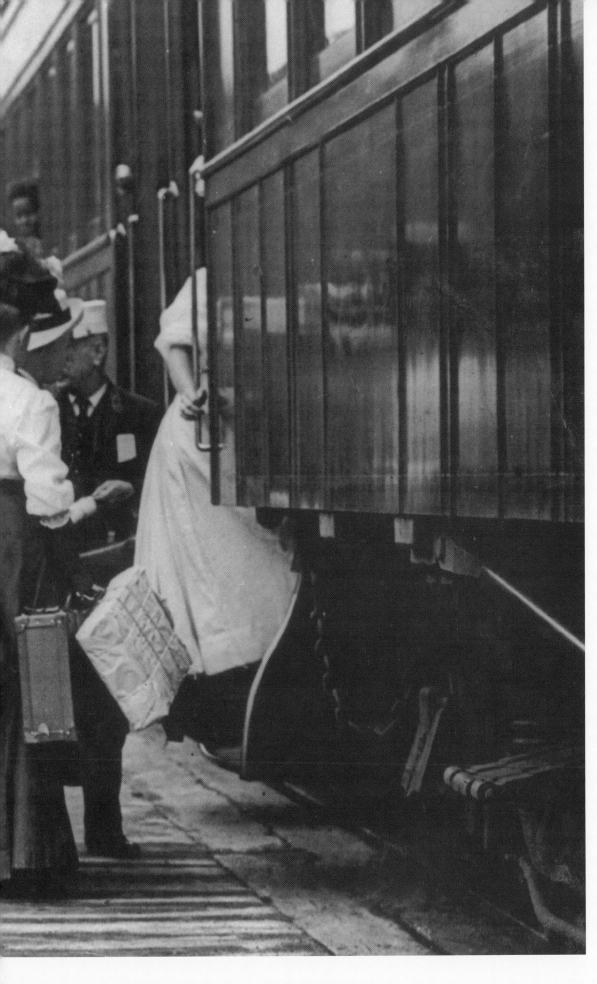

Passengers board a train at the Pennsylvania Railroad Depot at East 55th Street and Euclid Avenue in 1908. *Western Reserve Historical Society*

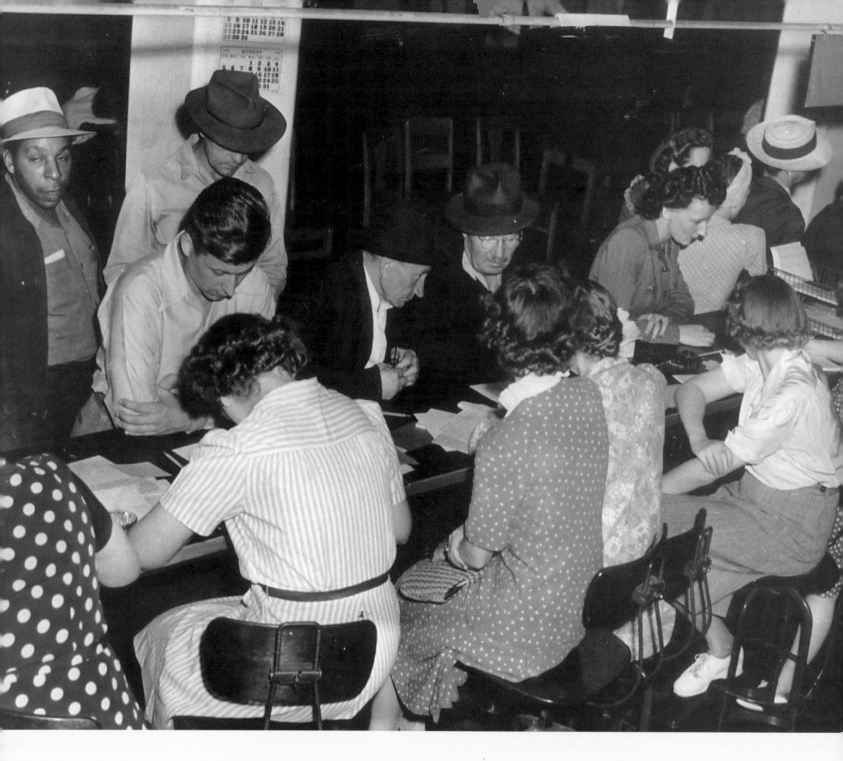

Applicants line up at the unemployment bureau in 1945.
Cleveland State University, Cleveland Press Collection

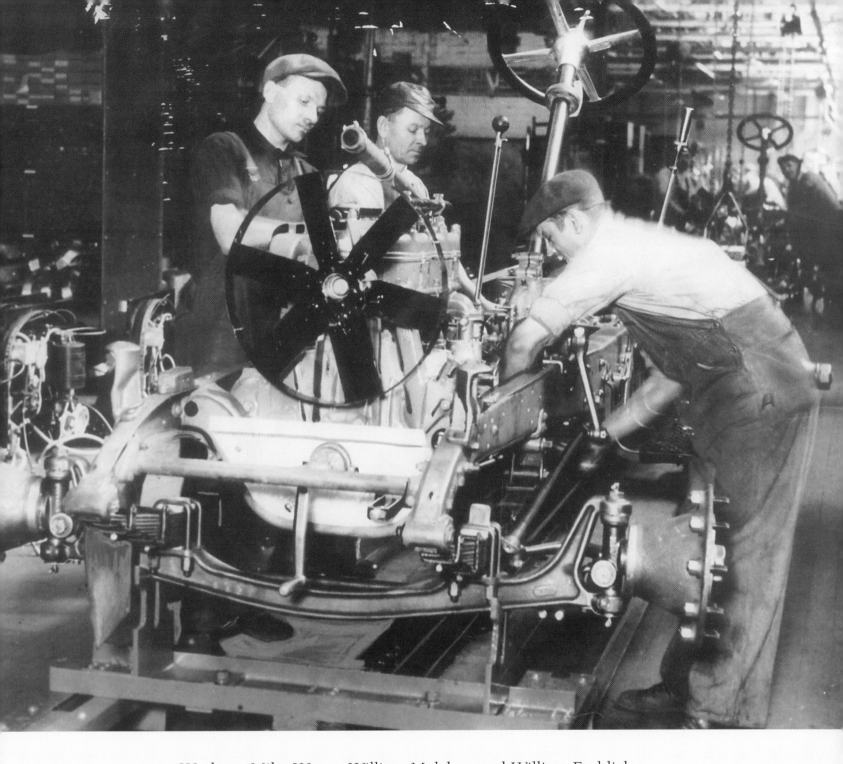

Workers, Mike Wozar, William Molchan and William Frohlich, assemble a truck at Cleveland's White Motors Factory in 1928.

Cleveland State University, Cleveland Press Collection

Workers — one of them holding the radical newspaper *Daily Worker*, sit in front of a statue of Cleveland Mayor Tom L. Johnson in 1930. Johnson was a popular mayor of the city early in the century, sympathetic to the voices of workers and disenfranchised citizens.

Cleveland State University, Cleveland Press Collection

Teen-agers earned summer money operating ice cream carts in Cleveland's expanding suburbs in the 1940s and the 1950s.
Western Reserve Historical Society

The African-American "gandy dancers," like those shown in this 1940 photograph, laid rail lines before machine-driven tools made their labor obsolete in the 1960s. As they worked, gandy dancers sang to break the monotony and to communicate with one another. Their rich songs sounded, in the words of folklore specialist Alan Lomas, "so wild and sweet that the mockingbirds in the nearby bushes stopped to listen."

Western Reserve Historical Society

The Detroit Superior Bridge
(now the Veterans Memorial Bridge) experienced tremendous traffic volume that was heightened during periods of road repair as in this instance in 1938. In 1930, with traffic reaching a volume of 70,400 automobiles a day, the bridge was being called the nation's busiest.

Cleveland State University, Cleveland Press Collection

Workers at White Motors built custom-made trucks for customers.
The factory shown here about 1930 did not use the typical mechanized assembly line;
instead a system of overhead conveyors and movable assembly was used.
Western Reserve Historical Society

The last truck produced at White Motor Corporation's
East 79th Street Plant rolls off the assembly line in 1978.
Western Reserve Historical Society

The world's first jet locomotive was created by a team of skilled workers at the New York Central Railroad's Collinwood Diesel Locomotive Shop in 1966.
Don Wetzel and Western Reserve Historical Society

White Motors was famous for its buses, such as this one on the streets of Cleveland about 1940. White buses were widely used in national parks, such as Yellowstone, from the 1910s through the 1930s.

Western Reserve Historical Society

one
chapter one

Waterways and Wilderness Trails:
A Crossroads with Potential

In the 18th century, the North American continent, abundant in natural resources and lightly populated by its native inhabitants, was regarded as a rich prize of empire by the global powers of the day. In the south and west, Spain held sway. In the north and east, France and Great Britain had both staked their claims. The American interests of these two nations increasingly clashed as the century progressed, and both tried to gain control over the heartland and its two great water systems, the Great Lakes and the Ohio River. In the wilderness that lay between French Canada and the British colonies, agents and traders from both sides bargained for furs and the loyalty of the various native populations.

In the early 1750s French initiatives to seize and fortify strategic spots in western Pennsylvania alarmed the British. This area was the gateway to the "Ohio Country" to the west, and French control would bar British access. Robert Dinwiddie, the lieutenant governor of the Virginia colony, sent two expeditions to western Pennsylvania in 1753 and 1754, the first to warn the French and the second to establish a military presence against them.

Both expeditions were led by a young, untested lieutenant colonel named George Washington and guided by the experienced woodsman Christopher Gist, who had served as agent and surveyor for the Ohio Company, a group of Virginia land speculators. On the first expedition Washington and Gist, making their way back through hostile territory after delivering Dinwiddie's message, braved the hunger, cold and icy rivers of winter in the wilderness. The two were fortunate to return with their lives. The second expedition ended with the French and their Native American allies defeating Washington's forces at Fort Necessity.

Yet there was something gained from these seemingly failed ventures. Washington came back to Virginia a tested soldier and leader with valuable experience behind him. How he built on that experience to marshal the American colonies to victory and independence is a well-known

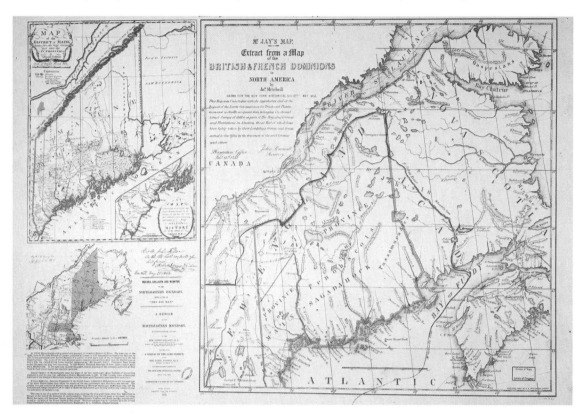

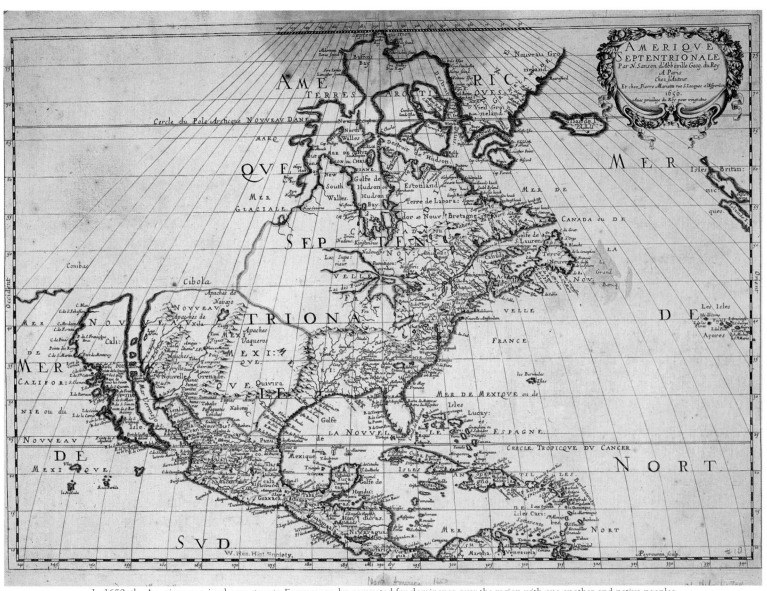

In 1650, the Americas remained a mystery to Europeans who competed for dominance over the region with one another and native peoples.
Mapping was an important tool in the political and military quest to control the continents.

Western Reserve Historical Society

story. But Washington was not only a military man, he was also a surveyor and land speculator with an eye for valuable property. The expeditions that brought him to the eastern edge of the Ohio country gave him a first-hand glimpse of the lands that lay to the west of Great Britain's colonies. Reports of scouts and agents like Gist, who had explored the region as far north as Lake Erie, further acquainted him with the territory. Washington recognized its economic potential as well as its strategic value.

The area surrounding the Cuyahoga River, in particular, attracted his attention. He envisioned it as the key link in a transport and trade route connecting the Great Lakes with the Ohio River and ultimately the Atlantic. In 1788, as the victorious 13 states were struggling to ratify the new nation's constitution, soon-to-be President Washington, looking toward future expansion, was already inquiring whether it would be possible to cut a canal between the northward-flowing Cuyahoga and the tributaries of the Ohio to the south.

Washington's vision of the region as a transportation corridor was not new. The area that would become greater Cleveland had long been a crossroads. In the Woodland

Leader of the Mohawk Iroquois, Thayendanagea, or Joseph Brant, insisted that the Connecticut Land Company pay $1,500 to the Iroquois Confederacy for the rights to the lands of the Western Reserve. Thayendanagea was painted by William Berczy in 1807. *National Gallery of Canada*

period, 1000 B.C. to 1000 A.D., early populations of Native Americans had built their villages and ceremonial mounds along the banks of the river. As archaeologists have discovered, these villages were not isolated settlements but interlinked communities that exchanged trade goods over a far-flung network. Northern Ohio peoples possessed axe heads made of Lake Superior copper and cups crafted of Gulf Coast conch shell.

By the time Europeans began to explore the New World, the older Woodland cultures had long since disappeared. In northeastern Ohio, they were at first followed by the peoples of what archaeologists called the "Whittlesey Tradition" (around 1000 A.D. to the mid-17th century). This classification was named after 19th-century lawyer-soldier-geologist Charles Whittlesey of the Western Reserve, who recorded a number of its sites, some of them along the Cuyahoga. The Whittlesey people remain something of a mystery to the present day, the remains of their settlements showing characteristics of both Iroquois and Algonkian cultures.

Also a mystery is the reason for their disappearance and that of the neighboring Fort Ancient peoples. The formation of the powerful New York-based Iroquois Confederacy and its military incursions into the Great Lakes-Ohio River region was undoubtedly an important factor. Certainly, the Erie, or "Cat Nation," who lived along the southeastern shores of the lake that today bears their name, were defeated and dispersed by the confederacy in the 1650s. There is debate, however, as to whether the Erie Nation's territory extended farther west than Pennsylvania. In any case, the Ohio country, although occasionally visited by hunting parties, was largely uninhabited by the end of the 17th century, at the same time as French and British commercial interest in the region was growing.

During the 1700s several Native American tribes — the Wyandots, Miami, Mingoes, Ottawa, Shawnee and Delaware — began to settle in Ohio. Some spoke Algonkian languages, while others were linguistically Iroquois. Some had been pushed out of their original territories by Iroquois or white aggression, while others apparently migrated voluntarily. The northeastern section of the state remained sparsely settled, perhaps because less powerful tribes wished to keep a safe distance between themselves and the Iroquois Confederacy.

An exception to this occurred during the 1740s when, ironically, the presence of whites attracted larger numbers of Native Americans to the banks of the Cuyahoga. In 1742 a French trader, Francois Saguin, opened a trading post five to eight miles up the river. He did so with the approval of the French authorities in Detroit, who were concerned about the activities of British traders and agents such as George Croghan. Although the French generally had better rapport with Native Americans than did the British, Croghan, described by historian George Knepper as a "semiliterate Irishman," was exceptionally skilled and successful in dealing with the tribes of the Ohio-Great Lakes region. He established a British presence at the Cuyahoga's mouth, opening a trading post there around 1745.

By this time, all of the native peoples in the area had long been in contact with Europeans and were growing dependent upon goods obtained through trade with the white man — including firearms, shot and powder for hunting — in their daily lives. Wyandots, Mingoes and Ottawas came to the Cuyahoga to exchange furs for such products. The trade carried on at these small wilderness outposts was in fact part of a global system of exchange, since furs purchased by Saguin and Croghan ended up in the markets of Europe.

Although the Cuyahoga posts were abandoned by 1750, and the Native Americans who had visited them ended up settling in other parts of the Ohio country, the area's importance for trade had been established, as evidenced by a 1755 map prepared by John Mitchell for the British Board of Trade. This map described the area from Sandusky to Cleveland as "Canahoque: The Seat of War, the Mart of Trade, & Chief Hunting Grounds of the six New York Iroquois on the Lakes & the Ohio."

A map by Lewis Evans published in Philadelphia in the same year showed a French trading house and a Mingo Indian town on the west bank of the Cuyahoga. Across the river was a village of "[Ot]Tawas" on a trail running from Pennsylvania to the Sandusky area. The printer of the Evans map was Benjamin Franklin, who in 1754 had already suggested that a fort be built "at the mouth of the Hioaga," where in addition "a port should be formed, and a town erected, for the trade of the lakes." Franklin maintained that the Great Lakes-Ohio River region, with its abundant "natural advantages," would "undoubtedly... become a populous and powerful dominion," and that the British should move in to fortify and settle the area before it fell into French hands.

At this time, northeastern Ohio had a network of Native American trails used mainly for hunting, seasonal migration and to an extent for war. White presence in the area increased their use for trade as well. These narrow paths, traced across the landscape by foot, left an indelible mark on the region's human and economic geography. In later years roads and railroads would follow the same routes, helping to determine patterns of settlement and industrialization. The Native American trails often ran along ridges, or paralleled and supplemented water routes, which were the best means of transportation. Those villages that did exist in the area were in many cases located where trails intersected with rivers. The river sites served both transportation and agricultural purposes, as native women planted the bottomlands with crops of maize, squash and beans.

Several trails and paths crossed or paralleled the Cuyahoga River. The Lake Shore Trail from Buffalo to Detroit followed the ridge along the southern shore of Lake Erie. The Mahoning Trail, which met the Lake Shore Trail a few miles east of the river, connected the mouth of the Cuyahoga with the confluence where the Ohio River begins and Pittsburgh stands today. Another branch of the Mahoning Trail crossed to the west side of the river, and via

In 1755 Benjamin Franklin published one of the first maps of the Great Lakes Region. Franklin predicted that an important city would arise at the point where the Cuyahoga River met Lake Erie. *Western Reserve Historical Society*

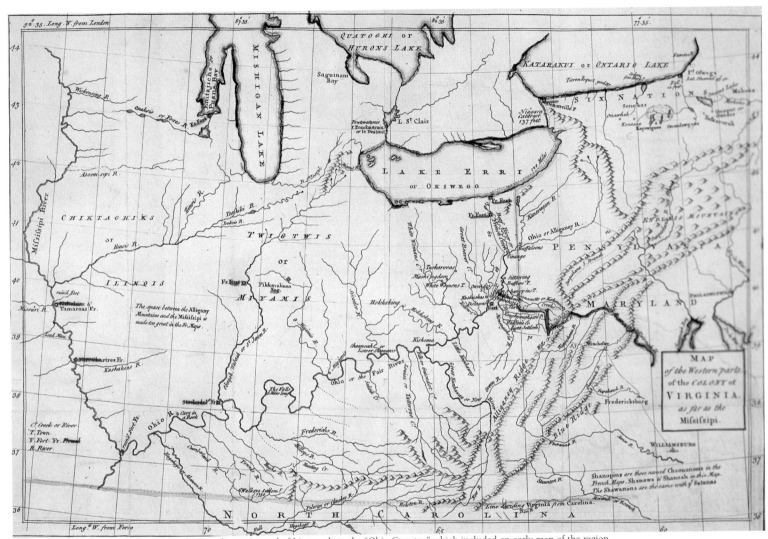

Washington kept a journal of his travels to the "Ohio Country," which included an early map of the region.

From a copy of the first published edition of Washington's journal in the Library of the Western Reserve Historical Society.

the Cuyahoga Path met the Lake Shore Trail near the river's mouth. The Muskingum Trail, which led into the southern interior along the Tuscarawas and Muskingum Rivers to the site of Marietta on the Ohio River, began at the Lake Shore Trail just east of the river and followed the river south as far as the portage path in today's Summit County. The Mahoning Trail and the Muskingum Trail both connected with this path. Less than 10 miles long, it crossed the divide between the Great Lakes and Ohio River watersheds. The Cuyahoga River thus formed part of a natural water transportation route between Lake Erie and the Ohio River — the exact route that George Washington considered important.

The expeditions of the young Washington and later of General Braddock were the sparks that set off the French and Indian War, the major conflict in the "Great War for Empire" between the two powers. In Europe, Britain and France were ranged on opposite sides in the Seven Years' War; the colonization of India was also at stake. Britain's victory ended the French empire in North America, with the 1763 Peace of Paris awarding Canada (and India) to Great Britain. This settled all questions of European sovereignty in the Ohio country. However, one party to the war had been left out of the peace process. Native Americans who had sided with the French had not surrendered, nor did they consider that France had a right to cede North American lands to the British. In the same year the treaty was signed, the Ottawa chief Pontiac organized a confederacy of tribes, which rose against British presence in what became known as Pontiac's Rebellion, capturing a number of British posts and laying siege to Detroit.

In 1764 the British sent two expeditions across the Ohio country to pacify the tribes in the area. The first, led out of Fort Niagara by Colonel John Bradstreet, traveled by boat across Lake Erie, stopping at both the Cuyahoga and nearby Rocky River on the way. The expedition had little military impact and suffered disaster upon its return across Lake Erie in mid-October. A sudden storm wrecked 25 of its 60 boats while they were attempting to land for the evening near the mouth of the Rocky River. Although there were no reported deaths, the remaining boats could not accommodate the expedition's 1,550 men. A substantial portion of the force returned to Fort Niagara by land, becoming the first large contingent of Europeans to cross

the greater Cleveland area. Their route to the east largely followed Native American trails. It took weeks to complete the journey, with bad weather continuing to dog the boats on the lake, while the overland party endured illness and food shortages. In subsequent years, Lake Erie storms, like the one responsible for "Bradstreet's Disaster," would claim many additional vessels and lives as well.

The second expedition, commanded by Henry Bouquet, traveled westward by land routes well to the south of the lake. Bouquet's show of force was more successful. He was able to dictate terms of peace to the Ohio tribes, which basically left the lands north of the Ohio River to the Native Americans, in return for their promise not to attack white settlers south of the Ohio. The 1768 Treaty of Fort Stanwix also designated a Native American reserve north and west of the Ohio.

This fit in with the general British policy of prohibiting settlement west of a "Proclamation Line" along the Appalachian frontier in an effort to prevent further native-white conflict. The British victory over France therefore did not have exactly the outcome that many colonial Americans had expected. Although the French claim was gone, the western lands still remained unavailable to speculators and settlers. The hated Proclamation Line, along with the British military presence necessary to enforce it (or attempt to enforce it), and the taxes levied to pay for that presence were key catalysts for rebellion in America. It was not until after the colonies had gained their independence from Britain and by the terms of the 1783 Peace of Paris gained control of the land westward to the Mississippi as well, that the Ohio country was officially open for settlement.

Even then problems of ownership still existed. The various former colonies had conflicting claims to the western lands. Connecticut based its claim to northern Ohio on its 1662 colonial charter, which granted it all lands from "sea to sea" between the lines of latitude (41 degrees to 42 degrees 2 minutes) defining its northern and southern borders. However, the rebellion that freed Connecticut and the other colonies from British rule reopened the question of who owned the western lands, forcing the new nation to settle the issue. The consensus was that the lands should become part of a single area, the sale and political development of which would be governed by a set of common rules.

Along with a team of surveyors, axmen and chainmen, Pease cut through the undergrowth and determined the land divisions of the Western Reserve for the Connecticut Land Company. This survey of the region dates from 1798.

Western Reserve Historical Society

Eventually, the states ceded their western claims to the new American Confederacy in the years leading up to 1787. The Northwest Ordinance of 1787 — arguably the most important piece of legislation passed by the weak congress established under the Articles of Confederation — set forth the procedure by which new states would be created out of the lands in the Northwest Territory, the area bounded by Pennsylvania, the Ohio River, the Great Lakes and the Mississippi.

Initially, the Northwest Territory lacked its northeast corner. When the states gave up their claims, an exception was made for Connecticut, which had already ceded claims to lands in New York and Pennsylvania. Connecticut thereby "reserved" for itself lands within its latitudinal boundaries from the Pennsylvania border to a line 120 miles west, while renouncing any claim to lands farther west. Connecticut's Western Reserve, as it became known, was estimated to contain some 3.3 million acres, and included several small rivers flowing north into Lake Erie, among them the Cuyahoga.

Connecticut's intention in retaining these western lands was not to settle them as an extension of the state but to sell them, catering to the speculative hunger for western land that colored much of the economic life of the old colonies and the new states. Connecticut officials knew about the land's potential through the descriptions of those who had traversed it, and the tales told by those already settling in the southern portions of the new Northwest Territory. At this point, however, sale of the land could not yet begin. It was still technically the property of the Native Americans.

As in 1763, the 1783 terms of peace disregarded the Native Americans, as the British agreed to pass on to their former colonies control of the land they had won from the French just 20 years earlier. Again, most tribes of the frontier area had allied themselves with the losing party in the conflict. Their choice of siding with the French in the earlier war, and then with the British against the colonials, was not an arbitrary one. The Native Americans had correctly perceived that the French, who were more interested in trade than in settlement, were less of a threat than the British, and subsequently that the far-off British government was less of a threat than the colonial rebels, who included the settlers encroaching on western lands.

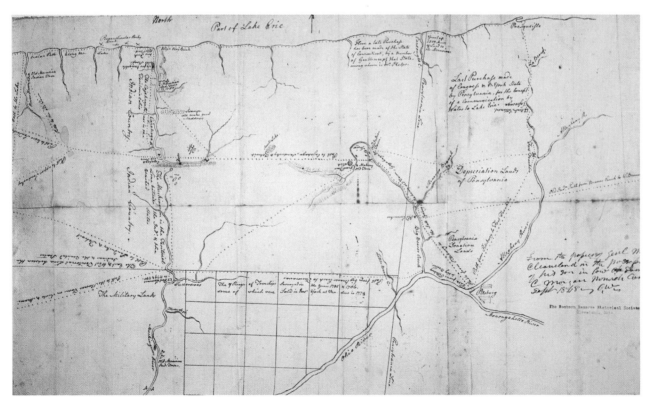

John Heckewelder was a Moravian missionary who settled along the Tuscarawas River in the 1780s and produced an early map of the region in 1796. *Western Reserve Historical Society*

The new American government did recognize that the native inhabitants had title to the land by right of possession, and by a series of treaties during the mid-1780s sought to "extinguish" that title. As Charles Whittlesey later observed, "although matters had the appearance of bargain and sale... the terms were those of a conqueror, dictating to the vanquished." The individual Indians who acceded to the terms of the treaties, however, were not authorized representatives of the tribes, who therefore did not feel obligated to give up their lands. The frontiersmen, on the other hand, believed that "the possession of the soil is evidently due to those who will cultivate it." In many instances, both sides ignored the boundaries drawn up by the treaties, and in defending what they considered their rights, committed senseless acts of brutality. In the 1780s

Respected for his eloquence, Sagoyewatha, or Red Jacket, represented the Seneca Tribe in council meetings of the Iroquois Confederacy and later represented the Confederacy in its land claims against whites. Charles Bird King painted this portrait of Sagoyewatha in 1828. *Albright-Knox Art Gallery*

the line of contact between Indians and whites ran through the eastern part of the Ohio country.

Although in the late 18th century the area near the Cuyahoga still remained a sparsely populated "neutral zone" between the Iroquois and the predominantly Algonkian peoples to the west, larger groups did inhabit areas to the south. Among them were Christianized Indians, mostly Delawares, who had been led to the Tuscarawas River area by two Moravian missionaries, David Zeisberger and John Heckewelder. The white Moravians and their native converts had, as Whittlesey put it, "the misfortune to be suspected by all parties," British, colonial, and native alike. In 1781 the Wyandots and non-Christian Delaware forced the Moravian converts to move farther west to keep better watch over them. The following year they allowed a small group to return to the Tuscarawas to harvest crops from the fields they had planted there. Falsely accused of murdering a white family, 90 of the Christian Indians — including 29 women and 39 children — fell in a massacre carried out by a force of nearly 100 frontiersmen.

Following this, the missionaries moved north with their surviving converts, first to Detroit and then in 1786 to a site on the Cuyahoga River which they named Pilgerruh (Pilgrim's Rest). Within less than a year, the experiment at Pilgerruh ended as Zeisberger, Heckewelder and their followers moved to New Salem, Ohio. Their short stay along the Cuyahoga, however, gave Heckewelder enough information to draft a map of the area. A copy of the map was later found among the papers of Moses Cleaveland, head of the party that surveyed the Western Reserve.

Battle eventually resolved the status of the eastern portion of the Western Reserve. In the first years after the establishment of the Northwest Territory, ill-trained, poorly equipped American forces had little success against their Indian adversaries, and in 1791 Native American warriors decisively defeated a contingent led by the territorial governor, Arthur St. Clair. Indian hopes of keeping their lands were dashed, however, when in 1794 General Anthony Wayne's troops defeated a coalition of Native American tribes at the Battle of Fallen Timbers near what is now Toledo.

Wayne proved to be as skillful at negotiation as at warfare, and a large delegation of tribal chiefs and leaders signed the Treaty of Greenville, which extinguished Native American claims to much of Ohio. The tribes ceded their lands in exchange for a payment (in goods) of $20,000 and $9,500 worth of annuities. The northeastern part of the treaty line ran up the Cuyahoga River and across the portage to the Tuscarawas, clearing Indian title to the portion of the Western Reserve east of the Cuyahoga. The treaty was signed in August 1795. On September 2 of that year, the newly formed Connecticut Land Company concluded an agreement with the State of Connecticut for the purchase of the Reserve.

In 1796 General Moses Cleaveland led the first surveying expedition to Connecticut's Western Reserve, sponsored by the Connecticut Land Company. Painted in the 1930s by Rolf Stoll, this portrait of Cleaveland was based on written descriptions because no images of him were known to exist at the time. *Western Reserve Historical Society*

Thirty-five purchasing groups representing 58 investors constituted the Company. Its members represented some of the wealthiest and most influential families in the state including the Mathers, Boardmans, Champions and Phelpses. Together they put up $1.2 million — in the form of mortgages rather than cash — for the land. They had every confidence it would sell quickly, allowing them to redeem their debt and make a profit. In fact, it looked like a bargain. At 40 cents per acre they had purchased much of the southern shore of Lake Erie, one of the five lakes making up the greatest freshwater surface in the world. The many rivers that fed the lake promised to be attractive sites for communities in an era when water, which could irrigate crops, turn mills and transport people and goods, was the key ingredient for growth. Now the investors had only to take stock of what they had bought, divide it into salable parcels and sell it.

To accomplish this they selected one of their own, Moses Cleaveland, to lead the first surveying expedition to the Western Reserve. Married to Esther Champion, the daughter of another investor, Cleaveland had invested $32,600 in the enterprise (his father-in-law had invested $85,675) and served as a board member of the company. A Yale graduate, lawyer and captain in the Revolutionary War, Cleaveland had a reputation for leadership, despite an appearance some of his contemporaries considered less than attractive: coarse features, swarthy skin and a "vulgar" manner. He would need all the leadership skills he could muster in the months that followed, as he assembled a surveying team and then led it through the wilderness to what men like Washington and Franklin had seen as a land of promise in the American west.

two

Boatbuilders and Innkeepers:
New England at the End of the Road

On the evening of July 4, 1796, Moses Cleaveland and a

company of 45 men, three women and four children celebrated the

nation's Independence Day and their own arrival in "New Connecticut."

The men fired off salutes and consumed "several pails of grog," after which

everyone, according to Cleaveland, "retired in remarkable good order."

Encamped near what is today Conneaut, Ohio, the party had just

completed an arduous trek of 68 days. Now their real work — surveying

the 3.3 million square miles of the Connecticut Land Company's

holdings — was about to begin.

Cleaveland and his surveyors had set off from Dover, Connecticut, on April 28. The first part of the journey, in the well-settled area of eastern New York, where established roads existed, presented no problem for the party's wagons. The leaders of the group reached Albany in three days and then traveled in relative comfort to Schenectady, where additional men were hired. From that point on the party moved

Seth Pease served as astronomer and surveyor on Moses Cleaveland's 1796 surveying expedition. *Western Reserve Historical Society*

through sparsely settled areas. It was split into two groups, one of which drove the expedition's horses and cattle overland. The other group, using water routes to transport supplies, went up the Mohawk River and portaged their boats to Lake Oneida, from which the Oswego River flowed into Lake Ontario. At this point the British still held forts in the Great Lakes area including Fort Oswego, and problems in gaining permission to pass this fort plus bad weather conditions on Lake Ontario delayed the waterborne party. The two groups reunited at Irondequiot, then separated again, meeting at the small settlement of Buffalo on June 17.

Here Cleaveland negotiated with representatives of the Six Nations of the Iroquois Confederacy. The Iroquois had technically given up claims to lands west of Pennsylvania in 1784, but they were still a presence in the area. The Connecticut Land Company proprietors, to ensure their own title and to prevent incidents that might discourage sale

and settlement of the Reserve lands, were prepared to pay the Six Nations to extinguish any remaining claims. Cleaveland provided whiskey and food in abundance before beginning serious bargaining on the third day of the meeting. The Seneca leader Red Jacket, renowned for his eloquence, made a speech through an interpreter:

You white people make a great parade about religion, you say you have a book of laws and rules that was given to you by the Great Spirit, but is this true? No.... Their whole wishes center here (pointing to his pocket), all they want is the money.... He says white people tell them, they wish to come and live among them as brothers, and learn them agriculture. So they bring on implements of husbandry and presents, tell them good stories, and all appears honest. But when they are gone all appears as a dream. Our land is taken from us, and still we don't know how to farm it.

The council ended, inevitably, with Cleaveland gaining his end for the modest payment of 500 New York dollars' worth of goods, plus two beef cattle and 100 gallons of whiskey. The Company could now be certain that Native American claims to the portion of the Reserve east of the Cuyahoga were completely extinguished.

Following the negotiations, the party moved on. A local guide, an African-American trapper named Joseph Hodge, accompanied them from Buffalo to the Reserve. The group included, besides Cleaveland himself, six surveyors, a commissary, a physician, a boatman, a cook, and 35 axemen, chainmen and rodmen, plus two hunter-traders, and two married couples. At this point the Reserve's first independent settlers — James and Eunice Kingsbury, their three children and their nephew — also joined the group.

On July 4, astronomer and surveyor Seth Pease found the inscribed stone that marked the northwestern corner of Pennsylvania. The boundary had been surveyed in 1786 and the markers were still in place and not yet fully obscured by new growth. Following the Independence Day celebration, work began in earnest on July 7 when the surveyors started the arduous task of dividing the land into 25-square-mile townships. Today's township roads, which run north-south and east-west at five-mile intervals across northeastern Ohio, in large part follow the lines laid down by the surveyors. Their neat regularity belies the fact that nothing but swamps, hills and forest existed there in 1796. Through this wilderness the surveyors, assisted by their chain- and rodmen, had to lay mathematically precise lines of division as the axemen chopped down trees and cut through the tangled underbrush ahead of them, all alike plagued by the heat, humidity and insects of summer.

With the survey of the Reserve under way, Cleaveland turned to another task. The Company had decided that a city should be founded at a central location along the Lake Erie shore. It was up to Cleaveland to determine the exact site of the "capital" of the Western Reserve. He and a small party began the search, coasting along the shore until they came to the mouth of the Cuyahoga River on July 22. They beached their boat at what is now the foot of St. Clair Avenue along the river. Near this point, the Lake Shore and Muskingum Trails intersected, and Cleaveland and his companions apparently set off along an Indian path. It must have been a relief, after weeks spent hacking their way foot by foot through trackless back country, to see a narrow but well-worn trail opening out off the banks of the river. They followed it up the bluff to a vantage point overlooking the wide expanse of the lake. To the west, the Cuyahoga wound its way southward.

After some hesitation, Cleaveland chose this site at the river's mouth as the location of the proposed city, probably based on information gleaned from early maps and commentaries which allowed him to conclude that it would "command the greatest communication either by land or Water." Although Cleaveland wished to name the town after the river, his surveyors insisted that it be named after their leader. Spelling of the town's name varied, but eventually became standardized as "Cleveland," without the first "a."

The new settlement was from the beginning envisioned as a city. Unlike many old-world urban centers, which had grown up naturally in favored spots where people gathered to farm, fish or trade, Cleveland was envisioned as a city from the very beginning. Its site, too, had been favored by nature, as the existence of the Indian trails showed, but it was planned and platted before a single settler arrived. The neat town plan devised by the surveyors imposed a pattern on the landscape, rather than following natural features. It owed something to an Enlightenment-era love of the rational and orderly, but more to the land developer's desire to sell off property as quickly and profitably as possible. The Western Reserve was, first and foremost, a commercial venture, and its capital city was laid out with this in mind.

To Cleaveland and his surveyors, the natural shape for a city was that of the New England town, centered on a commons. They gave their city a large commons of 10 acres, where the townsfolk would be able to graze their livestock, and a series of rectilinear streets, two of which (Superior and Ontario) divided the commons into four quadrants. Along the commons, which would become known as Public Square, and the inner streets, Cleaveland's men platted 222 2-acre lots. While part of the crew created the new capital,

Captain Allen Gaylord's sketch of the struggling settlement in 1800 documents the rough conditions faced by Cleaveland's surveying party. Prominent in his sketch was the surveyors' cabin — or "Pease's Hotel," as it was known. *Western Reserve Historical Society*

other parties continued to lay out the townships in the rest of the Reserve.

On October 21, 1796, with the first hints of winter in the air, Cleaveland and his men left for their homes in the east with much of the survey work not completed. Moses Cleaveland, who had a law practice and other interests in Connecticut, would never return to the Western Reserve. Another party, led by Seth Hart and Seth Pease, would come back the following year to complete the laying out of townships in the area east of the river. They also platted additional lots beyond the central 2-acre lots in Cleveland. These were 10 acres in extent, their greater size meant to compensate for the greater distance from the town center. Beyond the 10-acre lots, the rest of the township was to be divided into 100-acre lots. Having lots of standard sizes to sell at a standard price would simplify the sale process.

In the meantime, 11 people stayed behind to maintain a presence in New Connecticut. They included all three women who had come out with the surveying party plus their husbands, the Kingsbury children, and one single man. Only three people lived in the brand-new city, a young couple, Job and Tabitha Stiles, and Joseph Landon, who boarded with them in their cabin near the Cuyahoga. Here, they could watch over the surveyors' empty cabins and the Company's meager stores. Elijah and Anna Gunn (also spelled Gun) and the Kingsbury family settled in Conneaut, a few days nearer the east. Eunice Kingsbury, aged 27, and Tabitha Stiles, 17, were both pregnant.

It is difficult for Americans today, less than a day's journey by air from almost anywhere in the world and able to communicate instantaneously and continuously by telephone and Internet, to imagine the isolation in which these people lived that first winter. There were no roads, no postal service and no possibility of communicating with friends and family back east. Landon stayed for only two weeks under these

conditions (he returned in the spring with the second surveying party). His place in the Stiles cabin was taken by Edward Paine, who traded with the Native Americans west of the river. A few Senecas lived on the east side of the river, and the story goes that Indian women served as midwives when Tabitha bore her first child in January. Apparently, Tabitha, her baby and her husband survived the winter with few serious difficulties, perhaps because the presence of Paine and a location near the intersection of two major trails made it relatively easy to trade for food, particularly meat, with the Native Americans.

The Conneaut settlement did not fare so well. By November the Kingsburys were running out of food, and James was unable to find sufficient game to feed a family of six. He decided to go home to New Hampshire to obtain supplies, expecting the trip to take a month or so. In the east, Kingsbury fell ill but nonetheless set out on the return trip to his family, arriving in Buffalo on December 3. For the next three weeks he traveled through a continuous snowfall. His horse died and Kingsbury continued on foot with the few supplies he could carry, through snow sometimes up to his chin. He arrived home on Christmas Eve, to find that his wife, who had already given birth, was overcome by fever and unable to nurse her newborn. Soon out of food again, Kingsbury was forced to walk to Erie where he bought a bushel of wheat, dragging it back to his home on a hand sled. Despite these efforts, the baby, the first white child born in the Reserve, died in January.

The weather patterns of the region, not understood by settlers in those early days, had contributed to the Kingsburys' trials. The prevailing winds that swept across Lake Erie from the west picked up moisture along the way, in winter creating a "snow belt" where the shore curved northward at the eastern end of the lake. Cleveland was just far enough west to escape the worst of this lake effect snow. Although the Kingsburys and the Gunns could not have known this, they had no wish to remain in Conneaut. Even before the surveyors arrived the next spring, the Gunns had already moved to the banks of the Cuyahoga. The Kingsbury family soon followed.

Back in Connecticut, Moses Cleaveland had made his report to the directors of the land company. "While I was in New Connecticut I laid out a town on the bank of Lake Erie, which was called by my name, and I believe the child is now born that may live to see that place as large as Old Windham." Windham, Connecticut, with a population of 2,700 in 1790, was a sizable town by the standards of 18th-century America. New York was the young nation's largest city with a population of 33,131. It and only four other cities could boast over 10,000 people in 1790. Cleaveland was eventually correct in his prediction, but at the time the odds seemed against it.

Whether Cleveland could be termed a community during its first 14 years of existence is debatable. It did not have a large or constant population. Perhaps the most serious problem was "the ague": malaria, carried by the swarms of mosquitoes that bred in the sluggish waters at the river's mouth. Anyone who ventured down into the flatlands along the riverbed in summer was likely to contract the disease. Many members of the surveying teams experienced its debilitating fever and chills and treated themselves with an infusion of "Peruvian bark," or quinine. With few exceptions settlers came and then went, seeking healthier ground.

The Kingsburys were the first to flee the malarial lowlands, relocating on a ridge about six miles to the southeast at the end of 1797, only months after their move to Cleveland. In the following year almost all of the town's few residents suffered from malaria, and the Gunns and the Kingsburys, who remained relatively healthy, assisted the others as well as they could. The Stiles and the Gunns soon joined the Kingsburys on higher ground. The new settlement, near what is now the Woodhill Road-East 93rd Street area, became known as Newburgh and for a time outstripped Cleveland in growth.

A handful of the men who had come west as part of Cleaveland's surveying party returned to settle in or near the new town. One of them, Nathaniel Doan, came back in the employ of the 1797 team, which finished the job of surveying

the eastern part of the Reserve. In 1798 the Connecticut Land Company gave Doan a city lot on Superior Street in exchange for his agreement to reside on that lot as a blacksmith. The 36-year-old Doan returned to Connecticut for his wife and six children; the trip from the Reserve and back again took 92 days. Realizing that resident families formed the basis of a permanent settlement, the company also gave land to Tabitha Stiles (a city lot, a 10-acre lot, and a 100-acre lot), Anna Gunn (a 100-acre lot), and the Kingsburys (a 100-acre lot and 100 additional acres).

The next year, Doan also moved away from the river, not to Newburgh, but instead farther north along the heights, four miles east of Cleveland. The second surveying team had added three "highways," North, Central and South, radiating out from the center of the original plan, and Doan chose to locate along Central Highway (today's Euclid Avenue). He set up a new blacksmith shop, a tavern, a store and a facility for producing saleratus (sodium bicarbonate). This area (now the intersection of Euclid and Stokes Boulevard) became known as Doan's Corners.

The area's first tavern-keeper, Lorenzo Carter, a Vermont native who had arrived with his wife Rebecca in 1797, was seemingly immune to the annual ague. Immediately upon his arrival, he had chosen a spot near the mouth of the river and built a cabin large enough to accommodate travelers and drinkers. For him, the business potential of the site offset its drawbacks. He operated a ferry across the river, trading with the Native Americans who

cabin hosted Cleveland's first social dance on July 4, 1801. It attracted 20 men and 12 women from the surrounding area, including Gilman Bryant who took one of Nathaniel Doan's daughters as his date and left a recollection of the occasion:

I waited on Miss Doan, who had just arrived at the Corners, four miles east of town. I was then about seventeen years of age, and Miss Doan about fourteen. I was dressed in the then style — a gingham suit — my hair queued with one and a half yards of black ribbon, about as long and as thick as a corncob, with a little tuft at the lower end; and for the want of pomatum, I had a piece of candle rubbed on my hair, and then as much flour sprinkled on, as could stay without falling off. I had a good wool hat, and a pair of brogans that would help to play "Fisher's Hornpipe" or "Hie Bettie Martin" when I danced. When I went for Miss Doan I took an old horse; when she was ready I rode up to a stump near the cabin, she mounted the stump and spread her under petticoat on "old Tib" behind me, secured her calico dress to keep it clean, and then mounted on behind me. I had a fine time!"

lived west of the river and later with the new settlers there. In 1808 he constructed the community's first large boat, the 30-ton schooner *Zephyr*, which was used for coastal trading along the lakeshore.

So during the first years of the new century, a trio of tiny settlements existed within a few miles of each other just east of the Cuyahoga River. Eventually, Cleveland would absorb the other two. Already they were interconnected by economic and social bonds and by paths, trails and horse transport. Clevelanders reached Doan's settlement going east along Central Highway, which followed the Lake Shore Trail. Since this route continued on all the way to Buffalo, the highway was popularly known as the Buffalo Road. Doan's tavern-inn and blacksmith shop provided vital services on the trail. Going south from Doan's settlement along the old Mahoning Trail led to Newburgh. From Newburgh to Cleveland, the northernmost section of the Muskingum Trail — which became known as the Pittsburgh Road, and later, Broadway — completed the triangular route that connected the three settlements and defined what community existed in the Cleveland area in the years leading up to the 1820s.

Five years after Cleaveland's surveying party toasted the nation's birthday with pails of grog at Conneaut, the Carters'

Young Bryant and his father David had arrived in Cleveland in 1797. In 1800 the Bryants set up in the distillery business with a second-hand still brought from Virginia and began producing whiskey at the rate of two quarts per day. The Bryants were key figures in the local grain trade — their primary occupation was shaping grindstones that they quarried at nearby Vermilion. What their stones didn't turn into flour, they turned into whiskey.

Economic interests, as well as woodland trails, connected the Doans, the Bryants and the Carters. The three families performed jobs vital to Cleveland's pioneer economy. This economy was based on agriculture, and even those who had other occupations generally did a little farming as well. Carter, for instance, planted a few acres of corn near his tavern. The availability of a mill to produce flour was crucial in making the area a desirable place for settlers. Not only was flour a marketable commodity, it also made a great difference in household economy, replacing coarse meal laboriously pounded out by hand. The Bryants cut the stones for the area's first gristmill, established in the Newburgh area in 1799.

Once the Bryants had opened their distillery, tavern-keepers such as Carter and Doan could buy spirits locally. Early America was a hard-drinking culture, nowhere more so than on the frontier, with alcohol considered a near-necessity of life. It was also used as a medicine and as a trade commodity that was more portable than flour and could be bartered to Native Americans in return for skins to be sent east and meat for local consumption. The store at Carter's cabin did a great deal of business with Indians in the early years.

Two centuries later these occupations seem quaint, at best. But they formed the basis upon which a more advanced economy could grow. Nathaniel Doan's blacksmith shop, in particular, not only performed a vital service in the pioneer community and helped to maintain what links it had with the outside world but also pointed toward the future. At a time when people traveled on horseback or by oxcart, it functioned in the transportation sector as a service station and repair shop. It was also Cleveland's first metalworks, a forerunner of the massive iron and steel mills of later years.

The settlers themselves appear, on the whole, to have coped well with the difficulties of their daily lives, and even to have relished the frontier's challenges and opportunities. The Connecticut Land Company's field agent reported back in 1800 that "crops are extraordinarily good, and settlers healthy and in good spirits." But from the viewpoint of those who had predicted great things for the site at the mouth of the Cuyahoga River — and particularly from the viewpoint of the investors back east — the region's earliest years were dismal.

Ironically, the problem centered mainly around transportation, the factor that had seemed to offer the brightest promise. As long as Cleveland and the Western Reserve remained isolated from the population centers of the east they would not grow rapidly. The streets and lots so carefully plotted out by the surveyors would remain nothing more than lines on a map. Why should prospective settlers make the difficult journey to the Reserve when they could find open, fertile, more accessible lands in western New York?

Other considerations also discouraged settlement. In the first place, investment in land was safer where governance and ownership was clearly defined. Until 1800 no one could be certain whether New Connecticut was to be governed by the land company, the parent state or the new Northwest Territory. In that year an act of Congress resolved the issue,

granting political authority over the Western Reserve to the United States, although the Connecticut Land Company still held title to the land. At this point, the Reserve became part of the Northwest Territory, and in 1803 Ohio became the first part of the territory to attain statehood. Some potential settlers also held back because they feared attack or invasion. Memories of the Revolutionary War were still fresh, and the enemies from that conflict, the British and the Native Americans, were nearby — the British across the lake in Canada and the Indians in northwestern Ohio just across the Greenville Treaty line on the other side of the Cuyahoga River.

White settlers already present on the east bank of the Cuyahoga knew that they had little to fear from the Native Americans in the area, and indeed had benefited first from their help, and then from their trade. Nonetheless, until 1805 the portion of the Western Reserve west of the Cuyahoga could not be settled because Native American claims had not yet been extinguished in the northwestern quadrant of Ohio. To Moses Cleaveland's credit, he held to the letter of his agreement with the Indians, and except for

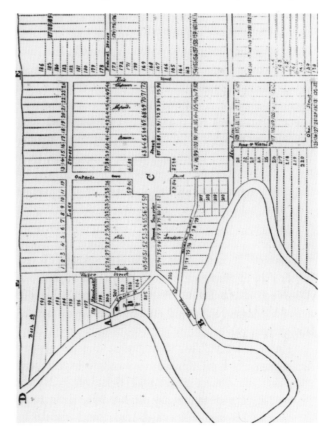

Amos Spafford served as a surveyor on Moses Cleaveland's surveying expedition of 1796. Spafford's "Original Plan of the Town of the Village of Cleveland, Ohio, October 1, 1796," was designed to facilitate sales and distribution of real estate. It followed a regular pattern of uniform lots and streets. *Western Reserve Historical Society*

a single traverse along the lakeshore to determine the extent of the company's lands, kept his surveyors on the east side of the river.

On July 4, 1805, representatives of the U.S. government, the Connecticut Land Company, and various tribes of western Ohio met and signed the Treaty of Fort Industry, in which the Native Americans relinquished their title to the remainder of the Reserve and lands to the south of it. Those who attended later related that "the Indians in parting with and making sale of the above lands to the whites, did so with much reluctance, and after the treaty was signed, many of them wept." With this treaty, Cleveland was no longer at the border between white and Native American lands. The British threat remained, however. Many people doubted the ability of the fledgling United States to protect Ohio and the Northwest Territory from possible British invasion.

Despite these problems, the sheer difficulty of getting people to the Reserve and, more importantly, of getting their products to outside buyers was still the major factor retarding the region's growth. Its potential would be fulfilled only when it had better connections to markets in the east or along the Ohio River. As land sales moved slowly, the mortgage holders of the Connecticut Land Company tried

If dense forests often proved a formidable obstacle to road building and settlement, this environmental resource — along with fertile farmland — eventually helped to make economic and social development of the region a reality.

to deal with the situation. In 1798 they had commissioned a road to the Reserve. The Girdled Road, as it was known, snaked its way from Conneaut to Cleveland through what are now Ashtabula, Geauga and Lake counties. It was not a magnificent feat of engineering. It consisted of a path cut through the woods by girdling trees, that is, stripping off a ring of bark all the way around near the base, causing them to die and eventually fall. The proprietors of the company could afford nothing better. Saddled with huge mortgages and slow sales, several found themselves facing financial ruin. The man with the largest investment in the venture, Oliver Phelps, eventually spent time in a debtors' prison.

In the early years, Cleveland did not even have regular postal connections with the outside world. In 1803 mail began reaching Cleveland from Pittsburgh via Warren, and in 1808 and 1809 regular mail routes connecting Cleveland with Erie and Detroit were established. The early carriers covered these distances on foot over the trails that threaded the woods and skirted the Lake Erie shore. The round trip between Cleveland and Warren took 10 days to two weeks. Faster service would depend on the construction of better roads.

Those who came to farm in Cleveland and the surrounding area certainly could not count on the Girdled Road as an efficient way to transport any surplus they might produce. They had two options. The first and easiest was to turn excess grain into hard liquor, which could be carried on horseback and traded locally or farther afield. The other was to ship their grain by boat to communities along the lakeshore.

During the first decade of the 19th century, an increasing number of boats entered the lakeshore trade, carrying grain, whiskey and potash (made from the many trees burned when fields were cleared). Many of them were constructed by house carpenters or general artisans, rather than by specialized shipwrights. In 1805 David Abbott built the 20-ton schooner *Cuyahoga Packet* on the Chagrin River. Carter's *Zephyr* joined the lake fleet in 1808, as did two small schooners, the *Sally* and the *Dove*, in 1809. The *Ohio*, completed on the Cuyahoga in 1810, was at 60 tons the largest locally built ship to that date. These vessels, along with smaller unnamed hulls, and boats from other ports around the lake, provided the transportation for a growing lake trade system.

1811, observed that Cleveland, "though dignified with the name of a city, remained a paltry village," with "only 16 dwelling-houses, 2 taverns, 2 stores, and 1 school." Melish, an impartial observer with a keen eye and an analytical bent, had one major recommendation for improving the city: cutting through the sandbar at the Cuyahoga's mouth and creating a harbor. This would solve two problems at once. It would get rid of the disease-breeding stagnant water and its "insufferable" smell, and it would immeasurably increase trade and prosperity.

Lake Erie's potential as northern Ohio's major transportation artery was partly offset by the danger of navigation there, especially for the small, sometimes poorly built craft in use at the time. Early on, settlers learned that storms rose and moved quickly over the lake and that its shallow waters turned treacherous at such times, as the Bradstreet expedition had discovered in 1760. In 1806 another ship foundered off the shore west of the river. The sole survivor was a fugitive slave named Ben. Lorenzo Carter nursed him back to health and is said to have helped him escape when his owners came to reclaim him.

Most immigrants to the Reserve came overland. Travel by foot and wagon was slow and toilsome but safer than venturing out upon the lake. A large percentage of the first deaths in Cleveland were by drowning. An entire family trying to cross from Buffalo to Cleveland perished near the mouth of the Cuyahoga when a sudden storm capsized their small boat.

By its very existence as a transportation corridor, the lake presented one other danger. It could serve as an invasion route for the British of Canada, only a short distance across open water. Although cross-lake international trade took place, the British posed a potential threat to the security of the region. Tensions between the United States and Britain had grown during the years of the Napoleonic Wars, fed by issues such as the impressment of seamen and trade blockades. During his travels through the region, Melish had noted two British war vessels on Lake Erie in 1811, one of which, "the *Queen Charlotte*, was built last summer, in expectation of a war, and carries 18 guns." The threat to the citizens of northern Ohio became real after June 18, 1812, when the United States declared war on Britain.

Hoping to conquer Canada, the United States instead almost immediately lost Detroit and suffered a disastrous

This was, however, a closed system, further limited by the fact that many of the area's inhabitants were self-sufficient farmers with no need for others' agricultural produce. Large urban populations lay to the east along and beyond Lake Ontario, but the falls at Niagara blocked access to these markets. Erie and Buffalo were the major stops for boats from Cleveland. They brought back manufactured goods, including glass, cloth and metalwares that were not yet produced in the Cleveland area. Prices for both agricultural and manufactured goods were high, due to the transportation problems, and cash was scarce. Goods were usually exchanged by barter. Whiskey very likely paid for some of the finery worn at the first ball at Lorenzo Carter's cabin.

The lake trade was helping Cleveland to grow, although very slowly. Only 57 people lived there in 1810. Its county, Cuyahoga, had a total population of 1,459, the smallest of any county in Ohio. The state's first settlers had come in along the Ohio River, and the southern part of the state was far more populous and prosperous than the northern. Cincinnati, for example, had 900 people in 1792, and by 1810 was a substantial town of 2,320. A Scottish traveler, John Melish, who came through the Western Reserve in

In June 1812 the United States declared war on Great Britain, and in September 1813 Commander Oliver Hazard Perry battled the British Fleet at Put-in-Bay.
Hazard announced the victory with the famous words, "We have met the enemy and they are ours."
This painting by Louis Chevalier depicts the burial of the dead from the Battle of Lake Erie.
Western Reserve Historical Society

defeat at the Battle of Queenston Heights on the Niagara frontier. These losses so close to home put all of the Reserve on high alert. Militias were organized in Cleveland and Newburgh, and women and children evacuated inland, as fears of British-instigated Indian uprisings swept through northern Ohio. Abbott's *Cuyahoga Packet* was captured by the British. In May 1813 a company of regular army troops arrived and built a fort and a hospital. On June 19 Clevelanders awoke to find a British fleet offshore, and began frantic preparations to resist the expected invasion. Fortunately for them, a sudden storm forced the ships away after they had approached to within a mile and a half of the town.

On September 10 Clevelanders heard cannon fire in the distance. The Battle of Lake Erie had begun, as a small fleet of American ships under Commodore Oliver Hazard Perry engaged the British Lake Erie fleet off the islands some 70 miles to the west of Cleveland. Perry's ships included the Cleveland-built lake trader *Ohio*, used as a supply vessel, and also three smaller craft, the *Porcupine*, *Trippe* and *Tigress*, built the year before on the Cuyahoga River near the portage. The Americans defeated the British at Put-in-Bay after a three-hour battle. James Kingsbury, by now a prosperous citizen and political officeholder, entertained Perry, who was his friend and Cleveland's hero, at his substantial frame house in Newburgh.

Perry's triumph, which cleared the lake of British power, was one of the few great victories for the American nation in a war studded with disasters, including the invasion of Washington and the burning of the White House. The Treaty of Ghent, which ended the war, nonetheless recognized the integrity of the American boundaries, settling any lingering doubts that some may have had about the lastingness of U.S. sovereignty over the

Northwest Territory, Ohio, the Western Reserve and Cleveland. A major political impediment to Cleveland's growth had been removed. Now, only the transportation problem held the city's economic potential hostage. This time a lawyer, rather than a military man, would step in to save the day for the struggling settlement on the Cuyahoga.

chapter three

Canals, Commerce and a New Diversity

On September 26, 1855, a new bookkeeper reported

for his first day of work at the commission firm of Hewitt & Tuttle, situ-

ated on Merwin Street in the riverside district of Cleveland known as the

Flats. From the office he could hear the sounds of the nearby docks and

busy streets. Conversations, shouts, arguments, the clop of horses'

hooves and the screech of steam whistles filled the air. Ships with their

masts silhouetted against the smoky skyline lined the river outside the

building. Boxes, bales and goods were piled on the wharves. Cleveland

was now a city, a city on the move. It was just the right place for

ambitious, 16-year-old John D. Rockefeller.

The predictions of the previous century had finally come true. The trappers and traders who had gathered to drink at Carter's tavern and barter pelts for whiskey or gunpowder would have found little in the prosperous, bustling mid-century city to remind them of the frontier settlement they had known. There, a few rough cabins sat in clearings among the trees, and a mill, a distillery and a blacksmith shop made up the manufacturing base. Cleveland had been transformed, largely thanks to one great structural improvement and one person who secured that improvement for the city.

Alfred Kelley was a nephew of Joshua Stow, a partner in the Connecticut Land Company who had accompanied the Moses Cleveland party of 1796 as commissary. Trained as a lawyer, Kelley came to Cleveland from Oneida, New York, in 1810 at the age of 21 and was admitted to the bar. He became a political power in the small community, serving in the state legislature during most of the terms from 1814 to 1822. There he began working to realize what so many had imagined — Cleveland as the central port of a waterway spanning the continent from the Atlantic Ocean to the Gulf of Mexico. Canal fever had struck Ohio, and Kelley not only did all he could to promote the building of a canal connecting Lake Erie and the Ohio River, but was determined that his adopted city should be the canal's northern terminus.

Canals were state-of-the-art transportation technology in 1810s America. England's canals had helped to foster the industrial revolution there, and early canals in the United States played major roles in opening up interior areas to settlement and trade. New York's Erie Canal, begun in 1817 and completed in 1825, linked Albany and Buffalo. This enabled boats to move people and goods from the harbor of New York City up the Hudson River and then across the state to the Great Lakes.

In itself, the Erie Canal had a great impact on Cleveland and the Western Reserve as a waterway connecting the Great Lakes with the Atlantic seaboard. For early settlers the journey from the east had taken a month or more as they moved what possessions they could carry by oxcart over miles of muddy, rutted tracks through the back country. Once the Erie Canal had opened, mail from Cleveland reached New York in as little as five days by a combination of stage and canal transport. Freight rates fell dramatically, to a tenth of what they had been. Agricultural products and salt from the Reserve could now reach eastern markets, and manufactured goods and luxury items from as far away as Europe began to appear in Cleveland's shops.

The Erie Canal also served as a pattern and an impetus for the construction of a trans-Ohio canal. The state set up a board of canal commissioners in 1822, which hired a surveyor to look at possible routes. The canal had to parallel natural waterways as far as possible, since they would provide its water. There was a choice of the Maumee, Sandusky and Cuyahoga rivers as the northern portion of the route for Ohio's canal. The foothills of the Appalachians made it impossible to build a canal any farther east.

Kelley, serving as one of the canal commissioners, realized that the state government's decision on the matter could make or break Cleveland's future. He was helped in his campaign for the Cuyahoga route by geography.

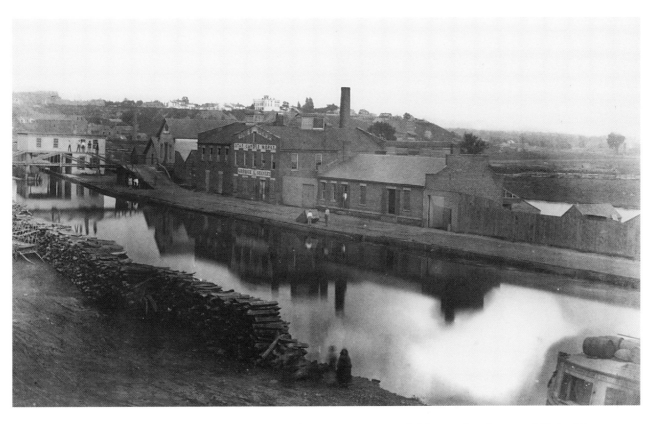

The Ohio & Erie Canal, shown in this 1859 photo, connected Lake Erie at Cleveland with the Ohio River at Portsmouth. Built at a cost of $4.3 million, the canal was 309 miles long and required 146 lift locks. *Western Reserve Historical Society*

Any possible canal would have to cross the ridge dividing the northern and southern watersheds. The Portage Lakes, at the portage on the divide between the Cuyahoga and Tuscarawas rivers, offered an ample water source at this difficult point. To clinch the choice, Simon Perkins offered free land for the canal's right-of-way and proposed to develop a new town, Akron, next to the canal. Perkins, the major landowner-speculator in the area, also happened to be a friend of Kelley's.

It took seven years to complete the 309-mile Ohio & Erie Canal from Cleveland to Portsmouth on the Ohio River. Alfred Kelley and one other commissioner, Micajah Williams, served as the project's managers, and started off by visiting the ongoing work in New York to familiarize themselves with the details of canal construction. Kelley gave up his law practice to personally oversee almost every aspect of the work on the Ohio & Erie Canal. Numerous small contractors, some more reliable than others, had been hired to complete small sections of the canal. Kelley carried a long iron pole that he used to probe newly packed embankments. With it he quickly exposed dishonest contractors who merely tossed earth over trees and debris rather than carefully building water-proof barriers of solid earth.

The effect of the Ohio & Erie on the economy of Cleveland and the Western Reserve was astounding. Upon the canal's opening, the price of wheat grown in the interior rose from 25 cents a bushel at best, to as much as 75 cents a bushel. Farmers finally had a market for their goods, and transportation costs on imports from the eastern states dropped. The first section of the canal, running between Cleveland and Akron, was completed in mid-1827. In the first half season of operation, the canal generated $1,000 in tolls. The following full year it generated $4,000. During 1833, the first full year after the entire length of the canal was completed, tolls exceeded $136,000.

Canal construction also focused attention on one of Cleveland's greatest problems. The canal was to end at the foot of Superior Avenue near the Cuyahoga's mouth. Sandbars blocked navigation between river and lake for all but the smallest vessels. The situation was embarrassing for Cleveland, the would-be hub of Ohio River-Great Lakes commerce. When New York Governor DeWitt Clinton had sailed in by way of Lake Erie to participate in the canal's

Brute labor — of men and beasts — made the canal into a reality. The canal was dug by laborers — many of them Irish — who earned 30 cents a day using simple tools such as picks, shovels and wheelbarrows. Boats travelling up and down the Ohio & Erie Canal were dragged from lock to lock by horses.
Western Reserve Historical Society

groundbreaking ceremonies in 1825, he had to be rowed ashore in a small boat because the ship that brought him could not clear the mouth of the river. As John Melish had noted, the sandbars both impeded commerce and created an unhealthy climate. For the canal to function and Cleveland to be cleared of the notorious ague-carrying mosquitoes, the harbor would have to be improved. It took federal aid to do so. Congressional grants of $5,000 in 1825 and $10,000 in 1827 financed the re-channeling of the river and the construction of a new 600-foot pier extending into the lake.

Clearing the river not only changed Cleveland's economic destiny, it changed the topography of the Flats forever. The original mouth of the river was nearly a mile to the west of its present location, the Cuyahoga making a long slow loop before entering the lake. Cleaveland had entered the site of his namesake city via this route. The new, direct river mouth cut straight through the peninsula to the lake, bypassing the last curve and leaving what became known as "Whiskey Island" to the west.

Packet boats traveling on the Ohio & Erie Canal carried large numbers of passengers. Travel by canal was not particularly fast — about four miles an hour, the speed at which the tow horse walked — but it was far more comfortable than journeys by road. The trip between Cleveland and Portsmouth cost $5 and took about 80 hours. A typical packet boat had two passenger cabins, one for ladies and one for gentlemen, where travelers could sleep at night. Weather permitting, the most pleasant place to be was out on the deck chatting with the crew and fellow passengers and watching the scenery go slowly past.

Freight, however, was the mainstay of canal traffic. The Ohio & Erie brought a wide variety of goods from the state's interior, including wheat, corn, pork, cheese, wool, stone, timber and ashes. Nineteen million pounds of goods traveled by canal in 1838. Cleveland reportedly received its first shipment of coal in 1828 when Henry Newberry brought a load by canal from his land near the portage and managed to find only one customer, a tavern-keeper who

agreed to try substituting coal for wood to heat his barroom stove. Soon, lake steamers were using coal to stoke their engines. The opening of the Pennsylvania-Ohio feeder canal in 1840 connected Cleveland with the coal-rich Mahoning Valley, and coal became a major commodity on the Ohio & Erie, with a million bushels arriving in Cleveland in 1845.

The canal was only one part of the transportation revolution that took place in Cleveland in the 1820s. The improved harbor also accommodated a boom in lake shipping. New boats for use in Lake Erie commerce were constructed at almost every port. In Cleveland, Levi Johnson, who had migrated to the community from New York state in 1809, was one of the more skilled and successful of the homebuilder-turned-shipbuilders. Johnson had his first experience of lake shipping during the War of 1812, when he and a partner ran the British blockade on Lake Erie to deliver foodstuffs to American troops in Detroit. When cannon fire sounded across the lake in 1813, heralding the Battle of Lake Erie, the 28-year-old Johnson and his crew were building Cleveland's first courthouse, on Public Square. Johnson put down his tools and led his fellow townspeople in cheering Perry's victory and the departure of the British threat.

Later that year, Johnson began work on a small schooner, *Lady's Master*, using timber from the woods beside his house on Euclid Street. He built another schooner, *Pilot*, in 1814. Twenty-eight yoke of oxen dragged the boat down to the water's edge, where Johnson christened it by breaking a jug of whiskey over the bow. He

DAILY LINE OF OHIO CANAL PACKETS

Between Cleveland & Portsmouth.

DISTANCE 309 MILES--THROUGH IN 80 HOURS.

A Packet of this Line leaves Cleveland every day at 4 o'clock P. M. and Portsmouth every day at 9 o'clock A. M.

T. INGRAHAM, *Office foot of Superior-street, Cleveland*,
OTIS & CURTIS, *General Stage Office*, do. } AGENTS.
G. J. LEET, - - - - *Portsmouth*, }

NEIL, MOORE & CO.'S Line of Stages leaves Cleveland daily for Columbus, via Wooster and Hebron.
OTIS & CURTIS' Line of Stages leaves Cleveland daily for Pittsburgh, Buffalo, Detroit and Wellsville.

The Ohio & Erie Canal stretched from Cleveland to Portsmouth at the Ohio River, 309 miles distant. The canal helped draw Cleveland more tightly into a regional economy and dramatically reduced travel times for people, goods or information. *Western Reserve Historical Society*

completed a larger vessel, the 65-ton schooner *Neptune*, in 1816. In 1824 Johnson was a partner in building the *Enterprise*, a 220-ton steamboat, the first to be constructed in Cleveland. The first steamboat on Lake Erie, the *Walk-in-the-Water*, had begun making the journey between Buffalo, Cleveland and Detroit in 1818, carrying passengers, cargo and mail. These three cities became the dominant ports on the Great Lakes.

Traffic and commerce at the port of Cleveland grew almost exponentially. In 1831, 355 ships arrived and departed. The number rose to over 1,000 by the end of the decade and, not counting steamboats, to 1,600 in 1844. Small, two-masted schooners, about the size of a modern tugboat, still predominated. The early steamboats,

wood-burning sidewheelers, were difficult to maneuver into the Cuyahoga River, even after the harbor improvements of 1827. They were also better suited for carrying passengers than freight. In 1842 the first screw-propelled steamer, the *Vandalia*, appeared on Lake Erie. The following year, Captain George Jones' shipyard launched the *Emigrant*, the first Cleveland-built steam propeller. With propellers located at the stern driving them through the water, these ships were more maneuverable and were also capable of carrying large freight cargoes. By mid-century, Cleveland was a leader in producing the wooden ships, both steamers and schooners, that sailed the Great Lakes.

In later years Clevelanders would not think of their city as a maritime center. A more diversified economy and the spread of the metropolitan area inland caused the city and most residents to turn their backs to the water, except for recreation. But in the 1830s and 40s, with railroads in their infancy and the era of the steel mill yet to come, Cleveland depended on waterborne commerce. Economic life centered about the docks, warehouses and shipyards that serviced the vessels traveling on the lake, river and canal. Shipmasters, sailors, canal drivers and dockhands mingled with merchants and farmers in the town center.

The less fortunate sailors led a hand-to-mouth existence and were sometimes stranded in port between voyages

without money. Cleveland's first relief agency was the Western Seaman's Friend Society, established to minister to the needs "of Sailors and Boatmen employed on the Western Waters." Benjamin Rouse, an agent of the American Sunday School Union, organized the society upon his arrival in Cleveland in 1830. Basically a Protestant mission, the society also operated a lodge to house and feed sailors. From this beginning grew the city's philanthropic movement, which later fostered innovations like the United Way and the community foundation and also helped create a significant nonprofit service sector that included several large hospitals. Rouse and his wife Rebecca Cromwell Rouse became focal figures in the mid-19th-century reform movement, active in founding numerous religious and social service organizations.

At the same time that canals and steamboats were transforming Cleveland from a backwoods trading post to a busy commercial port, overland transportation was slowly improving. During the 1810s and 20s, northeastern Ohio's first regular stage and mail coach lines began operating. It took 18 hours, including an overnight stop, to travel by stagecoach (in this case a springless wagon with a canvas cover) from Cleveland to Painesville, a distance of about 26 miles. At this time most mail routes were traveled on horseback with weekly deliveries from Buffalo, Pittsburgh and Columbus. Stagecoaches soon took over the major mail routes.

By the mid-1820s, the trip to Buffalo took 40 hours, with passengers paying a $6 fare. A few roads were good enough for wagons, including the relatively large Conestogas, to haul freight overland to Cleveland. These modest improvements in transportation made it possible to publish the town's first newspapers near the end of the decade. The weekly *Cleveland Herald* depended on wagon delivery of paper from Pittsburgh and horseback or coach delivery of mail containing news from the outside world. The editor himself delivered the paper on horseback, riding a circuit of 300 subscribers scattered throughout the Western Reserve.

Even in the era of stagecoaches and Conestogas, most intercity roads were still dirt tracks, dusty, muddy or frozen into solid ruts depending on the season. Stage passengers frequently had to get out and walk to lighten the load over difficult spots, or even help push the wagon if it was stuck

in a mudhole. The state of Ohio gave some minimal assistance in developing roads during the early 19th century, with important intercity routes like the Buffalo, Pittsburgh and Kinsman roads to the east and the road through Strongsville to the southwest designated as state roads. The state also chartered private companies to build or improve roads which those companies would then maintain as turnpikes, charging tolls to cover the cost of construction and maintenance. In the 1830s gravel-topped macadam roads and in the 1840s plank roads seemed to promise greater efficiency and comfort. Although an advance, these surfaces also soon deteriorated under the assault of wear and weather.

Streets within Cleveland were likewise unpaved. In the mid-1830s, Euclid Street, as part of the state's Buffalo Road, was covered with planks. In 1850, Superior Street, the center of the city's retail district, was the first street to be partially paved with stone. Most city streets were paved, if at all, only with gravel until near the end of the century. During the 1840s road taxes were paid in labor rather than money, with each townsman required to report "with a good and sufficient Shovel" for two days of work digging

In 1874 a bridge was proposed to facilitate cross-river traffic and commuting. Up until that point, bridges across the Cuyahoga River had been "low-level," necessitating being opened for every river craft that needed to pass. In 1878, after three years of construction, the 936-foot Superior Avenue Viaduct was completed with a pivoting center span. *Western Reserve Historical Society*

culverts, filling holes and spreading gravel. Sidewalks had theoretically existed since 1832 when a city ordinance forbade vehicles from trespassing outside the streets, but property owners were not required to pave them until the 1850s.

One improvement that did take place was the building of a permanent bridge across the Cuyahoga. In the early years, ferries operated by Lorenzo Carter and Elijah Gunn had linked the east and west sides of the river. As settlement west of the Cuyahoga increased, need for a bridge grew. The Center Street Bridge, opened to traffic in 1822, floated on logs and could be moved aside for boats to pass.

The new bridge connected Cleveland with another independent settlement just across the river. This settlement was incorporated as Ohio City (formally, the City of Ohio) in 1836, two days before the incorporation of its larger rival Cleveland. At the same time, a group of land speculators was building the first fixed bridge across the Cuyahoga, the Columbus Street Bridge, farther to the south. This bridge gave direct access to Cleveland from the main road south, bypassing businesses in Ohio City and setting off the "Bridge War" between the two communities. Ohio City residents boycotted the new bridge; Clevelanders removed their half of the floating bridge. The

west siders resorted to various means, including explosive charges, to attempt to destroy the new bridge. A group of Cleveland militiamen, headed by the mayor, came out to confront their rivals and a riot took place right on the bridge.

Eventually the courts ruled that both bridges should remain open, and in 1854 Cleveland annexed Ohio City by vote of the citizens of both communities. The Center Street Bridge was rebuilt and additional bridges constructed, but the Cleveland-Ohio City rivalry would be perpetuated by separate East and West Side identities down to the present day.

In 1834 the city marked another Fourth of July. From 1796 onward, "rum and gunpowder" had featured prominently in all local celebrations of that holiday. This year, things were different. Children from the county's Sunday schools marched with their teachers to the Presbyterian church, and after listening to a patriotic sermon, had a picnic of crackers and cake at the lakeshore. It was reported to be the largest gathering of children that Clevelanders had seen. In the town's earlier years, circuit-riding clergymen had despaired over the inhabitants' irreligious attitude, and despite its New England roots, Cleveland had no organized congregation until 1816, no school until 1817, and no church building until

1829. The Sunday school gathering of 1834 showed that a settled, orderly society had developed, with families and community institutions raising and educating the next generation of citizens.

For a brief period, Cleveland resembled the New England town of the surveyors' dreams. By the 1830s, the improved transportation connections had brought increased prosperity, a prosperity that the town's appearance reflected. No longer was Cleveland a raw frontier settlement. Although cows and pigs still roamed the unpaved city streets, smarter horse-drawn vehicles were beginning to replace the lumbering oxcarts of the early settlers. Some log cabins remained, but most Clevelanders now lived in frame houses. A few of the community's more ambitious structures, including the Kelley home near Water and Lake Streets and a new courthouse on Public Square, were built of brick. The square itself had finally been cleared of stumps and brush in the late 1820s, and young shade trees planted. This was somewhat ironic, since land only a little way east of the square was still heavily wooded,

just as the square itself had once been. There too, however, property owners were energetically felling fine old-growth trees to make way for the expanding city.

Most of the town's buildings were situated between Public Square, the Cuyahoga River to the west and Lake Erie to the north. Cleveland's first three church buildings — Episcopal, Presbyterian and Baptist — were located on or near Public Square. Around the square and to the north, houses stood in orderly, spacious lots on oblong blocks, in accordance with the original town plan. Nearly all of

Cleveland's retail shops were located along its principal street, Superior, which bisected the square and ran down to the river. Most of the city's tavern-hotels could also be found on Superior. The largest to that date, the Franklin House, opened in 1826 and catered to stagecoach passengers and ship captains. Just south of Superior's western end, the canal met the river, creating the heart of the city's commercial district. Wharves and warehouses, interspersed with a few small factories, lined the riverbank.

Much of the city's employment opportunity also centered here, in jobs related directly to transporting and unloading goods and buying and selling the commodities that moved ever more rapidly through the city. As the economy and society of Cleveland and the Western Reserve began to mature during the canal era, a more formal fiscal and legal framework became necessary. A handful of lawyers opened offices, and the city's first banks were organized. From these modest beginnings grew the service economy that would provide so much of northeastern Ohio's employment some 170 years later.

In addition to his role in canal building, Alfred Kelley was a pioneer in both banking and law in Cleveland. He served as president of the community's first bank, The Commercial Bank of Lake Erie. It is easy to take a cash economy for granted, but in the early years, there was a desperate shortage of money in the Western Reserve, as numerous visitors to the area noted. How could a major commercial port grow up in a town where people paid for goods in grain or whiskey? Cleveland needed money and a credit system to prime its economy. The Commercial Bank was founded in 1816 and provided loans for mercantile activities and dealings in real estate. It failed in 1820 as a consequence of the financial panic of 1819 but was reorganized and reopened in 1832, financing imports of eastern goods and exports of Ohio farm products during the heyday of the canal era. Both the Commercial Bank and the Bank of Cleveland, the city's second bank, were damaged by another panic in 1837. The Commercial Bank survived this time, but the Bank of Cleveland failed.

As the economy improved, the banking sector also recovered. Kelley, now a state senator, was instrumental in framing new banking laws for Ohio in 1845 that regulated and stabilized the state's banking system. The City Bank of Cleveland, chartered under the new rules in 1845, eventually evolved into National City Bank, still in operation at the opening of the 21st century. In 1849 the city's first mutual savings association, the Society for Savings, was established. In the middle of the next century it, too, would become a commercial bank, Society Bank, which following various mergers entered the 21st century as part of the Key Corporation financial institution.

Kelley had also been one of the community's first lawyers when he set up his practice in 1810. He soon acquired an office partner, the community's first physician, 23-year-old David Long. Born into a family of physicians in New York state, Long served as the only doctor for many miles around during his first four years in the city, riding out on calls to

The salesrooms of the Van Dorn Iron Works on Euclid Avenue in the 1890s showcased the many iron and steel products being made in Cleveland following the Civil War. *Western Reserve Historical Society*

isolated cabins scattered across the landscape. His profession, too, would take on an importance in the future service economy that undoubtedly would have surprised him. In his own day, he also ran a dry-goods store out of his home on Superior Street and joined Kelley as one of the incorporators of the Commercial Bank.

Kelley's legal profession had a particular significance in the years of expanding settlement, because lawyers were often involved in handling real estate transactions. The development of a separate real estate business specialty would come much later. The growth of commerce in Cleveland increased the need for lawyers, for example to draw up contracts or act for buyers and sellers in matters of dispute. Forty-six attorneys practiced in the city in 1837. In 1843 George Willey and John E. Cary founded a firm specializing in maritime law, a firm that later became one of the city's foremost under the name Arter and Hadden. Maritime law in fact became something of a local specialty as shipping expanded, and particularly so after 1855 when Cleveland became the seat of the northern District Federal Court, the venue for cases relating to maritime matters.

In the 1840s, Cleveland was clearly a destination with possibilities. It had grown rapidly, from 606 people in 1820, to 1,075 in 1830, and 6,071 in 1840. It was by this time a real community — and much larger than Old Windham, Connecticut, which had a population of 4,503 in 1850 compared to Cleveland's 17,034. The outlines of the New England town were still there, but urban characteristics were beginning to overshadow the rural. Public Square, now a city park rather than a grazing commons, was fenced to keep the cows out, and residents were forbidden to allow their hogs to wander the streets. Residential districts were growing up east and southeast of the square, and more and more houses and commercial buildings were built of brick or even stone.

On Superior Avenue it was now illegal to construct new wooden buildings. Three- and four-story brick blocks replaced the older frame shops, and several large new hotel buildings also went up on the street. Retail and commercial use took over additional areas north and south of Public Square, crowding out private dwellings. Although streets were still not paved, they were at least graded, and some attempt was made to provide better drainage by digging

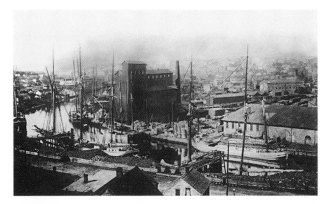

culverts. The beginnings of a public utility system were put in place in 1849, when both water and gas lines were first laid along the main streets.

By mid-century, Cleveland, described by a contemporary observer as "the great mart of the greatest grain-growing State in the Union," was poised to undergo another transformation that would create a city quite different from anything Moses Cleaveland and his surveyors could have expected. Already in the 1830s and the 1840s, some of the first elements of that transformation were present. Most importantly, transportation and commerce had made Cleveland an increasingly cosmopolitan community.

Many of those who came to find prosperity in Cleveland were, like John D. Rockefeller, people with deep roots in America. In 1843 Samuel Livingston Mather, son of one of the Connecticut Land Company proprietors, had come to the city to manage his father's holdings and practice law. Nine years later teen-aged Marcus Hanna arrived from New Lisbon, Ohio, when his father, who had recently set up in a wholesale grocery partnership, sent for his family to join him. Rockefeller's family, led by his father,

Cleveland had become a great market for Ohio's agricultural commodities by the 1840s as a result of the Ohio & Erie Canal.
In 1929 the bustling Northern Ohio Food Terminal attests to the continued importance of agricultural products to the region's economy,
which continue to flow through the market for wholesale customers such as grocery stores, hotels and restaurants.
Cleveland Press Collection, Cleveland State University

William, came to settle in Strongsville in 1853. Members of each of these families would figure prominently in the city's history, particularly in the areas of transportation and industry. All fit well into the type of community Cleaveland would have expected, at this point still made up mostly of people like Benjamin and Rebecca Rouse from Massachusetts, New Yorkers Levi Johnson and David Long, and Alfred Kelley, another Connecticut native.

Mostly, but not entirely. Canal construction had attracted a large Irish labor force to the area. Many of the Irish had worked on the Erie Canal in New York, and then moved on to the next project in Ohio. At first paid only 30 cents per day (the rate would eventually rise to $15 per month), the Irish, along with thousands of other workers, endured heat, dampness, cold and mud to construct the canal. Canal workers fell victim to malaria and in 1827 to a typhoid epidemic that swept through Cleveland. The epidemic left behind a "terrible depression of spirits and stagnation of business," according to Clevelander Ara Sprague (who neglected his own business for two months to help typhoid victims), to temporarily dampen euphoria over the canal project. Despite disease and depression, the laborers continued at their Herculean task, digging a 309-mile long ditch, six feet deep, 26 feet wide at the

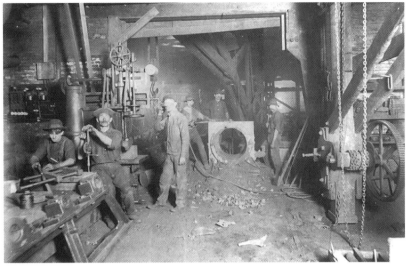

The interior of the Bowler & Company Foundry in the 1880s highlights the working conditions, environment and clothing of laborers in Cleveland's early iron and steel industries. These jobs were often dangerous, dirty and demanding. *Western Reserve Historical Society*

bottom and 40 wide at the top, plus the locks and towpaths that made the ditch a working canal.

When the project was finished, many of the Irish workers settled in the communities along the route, particularly the larger towns like Cleveland. There they became the unskilled laborers who unloaded and loaded the boats. To this day, Cleveland's stevedore union is dominated by people of Irish background. Roman Catholic, and mostly uneducated and unskilled, they received a cold welcome from the community's earlier Protestant settlers. The area in which Cleveland's earliest Irish residents lived, the riverside Flats, received a reputation as the city's first "bad" neighborhood. In 1826 Cleveland's first Catholic parish was organized there, and a church built in 1839. Although popularly known as St. Mary's on the Flats, the parish's real name was, appropriately, Our Lady of the Lake.

It is very likely that John Malvin, a canal boat captain, encountered the Irish in Cleveland. Although a Protestant and a native of the United States, Malvin, like the Irish, was an outsider. Born in Virginia, the son of a slave, Malvin made his way to Ohio. Finding Cincinnati far too southern in its racial outlook, he moved to Cleveland, which seemed more congenial, due to the antipathy of New Englanders toward slavery. He

Large numbers of immigrants, especially from Germany and Ireland, made their way to Cleveland in the years before and after the Civil War. In 1871 many German immigrants celebrated German victory in the Franco-Prussian War at Public Square. *Western Reserve Historical Society*

became part of the small but vibrant community of free blacks that existed in Cleveland; at the time just before the Civil War it numbered nearly 800 individuals.

Malvin purchased his canal boat *Auburn*, a passenger packet, in 1839. His crew consisted of three African-Americans (the bowman, a female cook and a steersman) and three whites (a steersman and two drivers). Although he moved with relative ease in the predominantly white society, Malvin still encountered prejudice. On one occasion a white female passenger took strong objection to being on a boat with so many blacks. She demanded to see the captain. When Malvin appeared her discomfort grew. Nevertheless, he and the crew did all they could to make her at ease during the several days she was on the boat. Finally, at the end of her journey she told him,

Captain, when I first came aboard your boat, not being accustomed to travel in this way, I supposed I must have acted quite awkward. Now, I must return my thanks to you and your crew, for the kind treatment I have received. I never traveled so comfortably in all my life, and I expect to go north soon, and I will defer my journey till you are going north, even if I am obliged to wait two or three days.

Malvin never saw her again.

"Awkward" encounters were to become more frequent as Cleveland became an integral part of an evolving national and global transportation system that made immigration from Europe easier. The Irish canal builders were soon joined by additional Irish immigrants, particularly after the Great Famine of the late 1840s. Even so, the Irish migration to Cleveland was small in comparison with the great influx of newcomers from what is now Germany. By the late 1830s Cleveland and Ohio City were home to several

German neighborhoods. Working mostly as artisans, craftsmen and shopkeepers, the Germans became the predominant ethnic group in Cleveland by the time of the Civil War. The appearance of a German-language newspaper, *Germania*, in 1847 showed that Cleveland was no longer monolingual.

Unquestionably, it was the city's growing economy that attracted immigrants. Simson Thorman came through the city in 1837 after trading furs west of St. Louis. He apparently liked what he saw and wrote a favorable report back to family members in Unsleben, Bavaria. In 1839 a party of Thorman's former neighbors, afflicted by "America fever," left Unsleben. They traveled to Hamburg, booked passage on the ship *Howard* and arrived in New York on July 12, 1839. The group traveled by boat up the Hudson River, and then from Albany to Buffalo on the Erie Canal. Late in the summer, having traveled across Lake Erie to Cleveland, they disembarked at the foot of Superior Lane. The immigrants from Unsleben were the first large group of Jews to come to Cleveland. Each found his way into the city's expanding economy.

One later group of immigrants from Germany was not so fortunate. Having made their way safely across the Atlantic, they lost their lives on Lake Erie, just 20 miles east of Cleveland, when the sidewheel steamer *Griffith* caught fire and went down on June 17, 1850. Nearly 300 of the 326 people on board died in the disaster. Cleveland's German residents came together after the disaster to arrange proper Christian burials for the immigrant victims.

In this period, wood- and coal-fired boilers on wooden ships constituted an even greater danger than storms and navigational hazards. For the shipping trade, losing vessels was part of the cost of doing business. Cleveland shipyard owners and employees depended for part of their incomes on building ships to replace those that were wrecked or caught fire. Tragedies like the *Griffith* disaster would spur movements to make lake shipping safer, but safety could never be taken for granted as ever increasing numbers of boats carrying passengers and cargoes sailed the fickle waters of Lake Erie. Maritime disasters would pepper the lake's history for decades to come, as it and those who sailed it helped build northern Ohio's economic fortunes.

On September 10, 1860, the citizens of Cleveland unveiled their first public monument. The date marked the 47th anniversary of the Battle of Lake Erie; the monument was a larger-than-life marble statue of the battle's hero, Commodore Oliver Hazard Perry. Thousands attended the unveiling ceremony and watched a re-enactment of the battle staged off the city's waterfront. The new statue stood right in the center of Public Square at the intersection of Ontario and Superior. Once nothing more than lines on a surveyor's map, these were now major thoroughfares. The city center, with its commons and its churches, was a lasting reminder of Cleveland's New England roots.

But Cleveland was no longer a New England community. Forty-four percent of its population of 43,417 was foreign-born. The entire area between Public Square and the Cuyahoga River was occupied by businesses, warehouses and factories. By opening the lake, Perry's victory had helped create the city his statue now graced. The era of canal boats and wooden lake steamers had been a crucial turning point in the city's history. However, it was already over. Clevelanders gathered downtown that day to honor Perry's victory could still see smoke on the horizon and hear whistles from the Flats nearby. These came not only from steamboats but also from a newer form of transport, one that would change Cleveland yet again, into an industrial metropolis with its fortunes riding on rails of iron and steel.

Wooden canal boats were limited by the size of the locks. Large-capacity freight boats were towed by mules in tandem and filled with the commodities that were the lifeblood of the region's economy. *Western Reserve Historical Society*

In 1850 several hundred people died when the steamer *Griffith* caught fire and sank. Such disasters became increasingly common with the accelerating development of industrial and transportation technologies. *Great Lakes Historical Society, Vermilion, Ohio*

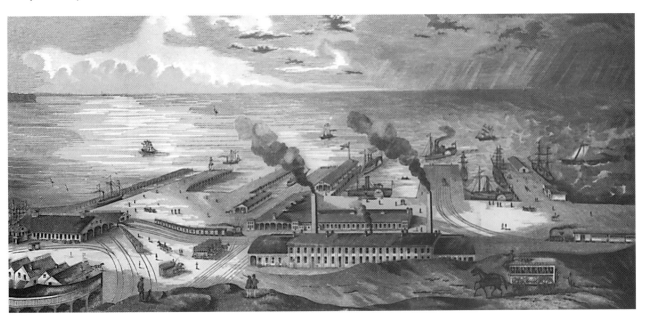

In 1850 the first railroad depot in Cleveland was built on the lakefront near West 9th Street. The *Cleveland Herald* predicted, "The whistle of the locomotive will be as familiar to the ears of the Clevelander as the sound of church bells." Soon the railroad would supplant the Ohio & Erie Canal, and through World War II, it would serve as the region's primary mode of transportation. *Western Reserve Historical Society*

four

Steam, Steel and Rails:
Foundations for an Industrial Century

On Saturday, December 6, 1884, a wet and muddy day,

1,500 men carrying shovels marched in procession with their wives and

children along Euclid Avenue. Their ancestries traced back to England,

Scotland, Wales, Ireland, Bohemia and Poland. These men, the iron and

steelworkers of the Cleveland Rolling Mill Company, were not on strike.

They had gathered at the mill, taken a special train to the Euclid and

Willson Avenue station and were walking the remaining two miles to

Lake View Cemetery, the city's finest burial ground. There, they would

dedicate a monument to their boss, Henry Chisholm, who had died three

years before.

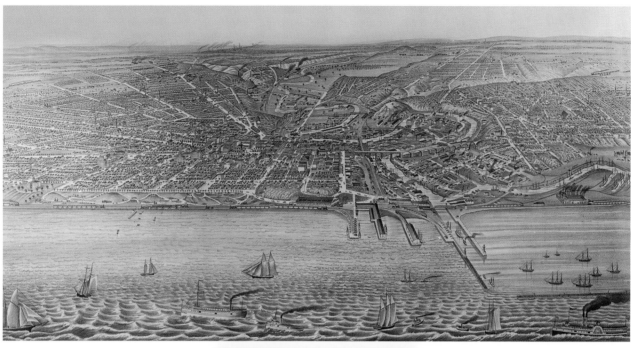

Marching down graveled and graded city streets, the procession followed the old route between Cleveland and Doan's Corners, where early settlers and traders had threaded their way along a woodland trail on horseback, bound for Nathaniel Doan's blacksmith shop. They had begun their journey in Newburgh, the third of the area's pioneer settlements. In the years since the turn of the century, each community had grown considerably. At the same time, Cleveland's boundaries were relentlessly expanding. The city annexed both Doan's Corners, with its numerous shops and small factories, and the heart of Newburgh, where the mill was located, in the early 1870s.

As men who worked iron and steel, the rolling mill employees were blacksmith Doan's occupational descendants. But they worked on a much larger scale. During the years just before and after the American Civil War, an enormous change in Cleveland's metalworking industry, and in its transportation network, took place. In bringing about this change, Henry Chisholm deserves as much credit as anyone.

His monument, which still stands near Lake View Cemetery's Euclid Avenue entrance, tells the story. Bronze panels on three sides of the pedestal depict scenes in the mills. Atop the pedestal, Chisholm's statue, also in bronze, shows him leaning casually on a steel mill roller. Framing the panels and the accompanying text are carved marble T-rails, the iron and steel tracks that carried Cleveland to industrial greatness. Each worker had donated a day's wages to the monument fund. An inscription on the back of the pedestal reads, in part:

Erected by 6000 employees and friends in memory of Henry Chisholm, Christian philanthropist and everybody's friend.

It was appropriate that a native of Great Britain, the birthplace of the Industrial Revolution and the steam locomotive, helped bring the industrial age to Cleveland. Henry Chisholm was born in 1822 in Lochgelly, Fifeshire, Scotland. He apprenticed as a carpenter and then immigrated to Montreal. In 1850 he came to Cleveland as a contractor to build part of the breakwater that protected the Cleveland and Pittsburgh Railroad's tracks from the erosive waves of Lake Erie. He also built piers, docks and even a ship, thus contributing to waterborne transportation, the dominant form at the time. However, he would make his reputation and his fortune in iron and steel, the basic material of railroads.

In 1857 Chisholm joined a business partnership with two other British immigrants, David and John Jones from Wales. The Jones brothers had started a small iron mill in Newburgh to roll railroad rails. While they would continue to manage the plant's day-to-day operations, Chisholm, who had become the principal investor, took over the firm's general direction and finances. By 1858 the mill was rerolling 50 tons of used railroad rails each day. Chisholm had both a shrewd sense of market trends and a talent for handling men. His management style would later be called paternalistic, but as a craftsman himself, he knew and understood his employees and they responded to this, as their contributions to his memorial showed. At the time Chisholm died, the Cleveland Rolling Mill Company was the area's largest employer, producing iron and Bessemer-process steel, much of which was purchased by the growing railroad industry.

Steam-powered railroads, first established in England, were the technological marvel of the early 19th century. The first steam railroad in the United States began operating in 1829. Within a decade, the once-novel form of transport had proven itself and was viewed as a solid investment. Unlike ships and canal boats, dependent on natural waterways, railroads could go wherever engineers could lay tracks. They were faster, 20 to 30 miles per hour for early passenger trains, versus 4 miles per hour for canal packets. And unlike lakes, rivers and canals, they did not freeze during the winter, an important consideration in the northern part of the country. Nineteenth-century civic boosters had despaired over Cleveland's yearly "hibernation"

in the pre-railroad era, when bad roads and an iced-over canal disrupted travel and commerce.

In 1836, only four years after the Ohio & Erie canal began full operation, Cleveland and Ohio investors chartered three railroad companies. One, the Ohio Railroad, was an impractical scheme to build an east-west trans-state route on a 100-foot roadbed raised on wooden pilings. The second would link Cleveland with Cincinnati via Columbus. The third would run between Cleveland and Pittsburgh. Each project came to a halt during the financial panic of 1837, although 63 miles of pilings were driven for the railroad on stilts.

Only after the financial recovery of the 1840s did Cleveland get its railroad. In 1847 backers of the proposed Cleveland, Columbus and Cincinnati line, struggling to raise subscriptions, turned to a familiar figure for help: Alfred Kelley. Kelley, now living in Columbus, agreed to become president of the venture. His name still held magic for potential subscribers, who flocked to invest money to build the road.

Construction of the Cleveland, Columbus and Cincinnati Railroad began in the late 1840s. At this date, construction materials still had to be brought in from outside. Some iron came from the eastern United States. Kelley, now devoting the same kind of personal attention to the railroad as he had to the canal, went to Wales to purchase additional iron for the rails. Older methods of railroad construction had featured oak rails surfaced with iron straps. Kelley insisted on use of the newer T-rails, solid lengths of iron.

The first train ran in Cleveland on November 3, 1849. By February 1851 the road had been completed to Columbus. Although the rails came from outside, the steam engines that traveled them were manufactured locally by Ohio City's Cuyahoga Steam Furnace Company. Also in February 1851, the Cleveland and Pittsburgh Railroad, another of the projects chartered in 1836, opened its Cleveland to Hudson section. Once complete, this road brought coal from the fields of southeastern Ohio

Chisholm, Jones, & Company was founded in 1857 by two Welsh immigrants, David and John Jones, who were later joined by the Scot, Henry Chisholm. The firm's Emma Blast Furnace is shown here. Western Reserve Historical Society

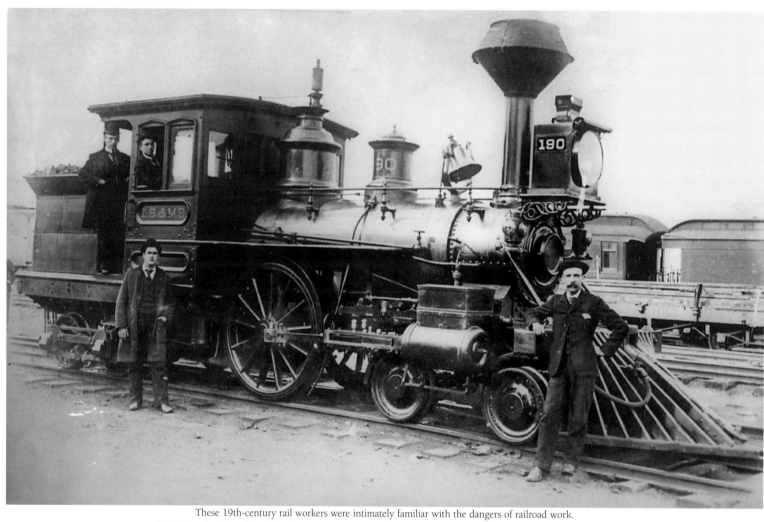

These 19th-century rail workers were intimately familiar with the dangers of railroad work.
In 1877 railroad workers throughout the nation went on strike demanding better wages and improved safety.
Western Reserve Historical Society

to Cleveland. Its trains not only carried coal but burned it in their engines, replacing wood as fuel.

These north-south routes were soon joined by lines that ran east-west across the city along the lakeshore. By the late 1850s a series of independent roads provided through connections to New York City and Chicago. Travel times fell dramatically. In 1853 "lightning trains" chugged between Cleveland and Cincinnati in eight hours, Cleveland and Buffalo in six and a half. By the eve of the Civil War, Clevelanders were a few days' journey, at most, from almost any major American city east of the Mississippi River. With the completion of the first transcontinental railroad in 1869, they and the goods they produced had a direct and swift connection to the people, ports and products of the Pacific coast.

As miraculous as these changes seem, they were only some of several significant effects railroads had on Cleveland. In the first place, railroads changed the city's layout and appearance. Moses Cleaveland's surveyors had created a town plan of neatness and order, combining Enlightenment rationality with New England practicality. By and large, the town had grown up according to this plan. Business, such industry as there was and most commerce were confined to the areas along the river and harbor. To the east extended the carefully platted square lots, where streets and properties existed in a world of north-south and east-west lines. To the west of the river, in Brooklyn Township and Ohio City, street and lot layout replicated the strict grid pattern. On both sides of the river, the geometric layout was interrupted only by ravines and valleys, and by the intercity roads — Pittsburgh, Kinsman, Buffalo, Detroit and Columbus — which tended to follow the natural features of the landscape, their routes in most cases determined by the Native American trails used in turn by the early settlers.

The railroads paid no heed to the surveyors' well-ordered plans and no respect to scenic values. The east-west routes between New York and Chicago cut off public access to the

lakefront across much of the city's shoreline. Elsewhere, rails also followed the most direct and affordable route, cutting across farm fields and roads. The route to Cincinnati began in one of the city's major valleys, Walworth Run, emerging to run diagonally southwest across streets, roads and properties. The Cleveland and Pittsburgh left the lakefront near what is now East 20th

The New York, Chicago and St. Louis rail passenger station located on Broadway was used until 1930.
Western Reserve Historical Society

Laborers working for the New York Central Railroad in the 1920s — the New York Central's Collinwood shops were a major employer in Cleveland.
Western Reserve Historical Society

Street and cut diagonally southeast, slicing across Euclid at what would become East 55th. Unlike the unpaved roads still prevalent at mid-century, the new iron roads were an intrusion into the landscape rather than a part of it. Locomotives were not, in fact, "iron horses" but something far different, and as they appeared with increasing frequency after 1850, the smoke, noise, speed and sheer size of the engines and trains forever changed the areas through which they ran.

In addition to the visual, auditory and psychological impact of the railroads themselves, the new form of transportation altered land use. Railroads freed entrepreneurs from having to locate warehouses, businesses and, most important, factories near the water. Cleveland expanded significantly as new enterprises were sited away from the more expensive real estate of the center city.

By the turn of the century, industrial areas had grown up along the rails at West 117th Street; all along the route of the Cleveland and Pittsburgh (later the Pennsylvania) Railroad on its way through to the southeast; and along the eastern lakefront, with the section from East 20th Street to Gordon Park lined with one factory after another taking advantage of the major rail lines to Chicago and New York. Industrial complexes employing the latest production technologies of the day stood on land where scarcely a generation earlier, farmers had sown and harvested their crops, with draft animals providing the only power. The factories that replaced this slow-paced rural life engendered noise, smoke and activity on a scale far surpassing that of the trains, which brought in raw materials and carried away manufactured products.

There was in fact a symbiotic relationship between the railroads and the goods they transported and the factories they served. It centered around iron, and later, steel. Cleveland's iron and steel industry developed in large part to meet the transportation sector's needs. The area's earliest factory and the first to use steam power, the Cuyahoga Steam Furnace Company, was established in 1827 on the west bank of the Cuyahoga River. The company used local iron ore, smelted at a site in what is now Westlake, to make gearing for grist and saw mills, as well as farm implements. By the 1840s, however, its main product was steam engines, initially stationary engines to power mills, but soon engines for the growing number of steamboats on the lakes, including the *Emigrant*, the first Cleveland-built steam propeller.

In 1849 Cuyahoga Steam Furnace began to construct steam locomotives, the first plant west of the Appalachians to do so. It built many of the locomotives used by regional railroads.

The Cleveland Rolling
Mill Company was
Cleveland's largest
employer in the
1890s, with more
than 8,000 workers.
*Western Reserve
Historical Society*

Eventually it would become a component of the American Shipbuilding Company. William Castle, a Vermont native who joined the Cuyahoga Steam Furnace Company as an accountant in 1843, became the firm's manager in 1859, overseeing its growth as a producer of railroad iron and a manufacturer of parts for lake freighters during the next decade. Meanwhile, Castle served as Ohio City's last mayor in 1853-4, and then, after annexation, was elected for a term as mayor of Cleveland.

Thanks to Henry Chisholm and David and John Jones, rails as well as locomotives were being produced locally by the end of the 1850s. At the beginning of the decade, Alfred Kelley had imported rail iron from Wales. Now, Welsh and Scottish immigrants had set up an iron mill in Newburgh, manned largely by natives of the British Isles. Under Chisholm's guidance, the mill took local iron production a step further. By 1861 it had constructed the first blast furnace in Cleveland to produce pig iron.

Brown hoists like these
were used to unload ore
freighters beginning in
the 1880s. Workmen
filled tubs with ore that
the machinery then
delivered to the docks.
*Western Reserve
Historical Society*

Realizing that steel was a far superior material for rails and other railroad-related applications, Chisholm and his ironmasters began investigating the Bessemer process for mass-producing steel, patented in England a few years earlier. In 1868 the Cleveland Rolling Mill began operating the first Bessemer converters west of the Appalachians; two men were brought over from England to supervise the process. By the 1880s the plant employed over 8,000 workers.

Chisholm and his partners were not alone in the field. For example, in 1852 William Otis and John Ford started a company to forge axles for railroad cars and steamship drive shafts. Their Lake Erie Iron Works was located in Ohio City, close enough to conveniently supply these products to the Cuyahoga Steam Furnace Company. On the lakeshore, at what is now East 38th Street, the Forest City Iron Company began producing boiler plate in 1855. Nearby, in 1873, Charles Otis, William's son, established the Otis Iron and Steel Company, a firm that pioneered the production of open-hearth steel in the United States. Its chief engineer, Samuel Wellman, would go on to invent a large number of devices for use in the steel industry, including chargers for the open-hearth furnaces that were used around the world. With his brother, Charles, and John Seaver, he founded the Wellman-Seaver Engineering Company, later Wellman-Seaver-Morgan, which designed steel mills and produced industrial equipment.

Ultimately, however, it was geography and geology that drove Cleveland's industrial development. In the 18th century, soldiers, politicians and land speculators had recognized the strategic and commercial advantages of the site at the Cuyahoga's mouth. But they could not have foreseen the iron- and steel-based industrial expansion that would take place in the second half of the 19th century, nor how perfectly situated Cleveland was to participate in that expansion. It was not until the 1840s that people became fully aware of the geological resources accessible to the city.

George Hulett invented the Hulett unloader, a device with a cantilevered arm and bucket for unloading iron ore and coal from lake vessels. Previously, 100 men worked 12 hours to unload 5,000 tons of ore, but four Huletts could unload 10,000 tons in less than five hours, requiring only 25 men. *Great Lakes Historical Society, Vermilion, Ohio*

In that decade, copper, silver and iron deposits were discovered in the remote country around Lake Superior in Upper Michigan. Clevelanders were quick to follow up on the news, and two of the city's foremost scientific men played leading roles in exploring the region and publicizing its mineral riches. The versatile Charles Whittlesey went to Lake Superior in 1845, soon after first word of the discoveries leaked out, and then made a mineral survey of the entire area for the U.S. government in 1847-51. In 1846 Glasgow-born John Lang Cassels explored the Superior ranges and claimed the "Cleveland Mountain" iron ore deposits for a group of Cleveland investors. Like Whittlesey, Cassels was a man of wide-ranging interests and activities, a chemist and physician who helped establish the area's first medical schools, as well as a geologist.

The discovery and exploration of the mineral deposits created nationwide interest, which initially centered on copper and silver, but soon focused on the incredibly vast deposits of iron. Although less glamorous than the California Gold Rush that began in 1848, the exploitation of the Lake Superior iron ranges had a much wider and longer-lasting impact, setting the United States on its way to becoming the world's greatest industrial power. Certainly it had an enormous impact on Cleveland.

The city received its first shipment of iron ore, six barrels carried in the hold of the schooner *Baltimore*, in 1852. The opening of the Sault St. Marie Canal between Lakes Superior and Huron in 1855 made the shipment of iron ore from the Superior ranges much easier and more economical. In August 1855 the brigantine *Columbia* docked at Cleveland with 132 tons of ore aboard, the first shipment of iron ore to pass through the new canal. The mass production of iron, however, depended not only on iron ore but also on limestone and abundant supplies of coal to stoke the blast furnaces. Again, Cleveland's location was favorable. Large coal deposits in the Mahoning Valley and the Massilon area to the south could be shipped north, at first by canal and then increasingly by railroad as the Cleveland and Pittsburgh and Cleveland and Mahoning lines were completed. The amount of coal coming into Cleveland increased dramatically. Limestone was also quarried nearby, notably in western Ohio.

Enterprising citizens such as Samuel Livingston Mather recognized the business opportunity the Superior ore deposits offered and soon began to purchase land for iron mines. The iron ore shipped on the *Columbia* belonged to the Cleveland Iron Mining Company, which Mather had helped found in 1850. Mather's company was one of the first to work the rich deposits of the Marquette Range. Eventually it would merge with the Iron Cliffs Company to form Cleveland-Cliffs Iron Company and put together its own transportation system consisting of railroads linking the mines with Lake Superior and a fleet of ore carriers to bring the iron to Cleveland. Later, the Cleveland-based Pickands Mather and Company, M. A. Hanna Company, and Oglebay Norton Company would also mine and transport the iron and coal that fed the city's industries.

In 1880, 750,000 tons of iron ore arrived in Cleveland. Six years later the total rose to 1 million tons. Such huge quantities had an equally huge impact on Cleveland's transportation and industrial development. Wooden schooners could no longer efficiently handle the traffic, so Cleveland's shipbuilders responded with a new type of carrier. The *R. J. Hackett*, a 211-foot, wooden, propeller-driven ship, was the first vessel built specifically for the iron ore trade. It had its pilothouse at the bow, still common practice for lake carriers. Peck and Masters constructed it in their yards along the Cuyahoga. In 1882 the Globe Iron Works launched an iron-hulled ship, the *Onoko*, a prototype of the ore carriers to come. In 1886 they built and launched the first steel-hulled bulk carrier on the lakes, the *Spokane*.

The new iron and steel boats were built from the iron and steel produced in Cleveland. Most were bought by the great ore houses for their own fleets. The Mathers, Hannas, Oglebays and Nortons of Cleveland not only operated mines, but also owned and managed some of the largest marine fleets in the country by the turn of the century. Cleveland became the center of the Great Lakes maritime industry, with 80 percent of the ore boats on the lakes controlled by Cleveland companies.

Arriving in port, the ore carriers had to be unloaded so the ore could be transferred to mills in Cleveland or elsewhere. Initially the work was done by hand. A worker pushed a wheelbarrow up a plank from the dock to the ship's deck and then rolled it down a plank to the hold. Someone filled the barrow. It was then pushed back up, out and down, and emptied. Workers repeated this process a barrow at a time until the ship was empty. It was grueling, inefficient and slow. It could take nearly a week to unload a single ship. Local legend has it that barbers refused to trim the beards of the mostly Irish force of "Terriers" who did the work, for fear of ruining their fine scissors on the iron ore dust embedded in the men's whiskers.

The Cleveland Ship Building Company was building ships in the 1890s. It was the forerunner of the American Shipbuilding Company, which was the largest shipbuilding firm on the Great Lakes by the 1950s. *Western Reserve Historical Society*

Steelmaking was rigorous physical work, performed in difficult conditions. This work crew at Otis Steel in 1938 suggests some of the conditions faced by workers in the region's steel mills. *Western Reserve Historical Society*

Clevelander George Hulett invented the Hulett ore unloaders shown here, in 1898.
Huletts could completely unload a ship in 13 hours — a task that had once taken nearly a week.
Cleveland Press Collection, Cleveland State University

After 1867, portable steam engines were used to speed up the task by hoisting buckets of material from the hold to the deck. By the 1870s a 400-ton cargo could be unloaded in a day. Then in 1880 Cleveland native Alexander Brown invented the Brown hoist, a mechanical device that allowed ore to be moved by machinery out of the hold directly to a dock or railroad car. Someone still had to fill the hoist's bucket when it was in the ship's hold. A further improved method appeared at century's end when another Clevelander, George Hulett, invented an electrically powered unloader that almost totally eliminated shovel work. The Hulett unloader's cantilevered arm could empty a carrier in 13 hours, removing 17 tons with each bite of its large buckets.

Huletts were used not only in Cleveland but in ports throughout the lower Great Lakes. Hulett eventually became an executive at Wellman-Seaver-Morgan, which manufactured the unloaders. Cleveland factories also built Brown hoists and many other types of machinery and major equipment used in the city's and the nation's docks, shipyards and steel mills. In the process, they consumed ever-larger quantities of iron and steel, creating a self-perpetuating cycle of increase.

By the eve of the Civil War, the elements for Cleveland's industrial revolution had come together. Coal

fields had opened up in Ohio, and iron ore was being mined around Lake Superior. Railroad connections east, west and south offered swift, year-round transport for raw materials and finished products. The Ohio & Erie Canal was all but obsolete. Beginning in the 1850s, first passenger and then freight traffic declined steadily. In 1850 canal tolls collected at Cleveland amounted to $90,874.20; by 1860 the figure had dropped to $16,156.99, partly due to decreased traffic and partly because toll rates had been lowered in a vain attempt to compete with railroads. The state began leasing Ohio's canals in the 1860s, and the system was allowed to deteriorate. The canal era had lasted for only two decades, but it had brought commercial

By the 1870s the Cuyahoga River at the Columbus bend found dozens of ships loading and unloading cargo along the flats, which were also connected via train to the nation's economy. The smoky haze of dozens of manufacturers reassured the city's growing population of their industry's health and pointed to a bright future.
Western Reserve Historical Society

The Wellman-Seaver-Morgan Company of Cleveland built many Huletts. At one time there were 77 of the giant machines in Great Lakes ports and 14 in Cleveland.
Great Lakes Historical Society, Vermilion, Ohio

prosperity to Cleveland. The money made during those years provided the necessary basis for investment in mines, factories and railroads, fueling the city's industrial takeoff.

The central event of 19th-century American history, the Civil War, did not change Cleveland's destiny. It did give an extra push to economic and industrial development, boosting the city's garment industry and the production of railroad iron in particular. John D. Rockefeller by now had his own commission partnership, which handled foodstuffs, and it also profited substantially during the war. Meanwhile the number of oil refineries in the city was growing substantially, and in 1863 Rockefeller entered the business.

Another cutting-edge venture of the day, telegraphy, marked a milestone in 1861 when the first transcontinental line opened. The first coast-to-coast message was sent by the chief justice of California to President Abraham Lincoln, reiterating the state's loyalty to the union. Communication could now travel instantaneously by wire, outstripping even the railroad in speed. Telegraphy in fact became vital to the safe and efficient operation of railroads. It gave train operators the ability to learn, at any particular moment, where trains were along hundreds of miles of track and thus plan where they might safely meet or overtake one another at siding or passing tracks.

A key figure in developing a nationwide network of telegraph lines was Jeptha Homer Wade, who had helped wire Cleveland to Buffalo, Detroit, Chicago and Cincinnati, as well as the iron ore district, by 1850. In 1856, Wade, as general agent for the Western Union Telegraph Company, into which his lines had been consolidated, moved permanently to Cleveland where he served as director of several railroad companies and invested in the Cleveland Rolling Mill.

Although less and less of a New England town with every passing year, Cleveland still had cultural ties to the northeast. Antislavery sentiment was strong in the city, and in the 1860 presidential election, Lincoln commanded a substantial majority of Cleveland's votes. Traveling by rail to Washington for his inauguration in February 1861, Lincoln stopped in Cleveland, arriving at Euclid Street Station to an enthusiastic welcome as local military units, public officials and workers from the city's shops and factories escorted him to the Weddell House on Superior Street.

The Standard Oil Company's Number 1 Refinery was founded by John D. Rockefeller in Cleveland in 1889. Following the Civil War, Cleveland became the center of the petroleum industry.
Western Reserve Historical Society

Following secession and declaration of war, even those Clevelanders who had voted against Lincoln rallied to the Union cause. About 10,000 men from Cuyahoga County, or two-thirds of those eligible, served in the military for at least part of the conflict. The new railroads sped them away from home, toward camps and the battlefields from which 1,700 would not return alive.

During the conflict and immediately after, the Cleveland community focused its philanthropic and voluntary efforts on wartime needs. The U.S. government had neither the ability nor the resources to outfit such a large force of civilians-turned-soldiers, and later to cope with the casualties of war. Private organizations stepped in to fill the breach. In Cleveland a group of church-women, headed by Rebecca Rouse, began their work five days after President Lincoln called the nation to arms. Their organization developed into the Soldiers' Aid Society of Northern Ohio, a pioneer branch of the U.S. Sanitary Commission (a precursor of the American Red Cross). They collected donations to supply clothing, food and medical materials to troops in Cleveland and in the field. They also cared for the sick and wounded and raised enough money to set up both a hospital

and a Soldiers' Home next to the city's Union Depot. The hospital received serious cases immediately off the trains, and the home provided lodging and meals for soldier's in transit.

Railroads brought the dead as well as the wounded home to Cleveland. And on a rainy day in April 1865, Abraham Lincoln's train again stopped in the city. This was the assassinated president's funeral train, carrying his body back to Illinois. Ninety thousand Clevelanders lined up to pay their respects at the catafalque set up on Public Square.

Following the war, life in Cleveland, as in the rest of the nation, gradually returned to normal. For three more years the Soldiers' Aid Society continued in operation, helping veterans process claims and find employment, and then in 1868 disbanded, its work done. The need for philanthropy was increasing, rather than diminishing, however, and in the postwar decades numerous agencies sprang up to deal with the problems faced by people living in an increasingly complex and crowded industrial city.

The jobs created by economic expansion and industrialization attracted new seekers of opportunity to Cleveland: young men and women from small towns and farms, eager to make their fortunes or at least get a taste of city life; and also, increasingly, migrants from Europe, lured across the ocean to America by tales of streets paved with gold. Steamships and locomotives brought them here, perhaps to work in factories that produced screw propellers, boilerplate or iron rails.

M.A. Hanna and Company, Brown Hoisting Machinery Company, Wellman-Seaver-Morgan, the Cleveland and Pittsburgh Railroad, Cleveland Shipbuilding — these and hundreds of other companies made up industrial Cleveland at the end of the 19th century. Several factors had come together to create this critical mass of manufacturing capability: the city's location in the center of the United States' eastern industrial market; its proximity to abundant natural resources; the transportation nexus that Cleveland industries had helped build; the entrepreneurial

and inventive skills of native or transplanted Clevelanders; and, not least important, the people who made up the city's burgeoning work force.

In 1860, 374 men worked in bar and sheet iron businesses in Cleveland. By 1884, 14,000 worked in iron and steel and related industries. Thousands of others worked on the ships, railroads and docks of Cleveland, and many more sold the groceries, brewed the beer, sewed the clothes and built the furniture to fill the needs of the city's growing population. The same transportation system that brought together raw materials to supply the city's industries also served to bring together, on the shore of an American inland sea, a global work force, both literally and figuratively changing the face of Cleveland.

C. B. Wons.

Grasselli and other chemical makers provided jobs to hundreds of immigrant workers such as those shown in this photograph from 1885.
In 1928 Grasselli Chemical Co. consolidated with the E.I. DuPont de Nemours Company.

Western Reserve Historical Society

chapter five

Local Connections for an International Population: Transportation, Travel Brokers and Neighborhoods

In 1866 a new union depot replaced the old station so many

soldiers had passed through during the recent war. Located on the

lakefront between Bank (West 6th) and Water (West 9th) streets and

built of sandstone quarried in nearby Berea, the new depot was the

largest building under a single roof in the nation when it opened,

thanks to the use of fabricated iron for roof supports and other structural

elements. The building's design took full advantage of, in the words of

urban historian Edmund Chapman, "the possibilities of the new materials

which accompanied industrialization."

Three hundred guests attended the dedication banquet on November 10, enjoying a menu that included over 100 items, ranging from fine wines to wild turkey, squirrel and bear meat. Amasa Stone, John H. Devereux, Henry B. Payne and L. M. Hubby, all current or past presidents of local railroads, delivered speeches. An architectural flourish on the depot building paid tribute to (and whether intentionally or not, made a pun on the name of) Stone, the most prominent of the group. His likeness, carved in sandstone, overlooked the eight tracks on the east side of the 603-foot-long trainshed.

The stone face would look down over a kaleidoscope of activity in the years to come. Within two decades it, along with the rest of the depot's exterior, had turned a grimy black from the smoke of countless railroad engines and nearby factories. It would observe a greatly increased volume of traffic coming through Cleveland on the lakefront lines, so that within less than two decades the depot was no longer adequate. Eventually, it would see a later generation of Cleveland's sons go off to fight in another war, this time on distant soil — but in the meantime it saw, above all else, hundreds of thousands of immigrants and migrants arrive in Cleveland to find work and build new lives.

One of those immigrants was a Czech, Frank Vlchek. An 18-year-old blacksmith, Vlchek left his home in Budyn, Bohemia, to come to Cleveland in 1889. His sister and brother-in-law already lived in the city. Vlchek traveled from the family cottage to the nearest railroad station by wagon. The train took Frank and two companions to Berlin. There they transferred to a special emigrant train

bound for Bremen, where they then waited in an emigrant hotel until their ship was ready to sail. Including a stop at Southampton, England, the voyage to New York took eight days.

Almost immediately, Vlchek caught a train for Cleveland. The last leg of the trip would take about 24 hours:

Our carriage was better than third class in Austria: in one corner there was a round stove and in a corner at the other end of the car stood a barrel of ice-water. The seats were comfortable, but too short to sleep on.... I was the only Bohemian in my car. It was jammed; among others there were four families from Hungary, with many children. The men had black mustaches, so long that they could have wound them round their ears easily. The women were small and plump, three young girls wore kerchiefs on their heads, which they tied in a knot under the chin. Several men took off their shoes and walked about barefoot; the stench in the carriage was very unpleasant.

The young blacksmith arrived at the union depot where he was greeted by his sister and brother-in-law. Most likely he was met and "counted" by a police officer at the

station. Since 1874, the city's police department had stationed special "emigrant officers" at the depot to tally and also assist the increasing number of foreign immigrants arriving in Cleveland. In 1889 the police counted 661 Bohemians, along with 4,000 individuals from 13 other places of origin. Had Vlchek's sister not met him, the officers would have helped him find his way to her home.

The Haymarket neighborhood began as a marketplace in the 1830s and later housed waves of immigrants. Shown here in the 1930s, the Haymarket covered about 4 acres near where Jacob's Field now stands. *Western Reserve Historical Society*

European immigrants between the 1880s and 1920 traveled on steamships, such as those advertised by the Hamburg American Line on these 1914 handbills in Hungarian and English. *Western Reserve Historical Society*

The lakefront depot was only one of several places that newcomers to Cleveland disembarked in the late 19th and early 20th centuries. Others got off the trains at the Erie, Wheeling and Lake Erie, or Baltimore and Ohio Railroad depots in the Flats, or at the "suburban" stations in Newburgh, in the Glenville district or on Willson Avenue (East 55th Street). Still others came not by train but by lake steamer. Steamers connected Cleveland to Buffalo, Erie and Detroit as well as to nearby vacation resorts, such as Cedar Point in Erie County. No immigrants came by canal, for by the post-Civil War era the comfortable but slow canal packets were a thing of the past.

Whether they were getting off a boat, train or wagon, immigrants arriving in Cleveland had reached the end point of a remarkable global transportation system. Just as the railroads, bulk carriers and Huletts efficiently moved millions of tons of ore and coal to Cleveland's factories, this human transport system moved millions of immigrants, largely from Europe, to the industrial cities of America during the years between the Civil and First World wars.

The system's key component was the transoceanic steamship and the competing steamship lines that evolved during these years. They included North German Lloyd and Hamburg America (German), White Star and Cunard (British), Compagnie Generale Transatlantique (French), Holland America and a variety of others. Each hoped to profit from this vast movement of people. Eventually their ships would transport over 20 million immigrants to the United States in the years before World War I. In their quest for market share, the various lines built ever larger and faster ships, improved accommodations in steerage, the class in which most immigrants traveled, and established

a network of ticket agents throughout Europe and the United States.

The agents sold not only passage on one of the line's ships, but also the tickets for rail connections in both Europe and America. Tickets could be bought in Europe or by someone in America for a relative coming from Europe. Agents also forwarded money for passage by issuing money orders. It was a highly organized system. Port cities such as Bremen and Hamburg thrived on the immigrant trade. In Bremen, for example, hotels, some run by the steamship company, existed specifically to accommodate immigrants until it was time for their boat to sail. At that point all passengers for a particular boat boarded a special train that took them to the harbor, Bremerhaven, where they got off and took small tenders out to board the vessel on which they would travel to America. Frank Vlchek's journey illustrates just how well the system worked. He traveled from a rural Czech village to Cleveland in a little under two weeks with no real problems along the way.

The steamship agents were precursors to today's travel agents. Cleveland directories listed a dozen to 20 agencies throughout the late 19th and early 20th centuries. More individuals not listed as agents sold tickets on the side while running other businesses such as groceries or saloons. Some agencies specialized in arranging trips for Americans to Europe or other destinations. For example, the Collvers agency helped many wealthy Cleveland families make arrangements for their "grand tour" of Europe in the late 1800s and early 1900s. It was on such a tour with his father, Randall, during the 1870s that young Jeptha Wade II, grandson of the telegraph pioneer, developed an interest in art. Eventually, he would be one of the incorporators of the Cleveland Museum of Art, donating collections and substantial funds to enhance its holdings.

For all but a few Americans, however, travel abroad was an expensive luxury far beyond their means, and most steamship agents catered to the immigrant trade. Generally, an agent was himself an immigrant and specialized in making arrangements for members of his own ethnic group, out of an office located in an immigrant neighborhood. Steamship agencies in Cleveland had names like Scepessy, Perczel, Bonelli, Akers and Folkman, Spira and Kniola, and were patronized by Hungarians, Italians, eastern European Jews and Poles, respectively.

Born in Poland in 1859, Michael Kniola was prominent in Cleveland's Polish community. Kniola provided economic services to recent immigrants and arranged steamship passages, organizing the Kniola Travel Bureau in 1890.
Western Reserve Historical Society

Immigrant women and children in front of Hiram House, a social settlement located at East 27th and Orange Avenue, c. 1915
Western Reserve Historical Society

Michael Kniola, a native of what is now Poland, came to Cleveland in 1880 after living for a few years in New Jersey. Like many Poles, he took a job at the Cleveland Rolling Mill. It is possible that he participated in the march to dedicate Henry Chisholm's monument. Whatever his feelings toward Chisholm, he had no intention of spending a lifetime in the mills. He studied English at night and saved money until, with the aid of his wife Anna, he was able to open a grocery store on Tod Avenue (East 65th Street) in the heart of the neighborhood Cleveland Poles called Warszawa. Soon he began to deal in money orders to Poland and "shifkarte," as steamship tickets were known in many ethnic communities. By 1890 he had sold the grocery to concentrate on travel brokerage.

Kniola had chosen a good time to enter the business, which was becoming more lucrative as the chain of immigration grew. People already in Cleveland would write letters home convincing relatives to come, who would in their turn persuade still more relatives and friends to make the journey. So long as economic times were good and Cleveland's industries were expanding, the prospects for immigration seemed endless. Moreover, many European migrants were so-called "birds of passage" rather than permanent immigrants. At least initially, they had no intention of settling in America, but came only to earn a certain sum of money before returning to their homelands.

Brokers therefore booked passage from Cleveland back to Europe as well as vice versa. Most of the temporary migrants were single men, bachelors or husbands and fathers who had left their families behind. If they decided to stay in America after all, there was more business for the travel agent in bringing over wives, children and fiancées.

Although they did not accumulate wealth on anywhere near the scale that industrialists like Henry Chisholm or Jeptha Wade did, Kniola and his fellow brokers generally became comfortably well-off and, more important, respected figures in their own communities. They were the men who could deal with the complexities of modern travel and, through the miracle of telegraphy, send money to the family back home, or arrange to bring a brother, son or wife

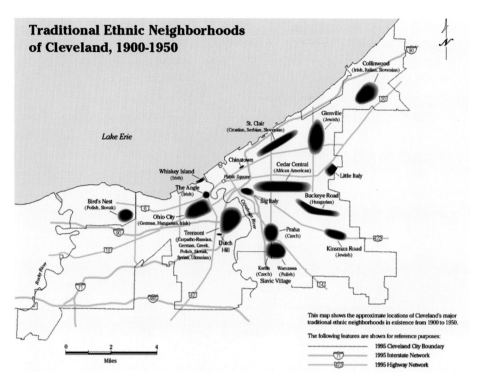

Traditional Ethnic Neighborhoods of Cleveland, 1900-1950

asked me to write to you and state the case, and to find out if you would permit the boy to come and stay with his parents. They are willing to do about anything and put up security if that would be necessary that he never in his life would become a public charge that they would also get some one in Europe to come along with him and bring him safely to the United States.

Your honorable body can no doubt appreciate the helpless condition the child is left in and the feelings of the parents on this side under the circumstances, especially as the parents are well able to care for him. The mother has been calling on me very frequently and requesting that I assist them in getting the child to this country. The helpless condition of the child is a constant worry to her which can only be relieved by having the child sent over here, and I am sure under the circumstance it would be a very charitable act.

Hoping you will give the matter your most favorable consideration, and thanking you in advance for any favorable conclusion you may come to I remain,

Yours Truly,
M. P. Kniola

halfway around the world to Cleveland. They had the linguistic skills and business know-how to deal with government officials or the "big people" in charge at North German Lloyd or the Baltimore and Ohio Railroad. The travel broker was the man who could sort out problems such as lost luggage or someone held up at the immigration inspection station. Kniola, for example, did not hesitate to contact the most important officials:

Jan. 17, 1902
Emigrant Commissioner
Ellis Island, N.Y.

Gentlemen:
There is a family by the name of Koslowski living in Cleveland, Ohio, for about nine years. They have one son in Europe about 12 years old, who was taken very sick a few years ago and lost his eyesight. This boy was left in Europe with his grandmother but a short time ago the old lady died and the helpless child is left there among strangers and has no [one] to take care of him. The parents are worrying very much about the boy, and would like to know if they could get him to come here to America to live with them. They have

Kniola's efforts elicited a response. Though bureaucratically noncommittal, the commissioner held out the hope that the child could enter the United States provided he had not been afflicted with the eye disease trachoma and that his family could guarantee his support.

Cleveland had, in fact, always been a city of migrants, with the majority of its population coming from other places. The city's first Cleveland-born mayor, William Case, was not elected until 1850. The earlier migrants had come mostly from elsewhere in the United States. By the time Case became mayor, immigrants from abroad, many of them Irish or German, had arrived in significant numbers, joining the American migrants and their Cleveland-born children. In the 1850s, Czechs began to arrive. Like the Germans or the British ironworkers, they were predominantly skilled artisans and craftsmen. They were also Cleveland's first Slavic group.

Following the Civil War the pace of immigration accelerated. As the century went on, and Cleveland's growing number of factories incorporated new technologies into their manufacturing processes, there was no longer a premium on skilled craftsmen. Most of the immigrants who came to the city during the late 19th and early 20th centuries worked as unskilled or semi-skilled industrial laborers. The pay, although low, was much better than what they could earn in Europe, and for that reason they endured the drudgery and danger of work in the mills, described thus by a Polish immigrant: "Great red-hot furnaces were standing in a row and next to each of them, there was a big hammer....When everybody started hammering, the noise was so great all day long... the red-hot bars of steel were pulled out of the furnaces by means of iron pincers."

At Cleveland Rolling Mill, second-generation steelman William Chisholm took over after his father's death. He did not have the elder Chisholm's talent in handling men. Ironically, two years before they had marched to Lake View Cemetery to memorialize the father, Rolling Mill workers had gone on strike against his son's management, demanding a union shop and union-set wage scale. Chisholm locked out the strikers, skilled men whose numbers included mostly British and Irish but also some Czech workers, and replaced them with unskilled laborers, mostly Poles and Czechs newly arrived in Cleveland. When Chisholm cut wages in 1885, the former strikebreakers themselves walked off the job. Even on a day-to-day basis, provided economic times were good and demand for workers high,

immigrants voted with their feet, changing jobs whenever there was a chance at a better wage.

In this way, some immigrants were able to save enough money to leave their factory jobs and become entrepreneurs. Travel agencies, groceries, saloons and other small businesses sprang up along the streets of the growing number of ethnic neighborhoods in Cleveland. These businesses required little start-up capital, and were usually housed in modest frame buildings, with the owner's family often living above or behind the shop. Along with churches or synagogues and meeting halls, they provided a focal point for the surrounding residential district. The ethnic neighborhoods were the paradox of the immigration experience. Having been carried thousands of miles by the latest transportation technology, many new

Butchers cut and dress meat in the cutting room of the Earl H. Gibbs Packing House at the Cleveland Union Stockyards in 1941. *Cleveland Press Collection, Cleveland State University*

Slovenian, Croatian and German women operate drill presses at the Cleveland Hardware Company in 1917. *Cleveland Press Collection, Cleveland State University*

A band of musical German immigrants — many of whom were probably skilled workers — pose outside their local tavern in the 1890s.
Western Reserve Historical Society

Clevelanders were now largely immobile. They lived in a walking world where the most important transportation technician was the cobbler.

For almost all of the 19th century, most immigrants and migrants to Cleveland had to live where they could walk to work. This, in combination with the chain of immigration, led to the concentration of people of one ethnic background or another in particular areas. Pioneering migrants would find jobs at a certain factory and then encourage others of their group to come and work for the same employer. Often they used their influence with a foreman or boss to get a brother or cousin a job. New arrivals lived with earlier arrivals, sometimes in boardinghouses run by immigrant wives.

The chain of immigration built neighborhoods of Hungarians around the plants that Cleveland Hardware and Eberhard Manufacturing had established along the Cleveland and Pittsburgh Railroad on lower Buckeye Road. Slovaks settled near the National Carbon Company plant at West 117th Street and Madison in Birdtown, a company development with side streets named Robin, Thrush, Quail and Plover. Poles accumulated in the area west of the Cleveland Rolling Mill while Slovenians built a neighborhood to the mill's

east side. Jews, Italians and later Greeks, Syrians and Lebanese lived near the produce and wholesale markets at the city's center where many of their number worked. Each neighborhood had such an economic nucleus, around which people and institutions gathered. The nucleus was in many instances a factory recently built on relatively inexpensive real estate along the railroad lines radiating out from central Cleveland. Rail lines also usually defined one of the borders of an ethnic community, with ravines and streets making up the remaining boundaries.

Since the immigrant settlements were located in newly developing areas, they initially had a semi-rural character, not so different from the way central Cleveland had looked in the 1810s and 20s. A collection of European rather than New

An Italian café along Woodland Avenue in the early 20th century reminded Italian immigrants of their homeland. *Western Reserve Historical Society*

Woodland Avenue was a melting pot of immigrants and migrants in the early 20th century. This grocer served Jewish immigrants from Eastern Europe. *Western Reserve Historical Society*

The Central Market dates from October 1856 but was destroyed by fire in 1949. Shown here in 1940, the Central Market was a hub of daily and weekly shopping activity for waves of migrants to Cleveland. *Cleveland Press Collection, Cleveland State University*

Vlchek described conditions in the Bohemian settlement along Broadway in 1889: "unpaved streets full of mud, no stone sidewalks." In the 1890s, a newer Polish neighborhood in the northeastern part of the city looked "pretty primitive; the streets have only just been laid out, and one wades ankle-deep in the alluvial sand or in the mud of the prairie."

Besides the mud on the streets, newcomers and visitors to Cleveland's immigrant settlements were also struck by their ethnic and linguistic apartness. "The extensive Hungarian quarter on the East Side is truly and clearly Hungarian. One can hardly hear another language spoken... Hungarian song can be heard in the streets, and newsvendors are shouting out the titles of Hungarian papers." Upon Vlchek's arrival in the Broadway neighborhood, he "everywhere... heard the Czech language." A Polish journalist visiting Cleveland's Polish districts remarked incredulously: "This is not America!" The immigrant neighborhoods were indeed insular, existing in part as voluntary cocoons that preserved culture. They eased the transition into an alien and often unfriendly society, which was as much of a wilderness to the new arrivals as the virgin forest along the banks of the Cuyahoga had been to the settlers from New England. But these neighborhoods also existed because it was impossible for workers to live elsewhere and commute to their jobs.

England villages was now forming around the outskirts of the city. After the turn of the century, these first neighborhoods grew crowded, as new immigrants continued to flood in and housing density was increased. But in the early years, residents typically lived in small wooden houses set on lots large enough for them to raise vegetables and poultry. Some even planted fruit trees and kept a cow or two. One of the city's Polish neighborhoods, known to its residents as "Krakow," was called "Goosetown" by outsiders. Hungarian immigrants could picnic or go berrying in woods and meadows adjacent to their east side neighborhood.

On the downside, city improvements were lacking. This was true of many Cleveland districts, but to men and women freshly arrived from the Old World, their new neighborhoods seemed crude and unfinished. Frank

Italian children played in the back yard of dilapidated housing along Lower Woodland Avenue —
the sort of residential neighborhoods into which so many new immigrants moved.
Western Reserve Historical Society

It was not that 19th-century Cleveland did not have any means of private or public urban transport. In the earliest years, this meant travel on horseback or in wagons

drawn by oxen. As the settlement grew and streets were extended and received rudimentary improvement, faster and more comfortable vehicles replaced the unsprung wagons. Those with wealth could afford a horse and carriage plus the stable, equipment, feed and, if desired, hired help necessary to maintain the outfit.

Horse-drawn public transportation also existed. In the 1850s, omnibuses, sometimes referred to as "urban stagecoaches," operated primarily to transfer travelers from railroad stations to hotels, but also carried local passengers. Teams of horses pulled large closed carriages along fixed routes several times daily, for a standard fare of up to 10 cents. Although some routes did extend as far as East Cleveland or the West Side, the omnibus had limited utility for longer distances because the city's unpaved streets were still bumpy, often muddy, and during snows nearly impassable.

Horse-drawn streetcars, which traveled on rails laid down in the road, offered a somewhat smoother ride and were less likely to get bogged down. As early as 1834 a horse-drawn car drawn along wooden rails hauled stone and other freight from a quarry in Newburgh to Doan's Corners, and then carried passengers between the Corners and Public Square via Euclid Avenue. Low ridership killed this pioneering street railway. Even a $50,000 subsidy from the county could not keep the line in operation after 1842.

Further population growth resulted in a revival of the streetcar by the 1860s. In 1860 two street railway lines owned by Harry S. Stevens, a former omnibus operator, opened for service. The East Cleveland line ran between Willson and Bank streets, mostly along Prospect. The Kinsman line also ran from Bank to Willson but used Kinsman and Woodland Avenue for much of the distance. Both lines opened in time for Clevelanders to use them to come downtown for the dedication of the Perry Monument. Within the next 16 years, another eight lines were established to serve the growing city.

The fare on Stevens' first streetcars was 5 cents. The driver stopped his team wherever passengers wanted to get on or off. Passengers sat on long benches in open-sided cars in the summer; in winter they rode in closed boxcars. Not all citizens supported street railways, objecting that they put pedestrians in danger and interfered with other traffic. To help quiet their fears, City Council set speed limits: five miles per hour on straightaways, a slow walk on curves. Although it would have been more logical for the East Cleveland line to use Euclid Avenue, it had to be

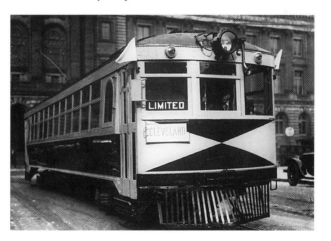

routed along Prospect between Erie (East 9th) and Willson streets. At this period, Euclid was Cleveland's most exclusive residential district, and its wealthy homeowners had enough influence to keep rails off their street until 1890.

All of the street railway lines and other forms of public transport that followed were until 1942 privately owned. Entrepreneurs would obtain franchises from City Council to lay rails on public streets and to operate the service on those routes. As the city grew and urban transport became a vital and lucrative business, the stakes on securing or

losing a franchise also grew. In Cleveland, as in other big cities, widespread bribery and corruption entered the politics of street railway franchising.

Although horse-drawn public transportation made it possible for modestly well-off Clevelanders to live farther from the city center, it did not enable many industrial workers to move to new neighborhoods. Horsecars were not only slow but expensive. Most workers rarely earned more than $400 per year in the period before World War I. A daily commute to and from work (assuming six working days per week and 50 weeks of work) would cost $30 per year. Most workers therefore used the cars only for special occasions.

Technological change eventually made public urban transport more efficient and democratic, and in addition more humane. Horses suffered carrying overfilled cars, particularly in the wintertime. They were also vulnerable to disease. During the "Epizootic" of 1872, a strain of equine influenza virtually immobilized local transportation for a month. Street railway operators began searching for more reliable ways to power their cars. Like San Francisco, Cleveland experimented with street railway lines on which cars were pulled by an underground cable connected to a central powerhouse. Two cablecar lines opened on Payne Avenue and Superior in 1890. The cars moved at 12 miles an hour, a marked improvement. The machinery was large and hard to maintain, however, and eventually the lines switched to an alternative system, in which electricity powered the cars rather than the cable.

Electrically powered streetcars first successfully operated in Cleveland in 1884. Within 15 years all of the

(Far left)
This interurban railway car, shown in 1920, ran between Cleveland, Lorain, Toledo and Detroit. In 1907 the Lakeshore Electric Railroad carried over 5 million passengers.
Western Reserve Historical Society

The Cleveland, Southwestern, & Columbus Railway, which was the second-largest interurban in the state at one time, connected Cleveland with Columbus to the south and Norwalk to the west. By the 1920s, the date of this photograph, the company was in a state of decline.
Western Reserve Historical Society

Although faster, the electric and cable systems were not necessarily cheaper than the horsecars. For many, they remained special-occasion-only transport. The owners knew this, and in order to generate traffic built attractions adjacent to their lines or ran new lines to existing attractions. In 1891 traction entrepreneur Frank Robison built League Park, Cleveland's professional baseball field, at East 66th Street and Lexington, along one of the cable lines he owned. Euclid Beach, the city's main amusement park, opened a few years later. Eight miles east of Public Square, it was accessible to most people only by streetcar.

The issue of the cost and availability of public urban transportation was of such importance that it engendered a political revolution in Cleveland. That revolution was led by an unlikely figure: Tom L. Johnson, a wealthy traction magnate. Johnson had become rich at an early age by running street railways, first in his native Kentucky and then in Indianapolis and soon, Cleveland. Despite a Santa Claus-like figure and a cherubic face, he knew all of the tricks regarding franchising and used that knowledge in battling his competitors, most notably Marcus Hanna, whose wealth came principally from coal and iron ore mining, but who had also invested heavily in urban traction. A routine railway commute between Indianapolis and Cleveland became Johnson's road to Damascus. During the trip he was sold a copy of Henry George's *Social Problems*, which he read from cover to cover. It converted him to the cause of social and political reform.

By the 1890s the former traction plutocrat was putting forth arguments that drew shocked and angry reactions from his fellows. He demanded, for instance, that services

lines were using the new mode of power. Although initial investments in power plants, poles, wires and cars were high, electric streetcars were fast, clean and efficient. They could also be very profitable. As the city grew in population — from 43,417 in 1860, to 261,353 in 1900 — it had to expand in size. It went from 7.325 square miles in 1860 to 34.34 in 1900. The numbers and the distances were attractive incentives to the "traction magnates" who owned the streetcar lines. They continued to compete for new franchises that would extend services to more distant areas, and to take over other companies. There were 22 different lines in Cleveland prior to 1893. In that year they consolidated into two massive private companies, The Cleveland Electric Railway Company, known locally as the "Big Con," and the Cleveland City Railway Company, or "Little Con."

such as urban transport and the provision of electricity be municipally rather than privately owned. Johnson ran for mayor of Cleveland in 1901, campaigning on a platform that included a 3-cent fare for public transit. The call met with immediate response from the public. Ordinary citizens who generally took little interest in politics and newly naturalized immigrants voting for the first time adopted Johnson as their champion. Elected that year, he spent four terms trying to achieve his goal. Through municipal leasing of the private railway system (now merged into a single company, inevitably nicknamed "ConCon"), he was able to implement the 3-cent fare in 1908. Full municipal ownership of the transit system did not come about until 1942.

In the meantime, through an arbitrated agreement known as the Tayler Grant, all transit services were given to a new franchise, the Cleveland Railway Company, which promised to provide services at cost and return a maximum of 6 percent to its stockholders. The new company succeeded in improving and extending service and making it more affordable than ever before. Within 10 years of its establishment in 1910, ridership jumped from 228 million to 450 million per year.

During this time the flood of European immigration had crested. Between 1900 and 1910 nearly 9 million new immigrants arrived in the United States. In the peak year of 1907 emigrant officers at Union Depot recorded over 17,000 new arrivals in Cleveland. The original ethnic neighborhoods could not contain so many people, even though houses were added to, divided and then subdivided to accommodate more families in cramped and often unsanitary conditions. Commercial and industrial development was also encroaching on residential areas in the inner ring of immigrant settlements.

Meanwhile, the first immigrants had gained a degree of financial security and were looking to move out away from the shadow of the factories. "I cannot remain here any longer," complained a Croatian clergyman living in the lakeshore industrial area just after the turn of the century. "Cleveland is always full of smoke gushing out of 2,500 factory chimneys in the city and forming a cloud. Since I have been here, the sky has not been clear over Cleveland for 24 hours at a time. Sometimes the atmosphere is so heavy that I can hardly breathe." The clergyman wanted to return to his homeland. But for most immigrants, a new neighborhood with cleaner, quieter, less crowded streets would be good enough.

Michael Kniola was an astute businessman. He had profited from the growing wave of immigration to Cleveland, first by arranging steamship passage, and then by brokering jobs with railways and steel mills for the new arrivals he brought to Cleveland. He ran a boarding house for those who had no place to stay. He also invested in property in and around the steel mills, selling lots to immigrants when they were ready to buy homes. In 1905 Kniola had listed himself in the city directory as a realtor, insurance agent and steamship agent. By 1910 he was listed only as a real estate agent and was promoting suburban development, banking on immigrants' desire to leave the factory neighborhoods. He

Elected to the first of his three terms as Cleveland Mayor in 1901, a portly Tom L. Johnson inspects the work of a city street repair crew in 1907.
Western Reserve Historical Society

Politician and Ohio leader Peter Witt was a consultant on mass transit for many cities. He served on Cleveland's City Council in the 1920s and twice ran unsuccessfully for mayor of Cleveland.
Western Reserve Historical Society

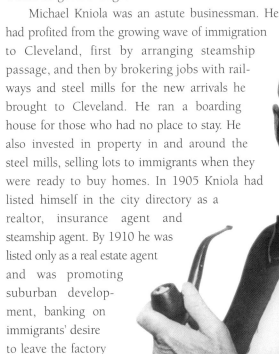

was first involved in selling property in the Corlett area, accessible via the new streetcar line along Broadway, and later promoted development of a "new Polish settlement" in Garfield Heights, again near a streetcar line.

Cleveland's system of electrified streetcars, operated by a private company under strict city regulation, made it possible for Polish immigrants to continue working in the Newburgh mills while buying their own homes in newer neighborhoods. This pattern was duplicated in immigrant settlements throughout the city. Slovenes, for example,

who had clustered around the Otis steel mills on St. Clair Avenue, began to move east to create new neighborhoods in Collinwood and Euclid. Jews moved out along Woodland and Kinsman Avenue with many commuting to jobs or businesses in the city by streetcar.

The outbreak of World War I would drastically reduce emigration from Europe. Real estate sales also slowed during the war years. Michael Kniola, looking for an alternative field in which to exercise his entrepreneurial skills, fixed on the American Puncture Proof Tire Company. He became the firm's vice president in 1917, casting in his lot with the latest in transportation technology, the automobile.

In first decades of the 20th century, the street railways were moving people quickly and efficiently within the city, while steam railroads took passengers as well as freight to destinations across the continent. Mass transit had given a greater number of Clevelanders greater mobility than ever before. The automobile would soon swing the balance back in favor of private transport, while playing a central role in the next phase of Cleveland's economic and social development.

In 1928 when this photo was taken, hopping on a streetcar required crossing a lane of traffic as streetcars, automobiles and pedestrians plied the narrow road.

Cleveland Press Collection, Cleveland State University

six chapter six

Rubber Tires and
a Revolution in the Making

Phillipston, Massachusetts, and Metzenseifen,

Hungary, are about 5,000 miles apart. Yet men from these two cities, who

met and combined their talents in Cleveland, helped initiate the next phase

of the transportation revolution. This came about through an unlikely

intermediate step: the sewing machine.

The sewing machine was patented in the United States in 1846 by

Elias Howe of Spencer, Massachusetts. In 1857 Thomas White of

Phillipston invented a small hand-operated machine. His "New

England Sewing Machine," selling at $10 a unit, proved popular. To

further increase sales, White needed to decrease shipping costs.

His plant in Templeton, Massachusetts, was too far from the growing markets of the Midwest. In 1866, he relocated to Cleveland where he could take advantage not only of location but of raw materials, including the iron and steel needed for the machines.

He also needed wooden cabinets in which he could house the machines attractively, so they might look less like a mechanical contraption and more like a piece of furniture in someone's sitting room or parlor. He found a source quite near his Canal Street plant in the Flats. The Theodor Kundtz Company on Elm Street produced fine cabinetry. Theodor Kundtz, who had learned woodworking from his father, had come to Cleveland from Metzenseifen in 1873. While White exemplified the New England heritage that had traditionally dominated the city, Kundtz was an early representative of the great wave of European immigrants that would swell Cleveland's population in the coming decades. Together, both men and their companies prospered. By 1886 White was producing 2,000 sewing machines a week, most of them housed in elegant and clever cabinets produced by Kundtz's factory.

Sewing machines were themselves a remarkable innovation. Sold to individuals and then to garment manufacturers, they changed the way clothing was made, spurring the development of the ready-to-wear industry at the same time as they revolutionized home sewing. The story goes that women's movement leaders Susan B. Anthony and Elizabeth Cady Stanton, on a train journey that took them across Ohio during the 1870s, noticed lights burning late into the night in many of the homes they passed. Women, having spent their daylight hours cleaning, cooking and tending children, were sitting up to sew their families' clothing, a stitch at a time. The suffragists decided to ally with manufacturers, including White, to promote both sewing machines and votes for America's hard-working women. Handbills appeared, printed on one side with a call for women's suffrage and on the other with a sewing machine advertisement.

The vote would have to wait. But sewing machines entered millions of American households during the mid-to-late 19th century, becoming the first widespread home appliance and ushering in the next century's consumer age.

As the White Sewing Machine Company continued to increase its sales, the founder's sons, Rollin and Windsor, convinced their father to diversify production. Using the plant's sophisticated metalworking equipment and the machining expertise of their employees, the Whites began to produce roller skates and bicycles by the 1880s. While skates were a recreational fad, bicycles had practical value as a means of personal transportation.

The bicycle craze in America began in earnest during the 1880s as the expensive and awkward "ordinary" bike, with its high front wheel, was replaced by the safety bicycle with two wheels of equal size. At first priced out of most people's reach, bicycles cost only $60 for some models by the early 1890s. They reached the peak of their popularity during that decade when an estimated 50,000 Clevelanders rode bicycles to work or for pleasure. For the middle class, they represented an affordable, efficient alternative to a horse or horse and carriage — there was no need for a stall, or for feeding, currying and cleaning. By the mid-1890s White was producing 10,000 bicycles per year with tires mounted on elaborately formed wooden rims manufactured by Kundtz.

While Thomas, patriarch of the business, countenanced his sons' interest in skates and bicycles, he refused to devote much time or production to their next enthusiasm, the automobile. They persisted, however. Practical automobiles had first appeared in Germany and France in the 1880s. The following decade some Americans began to take notice of what at first seemed only a toy. In 1895, nine of 22 vehicles entered in a Paris to Bordeaux race finished the 727-mile course, helping to convince Americans that motorcars had potential. And just as sewing machine and bicycle production had common features, bicycles and automobiles had similar components — for instance spoked wheels and steel frames. It was a logical step for a bicycle manufacturer to diversify into automotive production. Rollin White studied automobiles while attending Cornell in the late 1890s and then went to Europe to see at first hand the evolving industry on the continent. Although he had worked with Clevelander Walter Baker on an electric car, he became a firm believer in steam propulsion while there.

In 1900 the White Sewing Machine Company produced four steam-powered cars, each utilizing the special flash boiler (which allowed for the quick buildup of a head of steam) that Rollin invented. In 1901 the company produced

By the 1890s workers at the White Sewing Machine Company were building roller skates and bicycles as well as sewing machines. *Cleveland Press Collection, Cleveland State University*

Manufacturing work grew increasingly automated during the 20th century; a worker at the White Sewing Machine Company in the 1930s adjusts new machines on the testing line. *Western Reserve Historical Society*

193 cars for sale. By 1906, the year in which a separate White Motor Company split off from the parent organization to specialize in automobiles, annual production was 1,500 units. This was twice that of any other manufacturer in the world, according to the company's claims. The spoked wheels and much of the bodywork for these cars originated, of course, in the workshops of the Theodor Kundtz Company.

While Rollin White perfected his steam automobiles, other Clevelanders produced their own variants of the horseless carriage. In this era of experimentation, no one design or power source had been proven clearly superior, and Cleveland was a hotbed of automotive development. It had eager entrepreneurs, access to raw materials, skilled machinists and production traditions that allowed it to enter the new industry quickly. One of those traditions was carriage building, a more obvious precursor to automobile

Alexander Winton, the founder of the Winton Motor Carriage Company, can be seen steering his second experimental vehicle in 1897, the same year that Winton drove one of his cars to New York City.

Western Reserve Historical Society

manufacture than was sewing machine production. The first wagon and carriage builders were operating in Cleveland by the 1820s. By the end of the century over 50 firms produced hardware for, repaired or made wagons.

In 1895 Walter Baker, in company with Rollin White, John Grant and Phillip Dorn, started the American Ball Bearing Company to produce axles for horse-drawn vehicles. In 1898 Baker built his first electric automobile. It cost $850 and was advertised as "the Most Elegant Automobile Made." Within six years the company was building 400 units annually. Eventually Baker would merge his firm with a carriage-maker, Rauch and Lang, to produce electric automobiles under the name Baker-Raulang.

Neither Baker nor White could take credit for introducing automobile production to Cleveland, however. That honor belonged to Alexander Winton. Winton, a native of Scotland, came to Cleveland in 1884. He began building bicycles in 1891, using his own patented design. He stayed in the business for about 10 years, becoming enormously successful. However, he too fell under the spell of the automobile. Having worked on marine engines when he first came to the United States, he had a knowledge of motive power. He built his first car in 1896. Unlike those to be built by White and Baker, it was powered by an internal combustion gasoline engine. In March 1897 he incorporated the Winton Motor Carriage Company.

A born promoter, Winton drove one of his cars from Cleveland to New York City that summer in a trip that took nine days, or a little under 80 hours of actual driving. The publicity stimulated investment, and the company began producing a standard model in 1898. Up to this point, American companies had made cars to order. The sale of the first standard-model Winton in March 1898 "marked the beginning of the American automobile industry as a whole," in the words of historian of technology Darwin Stapleton. The car's price, $1,000, was high. However, another drive to New York, with a Cleveland *Plain Dealer* reporter along for the five-day ride, provided even greater proof of the Winton's quality. The stories from the road, syndicated in 30 newspapers, caught the nation's attention and are also said to have definitively established the French word "automobile" in the American vocabulary.

Winton, who was greeted by large crowds in New York, raised the price of his car to $2,000. Success was quick and enormous. His factory on Berea Road along the Cleveland to Chicago railroad tracks employed 1,500 by 1902. Three years later the company, which continued to introduce technical innovations in its cars, had sales branches in New York, London, Toronto and Honolulu. It had taken less than a decade for a new Cleveland-made product to go international.

Winton, Baker and White were only three of the more than 80 companies that built automobiles in Cleveland during the period 1896-1931. An edition of the *Cleveland Leader* promoting the city's first auto show in 1903 referred to Cleveland as "the leading automobile manufacturing city

The F. B. Stearns Company produced automobiles in Cleveland from 1898 until December 1929. In 1910, the year in which this Sedan was produced, the company manufactured over 1,000 cars. *Western Reserve Historical Society*

in the universe." Prior to 1904 and arguably up to 1908 Cleveland was at any rate the automotive capital of America, producing more cars annually than any other city. By 1909 automobile manufacturing had become the city's third-largest industry after iron and steel works and foundry and machine-shop production.

Despite this, in the first years of the 20th century relatively few automobiles competed with the estimated 10,000 horses, plus carriages, bicycles and trolleycars jockeying for space on Cleveland's streets. The first car seen in the city was reportedly an out-of-town vehicle that came through in 1894. In 1900 automobiles formed the centerpiece of a New Year's parade ushering in the new century. By 1901 there were approximately 150 automobiles in Cleveland. Despite the vehicle's potential, it was still basically a rich man's toy. The Cleveland Automobile Club was founded in 1900 by a group of men (including Baker, Winton and the Whites) described as owners of "self-propelled pleasure vehicles" in order to advance the "sport" of motoring. In 1902 the club began sponsoring auto races at the Glenville Race Track, a harness-racing track where wealthy Clevelanders had gathered to bet, socialize and show off their fastest horses since the 1870s.

The Cleveland Automobile Club was the nation's second automobile club and played a part in the founding of the American Automobile Association in 1901. By 1916 the Cleveland club had nearly 7,000 members to whom it provided information and other services. It also acted as an advocacy group to advance motorists' interests, for instance lobbying for better roads. The races and other competitions sponsored by the club helped attract the attention of the general public and increased the automobile's popularity. The growing number of cars on Cleveland's streets made speed limits necessary: 8 miles per hour in the city center, 15 in residential areas.

In 1900 Cleveland was America's seventh-largest city, with 381,768 people. It had grown more than twentyfold since 1850 when its population of 17,034 had ranked 37th in the nation.

Cleveland was now a major city and could not be run on a shoestring, as it had in the past when citizens used their own shovels to dig ditches and maintain the streets. Tom Johnson was mayor of Cleveland for most of the 20th century's first decade, and his administration and that of his disciple Newton D. Baker (mayor from 1912 to 1915) instituted numerous progressive reforms that led to increased organization and rationalization in all areas of civic life.

The 1903 "Group Plan" report, for example, proposed replacing a deteriorating area northeast of Public Square with a monumental grouping of public buildings centered on an open mall. Over the next decades, the Federal Building, Cuyahoga County Courthouse, Cleveland City Hall and additional public-purpose structures went up on the site, creating an imposing new civic center still in place at the beginning of the 21st century. In 1913 a City Planning Commission was appointed to oversee the city's streets, public works and public spaces, and to draw up a city plan. Johnson's long-held dream of a municipally owned electric plant came true in 1914 when the largest such plant in the nation began operating on Cleveland's lakefront.

Improvement of Cleveland's streets continued. In the 1880s bicyclists had begun campaigning for more paved roads, and now auto owners made the same demand. Brick or asphalt-paved mileage was gradually extended into residential and

The Winton Motor Carriage Company was a pioneer of the American automobile industry known for making cars like this 1899 buggy. The company was the first to sell a standard American-made, gasoline-powered automobile; its price was $1,000. *Western Reserve Historical Society*

outlying areas. Main arteries were widened, and additional street lighting installed. Also, beginning in the first decade of the 20th century, the city instituted systematic street-cleaning and refuse collection. Although most citizens and businessmen welcomed such improvements, they were less pleased when in 1906 the city's north-south streets were renamed according to a numeric system running east and west from Public Square. Old habits died hard, but the new system symbolized the Progressive-Era spirit of rationalizing reform in Cleveland.

Private as well as governmental agencies looked about for ways to organize the community more efficiently. In 1913 the newly formed Federation for Charity and Philanthropy held the city's first unified fund-raising drive, raising $126,735 during "Good Will Week." The Federation distributed the money among 55 separate charitable agencies, Catholic, Protestant, Jewish and nonsectarian alike. The well-organized campaign brought responses from a large number of small donors, benefiting the agencies; for their part, the donors could make a single contribution and know that it would go to legitimate charities examined and approved by the Federation. This unified system of fund-raising eventually developed into the United Way.

The business sector naturally joined in the quest for efficiency, with individual companies developing new

Created by Daniel Burnham, Arnold Brunner and John Carrere, the Group Plan Report of 1903 recommended the 500-foot-wide central mall and the placement of the seven major buildings surrounding it. *Western Reserve Historical Society*

mechanized manufacturing systems and setting up industrial research laboratories. One of the city's most innovative firms was a construction company, Samuel J. Austin & Son. Samuel Austin, trained as a carpenter in his native England, had come to Cleveland as a young man and set up his own contracting business in the 1870s, designing and building factory, residential and commercial buildings. In 1901 his son, Wilbert, an engineering graduate of Cleveland's Case Institute of Applied Sciences, joined the business, which was by now specializing in the construction of manufacturing plants.

The Austins were able to handle every aspect of factory design, engineering and construction for their clients. What came to be known as the Austin Method of "undivided

During the Depression, the Austin Company helped to build an automobile factory in the Soviet Union. The engineers and leaders of the trade mission are shown here in Gorky, the plant site, in the 1930s. *Austin Company Archives*

techniques in mass production, introducing the assembly line in 1913. Cleveland companies, on the other hand, generally concentrated on building well-styled, expensive cars that only a select few could afford. Almost overnight Detroit surpassed Cleveland as the nation's automotive capital. In 1914 Ford opened a branch assembly in Cleveland, with parts brought to the city by rail, and in 1922 General Motors established Cleveland's leading automobile factory, the Fisher Body plant. Alongside these branches of Detroit companies, Cleveland-based manufacturers continued to produce cars until 1931 when Peerless, the last survivor of a once promising local industry, closed its factory doors.

Cleveland's location and industrial history had apparently positioned it perfectly to dominate automobile manufacturing. It produced or had ready access to the "raw materials" of auto production — steel, glass and rubber — and had excellent transportation connections as well as a large industrial work force. But this time geography was not destiny. With the supremacy of Detroit firmly established, Cleveland became the second-largest manufacturing center in the American automobile industry, its production of automotive parts increasing at the same time as its production of Cleveland-designed cars declined.

What is fascinating about the history of Cleveland's early auto industry is not the number of cars produced or

responsibility" for a project eliminated the need for multiple contractors and streamlined the entire process from architect's drawing to finished building. In 1911 the company began work on Nela Park in East Cleveland, sometimes cited as the nation's first planned industrial park, which would house General Electric's lamp research and development programs (including development of high- and low-beam headlights in 1924). This major project added to the Austin firm's growing national reputation and led to Wilbert Austin's work on standardization of factory design, another milestone in industrial construction and another step toward rationalization and efficiency.

The drive for greater efficiency and organization brought benefits to early 20th-century Cleveland. But it also undercut the city's claim to leadership in automobile production from the moment the first Model Ts rolled out of a Detroit factory in 1908. Henry Ford had decided to build a reliable, no-frills car that would be inexpensive enough for many Americans to buy. To do this, he used innovative

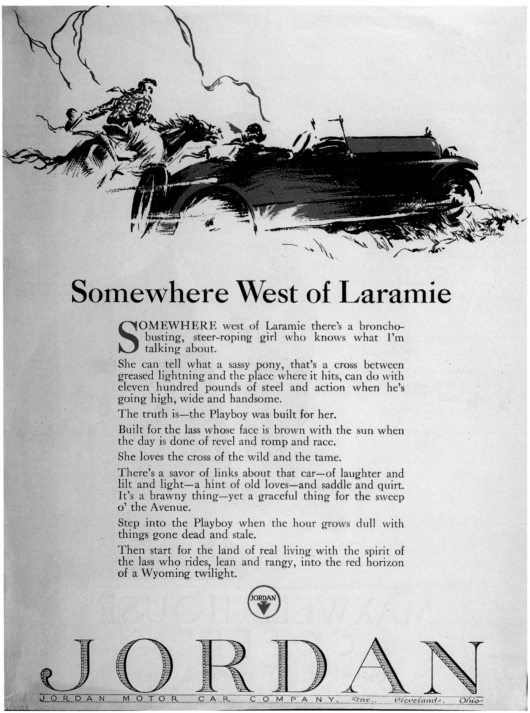

Somewhere West of Laramie

SOMEWHERE west of Laramie there's a broncho-busting, steer-roping girl who knows what I'm talking about.

She can tell what a sassy pony, that's a cross between greased lightning and the place where it hits, can do with eleven hundred pounds of steel and action when he's going high, wide and handsome.

The truth is—the Playboy was built for her.

Built for the lass whose face is brown with the sun when the day is done of revel and romp and race.

She loves the cross of the wild and the tame.

There's a savor of links about that car—of laughter and lilt and light—a hint of old loves—and saddle and quirt. It's a brawny thing—yet a graceful thing for the sweep o' the Avenue.

Step into the Playboy when the hour grows dull with things gone dead and stale.

Then start for the land of real living with the spirit of the lass who rides, lean and rangy, into the red horizon of a Wyoming twilight.

JORDAN

JORDAN MOTOR CAR COMPANY, Inc., Cleveland, Ohio

Jordan was one of many luxury-car manufacturers located in Cleveland during the early 20th century when the city was the center of the nation's automotive industry.
Western Reserve Historical Society

even the names of the companies and makes — Peerless, Stearns, Owens-Magnetic, Cleveland, Chandler and the rest — but the way the industry linked with existing industries and created new ones. This process illustrated in the clearest way possible the workings of the web of transportation and industry that made Cleveland a modern, viable and economically successful city.

Although very different industries, the automotive and garment sectors were related through the sewing machine. Cleveland is not usually thought of as a center of the clothing industry, but the city in fact had a thriving garment trade as early as the 1860s, and by 1920 was second only to New York City in the manufacture of women's ready-to-wear clothing. The sewing machine made large-scale production possible.

Many of the early entrepreneurs in the sector were Jews from Germany or Austria-Hungary. David and Morris Black, who had pioneered Hungarian-Jewish migration to Cleveland in the 1850s, were also pioneers in Cleveland's garment industry, starting production of women's coats, cloaks and dusters in 1874. Although they and others (including Kaufman Koch, whose company later evolved into menswear manufacturer Joseph & Feiss) initially contracted with home sewers or small shops, by the turn of the

century large factories were being established in the Flats and the warehouse district near the river. One of these, the L. N. Gross Company, was among the first to apply assembly line-type techniques to clothing production, with a worker specializing in one procedure or another rather than sewing an entire garment.

Just as important as the sewing machine in the growth of Cleveland's garment industry were the legions of immigrant laborers, many of them women. While immigrant men found employment in the city's auto plants, steel mills and machine shops, their wives and daughters worked long hours making shirtwaists, gloves or knitwear. In 1910 Cleveland's garment industry employed 10,000 people.

Although garment manufacturing was thus woven into the web linking the automobile with other Cleveland industries, most auto-related manufacturing took place in a man's world, a world of metal and machinery, grease and oil. Little could John D. Rockefeller have dreamed while clerking at Hewitt

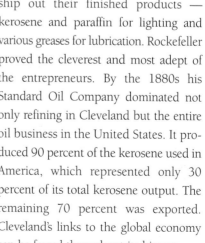

and Tuttle that he would eventually influence and benefit from a new transportation invention. But he did, decades after using the profits from his own commission company's wartime sales to invest in oil refining capacity.

Cleveland's role in the American oil industry was determined by geography and transportation. Its entrepreneurs took advantage of good rail connections to the great American oil fields in western Pennsylvania to ship in raw crude beginning in the 1860s. They used rail and water to ship out their finished products — kerosene and paraffin for lighting and various greases for lubrication. Rockefeller proved the cleverest and most adept of the entrepreneurs. By the 1880s his Standard Oil Company dominated not only refining in Cleveland but the entire oil business in the United States. It produced 90 percent of the kerosene used in America, which represented only 30 percent of its total kerosene output. The remaining 70 percent was exported. Cleveland's links to the global economy can be found throughout its history.

also had other, less obvious links to the automotive industry. For instance, to refine oil, Rockefeller and other producers needed sulfuric acid. Large-scale chemical production in Cleveland began when Eugene Grasselli moved his sulfuric acid works from Cincinnati to Cleveland in 1867 to serve the oil industry. The chemical industry in turn supported the development of a paint and coatings industry. Two of the sector's major companies, Glidden and Sherwin-Williams, had their start in Cleveland during the post-Civil War decade. Their varnishes (particularly Glidden's) and paints were used not only on houses, but also on railroad cars, wagons and eventually automobiles. Ready access to quality coatings made auto production in Cleveland easier.

Another chemical process industry both profited by and supported the automotive industry. Like oil refining, the commercial production of rubber had predated the automobile. First used to produce waterproof garments and footwear, rubber gained in importance with the invention of the pneumatic tire. Rubber-tired bicycles contributed to the cycling craze, increasing the market for tires and bicycles alike. The transition from bicycle to automobile tire was a natural one, and suddenly the rubber industry was booming. Akron, 40 miles south of Cleveland, became the rubber capital of the world, as four major rubber and tire manufacturing companies — B.F. Goodrich, Goodyear, Firestone and General Tire — located there. Once, the two cities had owed their growth and commercial prosperity to the Ohio & Erie Canal. Now, as producers of the basic materials rubber and steel, as well as tires, auto bodies and other essential components, Akron and Cleveland both looked to profit from the automobile.

Nuts, bolts and screws — fasteners had long been a product of Cleveland industry. Large ones held together ships, steam engines and locomotives produced in the city and elsewhere. Smaller ones went into roller skates, bicycles and eventually auto-

It is easy to move forward in time and see that Rockefeller both influenced and profited by automotive development through Standard Oil's production of gasoline, initially a next-to-worthless byproduct of refining. But he mobiles. Thomas H. Lamson, Isaac P. Lamson and Samuel W. Sessions had made carriage bolts in Connecticut before coming to Cleveland in 1869. Situated near the Cuyahoga River, their business expanded constantly as the Lamson and

Sessions Company made fasteners for a variety of implements and machines and for the construction trade, becoming one of the largest manufacturers in the sector nationwide.

Another major company in the field had its beginnings in 1900 when a group of investors organized the Cleveland Cap Screw Company to take advantage of the growing market for automotive and machine tool fasteners. By 1904 it was making automotive valves. Its products were so important that the Winton Motor Carriage Company took over the firm in 1905. Under the direction of general manager Charles E. Thompson, it became the Electric Welding Products Company in 1908 and produced chassis parts for the auto industry. Thompson bought the firm from Winton in 1915 and changed its name to the Steel Products Company.

The nuts and bolts that held early Cleveland cars together and the gears, crankshafts and camshafts that formed important parts of their engines and drivetrains had to be manufactured to precision tolerances and standardized sizes. Machine tools made this possible, and Cleveland made machine tools. Cleveland Twist Drill began operations in the city in 1876, manufacturing high-quality drills to cut cast iron and steel. Worcester Warner and Ambrose Swasey brought their partnership, Warner & Swasey, from Chicago to Cleveland in 1881. Here they produced turret lathes as well as some of the finest astronomical instruments in the country. Bardons and Oliver started operations in 1891, manufacturing both bicycle hubs and the machines to make them. The Cleveland Automatic Screw Machine Company, once part of White Sewing Machine, produced machines to make the screws that fastened sewing machines,

Automatic starters in automobiles created a huge need for storage batteries such as these being assembled at the Willard Storage Battery Company in 1930. *Cleveland Press Collection, Cleveland State University*

Workers assemble batteries at the Willard Storage Battery Company in 1930. *Cleveland Press Collection, Cleveland State University*

General Motors' Fisher Body Plant experienced frequent strikes and violence during the Great Depression as workers agitated for union recognition and better wages. In this photograph of the 1939 strike, workers overturn a car. *Cleveland Press Collection, Cleveland State University*

Elliot Ness (right), who was nationally known for leading the Chicago "Untouchables," was appointed Safety Director for Cleveland in 1935 to clean up the scandal-ridden police department. Here he poses with Cleveland Mayor Horald Burton. *Western Reserve Historical Society*

bicycles and automobiles together. The Lees-Bradner Company, founded in 1906, manufactured hobbing machines for the precision cutting of gears. These and many other companies took the steel produced in Cleveland and made it into machines. Those machines took more steel and made it into the parts that made automobiles.

The Eberhard Manufacturing and Cleveland Hardware Companies had long dominated the lower Buckeye industrial area, employing many of the Hungarian and Slovak immigrants who lived nearby. They specialized in making hardware, angles, steps, rails and other parts used in the construction of wagons and carriages. As the carriage industry waned nationally and locally in the face of the growing use of automobiles, these companies wisely began to produce items for the new industry. A nearby factory, established by an immigrant entrepreneur, was already doing the same.

Frank Vlchek's introduction to industrial Cleveland had spurred his ambition to be something other than a hired hand in a factory. Soon after his arrival in the city, a

The largest crowd ever to watch a baseball game in Cleveland witnessed the intercity championships between White Auto and Omaha Luxus in 1915 at Brookside Park. *Western Reserve Historical Society*

FINAL INTER-CITY CHAMPIONSHIP GAME—WHITE AUTOS

Czech friend had taken him on a "job walk" to search for work in the industrial Flats. He was distracted from his goal by disgust at the sight and smell of the heavily polluted Cuyahoga River as it flowed near the Standard Oil works. By the 1880s the river had become an open sewer for industrial and human waste. The young migrant was for a moment overcome by homesickness, thinking of the clear, tree-lined rivers of Bohemia. His friend had some advice: "My boy, you must forget Bohemia; you're in America now."

Rather than going to work for a major industry, Vlchek found employment in small blacksmith shops, where he became expert in hardening mason's tools. In 1895 he opened his own shop, capitalizing on and continuing to build his knowledge of masons' and other hand tools. His timing could not have been better. The need for wrenches, pliers and screwdrivers would expand enormously with the coming of the automobile. Almost every car sold in the early decades of this century contained not only a jack but also a full tool kit for tire and other repairs. The Vlchek Tool

Company began to serve this market, supplying the tools to automobile companies. As Detroit manufacturers such as Ford, Dodge and Chevrolet sold more and more cars, Vlchek sold more and more tools. He built a huge new plant in the lower Buckeye neighborhood to increase production capacity, and it employed hundreds of workers, many of them immigrants like himself.

Thanks to the automobile industry and his own expertise in hand tools, the Bohemian youth who had walked the Flats in search of a job was by the 1910s a wealthy man. Vlchek drove not an ordinary Ford, but instead a more expensive Willys Overland to his plant every day, not from a small frame house in the Quincy Avenue Bohemian neighborhood, but from a spacious residence in a new suburban development, Shaker Heights. As an immigrant turned automotive commuter, Frank Vlchek had set a pattern that many would follow. In the years after World War I, automobiles in particular, and other forms of transport to a lesser degree, would make Cleveland into "Greater Cleveland."

AHA "LUXUS" TEAM —— BROOKSIDE STADIUM · OCT. 10, 1915.
SCORE — 11 TO 6 IN FAVOR WHITE AUTOS —— ATTENDANCE OVER 100,000.

seven

Roads to a New Future:
The Making of a Greater Cleveland

Throughout the 19th century Cleveland grew by

annexing the smaller communities that lay outside its borders. Community

leaders, businessmen and citizens alike equated growth with progress. In

the late 1850s the Cleveland Board of Trade — predecessor of the city's

Chamber of Commerce, later the Greater Cleveland Growth Association —

called for the creation of industries so that Cleveland would not be

eclipsed in its progress by rival cities such as Pittsburgh.

Before it was dismantled in 1930, the traffic tower along Euclid Avenue was a favorite vantage point for photographers capturing street scenes, such as this view of Euclid Avenue looking west toward Public Square. *Cleveland Press Collection, Cleveland State University*

Their formula worked. The combination of geographic and economic expansion gave Cleveland the critical mass necessary to attract additional industry and population. As industry grew, wealth grew, and as wealth grew the central city could offer services such as water, sewers and police that were not available in the smaller communities. The social and cultural life appropriate to a major city also developed in Cleveland, as the same industrial wealth

endowed museums, universities, hospitals and charities. Recreational and sporting facilities gave Clevelanders greater opportunity to enjoy themselves, and fine buildings and parks enhanced the city's appearance. Beginning in the 1880s, the area just east of old Doan's Corners began to develop into a cultural and educational district that became known as University Circle.

When Cleveland legally became a village in 1815, its boundaries were formed by the Cuyahoga River to the west, Erie (East 9th) Street to the east, the lake to the north and Huron Road to the south. Little more than a century later, in 1922, the western boundary extended as far as the Rocky River valley. The eastern limit now stretched to East 200th Street, and the southern edge of the city was in places seven or eight miles from the lake. Doan's Corners and most of Newburgh were now part of Cleveland, as was its old west side rival, the City of Ohio. Once separate villages, Collinwood, Glenville, South Brooklyn, Corlett, East View and West Park had joined the center city in 1910, 1905, 1905, 1909, 1914 and 1922 respectively. The sprawling new community was held together by its transit lines and by an increasing number of well-paved streets.

Cleveland's expanding network of streets made travel by both automobile and rapid transit more convenient, encouraging the city's expansion beyond its borders as this 1925 street/transit map suggests. *Western Reserve Historical Society*

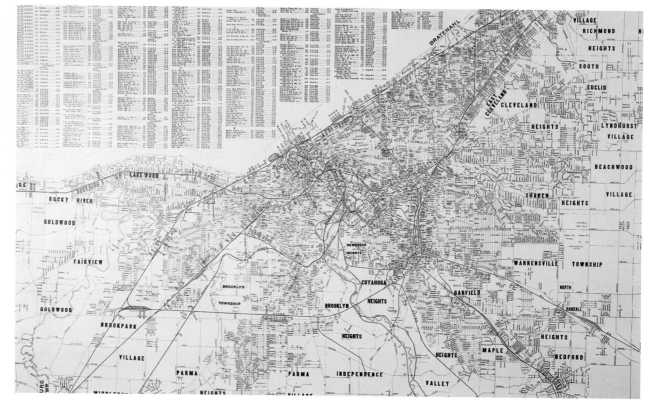

Cleveland, which surpassed Cincinnati to become the state's largest city in the 1890s, dominated northeastern Ohio. In 1860 its population of 43,417 had been only 24 percent of Cuyahoga County's total population. Fifty years later Cleveland's 560,663 people made up 88 percent of the county's population. By 1920 Cleveland's population had grown to 796,845, making it the nation's fifth-largest city. At the same time, however, its percentage of county population had slipped to 84 percent. Although this small drop might have seemed insignificant, it was in fact a sign of things to come. A major change in community structure was beginning to develop.

The city of Cleveland now had company. Four new suburbs, Cleveland Heights, Shaker Heights, East Cleveland and Lakewood, were rapidly growing around its periphery. Unlike earlier communities, they resisted annexation, providing an alternative to city life. Transportation and industry, the very factors that had made Cleveland grow and prosper, worked to transfer population and wealth from the central city to outlying areas. This had both positive and negative consequences and created a new metropolitan area, Greater Cleveland, which continued to increase in size and population partly at the central city's expense.

The fate of the city's grandest street was a case in point. Some had compared it to the Nevsky Prospect in St. Petersburg, others to the Champs Élysées in Paris or Berlin's Unter den Linden. From the 1850s until the turn of the century, Euclid Avenue was an elegant thoroughfare, home to the city's wealthiest people. Amasa Stone, John D. Rockefeller, Leonard Hanna and Henry Chisholm all maintained large homes on the tree-lined avenue. It was one of Cleveland's many neighborhoods, although a very exclusive one, devoid of the small shops and everyday hustle and bustle that characterized many others. By the 1900s, however, the world-famous street was in decline. Many of its residents were opting for new homes. Some built in the new Wade Park area at the eastern border of Cleveland. Others left to live year-round in their summer homes along the lake in Bratenahl Village. Still others moved far to the east, to the Chagrin River valley or beyond to Waite Hill in Lake County. The vacating of Euclid Avenue did not occur all at once but was a gradual process, with one or two families lingering on into the post-World War II years.

Dedicated in 1894, Soldiers' and Sailors' Monument stands in the foreground of this east-southeast view across Public Square in 1949. Euclid Avenue is at the right.
Cleveland Press Collection, Cleveland State University

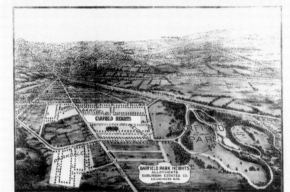

GARFIELD HEIGHTS
WILL HAVE
GRADED STREETS, WATER, SIDEWALKS, SHADE TREES, GAS AND ELECTRICITY

Located on E. 99th, 104th Sts. and Turney Rd. near Garfield Blvd. and adjoining Garfield Park.
The East 105th Street 3c Car Line runs direct to our Allotments, and Transfers to all Car Lines on the East Side

As developers built Cleveland's suburbs beginning as early as the 1920s, they placed them along streetcar lines and advertised this convenience to customers.
Western Reserve Historical Society

The factors that drove Euclid Avenue's residents away were the same that caused Michael Kniola's real estate clients to build homes in Corlett or Garfield Heights, and impelled Frank Vlchek to move to Shaker Heights. The industrial growth that brought wealth — whether the enormous fortune of a Rockefeller or the hard-earned savings of a factory worker — also brought overcrowding, dirt and noise. Certainly Euclid Avenue did not suffer from pollution to the same degree as areas near the steel mills or railroads, but the sights, sounds and smells of urban life inevitably encroached. Once the streetcar tracks so long resisted by the avenue's residents were laid in 1890, the exclusive quiet of the street was shattered. Also, as the commercial center of the city expanded eastward, engulfing Public Square and by the 1920s reaching beyond the new Playhouse Square entertainment district at East 14th

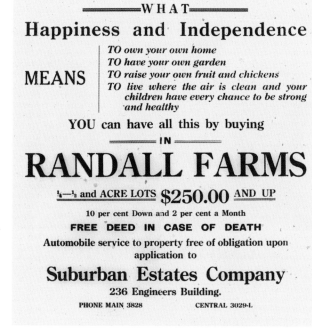

===WHAT===
Happiness and Independence

MEANS
TO *own your own home*
TO *have your own garden*
TO *raise your own fruit and chickens*
TO *live where the air is clean and your children have every chance to be strong and healthy*

YOU can have all this by buying
=== IN ===
RANDALL FARMS

¼—½ and ACRE LOTS **$250.00** AND UP

10 per cent Down and 2 per cent a Month
FREE DEED IN CASE OF DEATH
Automobile service to property free of obligation upon application to

Suburban Estates Company
236 Engineers Building.
PHONE MAIN 3828   CENTRAL 3029-L

Street, their property became more valuable for business than residential use.

While it was nice to have a small green lawn or garden in Garfield Heights, or to be far away from the sound of traffic in rural Chagrin valley, it was also pleasant to escape a city that had become unfamiliar and uncomfortable for many Clevelanders. Not only industrialization but the newcomers it attracted had changed the city, and not for the better as far as some longer-established residents

were concerned. They found urban ward politics dishonest or at least ungenteel and regarded their new neighbors with distaste that shaded into suspicion and sometimes hostility.

When the Irish first came to Cleveland, the larger Protestant community shunned them. Their neighborhoods in the Flats or later in Newburgh were not places where outsiders wanted to go, much less live. At least, however, they were at some distance, separated by geographical barriers or industrial development. When large numbers of Poles came to work in the Cleveland Rolling Mills after the 1882 strike, Irish, Welsh and Scots workers who lived in the area began to move away from the growing Polish settlement. And so it continued as new groups moved to the city. Eventually, as the trans-Atlantic steamships brought more immigrants and trains brought in farmers and new migrants from the deep South, the city filled out, and the empty spaces that once separated Slovenes from Italians, Hungarians from Slovaks, and immigrants from native-born disappeared.

By 1920 Cleveland had become a city comprised of villages, the neighborhoods that served as homes to the more than 50 ethnic groups in the community. Two-thirds of the city's population was foreign-born or of foreign parentage. The neighborhoods often translated into political wards, where ethnic politicians could use patronage to build a parochial power base. To older Clevelanders, the municipal government that resulted seemed more like a corrupt European assembly than a city council. The new suburbs offered not only a cleaner environment but one that was more "American."

O.P. and M.J. Van Sweringen were the sons of a wounded Civil War veteran. The father was unable to work steadily, and his family grew up in poverty in Wooster, Ohio. Around 1890, when the boys were eleven and nine respectively, the family moved to Cleveland in search of better opportunities. The boys, whose given names were Oris Paxton and Mantis James, received only an elementary school education, yet within three decades of their arrival they became the richest and most recognized men in

Greater Cleveland. They made their money as realtors, participating in and in fact shaping the suburbanization of Cleveland.

The real estate business depended on transportation links. Empty land could become new home allotments only when people could conveniently travel between work and residence. With the multiplication of streetcar lines and other improvements, the number of realtors in the area soared from 37 in 1871 to 175 in 1890. In 1892 this new field of commercial enterprise, previously wide open to all with guile, gumption and a drive to make money, began to organize and set standards through the establishment of the Cleveland Board of Realtors. As realtors, the Van Sweringens first worked in the new suburb of Lakewood.

Lakewood began to grow in the late 1880s when natural gas wells enhanced the value of land in the area. However, the real boom in development began after a streetcar line along Clifton Boulevard reached the suburb in 1903. Between 1890 and 1910, the village's population increased from 450 to more than 15,000. Although a portion of the population consisted of Slovaks and some Poles working at the National Carbon Company plant on West 117th Street, most new Lakewoodites were middle-class office workers and skilled craftsmen seeking escape from the crowded central city. Many were the descendants of early northern and western European immigrants.

Despite the town's growth, the Van Sweringens' real estate venture in Lakewood was a failure. After briefly leaving the field to pursue other jobs, they returned to land development in 1905, this time setting their sights on land to the east of Cleveland. Through options, they began to buy property that once formed the North Union colony of the United Believers in the Second Appearance of Christ, or the Shakers, as they were more commonly known. The brothers sensed potential in the area. Already, by the early 1900s, wealthy families were moving to the Wade allotments at the city's eastern edge. Middle- and upper middle-class families were moving across the city line to East Cleveland, which grew phenomenally, reaching a population count of 10,000 by 1910. A little to the south, developers Patrick Calhoun and John Harkness Brown bought land on the ridge overlooking University Circle. Their Euclid Heights subdivision began the transformation of the area colloquially known as Turkey Ridge into Cleveland Heights.

The success of each of these ventures hung on the availability of public transportation. Streetcar lines to East Cleveland and up Cedar Hill to Euclid Heights enabled new residents to commute downtown to work. So as the Van Sweringens accumulated land that had once belonged to the Shakers, they began to press the Cleveland Railway Company to extend its lines into their new development, Shaker Heights. The company did extend some lines, but not to the degree the Vans expected. They decided to do the job themselves by building their own transit line. That decision had a major impact on Cleveland's transportation history.

In order to provide a downtown terminus for their line, the Van Sweringens found that they had to buy a railroad in order to use its right of way into the city. The Nickel Plate Railroad, formally the New York, Chicago and St. Louis, had been founded in 1881, with the main line between Buffalo and Chicago completed in a record 18 months. It competed with the Vanderbilt-run New York Central, which dominated the east-west corridor between New York and Chicago. In short order the Central absorbed the Nickel Plate and quashed the competition. Under pressure from the government to end their monopoly, the Central's directors were eager to sell the line to the Van Sweringens, and the deal went through in 1916.

In this fashion, almost by chance, the brothers started on their way to becoming railroad tycoons. The Nickel Plate was the first of a large number of roads they would acquire in the 1910s and 1920s, building a huge railroad empire. That empire was run out of Cleveland, a town that

Completed in 1927, the Terminal Tower at 708 feet was the tallest building in the world outside New York City until 1967. The building housed a working railroad terminal and was also the main terminal for the Shaker Heights Rapid Transit and later for the crosstown RTA rapid line. *Western Reserve Historical Society*

Passengers got on and off the Euclid Avenue streetcar at Public Square. Such transit lines were important to the early growth of Cleveland's suburbs.
Cleveland Press Collection, Cleveland State University

had built and served as headquarters for many lines in the mid-19th century, only to see control of them pass to powerful interests in the east. It was a victory of sorts not only for the Vans but for the city.

Now that they had their transit line, the Van Sweringens needed a terminal. They felt that Public Square, the city's business hub, would be an ideal site for a combined rail and transit station. Cleveland officials, however, had other plans. The Group Plan called for a grand new railroad station to be built along the lakefront between city hall and the county courthouse on the north side of the mall. This station would replace the 1866 Union Depot, which was by the turn of the century so outmoded and run down as to be a civic embarrassment. An unofficial sign posted along the rail approach to the station purportedly told passengers arriving in Cleveland, "Don't Judge this City by this Station." World War I put all plans on hold, but in 1919 the Vans' desire for a union terminal on Public Square was put before the public. The referendum resulted in voters agreeing to switch the site for the city's new depot. It was a wise move, for the increase in traffic during World War I indicated that a passenger terminal right on the east-west mainline might create a major bottleneck.

Excavation for the Union Terminal project began in 1924. When the first train arrived in 1929, the 708-foot Terminal Tower was the world's tallest building outside of New York City. It would remain so until 1967, serving as a landmark for generations of Clevelanders. The tower and the complex of buildings it anchored had replaced over 1,000 decrepit structures. The Union Terminal project remains the largest building project ever undertaken in the city.

Almost overshadowed by all that came in its wake was the electric railway line the Vans had built to foster the growth of Shaker Heights. It was not technically a streetcar line, but an interurban. The Van Sweringens' Cleveland Interurban Railroad, or Shaker Rapid, was one of many long-distance electric railways that connected small- and medium-sized communities in northeastern Ohio. Although the primary use of electric traction was for street railways, entrepreneurs had quickly recognized additional possibilities for the new technology. The electrically powered rail cars were light and relatively cheap to construct. The rails on which they ran could be placed on lighter roadbeds. Service, unlike that of steam railroads, could be frequent. It cost far less to run a series of single electric cars on an hourly basis than it did to run a multi-car steam-powered train.

The first interurban line out of Cleveland was built to Akron in 1895. By 1910 Cleveland had six distinct systems connecting the city directly to Painesville, Columbus, Toledo, Chagrin Falls, Akron and a variety of smaller towns. Connections with other lines allowed passengers to travel all the way to Cincinnati, Indianapolis or even New York if they wished. Ohio had over 2,700 miles of interurban lines by the 1910s.

The technology allowed people with means to move beyond the new suburbs to what would become known as the exurbs. Gates Mills and Chardon in neighboring Geauga County were served by interurbans. The development of

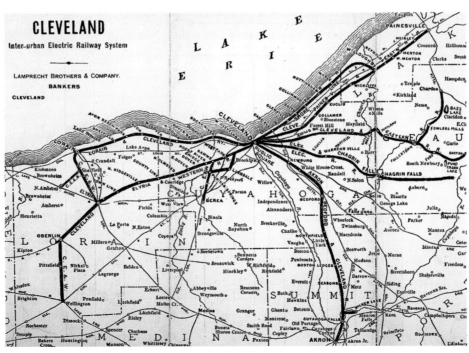

The system of interurbran railways that dotted Cleveland in 1900 began to disappear in the 1920s as the automobile became increasingly common. *Western Reserve Historical Society*

Interurban cars had comfortable, if not luxurious, interiors during the 1920s when this photo was taken of the Cleveland, Southwestern, & Columbus Railway.
Western Reserve Historical Society

Gates Mills as one of the area's most exclusive residential areas was due in part to interurban service.

The lines also benefited the less well-to-do. Farm families from Medina County to the southwest could now come in to the city for a day of shopping. Some Cleveland department stores such as the May Company and the Higbee Company cooperated with the interurbans in offering special fares to shoppers. A resident of the little town of Seville, Ohio, commented on the benefits the Cleveland, Southwestern and Columbus line provided to his community: "Shoppers can take advantage of Cleveland sales; farmers can expect their produce to arrive in city markets in good condition and everybody can enjoy an outing to a motion-picture show." The glory days of the interurban would be brief but significant. This form of transport, which connected the farm and the small town directly with the city, began eroding the division between rural and urban, eventually leading to the development of a regional northeastern Ohio identity.

Like other forms of transportation technology, interurbans and streetcars stimulated and supported a variety of industries. Of course, they drew heavily from the steel industry for rails, wire support poles, wheels and car bodies. One Cleveland company, G. C. Kuhlman, became a major manufacturer of interurban cars, with its products running on a number of local lines including the Shaker Rapid.

Cleveland's electrical industry perhaps gained the most from electric traction. The Brush Electric Company, established by Charles F. Brush, a local inventor noted for developing the arc lamp and improving the dynamo, provided equipment for the city's first street railways. The power plants that generated electricity for the cars often sold excess power to local industrial and residential consumers. This was particularly true in the case of interurbans, where the generating stations along the lines sometimes provided the first electric power for suburban and rural communities. Electric-powered transportation helped take Cleveland beyond the old steam industrial age and into the technologies of the dawning 20th century.

By 1939, however, only one interurban line, the Shaker Rapid, still operated in Cleveland. The remainder had fallen victim to a more individualistic form of transportation, the automobile. The car influenced the history and development of Cleveland during the 20th century more than any other form of transport. The suburbs, nurtured by streetcars and interurbans, reached robust adulthood only when automobile ownership became widespread. Ironically, it was Detroit, and Henry Ford in particular, rather than Winton, White, Stearns or any of the other local manufacturers, that put Clevelanders into the driver's seat. Affordability and reliability propelled the auto into the mass market.

By 1920 there were 92,600 passenger cars and trucks in Cuyahoga County. Ten years later there were 270,000 passenger cars in Cleveland alone. Despite the Depression, the number of cars in the county rose to 367,600 by 1941, with nearly two-thirds of the county's families owning a car.

Street paving accelerated in tandem with the rise in automobile ownership during the first two decades of the century, so that by the 1920s most of the city's streets were paved. Yet problems remained. Most streets had been laid out in the era of horse-drawn transportation. They often

The Blaushild Motor Company was one of many automobile dealerships in the Cleveland Metropolitan area. Here it promotes sales at a booth at a local African-American trade fair. *Western Reserve Historical Society*

proved too narrow for autos and the increasing number of trucks. The main thoroughfares that connected Cleveland to nearby suburbs and cities could barely handle the volume of traffic. East of Cleveland, Lee Road, Kinsman and Euclid were upgraded to four-lane roads, and on the other side of town West Lake Road received similar treatment. It was relatively easy to widen roads outside of the built-up city. It was less easy in the urban center where buildings hemmed in existing roadbeds. Streetcars trundling through the

narrow streets further complicated traffic patterns.

The river and its valley proved the greatest obstacle, however, as Clevelanders became more dependent on the automobile. In the region's earliest days, bridges crossed the Cuyahoga at river level. All had lift spans to allow for the passage of boats. But after Cleveland merged with Ohio City and both east and west sides grew in the years after the Civil War, it became impossible to conduct commerce by moving wagons down one steep bank, crossing the river, and then moving them up the opposite side. The city's first high-level bridge, the Superior Viaduct, opened in 1878. A second high-level span, the Central Viaduct, opened 10 years later. They accommodated both wagon and streetcar traffic. Below them in the Flats an increasing number of lift bridges carried the growing number of railroad lines across the river.

These bridges proved inadequate once the automobile arrived. In the space of 22 years, engineers oversaw the construction of three additional high-level spans: the Detroit Superior High Level (Veterans Memorial) in 1917, the Lorain-Carnegie (Hope Memorial) in 1932 and the Main Avenue (Harold Burton Memorial) in 1939. The engineers planned the bridges according to the traffic mix they envisioned. The Detroit-Superior incorporated trolley tracks on a lower-level platform. The Lorain-Carnegie was planned with a deck for trolley tracks, but it was not constructed. The Main Avenue bridge plans included no accommodation whatsoever for trolleys. By 1939 rubber-tired vehicles were set to triumph over rail transport.

The effect of new highways and bridges was enormous. After the completion of the Detroit-Superior bridge, the population of Lakewood rose to 40,000 in 1920. Lakefront property in the suburb sold for $15,000 an acre. Even in the middle of the Great Depression, traffic surveys counted 43,000 vehicles crossing the bridge during a 12-hour period. Although Shaker Heights retained the state's last interurban line, it too was basically an automotive suburb. In the 1940s, 75 percent of its principal income earners used automobiles to go to work. They and their families could also drive to shop at nearby Shaker Square, located just past the boundary with Cleveland, where the Shaker Rapid's two branch lines converged. Ironically, the Van Sweringen brothers, who had committed themselves to the railroad and the streetcar in building the Union Terminal, contributed to the development of automotive culture with the construction of the Shaker Square shopping center in 1927-1929. Considered the oldest "modern" shopping center in Ohio and the second oldest in the United States, Shaker Square featured off-street parking, a hallmark of the thousands of shopping centers, shopping malls and strip malls to come.

In the midst of these changes, there were places in Greater Cleveland where the past still seemed to live. In East Cleveland, a modern streetcar-automotive suburb, residents were treated once a week to the sight of horse-drawn garbage wagons. Hugh O'Neill, who had immigrated to Cleveland from Ireland in 1885, contracted with East Cleveland to provide the service beginning in 1916. O'Neill's horse-drawn wagons continued to collect the town's garbage until 1947. He hauled the garbage to a farm he leased in Solon, where he fed it to pigs, selling the pigs in turn to increase the marginal profit the city contract provided.

O'Neill was a man who loved horses. His knowledge of them had put him in good stead when he worked as groom and coachman at J.B. Perkins' Euclid Avenue home during the 1880s and 90s. Perkins and other wealthy Clevelanders turned to O'Neill for help in choosing the best horses for their carriages. After leaving the employ of the Perkinses in 1898, O'Neill went into business for himself as a horse dealer. However, by the early 1900s he found himself more often than not being asked to sell rather than buy horses, as the automobile fad caught on among Cleveland's elite. Realizing that the days of the carriage horse trade were numbered, O'Neill started a cartage business in 1905.

In the late 19th and early 20th centuries, most local transport of goods was by horse and wagon. The First World War changed that. During the conflict armies on both sides discovered that trucks could haul goods and men more efficiently than could horse-drawn wagons.

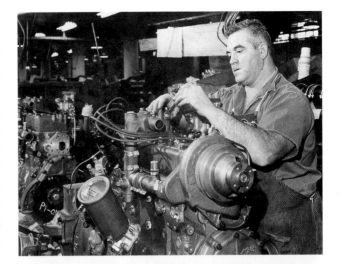

A worker at White Motor Corporation prepares an engine about 1960. *Western Reserve Historical Society*

In the 1950s employees at White Motors used a system of hanging conveyors to move parts, such as these heavy engine blocks, from station to station. *Western Reserve Historical Society*

Cleveland's White Motor Company, once a maker of expensive steam-powered automobiles, was by this time manufacturing gasoline-powered trucks. Their products sold very well, impressing even Czar Nicholas II of Russia.

Americans who had served in the war came back from "over there" with an appreciation of trucks. Many had been trained to drive them; some had learned to repair them. Returning home, a number of soldiers decided to go into business and bought trucks. Many worked individually as "gypsy" truckers, while others formed companies. By the mid-1920s there were over 400 truckers and trucking firms listed in Cleveland's city directory. Most moved goods within the city, but a few entered the intercity freight business. Truckers' voices were often the loudest in the call for new roads and improvements to the rudimentary highways that connected Cleveland to other cities.

Hugh O'Neill's allegiance to the horse did not blind him to the changes taking place in urban transportation. The fact that he ran a horse-and-wagon garbage business sometimes obscured the fact that he and his sons, Hugh Jr., William J. and F.J. (Steve) were at the forefront of the local trucking industry. While horse-drawn wagons collected the rubbish in East Cleveland, White-built dump trucks took it to the farm in Solon. The O'Neill family's Superior Transfer Company handled merchandise and package deliveries within Cleveland. By 1930 the brothers had put together Motor Express Inc., which specialized in inter-city trucking across northern Ohio. After their business merged with other consolidated trucking companies to create U.S. Truck Lines, the O'Neills became principal managers of that firm, which by the late

1930s was one of the largest and most profitable trucking companies in the United States.

Truckers working for the O'Neills were among those celebrating the completion of the Pennsylvania Turnpike in 1940. This high-speed, limited-access highway was what the "good roads" movement had been advocating. It not only provided a well-paved, relatively wide roadway, but its limited access system did away with dangerous and time-consuming interchanges and stop signs. Although Ohio's turnpike would not open until 1955, drivers of both trucks and cars were heartened by the fact that Cleveland had completed portions of its shoreway, a limited-access highway built on landfill along Lake Erie, by 1938. When the Main Avenue Bridge was opened the following year, Cleveland motorists were able to travel on a modern road almost nonstop from East 55th Street to Edgewater Park on the west side. Now they could look forward to the completion of the north-south Willow Freeway, which would speed traffic from downtown to the southern suburbs. The freeway's "cloverleaf," constructed at Granger Road in Independence, was the first such inter-change in Ohio when completed in October 1940.

On any given day in the late 1930s, however, most Cleveland drivers still traveled old streets. Nowhere was this more the case than on the commute between downtown and the suburbs on the Heights. Drivers had a choice of routes. Euclid, Cedar, Central and Carnegie avenues were the best, since Chester Avenue had not yet been completed through to University Circle. These streets took the drivers through or along the edge of Cleveland's major African-American neighborhood, Cedar Central.

African-Americans coming to Cleveland in the years before the Civil War had found a relatively open although certainly not prejudice-free society. In the postwar period John Patterson Green, the first African-American to hold political office in Cleveland, was elected justice of the peace in 1873, state representative in 1881, and state senator in 1892, even though the city's black population was small and dispersed at the time. As late as 1910 all but a small number of the census tracts on Cleveland's east side had at least some African-American inhabitants, while no tract was more than a quarter black.

By the late 1930s this pattern had altered drastically. Most African-Americans had been forced into the segregated confines of the Cedar Central neighbor-hood. In 1940, 95 percent of Cleveland's 84,504 black inhabitants lived there. In many cases

they, or their parents, had come to Cleveland as part of the Great Migration, a movement that saw hundreds of thousands of African-Americans flee the oppression and poverty of the American South in the years after 1890. Carried largely by train, the movement accelerated during World War I when war industries in cities such as Cleveland found their labor supply from Europe cut off at the same time demand for their products grew. With immigration from Europe restricted after the war, African Americans, along with migrants from Appalachia and immigrants from

John Patterson Green attended Central High School and was the first black to hold elective office in Ohio.
Western Reserve Historical Society

Cars pass across the old Main Avenue Bridge in 1938.
Cleveland Press Collection, Cleveland State University

THE FUTURE OUTLOOK LEAGUE

MILITANCY

The Future Outlook League was formed in 1935 to help obtain jobs for African-Americans residing in the Central area. The organization initially appealed to unskilled and semiskilled workers but later broadened its focus to include the entire African-American community.
Western Reserve Historical Society

Members of the Future Outlook League in 1938 — the organization promoted the use of pickets and economic boycotts with the slogan "Don't buy where you can't work" and won jobs for several hundred African-Americans. *Western Reserve Historical Society*

Newsboys gather in front of the Call & Post Building in the 1930s, Cleveland's principal African-American newspaper. *Western Reserve Historical Society*

Mexico, formed the bulk of the industrial migration to the north. Cleveland's black population was only 5,988 in 1900. By war's end it was over 34,000.

African-American migrants to the city in the years after 1890 carried with them many of the same hopes and fears as European immigrants, the modest hopes and fears of ordinary people: hope of getting a good-paying job, desire for a better life, sadness at leaving loved ones behind, fear of living among strangers. Those who had most to fear were, perhaps, single women, especially those brave enough to venture out on their own without family or other support to fall back on. They were in a minority in all migrant groups, but there were proportionately more single women among American migrants than among most European immigrant groups.

One of the most notable of these young women was Jane Edna Hunter. An African-American born in South Carolina, in 1905 at age 23 she boarded a train and left the South for Cleveland. A severe storm, accompanied by wind, heavy rain and hail, halted the train at Delaware, Ohio. For Hunter, the incident symbolized the risk of her undertaking, and she

later recalled being more exhilarated than daunted. "The storm, while it did not frighten me, to my imaginative spirit, standing on the threshold of a new adventure, suggested the turbulence and inclemency which I might encounter there."

Hunter had one great advantage that most young women migrants, black or white, lacked: a profession. She was a nurse, having graduated from the Hampton Institute in Virginia. Soon after her arrival in Cleveland she saw at first hand the pitfalls awaiting female migrants with no particular education or skills. On the portion of Cedar Avenue where she lived, she found newly arrived young girls being led into prostitution. She placed particular blame on "Starlight" Albert Duncan Boyd, a tavern and poolroom owner and politician, for taking advantage of the young migrants. This rude awakening to the realities of urban life changed Hunter's own destiny, leading her to devote herself to social activism. In 1911 she established the Phyllis Wheatley Association, a residence and training center for young black women coming to Cleveland.

Hunter's story does not, of course, encapsulate the full history of the African-American migration experience.

Members of St. James African Methodist Episcopal Church interviewed in 1986 remembered settling in areas of Central that were not troubled by disreputable figures like "Starlight." Some portions of the neighborhood were still integrated in the 1920s, presenting a contrast to what they had experienced in the South, and even on the trip north. While some came to Cleveland by automobile, most traveled by train. One of the church members remembered riding in a segregated "Jim Crow" coach as far as Cincinnati, and there transferring to an integrated car. Another, however, recalled riding in a segregated car all the way to Cleveland.

Cleveland itself was becoming more segregated by the year. Few of Cleveland's white residents saw any similarity between themselves, as immigrants or the descendants of immigrants, and the newer migrants. Interracial interaction was limited and took place mostly within a business or service context, for instance on the drive from downtown to the Heights. Commuters could stop for service at African-American-owned Kyers Shell Station at East 79th and Cedar or at one of Alonzo Wright's six Sohio stations,

An important Cleveland inventor, Garrett Morgan developed a safety helmet to protect the wearer from smoke and ammonia. He introduced his "Breathing Device" in 1912 and patented it in 1914. He can be seen wearing it here in 1916. *Cleveland Press Collection, Cleveland State University*

Garrett Morgan used the breathing device he invented to descend into the gas-filled tunnel beneath Lake Erie to rescue workers and retrieve bodies after the Cleveland Waterworks explosion in 1916. Local newspapers downplayed his role as hero, perhaps because he was African-American. *Western Reserve Historical Society*

the first of which was located at East 93rd and Cedar. There, customers' cars were not only filled up with gasoline, but received free radiator and tire checks and had their windows cleaned. Wright became Cleveland's first African-American millionaire by providing superb service to the city's growing number of motorists. His stations provided much-needed job opportunities for young black men. One of Wright's employees, Jesse Owens, would go on to earn worldwide fame during the 1936 Olympics.

Few, if any, of the thousands of drivers passing through Cedar Central or the city's other neighborhoods gave any real thought to the stoplights they encountered. The lights and the rules of the road were taken for granted by the third decade of American motoring. Yet they were part of an enormous set of changes put in motion by the automobile. Police departments such as Cleveland's had at one time focused on dealing with crime and with the minor problems occasioned by horse-drawn traffic. By the 1920s, 15 percent of Cleveland's police officers dealt with traffic and traffic movement. The police needed their own cars, not only to catch traffic offenders, but to keep pace with criminals, who found the new vehicle ideal for pursuing their illegal activities. By the next decade, under the leadership of Safety Director Eliot Ness, an increasing number of Cleveland police officers patrolled the streets in automobiles, all of which were radio-equipped.

Police departments in Cleveland and other cities initially assigned individual officers to stand at intersections and manage traffic using hand-operated lights and semaphores. In 1923 the nearby city of Willoughby tried out a new device, a lighted semaphore-type signal that had an intermediate caution position. It was an important advance in traffic signaling and its inventor eventually sold the rights to the General Electric Company. Combining this device with precedents drawn from railroad signaling, plus the long-life bulbs produced at its Nela Park facility in East Cleveland, General Electric would go on to develop the modern traffic light.

The inventor of that signal was Garrett Morgan, an African-American. Born in Kentucky, he moved to Cincinnati and then to Cleveland. He lived on Harlem Avenue, just blocks away from the route to the Heights. Yet while all of Cleveland was on the move, neither Morgan, a talented inventor, nor even Alonzo Wright, a highly successful businessman, could change neighborhoods easily, although both could have afforded to do so. Restrictive covenants governed who could move to areas such as the Wade allotment or Shaker Heights. Where there were no written restrictions, hostility to unwanted new neighbors accomplished the same purpose. Alonzo Wright moved to a home at 2985 Hampshire Road in Cleveland Heights in the 1930s. Someone promptly bombed the house. Wright endured, staying until 1947, at which time he moved to a 200-acre farm in rural Chesterland. In the intervening years, Cleveland industry and Cleveland transportation technology would help the United States and its allies win another world war, a war in which the issue of race and equality would loom large.

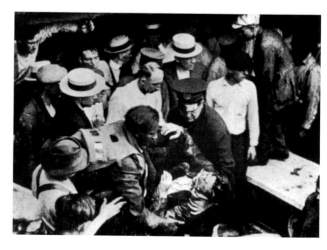

Garrett Morgan established the National Safety Device Company in 1914 and his other major invention, a traffic light (1923), was unique in using a third, cautionary signal between "stop" and "go." Morgan sold his traffic light to General Electric for $40,000 in 1923.
Here Morgan is pictured with the early light he invented.
Western Reserve Historical Society

chapter eight

The Sky Is No Limit:
From Curtiss to Glenn and Beyond

In 1882 William R. Hopkins, aged 13, left school to take a job in the Cleveland Rolling Mill in Newburgh. His parents had moved to Newburgh from Johnstown, Pennsylvania. The large family — there would eventually be 10 children — became a part of the close-knit Welsh community near the mills. Young William saved his earnings from the mills and used them to finance his studies. He was in his early 20s when he graduated from Western Reserve University's preparatory department, the Western Reserve Academy. Hopkins then went on to earn bachelor's and law degrees from the parent university.

all the major trunk lines entering the city — without crossing any major roads or streetcar lines at grade. Completed in 1912, it provided an ideal way to interchange freight and avoid the congested rail yards within the city. It provided an entire new string of industrial sites. Its route on the city's west side, closely paralleled today by Brookpark Road, would eventually become the location of the region's major automotive parts plants, the Ford engine facility and the General Motors stamping plant.

Hopkins also entered politics and was elected to his first term as a Republican member of City Council in 1897 while still in law school. Based on his political experience, but more importantly on his reputation as a "can do" businessman, Hopkins was appointed Cleveland's first city manager in 1924. The city manager form of government, which reduced the mayor to a ceremonial figurehead, lasted for seven years in Cleveland, until the citizenry voted to

He practiced law for only a few years before entering the business world full time. With his brother Ben, he began promoting and developing industrial sites around Cleveland. Hopkins made his reputation by promoting construction of a major transportation-related project, the Cleveland Short Line Railroad. A precursor to interstate highway ring roads, the 19-mile Short, or Belt Line, arched around Cleveland from Collinwood to Lakewood in a giant semicircle, intersecting

Watching Glen Curtis in his First Aeroplane Flight from Euclid Beach, Cleveland, Ohio.

return to the traditional mayoral system. It was an attempt to run the city in an efficient, businesslike manner and to overcome the divisiveness of ward and party politics. One of Hopkins' first tasks as manager was to find a solution to Cleveland's airport problem. The federal government was threatening to remove Cleveland as a stop on the national east-west airmail route unless it provided an adequate airport.

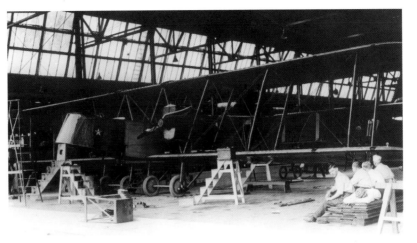

Workers at Glenn L. Martin are taking a break as they build bombers for the American military.
Western Reserve Historical Society

Twenty or even 10 years before, this would not have been a problem, for aviation was little more than a sideshow in the minds of most people. Clevelanders paid slight notice when the Wright brothers, fellow Ohioans, were the first to achieve powered flight in 1903. Aviation gradually caught the public eye, but more as a curiosity or attraction than a potential industry or form of transportation. Barnstorming aviators attracted the same type of interest that balloonists had when they made ascents in the 19th century. (Cleveland's first balloon ascent had taken place from the foot of Erie Street in 1851; the balloonist had charged spectators 25 cents apiece.) In August 1910 nearly 150,000 people lined the Lake Erie shore to watch Glenn Curtiss, one of the country's most noted aviators, make a round-trip flight between two lakeside recreation spots, Cleveland's Euclid Beach and Cedar Point in Erie County. It was the world's longest flight over water up to that time, and the *Cleveland Press* rewarded Curtiss with a $5,000 prize. In October Curtiss and other aviators put on an aerial display over Cleveland's lakefront as part of Cuyahoga County's centennial celebration. Native Americans, also participating in the celebration, were posed in the aircraft to create a tableau of northern Ohio's past and present.

The *Graf Zeppelin* flies over Cleveland and is framed with the Terminal Tower in this image by photographer Louis Van Oyen, c. 1930.
Western Reserve Historical Society

Curtiss' achievements impressed one young Clevelander so deeply that he decided to take up aviation himself. Al Engel, an employee of the city's water works, attended the Curtiss flying school at Hammondsport, New York, getting his "wings" in 1911. He crashed his first plane near Cleveland that year. Undaunted, Engel bought his second plane, the *Bumble Bee,* which he used for exhibition flights throughout northern Ohio. He also flew it at air shows in Buffalo and Chicago, and used it to deliver airmail at Lake Chautauqua, New York, in 1914. The outbreak of war in Europe that same summer had a sobering effect worldwide. Engel left the exhibition circuit and went to Spain, where he taught flying to army recruits. Aviation, no longer a frivolous pastime but dead serious business, had come of age.

World War I went on for two and two-thirds bloody years before the United States entered the conflict in April 1917. Long before that, however, American industry had been playing a role by supplying goods to the Allied Powers. Among the most important were trucks, autos, engines and engine parts. Cleveland firms like White Motor grew and prospered. By war's end White had sold 18,000 trucks to the European allies and the United States, helping the company to become the country's foremost truck manufacturer.

Peter DePaolo, a Thompson Products representative, makes a sales call at a service station in California in the 1950s.

Western Reserve Historical Society

What attracted the most avid public and business attention, however, was not so much the stalemate in the trenches of Western Europe, but the war in the air, as first airships and then airplanes played a more prominent part in the conflict. Inside every airplane and even every Zeppelin was an internal combustion gasoline engine, the power plant that created America's automotive revolution. The fact was not lost on the valve, engine block, fastener and machine tool manufacturers of Cleveland.

The United States entered the war far too late to develop and fly an effective airplane. Only the Curtiss-manufactured Jenny, used as a training aircraft, would see extensive service. American factories did, however, provide engines for European-designed airframes. The Liberty Engine was the nation's major aviation contribution. At its heart were valves, many of which came from Charles Thompson's Steel Products Company. The company, renamed Thompson Products, Inc., in 1926, would become the country's dominant producer of aircraft engine valves, and Thompson would become one of the chief promoters for the growth of the local aviation industry.

Thompson served as a member of the Cleveland Chamber of Commerce's Committee on Aviation. Established in 1918 as the Airplane Field Committee, the group sought to expand and continue the growth of aviation in Cleveland, looking both to wartime needs and to the postwar period when the expertise and industrial capacity developed during the war could be put to profitable civilian use. Just as the war taught Americans and Clevelanders how useful trucks could be, it also taught them the practical

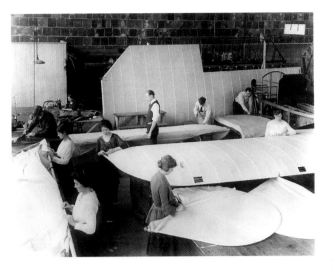

Women helped build the wings for bombers that the Glenn L. Martin Company supplied to the U.S. military in the 1920s.
Western Reserve Historical Society

value of airplanes. Thompson and the committee were determined to bring a major aircraft manufacturer to Cleveland. In 1918, when 10 industrialists had raised enough capital, designer and builder Glenn L. Martin agreed to build an aircraft plant in Cleveland.

Located at 16800 St. Clair, the plant and its adjacent airstrip were one of the nation's most important aircraft developmental centers in the 1920s. Martin produced the nation's standard bombers, the MB-1 and MB-2, as well as mail planes. Working with Martin were Donald W. Douglas, Lawrence Bell and James H. Kindelberger. They would go on to found, respectively, Douglas Aircraft, Bell Aircraft and North American Aviation, Inc.

In 1926 Martin fitted one of his planes with the "aerol strut" designed at the Cleveland Pneumatic Tool Company. This, the first hydraulic landing gear, was an adaptation of the Cleco-Gruss automotive shock absorber developed by Cleveland Pneumatic in 1918. The company's president, Louis Greve, had a board rigged up under the body of the plane, where he could sit and monitor the aerol's performance during repeated test flights. Cleveland Pneumatic continued to introduce innovations in landing gear design, and its products became the industry standard. With the combined presence of the Martin aircraft factory, Thompson Products and Cleveland Pneumatic, Cleveland occupied an apparently secure niche in the developing aviation industry.

After the war, airplanes were used primarily to deliver mail. Cleveland once again benefited from geography, as it found itself on the main New York-Chicago leg of the

A manager at Thompson Products demonstrates how to sell one of the firm's many automobile and aviation parts in the 1950s. Thompson Products employed an aggressive sales force that drove distinctive Thompson Products sales cars, equipped with products and promotional materials.
Western Reserve Historical Society

nation's developing transcontinental airmail-delivery system. The city's first mail flights took place a few weeks after the armistice was declared in 1918. Pilots used a grass airstrip at Woodland Hills Park near East 93rd and Kinsman for takeoff and landing. Equipment and weather problems

temporarily suspended the flights, but they resumed in May 1919, each plane carrying 850 pounds of mail. In September 1920 the route was extended beyond Chicago to San Francisco, making transcontinental service a reality. In 1922 airmail flights between Cleveland and Cincinnati were initiated. During this early period, U.S. Army pilots flew all the planes on these routes.

Given the city's now lively industrial and civic interest in aviation, it is not surprising that local leaders were dismayed when the government expressed concern over the adequacy of the Woodland Hills field. There was a real possibility that the city could be dropped from the airmail route. That was when William Hopkins stepped into local aviation history. He quickly identified a 1,040-acre parcel at Brookpark and Riverside roads, near the Short Line Railroad. Although eight miles from the city center, the area was flat and free from obstructions, a large and ideal site for an airport, city officials and Army Air Service officers agreed. With Hopkins urging immediate action, City

Council issued bonds to raise $1.25 million for the purchase and development of the site, and workers speedily cleared and graded the old farm fields. On July 1, 1925, Cleveland Municipal Airport hosted its first airmail flight. Hopkins had pushed the project through just in time, for in 1925 the United States Congress passed the Kelly Act, which turned the transport of airmail over to private companies. It was the dependable and substantial income from airmail that allowed entrepreneurs to offer passenger service and still make a profit.

In the first half year of its operation, 4,000 flights cleared the airport. In 1927, 14,000 flights used the field, which now had a terminal and the first control tower used

in the United States. An increasing number of planes accommodated passengers. Although Al Engel and other barnstormers had periodically carried passengers, the first regular service to Cleveland began on July 1, 1925, when Ford Commercial Air Lines, with a fleet of 14 trimotor planes, inaugurated passenger flights from Detroit. Stout Air Lines, also headquartered in Detroit, began Cleveland-Detroit service in 1927 and Cleveland-Chicago flights in 1929. The 100-minute flight to Detroit was expensive: $18 one way and $35 round trip. Stout offered bus service from downtown to the airport and until 1931 teamed with the Cleveland, Southwestern and Columbus Railway to offer combined interurban/air tickets from 10 Ohio cities, including Medina, Mansfield, Oberlin and Elyria. Stout, which had been founded by a toy manufacturer, would eventually become part of United Airlines.

The growth of aviation and air travel provided the Austin Co. with a new field for its design and construction business. Austin was by now gaining an international reputation. During the war, it had built military structures for the Army in France, and had constructed a major factory as part of Belgium's postwar reconstruction. Closer to home, the Austin Co. had built the Curtiss aircraft plant in Buffalo as part of that company's wartime expansion. Now, the Cleveland building firm took the lead in the design and construction of airport and airfield facilities, with Wilbert Austin developing a canopy door for hangars.

Although the popularity of air travel was growing, it was not for everyone, due more to the high cost of tickets than the fear of flying. This was especially the case in the 1930s when Cleveland, like most of the nation, was mired in the Great Depression. As a heavily industrialized city, Cleveland

At Cleveland Municipal Airport in the 1930s, passengers walked through gates on the tarmac to board planes, which were arranged around a makeshift barrier, as shown here. *Western Reserve Historical Society*

Florence Boswell ran a flight school at Cleveland's airport in the 1920s and 1930s. *Western Reserve Historical Society*

Rampant unemployment during the Great Depression spurred demonstrations, such as this one in 1935 by the Workers' Alliance of Cleveland. *Cleveland Press Collection, Cleveland State University*

was devastated by the Depression. Unemployment was at one point more than 33 percent. The steel industry and steelworkers were particularly hard hit, as demand for steel-based consumer goods such as automobiles, and industrial goods such as structural steel and railroad steel, plummeted.

By the 1930s three companies dominated the iron and steel industry in Cleveland. The first was a giant national corporation, United States Steel, which operated what had been the Cleveland Rolling Mills (by this time a subsidiary of the American Steel and Wire Company). This included the old plant in Newburgh, a newer facility in Cuyahoga Heights and the Central Furnace. The second company, Cleveland's Otis Steel, had expanded considerably during the 20th century, building a large new plant on the west bank of the Cuyahoga River. Jones and Laughlin of Pittsburgh would acquire Otis in 1942. The third and newest firm was Republic Steel, a Youngstown company that in 1935 took over the Corrigan-McKinney works established on the east bank of the river in 1909. At one point the third-largest steelmaker in the nation, Republic moved its headquarters to Cleveland in 1937.

As jobs were eliminated and wages cut, workers in the steel mills and other industries began to unionize to protect what they had left and to demand changes that would give them a larger share of the wealth produced by local industry. Unions were not new in Cleveland. Skilled workers had the longest history of unionization in Cleveland, with local typographers organized since 1857. Cleveland also served as the national headquarters for the Brotherhood of Locomotive Engineers, the most powerful of the labor organizations representing employees of the

massive railroad industry. However, workers in heavy industry and the automotive plants had not been able to organize effectively. Strikes, some violent, had rocked the local iron and steel industry in 1882, 1885, the 1890s and 1919, but the industry successfully quashed strong unions in the 1920s.

In the 1930s, however, with jobs and livelihoods in jeopardy and aided by the backing of the Roosevelt administration in Washington D.C., those Clevelanders whose labor ultimately made modern forms of transportation possible began to unionize. It was a tough battle. The head of Republic Steel, Tom Girdler, vowed that he would shut down the mills and "raise apples and potatoes" before he would allow his workers to unionize. The "Little Steel Strike" of 1937 ensued, affecting Republic plants in Cleveland, Youngstown and Chicago. Twelve people died, and not until 1942, under the order of the wartime government, did Republic allow its workers to unionize.

On Cleveland's east side, workers at the Fisher Body plant, a division of General Motors, staged a sit-down strike in 1936. It proved a model for others that would follow and led to the acceptance of the United Auto Workers as the company's union. By the early 1940s, the UAW had successfully organized White Motor, Willard Storage Battery, National Carbon and a variety of other area plants that produced automotive-related goods. The union had 40,000 members in Cleveland by 1942.

The pro-labor policies of the Roosevelt administration also helped those who drove the trucks and worked the docks at Cleveland food and freight terminals during the Depression. The Teamsters Union had first organized in

(Far right) Franklin Roosevelt was the first U.S. president to fly regularly; here Roosevelt can be seen passing through the city on his way to the Democratic National Convention in 1932.
Western Reserve Historical Society

Steelworkers pour molten steel into molds at Corrigan-McKinney in 1926.
Cleveland Press Collection, Cleveland State University

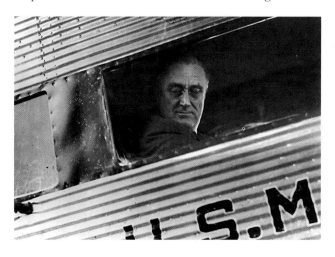

Cleveland in 1912. Despite the numbers of workers in the field, the union had only 3,500 members in the Cleveland area in 1933, when passage of the National Industrial Recovery Act guaranteed the right to unionize. By 1940 it had 24,000.

Unemployment, soup lines and labor violence characterized the Depression years in Cleveland, as elsewhere. Railroads saw the number of paying passengers fall while the number of nonpaying passengers — the unemployed riding on freight trains — increased. Many got off the trains along Cleveland's lakefront, settling in the "Hoovervilles," or shantytowns, that could be found along the tracks. One, along the lakeshore at East 13th Street, housed 200 men. Another had organized mail delivery. Yet another stood adjacent to the new Municipal Stadium, an embarrassment to the city until it was torn down.

Aviation, despite its still limited commercial importance, played a role in helping Cleveland temporarily forget, and eventually overcome, the economic troubles of the Great Depression. Beginning in 1929, Cleveland's airport played host to America's premiere air spectacle, the National Air Races. Once again it was the leaders of the local aviation industry, including Charles Thompson, who convinced the organizers that Cleveland was the best venue for the event. They managed to do so despite the fact that Cleveland's position in aviation had begun to slip. In 1929 Glenn Martin moved his plant to Baltimore where he had more space and a tidewater to test the patrol boats he was building. Eventually, he and other airframe manufacturers would move to the West Coast where sunshine and warm temperatures allowed for year-round aircraft testing.

The air races, which would return to the city in 1931, 32, 34, 35, 37, 38 and 39 and again after the war, featured stunts, closed-

course races, exhibitions and most of all excitement and a glimpse into the future. Its major events, the closed-course Thompson Trophy Race and the cross-country Bendix Race, provided an incentive for private developers to produce faster and better aircraft in an era when the government played a very small role in forwarding aviation technology. The tens of thousands who witnessed the races had a chance to forget the Depression and see the aviation heroes of the day, including people like Charles Lindbergh, Amelia Earhart and Jimmy Doolittle. The most recognizable hero of the races was undoubtedly Roscoe Turner. Mustachioed, dressed in a dashing, custom-made flying suit and accompanied by a mascot lion named Gilmore, Turner was a crowd favorite. Some 50 years after meeting him, one Cleveland woman still retained a

vivid recollection of the famous aviator, declaring, "He was a real hunk!" He was also a superb pilot, winning the Thompson Trophy in 1934, 1938 and 1939.

One of the races' greatest backers in the 1930s was Frederick C. Crawford, who became president of Thompson Products after Charles Thompson's death in 1933. Like Thompson (for whom he had worked since 1916), he used every possible opportunity to promote aviation in Cleveland and benefit those industries tied to it. As early as 1937 Crawford realized that memories of the automotive and aviation industries' beginnings were already fading. To preserve this important facet of industrial history, he founded the Thompson Auto Album and Aviation Museum, a collection of antique cars and airplanes that later became the nucleus of the Western Reserve Historical Society's Crawford Auto Aviation Museum.

Crawford's interest in the past did not distract him from looking toward the future, however. As president of the Cleveland Chamber of Commerce, he led efforts to convince the federal government to locate the National Advisory Committee for Aeronautics' new Aircraft Engine Research Laboratory in Cleveland. The campaign succeeded, with Cleveland winning out over 62 other cities when the government announced its decision in 1940. The laboratory was built at the eastern end of the Municipal Airport. The work done at NACA and at aviation-related industries in Cleveland would be critical in the coming five years as the United States entered World War II. It would also help lift the city out of the Great Depression.

When war broke out in September 1939 with the German invasion of Poland, it became obvious to most observers that aircraft would play a prominent role in the conflict. The German blitzkrieg showed how effective combined air and ground operations could be. The Battle of Britain, which followed, reinforced this view. Local industry began to increase production even before Pearl Harbor as the government began providing aid to Great Britain through the Lend-Lease program and also elevating its own level of preparedness. In 1941 a government loan enabled Thompson Products to build a huge new facility, the TAPCO plant, in suburban Euclid producing vital aircraft engine components. The company would remain a leader in defense and aviation manufacturing following the war, merging with the Ramo-Wooldridge Company of California in 1958 to form Thompson Ramo Wooldridge, later TRW, Inc., a Fortune 500 company and major international presence in transportation-related industries into the 21st century.

Along with Amelia Earhart, Jackie Cochrane was one of many women aviators who participated in the National Air Races. Cochrane won the Bendix Trophy.

Western Reserve Historical Society

Other companies linked to aircraft manufacturing also stepped up production during the war. Cleveland Pneumatic, the dominant supplier of aircraft landing gear for both commercial and military planes, built the world's largest landing gear factory in Euclid. In the spirit of wartime cooperation, Cleveland Pneumatic shared its technology with other companies, creating postwar competitors in its own field. (Purchased by B.F. Goodrich in 1993, the company remained the world's largest manufacturer of landing gear.) The Pesco Products Company built aircraft pumps, and the Aluminum Company of America, or Alcoa, greatly expanded production of aluminum forgings at its Cleveland plant, as lighter metals came in demand for wartime aviation. In 1943 the trade journal *Aerosphere* listed 189 regional companies that together supplied one-quarter of the aircraft industry's need for parts and materials.

William S. Jack was a native-born Clevelander and a longtime union member. A machinist, he had joined the International Association of Machinists in 1911 at age 23. In two years he rose to become the union's Cleveland district business agent. But Bill Jack was also a talented, if unconventional, businessman. From the 1910s to the 1930s he

organized and then sold several successful businesses, including the precursor to Pesco Products. In 1940 he teamed with Ralph M. Heintz to form Jack & Heintz in Palo Alto, California, to manufacture precision aircraft parts. Bucking the trend that saw aviation moving west, he moved the company east to his hometown.

During the war, Jack & Heintz became Cleveland's greatest success story and also its most desirable place of employment. It went from 46 employees in 1940 to 8,700 in 1944, with 35,000 on the waiting list. Employees were called "associates." They received free medical care and life, accident and medical insurance. Free meals and vitamin pills were available in the cafeteria and employees on break could have steam baths and massages. Music was piped to work areas. In return Jack & Heintz required employees to work long shifts, seven days a week. They were paid time and a half for work beyond 40 hours and could receive free vacations in Florida. The company was able to cut costs on government contracts, passing the extra money on to its employees as part of a profit-sharing plan.

Within a few short months the war moved Cleveland from unemployment to excess employment. More African Americans and people from Appalachia came north, drawn in waves to the industrial cities of the nation's heartland, as European immigrants had been drawn 40 years before. News filtered back to the mountains and bayous, to the coal mines and sharecroppers' fields, that there were good jobs to be had in wartime production. One West Virginia man who heard that White Motors was hiring got in his car and made the drive north on the strength of that rumor. He

During World War II, women entered Cleveland's steel mills in record numbers to help meet production goals for the war effort. Here welders take a break for the filming of a World War II propaganda film at Republic Steel. *Western Reserve Historical Society*

had no idea where White was, except that it was in Cleveland, and found the plant by asking people on the street. What he had heard back home turned out to be true, and his journey paid off. He was taken on to the White work force, joining thousands of employees now laboring to produce half-tracks and armored car, rather than White's usual commercial trucks.

White and other defense plants also tapped a labor source closer at hand to staff their production lines. Cleveland-area women played a vital part in the civilian war effort, leaving homes or poorly paid jobs as salesclerks or waitresses to work in industry. On a smaller scale, the same thing had happened during World War I, with women filling what were considered men's jobs: for instance, "conductorettes" worked on Cleveland streetcars until objections from the male-dominated street railway employees' union led to their dismissal after the war.

Many of the factory workers during World War II had husbands, fiancés or brothers in Europe or the Pacific, and this fact gave a personal significance to the impersonal routine of the defense plant assembly line. One of the jobs

women performed at White Motors was packing replacement parts in protective cloth and wax for shipment to the front, where army mechanics would use them to repair White-made vehicles. Recalling her wartime employment, one woman recounted how she and her co-workers would sneak notes in along with the parts to boost the morale of the soldiers who would unwrap them.

A similar spirit of patriotism pervaded Cleveland's largest wartime factory, the Cleveland Bomber Plant, built by the Department of Defense on Riverside Drive adjacent to the airport. In 1942 its 15,000 workers began producing the new B-29 bomber. To spur their own production efforts, employees gave their work areas names like "Iwo Jima" or "Guadalcanal."

On the other side of the airport, the scientists and engineers at NACA were working in their own way to bolster the country's airborne military might. NACA's initial work focused on the problems encountered by reciprocating aircraft engines at high altitudes. It helped solve cooling problems with the engines that would power the B-29. Its altitude wind tunnel was the most advanced in the world.

However, by the time the tunnel was completed and in full operation in 1944, the research concerns at NACA had changed. The facility began to concentrate on the development of turbojet engines. Germany and England had already built jets, and the new propulsion system was changing warfare over Europe. It promised to change the nature of air travel forever.

At Cleveland City Hall, transportation concerns were more down to earth. As Allied forces advanced across Europe and the Pacific and victory seemed within reach, local planners began to consider what the future Cleveland would look like. Concerned primarily with making the urban environment more livable, they proposed more parks and filled out the plans, initiated as early as the 1920s, for a series of limited-access highways leading through and out of the city. They hoped that by removing traffic from city streets and onto highways, they could make Cleveland neighborhoods quieter and more attractive. The biggest question was: would it be the city, state or federal government that paid the bill?

With the end of the war, Cleveland and its transportation system entered what might be considered a golden age, with almost all major categories of modern transport available in one form or another. Water transport, which had served Cleveland well since the settlement's earliest days, still functioned, mainly in the form of the massive ore freighters that continued to ply Lake Erie and the Cuyahoga. Although passenger transport on the lake had almost disappeared by this time, the Detroit and Cleveland Steam Navigation Company operated between those cities until 1951. A brief experiment with a troop carrier-turned-cruise ship, the *Aquarama*, extended passenger service into the 1960s.

The transportation marvel of the 19th century, the railroad, seemed unassailable. During the war, almost all troops had moved by train within the United States. In Cleveland 60 passenger trains a day called at bustling Union Terminal. After the war, railroads such as the New York Central totally modernized their passenger fleets in the assumption that ridership would continue to grow. Although the heavy demands of wartime traffic had played havoc with road maintenance, necessitating extra investment in repair and renovation, railroaders felt the future to be a secure one. They were confident that innovations like diesel power, slick streamlined styling and radio communication would stave off growing competition from trucks and automobiles.

On Cleveland's streets, the Cleveland Transit System (CTS), the public entity that had taken over the Cleveland Railway Company in 1942, carried several hundred million riders each year. CTS was by now operating a growing fleet of trackless trolleys and gasoline-powered buses in addition to streetcars. At the other end of the transportation spectrum, aviation proponents looked forward to the day

when the advances made during the war would fully affect passenger transport. Already, the workhorse DC-3s were being replaced by larger, longer-range four-engine planes such as the Lockheed Constellation. In 1945 Eastern Airlines, the major carrier in America, received permission

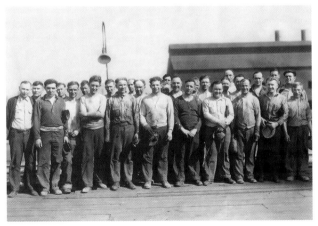

to enter the Cleveland market. It immediately began service to Miami.

The National Air Races resumed in 1946, returning to Cleveland each year through 1949. However, the postwar races had a different look. They were dominated by surplus warplanes such as the P-51 Mustang and the Corsair. No longer could home-built planes developed by enthusiasts compete successfully with those designed and produced under government patronage. Jets also appeared, pumping up the races' speed and excitement. Record after record was broken. But speed soon put a tragic end to the National Air Races in Cleveland. In 1949 Bill Odum's P-51 slammed into a Berea house, killing a mother and child as well as the pilot himself.

What put Cleveland in motion after the war was in fact not so much a matter of technological development as a shift in personal expectations. Servicemen born and raised within the confines of Little Italy or Warszawa had now spent several years in close company with fellow soldiers from varied backgrounds. Catholic sons of immigrants bunked with country boys from the South, trained with Jews from New York City, and served side-by-side with Protestants from upscale suburbs like Shaker Heights. Almost all traveled around the United States; many went abroad, and most returned. The old neighborhoods now seemed too small, as young men came back with broader horizons and a different sense of who they were or what they could be.

African-Americans from Cleveland served in large numbers in a war against fascism and racism. They served, however, in segregated units and returned to segregated communities. One veteran remembered his arrival back in Cleveland. He came in on the Pennsylvania Railroad, getting off at its East 55th and Euclid Avenue station. From there he walked straight back into the Cedar Central neighborhood, where much of the city's black population lived in its own separate, but not equal, community. Although glad to be home, he could not ignore the paradox of what he had fought for and what he returned to. African-American veterans and their children would no longer tolerate second-class citizenship.

Women who had worked at men's jobs in war industry plants felt similarly. Like the conductorettes of World War I, they gave up their jobs to the returning soldiers. Although

During the 1949 Thompson Trophy race, pilot Bill Odom crashed his highly modified P-51C racer into a Berea home, killing himself, resident Jeanne Laird and her 13-month-old son. The crash produced a flurry of ordinances in nearby communities that prohibited racing over their cities, effectively ending the National Air Races in Cleveland. *Western Reserve Historical Society*

(Both images, left) Work in Cleveland's steel industry paid well, even though the work was often hot, dirty and dangerous. Until the 1950s many sections of the mills often were segregated into all-black or all-white work crews, as these pictures taken at Republic Steel in the late 1940s document *Western Reserve Historical Society*

many did so gladly, marrying or joining returning spouses and starting families, their experiences as independent wage earners had given them a different perspective on life.

Despite contradictions such as these, the general mood was one of optimism, buoyed by victory and the joy of a safe return. The privations of war, slight as they had been in the United States, gave people a taste for the good things in life. At this particular time, the focus of most personal expectations was the purchase of an automobile. Savings from work in wartime industries and higher unionized wages now made it possible for most Clevelanders to buy a car. Auto sales boomed when the first new models came out after the war.

Personal mobility brought demographic movement away from the city and out to the suburbs. The Willow Freeway, completed in large part by 1950, enabled Clevelanders to move to the southern suburbs. The extension of the Memorial Shoreway into the Lakeland Freeway resulted in the growth of Euclid and other eastern suburbs. Even without limited-access highways, people moved in large numbers. Italian-Americans, for instance, left their Little Italy neighborhood at the western end of Mayfield

Road in Cleveland and moved east along Mayfield to Lyndhurst and South Euclid. The automobile, along with advantageous housing loans provided to veterans by the G.I. Bill passed in 1944, made this possible. The city hall planners who had seen highways as a way of enhancing life in Cleveland's neighborhoods now stood by and watched as the city started to empty on the roads they had promoted.

Cleveland's population reached a peak of 914,808 in 1950. This was only 66 percent of the county total, however. Shaker Heights, Cleveland Heights, East Cleveland and Lakewood had grown faster than their parent city, and they along with newer suburbs were home to an increasing share of Cuyahoga County's people. Areas that had been rural quickly changed character, evolving from village to city within a span of two to three decades. Parma, southwest of Cleveland across Brookpark Road, incorporated as a village in 1924 and a city in 1931, now had more than 20,000 residents. In the years 1951-1960, 12 suburbs — Bay Village, Mayfield Heights, Fairview Park, Parma Heights, Westlake, Brecksville, Broadview Heights, Independence, North Olmsted, Richmond Heights, Strongsville and Warrensville Heights — were incorporated as cities. In the same period, Cleveland lost population for the first time in its modern history, with the

city's 876,050 people making up little more than half the county total by 1960. The automobile had driven this demographic shift.

The new suburban homes and new commuter lifestyle seemed to say that the character of Greater Cleveland had

changed. Yet in another sense, the city had remained much the same. Its economic structure and its people's workday lives were to all appearances continuing in the same track as before the war. Most Clevelanders still held jobs in heavy industry. The city's steel mills entered the 1960s working at full capacity. Steel was critical in meeting the ever-increasing demand for consumer goods such as washers, refrigerators and especially automobiles. A unionized job at J&L or Republic was a ticket to the good life. Youngsters graduating from city high schools often chose to enter the mills rather than invest in a college education. The immediate returns seemed far better.

The automotive industry employed even more Greater Clevelanders than did the steel mills, although there were no longer any Cleveland-designed cars. Area workers instead made parts and assembled components and vehicles for the big three, Ford, General Motors and Chrysler. In 1963 Greater Cleveland had 59 motor vehicle parts and assembly plants producing products worth $559 million and employing 37,383 people, nearly 13 percent of the regional industrial work force.

George Lewis directed the National Advisory Committee for Aeronautics and was instrumental in bringing space research to Northeastern Ohio. The NASA facility near Hopkins International Airport held his name until 1999.
NASA Glenn Research Center

Many of these plants were now outside of the city proper, located along rail lines. The construction of Thompson Product's TAPCO plant in Euclid during the war presaged this. New modern factories were one-story structures that needed vast amounts of inexpensive real estate. For this reason, Ford established engine plants in the suburb of Brook Park in 1951 and 1955 and a stamping plant in Walton Hills in 1954. General Motors built a transmission plant in Parma in 1949. Chrysler would opt for a location in the next county, constructing a stamping plant in Twinsburg. Proximity to these plants, with their large numbers of jobs, made living in the suburbs even more attractive to many former residents of the central city.

The automotive row along Brookpark Road in the 1950s and 1960s, as an indicator of Greater Cleveland's industrial strength, was a reassuring sign of continuity with the city's past. A little farther down the road, developments at the airport and the NACA facility pointed to the future. In 1947-8 the NACA facility was renamed the Lewis Flight Propulsion Research Laboratory, as it continued its task of investigating jet and other promising propulsion technologies. In 1956 the airport opened a new terminal building to accommodate the growing number of airline passengers. The year before, American Airlines, a prime carrier into Cleveland, had purchased a fleet of 30 Boeing 707s, the first American commercial jetliner. The 707 and the Douglas DC-8 that shortly followed it changed commercial aviation. Flights were now quieter and faster. The world was shrinking, due in large part to jet technology. The scientists at Lewis Laboratory played a significant role in developing and refining this technology; the skilled workers at Thompson Products, who now added jet fan blades to their repertoire of transportation-related parts production, helped make it a reality.

In 1958 the NACA facility came under the control of the new National Aeronautics and Space Administration. NASA had been created to meet a Soviet Russian challenge in outer space: the 1957 rocket-powered launching of Sputnik, the first artificial earth satellite. The new achievement, with clear potential for military application, had badly shaken the United States. NACA scientists had, in fact, engaged in rocket technology research and development since the last years of World War II, when the success of the German V-2 rocket caught the attention of the aviation

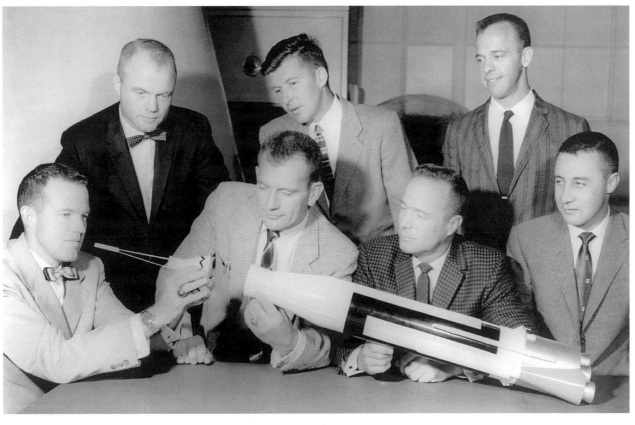

John Glenn (standing left) was among the seven Mercury astronauts in the 1950s as they trained for the first space missions. *NASA Glenn Research Center*

and defense community. However, rocket research had initially remained in the background, as the laboratory concentrated its attention on jet propulsion. The Sputnik launch and the creation of NASA changed this, placing a new and public priority on rocket development. Much of the staff at NASA's Lewis Laboratory in Cleveland would set their sights on outer space. When in 1961 President John F. Kennedy committed the United States to land a man on the moon before the end of the decade, activity at the facility accelerated further as it participated in the Mercury and Apollo space programs.

Back on earth, Clevelanders were enjoying their own modest form of mobility, traveling in their cars to Manners drive-in restaurants (a chain founded and based in Cleveland) and the new shopping malls in the suburbs. Television and radio reports brought news of the Cuban missile crisis and Project Mercury into their homes. Fellow Ohioan John Glenn's three earth orbits in the space capsule *Friendship 7* made banner headlines in Cleveland and across the nation in 1962. Space was a popular topic of conversation, and Clevelanders were proud of what their city was contributing in the effort to beat the Russians. Yet most still lived in the expectation that the familiar systems of transportation and industry built up over the past 100 years would go on more or less unchanged. That would not be the case, for a new global struggle was under way. In a shrinking world, Clevelanders could not escape its consequences.

A lakefront airport was first suggested in the 1930s. A facility finally opened in 1947 and was named after Mayor Thomas Burke in 1958. *Cleveland Press Collection, Cleveland State University*

chapter nine

Missed Connections and
Unforeseen Consequences

In October 1973 Clevelanders were forced to realize that

there were two sides to every advance in transportation. In that month

the Organization of Arab Petroleum Exporting Countries embargoed oil

shipments to the United States and other western nations that supported

Israel. The United States, once the chief oil-producing country in the world,

had become heavily dependent on cheap imported oil. This should have

seemed particularly ironic to Clevelanders, whose city had once been the

oil-refining center of the world. But in the years since Rockefeller's

Standard Oil had controlled the market, advances in drilling, piping and

transoceanic shipment had made it possible to sell foreign oil at prices

that made exploration costs for new domestic fields prohibitive.

Since the days of exploration, visitors and residents alike had dreamed of a time when a clear channel could be opened from the Atlantic Ocean to the farthest reaches of the Great Lakes, opening the region to global commerce. The completion of the first Welland Canal in 1829, which enabled waterborne traffic to bypass Niagara Falls, was an initial step. Only in 1959 was the dream fully realized. The St. Lawrence Seaway, opened that year, allowed large, ocean-going ships full access to the lakes. Cleveland and other Great Lakes cities looked forward to huge increases in commerce, with local products shipped at low cost to markets in Europe. What happened was essentially the reverse. European goods, particularly steel, began to pile up on the docks of Cleveland. Rebuilt factories, lower labor costs and government support in Europe had literally turned the tide in the flow of manufactured goods. Cleveland's industries now faced global competition at their doorstep.

Local manufacturers attempted to use a new link in the area's transportation system to their advantage in order

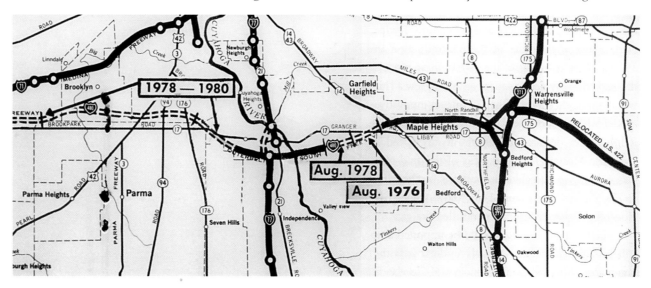

At the same time, the American infatuation with automobiles grew, driving up demand for the product and helping to make the United States by far the largest consumer of the world's oil production.

When the 11 OPEAC nations turned off the flow from their wells, the price of gasoline in Cleveland went from around 35 cents to over $1 per gallon. Shortages developed. Endless lines formed at those service stations that still had gasoline. The government took emergency measures, such as lowering the national speed limit to 55 miles per hour to lessen demand, and even discussed a plan for rationing.

Clevelanders quickly learned two lessons from the embargo. The first was that the current global battle for empire between the United States and the Soviet Union was not limited to the space race or even the threat of nuclear destruction, but could take other forms. Just as Britain and France had staked national prestige and imperial ambitions on gaining control over the distant Ohio country in the 18th century, the 20th-century superpowers fought their battle by proxy in the strife-riven Middle East, with the United States backing Israel while the Soviet Union supported several of the Arab states. Moscow stood behind the embargo.

The second lesson was recognition of just how dependent the city and region had become on the automobile. Greater Clevelanders unable or unwilling to pay the price at the pumps turned to public transportation, but the Cleveland Transit System was itself in a bind. Its last streetcar had run in 1954, and in 1963 it phased out the last of its electric-powered trackless trolley buses. With the exception of its rapid transit line, which had opened in 1955, it too was dependent on petroleum products.

CTS also lacked the resources needed to cope with the sudden demand. The system had last turned a profit in 1967. It was running annual deficits well over $1.5 million by the early 1970s. As more commuters deserted public transit for private automobiles, revenues dropped, and as revenues dropped, ticket prices were raised to make up the difference. Higher prices further decreased ridership, resulting in service cuts. It was a vicious downward spiral, which kept CTS from buying new or improved equipment. In any case, CTS was no longer an option for many Greater Clevelanders, since they had moved to suburbs with no public transportation service.

The growing popularity of the automobile, along with improvements in air travel, had also almost destroyed another link in Cleveland's transportation system, the passenger railroad. In 1973 only two trains served the city. One, operated by the new national passenger service, Amtrak, connected Cleveland with New York and Chicago. The other was a commuter train to Youngstown operated by the Erie Lackawanna Railroad. Commuters

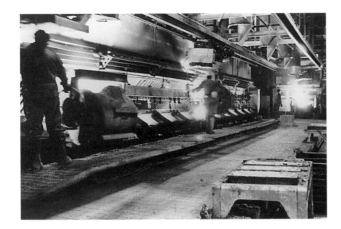

bound for suburbs southeast of Cleveland jammed its cars during the oil crisis.

The embargo's impact went beyond the immediate crisis of higher gasoline prices and stranded commuters. It began to affect Cleveland's basic industries as well. Small, fuel-efficient cars — not domestic automakers' prime product — were suddenly in high demand. Sales of larger American-made cars plummeted. Steel production, heavily dependent on the automotive market, also fell. While American makers rethought their products and retooled their factories, imported cars made their move. Compact, well-made imports had been working their way into the American market ever since the first two Volkswagens were shipped in 1949.

By the late 1950s the relatively inexpensive smaller European cars had become something of a threat. American manufacturers responded with the Ford Falcon, Chevrolet Corvair and Dodge Dart. Between the time of their introduction in 1960 and the gas crisis of the 1970s, these models did something typically American: they grew. (This was with the exception of the Corvair, an innovative model whose production life was cut short when Ralph Nader declared it "unsafe at any speed.") Even the Mustang, the pony car of the mid-60s, was growing to horselike proportions by the early 1970s. Volkswagens and Fiats, now joined by Hondas and Toyotas from Japan, filled the gap.

The fact that these cars could be imported and still undersell American models underscored the importance of transportation technology in Cleveland's

development. The shipping network that brought the cars connected to Cleveland only at its endpoint. It nonetheless affected the city, because its cost efficiencies, combined with those of the overseas car producers, made the product competitive.

Those efficiencies also governed the import of other products, particularly steel. When Cleveland soldiers left Europe or Japan after World War II, they left economies in ruin. Twenty years after the war the industrial base of those economies had been rebuilt, in the form of modern, efficient factories. Even with transportation costs factored in, Cleveland's steel mills found it hard to compete with products from Europe and Japan. Ironically, a highly touted regional transportation improvement made it easy to import steel and other products into America's industrial heartland.

The moulding line of the foundry at Ford's Brook Park facility fed America's increasing appetite for automobiles in the 1960s.
Cleveland Press Collection, Cleveland State University

During the 1970s and the 1980s, the deteriorating steel market led to the consolidation of the industry in Cleveland, closure of older, less-efficient mills and the loss of thousands of jobs. Here, a worker at Republic Steel toiled above the furnace in the 1950s, when the steel plants along the Cuyahoga River employed over 10,000 workers.
Cleveland Press Collection, Cleveland State University

Since the days of exploration, visitors and residents alike had dreamed of a time when a clear channel could be opened from the Atlantic Ocean to the farthest reaches of the Great Lakes, opening the region to global commerce. The completion of the first Welland Canal in 1829, which enabled waterborne traffic to bypass Niagara Falls, was an initial step. Only in 1959 was the dream fully realized. The St. Lawrence Seaway, opened that year, allowed large, ocean-going ships full access to the lakes. Cleveland and other Great Lakes cities looked forward to huge increases in commerce, with local products shipped at low cost to markets in Europe. What happened was essentially the reverse. European goods, particularly steel, began to pile up on the docks of Cleveland. Rebuilt factories, lower labor costs and government support in Europe had literally turned the tide in the flow of manufactured goods. Cleveland's industries now faced global competition at their doorstep.

Local manufacturers attempted to use a new link in the area's transportation system to their advantage in order

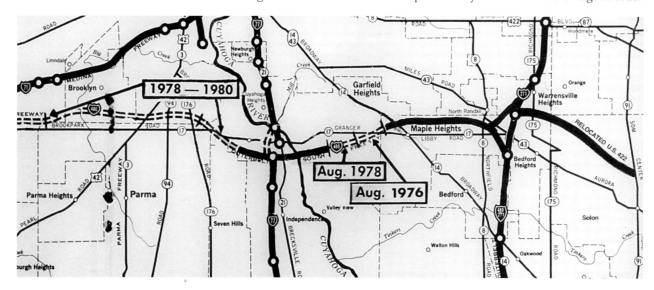

to meet the competition and increase profits. Until the late 1950s good rail and water transportation connections were essential to the success of almost every industrial enterprise. Cleveland and other Great Lakes cities had these connections. At this point, a viable alternative began to change the situation, as trucks increasingly challenged rail transportation for a share in carrying the nation's goods.

Improvement and expansion of the nation's highway system made this possible. As the number of new intercity highways grew, so did the percentage of freight carried by truck. When the federal government committed to the construction of an interstate highway system by passing the National Interstate and Defense Highways Act in 1956, the destinies of older industrial cities such as Cleveland changed forever. While the new emphasis on road transportation benefited some local companies, for example White Motor, it had a generally damaging effect on Cleveland's neighborhoods.

The Interstate Highways Act provided the necessary funds to build the network of toll-free, limited-access roads some Clevelanders had envisioned since the 1920s. The state-run toll road, the Ohio Turnpike, had opened along its full length in 1955, whetting the appetite of truckers and travelers alike for non-stop travel on multi-lane divided highways. By the 1970s much of the toll-free interstate system in the Cleveland area was complete, linking the city to Columbus and Cincinnati (I-71), southeastern Ohio (I-77), and points east and west (I-90). An outer

A Ford employee at Brook Park reads about the possibility of the plant being closed in 1980. *Cleveland Press Collection, Cleveland State University*

ring road (I-271) tied the system together. An inner ring road (I-480) would eventually complete the local network.

Cleveland's manufacturing industries had to cut their expenses to increase profits. The most obvious ways to do this were first, to invest in modern, more efficient plants and second, to lower labor costs. With highways in place and better truck services available, they could accomplish both at once by building new plants in areas of the country where unions were weak, labor cheaper, and taxes and other costs lower.

By the late 1950s and early 1960s, an increasing number chose to relocate outside northeastern Ohio. During the next 20 years dozens of plants would move to areas of cheaper labor or close entirely due to foreign competition. The American Stove Company, which had for years built Magic Chef-brand ranges in Cleveland, left its Harvard Avenue plant in 1958 and moved to Tennessee. One of the region's major manufacturers of fasteners, the National

Deindustrialization would hit Cleveland hard. Jobs were lost in nearly every manufacturing sector. Lines of unemployed workers, like this one in 1982, grew longer. *Cleveland Press Collection, Cleveland State University*

Workers build trucks at White Motors in the 1950s, meeting the increasing demand of an expanding trucking industry.
Western Reserve Historical Society

Screw Company, shut down its huge plant near Woodland and East 79th Street in 1969, moving to a new one-story plant in Lake County. Weakened by changes in both global and local transportation systems, the industrial web that held Cleveland's economy and its neighborhoods together was beginning to disintegrate.

The new transportation patterns did have positive effects as well. Trucking, always strong in northeastern Ohio, prospered with the growth of the interstate system. Hugh O'Neill's sons, Bill, Steve and Hugh, Jr., would use their long experience in the business to put together one of the nation's premiere trucking operations, Leaseway Transportation, in 1960. An innovative holding company, Leaseway combined the operations of 79 firms in a loose confederation. That confederation would eventually grow to 150 firms, so that at its peak in 1983 Leaseway would own 82,000 vehicles, employ 16,000 people and earn $1.3 billion in revenues.

In addition to the Leaseway companies, the "Big 5" of trucking in the 1950s, Roadway, Consolidated Freightways, Pacific-Intermountain Express, Yellow Freight and McLean Trucking, all served Greater Cleveland. It was only outside of the city, however, that an observer could get a real sense of the industry's size and scale, as most of the headquarters and service areas were located near I-77 between Akron and Cleveland in Richfield.

Many Clevelanders could see more trucks and heavy traffic than they wanted to without leaving their own back yards. The new highways cut through the middle of a number of established neighborhoods. They not only created high noise levels and pollution, but also severed the internal unity built up over the course of years. Many neighborhoods were affected. The Willow Freeway, which would become I-77, divided the Fleet Avenue portion of the Polish and

Czech community from Newburgh Heights. Large numbers of homes in Euclid, a relatively new suburb, were demolished in advance of the Lakeland Freeway. But nowhere else, perhaps, was the social damage as great as in Tremont.

Located just across the Flats from the southern part of downtown Cleveland, Tremont had at one time been home to some of the area's wealthier families, such as the Lamsons and the Sessions, who had constructed their

In 1937, about a decade before White motors was purchased by Volvo, the company's East 79th street plant produced its 600,000th truck. *Western Reserve Historical Society*

White Motors employees read about the possibilty of their plant closing in the Clevalnd Press on May 8th,1980. *Western Reserve Historical Society*

fastener factory nearby on Scranton Road. The neighborhood's main street, Jennings Avenue (West 14th), was lined with large houses. A central square, Pelton Park, provided green space. From 1851 to 1853 the area served as the home of Cleveland's short-lived first university and boasted street names like Literary, Professor and College. During the Civil War a military hospital and the city's largest training camp, Camp Cleveland, stood there. Known successively as Cleveland Heights, University Heights and Lincoln Heights (with Pelton Park becoming Lincoln Park), the neighborhood did not receive the name of Tremont until early in the 20th century.

By that time the area had changed completely. Now connected to downtown by the Central Viaduct, it was hemmed in by a growing number of heavy industries in the valley below, including (after 1912) Otis Steel's new Riverside works. Tremont became a prime residential area for the workers in those factories. Poles, Ukrainians, Slovaks, Carpatho-Russians, Syrians, Greeks and a host of other nationalities settled in the area, each building their own churches and meeting halls, each laying a special claim to the region. Residents gained a reputation for unorthodoxy, founding schismatic parishes or left-wing organizations.

Although smoky and noisy, Tremont inspired intense loyalty among the immigrants and children of immigrants who lived there. Some, including writer Raymond DeCapite, made life in the neighborhood the subject of novels such as *The Coming of Fabrize*. In a memoir and commentary on the neighborhood, Tremont resident Paul Ziats described the area with fondness.

It was a good neighborhood, a poor neighborhood, it was an ethnic neighborhood. It was not a ghetto, it was Cleveland, Ohio's notorious Southside... The area was serviced by a Cleveland railway streetcar running from the downtown, Prospect and Ontario Street, south past the Central Market house, across Central Viaduct Bridge to Fairfield Avenue and West 14th Street....The streetcar was called a "dinky" because it was driven by a one man combination conductor and motorman... By the early '20s the Southside settled within itself and became an enclave of industrious families striving to better themselves so that a brighter future could be given to their children than what the emigrant parents never dreamed of in Europe.

In 1959 a new bridge across the valley terminated in Tremont. It was the western end of the new Innerbelt Freeway. In the years that followed, hundreds of homes and businesses on the north side of Tremont were demolished to make way for the Airport Freeway (I- 71), which went southwest from the end of the innerbelt. When the freeway cut the area in two, many residents did what some of their neighbors had done earlier and opted for a life in the suburbs. They followed a standard route down West 25th Street to Parma, Parma Heights and other suburbs of the southwest side. By 1980 Parma was the second-largest city in the county, with a population of 110,000, nearly one-fifth as many people as the central city. More than 36,000 people had lived in Tremont in 1920. In 1980 barely more than 10,000 residents remained.

As shifts in regional transportation and improvements in global transport led to a partial de-industrialization of northeastern Ohio, those same systems brought more people hoping to work in the area's industrial plants. The change in the region's economy would be clear only in hindsight. Throughout the 1950s and 1960s, when opportunities for unskilled labor in northeastern Ohio were beginning to diminish, large numbers of people expecting to find work in factories and mills continued to move to the area. Some came from Europe, largely under special programs that allowed people displaced during World War II and its aftermath to immigrate to the United States despite the still highly restrictive overall immigration policy.

Most new Clevelanders of the period, however, came from within the United States. The second internal "great migration" brought tens of thousands of African-Americans seeking freedom and opportunity in the north. Buses and automobiles, using the growing highway network, carried much of this migration. In the 20 years from 1950 to 1970, Cleveland's black population increased from 147,850 to 287,850. Other migrants came from the American commonwealth of Puerto Rico. The United States Steel plant in Lorain, Ohio, had brought the first large group of Puerto Ricans to northeast Ohio during World War II to fill jobs in its mills. Some moved eastward to Cleveland. By the 1950s others were coming westward from New York City, which was growing into the center of the continental Puerto Rican population following the establishment of regular air service between it and San Juan in the late 1940s.

What the new migrants found instead of plentiful high-paid industrial jobs was a climate of diminishing opportunity, along with prejudice and segregation. A large portion of the city's African-American population had no choice but to live as tenants in the deteriorating buildings of neglected inner-city neighborhoods. Whites departed for the suburbs, their flight accelerated by some real estate dealers using "blockbusting" tactics to take advantage of the situation. Ninety-percent white in 1950, the east side Hough neighborhood was three-quarters black only 10 years later. Like many older American cities, Cleveland experienced what is euphemistically called "urban unrest" during the 1960s. Riots in Hough in 1966 and the Glenville area in 1968 resulted not only in loss of life and millions of dollars' worth of property damage, but took a

psychological toll as well, raising doubts about the city's ability to exist as a unified community.

The riots also put Cleveland in the national news, dismaying those who believed the city's future depended on positive perceptions in markets across the country and the world. During the 1950s, when general prosperity masked growing urban problems, civic leaders and the local media had promoted Cleveland with a slogan: "The Best Location in the Nation." Although the phrase itself might be modern, the idea echoed opinions expressed by Washington and Franklin nearly 200 years before. Now, for the first time since the pre-canal days, some began to doubt its truth.

In 1969 the city's image would deteriorate further with national news coverage of a spectacular fire on the Cuyahoga River. An oil slick under a railroad trestle burst into flames, igniting the trestle and growing into a five-story-high conflagration. Although it was brought under control after only 20 minutes, the damage had already been done in terms of negative publicity.

Firefighters extiguish a fire on the Cuyahoga River in 1952.
Cleveland Press Collection, Cleveland State University

The river had in fact burned many times before. A small river fire helped the city greet the new century on New Year's Day in 1900. A larger blaze inconvenienced industry during the Korean War in 1952. Neither attracted much attention. Transportation and manufacturing had ravaged the local environment for years, but this was considered the necessary price of progress. Government officials, anxious to see the city grow and prosper, refused to hinder industry in any way.

Broadway and Dille Avenue are covered by red dust in 1968. The billowing smokestacks that had once attracted immigrants to Cleveland's booming economy began to drive them to the suburbs after World War II.
Cleveland Press Collection, Cleveland State University

Average citizens, too, while aware of pollution, for the most part simply lived with it in the years between 1850 and the 1960s. Early settlers lamented the pall of factory and railroad smoke that covered the city by the 1860s. For steelworkers and their families living near the mills in the late 1800s, factory smoke, however unpleasant, spelled jobs and wages. They made few public complaints, although for women in particular it was a major nuisance, making it difficult to keep their homes clean or hang laundry out to dry. A woman who lived on the southeast side in the 1880s noted that the strike at the Cleveland Rolling Mills did the neighborhood a favor by clearing the air for a time.

Smoke abatement finally became a matter of debate beginning in the late 19th century, although little was done at the official level. At the individual level, the new mobility offered first by streetcars and then by autos gave middle-class and some working people the option of escaping the smoke by leaving the city. During World War II, when Cleveland feared a possible enemy air attack, it turned its ability to pollute into a defense tactic. The city tried a test "smoke out," in which factories and homes (many still burning coal for heating) pumped out as much smoke as possible to obscure targets on the ground.

Water quality, which had a more obvious effect on health, had attracted somewhat more concern. From John

Melish to Frank Vlchek, observers had left written records of their disgust at the smell or sight of the Cuyahoga River. Although the malaria of the early period was a natural phenomenon, as the human population grew and untreated waste went directly into the river, diseases like typhoid became a serious problem. By the early 1900s, Cleveland had developed a sewer system that kept the worst of human waste out of the river and the lake beyond. But the Cuyahoga still was an industrial sewer. Cleveland answered the problem by progressively moving its drinking water intake farther out into the lake as the water pollution grew.

The river's lower reaches contained such a brew of pollutants by the 1960s that one firm's chemists hit upon the idea of using its waters as a test for industrial coatings. They suspended painted test panels from wires in the Cuyahoga, just down the bank from

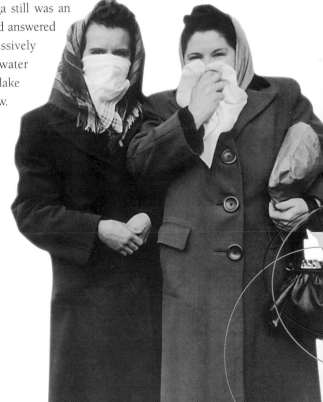

Stephanie and Nettie Nowak cover their mouths with handkerchiefs to shield their lungs from toxic air in 1946.
Cleveland Press Collection, Cleveland State University

the establishment of the Environmental Protection Agency were a legacy, in part, of the fire and the "dead" lake.

In other ways, too, solutions to the problems of the 1960s were developing. Cleveland began making changes in its transportation system in order to address its place in the evolving global economy. On November 15, 1968, Carl B. Stokes helped dedicate the Cleveland Transit System's new rapid transit connection to Cleveland Hopkins International Airport; with its opening, Cleveland became the first American city to connect its airport with the central city by light rail transit. Stokes himself represented a major change in Cleveland's history. His parents, Charles and Louise Stokes, had come to Cleveland as part of the first great migration from the south. In 1967 he had been elected as the city's first African-American mayor, becoming the first African-American mayor of a major U.S. city.

their laboratories. When the river ate through the wires, dropping the panels to its murky bottom, the procedure had to be changed. The tests were moved inside, with a lab worker sent down to the river daily to collect buckets of water for the purpose. This same water source flowed directly into Lake Erie, and its pollutants severely affected the fish population. In 1970 the state government banned the consumption of certain lake fish because they contained high levels of industrial mercury. Lake Erie was dying or dead.

Yet the ability to recognize problems was a first step in dealing with them. Clevelanders joined in the first national Earth Day events in April 1970. The Cuyahoga River fire, as a widely publicized symbol of the nation's environmental crisis, helped galvanize the environmental movement and bring about governmental action to reduce pollution and protect the country's natural heritage. Both Earth Day and

Seven years later, after the transit line to the airport opened, in the aftermath of the oil crisis, the voters of Cuyahoga County approved a 1 percent sales tax increase to finance the operation of a new, unified countywide public transportation system. Created out of the Cleveland Transit System, the Shaker Rapid and several suburban systems, the Regional Transit Authority (RTA) promised reduced fares and better service for the entire county. It seemed that a lesson had been learned.

Councilmen Katalinas, Sienkiewicz and Pilch examine a white cloth that was covered with oil after being dipped into the Cuyahoga River in 1964.
Cleveland Press Collection, Cleveland State University

Ten

Cleveland and the Global Village:
The Challenge of the 21st Century

As the 20th century drew to a close, half a million people

called the city of Cleveland their home. Over a million and a half more

who lived in the surrounding area identified themselves more or less

strongly with the central city. Whether or not they actually considered

themselves Clevelanders (and many did), most watched the same local

television channels and cheered for Cleveland sports teams. The

Cleveland metropolitan area, as of 1990 the 20th largest in the United

States, stretched east into Geauga, Lake and Ashtabula counties, south

into Medina County and west into Lorain County.

This regional city was created by the interstate highway system, which allowed businesses and commuters to spread across the area in a mobile and diffuse economic base. Commercial and industrial nodes had grown up at numerous locations, most often the intersections of interstates and major secondary thoroughfares. It took less than 30 years for interchange areas like Chagrin Boulevard at I-271 and Rockside Road at I-77 to evolve from semi-rural crossroads to hubs of commerce with hotels, multi-story office buildings and the ubiquitous national fast food and retail establishments of late-20th century America.

At the same time as economic and demographic diffusion continued, a counter-trend was focusing attention on the lakefront and river at the city's heart in an entirely new way. Lake Erie and the Cuyahoga River had attracted early explorers and traders to the area two centuries before and had been seized on by the canal-builders, merchants, shipowners, industrialists and railroad men who followed. They straightened the river and dredged the harbor to make way for their ships, built their warehouses and factories along the Cuyahoga's banks, and ran their tracks and trains along the lakeshore. In doing so, they cut off public access to much of the city's waterfront. Putting it to commercial use, they disregarded and in many cases degraded its scenic and recreational value. As Cleveland's economy shifted from industry to service in the late 20th century, civic leaders hoped to combine business and pleasure. The lake and river were to be central features of a vibrant, renewed downtown and a new image for Cleveland in the period after the 1970s. It was an image designed for national and global consumption.

The half decade following the oil crisis of 1973 saw Cleveland edging away from total economic dependence on heavy industry. At the same time, government officials and area residents were becoming more aware of the interdependence of the central city and the surrounding region. Even before the establishment of the Regional Transit Authority, a regional sewer and water treatment system had been created in 1972. As the city and its neighboring suburbs

The flats along the Cuyahoga River became a center of Cleveland's new service economy in the 1980s
as tourists and residents alike flocked to the river's shores for nightlife, restaurants and shopping.
Convention and Visitors Bureau of Greater Cleveland, Photo by Louie Anderson

sought additional revenues to offset those lost when housing values declined or industry left, as well as to meet increased costs, a regional income tax system evolved. Regional government was, however, out of the question and remained so.

For Cleveland itself, the troubles of the 1960s continued into the 1970s, affecting the city's politics and economy alike. Revenues declined, forcing Cleveland deeper and deeper into debt. The city administration and the business establishment came into conflict. Distrust finally led to a fiscal crisis at the end of 1978, with the city unable to pay the interest on its bonds and local banks unwilling to extend further credit. Cleveland went into default, the first major city to do so since the Depression.

Anxious to halt the decline in the city's image and fortunes, area executives realized that they would have to sell the city to

The Great Lakes Exposition drew thousands of visitors to Cleveland at the height of the Great Depression in 1936. *Cleveland Press Collection, Cleveland State University*

prospective businesses and citizens as attractive and viable. In 1978 *Plain Dealer* publisher Thomas Vail initiated the "New Cleveland Campaign." Using advertisements in national magazines and working with the Greater Cleveland Growth Association, the campaign did not try to disguise the fact that Cleveland had had problems, but stressed the city's successes in moving away from them. Images used in the advertisements focused on the appeal of lakefront living and on the entertainment district slowly evolving in the Flats district along the river.

The Cuyahoga's transformation from fire hazard to nightlife hot spot was a significant step in Cleveland's turnaround from "mistake on the lake" to "comeback city." Some

Clevelanders, attracted by the industrial ambiance of the Flats, were already frequenting bars such as the Flatiron Cafe in the 1970s. The Higbee Company proposed to develop an area along the river with a complex of shops and restaurants to be called Settlers' Landing. The name was a tribute to Moses Cleaveland and the first exploring party, who were said to have come ashore nearby. Although this particular project was never built, the idea helped raise awareness of the riverfront's possibilities. (Efforts to preserve the site as a memorial to the early settlers eventually resulted in the creation of Settlers' Landing Park, dedicated during the city's bicentennial in 1996.)

The district's popularity grew, and new entertainment venues and restaurants opened. Office workers and suburbanites now rubbed elbows with stevedores and industrial workers. Within 20 years, the once disreputable "Under the Hill" zone in Cleveland's industrial heart had become a trendy area of bars and clubs.

By the 1990s, activity on the river clearly indicated the change. The Cuyahoga still served as a shipping lane for freighters bringing iron ore, stone and other cargoes to the docks along its banks. But these ships now competed during the warm weather season with hordes of small pleasure boats that cruised the waterway or tied up at the docks of restaurants and bars. The river and lake had become focal points of a recreational boom in northeastern Ohio. Over 30,000 craft, the vast majority pleasure boats, were registered in Cuyahoga County alone in 1986. Thanks to new environmental rules, the river was clean enough for boating, while out on the lake, large numbers of people were able to fish from boats or the shore and safely eat what they caught. The waterways that had signified empire to the French and British and commerce to John D. Rockefeller and Samuel Mather were now used by Cleveland's promoters to represent a marketable urban lifestyle.

As the waterfront became more attractive, it was increasingly developed for recreational and tourist use. As early as the 1920s and 1930s a portion of the lakefront beyond the railroad lines had become accessible when sections north of downtown were filled with earth and opened for nonindustrial development. The construction of Cleveland Municipal Stadium in 1931 was a major milestone in attracting people to the downtown lakefront. In 1936 the Great Lakes Exposition opened on the new land to the east of the stadium. Running through 1937, the expo brought hundreds of thousands more people to the lakeshore. Ten years after the exposition closed, the city opened its second airport, Burke Lakefront, on part of the site.

During the 1980s Cleveland civic and political leaders fixed upon the downtown lakefront as a focal point for the city's urban renaissance, looking for precedents to lakefront development in Toronto and Chicago, as well as waterfront development in Baltimore. Cleveland Tomorrow, a private civic organization created in 1981, played a key role. The membership of the organization consisted of the chief executive officers of the 50 largest companies in Cleveland. Its initial goal centered on bringing new businesses to Cleveland and improving conditions for those already in the city. It also worked to build the amenities that would hold businesses and their employees in the city. Its efforts helped bring about a total rehabilitation of the lakefront. A new inner harbor for pleasure boats was constructed. The national Rock and Roll Hall of Fame and Museum opened at a site adjacent to the inner harbor in 1995 and the Great Lakes Science Center at the north end of the harbor in 1996.

By that time, Cleveland Tomorrow was devoting much of its effort to marketing Cleveland as a major tourist destination. A variety of downtown projects completed in the 1980s and 1990s would, it was hoped, provide a critical mass of attractions and amusements to tempt both out-of-town visitors and suburban residents to spend leisure time and money in Cleveland. These included the rehabilitated theater district on Playhouse Square and two new indoor shopping venues, the Galleria and Tower City Center. Tower City was in fact a reconfiguration of the former Union Terminal and included one of downtown's several new hotels as well as retail and office space. While RTA's transit lines still used the lowest level of the terminal, the last passenger train had come through in 1977.

On the site of the city's old market district nearby, the Gateway professional sports complex, financed in part by a countywide "sin tax" on tobacco and alcohol sales, had opened in 1994. The Cleveland Indians baseball team left Municipal Stadium to play their games at the new Jacobs Field, while the Cavaliers basketball franchise moved back downtown after a 20-year stay in exurban Richfield. By the turn of the 21st century, the lakefront had changed even further, with a new football stadium replacing the old Municipal Stadium in 1999 and plans in place for Civic Vision 2000, a detailed agenda to add hotels and other attractions to the lakefront. These included the new Crawford Museum of Transportation and Industry, a descendant of both the Western Reserve Historical Society, Cleveland's oldest cultural institution, and the automobile collection begun by Frederick Crawford in the 1930s.

The idea that Cleveland could become a tourist destination would have been laughable as recently as the 1970s. In much earlier days, mid-19th century visitors to Cleveland were impressed by

the community's commercial bustle, its pleasant setting on the lake and the large numbers of trees along its streets, so many that it was referred to as the Forest City. In the years that followed, Cleveland would host a large number of conventions, but only as a minor sideline to the city's real business, which was industry. The Public Auditorium, completed in 1922, kept the city in the national market for major conventions and was expanded and updated by the addition of an adjacent underground convention center in the 1960s.

The image rehabilitation and the development of waterfront attractions during the 1970s and 1980s were also undertaken with the convention trade in mind, but with a new emphasis on nonconvention visitation by individuals and families as well. By the 1990s the vast majority of American families owned automobiles. Air travel, once enjoyed only by the relatively well-to-do, had become more affordable with the introduction of larger capacity aircraft. The first wide-body jet, the Boeing 747, entered service in 1967. Even more important was federal deregulation of the industry in 1978, which resulted in increased competition and lower fares. Cleveland-Hopkins International Airport added new concourses in 1968 and 1978 to keep up with the traffic. In 1988 Continental Airlines, one of the companies that had emerged from the mergers and failures occasioned by deregulation, selected Hopkins as a major hub. Its traffic volume through

Hopkins increased enormously, and in 1998 it totally rebuilt one of the airport's concourses. In 1999 more than 13 million airline passengers used Cleveland-Hopkins.

The growth in air travel surprised no one. It was considered a natural consequence of progress, and Cleveland officials had floated various plans for expanding airport capacity. In 1966 Cleveland mayor Ralph Locher proposed that the city consider building a new airport on an artificial island in Lake Erie. The NASA Lewis Research Center became involved in the discussion, and in 1969 Abe Silverstein, the center's director, presented an initial plan for a $1.185- billion project to construct a jetport in the lake one mile north of Cleveland. Funding from the Federal Aviation Administration and the Growth Association resulted in an in-depth study, which raised questions about the cost-benefit ratio and the practicability of an airport that would be subject to the erratic weather patterns on the lake. Although the plan was abandoned in 1978, the need for a larger regional airport continued under discussion.

While plans for the "Lake Erie Jetport" were being debated, Süleyman Gökoğlu was a university student in Istanbul, Turkey, preparing to become a chemical engineer. In 1978 he came to the United States to pursue a doctorate at Yale, where his graduate studies were supported by NASA research grants to the university. He had heard of NASA and the space race while a child in Turkey, but never expected to be part of what he considered a "dream place." Yet, in 1982 Gökoğlu joined Cleveland's NASA facility as a contractor, working on improving combustion efficiency in jet engines, an area that had important applications for improving fuel economy in civil aviation. Within six years he had become a United States citizen and a government employee at NASA; by century's end he had settled with his family in suburban Brecksville and was working in microgravity research, an integral part of NASA Lewis' role in the creation of the new international space station.

Gökoğlu's work at NASA illustrated two major factors in Cleveland's move to a new economic base and a new century. NASA, dating back to its origins in NACA, had begun as an institution focused on specific transportation technologies. It had evolved into an enterprise in which its highly skilled engineers and scientists began to examine other technologies or to see how transportation-related innovations might find other uses.

This evolution was spurred in part by NASA's need to remain relevant in the late 1970s and 1980s as government funding

In 1948 the NACA Aircraft Engine Research Laboratory was renamed the Lewis Flight Propulsion Research Laboratory and became part of NASA in 1958. In 1970 famed rocket scientist Dr. Werner Von Braun toured one of the facility's wind tunnels. *NASA Glenn Research Center*

In 1945, National Advisory Committee for Aeronautics (NACA) scientist Abe Silverstein demonstrated the operation of a model ram jet aircraft engine at what was then the NACA Aircraft Engine Research Laboratory in Brook Park. Silverstein went on to win a Guggenheim Medal and was the director of research at the center from 1961 through 1969. *NASA Glenn Research Center*

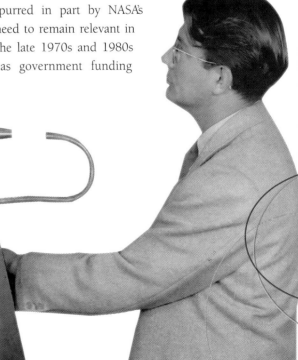

DRAG THRUST

NACA MODEL OF RAM JET ENGINE

for the space program decreased. Shortly after the energy crisis of 1973, the agency began experimenting with alternative energy sources. NASA Lewis set up a series of windmill-driven electric generators at its Plum Brook facility near Sandusky to examine the viability of wind as a power source. Building on its expertise in solar cells (an essential component of almost all spacecraft), it began to investigate their utility in terrestrial applications. NASA Lewis scientist Louis Rosenblum set up solar electricity generation facilities in a Native American village in Arizona in 1979 as a part of this program. Süleyman Gökoğlu's work in microgravity research similarly had benefits beyond space exploration, since studies of combustion in the zero-gravity environment of outer space held the promise of increased efficiency in the use of fossil fuels on earth.

The presence of a Turkish-born scientist at NASA was indicative of another major change that characterized Cleveland at the end of the century. The city's population had become more diverse than ever, a phenomenon driven in part by transportation developments and changes in American immigration policy. In 1967, the year that the first wide-body 747s went into service, the Immigration Act of 1965 took full effect. It opened immigration to all nations, unlike the previous

laws that had tightly restricted the flow from southern and eastern Europe, Asia, and the Near and Middle East. After 1967 anyone with skills needed in the United States or with close relatives already resident in cities such as Cleveland had a chance to immigrate.

Perhaps nowhere were the results of this convergence of changing immigration patterns and inexpensive and rapid global transportation more apparent than in health care. Well before the end of the century, health care had become the leading sector in the region's evolving service economy. In the 1980s and 1990s individual health care institutions grew partly through consolidation, merging with smaller hospitals to form large health systems.

Many of the professionals working in Cleveland's health care sector in the last quarter of the 20th century were recent immigrants. Physicians from India and Egypt and nurses from the Philippines found a ready market for their skills, as Medicare and Medicaid, also initiated in the mid-1960s, increased the demand for health care providers. By the 1990s the number of Indian-born physicians in Cleveland had grown to the point where they established their own professional organization. The city's growing diversity was also represented in health care administration. In 1992 University Hospitals named Iranian-born Farah Walters as its president and chief executive officer, making her the only woman to head a Cleveland hospital at the time.

Ethnic diversity, on a more limited scale, had been a factor in the founding of Cleveland's earliest permanent hospitals, the basis upon which the towering health care edifice of the late 20th century was built. By 1865 Cleveland's Roman Catholic community, made up mostly of Irish and German immigrants, was large enough for Amadeus Rappe, the city's first Roman Catholic bishop, to initiate the founding of a Roman Catholic hospital, St. Vincent Charity. Protestants reacted by organizing their own "Protestant Hospital" in 1866. Eventually named Lakeside Hospital, it became the nucleus of University Hospitals, one of the two superpowers of Cleveland's health care sector at the close of the 20th century. The other, The Cleveland Clinic Foundation, was established in 1921 by George Crile, a flamboyant and nationally known surgeon formerly on Lakeside's staff.

Meanwhile, numerous other hospitals had been founded, most as private, philanthropic ventures. Many of them tended the casualties of Cleveland's industrial economy. A "Railway

Hospital" cared for railroad workers injured on the job. The city's second Catholic hospital, St. Alexis (later St. Michael's) on Broadway Avenue, was founded in part to care for men maimed and injured in the adjacent steel mills and factories. In this pre-health insurance era, some hospitals raised funds by encouraging employers to endow beds where their sick or injured employees would be sure to receive care.

Beyond this, every major hospital in 19th-century Cleveland was supported with donations from those who had made fortunes in the industrial economy. The Mather family supported Lakeside Hospital. Francis F. Prentiss, the founder of Cleveland Twist Drill, was the key figure in the establishment of St. Luke's Hospital. The trustee and donor lists of these and other institutions read like a roll call of Cleveland industrialists. By the late 20th century, donors who themselves came out of the new service economy provided part of the funding for a surge of hospital expansion. For example, Cleveland-area financier Alfred Lerner, chairman and CEO of the MBNA Corporation, one of the nation's largest credit card issuers, made multimillion-dollar donations to both University Hospitals and the Cleveland Clinic.

By this time the reputation of Cleveland's medical centers had spread beyond the region and even the nation to reach across the globe. Although the service economy's products were in most cases less exportable than manufactured goods like steel or autos, jet transport made it possible for Cleveland's health care providers to serve patients from around the world, who visited the city to receive "world-class" health care in cardiothoracic surgery, cardiology, oncology and other specialties. Several heads of state or government including the president of Brazil, the prime minister of Egypt and King Khalid of Saudi Arabia, came to the Cleveland Clinic for medical treatment. The king subsequently provided support for the Cleveland Islamic Center, which served the area's increasing number of Muslims.

University Hospitals similarly treated patients from around the world. The renown of its pediatric facility, Rainbow Babies' and Children's Hospital, caused families and sponsors to bring children and young people to the city for treatment they could not receive at home. University Hospitals surgeons operated on patients ranging from a Lithuanian teen-ager born with severe facial defects, to a 7-year-old Russian boy badly scarred by fire, to a Palestinian toddler whose skull was seriously injured in a fall.

A worldwide network of physicians who had received advanced medical training at University Hospitals or the Cleveland Clinic reinforced the global connection. Both institutions opened international centers to keep pace with the needs of their growing international clientele. The centers provided one of their most important services, translation, by keeping on hand a cadre of translators. Since few Americans without roots in the countries in question could speak fluent Portuguese or Arabic, for example, many of the translators were immigrants or children of immigrants, who represented Cleveland's new diversity. One of the Cleveland Clinic's translators, Marcelle Baaklini, had come with her family to

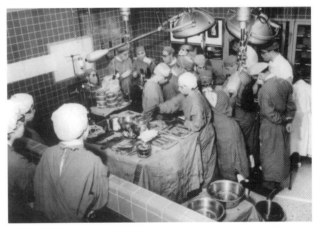

The first stopped heart operation was performed at the Cleveland Clinic in 1956.
Cleveland Press Collection, Cleveland State University

The Fourth General Hospital, University Hospitals of Cleveland Lakeside Unit, sent physicians and nurses to serve in the Pacific theater during World War II. This photograph shows nurses from Cleveland on their way to Manila in 1945, extending the reach of the city's hospitals globally.
Stanley A. Ferguson Archives, University Hospitals of Cleveland

the United States from Lebanon to escape that country's civil war. A student at Case Western Reserve University, she also exemplified the growing diversity in local institutions of higher learning.

Many students were not immigrants, but rather international visitors, drawn to Cleveland's universities to receive education, just as patients were drawn to its hospitals for medical treatment. Like health care, higher education in

northeastern Ohio had become a major economic factor in the postwar years, and like health care, local higher education had intimate links to the city's industrial and transportation heritage. Most of the early local schools had denominational roots: Western Reserve College was associated with the Presbyterian and Congregational churches; Baldwin-Wallace, Methodist; Oberlin, Congregational; John Carroll, Ursuline and Notre Dame, Roman Catholic. In many cases they struggled to survive until the city's industrial expansion brought greater wealth to the area and to the men and families who would serve as the schools' benefactors. Amasa Stone, the city's leading railroad entrepreneur in the years after the Civil War, provided the support for Western Reserve College's move to Cleveland in 1882. Later, the Mather family gave substantial funds to the college.

Nowhere, however, was the link between higher education and industry closer than on the campus that stood next to but separate from Western Reserve's during the years 1885 to 1967. Philanthropist Leonard Case, brother of Mayor William Case, established the Case School of Applied Science to provide the technical expertise that modern industrial communities like Cleveland would need in the late 19th century. It trained engineers, chemists and electricians who found careers in the expanding local and national industrial economy.

Some, such as chemical engineering graduate Kent H. Smith, would develop major companies linked to transportation.

With his brothers Albert and Vincent and two other associates, Smith founded the Graphite Oil Products Company in 1928. This became the Lubrizol Corporation, a Fortune 500 company and a major innovator and manufacturer in the field of additives for the oils and lubricants used in transportation and industry. Lubrizol and the Smith family, in turn, repaid Case and later Case Western Reserve University with extensive financial support that allowed the institution to create new academic programs serving the needs of a changing economy.

As technology and society grew more complex in the years after World War II, the need for higher education and post-high-school career training grew. This, along with the egalitarian belief that every young American had a right to a college education, led to the establishment of less expensive public-supported institutions: Cuyahoga Community College in 1963 and Cleveland State University in 1965. This revolution in education gave the region a range of educational opportunities for students of all economic backgrounds with almost any academic or career interest, and, as it turned out, attracted international as well as American students.

Students from abroad had in fact been coming to Cleveland for years. In the 1930s there were enough guest Chinese students in the area to occasion the creation of a Chinese students' organization. It was not until after World War II, however, and particularly after the 1960s, that Cleveland's campuses became increasingly international in character. Some students were supported by scholarships from their governments, while others came on their own. All were attracted by the opportunity to study medicine, accounting, engineering or other disciplines at schools that had built international reputations. The schools welcomed the international trade in students, who not only brought additional diversity and talent to their campuses, but also helped build enrollment and pay the growing costs of running a modern university.

Paramjit Singh was one of the first Asian Indians to settle in Cleveland. A mechanical engineer, Singh had come to the city in 1962 as a trainee working on a joint venture between the McDowell-Wellman Engineering Company (descendant of Wellman-Seaver-Morgan, the company that built the Hulett unloaders) and an Indian firm. He also enrolled in the MBA program at Western Reserve University.

As an observant Sikh, Singh with his turban brought cultural diversity to campus in a visible way (although at the time many Clevelanders were unsure exactly which culture the turban represented). He was one of a few dozen Indian students then attending Cleveland universities. Proximity to Western Reserve and Case was the chief reason that the area's first Indian neighborhood, although a rather amorphous one, was located just above University Circle in Cleveland Heights, the suburb that is still home to the group's community center. Although his turban was acceptable to the school during his course of study, it took some effort for Singh to convince the administration to allow him to wear it, rather than a traditional mortarboard, at graduation. Param Singh would stay on in Cleveland after graduation, passing state examinations to obtain a professional engineer's license in 1966, marrying and becoming one of the key figures in the Asian Indian community as it grew larger in the years after immigration reform.

The region's colleges and universities had additional impact on transportation and industry as the technological complexity of those areas increased, advanced by research and development programs carried out either by industry itself or in university laboratories, often funded by government grants. Almost all area universities in

their science and technology courses explored the properties of fuels and structural materials with transport-related applications.

After the 1970s, special emphasis was placed on the development of polymers, with the intent of creating a "polymer corridor" or "polymer valley" in the area between Akron and Cleveland. The seed or catalyst for this was the Akron area's key historical role in the tire industry. As tire production moved to areas with cheaper labor, polymer development, which grew out of regional expertise with rubber and its synthetic substitutes, seemed a logical move.

Other universities, particularly Case Western Reserve, received government research grants to develop technologies needed by the aerospace and defense industries. A program at John Carroll University's Boler School of Business focused on the role of transportation in business, with courses in the fundamentals of transportation and business logistics.

The consequences, rather than the technology, of transportation were studied at Cleveland State University's Levin College of Urban Studies. The tremendous regional expansion that had taken place in the last three decades of the century had negative as well as positive effects. In the absence of regional government, cities such as Cleveland and East Cleveland lost revenues as industries, people and the taxes they paid continued to move away. The areas to which they moved, opened by the construction of

Born in India, Paramjit Singh is one of a new generation of immigrants to Cleveland who are coming from Asia and Central America. Opportunities abound at institutions like CWRU, where Singh, shown along with his friend Ajeet Singh Sood, graduated in 1965. *Paramjit Singh*

new multi-lane limited-access highways, rapidly changed from open farmland to suburban subdivisions.

The situation in Geauga County during the 1990s was a case in point. When U.S. Route 422 was upgraded to a limited-access highway, connecting the area beyond the southeastern suburbs directly with the interstate system, it opened large tracts of rural land to development. Urban sprawl, which had turned some Medina County townships and communities into Cleveland suburbs during the 1980s, now threatened to overwhelm Geauga County. Its population increased by approximately one-third in the last 20 years of the century. The area's Amish residents, who once found the county a haven for their pre-industrial lifestyle, increasingly saw subdivisions encroaching on their farms and cars forcing their horse-drawn buggies off the roads. By the early 1990s they began to leave for more rural areas in Kentucky.

Sprawl also brought more traffic and air pollution to the entire area. Strict vehicle testing programs helped bring automotive emissions under control beginning in the late 1980s. But those advances began to be offset by consumer demand for large pickup trucks and sport utility vehicles, which did not have to meet automotive emission standards and had low fuel-economy ratings. In snow-belt areas such as Geauga and Lake counties, many of the new residents opted for an SUV, ostensibly for the sake of getting reliable winter transportation, but also because SUVs were trendy. In some ways the end of the century seemed to indicate that the lessons of the 1973 energy crisis had been forgotten.

In other ways, however, turn-of-the-century Greater Cleveland moved toward what many thought was a more efficient, environmentally friendly and genuinely urban lifestyle. The city's core neighborhoods, depopulated by the middle-class automotive flight to the suburbs in the 1950s, became home to new migrants and immigrants who found them more affordable. For every immigrant who came to the city with education and training applicable to

the post-industrial economy, dozens of others arrived by car, bus or airplane without special skills. Many were refugees of conflicts in distant parts of the world, like El Salvador, Vietnam and the Middle East. They transformed older neighborhoods into new communities. Detroit Avenue west of West 117th Street became a center of the Arab-American community. Jews from the former Soviet Union made Coventry Road in Cleveland Heights a little Moscow, while Spanish-speaking immigrants from Mexico, Central America and South America, along with Puerto Rican migrants, refashioned neighborhood life on the near west side.

In other places former residents returned from the suburbs to the city. Nowhere was this more spectacularly evident than in Hough, where many African-Americans returned to the once devastated neighborhood, moving into upscale developments such as Lexington Village or building large new homes on Chester Avenue and the streets that connected it to Hough Avenue. Downtown, young singles and couples, many of whom worked for the city's hospitals, banks and law firms, bought condominiums and loft apartments in the warehouse district, creating a neighborhood centered not on ethnicity but on lifestyle. By century's end, Tremont, too, was becoming home to an increasing number of young professionals who enjoyed the ambiance and convenience of urban life.

Suburban growth created traffic headaches and greater dependence on automobiles as city and regional planners sought to alleviate congestion with an improved freeway system. Cleveland Press Collection, Cleveland State University

Those who moved back to the city took some strain off the local highway system. Still, traffic engineers continued to add new lanes to old freeways such as I-71 and I-271 to accommodate the ever-growing number of cars. On the other hand, the issue of improved mass transportation was receiving more serious consideration. During Cleveland's bicentennial year in 1996, RTA constructed a new light rail line, linking Tower City to the increasing number of attractions on the lakefront. With the completion of the Waterfront Line, it became possible to travel by light rail from the eastern reaches of Shaker Heights almost to the door of the

Built in 1995, the Rock and Roll Hall of Fame became a centerpiece along Cleveland's revitalized lakefront.
Cleveland was chosen as the site for the Hall in 1986 after a year-long lobbying effort touting the city's important role in the history of rock-n-roll,
highlighted by Cleveland disc jockey Alan Freed's promotion of early rock music and the Moondog Coronation Ball of 1952.
Convention and Visitors Bureau of Greater Cleveland, Photo by Louie Anderson

Rock and Roll Hall of Fame. An enclosed walkway connecting the Tower City stop to the Gateway sports complex encouraged many suburbanites to leave the car at home and travel to the game by rail, much the way their grandparents had done when going to games at League Park.

Further experiments in rail commuter service were tried on existing heavy rail lines between downtown and Lake County. The possibility of opening this and other suburban routes to the southeast and the west was being given serious consideration in the late 1990s, as was the extension of the Waterfront Line to the Cleveland State campus area and the creation of a "dual hub corridor" light rail link between downtown and University Circle.

Greater Cleveland's people had always been concerned primarily with how they would live, travel and interrelate within their own community. This was as true at the end of the 20th century as it had been at the end of the 18th. Their jobs, their automobiles, the price of public transportation and the safety and quality of life in their neighborhoods were immediate and necessary issues. But even everyday, close-to-home concerns reflected Clevelanders' increasingly intimate

link to the wider world. By the end of the century, many of the parts for their cars, much of the clothing they wore, the out-of-season foods they enjoyed, and even some of the sports heroes they cheered at Jacobs Field or Gund Arena had come from abroad. The light rail cars that took them to those games or to the Tower City shops or the Rock and Roll Hall of Fame had come from the Breda Company in Italy.

The basic global ties that had been created when French and British traders set up shop along the Cuyahoga, bartering for furs from the North American heartland to send back across the Atlantic Ocean, had developed into an all-encompassing network, because transportation and communication had put the entire world in fast and relatively inexpensive motion. Now that the furs were gone, labor costs were lower elsewhere, and transportation was varied, flexible and largely independent of waterways and similar geographic advantages, what would serve to keep the economy of Cleveland on the move?

The answer is to be found in the past. At first glance, the late 20th-century economy seemed to have little relation to that of earlier years. In 1985 a listing compiled by *Crain's Cleveland Business* showed the Ford Motor Company, the Goodyear Tire and Rubber Company, The Cleveland Clinic Foundation, and LTV Steel (successor to the former Republic Steel and Jones and Laughlin Corporations) as the first, second, third and fourth largest nongovernmental employers in northeastern Ohio. By 1995 the Cleveland Clinic and University Hospitals Health System were Cuyahoga County's first and second largest private employers. Only the federal and county governments had more workers.

By 1999 the Cleveland Clinic Health System, with nearly 20,000 employees, and University Hospitals Health System, with 13,000, had outstripped government to become the

LTV steel maintains its international headquarters in Cleveland, continuing the steel industry's long presence in the region. Shown here is Republic Steel's contribution to the Great Lakes Exposition, some 50 years before it was purchased by LTV. *Western Reserve Historical Society*

county's largest employers, public or private. Of the top 10 private employers, only two represented Cleveland's traditional manufacturing base (Ford, 4th, and the LTV Corporation, 6th). Two were in health care, two in financial services (KeyCorp, 3rd, and National City Corporation, 7th), and one each in insurance (Progressive Corporation, 5th), education (Case Western Reserve University, 8th), communications (Ameritech, 9th), and grocery retailing and distribution (Riser Foods Company, 10th).

The legal profession was another leading sector in the city's new economy. During the 1980s and 1990s, Cleveland's corporate law firms had grown substantially, establishing a national and even an international presence. Jones, Day, Reavis & Pogue, with over 1,300 attorneys, was the third-largest firm in the country at the end of the century and had 23 offices worldwide. Squire, Sanders & Dempsey and Baker & Hostetler also ranked among the nation's 50 largest firms. All three had been founded in Cleveland during the late 19th or early 20th centuries, and each continued to maintain its largest office in the city, although their scope made them in fact national or international firms.

Overall, the situation at the turn of the 21st century seemed a far cry from the time when Cleveland's claim to fame had been its industrial output, and steel mills and railroads had dwarfed all other enterprises. There was, however, a direct economic connection between the old and the new Cleveland. The banks, law firms, hospitals, universities and cultural attractions that formed the base of the modern service economy all sprang from the wealth created from an industrial economy made viable by transportation, which in turn was based on location.

There was also a direct human connection, one that many people could trace in their own lives. At the close of the 20th century, lawyer José C. Feliciano, president-elect of the Cleveland Bar Association, was a partner at Baker & Hostetler. Feliciano had arrived in Cleveland from his native Puerto Rico as a small child in the 1950s. His father worked for many years at White Motor, part of the city's traditional industrial base. Graduating from the Cleveland-Marshall School of Law at Cleveland State University, Feliciano was within a few years appointed Cleveland's chief police prosecutor, and later joined Baker & Hostetler.

197
Chapter Ten

Cleveland's skyline has changed much since this image was taken in the early 1950s.
However, the Terminal Tower still remains the most distinctive building associated with downtown Cleveland.
Cleveland Press Collection, Cleveland State University

His civic activities, which included founding the Hispanic Community Forum as well as membership in the New Cleveland Campaign, demonstrated the dual connection to ethnic heritage and the Cleveland community that was a fact of life for so many of the city's residents, both past and present.

As a lawyer, Feliciano was part of a lineage running from Alfred Kelley to Mayor Newton D. Baker (a founding partner of Baker & Hostetler) to the national corporate firms of the modern period. Through his family's journey from Puerto Rico, he was linked to the long line of migrants and immigrants who had come to make their living and their home in the city. Through his father's work at White Motor, he was connected to Cleveland's tradition of transportation-related manufacturing, while Feliciano's own career in the law exemplified a new phase in the city's economy. Many Greater Clevelanders, both civic leaders and average citizens, could look at their own stories and see similarly rich and complex ties to the network of transportation, migration, industry and community that had created the city they lived in.

As the new millennium dawned, it was easy to see that in the near-term future, automatic teller machines, corporate legal advice, bypass surgery, academic degrees and museum exhibits would have a large part in keeping Cleveland's economy in motion. But transportation, which brought together people with their talents and their aspirations and connected the city with the rest of the world and beyond, was still the vital link in the system.

(Left and bottom) Immigrants from all over the world, including Mexico, Central America and South America, continue to stream into Cleveland. The Hispanic community holds an annual festival at St. Michael's, an immigrant church that once served German and Czech immigrants.
Photos by Herbert Ascherman, Jr.

CONCLUSION

When John Herschel Glenn became the first American to orbit the earth in 1962, he helped pull the United States even with the Union of Soviet Socialist Republics in the race for a new empire in space. Thirty-six years later, Glenn, after serving four terms as a U.S. senator from his native Ohio, again orbited the earth as a crew member of the space shuttle *Discovery*. In both instances, northeastern Ohio, by virtue of the work done at the Lewis Research Center, helped John Glenn into orbit. It was fitting therefore that the center was renamed the NASA John H. Glenn Research Center at Lewis Field in 1999.

By that time, however, the center was no longer a player in a quest for a cosmic empire, but rather working in alliance with its former adversary. At the end of the 20th century, NASA Glenn was a key center for the development of an international space station, a project in which European nations and Russia, the heir to much of the former Soviet Union, were America's partners. The expertise at Cleveland's NASA facility reflected the city's cultural makeup, with American-born employees of many backgrounds — African, Asian, European and Latin American — working with colleagues who had come from dozens of nations, as different as Ukraine and Taiwan, Turkey and China, India and Lithuania, to settle in Cleveland.

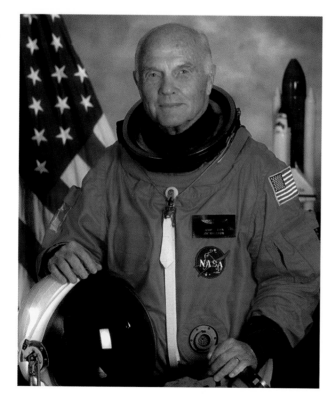

A native of Ohio, John Glenn was the first American to orbit the earth and was later a U.S. senator from Ohio. He returned to space in 1998, and the NASA Lewis Research Center was renamed the NASA Glenn Research Center in 1999 in his honor.
NASA Glenn Research Center

The international space station connected this typically American blend of talent with that found in the country's former adversary, Russia, and in its current economic competitors in the European Union. This grand joint project would, it was hoped, provide a platform for extended exploration of space and also for the development of products to solve problems on earth. The NASA Glenn Research Center, located on what was once Western Reserve farmland, between the Rocky River and the city's first major airport, near busy Brookpark Road and a former interurban route, within earshot of a diesel horn on the old Short Line Railroad, was living proof of the continuing role of motion in Cleveland's history, a history in which a lake, a river and Native American trails ultimately led to a portal to outer space.

While the international space station and the new economy focused Clevelanders' attention on the future, they were also reviewing their city's past as the 21st century began. With more than 200 years behind it, Cleveland was the work of many generations of people, ideas and machines, and had a history worth keeping. Alongside the career historians and curators, a small but dedicated cadre of area residents devoted themselves to preserving Cleveland's past, in a number of different ways. Some collected oral histories or set up

In addition to the ore freighters that continue to pass under the lift bridges along the Cuyahoga River, pleasure boats are a regular site along its banks.
The river has become a center for tourism, business and history.
Photo by Herbert Ascherman, Jr.

look at the canal not as a transportation anachronism, but as a historic component of the region's new service economy. The organization wanted to create a recreational and interpretive corridor along the Cuyahoga River portion of the canal and on across the watershed to the Tuscarawas River from Cleveland to Akron to Zoar, a historic site in Tuscarawas County, and possibly farther south.

Once stopping points along the major north-south economic artery of the state, many canal towns had lost their importance when railroads and then highways diverted traffic away from them. For years portions of the canal route remained pastoral and forgotten. Towns such as Peninsula and Everett seemed lost in time.

By the 1970s, urban sprawl, creeping south from Cleveland and north from Akron, threatened to overrun the entire area, sacrificing landscape and history alike. This was also the period when the environmental movement was gathering force, heightening people's interest in protecting open land. U.S. Rep. John Seiberling of Summit County spearheaded the effort that created the Cuyahoga Valley National Recreation Area in southern Cuyahoga and northern Summit counties in 1974. One of the country's earliest urban national parks, the CVNRA, which included a portion of the old canal route, protected the area from further development.

neighborhood museums, while others worked to restore historic buildings or industrial artifacts. Tim Donovan had an even larger goal in mind. He wanted to preserve an entire canal.

While George Washington had dreamed of a canal yet unbuilt, Donovan, from Irish immigrant and dockworker ancestry, dreamed of a canal reborn. As director of Ohio Canal Corridor, he and the organization's founders, Tom Yablonsky and Jeff Lennartz, did not for a moment imagine canal freighters once again hauling goods along the Cuyahoga valley and packet boats ferrying Clevelanders to Portsmouth, competing with the big rigs and private automobiles on I-77. The Ohio & Erie Canal, the engineering marvel of the 1830s, had been abandoned in 1913. Ohio Canal Corridor would

By the mid-1980s, northeastern Ohio's national park was a favorite spare time destination. Bike trails, nature centers and a scenic railway running between Akron and southern Cuyahoga County attracted thousands of local residents and visitors every weekend. Ohio Canal Corridor was founded in 1985 as part of the National Heritage Corridor movement, which aimed to preserve the country's industrial past as well as its natural landscape. The abandoned Ohio & Erie Canal could become a highway for enjoyment and for understanding the past, along a route that stretched well beyond the park's borders and included urban areas. Supporters of canal corridor preservation looked forward to the time when visitors could retrace the route that John Malvin and the other canal boat captains had traveled nearly a century and a half earlier. Interpretive signs and stations would help them understand what they passed, whether it was the canal itself or living legacies of the past like American Steel and Wire's Cuyahoga Works or the Tremont neighborhood.

Ohio Canal Corridor also envisioned the Cuyahoga Valley Scenic Railroad entering downtown Cleveland along the tracks of the old Baltimore and Ohio Railroad. Once, steam locomotives had hauled coke and coal to the city's steel mills along those tracks. Now an excursion train would bring tourists to the attractions near the river and lakefront, including the new Crawford Museum of Transportation and Industry. The canal corridor was an ambitious scheme, and by the early 21st century was becoming reality. In 1993 the CVNRA had opened the Ohio & Erie Canal Towpath Trail, tracing the route and history of the canal within the park. Soon money from the National Park Service was building new pathways along the canal outside of the National Recreation Area's boundaries and supporting research for interpretive stations.

Many years had come and gone since Native Americans walked the paths along the banks of the Cuyahoga. Moses Cleaveland spent a single summer and went back to Connecticut. A handful of settlers and traders stayed behind in the settlement that bore his name. The Ohio & Erie Canal brought prosperity and made Cleveland a city, and then disappeared. Lake freighters, railroads and steel mills combined to form the infrastructure of a massive industrial base, animated and made to work by the hundreds of thousands of migrants and immigrants who poured into the city. The new mixture of peoples created a cultural mosaic that would only become more diverse with time.

The economy, too, would grow more diverse, partly due to innovation, as Cleveland's factories began producing automobiles and aircraft — and partly due to necessity, as those very innovations made the world a smaller place and Cleveland's original geographic advantages less important. The city adjusted. Alongside the new economy, industry still remained — and so did people. Alongside the new

immigrants from all corners of the world, descendants of Native American nations and New England settlers, of European peasants and African villagers, coal miners' daughters and steelworkers' sons, all continued to live and work in a community no longer confined within a single city's limits, but spread across an entire metropolitan area.

Now, more than two centuries after the first trading posts went up along the Cuyahoga, northeastern Ohio's residents, each carrying inside an individual story of migration, settlement, family and work, can once more set out along paths that mirror the route of the Native American trails. Their journeys, by foot or by bicycle, as weekend tourists, amateur historians, birdwatchers or seekers of physical and spiritual well-being, are as much a part of the regional economy as the furs and game carried by the Senecas, the ingots and rolled steel of the industrial heyday, and on down through the products of more recent years, from auto bodies to aircraft engine valves to plans for an international space station. All alike have traveled a network of transportation, industry and time, to create the history of a community in motion.

Even as Cleveland was becoming a "service economy," manufactured products continued to pour from the city's manufacturing concerns. In 1960 New Zealanders transformed a Warner & Swaysey "Gradall" earth mover into "Wog the Clown" for a community parade. *Cleveland Press Collection, Cleveland State University*

The Sherwin Williams Plaza provided an important theatrical venue at Cleveland's Great Lakes Exposition. Although the Great Lakes Exposition celebrated Cleveland's industrial heritage in 1936, its emphasis on spectacle, theater and tourism predicted how Cleveland of the 21st century would reconstruct the lakefront. *Western Reserve Historical Society*

Nighttime accentuates the beauty of Cleveland's constantly evolving urban skyline.
All photos in this essay by Robert A. Eplett

Past and Present Come Together in Cleveland

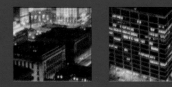

A drive or walk through Cleveland's streets finds the old historical city coexisting, side-by-side, with the new and future city. Although the industrial architecture of the past remains on display, these older buildings are being retrofitted for action in a service economy. Entertainment, arts and shopping now attract suburbanites downtown; regional development centers on sports and museum complexes. Likewise, where immigrants once came to work in the city's factories and steel mills, the region's newest migrants are drawn to its universities, hospitals and the professional service sector.

Just to the north of Gateway, Huron Road bustles with activity as visitors to the Gund Arena and Jaco
Field patronize the new shops and restaurants in the area.

Stunning 19th-century brick buildings, many former warehouses and offices, form the basis of the warehouse district along West 9th Street.

By the 1990s, once-empty warehouses along West 9th Street
were being rapidly converted into modern loft apartments, and a region that once centered on
business had become one of the city's most desirable neighborhoods.

Loft apartments have become a desirable place to live in Cleveland's warehouse district.

The intersection of East 9th, Huron and Prospect bustles with traffic in this view looking toward Playhouse Square.

Downtown Cleveland rises beyond the city's lakefront, the site of the Rock and Roll Hall of Fame and Museum and the Great Lakes Science Center.

A building that once
housed a power plant for
an electric street railway is
now an entertainment
center along the Cuyahoga
River in Cleveland's Flats.

(This page and opposite)
Suburban areas such as Rocky River, Lakewood and Shaker Heights offer a wide variety of elegant, older residences as well as new modern construction for Greater Clevelanders.

(This page and opposite)
New suburban homes such as those in Rocky River and the western suburbs are now complemented
by new construction within the city, including homes in developments such as
Beacon Place on Cleveland's east side.

The new Kelvin Smith Library is the electronic learning center of Case Western Reserve University in University Circle.

Ford Drive in University Circle is the site of a number of Case Western Reserve University's professional schools as well as the Glidden House hotel.

A former Wade Park residence, the Glidden House, is now the site of one of University Circle's finest hotels.

The Fine Arts Garden
of the Cleveland Museum
of Art is one of the focal
points of Cleveland's
cultural center,
University Circle.

Cleveland State

University's convocation center provides an ideal downtown setting for conferences, meetings and, of course, the university's graduation ceremonies.

Echoing the area's early history, a restored 19th-century house and gardens stand along Chester Avenue behind the Dunham Tavern, a former stagecoach inn on Euclid Avenue.

The Cleveland Botanical Garden is situated on Wade Oval,
the major green space in University Circle.

The Church of the Covenant is one of several major churches and temples
to be found in Cleveland's University Circle.

Situated just east of University Circle, Lake View Cemetery is the resting place for many
of the entrepreneuers who built the foundations of Cleveland's industries and transportation companies.

(This page and opposite)
Jacobs Field is part of the downtown Gateway complex and home of the Cleveland Indians,
one of the American League's original franchises still playing in its original city.

With a signature building by I.M. Pei, the Rock and Roll Hall of Fame and Museum has become the new landmark on Cleveland's downtown lakefront.

Filled with hands-on exhibits, the Great Lakes Science Center is a major destination for many families visiting the city's lakefront.

The area under the Detroit-Superior (Veterans' Memorial) Bridge provides part of the urban/industrial ambiance of the Flats entertainment district.

The plaza outside the Rock and Roll Hall of Fame and Museum provides a pleasant setting for relaxation and a light snack.

The Cleveland Browns

Stadium is the newest

landmark on the city's

revitalized lakefront.

Tour boats and pleasure boats have joined freighters on the Cuyahoga River as it winds its way through the Flats entertainment district.

Occupying space that once saw the coming and going of passenger trains at the Cleveland Union Terminal, Tower City Center is now one of downtown Cleveland's most popular shopping and entertainment venues.

Highlighted by the nighttime lights of Jacobs Field and those along East 9th Street, the statue of Bob Feller, the Cleveland Indians' legendary pitcher, graces the plaza outside the ballpark.

Partners in Cleveland

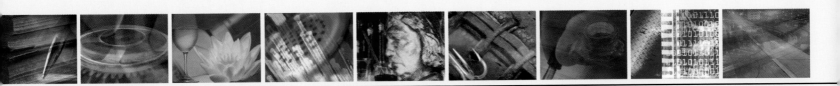

Cleveland: A History in Motion

ARTS & CULTURE

Cleveland's museums, galleries, theaters, performing arts centers and their surrounding neighborhoods support a thriving cultural community.

University Circle Incorporated

Picture a beautiful parkland setting complete with a lagoon, expansive green space and handsome park benches. Add landmark buildings (old and new), a delightful children's garden and creative banners announcing all that there is to see and do. Stroll through a historic residential neighborhood, enjoy the carriage house-turned-restaurant ambiance of a local eatery and take in the array of outdoor sculpture. Now, include in this setting the largest concentration of cultural, medical, educational and religious institutions in the world and you have University Circle.

A truly extraordinary urban district, University Circle is located five miles east of downtown Cleveland. Just one square mile in size, it is home to more than 40 institutions, several of them among the world's finest. Annually, the Circle's institutions attract more than 2 million people seeking educational opportunities, health care, entertainment and cultural or spiritual enrichment. University Circle is also the home of University Circle Incorporated (UCI), the nonprofit planning, service and development organization established in 1957 and dedicated to ensuring the excellence of this important place.

1796-1890: The Circle is Settled and Named

UCI exists to serve University Circle. Hence, the story of UCI starts with a history lesson that begins in 1796 when Moses Cleaveland, leading the first expedition party of the Connecticut Land Company, founded the city of Cleveland. In 1797, Nathaniel Doan, a member of the second surveying party from the Connecticut Land Company, arrived in Cleveland. Shortly thereafter, Doan decided to pack up his wife and eight children and move to a woodland area five miles east of town. The area they settled became known as Doan's Corners, where Nathaniel built a log hotel and tavern that quickly became a routine stop for travelers between Buffalo and points west. Doan later built a store and baking soda factory and was soon joined by other merchants and small industries, as well as a church and post office. Doan's Corners grew rapidly and leading citizens

Severance Hall (home of The Cleveland Orchestra) and The Cleveland Museum of Art are but two of the illustrious institutions that make the Circle an incomparable cultural district.

of the day, recognizing the area's potential, laid the groundwork for a neighborhood that would distinguish Cleveland from all other cities.

Several events shaped the development of this area, which would only later come to be known as University Circle. In 1882, Jeptha H. Wade, founder of the Western Union Telegraph Company, donated 75 acres of land to the city of Cleveland for a public park and an art gallery. During the same year, a donation of $500,000 and 43 acres of land by railroad tycoon Amasa Stone allowed Western Reserve University to move from rural Hudson, Ohio. In 1885 the Case School of Applied Sciences relocated to Doan's Corners from downtown Cleveland as did The Western Reserve Historical Society more than a decade later. A streetcar line was built to serve Euclid Avenue and destinations east of downtown. The circular trolley turnaround at East 107th Street became known as the University Circle stop — and so the bustling, collegiate neighborhood was given its name.

1900-1930s: Mansions, Music and More

By 1900 the schools and beauty of the area attracted other institutions, and an educational and cultural district of note was in the works. The Circle soon became the preferred neighborhood for Cleveland's leading families, who now lived in proximity to the institutions they supported. The Cleveland Music School Settlement was established in 1912. The Cleveland Museum of Art opened in 1916 on land donated by Jeptha Wade. The art museum overlooked an old pond where the Doan Children had once ice-skated. In 1921 this pond was rebuilt and renamed the Wade Lagoon. Loew's opened one of the most elegant theaters in the country at East 102nd Street and Euclid Avenue where it joined other movie houses to create a new theater district.

of University Hospitals, " ...after nearly 20 years of Depression and war, the institutions in University Circle faced a mammoth need for expansion and improvement... the city's population had grown... people were enjoying more leisure time and were looking for worthwhile ways of spending it... museums, libraries, and concerts were filled as never before... however, expansion was more than a matter of money or determination because there just wasn't enough room, and because the area was becoming built up like a patchwork quilt."

Enter one of Cleveland's most spirited civic leaders, Mrs. William G. Mather, who recognized that University Circle was at a pivotal point. Her vision and generosity made possible the hiring of the renowned Boston planning firm of Adams, Howard & Greeley, and after a rigorous

By the late 1920s, however, traffic and congestion drove out many affluent families who moved further from town to more bucolic surroundings. Still, the Circle continued to grow. The Cleveland Orchestra found a permanent home when Severance Hall opened in 1931, the same year that University Hospitals was dedicated.

1950-1960s: A Master Plan for University Circle

By 1950, 34 institutions had chosen University Circle as their home — but the Circle was facing some serious challenges. In the words of Stanley Ferguson, the president

18-month study, the 1957 University Circle Master Plan was issued. The Plan not only gave direction for the Circle's orderly growth, it did something inspiring: it reaffirmed that Cleveland had succeeded in creating the most impressive concentration of educational, medical, and cultural institutions in the country.

Perhaps the most important recommendation made was to "establish a central organization to administer the Plan and give it some real authority." And so with full institutional support, the University Circle Development Foundation (the predecessor to University Circle Incorporated) was formed by three charter members:

University Hospitals, Western Reserve University and The Case Institute of Technology. Initial efforts were focused on creating a land bank to purchase and hold available land needed by institutions for expansion. The land bank was initially capitalized by two fund-raising campaigns in the early 1960s that raised $11 million.

Soon, services that could be provided more efficiently if done collectively — parking, shuttle bus service, public safety, architectural review and landscaping of common areas — were added. Established in 1959, the University Circle Police Department was one of the first private police units in the country. The stability provided by these services gave new confidence to the institutions and the Circle's growth skyrocketed.

By the late 1960s, however, urban sprawl had accelerated on a national basis and was beginning to leave urban decay behind it. It was a decade of concern about many issues, including the Vietnam War, mounting urban

and social problems, and institutional change — all of which affected University Circle. At the time of the historic 1967 federation of Western Reserve University and Case Institute of Technology into Case Western Reserve University, intense campus unrest was in the wings. A year earlier, four days of rioting in the nearby Hough neighborhood had occurred, followed in 1968 by a confrontation in the adjacent Glenville neighborhood that left seven people dead. "It was not an easy time for University Circle," remembered Joseph D. Pigott, UCI President from 1970 to 1989.

But while the riots were devastating and campus turmoil unsettling, there was a positive outcome: the University

Circle Development Foundation, community leaders and the institutions came together and acknowledged that the future of the Circle and its surrounding neighborhoods were mutually dependent and required a cooperative effort. As one staff member noted: "We couldn't be an island with a moat around us. We wouldn't have survived." And despite the times, six new institutions located to the Circle and major physical expansion to existing institutions continued.

1970s: A New Direction for UCI

In 1970 the University Circle Development Foundation was reorganized as University Circle Incorporated (UCI), with greater emphasis on strengthening ties between the Circle and its adjacent neighborhoods. To this end, UCI co-sponsored several housing projects in Hough that yielded more than 1,100 units of housing between 1972 and 1984. UCI also began to work more

closely with neighborhood organizations to broaden access to community resources. In addition, priority was given to improving relationships with Circle institutions, the private sector and the public sector at all levels — city, state and federal.

Created in 1973, UCI's acclaimed Community Education Department was designed to be a bridge between the neighborhoods and the Circle institutions — a wonderful collaboration that thrives today. Annually, more than 35,000 students benefit from the multiprogram effort that introduces children (and their teachers) to Circle resources. The Cultural Education Program, for example, arranges field trips to Circle museums, theaters and concert

(Photo next page)
UCI's community outreach efforts bring thousands of Cleveland schoolchildren to Circle institutions each year.
Photo by Don Snyder

(Photo last page)
The beautiful Wade Lagoon and the many architecturally noteworthy religious institutions are among University Circle's most beloved landmarks.
Photo by Don Snyder

(Far left)
Since 1959 the University Circle Police Department has been dedicated to maintaining public safety in the Circle.
Photo by Don Snyder

Restaurants, a coffee-house and a mansion reinvented as a guest inn add to the ambience of this neighborhood.
Photo by Diane Hansson

halls for the students of more than 30 area schools each year. UCI not only prepares the master schedule, but also pays admission fees and arranges door-to-door transportation. A relatively new endeavor, the Early Learning Initiative, is noteworthy for its focus on preschool children. Modeled after a program created by the Smithsonian Institution, the Early Learning Initiative unites five preschools in the Circle area with 10 Circle cultural institutions and includes a curriculum that prepares the students for their visits to the participating locations.

1990s: Extraordinary Investment and an Updated Master Plan

While the vision to build such a concentration of institutions began with the artistic and cultural sensibilities of the late 19th century, University Circle quickly became a center of world-class accomplishment as well as an economic force. The institutions had long pursued innovative approaches to major issues facing the region and the nation, and to support their diverse missions, they planned to invest more than $500 million in new and improved facilities in the 1990s. Given the scale of this investment, it was time to look holistically again at the Circle and develop a plan for future physical development.

Together with a team of nationally recognized consultants, UCI and the Circle institutions collaborated to develop the 1990 University Circle Master Plan. The Plan

served as a guide for physical planning and development concepts, design guidelines, and recommendations for functional elements — pedestrian circulation, parking, and traffic. One of the most tangible projects that resulted from this effort was the extensive wayfinding system that is composed of more than 100 signs to help visitors find their destinations throughout the Circle.

1990 is also significant in UCI's history because it marked the first year of Parade the Circle Celebration, which has grown to become one of Cleveland's most popular community events, drawing more than 30,000 people each June. Created to showcase the scope and diversity of all the Circle has to offer, the event features a spectacular art parade coordinated by The Cleveland Museum of Art, as well as entertainment and activities presented by more than 30 Circle institutions. In keeping with the spirit of inviting the community to enjoy the Circle, UCI established Holiday CircleFest in 1993. A holiday open house in December, complete with special activities, entertainment and unique shopping, has become a Cleveland tradition for many families.

With the building of new major attractions in downtown Cleveland, including the Rock and Roll Hall of Fame and Museum and the Great Lakes Science Center, Cleveland is enjoying a renaissance as a tourist destination. To take advantage of this momentum, a consortium of six of the Circle's major attractions came together to form the University Circle Tourism Initiative and created the promotional campaign: "So Many Choices. One Amazing Place."

Well-planned community development has been essential in the successful growth of University Circle. Between 1957 and 1999, about $120 million worth of property passed through UCI's land-bank operation. According to the Urban Land Institute in Washington, D.C., "The UCI land bank has been the single most important factor in the dramatic growth of the University Circle institutions and is closely linked to the subsequent emergence of University Circle as a major economic force in Cleveland and northeast Ohio."

2000 and Beyond: Shaping the Future

With its land-banking function for institutional expansion nearly complete, UCI's plans at the turn of the century are focused on creating a dynamic neighborhood with more texture. To foster change, UCI and its constituencies determined that a new approach to Circle development was needed. Despite a long list of many appealing features, the Circle, as a whole, lacked coherence to make it an attractive destination in its own right.

Accordingly, in 1999 UCI launched a new planning effort called *Shaping the Future of University Circle* that will guide the Circle toward its goal of becoming one of the premier urban districts in the world. The planning process involved many members of the Circle community, as well as individuals from the greater community. Public input offered at three well-attended Town Meetings and a research project that was done regarding the image and perception of University Circle completed the process.

Great aspirations combined with specific initiatives outlined in the plan are represented by four core values of vitality, beauty, accessibility and community:

Vitality will be achieved by continued institutional strength and innovation; the building of many more residential options; increased tourism; and new business

development that builds on the research and technology-transfer potential that exists in the Circle.

Beauty will be heightened by an increased sensitivity to the impact of urban design; the improvement of the Circle's gateways; the addition of details that will make the Circle more pedestrian-friendly; and the promotion of public art.

Accessibility will be enhanced by the creation of amenities for visitors such as improved signage, maps and information brochures; welcoming and easily used public transportation; redesigned streets that are attractive and navigable; and adequate parking.

Community will be attained by creating activities to welcome people to the Circle, including educational programs, Circle-wide community events and marketing efforts; by a physical development strategy that reinforces the Circle as a welcoming cultural district for the community; and by a recognition that the Circle's future requires collaboration.

Some examples of specific projects that will greatly improve the Circle in the coming years include the Euclid Corridor Improvement Project. This $292 million transit improvement project will use electric trolley buses to move passengers from Public Square to the Circle and beyond. A streetscape design for the Circle's portion of Euclid Avenue includes traffic-calming measures and extensive pedestrian-oriented improvements. Also, sites for new housing options, from townhouses to apartments, have been identified throughout the Circle — on main arteries and on spaces tucked neatly next to institutions. Many exciting institutional projects are already in the works, beginning with the magnificently renovated Severance Hall. Around the corner, Case Western Reserve University is building the Peter B. Lewis Campus of the Weatherhead School of Management, designed by world-famous architect Frank O. Ghery. The Cleveland Museum of Art has unveiled a master plan that sets the stage for an ambitious expansion program and a three-story glass house will be the centerpiece of Cleveland Botanical Garden's growth. These are but a few of the developments that will soon be tangible proof of the Circle's progress.

"The most important goal," notes UCI President David T. Abbott, "is for us to create a community that has a greater sense of place and is an attractive place to live, to visit and to enjoy in many different ways."

Fine Arts Garden Commission

First Church of Christ, Scientist

Gestalt Institute of Cleveland

Hallinan Center

Hanna Perkins School

Hope Lodge

Judson Retirement Community

The Junior League of Cleveland, Inc.

Maximum Independent Living

The Mt. Sinai Health Care Foundation

Mt. Zion Congregational Church

Musical Arts Association

Ohio College of Podiatric Medicine

Ohio Montessori Training Institute

Pentecostal Church of Christ

Ronald McDonald House of Cleveland, Inc.

Saint Luke's Foundation of Cleveland

The Sculpture Center

The Temple-Tifereth Israel

University Circle Housing, Inc.

University Hospitals of Cleveland

The Western Reserve Historical Society

The Bonfoey Company

The Bonfoey Company has been building a legacy of quality in downtown Cleveland since 1893. The gallery provides a variety of specialized services, such as appraisals, distinctive framing, carving, gilding, art restoration and fine art shipping, in addition to carrying 19th- and 20th-century paintings and prints. It is also a showcase for the finest contemporary works that emerge from the regional and national scenes. Throughout the dark days when Cleveland seemed to be a fading city, The Bonfoey Company maintained a faithful presence. Many other key businesses at that time had begun a flight to the suburbs or escaped the Cleveland area altogether. Bonfoey, however, dug in its heels and quietly lived a commitment to its city.

In 1890 Asher D. Bonfoey was a violinist for the Euclid Avenue Opera House. He made a frame for a valentine he gave to his wife, Della, an accomplished seamstress. Friends were so impressed by the beautiful framing that he started creating frames for them as well. Increasingly, he expanded his craft into a full-time family business. In 1893 he officially opened doors for service in a store located in the heart of downtown, on Erie Street, now known as East Ninth. In 10 years Bonfoey moved again to East Fourth Street and Prospect and operated business there for six decades. George R. Moore joined the business in 1927, and

All photos by Wetzler Photography

by 1938 he took ownership from Bonfoey. He was involved in the daily operation, and his son, Richard, joined the company in 1955. In 1971 Richard became president. The business is still owned by the Moore family.

In 1963 Bonfoey moved once more to its current location on Euclid Avenue in Playhouse Square. There are several nooks and crannies winding through this old building, which was reportedly once home to a speakeasy during the Prohibition era of the 1920s. A visitor might find a textile expert in one room carefully restoring an antique hanging that will be framed with equal care and expertise by another in the room around the corner. An area of more than 6,000 square feet accommodates the backroom workspace. Bonfoey stocks over 1,000 different mouldings, the largest selection in the area, from which any frame imaginable can be custom-made with the support of the most modern equipment available.

The experienced staff at Bonfoey's represents quality. Most of the employees have been with the company from 10 to 25 years. Customers and artists are nurtured in an environment of knowledgeable service and artistic direction. Appraisals for insurance or estates are given by professionals with exceptional backgrounds in art and art history.

Apprentices are trained onsite in every phase of framing, art restoration and conservation. Each is a skilled artisan. Original designs and hand carving are a trademark service that The Bonfoey Company offers to its clientele. Whether it is the slow process of applying gold leaf to a frame or restoring a 19th-century painting to its original patina, the gallery and workrooms evoke a buzz of diligent and thoughtful artists whose work is born of their own personal passion.

In the 1970s Bonfoey recognized the potential of the local art scene while other gallery owners relied on the established markets of New York and other major cities. It was the first commercial gallery to present and promote Cleveland artists, and continues to showcase local and regional artists. Douglas Lucak, Gary Bukovnik, Linda Butler, Lawrence Channing, Kenneth Dingwall, Janos Enyedi, Mary Lou Ferbert, Kathleen Hammett, Patrick Kelly, Judith McMillan, Ed Mieczkowski, Ken Nevadomi, John Pearson, Christopher Pekoc, Stephen Pentak, Phyllis Seltzer and Phyllis Sloane are among the many local artists represented by The Bonfoey Company. Bonfoey installs as many as eight to nine exhibitions a year, each celebrated by a reception for the artist on opening day. As a vital member of the Cleveland arts community, the Bonfoey Company participates in many programs and events. Annually it donates framing for the auction that benefits Cleveland

WVIZ Public Television, along with $75 to $100 gift certificates. It is an active participant in the Art Song Festival, a benefit for the Cleveland Music Institute, providing an exhibition for the event, which occurs every other year.

The Bonfoey Company has been a core element in the renaissance of downtown Cleveland with its art, service and dedication to the community.

The Cleveland Museum of Natural History

Within the park-like setting of University Circle on Wade Oval Drive is The Cleveland Museum of Natural History — one of the finest institutions of its kind in North America. It is noted for its collections, research, educational programs and exhibits. The collections encompass more than 1 million specimens and research focuses on 10 natural science disciplines.

On the average, the museum attracts more than 250,000 visitors, including 72,000 schoolchildren, annually. Students learn in galleries, classrooms and laboratories. Members,

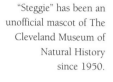

"Steggie" has been an unofficial mascot of The Cleveland Museum of Natural History since 1950.

their families and the public broaden their perspectives of the natural world through permanent and changing exhibits, educational programs, lectures and weekend activities, including animal and planetarium shows.

For many visitors, the most memorable exhibits are in Kirtland Hall of Prehistoric Life. Most famous is "Lucy," a 3.2-million-year-old female skeleton discovered in Ethiopia by a former museum curator. A visual record of evolution from *Australopithecus afarensis* to modern *Homo sapiens* is on display adjacent to Kirtland Hall. The museum is also celebrated for its Hamann-Todd Osteological Research Collection of 3,100 modern human

skeletons and over 900 non-human primate skulls and skeletons, used by researchers worldwide.

Other popular exhibits in the Hall are "Happy" and "Dunk." The plant-eating dinosaur, *Haplocanthosaurus delfsi*, lived about 160 million years ago and is one of the most complete mounted sauropods on exhibit anywhere in the world. *Dunkleosteus terrilli* is a huge armored fish that swam in the tropical sea that covered this region 360 million years ago.

For visitors who prefer diamonds to dinosaurs, the museum's Wade Gallery of Gems & Jewels is a must-see. It showcases more than 1,500 precious stones, jewelry and lapidary artwork from the museum's extensive collection, considered to be one of the finest museum collections in the nation. Adjacent to this gallery is PLANET e, the Reinberger Hall of Earth and Planetary Exploration. It contains high-tech interactives, real and replicated rock formations, a simulated earthquake and space imagery from NASA.

Other galleries feature prehistoric life in Ohio since 10,000 B.C., artifacts from nine different cultures, and modern-day Ohio animals and plants. The museum is also home to Balto, the internationally famous dog that helped save the diphtheria-stricken town of Nome, Alaska. He is on display about once a year. In addition, the museum has an observatory and planetarium, a Discovery Center, a 60,000-volume library, museum store, cafe and outdoor gardens.

The institution is also a major player in conservation programs to protect ecologically significant land for the future. The museum is one of the largest land trusts in Ohio, with over 3,000 acres of nature preserves under its stewardship.

The museum's scientific areas of research in the laboratory and field are: archaeology, botany, cultural anthropology, invertebrate paleontology, invertebrate zoology, mineralogy, paleobotany, physical anthropology, vertebrate paleontology and vertebrate zoology.

For nearly 80 years, The Cleveland Museum of Natural History has stayed true to its mission to instill an understanding and appreciation of life on Earth and the cosmos beyond.

Cleveland Opera

To open its 25th-anniversary season, Cleveland Opera presented the most celebrated singers in the world — José Carreras, Placido Domingo and Luciano Pavarotti — at Cleveland Browns Stadium. Pavarotti had entertained Cleveland audiences for the opera's 10th and 20th anniversaries as well. The company has featured other international stars such as opera singers Roberta Peters, Sherrill Milnes and Jerome Hines and, in specialty roles,

Theodore Bickel, Werner Klemperer and Bebe Neuwirth. But as 30,000 people rose to cheer "The Three Tenors" after their performance with the Cleveland Opera Orchestra, there was no doubt that the company had come of age.

Founded in 1976 and initially performing in a suburban school, the fledgling group played a significant role in the renaissance of downtown Cleveland. The opera company helped design the specifications for the entirely new stage at the State Theatre in Playhouse Square, transforming the historic 1921 movie palace with its tiny vaudeville stage into one of the finest opera houses in the country. The restored theater made its debut in the 1984-85 season, opening with the touring Metropolitan Opera of New York. Cleveland Opera proudly and successfully shared the same stage in only its 9th year of operation.

Under the dynamic leadership of founder and General Director David Bamberger, Cleveland Opera wins national and international acclaim for outstanding performances and for innovative programming in a range of styles that few opera companies dare consider. In the 1980s the company mounted the first professionally staged Gilbert and Sullivan

operetta and, with *Kiss Me, Kate*, the first professional production of a classic musical to be seen in downtown Cleveland in a quarter of a century. Cleveland Opera commissioned Stewart Copeland, the founder and drummer of the rock band The Police, to compose his first opera, *Holy Blood and Crescent Moon*. The 1989 world premiere drew audiences from around the world and press coverage from as far away as Los Angeles, Tel Aviv and Mongolia.

Cleveland Opera reaches a large audience beyond those who attend its productions at the State Theatre. The company won an Emmy for its televised version of Benjamin Britten's children's opera, *The Little Sweep*, and for many years was one of the few companies in the United States with productions regularly broadcast on radio.

Through its education and outreach program — Cleveland Opera On Tour — the company serves more than a dozen states from New York and Florida to Texas and Wisconsin. Each year, this program, which earned the 1998 Ohio Governor's Award for Arts in Education, enriches the lives of at least 80,000 children through approximately 350 events. Under the guidance of Cleveland Opera On Tour Music Mentors, elementary school students have written and produced more than 100 operas. Cleveland Opera is further distinguished by being Ohio's only major performing arts organization to bring the joy of live musical theater to senior citizen centers. By working in these programs, young professional singers gain the experience that has led many of them to successful national and international careers.

Kaori Sato as Cio-Cio-San and Michael Rees Davis as Lieutenant Pinkerton in Cleveland Opera's 2000 production of *Madame Butterfly*. *Photo by Roger Mastroianni*

The Three Tenors, joined by Maestro Marco Armiliato, enjoy the applause of the 30,000-strong crowd following their concert to kick off Cleveland Opera's 2000/2001 25th-anniversary season. *Photo by Roger Mastroianni*

The Cleveland Orchestra

Long considered one of America's great orchestras, The Cleveland Orchestra stands today among the world's most revered symphonic ensembles. For more than four decades, it has performed to critical acclaim around the globe. Music Director Christoph von Dohnányi's imaginative programming, exacting musicianship and the orchestra's traditionally high standard of performance have earned the praise of critics everywhere. Dohnányi and Cleveland, said *The Washington Post*, are "perhaps the most magnificently coordinated and mutually complementary teaming... since the late Herbert von Karajan's best days with the Berlin Philharmonic."

"Visually the new stage is stunning... Severance Hall sounds as seductive as it looks." (*The New York Times*, January 10, 2000) Photo ©2000 by Roger Mastroianni

Such world-class stature had a modest beginning, when in 1901 Adella Prentiss Hughes began presenting concerts by visiting orchestras. A forceful woman with business acumen and leadership ability, Hughes founded the Musical Arts Association (MAA) in 1915 with the goal of furthering the interest of music in the community. Desiring to establish an orchestra for Cleveland, she secured conductor Nikolai Sokoloff as music director, and The Cleveland Orchestra gave its debut concert on December 11, 1918. Three years later, the Orchestra performed at Carnegie Hall and aired its first national radio broadcast. The Orchestra initiated an extensive domestic touring schedule, educational concerts, commercial recordings and radio broadcasts.

For many years, Hughes solicited donations from wealthy Cleveland philanthropists to build a concert hall. On the 10th anniversary of the orchestra's inaugural concert, MAA President John Severance and his wife, Elisabeth, pledged a million dollars toward that goal. In February 1931 Severance Hall opened and was immediately acclaimed as one of America's most beautiful concert facilities. With its majestic Georgian exterior, Severance Hall contains two elegant performance halls and exquisite public spaces that exhibit Art Deco, Egyptian Revival and Neoclassical design. Beginning in 1998 Severance Hall underwent a major renovation, restoration and expansion. It reopened in January 2000 to rave reviews worldwide.

Nikolai Sokoloff's successor as music director was Artur Rodzinski (1933-43), whose tenure included the presentation of 15 fully staged operas. Erich Leinsdorf (1943-46) followed Rodzinski, although much of his directorship was in absentia while he served in the U.S. Armed Forces during World War II.

Under George Szell (1946-70), The Cleveland Orchestra entered a period of dramatic and sustained growth. With its first tours of Europe and Asia and its acclaimed recordings, it became recognized as one of the world's top orchestral ensembles. Blossom Music Center, the orchestra's summer home, opened in 1968, permitting the expansion of the orchestra's season to a year-round performance schedule.

Lorin Maazel (1972-82) continued the orchestra's international touring and recording activities while broadening the ensemble's repertoire. During the tenure of Christoph von Dohnányi, who became music director in 1984, the orchestra's subscription season was expanded to accommodate the largest audience in its history. The Cleveland Orchestra reaches out to a broad audience by offering jazz performances, popular family programs, free concerts, and through The Cleveland Orchestra Youth Orchestra and Chorus. In June 1999 Franz Welser-Möst was appointed as successor to Dohnányi beginning with the 2002-03 season.

The Cleveland Play House

Founded in 1915, The Cleveland Play House is the oldest resident professional theatre in the United States. Paul Newman, Joel Grey and Jack Weston are among the many actors whose careers began at The Play House, which also operates the nation's oldest community-based theatre-education programs.

1970), Richard Oberlin (1971-1985), William Rhys (1985-1988), Josephine Abady (1988-1993) and Peter Hackett (1994-present).

Under Hackett's leadership a strong emphasis on new-play development has resulted in numerous world premieres and ongoing support of a growing list of regional

The Cleveland Play House was designed by world renowned architect Philip Johnson.
Photo by Barney Taxel

A selection of the over 70 world and American premieres produced by The Cleveland Play House:

The Pleasure of Honesty,
Luigi Pirandello
You Touched Me,
Tennessee Williams
A Decent Birth,
William Saroyan
Command,
William Wister Haines
Mother Courage,
Bertolt Brecht
Simone, Ben Hecht
The Effect of Gamma Rays on Man-In-The-Moon Marigolds,
Paul Zindel*
The First Monday in October,
Jerome Lawrence and Robert E. Lee
Translations, Brian Friel
Ten Times Table,
Alan Ayckbourn
The Archbishop's Ceiling,
Arthur Miller
The March on Russia,
David Storey
The Enchanted Maze,
A Russian Romance, and
The Emancipation of Valet Du Chambre,
Murphy Guyer

* 1970 Pulitzer Prize Winner

In the early 1900s Cleveland theatre featured mostly vaudeville, melodrama, burlesque and light entertainment. But a select group of Clevelanders sought plays of substance on timely topics. Together, they formed The Play House and found a home in a farmhouse donated by Cleveland industrialist Francis Drury. Ultimately, Drury helped fund its permanent home at East 85th and Euclid Avenue.

The original Play House was built in 1927 to house two theatres. In 1949 The Play House opened the 77th Street Theatre in a converted church, which featured America's first open stage — the forerunner of the thrust stage that was popularized in the 50s and 60s. In 1983 the 77th Street Theatre closed, a significant Philip Johnson-designed addition to the original facility opened and The Play House became the largest regional theatre complex in the country.

Notably, The Play House has had only seven Artistic Directors since 1915: Raymond O'Neil (1915-1921), Frederic McConnell (1921-1958), K. Elmo Lowe (1959-

and national playwrights. His new programs include The Next Stage Festival of New Plays, an "associate artists" program that has created a core group of visiting and resident artists, and a master of fine arts program in acting with Case Western Reserve University. Education remains a high priority and, each year, more than 35,000 students attend productions, as well as drama and playwriting classes.

Internationally, The Play House has made its mark with the Full Circle International Theatre Exchange Program, the only program of its kind in the country. The Exchange was established to celebrate Cleveland's ethnic diversity, and has enabled The Play House to host or exchange productions with the National Theatres of Hungary, the Czech Republic and Slovakia, as well as Russia's Volgograd Theatre.

Throughout its rich history, The Play House has remained true to its mission of producing plays and operating educational programs of the highest professional standards that enhance the quality of life in Northern Ohio.

Don Drumm Studios & Gallery

Modern technology and its materials have found a place of harmony with contemporary artists and craftspeople. On an Akron side street near downtown, and in the shadow of the University of Akron, in a working class neighborhood of humble proportions, Don and Lisa Drumm have filled two buildings with a maze of 10 rooms to create the Don Drumm Studios & Gallery and the adjacent Different Drummer Shop & Gallery. Three generations of metal workers that include the artist himself provide the driving force behind Don Drumm's work and his expression of it through the studio and gallery he established in 1971.

In the mid 1950s Don Drumm was a pre-med student at Hiram College, a small liberal arts college less than a half-hour's drive west from his hometown of Warren in Ohio's northeast corner. His grandfather had been a blacksmith; his father, a welder and mechanic. When Drumm abandoned his path toward medicine to pursue art at Kent State University midway through college, his parents were not disappointed at his choice. The fact that he was the first in the family even to attend college was what pleased them. For them, his happiness was their concern. A heritage that merged his interests in art and sculpture with his respect for metal work, as well as the happy life his parents hoped for him is an almost tangible quality that greets visitors entering the shops. Drumm's sculptures grace the outdoor patio area, while the small, exquisitely laid-out displays inside seem more like those in someone's home rather than part of the largest American crafts gallery between New York and Chicago.

In 1958 Drumm pioneered the use of cast aluminum as an artistic medium, and began his work of creating one-of-a-kind sculptures for private homes, public parks, businesses, educational institutions, museums and cities that he continues to this day. By 1971, having served for six years as an artist-in-residence at Bowling Green State University, he and his wife, Lisa, a former teacher and artist in her own right, were raising three daughters. Their plan to open a shop was both a practical approach to the life they wanted to lead, and part of a vision they shared to enhance and further the promotion of American design and crafts, in addition to their own work.

Don Drumm Studios & Gallery features a wide variety of handcrafted art objects, both functional and decorative, that range from a dollar to thousands of dollars, and includes work in glass, ceramics, jewelry, metal, textiles, sculpture and graphics. The Different Drummer Shop & Gallery next door features Lisa Drumm's handcrafted dolls and collections of wood, jewelry, leather, weaving and art clothing imported from around the world, along with a back room filled with unusual toys.

Thirty years later their successful endeavor thrives. The work of Don and Lisa Drumm, with an active group of approximately 800 other artists, continues to present a showcase of beautiful, sometimes useful objects of art in a place respected as one of the top 10 galleries in the United States.

One of the first artists to use cast aluminum as an artistic medium, sculptor Don Drumm is pictured here with his wife, fabric artist Lisa Drumm. The large sun wall sculpture is part of Drumm's extensive collections in aluminum and pewter, which include jewelry, sculpture, furniture, home accessories and cookware.

Artists Don and Lisa Drumm opened a one-room gallery in 1971 to sell their work and works by a few friends. Today Don Drumm Studios & Gallery is recognized as one of the finest American craft galleries in the country, encompassing two buildings and representing over 500 top professional artists/craftsmen.

Playhouse Square Foundation

The second-largest performing arts center in the United States is in Cleveland in Playhouse Square Center. Just as this theater district — along Euclid Avenue from East 12th to East 18th streets and between Chester and Prospect avenues — was the core of Cleveland's entertainment scene in the beginning of the 20th century, so it may once again be the nucleus of a revitalized downtown well into the new century.

In the early 1900s Cleveland was a center of industrial activity for enterprising capitalists. People were clamoring for entertainment and entrepreneurs began developing the spots for after-hours amusements. Between February 1921 and November 1922, the State, Ohio, Hanna, Allen and Palace Theatres opened, some with full orchestra pits and the largest having over 3,600 seats. They were designed for legitimate theater, silent movies or vaudeville and hosted stars such as Fred Astaire, Jack Benny, Judy Garland, the Marx Brothers and Mickey Rooney. Eventually the theater district boasted 12 playhouses, and local newspapers christened the area Playhouse Square.

But its heyday did not endure. Vaudeville had disappeared by 1935; the Great Depression changed the tone of American culture; the postwar suburban sprawl drew people away from downtown; television as entertainment emerged as a formidable force; and the buildings themselves began to show their age. By the 1960s and 70s most of these theaters either had been torn down or abandoned and the streets of downtown Cleveland went quiet after the work day ended.

In 1970 the State Theatre was visited by Raymond Shepardson, a board of education employee looking for a conference space. The splendor of the abandoned theaters, whose magnificent lobbies had been homages to luxury and elegance — though now unkempt and tarnished — convinced him that the theaters were worthy of preservation from the wrecking ball. With minuscule budgets, Shepardson initiated small-scale productions in the State Theatre, and it was enough to spearhead a campaign for restoration. Before the end of the decade, the surviving theaters — Allen, Ohio, State and Palace — had been listed in the National Register of Historic Places and Playhouse Square Foundation had been established. Between 1982 and 1988 the Foundation organized a professional management team that procured $40 million, and full restoration was undertaken. The Playhouse Square Center was inaugurated in 1984, and the last of the four adjoining theaters, the Allen, was reopened in 1998. The Hanna, closed since 1989, was acquired by Playhouse Square Foundation in 1999.

Playhouse Square Center is home for several resident performing arts companies: Great Lakes Theater Festival, DanceCleveland, Cleveland Opera, Ohio Ballet and the Tri-C Cultural Arts Series. Programming is varied and diverse, from Broadway touring shows to urban contemporary theater and dance. It can accurately be described as offering something for everyone.

Although its primary mission is to save the historically significant theaters and to operate them, Playhouse Square Foundation has been instrumental in developing adjacent areas to further stabilize the theater district. For example, it helped locate a new 205-room hotel in a neighboring block. Long-term plans call for modifying the features in front of the theater doors: widening sidewalks, planting mature trees, adding colorful neon signs and banners, rerouting vehicular traffic and otherwise enhancing the space for pedestrians.

The Grand Lobby of the Palace Theatre, home of the Broadway Series

BUILDING A
GREATER CLEVELAND

Cleveland real estate development, management and construction companies, and local unions shape tomorrow's skyline, providing and improving working and living space for area residents.

R.P. Carbone Company

In Italian, Carbone means coal. When young Rosario Pasquale Carbone came to this country in 1920 with his bride, he built a reputation that he was made of "hard," not "soft" coal.

A graduate of the Royal Technical Institute of Rome with a degree in engineering and construction, Carbone served as a chief engineer for the Italian government after

One of the firm's first educational projects, Cleveland's Bolton School, 1936

World War I. When he and his wife came to visit relatives in Cleveland, it became a 57-year "visit" when Carbone realized the opportunities available and took advantage of them.

The city was growing, and there was need for talented bricklayers and masons, skills Carbone had mastered in Italy. He tried a couple of partnerships, but when those didn't work out, he formed R.P. Carbone in 1926.

It seemed as if all his dreams might go for naught when the Great Depression hit three years later, but Carbone focused his energies on Cleveland's changing infrastructure, working on several school additions for the board of education. The company's big break came just prior to World War II when the firm was asked to build two major projects at Cleveland Hopkins Airport for the National Advisory Committee for Aeronautics (NACA), which eventually would become the National Aeronautics and Space Agency.

As the business continued to grow, so too did the family commitment to the firm. Carbone's two sons, Alphonso and Dominic, joined the company after the war and remained until their deaths. Eventually their children and grandchildren also would join the firm. In

From elementary school to university — Cleveland State's Convocation Center

the construction industry, where 85 percent of second-generation companies fall by the wayside, having the fourth generation involved is an amazing record.

Boom times continued in the late 1940s when the company built the state's first postwar public school. The firm also won the contract for a new Euclid high school, at an amazing — for 1948 — $4 million. About the same time, the company built its first school in Medina, and it is still working with that school system.

Work on educational facilities was not limited to public schools, as the company was hired by the Catholic Diocese of Cleveland to build parochial schools and churches to meet the needs of a population that was moving to the newly emerging suburbs. One of the firm's biggest jobs was constructing the multimillion-dollar Borromeo Seminary campus in Wickliffe for the diocese in the early 1950s.

During this period Carbone, who had a sensitivity to minorities because of the discrimination he himself had suffered, sponsored the first minority individual for membership in the Bricklayer's Union. That kind of commitment has remained through the years. Two decades later, the firm sponsored the first female in the local.

And in the 1980s the company began an internal apprenticeship-training program for minorities, providing them with an opportunity to work toward a vocation in the construction industry. For its efforts and commitment to minority business and equal-opportunity employment, the company was honored by the city of Cleveland.

Throughout the 1960s R.P. Carbone continued its relationship with the church and education, erecting the first six building on Ursuline College's suburban campus. During the decade the company worked on such parochial schools as Regina, St. Augustine and Cleveland Central Catholic, but also did public school work for the Cleveland, Mayfield and South Euclid-Lyndhurst school systems.

By the late 70s there was change in the air — Not with the kind of clients the company served, but with the procedures for serving them. The company expanded beyond basic bricks and mortar into construction management, packaging an entire project from sending out the bids to overseeing construction.

Not only did the scope of the company's work continue to grow during the decade, so too did the family commitment when the third Carbone generation, brothers Ross and Vincent and cousin Rosario, joined the firm. Dominic came aboard in the early 1980s and Carmen in the 1990s.

Even as the firm's role changed, clients' reliance on the company remained the same. In 1972 the company worked on the Medina high school, continuing a relationship established 20 years earlier. In 1995 the firm was hired to work on the middle school and at the end of the 20th century was working on a five-year, $88 million upgrade and expansion of all schools in the community. A similar situation existed in East Cleveland. The company worked on a high school addition in the 1970s and in the late 1990s was awarded the assignment of upgrading every building in the system.

Among the firm's other major projects have been the Temple on the Heights complex in Pepper Pike and

renovation of the Cleveland Convention center in the 1980s. It was a decade of challenge, for during that period the firm worked with Cleveland native Philip Johnson, internationally famed architect, on the $14 million Cleveland Playhouse renaissance.

In the late 1990s Carbone served as construction manager for Cleveland State University's convocation center and mega block project that included development of the College of Business, College of Urban Affairs and College of Law.

Some of Carbone's other major projects include work on the Teamsters headquarters, Third Federal Savings and Loan operations center and conversion of Severance Town Center from an enclosed mall to a strip center. The firm also had primary responsibility for the four-year restoration of the historic Powerhouse in Cleveland's Flats district. It also had restoration responsibility for turning a portion of the Bolton estate in Lyndhurst into guest quarters for TRW.

Just as the scope of the company's work has changed over the years, so too has its geographic scope. In addition to activities in northeastern Ohio, the firm's work can be seen in Alabama, Arizona, Louisiana, Florida, Nevada, Texas, South Carolina, North Carolina and Mississippi. And some of that work is being planned by Allison, the fourth Carbone generation to take an active part in the business.

A newspaper article has quoted Ross Carbone, one of Rosario's grandsons and his namesake, as saying, "As much as technology changes our industry through computers and such, you still lay one brick at a time." That's how R.P. Carbone has built such a solid foundation over the years — brick by brick.

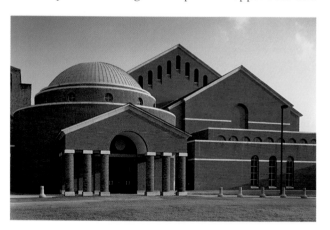

The company worked with internationally famed architect Philip Johnson on the $14 million Cleveland Playhouse renaissance.

Kelley Steel Erectors, Inc.

Kelley Steel Erectors, Inc., founded over 40 years ago, has combined skilled workers with quality machines to lift, lower and place over 2 million tons of structural steel and precast concrete panels in structures all over the world. What began as a small steel-erection company in 1958 has grown to become one of the top steel-erection and crane-rental companies in the United States.

Kelley Steel is the brainchild of Garen N. Kelley, the company's founder and current chairman of the board. Originally from Wheeling, West Virginia, he served for three years in the second division of the United States Marine Corps during World War II and was stationed in the South Pacific. When he returned in 1941 he began a career in steel erection by working as a steel superintendent for several large general contractors, including Hunkin and Conkey, and Sanders and Porter. He supervised a wide range of jobs all over Ohio and Western Pennsylvania, such as structural steel erection, the placement of reinforcing steel for concrete, machinery setting, millwright work and heavy rigging.

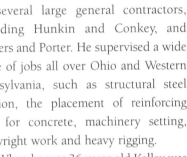

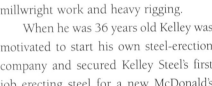

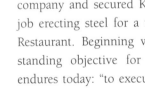

Garen N. Kelley founded Kelley Steel Erectors, Inc. in 1958 after working as a steel erector for over 15 years.

When he was 36 years old Kelley was motivated to start his own steel-erection company and secured Kelley Steel's first job erecting steel for a new McDonald's Restaurant. Beginning with that first job, he created a standing objective for every Kelley project that still endures today: "to execute the job properly in minimum time and at the lowest cost, to avoid interference with the owner's operations and to finish the project ahead of schedule when material is available."

It is an objective that helped propel Kelley Steel to become a prominent leader in the construction industry. Today, it self-performs a variety of industrial and commercial construction services for the steel, power, manufacturing, chemical, mining and environmental industries under the leadership of Garen N. Kelley's son, Michael J. Kelley, current president and CEO.

Michael Kelley began working for the company at the age of 15 as a boilermaker in the construction of steel mills. By the time he was 18 years old he was a member of

the ironworkers' union and was working for Kelley Steel on projects all over Ohio, Western Pennsylvania, Florida and Illinois, specializing in steel mills, power houses and high-rise construction. Kelley joined the company full time at the age of 21. He eventually stopped working at the construction sites and moved into administration and management. He became the company's president in 1992.

A surge in the construction of high-rise buildings in the 1960s helped the company steadily grow during its early years. Just a few of the buildings Kelley Steel erected in the Cleveland area during the 1960s and early 1970s include the precast facade on Cleveland State University's Library Tower, the IMG building downtown (formerly the Cuyahoga Savings Association building), the Tower East office building in Shaker Heights, John Kennedy School, the Bond Court building downtown, Glenville High School, the Diamond Shamrock building downtown and St. Ann's Hospital in Cleveland Heights. The Crystal Towers residential building in East Cleveland was one of the company's first large projects. The 27-story building required the erection on 2,500 tons of structural steel and the placement of 750 tons of reinforcing steel, all wire mesh, all metal deck and precast concrete panels. The 24-story Central National Bank building downtown was another large project that involved 4,700 tons of structural steel and placement work. The company also began working on projects in the Western Pennsylvania area during the 1960s, including the Seneca Power Plant in Warren, which it erected in 1967, and the 27-story Allegheny Tower apartment and office complex in Pittsburgh, which involved the erection of 2,500 tons of structural steel.

During the 1970s Kelley Steel focused mainly on the construction of power stations and steel mills. It erected every Cleveland Electric Illuminating Co. (CEI) power plant along Ohio's Lake Erie shore, including the Ashtabula, Eastlake, Lakeshore and Avon Lake plants, the latter of which involved the erection of approximately 7,000 tons of structural steel and the placement of all reinforcing steel. When Kelley Steel erected CEI's Perry Nuclear Power Plant, it required the hoisting and placement of 600-ton condenser sections. The company also erected several major power stations along the Ohio River. The three in West Virginia were the Ft. Martin Power Station in Morgantown; the Pleasant Power Station in Willow Island, for which it erected approximately 40,000 tons of structural steel and placed 16,000 tons of reinforcing steel, grating and decking; and the Harrison Power Station in Haywood, for which it erected 27,000 tons of structural steel and placed 16,000 tons of reinforcing steel.

In addition Kelley Steel branched out by erecting power stations in Florida. It erected approximately 8,000 tons of structural steel for the Seminole Electric Power Station in Palatka, Florida, and over 11,000 tons of structural steel for the St. Johns River Power Park in Jacksonville, Florida. The St. Johns project also required the company to install pulverizer mills and soot blowers, and to hoist a 420-ton main steam drum 232 feet above the ground.

The steel mills Kelley Steel erected during the 1970s were often very large jobs. The largest involved the erection of 58,000 tons of structural steel, which is three times the amount needed for a 46-story high-rise building. In Cleveland the company erected the Republic Steel hot strip mill, which involved 27,000 tons of structural steel, three furnaces and all overhead cranes.

By the 1980s Kelley Steel had solidified its reputation as a reliable and hard-working company. It was rewarded with some high-visibility projects, including the current British Petroleum (BP) Building (formerly the Standard Oil Headquarters building) in downtown Cleveland. The 630-foot-high company headquarters required the erection of 22,000 tons of structural steel as well as an 8-story atrium composed of heavy pipe trusses. In addition the company erected 18,000 tons of structural steel for the famous 65-story 900 North Michigan Avenue high-rise building in Chicago, Illinois, where the many challenges included high winds and blizzard conditions.

Some of Kelley Steel's more recent projects include major league stadiums such as the those for the Miami Heat, the Florida Panthers and the scoreboard for Cleveland's Jacobs Field. Other projects completed during the 1990s include the Marriott Hotel in Key Tower downtown and several Ohio correctional facilities. It also moved into the New York market when it placed a crane on the 90-story Trump Residential Tower, the tallest residential building in the world.

The company's past list of projects also includes some unusual and especially challenging ones, such as the placement of a large conveyor system and machinery for Standard Slag Co. in Marblehead, Ohio. It also completely assembled 36 oil rigs in 18 months for Ingals Ship Building in Pascagoula, Mississippi, for which its massive crane with 480 feet of boom would set 118 tons at one lift 400-feet high to the top of the platform.

Cleveland's McDonald & Co. building was one of Kelley Steel's early high-rise projects.

Another one of Kelley Steel's early projects was Cleveland State University's Library Tower, built in the early 1970s.

Kelley Steel erected three power stations along the Ohio River in West Virginia, including the Harrison Power Station, shown here.

Kelley Steel erected the Perry Nuclear Power Plant for CEI.

Kelley Steel's reputation and expertise in its field has led it to increasingly larger projects with larger tonnage, as well as to a larger market area. It has managed and self-performed projects from Maine to Miami and all over the U.S. East and Midwest. Its strong relationships with repeat customers have led to some international jobs for the company, including the construction of an ore unloader in Liberia, Africa, and expanding the pacific Canal Zone in Panama.

There are many reasons why Kelley Steel is successful, including careful planning, hard work and quality service. Since it erects a building's structure and therefore sets the pace on a construction project, it also enforces a strict adherence to timelines and budgets. Safety precautions are not compromised, but instead are diligently exercised. The company has an enviable safety record and has received safety awards from nearly every state in which it has operated.

Kelley Steel is also innovative in its approach to projects. Every one is performed differently according to what is best for the individual client. It effectively communicates with its clients and other project contractors, making their needs the company's main concern. This close working relationship and high level of service save its clients both valuable time and money. In addition Kelley Steel maintains the equipment and manpower needed to perform large projects, in particular those categorized by what it calls "the three Ds" — dirty, dangerous and difficult.

Another key to the company's continuing success is its ability to think long-term and subsequently to reinvest in its resources. Not only does it reinvest its profits in equipment; it also reinvests in what it considers its most valuable resource — its employees. It realizes that it cannot accomplish its objective without an experienced and talented staff.

By refusing to subcontract its jobs, the company not only maintains quality control, but also supports the unions. Employees, who have numbered anywhere from 200 to 5,000 over the years depending upon the amount of projects, are all members of a union, whether they are ironworkers, boilermakers, pipefitters, sheet metal workers, operating engineers, millwrights, carpenters, laborers or teamsters. And every one of the company's job superintendents has more than 20 years of experience on all types of steel work.

While Kelley Steel has stayed focused on its niche of the erection and placement of structural and reinforcing steel and concrete panels, it has also consistently been able to forecast and react to upcoming trends in the market. The company has remained versatile and open to change, phasing in other services as it saw a need for them in the construction industry.

In the mid-1980s Kelley Equipment Company, Inc. was founded to rent and lease Kelley Steel's many specialized cranes and other equipment to general contractors. The company owns some of the finest, largest and most modern steel-erecting equipment in the business, including crawler, truck, climbing and hydraulic cranes with capacities from 12.5 to 600 tons and with boom lengths that range from 20 to 500 feet. Its largest is the 4600 Manitowoc RINGER®, which has a capacity of 600 tons. Also impressive is its Manitowoc 2250, which combines a 300-ton crawler crane with conventional and luffing-boom configurations. With an overall erection time of four hours, the crane is the premier, state-of-the-art crawler crane in the industry.

In addition to cranes Kelley Equipment offers carry-alls, low boys, flat beds, gang busses, field trailers, dozers, welders, air compressors, pumps, snow blowers, heaters and hoists. It can also provide contractors with temporary personnel such as structural engineers, supervisors, foremen, operators and mechanics. All equipment is stored, repaired and maintained out of either its Cleveland office or the company's second office in Clearwater, Florida, both modern facilities that boast 200,000 square feet of climate controlled warehouse space.

During the 1990s Kelley Steel added even more services to its list of specialties. Today, that list includes the fabrication and installation of steel, pipe and sheet metal; the placing of metal and precast concrete decking; the setting of machinery and equipment; millwright work and turbine erection; boiler and condenser erection; and blast furnace erection. The company is qualified to do code work on repairing boiler, pressure piping and pressure vessels. It also carries a Certificate of Authorization from The American Society of Mechanical Engineers and is approved by the National Board of Boilers and Pressure Vessel Inspectors.

Kelley Steel will be reaching even higher in the future. The company's plans include more international projects for select

Kelley Steel has erected a wide variety of projects all over the United States, including the World Golf Hall of Fame in St. Augustine, Florida.

clients, possibly even expanding to include a worldwide office and more affiliate offices. It is also considering an expansion into the marine market, which would entail building, barging, owning and managing large ships for overseas transportation.

Since it was incorporated in 1958, Kelley Steel has handled a wide variety of jobs, both large and small, and some of the largest and toughest projects in the country. But whether the structure required only 100 tons of steel or more than 58,000 tons, it was given the attention it needed to stand strong for many decades to come by a company that has stood strong for over four of them.

(Below left)
Kelley Steel erected one of Cleveland's tallest buildings, the 46-story BP Building.

For the 900 North Michigan Avenue Project in Chicago, Kelley Steel erected all structural steel and metal decking.

Roth Construction Company

When fire, ice, snow, storm, vehicle impact, vandalism or burglary damages a person's home or business, the loss they feel can be devastating. The company charged with repairing the damage is not just rebuilding materials, but fixing lives. Roth Construction Company realizes it is providing a service its client had hoped they would never need and is sensitive to their need for professional service, quality workmanship and adherence to a schedule.

Roth Construction is an independent, family-owned business that has been serving the insurance repair industry since 1967. It performs only insurance referral work, and according to Roth, it is a preferred contractor for the 30 largest insurance carriers in the state of Ohio, including State Farm, Nationwide, Metropolitan and Travelers Insurance. The company is fully licensed, bonded and insured to perform all types of construction restoration in over 40 communities. From a small one-room fire to a major factory restoration, Roth Construction can rebuild it as long as the structure is intact enough to be brought back to life.

Now a leader in its field, the company was at first reluctant to enter the insurance repair industry. It was over 30 years ago when 22-year-old Robert Rothacker founded Roth Drywall Company, a drywall-contracting business. It performed such large projects as the Old Colony Lumber store in Mentor and the Central National Bank Building in downtown Cleveland, where over 1 million feet of drywall was hung and finished. Eventually, painting and installation were added to the company's list of services.

About five years after the drywall business had started, Rothacker's insurance agent, Randy Tahsler, of Motorists Insurance, had a client who needed shingles repaired on his roof. Rothacker wanted his company to focus only on drywall and objected to the work but got the job completed nonetheless. That soon led to other small insurance jobs and inevitably the company's first major fire-damage contract. The client was Ms. Gosnell, who had suffered a bad basement fire. The job was memorable because the basement was full of jars of canned sauerkraut and pickles that ripened quickly after being exposed to the hot summer weather for over two months. Ms. Gosnell became a familiar face around Roth Construction. For over 10 years, she delivered homemade cookies and cakes to the company's first office in Cleveland and even to its second office in Lakewood.

After a few years of performing both insurance and drywall work, the company phased out the drywall contracts and changed its name to Roth Construction Company to reflect its new focus on the restoration of homes and businesses. The company grew steadily, one happy customer at a time, from a small office attached to Rothacker's home with a staff of eight to a thriving multimillion-dollar business that employs over 100 people in four offices.

Roth Construction moved to its current main office in an industrial park on Cleveland's West Side in 1988. It serves four Cleveland-area counties, including Cuyahoga, Lake, Geauga and Northern Summit. Rothacker's two children became involved in the company by working there during the summer months of high school and college. It was 1990 when his daughter, Lisa Rothacker, joined the business permanently after a previous career as a mall

Founded in 1967, Roth Construction Company's main office has been located in an industrial park on Cleveland's West Side since 1988.

developer. She is currently the company's vice president and marketing director. In 1995, his son, Jack Rothacker, a structural engineer, joined the business as well. He currently serves as president of both Roth Construction West and Roth Cleaning Company.

The company grew to include a second office in 1997 when it opened Roth Construction Company West in Elyria, serving Lorain, Huron, Medina, Erie, Eastern Sandusky and Eastern Ottawa counties. At the same time, it started a separate business, Roth Cleaning Company, also located in Elyria. The cleaning company is a full-service contents-cleaning and restoration company that specializes in water extraction, smoke damage, odor control, carpet cleaning, dry cleaning and uphol-stery cleaning. It also performs strictly insurance referral work for both the residential and commercial markets. Belongings are packed, transported, cleaned with the most advanced cleaning techniques available and promptly redelivered.

In 1998 Roth Construction expanded yet again when it added a third office in Columbus. It serves Franklin, Delaware, Western Licking, Northwestern Pickaway, Union, Madison and Northwestern Fairfield counties. Though young, it is already prospering and exceeding all expectations.

Both Roth Construction and Roth Cleaning Company offer 231/2-hour emergency service. Just one call day or night immediately dispatches a crew to secure the property and help prevent further damage. A project representative, estimator and foreman are then assigned to the loss. They work as a team with the customer and their insurance representative to assess and coordinate a smooth restoration process. Though an insurance company is paying for its services, the company works directly with the insured and considers them the customer. Whether it works with them in person, on the telephone or by mail, it feels privileged to have the opportunity to serve its customers and realizes that they are the most important part of its business.

It is this sensitivity to the needs of the property owner that has helped make Roth Construction so successful, and it stems from the owner's real-life experience. A few years after he started the company, president and owner Robert Rothacker had a small fireplace fire in his home. Though the damage was minimal, he experienced the devastating psychological ramifications of having one's home damaged and having to deal with the necessary repairs.

Roth Construction begins a residential claim by first assessing the entire structure and the damage, then recording even the smallest, but most significant, details.

Professional service and quality workmanship have made Roth Construction Company a leader in Northern Ohio's insurance repair industry.

It aims to uncover hidden damages that can cause mon-umental problems after the job is completed. It submits restoration recommendations based on the customer's needs and researches the neighborhood's zoning and building ordinances.

Each damaged item is then inspected and tested prior to cleaning and restoration. The company restores the items using a variety of deodorization techniques, ultrasonics and environmentally safe solvents for unmatched results. For porous items such as books, upholstery and textiles, it uses an ozone room specifically designed for medium-to-severe odor removal. A three-step dry-cleaning process is used for extremely smoky but salvageable fabric items.

Smaller items are cleaned on the premises with the company's fully equipped, contents-cleaning vans, saving time and money. Walls, ceilings, floors, carpeting and woodwork are then cleaned and restored. Roth Construction's many repair services include carpentry, painting, odor control and finish trades — everything except electrical and plumbing work. High-pressure water cleaning and sandblasting capabilities help complete exterior cleaning requirements. While the home is being restored, the company will catalogue and inventory every salvageable possession, wrap and pack it, and move it to a 20,000-square-foot, secure, climate-controlled warehouse at its main facility. Once all repairs are complete, it will return them, cleaned, to their original location.

Key to Roth Construction's success is its "Unlimited Property Protection Plan," a promise of professional workmanship and quality materials, and its several layers of guarantees. It guarantees its work 100 percent for one year

In 1997 Roth Construction Company West opened in Elyria, sharing building space with Roth Cleaning Company, a full-service contents-cleaning and restoration company.

from the date of completion. If any work or product is found defective, it will promptly correct it without any cost to the property owner. Roth Construction guarantees it will meet its scheduled completion date. In cases where a customer must vacate their home, Roth Construction's Tenantability Guarantee stipulates that if they are unable to reoccupy their property by a specified date, it will pay the

homeowners for their additional living expenses. On fire losses it also issues an unconditional smoke and odor removal guarantee for the life of the structure.

Though the Cleveland office averages 1,750 jobs a year, it follows up on every one to make sure the customer is pleased with the results. It further solidifies its commitment to quality work by utilizing its own employees for construction work instead of subcontractors so that a high standard and attention to detail is maintained. The company also employs in-house engineers and skilled uniformed craftsmen, and only top-quality, name-brand products are used in its jobs — all of which leads to its long list of client recommendations.

There are very few construction companies that specialize only in fire-damage reconstruction and even fewer that are priced as competitively as Roth Construction. But the company is not only the leader in residential reconstruction, it has over 34 years of experience as a leader in commercial reconstruction as well. When working with a business whose survival is dependent on being able to open its doors to customers, quality work and a guaranteed completion date is even more critical. Roth Construction will restore a business' structure, inventory and equipment to peak condition. It will also move, store and clean warehouse contents for the duration of the project. All work is coordinated by Roth employees, eliminating the need for the involvement of another party and keeping costs low for the insurance companies.

Roth Construction handles all types of commercial reconstruction, including, but not limited to, restaurants, bars, groceries, retail, office, light-industrial and lodging structures. Recently it performed a number of jobs for the U.S. government, including the decontamination of over 200 homes in Lorain and Elyria. It also traveled to Detroit, Michigan; New York, New Orleans and Memphis to perform

Roth Construction
Company expanded
yet again in 1998 when
it added a third office
in Columbus.

government work. Another recent restoration performed by Roth Construction was a church in Cuyahoga Falls that had extensive damage.

In 1989 it tackled a large restoration project for Nationwide Insurance when it performed emergency repairs on North Olmsted High School when it was partially destroyed by fire. Timing was paramount. The enormous job had to be completed within 90 days because students were being bused to temporary classrooms at Cleveland's I-X Center. Conventions at the I-X Center help sustain Cleveland's economy and some were scheduled to take place after the 90-day deadline.

Roth Construction employees coordinated the work with other repair companies and completed the job seven days prior to the deadline, finding ways to meet safety requirements and cleaning every item in the school. More recently, it worked on the reconstruction of another high school damaged by fire, Cleveland Heights High School.

One of Roth Construction's most valuable resources is its employees. Knowledgeable, considerate, friendly and helpful, the company treats them as family. It rewards hard work with good wages and benefits, the necessary tools and equipment for their job, an understanding of their personal

lives and a show of appreciation, such as the recently implemented incentive program. Many employees have been with the company for over 15 years.

As a member of the Better Business Bureau, the National Institute of Restoration, Inc. and ASCR, Roth Construction stays on top of industry practices and changes. Always involved in the Cleveland community, Robert Rothacker was listed as one of the finalists for the Man of the Year Award with *Crain's Cleveland Business*. In addition, he has served as an advisor for Cleveland State University on special projects designed for training insurance adjusters in construction.

Roth Construction's future plans include staying up to date with continual changes in the insurance business, including mergers, acquisitions and the increased use of third-party administrators. It also intends to keep up with technological advances that affect its industry, including e-commerce, insurance carrier software programs and the use of digital cameras for estimates.

What Roth Construction doesn't ever intend to do is to stop caring about its customers and working as hard as possible to turn their devastating experience into a positive one — turning a destroyed house into a home again.

Carnegie Management and Development Corporation

A practicing physician and his wife are panic stricken by a real estate investment turned sour. Ten years later, their misfortune has turned so successful that the physician trades in his stethoscope for a tie.

It is the story of the founding of Carnegie Management and Development Corporation. Rustom Khouri, D.P.M., M.D., had a thriving practice as a foot specialist and decided to invest in some commercial real estate property. He and his wife, Mary, were very excited about the investment's potential profits until Dr. Khouri drove by the building the day after they had purchased it and saw that the main tenant had vacated overnight. Stuck with a high mortgage payment, Dr. and Mrs. Khouri took a real estate course to try to salvage their investment. Mary then started branching out by buying and leasing small buildings while Dr. Khouri continued his medical practice.

One of their first acquisitions was the University-Cedar Medical Center on Carnegie Avenue and 105th Street in 1984. That same year they incorporated their real estate company and named it Carnegie Management and Development Corporation, after the building that was serving as its first headquarters.

Dr. Rustom Khouri and his wife, Mary Khouri, founders and owners of Carnegie Management and Development Corporation

The Chagrin-Lee Center in Shaker Heights, Ohio, was another one of the company's early redevelopment projects and helped catapult it onto the Cleveland-area development map. This led to Carnegie's development of several office buildings along the I-90 corridor in Westlake, Ohio, that reshaped the central Westlake office district.

Carnegie continued to grow and in 1986 made its first major investment in Cleveland's Flats entertainment district. It became one of the first companies to redevelop in the area when it acquired Fagan's in the Flats. The company's $2.5 million redesign ensured the restaurant and nightclub's status as the largest and busiest complex on the area's east bank. Carnegie was also the driving force in partnerships that purchased Sycamore Slip, Nicky's Marina and Restaurant, the Rumrunners complex and the old Rose Metal Works properties in the Flats, establishing the longest continuous span of active waterfront property in the area with one owner.

In the late 1980s Carnegie also entered into environmental developments. Foreseeing the industry's large growth potential, it formed partnerships with several national auto-emissions testing companies in Arizona and Florida. It developed and built 14 sites in Arizona and six larger, multipurpose facilities in Florida. The buildings set a national standard and led to the company's development of testing facilities in Ohio in the 1990s that were awarded the 1996 Merit Award for Creativity in Concrete and Masonry Design.

The economic recession of the late 80s and early 90s found many Cleveland-area developers in the pre-construction phase of projects that couldn't be finished due to a lack a financing. One such project was the Medina Point Shopping Center in Medina, Ohio. The developer had problems with the site and had only one lease — with Sears Roebuck and Co. — which it was going to lose if construction of the project didn't commence in 45 days. Carnegie was financially strong enough to buy the project and successfully completed it on time. Sears was so pleased that it named Carnegie as one of its preferred developers in the Midwest area, catapulting the company into the retail shopping center business. Since then it has developed, owns and manages more than 15 shopping centers with Sears as a tenant.

The company prides itself on the simultaneous development of multiple sites at any given time. In recent years it typically had between five and 10 retail projects in the pre-construction or construction phase at one time. Its retail portfolio spans more than 10 states, and in Ohio alone, the company's holdings span more than 40 communities.

Dr. Khouri retired from practicing medicine in 1993 to devote his time solely to the company. He and Mary decided to take a chance on its continuing success. They reinvested their profits, didn't take a paycheck for themselves and tripled their staff so they could devote themselves to establishing new business. They currently have 40 full-time, highly skilled professionals at the company headquarters.

In the late 1990s Carnegie embarked on a new growth market — the development of larger headquarter-type office/research buildings. It recently developed the headquarters for Gliatech, a Beachwood, Ohio, biomedical research company. Carnegie stepped forward to do the project to help ensure the company remained in Northeast Ohio. It's only the first of many single-user headquarters in the company's future as the only developer member of the Edison Bio-Tech Group.

Carnegie entered the residential property arena with the development of upscale Quail Hollow in Westlake. That experience led to the company's most well-known and prestigious residential development — Red Tail in Avon, Ohio, which began in 1994 through its subsidiary, Carnegie Residential Development Corporation. The over 500 acres of land contain 630 elegant homesites and an 18-hole championship-caliber golf course that was played by golf legends Sam Snead and Bob Goalby prior to its opening. Carnegie also owns and manages several luxury apartment buildings throughout Cleveland's neighborhoods.

Both Quail Hollow and Red Tail are successful because of Carnegie's thorough market research and analysis. In fact, it will not proceed with any project unless it is assured that it meets the community's needs. As a result, not only do the developments succeed and spur further community growth, but the company gains respect from mayors and other prominent city leaders who often request its services. Community leaders are not the only ones who ask Carnegie to come back. It is estimated that 95 percent of the company's projects are repeat business from satisfied clients.

Carnegie and the Khouris also support community betterment through numerous charitable endeavors. The company donates to a wide variety of community-based charities, including United Cerebral Palsy and the Ohio Cancer Society. When the company built a new home for the Westshore Montessori Preschool, one of several preschool and daycare centers it has developed, it donated the

Carnegie Center houses the corporation's headquarters and is just one of several office buildings it developed along the I-90 corridor in Westlake, Ohio.

necessary land when the school's initial financing fell through. In 1999 the Dr. Rustom and Mary Khouri Foundation was established to focus on the needs of child education and development.

Carnegie and the Khouris have made a difference in Northeast Ohio, whether spearheading the development of the nationally known Flats, helping to create a biotechnology park, defining an emerging suburb or reshaping a community with a world-class project. Whatever Carnegie does, it works very hard to do well — and even harder to do right.

Good people, good intentions and hard work define Carnegie and explain how calculated ventures, not unlike that little real estate investment back in 1983, are sure to have successful results.

Forest City Enterprises

It was 1921 when entrepreneur Charles Ratner launched Forest City Enterprises, a company that provided lumber to homeowners for the construction of garages. At first glance that would appear to be a safe, conventional business; it's not until you consider how many automobiles were actually on the road in 1921 that the vision and magnitude of this venture becomes apparent.

Now owned and operated by third and fourth generations of the Ratner, Shafran and Miller families, the company has quite literally inherited the passion of its founders. They have parlayed that spirit into hundreds of successful ventures, the result of which is a thriving, $4 billion real estate development enterprise — one of the largest commercial and residential developers in the country.

Based in Cleveland from its inception, Forest City Enterprises (FCE) followed a rapid and progressive path of growth. Founding father Charles Ratner was soon joined by brothers Max and Leonard and sister Fannye Shafran and her husband, Nathan Shafran, and together they ventured from one business enterprise to the next, building step-by-step on their strengths and experience to ultimately create a full-service real estate development organization.

The grand opening of Tower City Center in 1990 transformed the Terminal Tower into a dynamic entertainment and retail complex visited by thousands every week.

The Terminal Tower (before renovation), the tallest building in downtown Cleveland, was a city landmark, but little more.

From residential garages in 1921 came the selling of garages to commercial customers, and then to contractors. In the 1930s the company began to buy and sell large amounts of land to developers.

Able to provide lumber and construction services, the company's Land Development division was established in 1946, giving it an additional competitive edge. This business dovetailed nicely into its residential development business in 1947. This segment of the business prospered during the fifties and sixties, when Forest City Enterprises became a major developer in burgeoning suburbs like Brook Park, Parma and Eastlake, Ohio.

Soon, the company had more land than its builder-customers could use for housing, so it began to turn its lumberyards into retail stores. Forest City's first real estate

development property, a retail shopping center on East 185th Street, was completed in 1939, and its first enclosed mall in 1962. In 1960 the company went public, with 80 percent of the business still lumber-related. During the 1980s the company sold the retail business and made a commitment to becoming a national real estate developer.

Forest City Enterprises has become increasingly recognized as one of the largest urban developers in the country, a unique niche that has earned it a national reputation for making significant lifestyle differences for thousands of people in major metro markets across the country.

One of the most difficult and publicized of such endeavors took place in Cleveland in 1986 when the company announced its planned renovation of the Terminal Tower. At the time, the Terminal Tower was an underutilized downtown structure in desperate need of revival.

But Forest City had a vision and believed that the time was right for a "return to the city." FCE developed a strategy that laid the foundation for customer-friendly, accessible attractions that people would want to visit. The result, of course, was the 1990 grand opening of Tower City Center, the polished, sophisticated megacenter that serves as the crown jewel of Cleveland's much-touted renaissance.

Flanked by FCE-owned properties including The Ritz-Carlton Hotel and the historic M.K. Ferguson Plaza (formerly the central post office of Cleveland), Chase Financial Tower and Skylight Office Tower office buildings, Tower City Center has grown progressively in scope and customer traffic since its debut, and has received increasingly dynamic tenants, including the long-coveted Hard Rock Cafe in 1998.

This philosophy, or what FCE refers to as the "City Strategy," of helping to bring interest — and residents — back to the city has been one that Forest City has spread throughout many urban areas of the country, including similar endeavors in Charleston, West Virginia; Pittsburgh; San Francisco; Boston; and Denver. These projects have helped to breathe life back into those downtown areas, as well.

Forest City has been a major developer in all five boroughs of New York City. Investments have paid off manyfold. Of recent prominence is the company's dramatic 42nd Street entertainment/retail complex in the heart of Manhattan, which includes a 460-room hotel, and its Battery Park City multi-use project that combines an Embassy Suites hotel with retail and entertainment venues. Both projects are expected to revitalize tourist traffic in two districts of the city which had become virtually off-limits due to crime and a lack of viable activities.

In one of its most recent ventures, Forest City was selected by the board of Stapleton Development Corporation as its development partner for the revitalization of a 7.5-square-mile parcel of land that was formerly Denver's Stapleton International Airport. The 4,700-acre Stapleton site currently represents one of the largest urban infill projects in the United States and, potentially, the largest development project ever undertaken by Forest City.

Forest City Enterprises has an ownership interest in 42 shopping centers totaling 16 million square feet of retail space, 35,000 residential units in 115 apartment communities, as well as 7 million square feet in 24 office buildings and nearly 3,000 hotel rooms.

Some of FCE's most important developments have been in Cleveland, where about 500 of its 3,500 employees operate from its Terminal Tower headquarters. Forest City's other notable commercial properties in the Cleveland area include the Halle Building and Signature Square office park in Beachwood, as well as numerous retail centers, including Chapel Hill, Golden Gate and Midtown.

For FCE, real estate development is not just about bricks and mortar, but the ability to reach people and change their lives. For that reason, the company considers its senior housing developments among the accomplishments of which it is most proud. In total, the company has provided some 80,000 senior housing units to people across the country.

The Hard Rock Cafe, an 11,000-square-foot tenant of the Tower City Center complex, receives a steady stream of patrons from the "Rock-and-Roll City."

In particular, FCE is very excited about its new senior-housing facilities, congregate-care and assisted-living facilities designed to provide superior care for the country's fast-growing aging population. A 300-unit care facility was launched in New York in 1998, joining two other such facilities already in existence and the development of five others in the New York metropolitan area.

Born from an innovative idea and driven by an entrepreneurial spirit, Forest City Enterprises has thrived for nearly 80 years. The company hasn't forgotten its rich heritage, and has used that spirit to guide its future. Forest City knows where it came from — and where it's going.

The Great Lakes Construction Company

Anyone who has ever visited Tower City, shopped at Southpark Center, hiked over the new Cleveland Browns Stadium pedestrian bridge, or appreciated the Jennings Freeway shortcut that links I-90 and I-480 has witnessed the craftsmanship of The Great Lakes Construction Company firsthand and probably never knew it. On many projects, Great Lakes Construction is involved in the earliest stages — literally from the ground up. The company is known for its general contracting capabilities, including site improvements, excavations, major industrial-plant and commercial-site construction, power plants, public works, highway and bridge projects, and mine-site reclamation. The placement of reinforced structural concrete is its specialty.

Great Lakes Construction is one of Cleveland's premier civil contracting firms, with more than $70 million in sales. The company was founded in 1948 by Frank Converse Jr., a graduate in civil engineering from Case Institute of Technology who managed the technical side of the business, and Art Cushing, an operating engineer/crane operator with a keen eye for construction. Two other key players in the early years were John Marano, lead estimator, and Carroll Nelson, head of operations.

The company started with a handful of employees working out of a trailer beneath the Detroit-Superior Bridge in Cleveland's Flats. Early projects grew out of a tremendous post-World War II demand for new roads and housing where Great Lakes earned its stripes as an excavation expert. The company rapidly moved into sewer and impoundment projects, highway alignments, heavy earthmoving and concrete paving.

One of the biggest breaks for Great Lakes Construction came late in 1957, when the firm successfully bid on its first section of interstate highway, a portion of I-77 in downtown Canton, Ohio. Interstate projects have composed the nuts and bolts of Great Lakes' business ever since. The Jennings Freeway project, for example, was a $50 million project that included excavation work, intricate bridgework — some with concrete piers standing 50-feet tall — and six lanes of concrete pavement.

In the early 60s the company stretched in a new direction after winning its first major bid in the private sector. The project was a large site preparation and earthwork job at a power plant for American Electric Power (AEP) in Brilliant, Ohio. Great Lakes has since completed many more contracts for AEP over the years, including a 15-mile coal conveyor system in the early 1970s and nuclear power plant construction in Ohio and Michigan.

The first senior management change in the company's history occurred during the late 70s when Bruce Gilbert, a young Harvard MBA who had joined Great Lakes in 1968, was named chief operating officer and president. Six years later, Frank Converse retired and Gilbert was appointed CEO. Converse sold his 40 percent ownership back to the company, which had become an employee-owned company, also known as an Employee Stock Ownership Plan or ESOP.

At about the same time, Great Lakes' project pendulum swung back to interstate construction, offsetting a downturn in power plant construction

The pedestrian bridge at the Cleveland Browns Stadium is one especially colorful example of Great Lakes Construction rehabilitation work.

Far and away one of the longest projects in Great Lakes' history is this 15-mile coal conveyor system built in the early 1970s in southern Ohio.

and a retrenchment of the steel industry. In the 1980s and early 90s, Great Lakes completed the final sections of I-480 around Cleveland, I-675 around Dayton and the Southern Tier Expressway through Pennsylvania.

By late 1997 the third management change in the company's history was announced when another young engineer with an MBA, George Palko, was named president and Bruce Gilbert became chairman. "George's appointment illustrates the opportunity any new engineer has at our company that he can't get at a family-owned business — the opportunity to be the company president at age 34," Gilbert notes.

Great Lakes' senior management takes great pride in the opportunities afforded its employees. New employees can participate in the ESOP after one year. They're vested in five years. ESOPs aren't unusual in the construction industry, but a company that is 80-percent ESOP owned is exceptional, since many firms tend to be family-owned. Great Lakes also has a board of directors including five members with no construction-industry ties who bring an outside perspective to the business.

Senior management also takes pride in its employees' credentials. The firm has more graduate civil engineers per employee than any of its competitors. Moreover, Great Lakes employees are known to go the extra mile through volunteer work with groups such as Habitat For Humanity and the local Boys Clubs and Girls Clubs. Appropriately, when the Cleveland Children's Museum first opened in University Circle, Great Lakes donated funds for the Over and Under Bridges exhibit in which children can build their own spans or see the inner-workings of scaled-down swing and lift bridges.

Today, Great Lakes Construction is positioned to serve clients from a new headquarters completed in early 2000. The 55,000-square-foot facility includes the company's main offices, warehouse, equipment maintenance shop and storage. It is situated on 33 acres in Hinckley, Ohio, south of Cleveland off Interstate 71. Great Lakes had long outgrown its previous location in Independence, where it had been headquartered since 1956.

Current projects include adding a third lane on inter-states in Ohio and a return to more private-sector work. Great Lakes Construction wants to increase its presence and capabilities in the local market through growth in current fields and through diversification in areas that will complement its current business. The firm also wants to increase its service to private customers no matter where they're located. Great Lakes' quality record and on-time delivery speak for themselves. "We also understand and appreciate projects with a sense of urgency," Gilbert adds.

Perhaps the best example illustrating how Great Lakes operates under pressure is a project the company took on for Conrail in the mid-1980s. The call came in on a Friday night. Twin, 40-foot-diameter culverts were failing along Conrail's main line between Albany and Chicago. Great Lakes and Conrail struck up an agreement over the phone and a seven-day-a-week, round-the-clock project began that lasted four months. Great Lakes excavated over 100 feet down to the culverts, diverted a river, rebuilt the culverts and replaced all the dirt to support the tracks.

"We think we have a lot to offer the private sector," Gilbert says. "We're technically more capable than other contractors and have an eye on the right target."

Great Lakes was proud to be the builder of Cleveland's last new freeway, S.R. 176 (Jennings Freeway), which connects I-480 to downtown Cleveland.

International Brotherhood of Electrical Workers Local 38

When International Brotherhood of Electrical Workers Local 38 members give the directive to "let there be light," that light can appear in an instant. It doesn't matter that the source of illumination is artificial and requires a lot of copper wiring, hook-ups and complicated circuitry. The significance is that these men and women can get people out of the dark. By extension, they can prolong daylight hours after nightfall and light up cities and monuments for auspicious celebrations.

These masters of light and power are electrical workers, who quite literally have their hands on the power switch. And locally, members of Electrical Workers Local 38 in Cleveland have been lighting the city for more than a century. They wire nearly every public, private and commercial building project in the metropolitan region. Members of the local are "inside" electrical workers, meaning they wire the interior of buildings during every phase of the construction process.

"We're there from the very beginning, when they're scraping the earth," says Thomas R. Whittaker, President of Local 38. "We're there stringing the temporary lighting and power so the other workers can work. We're there at the end, after the building is completed, putting the finish covers on the lighting fixtures and other electrical equipment. We maintain good relations with our customers and often continue to do their maintenance and any additional work requested by them."

The process hasn't always been that controlled and surefire. There was a period during the late 19th and early 20th centuries when just getting an electrical current to flow, for those early electric projects, was a life-and-death proposition. Yet these electrical workers, who were mostly linemen at the time, understood that they were destined to wire more projects throughout the nation that could be bigger and likely more dangerous. They were brought together by an 1890 exposition in St. Louis. Linemen came together from across the country to wire and erect exhibits for the exposition, which was to feature new electrical wonders.

The linemen began to share similar concerns about wages and safety in this emerging occupation. Lighting was generally an outdoor phenomenon then, with lights being used to illuminate dark streets and lots. But the potential for indoor expansion was not lost on companies seeking to become providers of electricity. With the exposition as a backdrop, the linemen in 1891 formed the National Brotherhood of Electrical Workers. It became the International Brotherhood of Electrical Workers in 1899 to admit Canadian workers. A Cleveland local was started in 1892 but folded about two years later during an economic depression. In 1895 Local 38 was chartered.

To meet a burgeoning demand for electric service, companies needed linemen to scale tall wooden poles and string electrical wire. No standard safety or training procedures were in place to protect these linemen from electrical shock. In some areas,

Wiring services were provided by these union electrical workers to the Mary Crest School in Cleveland in 1953.

These Local 38 electrical workers were members of the line crew for the old Doan Electric Company in Cleveland in the 1940s.

50 percent of electrical workers died from either electrocution or deadly falls. Many workers earned 20 cents an hour for workdays that could last 12 hours. Conditions were ripe for union organizing.

The early years of Local 38 coincided with a building boom in the city. While lighting in a home was still a luxury, electricity was being ordered for street lamps, commercial complexes and structures like the historic Old Stone Church on Public Square. Electricians later got a chance to showcase their skills at the Great Lakes Exposition of 1936-1937 along the city's lakefront.

Downtown development in the 1960s provided new work opportunities. The construction of two nuclear power plants in the region helped provide employment in the 1980s. The 1990s was one of the most favorable work periods for the union, with the addition of major hotels, office complexes and sporting arenas in the city and region. The workers have responded with their own displays of generosity to the community. Some provide free wiring services to area nonprofit organizations such as churches and small museums.

Throughout their history, electrical workers have experienced little of the turmoil encountered by union workers in other areas of the construction and manufacturing industries. Disagreements have existed, but the IBEW construction locals have not called as many strikes or engaged in many instances of public discord with contractors. In fact, the IBEW locals have a no-strike policy that is almost as old as the local union. For decades, disagreements have been handled through mandatory arbitration after more routine negotiation tactics have failed. Also, it doesn't hurt the union's bargaining power to be in close proximity to the light switch.

Like many unions, Local 38 is enjoying a period of revitalization. Membership is on the upswing. The union has more than 2,000 members, 200 more than a few years ago. Its membership consists of 1,900 electricians, 150 teledata workers to specifically wire telecommunication systems and 25 residential workers. In addition to the pension and health benefits, a major selling point for

Veteran electrical workers gathered for an "Old Timers" picnic in 1999. An "Old Timer" is a member with 25 years or more in Local 38.
Photo By Ken Busch

the union is that it offers job security. Unions are aware of jobs that may not be known to nonunion members. Contractors benefit as well from a strong union. They can tap into a pool of skilled workers for projects rather than seek workers through advertisements or other referrals.

Being able to offer skilled workers to projects is a source of pride for the union. Apprentices take part in a five-year training program that includes lessons in CPR and federal safety regulations. Where once there were no standard safety practices, workers now wear hard hats and carry their own equipment to test electrical currents at their work sites. Journeymen are provided ongoing training to keep abreast of new developments. Training for all workers is adjusted by the union and management to meet the changing needs of the market.

Advancements in technology are bringing about many changes, one of which is using computers to manage huge energy-management systems. Companies are seeking more efficient systems to operate their department stores, offices and recreational facilities. These systems not only control the lighting, but also burglar and fire alarms, and heating and cooling systems. As manufacturers provide these systems, electrical workers must be trained to install them. As Sam J. Chilia, Business Manager of Local 38 says, "We're doing a lot more than putting an outlet in a wall these days."

Electrical workers install underground pipe banks that will contain electrical cables for the structure.
Photo By Bob Cooper

Iron Workers Local 17

In the end, a towering structure may be swathed in granite, marble, mirrors or brick — perhaps accentuated with arched, stained-glass windows or the sculpted faces of national leaders. But at one time, before the structure and its elaborate ornamentation became evident, all that stood on the lot was a gawky skeletal system made of steel beams and girders.

The workers who put that system together were ironworkers, the aerial cowboys of the construction industry. People crane their necks to see them walking — all too casually, it seems — on top of narrow beams several stories above the ground in hard hats, blue jeans and work shirts. There is no readily apparent means to keep them from toppling over onto the gravel and other debris below. Yet they tower above, fastening those metal fixtures together to form the skeleton that will support the building shell, that they also erect, for office complexes, skyscrapers and sports stadiums. It's a job fraught with potential hazards, one that ironworkers are proud to have.

"It takes a certain type of individual to walk on those iron girders up in the air," says Gary Dwyer, financial secretary/treasurer and business manager for Iron Workers Local 17 in Cleveland. "We are in a very dangerous business, and have the most dangerous job among construction workers. We're like the U.S. Marines Corps, small and elite, with a lot of pride and dignity."

That assured bit of swagger from the workers comes from a century of developing resolves about work-related issues that are as steely as those girders. Iron Workers Local 17 is a founding member of the International Association of Bridge, Structural & Ornamental Iron Workers. Both the local and international groups were founded in 1896, but for financial reasons, the local wasn't able to secure all of its required charter documentation until five years later, in 1901.

Union members have weathered some turbulent years of organizational growth, including strikes against contractors over pay and work conditions, clashes with anti-union politicians, and wariness from the general public over the outspokenness and aggressiveness of union workers. The aggressiveness shown by union members in the early years was needed to draw attention to the plight of ironworkers, Dwyer explains.

Early union organizers came together as much to provide burial assistance to the families of a deceased co-worker as to fight for more pay and safer work conditions. The likelihood of the death of an ironworker in the construction of bridges and tall buildings was an accepted occupational hazard. During those early years, the use of the stronger, lighter steel was replacing iron, stone and wood as the construction material of choice. Knowledge about and implementation of safety procedures lagged behind the burgeoning use of new construction processes, building designs and techniques.

The accident and mortality rates for ironworkers were high. They often worked for about 10 years on various construction projects before being either sidelined with a crippling accident or killed on the job. Dwyer recounts instances where men lined up along the perimeter of major projects to await their turn at a job, because one of the workers was likely to fall to his death at a moment's notice. During those early organizing years, hours were long and pay consisted of a few dollars a day. Union organizing efforts intensified in the late 19th and early 20th centuries. Animosity between ironworkers, unions in general, and contractors over pay and work conditions has been palpable over the ensuing decades.

As recently as the 1980s, unions often found themselves in an unfavorable climate, especially politically. But the pendulum has been swinging the other way on many fronts. New mandatory safety practices are in place as a

Cleveland Browns Stadium began taking shape along Lake Erie after ironworkers assembled steel beams and girders to form the shell of this football arena.

result of the 1970 federal Occupational Safety and Health Act. Ironworkers now must use harnesses and safety wires for certain tasks. Project inspectors are on site, and training programs are required for apprentices.

Because business in Ohio is very good, these "sky walkers" are enjoying some of their best days. The changing skyline in Cleveland over the last several years is testament to that. Downtown is marked with major hotel and office structures. There is an outdoor football stadium, an outdoor stadium for the baseball team and an arena for the basketball team. Ironworkers have helped set those foundations. They are involved in building and bridge projects in 11 northern Ohio counties. Some 1,200 of the union's 2,000 workers are on the active duty roster. The others are retirees.

Not only is business good, but relations with contractors are just as good. The hard lines on issues, bluster and strikes of yesteryear have given way to more peaceful negotiations. Time, more savvy about addressing issues and the desire to leave the turbulence of union strikes

behind have helped promote a spirit of cooperation between these old adversaries. This has been the case especially for Local 17 in the 1990s. Representatives for the union and its contractors have stepped up their efforts to work together to resolve disputes. They understand that they share common concerns, namely completing a project, erecting sound structures, ensuring the safety of workers and making money.

Now that relationships with contractors do not require as much time and energy anymore, the union has been able to focus more attention on its members and prospective members. A new training center for apprentices joined the union headquarters site. In addition to providing job training, the three-year program also gives apprentices the opportunity to hear from experienced veterans about their work experiences. The program helps reinforce familial ties in the union. Many workers are third- and fourth-generation ironworkers, and the journeymen want to instill a sense of commitment to hard work in their sons and other prospective ironworkers, Dwyer says.

Also, more energy is being devoted to organizing nonunion workers. The higher regard with which unions are now held, because of the health-, death- and accident-related benefits unions offer, is helping recruitment. Unions have fought for and won wages that are more commensurate with the perilous work they perform, putting them squarely in the middle class. "These are exciting times right now for unions," Dwyer says. Their members are practically walking on air.

The towering steel skeleton of what is now the Key Tower office complex in downtown Cleveland was erected by ironworkers.

The intricate pattern of steel, assembled by iron-workers, is the basis of the Rock and Roll Hall of Fame and Museum in Cleveland.

The Richard E. Jacobs Group, Inc.

The Richard E. Jacobs Group has built a solid reputation of quality and integrity in commercial real estate development and property management since 1955. In that time, hundreds of millions of people have come in contact with The Jacobs Group where they shop, where they work, when they travel and when they spend some well-earned leisure time, probably not even aware they were benefiting from a Jacobs Group property.

In northeast Ohio, shoppers know The Jacobs Group as SouthPark Center in Strongsville, Westgate Mall in Fairview Park, Midway Mall in Elyria and The Galleria at Erieview downtown. Office workers come in contact with The Jacobs Group at Key Center, McDonald Investment Center and the Tower at Erieview in downtown, as well as Chagrin Highlands in greater Cleveland's eastern suburbs. Hotel guests have enjoyed its Marriott hotels, as well as several Courtyard, Towne Place Suites, Residence Inns and Spring Hill Suites hotels throughout Ohio. At its height, The Jacobs Group owned and managed over 46 million square feet of commercial real estate in 16 states from coast to coast.

Born in Akron, the Jacobs brothers were drawn early in their careers to commercial real estate development. For a time during the 1950s, they worked with another fledgling real estate developer, Edward J. Debartolo Sr., on a new development concept at the time called a "shopping center," a very novel idea that the Jacobs brothers helped pioneer.

In the late 1950s, the Jacobs brothers began a series of partnership retail developments with Clevelander Dominic Visconsi, which eventually grew into Jacobs, Visconsi & Jacobs Co. (JVJ).

Northland Mall in Columbus was JVJ's first regional mall, opening in 1964 as an open-air center. As the mall concept evolved, the company opened its first fully enclosed center, Midway Mall in Elyria, Ohio in 1966. By the early 1980s, JVJ had developed and operated over two dozen malls in several states, with numerous additional projects in various developmental stages. Throughout the 70s and early 80s the mall business flourished and the Jacobs brothers played a prominent role in the industry's dramatic growth, ultimately growing its mall portfolio to a total of 39.

Besides being brothers, the Jacobs were well-matched business partners. David, the older of the pair, developed a strong expertise in engineering, design and construction, while Richard became the consummate negotiator, assembling sites and overseeing operations. JVJ also became well known for the quality of its in-house capabilities, which spanned the entire spectrum of development and management.

By the mid-1980s the company began to branch out into other forms of commercial real estate. It acquired the 40-story Tower at Erieview in downtown Cleveland, along with an adjacent plaza area and underground garage, providing JVJ with an opportunity to apply its highly honed skills to the management of a major office property. It also brought the bold opportunity to develop a unique urban shopping complex — the first major retail development in downtown Cleveland in nearly 50 years. The Galleria at Erieview opened in 1987 and is widely recognized as a catalyst in the development of downtown Cleveland.

A series of acquisitions of downtown high-rise office buildings soon followed. By the early 1990s the company had developed and opened the landmark Society Center (now Key Center) which includes a 57-story office tower, the tallest building between New York and Chicago; the full

The Galleria at Erieview opened in 1987 and its success provided a catalyst for further development in downtown Cleveland.

service Marriott Hotel; the refurbished historic Society for Savings building; and an adjacent underground garage beneath the beautifully restored Memorial Plaza and fountain.

By 1991 JVJ had become The Richard & David Jacobs Group, since Dominic Visconsi had begun to focus more on outside development projects. With David Jacobs'

untimely death in 1992, the company became simply The Richard E. Jacobs Group, with Richard continuing to provide the overall continuity for the company he and his brother had carefully nurtured for so many years.

In the late 90s the Jacobs Group embarked on the development of a major corporate community known as Chagrin Highlands. The 650-acre site will ultimately consist of approximately 3.5 million square feet of office space, up to 250,000 square feet of retail and roughly 1,000 on-site hotel rooms. The project's first office building, One Chagrin Highlands, opened in August 1999. A similar 500-acre project in eastern Lorain County known as Avon Vista, was also begun by the company in 1998.

The Jacobs Group began building its hotel portfolio in the early 1980s with the development of several full-service, suburban Marriott Hotel properties in Cleveland, Columbus, Buffalo and South Bend, Indiana. By the late 1990s the hotel portfolio's emphasis had shifted to suburban limited service and extended-stay hotels, most carrying Marriott chain names. At its peak, the company's hotel portfolio included approximately two dozen hotels in

four states, including the luxurious Pier House Resort in Key West, Florida.

One of the Jacobs brothers' proudest business accomplishments had nothing to do with commercial real estate — at least not on the surface. In the mid-1980s, when the Cleveland Indians were in danger of being sold and moved from the city, Richard and David Jacobs stepped forward and purchased the baseball team. But that wasn't all they did. The Jacobs brothers then launched an elaborate program to strengthen the team's talent by greatly enhancing its minor league and scouting system and signing talented young players to long-term contracts.

Using his extensive resources, Richard Jacobs also spearheaded the development of the impressive Jacobs Field ballpark, which opened in 1994 as a part of the Gateway project in downtown Cleveland. It quickly became the model for every major sports facility in the country and the entire Indians organization, infused and revamped in the Jacobs management style, became the envy of professional sports teams everywhere. An unprecedented series of multiple season-long sell-outs at Jacobs Field soon became the norm. The team became a perennial playoff contender, winning the American League Central division from 1995 through 1999, going to the World Series twice — in 1995 and again in 1997. The Indians also became the first in Major League Baseball to offer publicly traded stock in the team. By early 2000, the 14-year Jacobs era of ownership of the Indians had come to an end with the sale of the team to fellow Clevelander Larry Dolan.

Long ago The Jacobs Group recognized that many factors contribute to the quality of the everyday life experiences of its many and varied customers — whether it's shopping at the mall, working late at the office, a comfortable hotel bed after a long day or even a sunny day at Jacobs Field.

In the process, the company has forged a strong historic legacy in the Cleveland area inscribed by landmark places, each the site of countless personal experiences and remembrances which endure today.

SouthPark Center in Strongsville is the newest of the four Jacobs Group malls in the Cleveland area.

Jacobs Field in downtown Cleveland is home to the champion Cleveland Indians and the envy of professional sports teams across the country.

S. Rose Office Interiors

It is often true that for long-standing businesses, things change but mission and philosophy are always the same. This is true for S. Rose Office Interiors. Its products and services have dynamically changed over the past 71-plus years, but its commitment to service, innovation and excellence is just as strong today as it was yesterday.

The company was started by Samuel Rose, who was in the home furniture business before the stock market crash of 1929. Starting over, he began selling used office equipment in addition to home furnishings. He found that he preferred selling to business people rather than domestic-use buyers and phased out home furnishings. In those days, S. Rose was located in the old Merchant's Bank building at East 4th Street and Prospect.

During World War II, the company moved to its present location near 12th Street and Prospect. Samuel Rose, at the age of 50, retired in 1945, leaving the business to his two sons, Dick and Bob. The brothers Rose expanded the business to include office machines such as typewriters, adding machines and comptometers. Once the machines became a full part of the S. Rose inventory, servicing and repair of the machines became a new aspect of customer service for the firm.

Dick and Bob Rose began to understand that the selling of product, and the service of that product, doesn't necessarily deliver the "foot traffic" that is needed to grow a business. Unlike their competitors at the time, they decided to cultivate and

S. Rose Office Interiors asks, "As much as you work around office furniture, shouldn't it be designed to work around you?"

focus on developing relationships with large corporate entities like Cleveland's TRW and Lincoln Electric. They embodied the firm's mission to deliver service, commitment, innovation and excellence in a way that was different.

In 1958 Bob Rose suffered a fatal heart attack. Dick Rose was left to run the business. During the 1960s, Dick Rose discovered that used furniture was becoming less profitable as it became more costly to refinish. S. Rose's facility was becoming filled with old furniture that wasn't selling. Dick decided to "institutionalize" the used furniture line of the business, moving the used furniture to a Midwest clearing facility. This type of management leadership ensured that the firm kept growing, "slowly but surely."

With the death of his brother on his mind, Dick Rose retired in 1972 at the age of 50. "I remember my brother passing away at the age of 38 and I figured that's not going to happen to me. If I die, I'm going to die on the tennis court!" the now 78-year-old says with a chuckle. Rose decided to give the business to his eldest son, Clark. His other son, Howard, would later join the firm as secretary/treasurer. "I've taken such great pride in watching the business grow. It's something you don't realize until you are a father. To see what is happening with your children, it's just beautiful to watch."

Dick Rose raised sales volume by 50 percent over his father, Samuel Rose. He believes that Clark has improved business by 100 percent since taking over the firm. Clark learned the business by the "throw the baby in the water" method, much the same way his father had. On his very first job, his father sent him out of town alone to uncrate and place a customer delivery. Since that time, Clark Rose has grown and positioned the firm to be a leading force in full-service office furnishings, working with mid- to high-end products and services.

Among the first initiatives taken by Clark was to expand the design department. Even though Dick Rose had begun to offer design services, Clark recognized the demand for a more aesthetic approach coupled with a greater expertise with space planning and design. Just as his father and uncle had always pushed the firm to think beyond the common, Clark became an early advocate for what is now commonly referred to as the focus of ergonomics: enhancing worker productivity by enhancing the workplace environment. "We've taken the science of ergonomics to heart here at S. Rose with our selection of products and our ability to design around the worker," notes Clark Rose.

Today, S. Rose Office Interiors takes a team approach to serving its corporate accounts, often even teaming up with major suppliers to S. Rose, including industry leader Haworth. This means that current and prospective clients have the opportunity to preview and try out the very latest products in either S. Rose's facilities in Cleveland and Akron or by flying with S. Rose professionals to Haworth's intense corporate headquarters in Michigan. "We are able to deal on a global basis today," observes Clark Rose. S. Rose belongs to the Workplace Alliance, a national group of 30 of Haworth's best dealers in the country. The members benchmark one another and help each other provide intermarket services, delivering and servicing needs around the country. That means a corporate account headquartered in Cleveland can receive delivery and installation services anywhere in the world.

S. Rose Interiors had about 12 employees when Clark Rose took the reins. It now has over 50 employees and a location in Akron, Ohio. The Akron location is the company's flagship franchise. Called Office Furniture USA, it is the fastest-growing franchise of its kind in the country. Office Furniture USA allows small business enterprises to buy high-quality office furnishings at a price point usually reserved for multinational corporations. Today, S. Rose's services include storage facilities and warehousing, asset management, space planning and furniture design in addition to its traditional sales, installation and servicing of office furnishings.

Clark Rose sums up his mission and philosophy simply. "This is a business that is based on repeat business. You must have the trust of the client and give them the value they're looking for. The way I define value, it's like the three legs of a stool: you have to have the quality; you have to have the pricing; and you have to have the service. And if any one of those is lacking, there is no reason for a customer to deal with you. If we can perform 100 percent on each of those segments, we will have the opportunity to serve a client for life."

The Schloss Paving Company

When he founded his paving company in 1935, William L. Schloss already had over 40 years of experience as a pioneer in the asphalt industry. Combining that expertise with a vision to better serve a world driven by increasingly advanced technology, he shaped Cleveland's history with a business that has entered its fourth generation of operation.

The Schloss Paving Company is the oldest company of its kind in the Cleveland area and has literally laid the foundation for progress. Beginning with brick and then moving into asphalt, Schloss has paved every street in the city during its history. Most significantly, it handled the original brick paving of Euclid Avenue, then went back years later and paved over the brick in order to meet the modern-day traffic needs of a growing metropolis. Whether it was the building of the Ohio Turnpike, the surfacing of the interstate highways in the 1970s or the development of every major highway in northeast Ohio to the Pennsylvania line, Schloss has been there with the latest techniques, materials and equipment.

William Schloss first entered the asphalt business as a young man in his native New York, where he was born to German immigrants. He worked for other companies there, learning how to use the mixes and equipment and teaching others the trade. While employed by the Cleveland Trinidad Company, he even spent time applying his trade in Cuba and Jamaica. It was Schloss' groundbreaking idea to utilize asphalt along the Mississippi River to maintain erosion control, now in successful operation for decades.

When Schloss died in 1944, his son, Raymond Sr., left his post as a Navy pilot and came home to serve as company president, assisted by his two brothers, Harold and Edward. The business thrived with Raymond's capable direction. Under his leadership, Schloss Paving continued to innovate the industry as it grew into a custom-service operation. Among its many distinctions, Schloss was the first in its field to experiment with tar asphalt, was the original contractor for the new Burke Lakefront Airport in 1958 and was a leader in the rebuilding of the Hough neighborhood's development plan following the devastating riots in 1967. Upon his death in 1997, his son, Ray Jr., moved into the presidency, as his three brothers stepped into equally challenging roles. Christopher and Carl serve as vice presidents and Peter as superintendent. Their business partner, Thomas Roland, is treasurer. The sons and nephews of the next generation are quickly moving into the business, working summers while finishing school.

Currently, The Schloss Paving Company is impacting the industry in a variety of ways. With two asphalt plants located in Geauga and Cuyahoga Counties and the sand and gravel pits in Portage County, Schloss operates primarily in the area's four surrounding counties: Cuyahoga, Lake, Geauga and Ashtabula, with occasional work down into Summit and Medina Counties. In addition to its paving operations, Schloss became an authorized dealer in 1998 for Streetprint, a method of texturing pavement to look like

The William L. Schloss Paving Co., 1936

brick. The primary focus of the business has been government road work, including Interstates 71, 77, 90 and 480, in addition to the Turnpike, but extends to parking lots, shopping centers, subdivision and even private driveways. With the newly founded commercial division, Schloss looks forward to yet another area where it might continue to innovate the industry.

Schloss manages to excel as an employer with a low-key philosophy, based on a work ethic of honesty and integrity. With as many as 125 employees working during the peak season when road work is at its most challenging, the company expects the best from them, and offers the best of itself in return. Many employees stay a long time, sometimes their entire careers, and it is not unusual to find more than one member of a family working at any given time. In its efforts to provide the best possible preparation for the demands of the custom paving market, Schloss offers extensive employee training, in-house workshops and bimonthly meetings that help everyone keep up with industry technology. Schloss maintains a full-service maintenance shop and quality-control lab at each plant facility and often experiments in mixes, performing many of its own lab tests.

In 1997 Schloss installed a state-of-the-art wash plant at its sand and gravel facility and tripled production in only one year. Environmentally conscious, Schloss boasts the "cleanest gravel in Portage County." Also, the company acts as a good neighbor at its asphalt plant bordering on a residential subdivision, addressing any problems that might arise as quickly as possible. Anticipated increases in the production of aggregate (sand and gravel) bring expectations that the company will increase its profit margin.

Schloss' pace with the future persevered in April 2000 when the company opened a state-of-the- art asphalt production facility at its main site in Garfield Heights. As the largest in the city, the new plant meets Environmental

Protection Agency standards and has a production rate of 400 tons per hour.

Schloss is a member of several professional associations, including Flexible Pavements of Ohio, the Ohio Aggregates Association, Ohio Contractor's Association, the American Society of Civil Engineers and the Greater Cleveland Growth Association. Its long partnership with the Ohio Department of Transportation (ODOT) reached a pinnacle in the spring of 2000 when Schloss and ODOT were honored as the first recipients of the Master Craftsman Award, presented by Flexible Pavements of Ohio. The newly created award recognizes excellence in craftsmanship exhibited by extended performance of hot-mix asphalt pavement construction and cited the resurfacing of Interstate 71, which was built in 1981 and 1982. Schloss has been recognized throughout the years with other awards, including Flexible Pavement's "Smooth Pavement Award" in 1980 and again in 1998 for the Green Road project in Cuyahoga County.

As a company striving to provide only the best, Schloss extends its kind hand to various local projects, particularly in Garfield Heights, Maple Heights and the other areas where its plants are located. The proud Schloss traditions of vision and service to the greater Cleveland community are destined to enhance its progress throughout the new century.

The Schloss Paving Company today

The Brewer-Garrett Company

During his varsity wrestling days at the University of Michigan, Lou Joseph was a bulldog. Seizing upon an opponent's weakness, the 150-pound grappler would move in fast for the takedown and pin. Coach Dale Bahr remembers Joseph as a motivator, inspiring his teammates to reach greater heights.

A shattered elbow and President Carter's boycott of the 1980 Olympics shattered Joseph's dream to compete internationally, so he transferred his passion, drive and leadership skills from the mat to the business world. Hired as the first sales rep at The Brewer-Garrett Company, a Cleveland mechanical engineering firm in need of new blood, the cocky 22-year-old hit the ground running, infusing the company with the excitement of a pennant race.

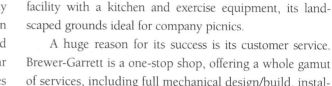

Over the past 18 years Joseph has transformed Brewer-Garrett into the shining star of the mechanical contracting business through proactive marketing and customer solutions, beating up on the competition time and time, again. Since Joseph took over the company reins in 1991 as president and CEO, Brewer-Garrett's revenues increased more than 300 percent.

Joseph's passion is infectious to his team of 350 employees at Brewer-Garrett's expansive 50,000-square-foot office and plant facility on Eastland Road in Middleburg Heights. He treats his employees like family, equipping the facility with a kitchen and exercise equipment, its landscaped grounds ideal for company picnics.

A huge reason for its success is its customer service. Brewer-Garrett is a one-stop shop, offering a whole gamut of services, including full mechanical design/build, installation, planning, service, plumbing and applications. Its high-tech computers are capable of remote monitoring.

Joseph was just 1 year old in 1959 when entrepreneurs Bill Brewer, Bill Garrett and Julius Jihasz pooled their resources and founded the Brewer-Garrett Co. After its first year of business, the company realized $300,000 in revenues. In 1962 Brewer-Garrett's "Big Three" landed a large contract renovating the headquarters of Cleveland's White Motors Co. and soon afterward relocated its operations from a storefront on Hamlet Avenue to larger quarters on Scranton Road.

Bill Garrett was in the right place at the right time in 1964 when he found a solution to a dripping air conditioner in the office window of a disgruntled Crawford Fitting Co. executive. That kind of quick-response customer relations laid the groundwork for Brewer-Garrett's success.

In 1982, Brewer-Garrett hired Joseph away from Honeywell to become the company's first sales rep, but Joseph had a much larger role in mind and began to formulate his vision for the future. Since Joseph was named president in 1991, Brewer-Garrett has realized a 29 percent increase in sales and a whopping 40 percent growth in profits.

Brewer-Garrett's larger accounts include $2.5 million in upgrades for Cuyahoga County government buildings, and to date the company has installed energy-management systems in office towers, banks, stores, warehouses and other facilities.

These days Joseph wrestles with staying on top of the competition and expanding the Brewer-Garrett success story to other cities. Those who know Joseph well won't bet against him.

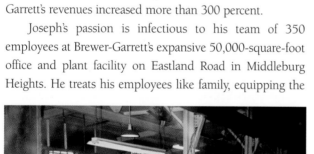

Cleveland Plumbing Industry

At the beginning of the 20th century, Cleveland's plumbing contractors formed an organization to balance the growing influence of labor unions.

Founders of that trade association, today known as the Cleveland Plumbing Contractors Association (CPCA), would be astounded to learn that their successors work closely with Plumbers Union Local 55 and that there is an excellent labor-management relationship that benefits both.

The relationship was strengthened with the creation of the Cleveland Plumbing Industry Fund (CPI) as part of a collective bargaining agreement in 1963. According to CPCA Executive Director Thomas Wanner, CPI is purely a management organization that provides educational and promotional services for plumbing contractors who contribute to the fund. It promotes the industry and serves as a human resources "department" for its 100 or so contractor members in northeastern Ohio who can't afford such a department.

CPI provides technical information to its member contractors; offers business, code, technology and safety classes; informs them of code changes, new products and new procedures; provides legislative liaison at the local and state levels; and maintains a close relationship with various governmental agencies to help improve plumbing conditions and provide input into policies that affect the industry.

But how does this help the union?

Plumbers Local 55 Business Manager Jim Sullivan points out that there are direct and indirect advantages to the relationship. The union provides the best trained, experienced and productive plumbers, and CPI provides the best qualified and reliable contractors. It is a relationship that benefits everyone — especially customers and the general public.

Sullivan, who represents the 1,347-member union, boasts about the state-of-the-art training center, which includes many programs the public wouldn't associate with plumbers. One of these programs is the mini-hospital that includes patient rooms, a nursing station and a simulated operating room where plumbers learn to install medical gas piping.

This specialized training program, which results in a state certification, is just one of many licenses and certifications Local 55 plumbers received during their five-year apprentice program, which includes 800 hours of classroom training and 8,400 hours of on-the-job training.

Although many CPI members work exclusively on commercial installations, there is growing interest in promoting residential plumbing. CPI is so confident of the value in using professionals, it offers a five-year warranty on new home plumbing installations. That same message is being told in radio and television commercials and newspaper ads.

The plumbing industry's motto is "the plumber protects the nation's health," and a publication from the Mechanical Contractors Association of America states that plumbers have saved more lives than the medical profession because of clean water and safe sanitation.

CPI and Local 55 both are proud of the community work they perform together. Volunteer projects that benefit community and social service organizations consume a great deal of their time and resources. Of course, their joint efforts to recruit minorities and females into the trade cannot go unnoticed.

Whether it's promoting commercial or residential work, CPI's primary goal is promoting professionalism.

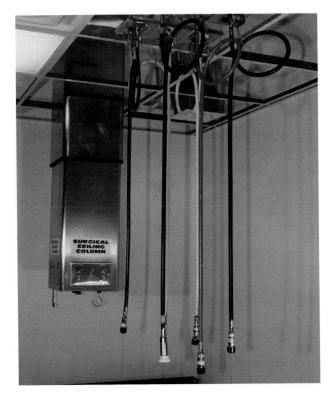

Specialized training needed to install medical gas piping leads to a state certification.

Coleman Spohn Corporation

The time and the environment could not have been any more different.

When the two-man Spohn Company opened as a residential heating company in 1911, Cleveland had grown to become the nation's sixth-largest city. Natural gas was replacing artificial gas for heating and cooking, and the market potential seemed unlimited. The firm grew to become a major installer of HVAC and plumbing systems in the private market.

By the time the ColeJon Corporation, a minority-owned enterprise, was founded in 1976, local newspaper headlines were decrying the city's shrinking population. As a result, ColeJon stayed away from the private marketplace and built its reputation in the public arena, designing, installing and maintaining mechanical systems in high-rise office buildings, hospitals, utility complexes and government centers.

Each company continued to serve its specialized market until 1994 when the two joined forces, creating Coleman Spohn Corporation, an enterprise that has become one of the largest minority-owned firms in Ohio and the largest minority-owned mechanical contractor in the Midwest. Historically the company has served the northeast Ohio area, but recently Coleman Spohn expanded its market to Pittsburgh, where it opened an office.

The ironic part of the firm's work, which has been integral to the success of such Cleveland-area facilities as the Cleveland Browns Stadium, Rock and Roll Hall of Fame, Chrysler's Twinsburg plant, Gund Arena, Key Tower and Cleveland Hopkins International Airport, is that rarely — if ever — is it seen or heard about by the general public — until something goes wrong. With Coleman Spohn, chances are it won't. But just in case, the company has a fleet of 12 service trucks available around the clock, seven days a week to respond to emergencies.

Successfully installing state-of-the-art HVAC equipment and maintaining it is the result of having a professional work force capable of meeting the diverse needs of both public and private-sector clients. The company has 70 union plumbers, pipe fitters and sprinkler fitters (those who install sprinklers) on the job.

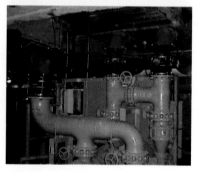

Coleman Spohn never has overrun a contract nor had a contract terminated for default or failure to perform.

Success also is the result of following company president Lonnie Coleman's corporate philosophy of combining customer satisfaction with cost control. That philosophy translates into reality when one learns Coleman Spohn never has overrun a contract nor had a contract terminated for default or failure to perform.

It is that kind of record that has led to awards for business performance from the Small Business Administration and the Ohio governor's office, among many other recognizable achievements.

But the company is just as proud of its maintenance program as it is of its mechanical installation activities. Because today's high-tech equipment may be "temperamental," Coleman Spohn has created a complete preventive maintenance program for its clients that protects their mechanical infrastructure against failure through ongoing and continuous vigilance.

By successfully blending old-fashioned integrity with the latest mechanical know-how — utilizing computer hardware and software to constantly monitor and provide essential management information, and maintaining one of the few Web sites in the mechanical contracting industry — Coleman Spohn continues to provide the kind of quality work its corporate predecessor began providing in the second decade of the 20th century.

Nine years ago, the partners of CRESCO (Corporate Real Estate Service Consultants) did what many people only dream of doing. They took their years of experience, their knowledge and expertise in the commercial/industrial real estate business and started a company of their own where they could do things the way they believed they should be done.

The company's phenomenal success indicates they're doing something very right, indeed. CRESCO's long and growing client list is owed not only to the team's experience, but to the personalized service they bring to their customers — service that goes well above and beyond the call of duty.

CRESCO is a full-service commercial real estate brokerage firm, providing services including sales and leasing of commercial/industrial property, land sales, development, tenant representation, consulting and property management. The bulk of its business takes place in northern Ohio, but through affiliations with organizations like CORFAC International, the company accommodates clients' real estate needs on a global basis.

Owned and operated by founding partners Joseph Barna SIOR and Fred Christie SIOR, along with Armand Aghajanian, who joined the firm four years ago, CRESCO maintains a teamwork approach to the business that allows it to offer superior service to its clients. It provides easy access to information for any customer with no delays, because all three partners keep up to date on each account, a practice virtually unheard of in the more competitive environments of larger firms.

The partners have been careful to avoid the trappings of traditional commercial/industrial real estate firms. Instead, they emphasize the customer service policies they consider most important, including regular communication about the progress of an assignment, as well as predictions of what can be expected in the next 60 days.

Additionally, CRESCO has created one of the most sophisticated and up-to-date databases in the industry. A touch of a button brings a complete and current list of all properties being sold, leased or built that CRESCO can provide to its clients at a moment's notice. A wealth of background information allows it to also match its clients' needs to the right space as soon as it becomes available. Property sheets, including a photo of the site, detailed information and a map are e-mailed to clients and brokers regularly.

Service, reliability and professionalism are the keys to the real estate business, the partners contend. It's the firm with the best information and the fastest response that will get the business; the firm with the best service and professionalism will keep the customer coming back.

CRESCO's Independence office is the third location the company has utilized as it has grown. The firm manages over 1 million square feet of space and represents another 3 million square feet of multi-tenant product, in addition to larger single-use freestanding property. Its client base consists of small entrepreneurs looking for 5,000 square feet of space to huge industrial manufacturers seeking hundreds of thousands of square feet in the manufacturing, warehousing or distribution sector.

Ultimately, real estate is a business of referrals. CRESCO's client list has grown by leaps and bounds in its nine-year history. And that, the partners are proud to point out, speaks volumes about the quality and integrity of service the company has been able to achieve. Their way does, in fact, appear to be the right way.

Partners Armand Aghajanian, Joseph Barna SIOR and Fred Christie SIOR of CRESCO, a full-service commercial real estate brokerage firm, attribute their exceptional growth to the reliable, personalized service they provide their clients.

D-A-S Construction Co.

Quality in building was not the only consideration that John A. Pumper had in mind when he started his own company in 1986, but it was the primary one. As a skilled carpenter for over 30 years, Pumper envisioned a business that would rise from a foundation similar to the one on which he had built his family. He knew that both required vision, patience, caring and commitment. When Pumper began his family-operated business, he even named it for the family members who inspired him to do so. D-A-S takes its name from the initials of his wife, Anna, and sons Steven and Daniel, a constant reminder of the values underlying the company's success. In 1994 Jeff Troxell joined D-A-S as a partner and vice president of business development; and in 1995 John David Pumper joined as a partner, serving as treasurer and chief financial officer.

The key to the success of D-A-S Construction is a simple philosophy of establishing and retaining a satisfied clientele by providing reliable service and quality solutions. The management's attention to detail, from a project's inception to completion, is the factor that brings D-A-S repeat business from satisfied customers. The company takes care to maintain a satisfied employee roster. Skilled and loyal workers who have an active, consultative role in projects have enabled D-A-S to grow and expand its market without sacrificing quality.

D-A-S focuses its attention on commercial and industrial building and renovation in a variety of industries, including banking and financial businesses, medical institutions, industrial buildings and complexes, office and professional buildings, retail establishments and restaurants. The list of projects covers the entire metropolitan Cleveland area, from downtown to the eastern, western and southern suburbs, as well as other locations around northeastern Ohio. Clients have included Metro General and University Hospitals; Marconi Medical Systems; B.F. Goodrich; Bob Evans; Firstar; Bank One; Ohio Savings; Fifth Third; The Bond Court; One Cleveland Center; Park Plaza; Huntington; BP office complexes downtown; the Cleveland Airport Marriott; Camp Manufacturing; Paine Weber; GTE; and others. In 2000 the project to renovate the 74,000-square-foot clubhouse as well as five additions at the Lakewood Country Club especially highlighted the D-A-S commitment to excellence. The in-house carpentry staff, which provides custom cabinetry and fixture-construction capabilities, further enhances the creative edge that keeps D-A-S a leader in area construction.

D-A-S is a member of several professional associations, including the Building Owners and Managers Association (BOMA), the National Association of Industrial and Office Properties (NAIOP), the Institute of Real Estate Management (IREM), the Construction Financial Management Association (CFMA) and the Greater Cleveland Growth Association, which awarded D-A-S the distinction of "Outstanding Growth Company" in 1998. It has been a Weatherhead 100 Award recipient consecutively since 1995 and listed among the Weatherhead top 25 Family Business recipients since 1998.

D-A-S participates in a number of area charities, most notably, Youth Challenge, an area organization that provides physically challenged youth with opportunities for sports and recreation.

(Left to right) Steven W. Pumper, Jeffrey J. Troxell, John A. Pumper, John D. Pumper, Anna Pumper and Daniel A. Pumper

Developers Diversified Realty Corporation

Cleveland-based Developers Diversified Realty Corporation, one of the nation's leading developers, owners and managers of community shopping centers, opened its doors in 1965 as Developers Diversified Group (DDG), but its roots go back to the 1950s when an enterprising young lawyer named Bert Wolstein took an interest in land development. This interest led to the development of more than 1,000 homes in Twinsburg, Ohio. In 1958 Wolstein took a job as project manager for Cleveland's Great Northern shopping center, and by 1965 he had entered the development business full time and formed DDG.

In its early years DDG developed freestanding Kmart stores and Kmart-anchored shopping centers. In 1977 DDG's activities expanded to include the development of JC Penney-anchored shopping centers in the Midwest.

After honing their skills as attorneys at the Cleveland law firm of Thompson, Hine and Flory, Scott Wolstein and James Schoff joined the elder Wolstein in 1981 to create Diversified Equities (DE), which began an era of property acquisition and equity capital formation.

While DDG continued developing shopping centers, DE continued its aggressive acquisition, expansion and development efforts through the late 1980s, concentrating on Cleveland-area projects including Barrington in Aurora, Ohio, an upscale residential community around a Jack Nicklaus-signature golf course. The company also developed the Renaissance Building, a multistory downtown office tower that helped spark the rebirth of Cleveland's theatre district and began a multiphase development on the east bank of the Flats in downtown Cleveland.

With its February 1993 Initial Public Offering (IPO), DDG and DE marked another major milestone by merging to become Developers Diversified Realty Corporation (DDR), listed on the New York Stock Exchange and operating as a Real Estate Investment Trust (REIT). Since going public DDR has seen its assets increase from $395 million in 1993 to over $2.3 billion in 1999. In that same time the total return on shares purchased at the DDR IPO has risen 71.8 percent and the company's owned shopping center space has grown 274 percent.

In 1995 DDR's portfolio dramatically increased when it acquired more than $500 million in community shopping centers from Homart, the retail development subsidiary of Sears. Bert Wolstein retired from DDR in 1997 to pursue other business ventures. Scott, then president and CEO, succeeded his father as chairman. In

DDR associates itself with the nation's premier retailers.

1998 DDR accelerated its growth by acquiring three more community shopping center portfolios, expanding its presence in Ohio, Utah and Missouri.

Today DDR owns and manages 206 properties in 40 states, including 34 in Ohio, representing over 47.7 million square feet. The company continues to seek development opportunities throughout the United States and has many projects currently under construction.

DDR has assembled a team of shopping center industry experts and currently employs more than 290 people, 156 of whom are located at its suburban Cleveland headquarters in Beachwood. DDR plans to continue building premier open-air community shopping centers occupied by the nation's most successful retailers. As DDR enters the 21st century, the company looks forward to continued success as a shopping center industry leader and innovator.

Donley's, Inc.

Donley's origin dates to 1895 with the partnership of James and George Donley as material suppliers to the construction industry. In 1941 Ernest F. Donley's Sons, Inc. was established as a general construction firm. Over half a century later, the family-owned company has become one of Ohio's foremost general contractors, construction managers and design/builders.

Terry Donley, current CEO, is the third generation of Donleys to manage the company. His son, Malcom (Mac) Donley, current president and chief operating officer, represents the fourth generation.

Throughout its history, Donley's has maintained a reputation for integrity and high-quality workmanship by offering tailored delivery systems, adhering to timetables

Donley's executive officers include (from left): Malcolm (Mac) Donley, president and COO; Terry K Donley, CEO; and Don Dreier, executive vice president.

and never hesitating to take on and successfully manage the risk of construction. Its project portfolio reflects largely repeat clients from some of Northeast Ohio's most prominent companies and organizations, including Allstate Insurance and Case Western Reserve University (CWRU).

Donley's growing list of health care clients includes almost every major provider in Northeast Ohio. It has managed multiple projects for University Hospitals, The Cleveland Clinic, Mercy Medical Center and Lake Hospital System.

Donley's delivery systems (role on projects) is split evenly between construction management, lump-sum general contracting and negotiated general contracting.

It also manages a growing number of design/build projects, such as Lake Hospital's Mentor Campus, the Akron Offices of Ernst & Young and several large parking facilities.

Though it has successfully expanded, Donley's roots remain anchored in concrete. It is the market leader in the construction of concrete parking facilities and has completed over 80 garages, including showpiece facilities for University Hospitals and Cleveland Hopkins International Airport.

Donley's expertise in self-performed concrete construction includes many high-profile Cleveland projects such as Jacobs Field and CWRU's Peter B. Lewis Weatherhead School of Management Building. Both projects would test the capabilities and resources of any major construction firm. The concrete work on Jacobs Field required more than 75,000 cubic yards of concrete. The Peter B. Lewis Building, the brainchild of world-renowned architect Frank Gehry, boasts a provocative "flowing ribbon" design demanding cutting-edge construction techniques. The project is currently under construction with Donley's custom form design and concrete placement to be completed in late 2000.

Donley's capabilities also extend to concrete restoration. Among its recent restoration projects is Akron's Firestone Stadium, home to the Akron Racers women's professional softball team. To restore this landmark 74-year-old facility to its former glory, it performed extensive concrete and masonry restoration.

As a member of the Construction Employers Association and with Terry Donley as president, Donley's hires only union labor and sits on a number of pension boards. It also supports local charities through financial donations and service as board members and volunteers.

Donley's future includes many exciting developments, such as using the Internet for better communications. The company is currently creating project specific Web sites so that the owner, contractor, architect and others involved can access current project information. It also plans to grow its work as a construction manager and general contractor and to expand its parking garage construction work beyond Northeast Ohio, all while preserving the company's hard-earned integrity for the next generation of Donleys.

Gleeson Construction, Inc.

The art of fine architectural woodworking has become a rare commodity, and woodworking contractor Gleeson Construction occupies a distinctive niche within the construction industry. The company's skilled craftsmanship and attention to detail is evident as Gleeson's premium-quality woodworking acumen graces many of Greater Cleveland's most prominent landmarks, hotels, hospitals and corporate headquarters.

Gleeson Construction is truly a family business. Vincent P. Gleeson, the company's patriarch and CEO, apprenticed as a carpenter in his native England in 1942. He immigrated to New York City in 1951 and then spent a year in Cleveland before returning to England. He came back to America in 1956, settled in Lakewood with his wife, Alice, and started the company in 1960.

During its first decade, Gleeson Construction specialized in small and medium-sized construction projects, then turned its sights toward larger jobs in the late 1960s. The company performed work on retail development and Howard Johnson's hotels throughout Ohio, Michigan and Pennsylvania during this period. It added hospitals to its portfolio in 1969, starting with work at Bedford Hospital, and worked on its first major Cleveland Clinic project in 1970. Vincent's brother, Michael B., emigrated from Denmark in the early 60s and joined the company in the mid 60s, while Vincent commuted monthly between Cleveland and England in 69 and 70 before settling in Solan in 1971.

As the 1970s progressed, Gleeson Construction took on larger commercial projects, including hospitals, schools and corporate work. The company's skillful woodworking graces the headquarters buildings of TRW, Huntington Bank, Parker Hannifin, Union Carbide, BP America and Eaton Corporation. The company also expanded into the furnishing, coordinating and engineering of architectural woodwork, institutional casework and specialty items as prime contractor. In the 1970s and 1980s, the company began expanding outside the state of Ohio, performing packages in West Virginia, Iowa, Michigan, Pennsylvania, Illinois, New York and Indiana.

Vincent's son, Michael, graduated from Solon High School in 1977 and began working full time for the company. He attended Cuyahoga Community College and Cleveland State University at night, earning an associate's degree in architectural technology. As company president he now oversees all operations, working closely with the company's highly experienced team of craftsmen and project managers. Michael's brother, Mark Gleeson, is the company vice president and operations manager and oversees field operations, including quality control and manpower.

Gleeson Construction's reputation for excellence continued to grow in the 1990s after it installed exhibits at the Rock and Roll Hall of Fame & Museum and the Great Lakes Science Center. Other major clients include the Gund Arena, the Federal Reserve Bank, the Federal Court House, the Ritz Carlton Hotel, Marriott City Center, Nordstrom, Cleveland Clinic, University Hospitals, CWRU, CSU and Playhouse Square. In addition, the company has performed work on dozens of corporate, bank and law firm offices. The company is a member of the Architectural Woodwork Institute and has received over 30 awards for superior-quality craftsmanship.

Through its four decades of steady growth, Gleeson Construction has maintained its unassuming nature. "We have established a reputation as a 'quiet company' that provides superior-quality work with integrity," says Michael Gleeson. "It has inspired strong loyalty from clients and employees alike, many of whom have stayed with the company for much of its history, and with whom we look forward to working in the future."

Ritz Carlton Hotel

Harrington Electric Company

On September 5, 1999, fans packed the new Cleveland Browns football stadium. Music blared, the crowd roared. Concession patrons watched strategically placed video screens, never missing a play. All these sights and sounds were made possible thanks to the work of Harrington Electric Company. The company's more than 90 years of doing business in Cleveland began with its founding by William Harrington in 1907. Bill Harrington did a great deal of work installing electrical systems in schools, churches, department stores and telephone utility buildings in those early years. Today, projects like the Cleveland Browns Stadium, where the company installed all the broadcast television, fire alarm, security and telecommunications systems, have brought a new era of high-tech work for the local business landmark.

When company Chairman and CEO James Morgan Sr. purchased Harrington back in 1971, the company was the oldest existing electrical contractor in the city. "We are the third family to own the company," he says. In those days Morgan worked for the second family, and when the father died, his two sons took over operations. When the siblings decided to sell, they offered the firm to two employees — one, an estimator, and the other, Morgan, a supervising field electrician. "There were not many people working there at the time so it made it easy for me and the other fellow to get in." Morgan took the lead in the business end of the purchase, a role he continued to play after closing the deal. Five years later he bought out his partner. "I have controlled the company for 28 years now. When I took over operations we were down to about a dozen people. Now we have between 150 and 200, so there's been a lot of growth in the business."

The company's controlled but continuous growth is being maintained by the current president, Morgan's son, Tom. He joined the firm in 1978 with a degree in electrical engineering from the University of Cincinnati. Morgan's son, James Jr., now executive vice president and responsible for financial matters at the company, also joined the company in 1978 with a master's degree in management from Case Western Reserve University. Since that time the company has grown not only in size, but in capabilities as well.

The Tele/Data division designs and installs structured cabling systems including voice data communications, local area networks (LANs), audio/visual, fire alarm and security systems. In 1998 the company began offering TEGG predictive and preventative maintenance service. The year 2000 witnessed the creation of the Harrington Electric Drive Service division, which offers predictive, proactive and preventive maintenance for static control drives. These drives are often used to regulate production line speed or temperature controls on air conditioning units.

Harrington Electric Company looks forward to growth in the area of custom design/build, a service for which the national demand is growing. But at the core of the company is its philosophy. Says Jim Morgan Sr., "Our mission is to provide the highest quality electrical services to our customers, to provide a pleasant atmosphere for our employees and to provide continuous work for our electricians in the field."

In 2000 Harrington Electric Co. completed another landmark construction project, the renovation of Severance Hall, home to the world-famous Cleveland Orchestra.

Workers put the finishing touches on the Cleveland Browns Stadium.

Koltcz Concrete Block Co.

In 1938 Cleveland had more than 101,000 residents — about one in 10 of its more than 900,000 population — on relief. Among those who were not, and who in fact started a business that Depression year, was Polish immigrant Michael Koltcz. Koltcz, who came to this country in the early 20s, went to work for a foundry in Fremont, Ohio. When the foundry moved to suburban Bedford, Koltcz moved with it.

In 1925 he started his own masonry contracting business. For a dozen years he maintained the tough daily grind, a grind that stopped in November when the weather turned cold and didn't resume until spring. It was half a year of limited, if any, business; half a year of limited, if any, income.

During the winter of 1938, rather than wait for warm weather, Michael and his two sons, Stanley and Anthony, decided to spend the time making masonry block in their backyard. Initially made only for their own use, they ran out of their homemade block before the first season was over.

Increasing their backyard production but still maintaining the masonry business led to complaints from their fellow masons, who felt they were at a disadvantage. The senior Koltcz agreed to stop doing masonry work if the unhappy masons would buy their block from him.

It obviously worked. Today, Michael's grandson, Stan, is the third generation to head the Koltcz Concrete Block Co., one of only five such firms active in Cuyahoga County. When the company was founded, there were 25 block plants in the county.

There have been quite a few other changes, also. From the family's backyard the company moved to a two-acre site on Northfield Road in Bedford in 1940, where it remained until 1995. It then moved to an 8-acre location in Oakwood Village, but the Bedford location still serves as a storage and warehouse area.

Michael and Stanley's two-man operation has grown to 28 full-time, year-around employees, but it still only takes two men to turn out the block in an environmentally clean procedure. That's two men a shift, three shifts a day, six days a week working computerized equipment that can turn out 32,000 8-inch-equivalent "lightweight" blocks daily. (An 8-inch equivalent is a block that is 8 inches by 8 inches by 16 inches.)

Using lightweight blocks, which weigh only 26-27 pounds compared to 35-pound heavy blocks, means a worker gets to walk home rather than crawl home at the end of the day, according to Stanley Koltcz, who still comes to the office.

Because the company's block is a basic building material, not necessarily an esthetic one, 75 percent of the company's market is wholesale, primarily throughout northeastern Ohio.

Although it manufactures only block — in more than 125 sizes and shapes — Koltcz does sell such related products as pavers, face brick, chimney material, masonry supplies, color mortar, cultured stone, drain pipe and associated hand tools. But in the aggregate, it's concrete that's been the building block to success for the company.

By 1942 the business had expanded to the point where additional workers were added to the family's backyard operation.

The firm's Oakwood Village headquarters, built in 1995

Sheet Metal Workers Local 33

The itinerant tinsmith of colonial America, with toolbox slung over his shoulder, would not recognize today's sheet metal worker. Nor would that 18th century rover with his tinsnips, soldering iron, tongs, vise and hammer — tools necessary to mend a household's dippers and basins and recast broken spoons — recognize today's computer aided design techniques.

The processes, markets and training are different, although the basic material remains the same. But today it is being shaped to meet the advanced needs of homeowners, commercial firms and architects.

In the Greater Cleveland area, the descendants of those colonial tinsmiths are members of Local 33 of the Sheet Metal Workers' International Association, an organization that got its start in Toledo in 1888 as the Tin, Sheet Iron and Cornice Workers' International Association. In 1897 it became the Amalgamated Sheet Metal Workers' International Association, a name it retained until 1903 when another merger made it the Amalgamated Sheet Metal Workers International Alliance.

It was under that name that Local 65 was organized in Cleveland in 1913. For three-quarters of a century Local 65 flourished as part of the International (which changed its name to its current Sheet Metal Workers International Association in 1924). In 1988 a merger of

five area locals in northern Ohio — to eliminate duplication of efforts and to put more organizers on the street — resulted in the creation of Local 33.

That change expanded the organization's jurisdiction well beyond Cleveland. As a result, Local 33 expanded to cover 40 northern Ohio counties; most of West Virginia, including Parkersburg, Charleston and Wheeling; two counties in Michigan contiguous to Toledo's Lucas County; and one in Pennsylvania, adjacent to Youngstown's Mahoning County.

Another activity yesterday's tinsmiths would not recognize is the union's five-year apprenticeship program. With eight training sites located throughout the local's jurisdiction, apprentices undergo extensive training. As extensive as it is, only a portion can be taught. It's possible to teach them math and computer usage. But because sheet metal workers also are artisans, it is impossible to teach them how to visualize the end result. Sheet metal workers are proud of the fact that theirs is the only trade in which the workers fabricate from flat steel to finished product and then install what they create. Other trades purchase what they need and then do the installation.

And more and more frequently, Local 33 members are installing those finished products in residences. For years, residential work was the backbone of the industry. As the housing market stalled in the 50s and 60s, the trade's market increasingly turned toward the commercial side. As housing starts increased in the 1990s, HVAC (especially air conditioning) became increasingly important and residential work began to recapture some of the glamour it once had.

The sheet metal artisan's work can be seen in everything from stainless steel kitchen equipment to architectural and building design. In Cleveland it is evident on church roofs such as St. Vladimir's, and at Jacobs Field, the Browns Stadium and the Rock and Roll Hall of Fame.

It's the kind of craftsmanship that enables the almost 5,000 members of Local 33 to show their "mettle."

Sheet metal fabrication dates back centuries, to the days when soldiers battled in iron body armor. Cleveland's sheet metal companies missed out on the days of knights in shining armor. Instead, they have evolved from designing and fabricating copper roofs to creating complex duct work that maintains livable temperatures in today's homes and office buildings.

To maintain quality and safety standards, the industry began to form organizations to develop product and workmanship standards.

Today, the watchdog organization is the Cleveland chapter of the Sheet Metal and Air Conditioning Contractors' National Association. It was created in 1961 by the merger of the Sheet Metal Employers Association and the Cuyahoga County Sheet Metal Contractors Association.

The Cuyahoga County group came together in 1934 when a group of small sheet metal contractors recognized the need for an organization that would help educate them on planning and installing the then-new residential air-conditioning systems. The group also initiated a certification and inspection program that would give builders a guarantee that heating-system work was carried out according to industry standards.

As A.J. Tuscany, the group's secretary, stated in 1938, "The sheet metal industry had come to a very low point. There is nothing in the building code of Cleveland covering warm air heating or winter air-conditioning installations. We have formulated a code to be followed in these installations."

The group aligned itself with the Sheet Metal Contractors National Association, founded in 1943, and tied together contractors from across the country. In the years during World War II and immediately after, the national association grappled with issues such as the availability of metal products because of their use in war material.

After the 1961 merger of the two local groups, the new organization created a trust fund to create minimum standards for materials and craftsmanship for the industry, responding to a wave of shoddy workmanship and substandard materials that had crept into the industry during recessionary times. The new standards assisted engineers and architects and were incorporated in many municipal building codes in Ohio.

Training skilled workers has always been a commitment of the industry. It has created apprenticeship programs in cooperation with the sheet metal workers' unions that have trained the finest workers since 1927. Today's Sheet Metal Apprenticeship Program is implemented by the independent Joint Apprenticeship & Training Committee of Cleveland. It is a five-year curriculum including classroom instruction and a minimum of 8,000 hours of on-the-job training. Apprentice graduates are prepared. With additional classroom work they can earn an associate degree.

When close to 40 apprentices graduate each year, their pride is passed to another generation. They can perform precision computer-aided design. The program also utilizes instruction to teach computer-assisted drafting, pattern development, pattern layout, welding and safety.

Recent sheet metal apprenticeship program graduates are in very high demand. Workers can expect to receive an excellent wage and benefits package. Those who become sheet metal workers have made the choice to be true achievers with a lifetime of security.

SMACNA/Cleveland is proud to have recently celebrated the 40th anniversary of the Sheet Metal Promotion Plan.

Turner Construction Company

Cleveland has often been described as America's comeback city, transformed in recent years from a rust-belt runner-up into a shining modern metropolis with a diverse and dynamic economic base.

At the center of this continuing metamorphosis is Turner Construction Company, which has managed new construction and renovation of the spectacular buildings that have helped to propel Cleveland and Northeast Ohio to international acclaim. Among these are the Rock and Roll Hall of Fame and Museum on Cleveland's downtown North Coast Harbor and the 63-floor Key Tower, the tallest building in Cleveland and in Ohio. Turner also built the 21,000-seat Gund Arena, home to the Cleveland Cavaliers of the National Basketball Association.

But it has not only been majestic new buildings that have powered Cleveland's ascendancy. Arts and culture have infused the community, too. Turner led the restoration of the downtown Playhouse Square Center, the largest theater restoration project in America. Today, Playhouse Square Center's showcase theaters — Palace, State, Allen and Ohio — make up the second-largest performing arts complex in America, behind only New York's famed Lincoln Center.

Turner also renovated the main building of the nationally recognized Cleveland Public Library — one of America's largest open-stack libraries — and built a new 10-story library annex named for retired U.S. Representative Louis Stokes.

Also at the vanguard of Cleveland's growth has been the expansion of its world-class medical institutions. Turner has built a new eye institute, research institute, cancer center, emergency room and other key facilities at the Cleveland Clinic. At University Hospitals, its work includes construction of a 244-bed, eight-story addition to the distinguished Rainbow Babies & Children's Hospital, Westlake Medical Center and Chagrin Highlands Ambulatory Care Facility.

Turner opened in Cleveland in 1962 with the construction of the 38-story Galleria and Tower at Erieview. This magnificent emerald tower has served as its local office since its completion. Today, the company offers Northeast Ohio a large, experienced staff that blends diverse knowledge of building disciplines: architectural, structural, mechanical and electrical. Other recent and current project experience includes:

- The City Club of Cleveland
- Brunswick City Schools Districtwide Improvements
- Avon Lake City Schools
- New U.S. Courthouse
- New Strongsville Recreation and Senior Complex
- New Cleveland Clinic Cole Eye Institute
- Warrensville Heights City Schools
- New Cleveland Clinic Crown Centre II Suburban Medical/Office Building
- Cleveland Clinic Lerner Research Institute
- Cleveland Public Library — New Annex & Main Building Renovation
- Middleburg Heights Community/Service Centers
- Thompson, Hine & Flory Law Offices
- Theater Renovation at Playhouse Square Center
- Courtyard by Marriott
- Avon High School
- Cleveland Clinic Taussig Cancer Center
- Metropolitan Plaza

Turner's staff not only contributes to the success of each project, but also to the community, participating in such organizations as the Boys and Girls Club, Youth Force 2000, Esperanza, the Urban League, Leadership Cleveland, Harvest for Hunger and Habitat for Humanity. Staffers also sit on various not-for-profit boards, including the Cleveland Board of Education.

Gund Arena

BUSINESS
& FINANCE

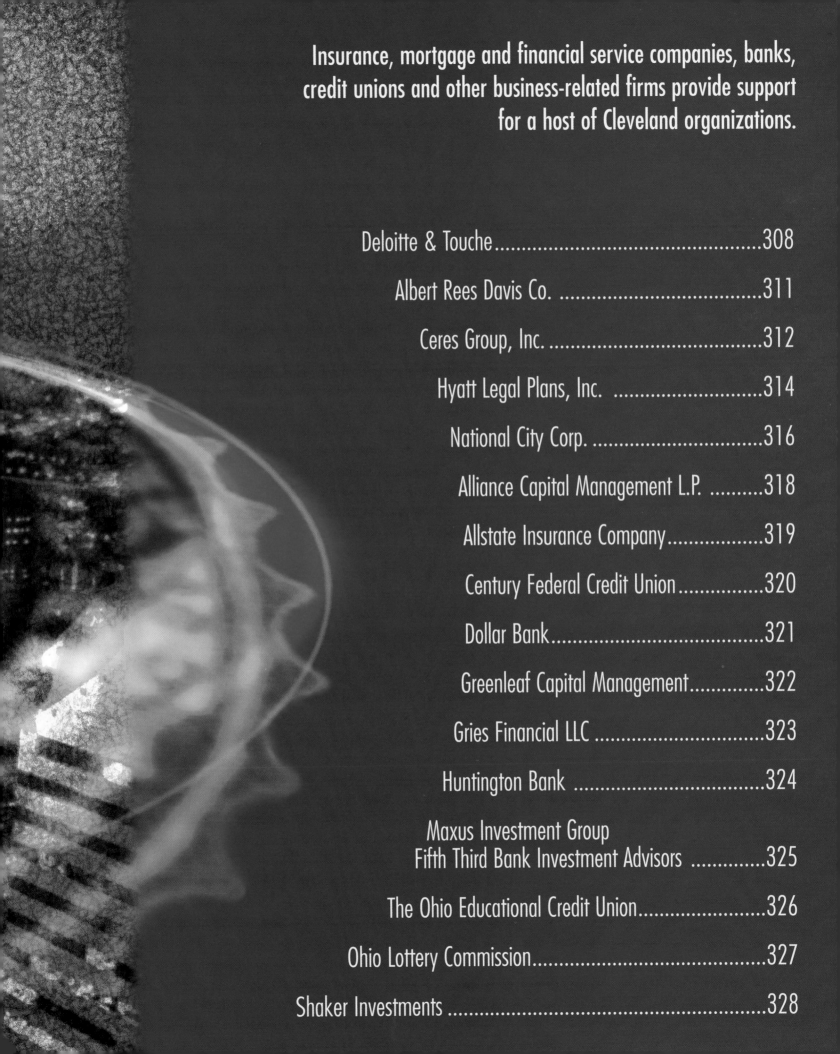

Insurance, mortgage and financial service companies, banks, credit unions and other business-related firms provide support for a host of Cleveland organizations.

Deloitte & Touche

Deloitte & Touche, one of the nation's leading professional services firms, provides clients with assurance and advisory, tax and management consulting services through over 30,000 employees in more than 100 U.S. cities. Deloitte & Touche is part of Deloitte Touche Tohmatsu, a global leader in professional services with over 90,000 employees in more than 130 countries. Its mission is to consistently exceed the expectations of its clients and its people.

The Cleveland Connection

The northeast Ohio practice has grown more than 50 percent in three years. Employing more than 500 people, the Cleveland practice ranks as the 13th largest in the country. Locally the client base primarily consists of manufacturing and real estate companies.

During Cleveland's renaissance, particularly from 1980 to 1987, the northeast Ohio practice served as the city's financial supervisor. James Delaney, Managing Partner of the Cleveland office for 19 years, was appointed to serve as financial supervisor for the state commission, which was instrumental in restoring and persuading companies to remain in the region. The firm also provided consulting services in the development of several major sites, including Gund Arena, Jacobs Field, the Rock & Roll Hall of Fame and Museum, and the Crawford Historical Society. It continues to maintain its position as a strong supporter of Cleveland's downtown and neighborhood redevelopment.

Deloitte & Touche's commitment to the community is also reflected through a spirit of volunteerism. All employees participate in fundraising events throughout the year. Many of them hold significant positions in such noteworthy organizations as United Way of Greater Cleveland, John Carroll University, Playhouse Square Foundation, Case Western Reserve University, West Side Ecumenical Ministry, the Cleveland Zoological Society and the Greater Cleveland Growth Association. Office Managing Partner Patrick Mullin has played an active role in the redevelopment of Euclid Avenue and the Playhouse Square district, as well as serving on boards for the Western Reserve Historical Society, the Downtown Cleveland Partnership, the City Club of Cleveland and the Cleveland Zoological Society.

Located in Cleveland's prestigious Key Tower, Deloitte & Touche's northeast Ohio practice has grown by 50 percent over the past three years and ranks as the 13th largest within the firm.

Exceeding EXPECTATIONS

The firm is particularly proud of its efforts on behalf of the United Way. From 1997 to 1999, while John Bava was Cleveland's office managing partner, employee campaign contributions increased by 40 percent each year.

The People

Deloitte & Touche's commitment to its people is exemplified by its Initiative for the Retention and Advancement of Women. The business imperative for the Women's Initiative was determined in 1992, when the leadership of the firm formed a task force to investigate why the presence of women was not sufficiently reflected at the partner level, and why women were leaving the firm at a higher rate than men. The task force found that women were leaving because of perceived obstacles to their career advancement and because of the difficulty of balancing their career and personal lives.

Today, the gender gap in turnover has been virtually eliminated, and the retention of both women and men is at an all-time high. By retaining and advancing highly talented women, Deloitte & Touche has improved continuity of client service, responded to the changing demographic of its clients and people, reduced costs related to turnover and created a competitive advantage.

Deloitte & Touche has been recognized as a progressive, individual-oriented firm with a culture that encourages flexibility, enables people to realize their potential and promotes a work/life balance. Its efforts have been rewarded by recognition such as its No. 8 ranking on *Fortune* magazine's 1999 list of "The 100 Best Companies to Work for in America."

Deloitte & Touche has taken a leadership role in human resource practices and is committed to remaining a leader in this arena. The development and subsequent annual distribution of the Human Resource Standards Survey not only gives the firm a competitive hiring edge, but it provides the information that is necessary to continually grow and respond to the needs of its employees.

The firm adheres to a set of client service standards that defines its philosophical and practical approach to client engagement planning, performance and assessment.

In response to an increasingly complex business environment and the growing needs of its clients, Deloitte & Touche works to continually broaden its range of services and specializations. These services combine insight, business knowledge and industry experience.

Deloitte & Touche serves clients through three functional areas and numerous specialized practices.

Assurance and Advisory services begin with expressing an opinion on clients' financial statements and extend to offering a range of value-added services. Deloitte & Touche helps its clients achieve business objectives, strengthen their internal controls and management processes, and improve profitability.

Tax consultants formulate strategies to support management objectives and minimize the tax implications of complex business transactions. In providing compliance services, the firm draws on its knowledge of complex tax laws, rules and regulations to help clients meet their tax filing and documentation obligations. It uses advanced computer technology to identify tax-saving opportunities and to prepare tax returns accurately and efficiently. Its Washington National Tax Group advises and represents clients on legislative and regulatory matters and provides timely, insightful analysis on the latest developments in Congress, the IRS, the Treasury Department and other government agencies.

Deloitte Consulting, the management-consulting practice, offers services that range from strategy development to the implementation of information services. The firm contends that no other management-consulting firm has an equal capability and track record of taking strategy through to action. Its services cover the full scope of management functions, focusing on financial management, information technology, operational improvement and strategy development.

In addition to traditional services, Deloitte & Touche offers clients specialized practices in several areas, including Human Capital Advisory Services, Enterprise Risk Services, Dispute Consulting Services, Real Estate Consulting, Mergers & Acquisitions and Management Solutions & Service.

A History of Growth

For more than 100 years, Deloitte & Touche has been delivering outstanding client services by pioneering breakthrough initiatives — employing best business practices through state-of-the-art technology used by highly qualified professionals. The firm traces its roots back to 1895 when Charles Waldo Haskins and Elijah Watt Sells formed an accounting partnership in New York City. Both men were influential in developing regulations regarding auditing and accounting standards in New York State and helped to found New York University's School of Commerce, Accounts and Finance.

While Haskins and Sells were establishing their business in New York, William Welch Deloitte was already running a thriving accounting practice in England and America. He began his career at age 15 as an assistant in London's Bankruptcy Court and eventually set up his own practice in 1845 at age 25. Deloitte expanded his practice to America in 1893 and began auditing a growing soap-and-candle business, Procter & Gamble, which remains a client today.

In 1899 Scotland native George A. Touche established a practice in London. A true Renaissance man, Touche became a member of parliament, an alderman and a sheriff of London. After several trips to the United States, he recognized the potential for business here and joined forces with John Niven, forming Touche, Niven & Co. in New York in 1900.

Philip S. Ross, another Scotsman, left home in 1858 at the age of 26 for Canada and eventually opened an accounting business in Montreal, serving small clients — many of which would go on to become corporate giants.

Through a progression of mergers and working relationships, these four prominent firms would work together over the next 75 years, becoming two firms, Deloitte, Haskins, & Sells and Touche Ross & Co. These two firms merged in 1989, creating Deloitte & Touche.

Clearly, Deloitte & Touche is among the best. The firm serves as distinguished auditor, tax advisor and consultant for a significant portion of the nation's most influential businesses. To maintain a progressive, growth-oriented culture, it diligently promotes its Mission, Shared Values and Practice Standards. Deloitte & Touche will continue to progress and succeed by building upon the firm's strong foundation and by continually striving to reach one of its most important goals — to consistently exceed the expectations of its clients and its people.

(Left to right)
Bailey
Deloitte
Haskins
Niven

(Left to right)
Ross
Sells
Smart
Touche

Albert Rees Davis Co.

With the trend to mergers, acquisitions and downsizing, a company that successfully stays in business for 100 years is an exception in today's business world.

The Albert Rees Davis Co., an independent insurance agency, has gone beyond the century mark, having been founded in 1890. More remarkable, it has remained a family business the entire time. And interestingly enough, it still is run by Albert Rees Davis — not the original, but his nephew, also named Albert Rees Davis. More commonly known as "Bud," he's the third Davis to preside over the agency.

The "original" Albert Rees Davis came to Cleveland from Youngstown in 1886 and four years later established the insurance company bearing his name. It was the same business his father had been running in Youngstown, but Albert felt there were more opportunities in Cleveland.

Once the business was established in downtown Cleveland, Albert began establishing himself in the community's cultural circles. From 1907 until his death in 1919 he served as conductor of the Singers Club, a male chorus; was a board member and first president of the Music School Settlement; was a director of the Tuesday Musical Club of Akron; was organist and choir master of Grace Episcopal Church; and was a founder and member of the Hermit Club, a meeting place for those with talent in, and appreciation of, the performing arts.

After Albert's untimely death, his brother, Charles, a mining engineer by training and education with no background in insurance sales, returned from Colorado where he had gone for his health, and took over the agency. He in turn brought his sons, Albert Rees and Willis, into the firm. Eventually, they brought their sister, Elizabeth Wellman, into the company.

Albert "Bud" Davis joined the company on a part-time basis just prior to World War II. Among his innovative ideas to gain business was making contact with a Welcome Wagon representative. He paid 50 cents for each name, and in the evenings would call on these new homeowners since it was obvious they needed insurance. During the first year he garnered 1,000 accounts.

After the war Bud joined the business full time and the client list no longer was culled from the Welcome Wagon roster. Among the firm's clients were such major corporations as Bonne Bell and Stouffer's, and the firm now meets the needs of thousands of individuals, families and businesses in 18 states.

Although the firm has continued to grow, it has had only as many offices — three — as presidents during its long life. After many successful years in downtown Cleveland, the company moved to Shaker Heights in the late 1960s. A changing neighborhood and a growing business required a third move to its current Shaker Heights location in a high-rise office building where it shares space and technological facilities with several other firms.

Continuing the well-established family tradition, Bud's sons, Bill and Michael, have been with the agency for many years. Their participation ensures the company will continue to meet the needs of its diverse clients well into the future.

Company founder Albert Rees Davis.

Albert Rees "Bud" Davis, flanked by sons Bill (left) and Michael.

Ceres Group, Inc.

Ceres was the mythological Roman goddess of agriculture who symbolized vibrancy and growth. These are two attributes that Ceres Group, Inc. has in common with the goddess.

A major employer in the Cleveland area, Ceres Group has been a leader focused on growth throughout its history. Initially known as American Central Life when it was formed in 1964, the company grew to become one of the nation's leading providers of accident and health insurance for business owners with one to 25 employees. The firm's early success was to a great degree the result of its pioneering efforts in promoting a preferred-risk concept in which healthy, low-risk people paid lower premiums.

In 1976 the company was reorganized as Central Reserve Life Corporation, with Central Reserve Life Insurance Company as its principal subsidiary.

During the 1980s the company was recognized by *Forbes* magazine for its achievements and was listed No. 1 in a ranking of the 100 fastest-growing Nasdaq companies, based on earnings over a five-year period.

For 1994 the company was listed in "The Beacon Journal 100" as one of the best-performing companies in Ohio. And *The Plain Dealer* in 1995 named the company among the top 100 "Best Companies in Ohio."

By 1996, the company had grown to 13,000 agents, had revenue of $265 million, assets of $119 million and was insuring 230,000 people. At that time, the company offered health insurance in 35 states, with the majority of its business in Ohio, Indiana, Michigan, Pennsylvania and North Carolina.

In 1998 a group of investors came to Central Reserve Life Corporation. Along with a new name, Ceres Group, Inc., the investors brought a $40 million equity capital infusion, additions to senior management and a new beginning for the company.

The new growth plan called for Ceres to expand its distribution and add accident disability, cancer, critical illness, dental coverages and senior health and life insurance products. The initial goals outlined by management in 1998 included doubling revenue by acquiring insurance businesses and substantially increasing its base of brokers.

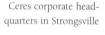

Ceres corporate headquarters in Strongsville

In the fall of 1998 the company announced that it would purchase Continental General Insurance Company in Omaha, nearly doubling Ceres' size. Continental had products and a distribution system for seniors, one of the growth markets Ceres had targeted. By 2020 it is estimated there will be more than 53 million Americans 65 and older. By then, the U.S. average life expectancy will be 86 years and total long-term care expenses are projected to be nearly $260 billion annually.

Other acquisitions completed in 1999 included Provident American Life Insurance Company and United Benefit Life Insurance Company. Ceres also acquired Pyramid Life Insurance Company, a major player in the senior insurance product market, in 2000.

Maintaining its reputation as a consolidator, the company announced additional acquisitions that would enhance its efforts in other markets. Among them were acquisitions of blocks of business of Central Benefits

Home page of the company's unique QQLink.com Web site

From its origins in the 1960s, Ceres has grown by changing and adapting to market needs and market opportunities.

Mutual Insurance Company and American Chambers Life Insurance Company. American Chambers also provided Ceres with an affinity relationship with more than 3,500 chambers of commerce across the country.

As the Ceres Group continued to expand its basic health insurance capabilities, it also took advantage of changing technologies, working to transform an old-commerce company into one with e-commerce capabilities.

In 2000 Ceres introduced QQLink.com, the company's own innovative business-to-business online connection. Ceres provides participating agents with Web sites and links to QQLink.com for online quoting and application processes. The company will market insurance and financial products directly to consumers, enabling them to buy online health insurance policies and other products from Ceres Group companies and unaffiliated companies.

However, unlike other firms offering direct Internet sales to consumers, Ceres will pay agents a commission for every policy sold through their Web sites, an approach that has been well received by agents concerned about the changing industry.

Of the 50,000 independent agents across the nation serving more than 600,000 Ceres consumers in 49 states in mid-2000, about 5,000 were expected to take advantage of the QQLink.com program by year end 2000. It is anticipated that eventually more than 25,000 agents across the nation will utilize QQLink.com. With unique and exclusive prospecting programs and strategic alliances with other companies to enhance the scope of the Internet program, Ceres expects QQLink.com to be an important factor in its continuing growth and development.

Ceres also will continue to expand its marketing efforts in the growing and affluent senior marketplace through its Senior Health Division, headquartered at Pyramid Life, near Kansas City.

From its origins in the 1960s, Ceres has grown by changing and adapting to market needs and market opportunities. Early in the 21st century it had grown to an $800 million revenue company with over $850 million in assets.

Even though Ceres has been successful, the firm realizes that yesterday's achievements do not ensure success for the future. Rather, it is the firm's forward thinking, inspired by the Roman goddess, that will continue to make its growth policies dynamic and exciting.

Hyatt Legal Plans, Inc.

According to a recent survey by the American Bar Association, a full 50 percent of moderate-income families require some type of legal assistance at least once in the course of a year.

Unfortunately these families rarely receive the legal services they need. Many people admit to being intimidated by the judicial system. Others are afraid of the cost, and some simply don't know how to find a helpful attorney.

Enter Hyatt Legal Plans and the concept of group legal plans. Armed with a full menu of legal services, affordable rates and easy access to qualified attorneys, Hyatt has created the simple solution to all these problems.

Following the same basic tenets as medical, dental and optical employee-benefit programs, group legal plans capitalize on the strength of group purchasing power to provide employees with low rates and convenient access to legal services.

Cleveland-based Hyatt Legal Plans has quickly become the largest of such providers. Recognized for its outstanding growth potential, the company was spun off from Hyatt Legal Services in 1989 as a separate operating entity and continued to thrive during the 1990s as the concept was planted and took root.

When the company formed a strategic business alliance with MetLife, which purchased Hyatt Legal Plans in 1997, things really began to happen. MetLife now includes legal services in the portfolio of employee-benefit programs it offers to companies nationwide. This enhanced distribution, coupled with Hyatt's stringent adherence to the highest-quality customer service standards, has served to triple Hyatt's business within the past three years.

This monumental growth has helped to bring Hyatt's employer-based group legal plans to over 1 million employees and their families across the country through more than 350 sponsor companies.

Organizations with as few as 200 employees all the way up to Fortune 500 companies have signed up to provide employees and their families with group legal benefits as part of a comprehensive benefits package. Because the plan is easy to administer, it has become increasingly popular with corporate benefit managers looking to provide important "work-life" assistance programs to employees and to help them compete for talent within an industry or region.

Participating firms include industry-leading organizations such as American Express, AT&T, Caterpillar, Frito-Lay, Lucent Technologies, PepsiCo, Nabisco, Ralston Purina, America Online, Shell Oil Company and the University of Michigan. Ohio organizations that sponsor a Hyatt legal plan include American Electric Power, Case Western Reserve University and Rockwell Automation.

Employees have responded equally favorably to the opportunity to receive customer-friendly legal services at low rates. The services utilized most frequently by participants are the creation of wills and trusts, real estate transactions and general office consultations, including advice on adoptions, premarital arrangements, credit and consumer issues and traffic violations. Employment-related disputes are not covered.

Other services provided under the basic plan are consumer protection; defense of civil lawsuits; document preparation and review, such as mortgages and affidavits; name changes; eviction defense; juvenile court defense; and personal bankruptcy.

Plan participants receive unlimited telephone advice and office consultations with an attorney of their choosing. There are no co-pays, dollar caps or waiting periods. They may also elect to utilize an out-of-network attorney and

The management team of Hyatt Legal Plans, Inc. is dedicated to maintaining the company's strong leadership position.

will be reimbursed for applicable fees. Payroll deductions are typically administered, making the process simple and familiar for employees.

Employees may receive service from any attorney anywhere in the country; a participant who gets into a car accident while traveling in another city will have full access to the legal services he or she needs from a local law firm within the network. Personalized assistance in identifying nearby attorneys is available through Hyatt's fully staffed client service center and its Web site.

Hyatt maintains a network of over 9,200 attorneys operating from 3,500 firms across the country. The company continually augments its membership of qualified attorneys as its employee participation grows. Criteria for new firms includes a breadth of legal experience and practice, as well as their desire to be a part of the network and a promise to live up to the rigorous customer-service standards set by Hyatt.

Member law firms must guarantee to have their phones staffed adequately, to return participants' phone calls in a reasonable amount of time, as well as to provide professional legal services. Participants are encouraged to contact Hyatt's corporate office with issues regarding the individual legal services they receive.

For this reason, Hyatt maintains a full staff of personnel dedicated to working with corporate sponsors and individual participants, and on-staff attorneys who maintain an ongoing

The nation's leading provider of group legal plans

Through participation of industry-leading organizations like these, Hyatt helps bring group legal plans to over 1 million employees and their families.

dialogue with network attorneys to assure the highest quality of service and open communications.

Most group legal plans are entirely employee-funded; a few programs are partially funded by the employer. Upon initial offering, typically 10 to 15 percent of employees within an organization elect to participate. Hyatt considers this to be quite high for a voluntary program. As word of mouth about the value of the program spreads, more employees sign on.

The key to the success of the program, Hyatt contends, is to make it simple and affordable. Plans typically cost less than $200 a year, a fee most people believe will more than pay for itself upon the first transaction.

In addition to being distributed by the MetLife sales force, Hyatt maintains its own staff of sales personnel that contacts organizations that are not MetLife customers to spread the word about the value and benefit of group legal programs.

Hyatt Legal Plans has also developed an Individual Plans business which is experiencing rapid growth. Customers of consumer finance companies, banks and other financial institutions are now being offered the opportunity to sign up for Hyatt's individual legal plan, called LawPlan, which provides the advantages of quality, easy-access legal services at affordable rates.

The individual plans program is being explored by MetLife as a value-added program offered by that company's individual insurance agents.

Hyatt clearly believes that the concept of group legal plans is an idea whose time has come. With its exceptional growth and ever-expanding membership, evidence is decidedly mounting in its favor.

Hyatt Legal Plans maintains a full staff of customer service professionals to assure fast and effective customer response.

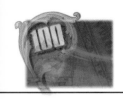

National City Corp.

In 1947 Wooster Rubber Company — best known for its bath mat — needed $42,000 to run an ad in *Ladies Home Journal*. Company executive Donald Noble went to talk with his banker at National City Bank about a loan. Ed Dekker, a National City vice president, suggested the company issue preferred stock instead. The move helped drive forward the Wooster, Ohio, housewares firm, which later changed its name to Rubbermaid Inc.

"If you want to describe National City in one word, it's service," said Noble years later, after he had become Rubbermaid's chairman and chief executive officer.

Rubbermaid is just one of countless businesses that have benefited from the sound advice and high-quality services that have been constant throughout National City Corporation's history.

What began as a small banking house on Cleveland's Superior Street in 1845 is today one of the largest financial services organizations in the country, offering trust, processing and investment management services in addition to the more traditional business and consumer banking services. As a leader in a highly competitive environment, National City has evolved significantly along the way.

"Today, you have hundreds of choices if you want an IRA, a credit card or a money-market account," says chairman and chief executive officer David Daberko. "It's not a monopoly or oligopoly like it once was, when you had to do your banking at the branch down the street."

Through it all, National City has endured by remaining faithful to its core values — which include high-quality

lending, cost control and strong commitments to its employees and communities. The result is a consistent record of growth — in earnings, employees and customers served.

City Bank of Cleveland came to life on July 1, 1845, in a small office in the Merchant's Exchange Building on Superior Street, just up the hill from the Cuyahoga River. A few days later cashier Theodoric C. Severance ordered $14,288 in currency from the state treasurer, 95 percent of the capital the bank's stockholders had deposited with the treasurer. Soon, Severance and bank President Reuben Sheldon were making loans for as little as 50 cents and up to thousands of dollars.

In the next few years, the city and the bank would be at the center of a commercial and industrial explosion. Geologists and surveyors from Cleveland were investigating the copper and iron ore deposits in the upper reaches of Michigan. In short order, the Cleveland, Columbus and Cincinnati Railroad was completed and tied into lines stretching to Chicago, Pittsburgh, Buffalo and points east; the first stockyards and slaughterhouses were opened; and a Clevelander named John D. Rockefeller was thinking about investing in oil refining.

In 1865 the bank received a national charter and took the name National City Bank of Cleveland. By the end of the Civil War, National City had capital stock of $200,000. Leading the bank in those years was John Whitelaw, who had joined the bank in 1857 as a messenger. In 1862 he became cashier and then president in 1889, serving the bank until his death in 1912.

In 1888 the Perry-Payne Building opened on Superior with the bank as one of its first-floor tenants. At the time, the city had more than 100 banks.

During this time, according to former director Edgar A. Hahn, National City came to be known as the "Stockyards Bank." Whitelaw had been an organizer and first president of the Cleveland Union Stockyards Company and had wooed a number of the packing houses as the bank's customers.

After Whitelaw's death, his controlling interest was sold to a syndicate of businessmen who increased National City's capital. In 1913 the bank moved into larger quarters

An artist's view of Cleveland's Superior Street in 1845. The City Bank of Cleveland operated from the Merchants Exchange Building on the far left.
Photo by Rebman Photo Service

in the Leader-News Building (now the Leader Building) at East Sixth Street and Superior Avenue. Assets by May 1913 were $4.5 million.

In the years after World War I, Standard Oil Company of Ohio and the East Ohio Gas Company were significant customers. Along with the long-time stockyards business, these natural gas and oil companies gave the bank a strong base of commercial business. "An atmosphere composed of the effluvia of stockyards, natural gas and oil refining establishments may have a connotation somewhat offensive to one's olfactory sense, but to us at National City it was sheer heavenly fragrance," Hahn recalled at a company dinner in 1954.

On January 1, 1921, the growing bank paid $1 million for the Garfield Building at East Sixth Street and Euclid Avenue that would be its next home.

Despite all of this growth, National City was a notch below the city's largest banks. While its assets were in the $30 million range, Cleveland Trust Company, Union Trust Company and Guardian Savings and Trust Company each had assets of over $100 million. All had grown rapidly during the 1920s by lending to speculative real estate ventures and through mergers and acquisitions. The more conservative National City had remained on the sidelines. In its entire history to that time, the bank had never made an acquisition.

In the wake of the stock market crash of 1929 and the Great Depression that followed, cash was in short supply and many banks struggled. National City, however, remained strong as the only Cleveland bank to maintain a standing offer to allow depositors to withdraw 100 cents on the dollar. After President Franklin D. Roosevelt declared a bank holiday in 1933, Union Trust and Guardian Savings and Trust never reopened; they were unable to pay their depositors. National City reopened without any restrictions on depositors and soon took over what little remained of those two larger, failed institutions. By 1934 assets reached $121 million.

National City never looked back. It opened a full-service trust department and

its first branch office in the Terminal Tower complex in 1933. The expansion continued after World War II with more branch offices and rising assets. By the 1960s the bank had 24 branches and assets exceeding $1 billion.

By the 1980s it was clear that banks would soon be allowed more freedom to expand geographically than they ever had before. National City Corporation was created as a holding company in 1973 to take advantage of this new-found freedom through acquisitions. In 1984 National City took its first big step with the purchase of BancOhio Corp., the leading banking company in Columbus. The merger doubled National City's size.

Now, many acquisitions later, National City is an $85 billion asset company providing consumer and commercial financial services in Ohio, Michigan, Pennsylvania, Kentucky, Indiana and Illinois. It has acquired 16 banks in 25 years. The largest was First of America Bank Corp. of Kalamazoo, Michigan, which had $21 billion in assets.

And there is still potential for further growth.

"In the next five years I expect to see more changes in this business than I have in my entire career so far," says Daberko. "Changes in delivery, changes in customer demographics, changes in products offered and changes in the way we market those products. These changes will be driven by competition and customer service. They will be built on advanced information management technology — and delivered in many ways — including via our very friendly tellers."

This photo of depositors waiting for National City to open for business during the bank panic of 1933 ran in newspapers across the country. On February 27, 1933, a day when many banks in Cleveland and elsewhere limited depositor withdrawals to as little as 5 percent of deposits, National City was the only local bank to pay 100 cents on the dollar. National City closed temporarily when President Franklin D. Roosevelt declared a bank holiday but continued to allow unrestricted deposits and withdrawals when the holiday ended.
Cleveland Press Collection, Cleveland State University NCB Historical Archives

Alliance Capital Management L.P.

Though the Cleveland office of Alliance Capital Management L.P. is one of 32 Alliance offices around the globe, its expertise in investment management has greatly affected the local community. As Cleveland's largest independent money manager, Alliance has helped institutions such as the Western Reserve Historical Society, Rainbow Babies & Children's Hospital and The Cleveland Society for The Blind to not just survive, but thrive.

Alliance began in 1962 as the investment advisory department of Donaldson, Lufkin & Jenrette (DLJ). It became a subsidiary of DLJ in 1971 and opened an office in Cleveland in 1975 by acquiring the Alexander, Van Cleef and Wood Company (AVW). AVW was started in 1923 by Principals Rob Roy Alexander and Frank Van Cleef and was one of the first firms in the country to offer investment advice independent of a bank.

In 1985 Alliance and DLJ were purchased by The Equitable Life Assurance Society of the United States and operated as an independent subsidiary. The firm went public in 1988 as a master limited partnership and was listed on the New York Stock Exchange.

The business of Equitable Capital Management Corp. was transferred to Alliance in 1993, adding more than $36 billion in assets under its management. Today, Alliance is the largest publicly traded asset manager in the United States, with over $400 billion in assets under its management, $7 billion of which is managed by the Cleveland office. The firm's focus is the management of investment assets for large corporations, public-employee pension funds and endowments and foundations.

Alliance's clientele list consists of 35 Fortune 100 companies and public retirement funds in 34 states, plus hundreds of national and international corporations, foundations and financial institutions. Eighty percent of the business at the Cleveland office emanates from institutional customers, and the remaining assets have been entrusted to Alliance by families in the Northern Ohio area. Its distinguished list of clients, many of which have been with Alliance for over 20 years, includes B.P. America, Nestle´ U.S.A., Ohio Northern University, Medical Mutual of Ohio, TRW Inc., University Hospitals and the Jennings Foundation.

There are many reasons these corporations and foundations trust Alliance. The firm has a strong commitment to in-depth research and a strong culture of communication between its offices. In fact, every business day at 9 a.m. EST Alliance links all its domestic and international portfolio managers and research analysts for a review of global markets and a discussion of topical company research. This helps maintain the firm's traditional focus on companies with superior prospects for earnings growth and shareholder returns.

Recent technology has significantly affected how Alliance conducts its business. Its worldwide network and instant international communication capabilities allow the firm to stay informed.

The more than 170 investment professionals at Alliance average seven years with the firm and 13 years of investment experience. They combine to form a reliable team equipped with research capabilities and trading expertise well beyond what each one could resource independently. And since Alliance bases its fee on the market value of its portfolios, it essentially has the same objective as its clients — to make the funds appreciate in value.

With Alliance Capital Management, clients in Cleveland literally have a world of resources working for them.

One of the many valuable resources at the Cleveland office of Alliance is the executive team. (Left to right, standing) Geoffrey C. Hauck, vice president/portfolio manager, David P. Handke, Jr., senior vice president/portfolio manager, David E. Jerome, senior vice president/portfolio manager. (Left to right, seated) Peter W. Adams, senior vice president and manager, Sarah M. Dimling, vice president/portfolio manager, Albert J. DeGulis, senior vice president/ portfolio manager

Allstate Insurance Company

It was 1930. The Great Depression was closing businesses and the automobile was fast becoming a mainstay of American life. Robert E. Wood, president of Sears, Roebuck and Co., was on the 7:28 train for Chicago when a fellow passenger suggested that Sears sell auto insurance through the mail. After convincing the Sears Board of Directors to finance the idea and borrowing a name from a tire sold in the Sears catalog, Wood began Allstate Insurance Company on April 17, 1931. Almost 70 years later Allstate is the nation's largest publicly held personal lines insurance company, with 13,000 agents in the United States and Canada.

Though Allstate lost money its first year, by the 1933 Chicago World's Fair the small card table in the corner of the Sears exhibit set up by the company's first agent was swamped with applications. Agents were placed in Sears stores that same year.

In 1950 an Allstate sales manager created the well-known slogan — "You're in Good Hands" — and the next few decades were a time of dramatic company growth. It added property, casualty and life insurance to its list of services and by June 30, 1995 became a totally independent company when Sears spun off its remaining shares to its stockholders.

Allstate's innovative customer services began in 1952 when it opened the first drive-in claim office and revolutionized the way auto claims are handled. Today, the company continues its unprecedented service with the industry's first multi-access approach to insurance products and services. Allstate customers can buy or service their insurance in person at an agent's office, by phone, over the Internet or through the mail — whichever is most convenient for them. And its committed and educated agents are always available "live."

Allstate also realized early on that insurance companies should help communities and has had a major positive impact, both financially and in the quality of life, on almost every community in the country. The Allstate Foundation was created in 1952 to support and improve neighborhoods, schools, communities and nonprofit organizations. One of the more than 1,000 programs the foundation supports is the Neighborhood Partnership Program, which helps urban neighborhoods become stronger, safer and more economically viable.

The program has been beneficial to the recent revitalization of Cleveland's inner-city Fairfax neighborhood. Cleveland was one of only seven cities in the country chosen to receive a large grant through the program. In 1997 $4.3 million was awarded as part of a five-year plan to improve the neighborhood through a partnership with the nonprofit Fairfax Renaissance Development Corporation. The funds, along with a dedicated team of Allstate agent and employee volunteers, have improved homes, built playgrounds, and supported after-school tutoring programs and senior citizen computer labs, among other accomplishments. Allstate also supports several other Cleveland community organizations, including the Cleveland Neighborhood Housing Service, the Urban League, and the police and fire departments.

In addition, Allstate has often been recognized for its supportive work environment and dedication to its employees, including being named one of *Working Mother* magazine's 100 best companies for working mothers for the 10th time in 2000.

A company that cares — for its customers, its community and its employees — Allstate's future is undoubtedly "in good hands."

Cleveland Mayor Michael White helped cut the ribbon that symbolized the initiation of Allstate's Neighborhood Partnership Program. Allstate donated $4.3 million to help Cleveland's neighborhoods.

Century Federal Credit Union

In 1948, 100 years after the inception of the credit union business in the United States, nine individuals followed their dream to form a not-for-profit cooperative aimed at placing its members before the bottom line. Each of the founding fathers invested $5 into the new venture, and Century Federal Credit Union was born.

Century Federal Credit Union's executive management team believes in people helping people. (Standing, left to right) Glenn Keeney, director of human resources; Pete Romano, lending manager; (seated, left to right) Nick Nero, director of MIS; Mike Bower, CFO; Russ Fisher, CEO; Lisa Zelek, director of marketing; Rose Lorenz, director of branch operations

It was the post-World War II era, and like most people, the first Century Federal members were chasing the American dream. Young families needed help with down payments on homes and loans for new cars.

Those dreams haven't changed much over the years. Neither has Century Federal's commitment to helping its members borrow and save. For more than 50 years Century Federal has offered its members lower rates on loans and credit cards and higher rates on savings. It is this commitment that has led to Century Federal's growth as the largest credit union in Greater Cleveland.

"Century Federal operates on the premise of people helping people," says Russell W. Fisher, Century Federal executive manager, from his office in the Anthony B. Celebreeze Federal Building in Cleveland.

Unlike other financial institutions that exist to benefit their shareholders, Century Federal, with its all-volunteer board of directors, focuses on offering quality services, Fisher says. Century Federal exists solely to serve its members.

Century Federal employee volunteers take phone calls on behalf of the Children's Miracle Network Telethon in conjunction with Rainbow Babies and Children's Hospital of Cleveland.

"Our members are very loyal to their credit union," says marketing director Lisa M. Zelek. "We've been there for them when they bought their first car, their first home and took out their first college loan."

Century Federal doesn't take the next generation for granted. The credit union has taken a lead role in teaching children and young adults how to manage their money in the future by first building smart savings habits. Century Federal has developed programs with the objective of education for children and young adults up to 19 years of age.

Century Federal also takes pride in its volunteerism and charity work. Its Cleveland employees have donated funds and participated in the nationally acclaimed Harvest for Hunger, Habitat for Humanity and the Children's Miracle Network Telethon in conjunction with Rainbow Babies and Children's Hospital.

In September 1998 Century Federal employees and their families joined the Race for the Cure for Breast Cancer, participating in the fund raiser following the death of a fellow employee to breast cancer. The event drew 10,000 people with a shared mission of eradicating breast cancer as a life-threatening disease.

Century Federal Credit Union prides itself on providing an array of quality products and services for its members and plans to enhance that tradition in the years to come.

In an age of megamergers in the banking industry, Dollar Bank has bucked the trend. Although it has grown to more than $3 billion in assets, it remains a mutual institution committed to remaining independent and dedicated to meeting the banking needs of the people and businesses of Northeast Ohio.

In 1855 founder Charles Colton departed from banking tradition by establishing a financial institution that was dedicated to serving all people regardless of their means. That dedication remains evident today.

In the 1970s Dollar Bank was one of the first in the nation to offer interest on checking accounts and pioneered telephone banking. More recently, its NetBanking online banking system won praise from customers across the region and national experts alike.

Dollar Bank has worked hard to differentiate itself from many of its competitors. Believing that banking is a personal business of trust, Dollar Bankers actively pursue their mission to treat every customer as if he or she were the bank's only customer — from software entrepreneur to single mom.

Consumers can choose from a wide range of traditional products offered by Dollar Bank. The bank is one of a select few that still offers all customers no-minimum checking accounts, free online banking and extended hours every day. Its NetBanking service garnered the bank a 1998 *Computerworld* Smithsonian Award for Technical Innovation by offering customers a simple, secure and convenient way to manage their finances on the Internet without the need to purchase additional software. Dollar Bank doesn't even levy surcharges on competitors' customers in Cleveland who use its automated teller machines.

Dollar Bank is proud of its reputation as a people's bank. Its Private Banking department is respected by a growing number of high net-worth clients. At the other end of the economic spectrum, low- to moderate-income borrowers can receive free credit counseling to help them overcome credit problems and become homeowners.

By stressing personal service to corporate clients, Dollar Bank has developed a diversified customer base that includes low- and high-tech manufacturing companies, professional corporations, retail operations and specialty service firms. Its Commercial Real Estate Department has a national reputation for handling everything from small projects to major multifaceted developments.

Whether dealing with individuals, small businesses, corporations or nonprofits, Dollar Bankers approach every relationship neighbor to neighbor.

Charles Colton, founder

Dollar Bank is proud of its reputation as a people's bank.

Greenleaf Capital Management

Cleveland is a city with strong and deep roots and a bold and promising future. Since 1976, Greenleaf Capital Management has been a part of Greater Cleveland's dynamic development. Many of the region's most successful individuals and organizations have entrusted Greenleaf to manage and grow their assets.

Many of the region's most successful individuals and organizations have entrusted Greenleaf to manage and grow their assets.

Located in prestigious Shaker Heights, Greenleaf Capital Management is named for Geof Greenleaf, who founded the company on the basis of experience acquired at McKinsey & Company and Merrill Lynch. Partners Ensign J. Cowell and S. Sterling (Ted) McMillan III joined the firm in 1980 and 1986, respectively. A broad-based professional staff supports them in managing

(Left to right) Greenleaf Capital Management investment management and counsel partners: Ensign J. Cowell, CFA; Geofrey J. Greenleaf, CFA; and S. Sterling (Ted) McMillan III

Depth of experience, commitment to forging lasting personal relationships and a wholistic approach to financial management make Greenleaf uniquely qualified to create and preserve wealth.

accounts ranging from individual trusts to corporate and individual retirement plans.

Greenleaf's distinctive difference is the highly personal approach it takes to each client's financial situation. Every portfolio is custom crafted, and beyond investment services, Greenleaf helps to coordinate estate planning, gifting and other needs. "We are dedicated to doing the best for each client. Quality work and helping clients meet their personal objectives set us apart," says Geof Greenleaf.

Besides trading in public stocks and bonds, Greenleaf offers a selection of products extending into private sector investments and ventures. "These added services attract clients who are looking for something a bit different from the typical investment firm," says Ted McMillan.

Not surprisingly, Greenleaf's partners spend a good bit of time out of the office, meeting with clients, listening to their needs and wants, and then acting accordingly. "Our clients value our experience and the fact that we know how to infiltrate the smoke screens that management and investor relations people frequently put up," says McMillan.

Depth of experience, commitment to forging lasting personal relationships and a wholistic approach to financial management make Greenleaf uniquely qualified to create and preserve wealth. By strengthening its clients, Greenleaf Capital Management helps fortify the already-vital Greater Cleveland community.

Sally Gries was destined to start and build Gries Financial LLC (GFL), the first and largest female-owned investment management firm in Ohio. An avid reader of the *Wall Street Journal* since her teen-age years, only a career in finance and investments would satisfy her. Thirty years ago, the male-dominated profession provided limited opportunity for women, so her first jobs were in bonds and backroom operations — firms discouraged women on the floor working with stocks. After 10 years Gries determined to start her own company. Two decades later Gries is the CEO of GFL, which has grown to 25 employees with expertise in comprehensive financial planning and investment management.

It was 1978 when Gries founded the firm to respond to the unmet needs of wealthy individuals for independent, fee-only financial and investment advice. One of her first clients was Richard B. Tullis, CEO of Harris Corporation, who grasped immediately the value of a totally objective, comprehensive financial advisory service. The firm grew quickly during the 1980s as client referrals and increasingly complex tax laws and investment products led to a heightened demand for GFL's expertise.

GFL offers a full spectrum of wealth management services to high-net-worth individuals and families. Its approach to managing finances is comprehensive. Clients trust the firm to be proactive and to bring a client's financial issues into focus by developing financial plans that integrate advice from all of the client's advisors so they can work together toward the same goals.

GFL expanded its investment management services to include larger institutions in 1994 when it was selected by Northern Trust Global Advisors to manage retirement funds for a large telecommunications corporation. It was one of only 19 firms chosen out of over 200 women and minority "emerging" money managers. Since then, institutional clients have grown as a result of superior performance and increased offerings.

GFL's mission is to have a positive impact on its clients' well-being. It is committed to excellence in its relationships with clients and in the performance it achieves for them. The firm invests heavily in experienced portfolio managers and analysts and uses state-of-the-art technology that adds an element of science to the art of investing.

Gries believes very strongly in community service and encourages this among all her employees. Each year the staff raises money for the American Cancer Society through its participation in the Relay for Life event. On various company anniversaries the firm planted trees in the city and dedicated and landscaped a city park. Gries serves on many boards of philanthropic institutions with special emphasis on Case Western Reserve University, Hawken School and the Holden Arboretum.

Many factors ensure GFL's continuing success. The demand for objective money management services is being fueled by a growing and older population and shifts in retirement law that place more responsibility on individuals for their financial security. People increasingly prefer investing to savings.

GFL plans to continue growing, responding to the needs of its clients and the Cleveland community. The firm's passion for helping clients meet their financial goals combined with its community involvement makes it stand out among its peers.

Pictured is the Management Committee at Gries Financial LLC: (left to right) Stewart L. Don Rice, executive vice president; Edward J. Bell, vice president; Paula S. Peck, vice president; Sally Gries, chairperson, president and CEO; Robert M. Leggett, chief investment officer; and Jeffrey H. Palmer, vice president.

Huntington Bank

The magnificent barreled-ceiling lobby of the Huntington Bancshares, Inc. Cleveland headquarters, hailed as a structure of major architectural significance, has overlooked nearly a century and a half of banking history in the city. Reputed to be the largest banking room in the country and perhaps the world, the building, constructed in 1924, originally housed the Union Trust Company.

Born of the merger of the Bank of Commerce (established in 1853 to serve the town's growing business community) and several major banking groups, Union Trust supported increased business growth in the city. The Depression era forced the closure of Union Trust, but from the financial wreckage rose the Union Bank of Commerce to help the Cleveland business community back to its feet. In 1954 the bank entered into retail banking and in 1957 changed its name to Union Commerce Bank.

It was both its strength and reputation that made the institution a prime merger target. In winter 1981 Huntington Bancshares, Inc. made an offer to buy controlling interest in Union Commerce. The Columbus, Ohio-based firm — the seventh-largest banking institution in the state — was trying to establish a strong competitive foothold in Cleveland. However, Union Commerce management ignored the offer. So Huntington changed its strategy in February of 1982 and took the offer directly to

Historic lobby of Huntington Bancshares, Inc. Cleveland headquarters.

the shareholders. In the end, the Columbus firm purchased Union Commerce for over $84 million in cash and stock, making Huntington Bancshares, Inc. the fourth-largest bank holding company in Ohio.

Huntington Bancshares, Inc. was founded in 1866 by P. W. Huntington and incorporated as The Huntington National Bank of Columbus in 1905. With a penchant for conservative business practices, the bank remained stable through hard economic times and in 1933, when all banks were closed for four days by government order, Huntington's stability allowed it to reopen within 10 days. In 1966 the institution was renamed Huntington Bancshares, Inc. and established as a holding company, one of only three in the state. At that time Ohio banks were only allowed to merge with other banks in their county and limited to combinations that would not reduce competition. However, bank holding companies could acquire banks anywhere.

In 1976 the Huntington Mortgage Company was formed, and in 1977 The Huntington Leasing Company was established. A change in Ohio's banking laws in 1979 allowed 15 banks to merge into one — The Huntington National Bank, with 97 offices across the state and assets of nearly $2.5 billion. In 1992 the bank brought technological banking to its customers through Direct Bank with personal bankers and 24-hour telephone access to account information. Nineteen ninety-four brought 24-hour access offices, and in 1996 Web Bank was introduced.

In addition to providing legendary service to its customers, Huntington is committed to improving the quality of life in each community. Through supporting numerous initiatives Huntington is able to benefit children, health, economic development, social services, housing, education and the arts. Organizations receiving financial support from Huntington gain both a partner and a friend. The Huntington also encourages employees to engage in philanthropic efforts and volunteer activities, which are taken into consideration during performance evaluations. Even as the company continues its second century of making banking history with recent acquisitions in Florida and Michigan, it will retain its traditions of customer-driven products, service and civic responsibility.

Maxus Investment Group
Fifth Third Bank Investment Advisors

For 27 years, the advisors of Maxus Investment Group have been looking for strong values — in the stock market and in their business. And for 27 years the company has found and delivered significant value to its clients. As a result, the Maxus Investment Group has become one of the region's leading investment advisors for both individuals and institutions. Its investment approach emphasizes asset value over earnings projections. This value approach has earned the firm a national reputation for quality management.

Maxus' success also earned the attention of Fifth Third Bank, one of the strongest banks in the country. Ranked by Salomon Smith Barney as the No. 1 Bank in the United States for the past nine years, Fifth Third Bank announced a plan in October 2000 to acquire Maxus. The purchase will add Maxus' prowess in investment management to Fifth Third's exceptional array of financial products and services.

"In joining forces with Fifth Third Bank, we will be able to grow our money management services through many new avenues," said Maxus Chief Executive Officer, Richard A. Barone. "Fifth Third will prove to be a great strategic partner for us."

In October 2000, Fifth Third Bank announced the acquisition of Maxus.

At present, individual and commercial clients have invested their trust and more than $2 billion in assets with Maxus. In return, the firm offers clients a comprehensive range of investment services including private portfolio management, online brokerage services and mutual funds.

Established in 1973 by Richard Barone, Maxus was founded to build wealth and security for an elite clientele through a uniquely successful value management style. Maxus began offering value management to a broader client base in 1985 when it introduced the first Maxus Fund (now the Maxus Income Fund). The company's vision for investing and unparalleled client service led the company to grow at a rapid pace.

A significant event in the history of Maxus was its merger with Gelfand Partners Asset Management, a $750-million investment firm. The combination of the two firms resulted in a company with a strong base of high net worth individual and institutional clients. By uniting the respective strengths of each firm, Maxus has been able to further grow their clients' wealth.

The Maxus Family of five mutual funds has received national recognition by offering a variety of niche, value-oriented funds that offer strong returns at low risk. The

Maxus Investment Group has become one of the region's leading investment advisors to both individuals and institutions. Its investment approach emphasizes asset value over earnings projections.

Maxus Income Fund concentrates on bonds and other debt securities. The Maxus Laureate Fund includes shares of other carefully selected mutual funds. The Maxus Ohio Heartland Fund focuses on small and medium-sized companies in Ohio. Its fifth fund, the Maxus Aggressive Value Fund, invests in smaller, undervalued companies. Over the years, Maxus Funds have become a significant portfolio piece for investors.

The goal of many financial advisors is to be able to offer a wide range of financial services to clients. As Maxus becomes a part of Fifth Third Bank Investment Advisors, the firm looks forward to achieving that goal and significantly expanding services. "Teaming up with Fifth Third will be a great service to our customers. Building on the strength of the bank will allow us to assist virtually any financial need our clients may have, whether it's finding a mortgage or retirement planning," said President and COO Fred D. DiSanto.

The Ohio Educational Credit Union

The school district cut its operating budget by $2 million. PTAs decried the overcrowded classrooms and urged greater pay for teachers. Banks were closing their doors, and two never reopened. Teachers were so concerned with the situation they formed the city's first teacher's union. It was 1933 and Cleveland and the nation were in the midst of the Great Depression.

Cleveland teachers took another major action that year when they got together to form The Cleveland Teachers Credit Union. The nonprofit group was created by teachers to help teachers during economic hard times.

One of Ohio's first credit unions, that initial group has grown in membership and geographic diversity. Today, known as The Ohio Educational Credit Union (OECU), it serves more than 540 organizations with 27,000 members. Its name also typifies its growth from its Cleveland birthplace. Although most of the organizations it represents are in northeast Ohio, it has 14 centers to serve its membership, as far away geographically as Zanesville in Muskingum County.

Another symbol of its growth is the organization's headquarters, completed in 1997. The 27,000-square-foot, three-story facility in downtown Cleveland is a far cry from the Cleveland Teachers Credit Union's first home in old Lincoln high school on the city's west side.

Even though membership has grown tremendously, the OECU's basic philosophy remains the same — to serve its members by establishing and enhancing their financial well-being. But those members are no longer only public school teachers. The credit union's charter allows it to provide financial services to any educational organization and its faculty, staff, students and their families. As a result, the membership roster represents a diverse group of organizations ranging from teaching hospitals to community colleges to private and public colleges and universities.

Because the OECU is a nonprofit, member-owned cooperative, it does not have to pay shareholders. Rather, its volunteer board of directors does everything possible to make certain that funds are used to provide as many member benefits as possible, whether they are higher savings rates, lower loan/lending rates or expanded services. And as the credit union's members have become more financially sophisticated, that range of services continually expands.

Today, known as The Ohio Educational Credit Union (OECU), it serves more than 540 organizations with 27,000 members.

According to Jerry Valco, the credit union's CEO, it's all part of that original philosophy of members helping members. He further points out that changing, competitive markets call for changing ideas, and as needs change, the OECU is constantly looking to change its portfolio of services to meet the changing needs of that market and of its members.

For several years The Ohio Educational Credit Union has been offering three $1,000 scholarships annually. Any credit union student member who meets certain academic criteria can apply, and a committee selects the recipients after careful consideration.

Another indication of the credit union's commitment to its members is its affiliation with American Share Insurance Corporation, which insures member's accounts to $250,000, compared to the government's $100,000 maximum.

It is another positive selling point for credit union membership, but since its inception in 1933, The Ohio Educational Credit Union (and its predecessors) has been selling itself very well by maintaining its basic philosophy of mutual assistance.

This 27,000-square foot, three-story OECU downtown headquarters is a far cry from the original Cleveland Teacher's Credit Union's first home in a high school.

The first lotteries were created by the Roman emperors. It took Ohio a great deal longer to hop on the bandwagon.

It was not until 1973 that Ohio voters, by a 3-to-1 margin, passed a constitutional amendment authorizing the state to conduct such an activity. The force behind the concept of the lottery and legislation that required the issue to be placed on the ballot was State Senator Ron Mottl. Although many reasons have been advanced for passage, among the more universally accepted is the fact that neighboring Michigan and Pennsylvania had lotteries and were siphoning off Ohio dollars.

Issue One, as it was known, was promoted as a means of generating additional revenues that could be used for keeping taxes down and helping Ohio's public schools, among other uses.

The original legislation called for the governor to appoint five commissioners to run the agency. Lottery management was reorganized in 1980, with a director given authority over daily operations. The commission itself was expanded to nine members, and its role changed to one of advice and consent.

In 1983 the Ohio legislature earmarked lottery profits for education. Voter approval of a constitutional amendment in 1987 made the legislative action permanent.

As the lottery's role was changing, so too were the games being played.

The first game, Buckeye 300, was a weekly 50-cent game. In 1974 the first millionaire drawing was held. These were passive games with numbers

preprinted on each ticket; players compared their numbers with those drawn. In 1976 Ohio Instant Lottery became the state's first instant game offered. Because of limited technology, redeemed tickets were hand counted by the

The largest payoff was a $50 million Super Lotto prize.

Lottery staff and more than 9,000 agents had to hand count the number and prize amounts for each winning ticket sold at their store.

A computerized instant-gaming system was brought into play in the 1980s, providing greater accountability and allowing for a steady increase in the number of instant games that could be sold. Now, up to 40 instant games are in play at any one time, ranging in cost from $1 to $10 specialty games.

As the price of playing has gone up, so too have the rewards. The largest payoff was a $50 million Super Lotto prize. Consumer interest has been regularly piqued with "Cash Explosion Double Play," a weekly television show that began in 1987 and normally has the No. 1 rating in its time slot.

Technology played an important part in enhancing Lottery games in the 1980s. State legislators are considering new concepts that are becoming popular due to technological advances.

In the future, it may be a case of "it's not whether you win or lose, it's how you play the game."

Shaker Investments

"Our goal is to be best at what we're doing," says Edward Hemmelgarn, founder, president and CEO of Shaker Investments. "That is important to us and important for Cleveland. We like Cleveland very much; it's a great place to do business."

Consistently ranked by performance in the top 2 to 3 percent of all U.S. investment management firms by Nelson Information, Shaker Investments provides investment management services to institutions and high-net-worth investors. The company's investment philosophy takes advantage of the stock market's inefficiency in valuing growth companies to buy superior companies at bargain prices. The strategy appears to be working well, as the firm currently manages $1 billion in assets, representing more than 1,000-fold growth since its inception in 1991.

Hemmelgarn's fascination with investment management is a direct consequence of his own personal investment efforts during the 1980s. In 1991 he started Shaker Investments and began to manage investments for others, beginning with family and friends. Believing that prospects were better off as clients, he began spreading the word on his investment strategies and results. Assets grew and David Webb, an investment manager formerly with Primus Venture Partners, joined the firm In December 1993. By early 1994 assets under management had increased six-fold and Adam Saloman, formerly of E.M. Warburg Pincus, came on board that October. Staffing and administration then became an issue and Karen Gilmore joined the firm in November 1994.

A former financial officer with Ameritrust Bank and consultant with Ernst & Young, Hemmelgarn is not one to measure success exclusively in terms of money. He is extremely proud of the team he and his partners have built. "Our assets walk out of the door every night," he says. Surprisingly, the members of his corps of 27 professionals do not all hail from the financial management arena. Some have expertise in genetics, biotechnology and engineering and learn the ins and outs of investment management on the job.

Hemmelgarn's entrepreneurial outlook has made the company extremely proactive in its dealings with clients. The firm takes pride in making money for clients and providing a high level of personalized service. Clients receive reports on a quarterly basis, while individual communications requests are handled immediately. The company tends to avoid reports written in complicated financial terms. "There shouldn't have to be any prior knowledge," says Hemmelgarn. "When a client looks at that piece of paper, they should be able to find out what's happened. They shouldn't have to put information together from 18 different sources." Representatives at Shaker Investments make themselves available to talk any time a client feels the need, and they meet at least once a year with those clients who want it on a regular basis.

Although a significant amount of the assets managed by Shaker Investments comes from outside Cleveland, the company has no intention of moving its base of operations to another location. It takes pride in contributing to this community and its people. "Although Cleveland is not thought of as one of the investment capitals of the world," says Hemmelgarn, "based on what we've done, Cleveland is becoming one of the investment hotspots."

The three principals of Shaker Investments are (left to right) Adam Saloman, David Webb and Edward Hemmelgarn.

EDUCATION

Cleveland libraries and educational institutions, and businesses that support them, provide citizens of all ages with learning opportunities in diverse subjects and environments.

John Carroll University

John Carroll University (JCU) began its history as St. Ignatius College, a small school founded near the west bank of the Cuyahoga River by German Jesuit missionaries in 1886. In the years that have unfolded since its creation, John Carroll changed its name, moved to University Heights (1935), and grew to be one of the Midwest's finest comprehensive regional centers of higher learning. Today, the university's undergraduate programs, which are solidly grounded in the liberal arts, serve 3,500 women and men in the College of Arts & Sciences and the John M. and Mary Jo Boler School of Business, giving JCU the largest undergraduate enrollment of any of northern Ohio's private universities. The institution named for America's first Catholic bishop also prepares nearly 1,000 students annually for master's degrees in business, education and other disciplines of Arts and Sciences.

John Carroll has experienced enormous changes since it came to life in a wooden schoolhouse in 1886. The present neo-Gothic campus on 60 pastoral acres began taking shape in the depths of the Great Depression. The Boler School of Business, which is highly regarded for its programs in areas such as accountancy, logistics and finance, was founded in 1945. Enrollment rose rapidly after World War II. Coeducation at the undergraduate level arrived in 1968, the same year that governance of the institution, previously held by the Society of Jesus, was given to a primarily lay board of trustees.

Amidst change, John Carroll's mission has been constant: the university exists to prepare young women and men for service to others and leadership in society. *Men and Women for Others* is the central principle of Jesuit education, a system which arose from St. Ignatius of Loyola's divine imagination and practical vision 450 years ago. It is now viewed as one of the world's finest educational traditions. Jesuit colleges and universities operate in 38 nations today and number 138 institutions in all. In the United States, there are 28 Jesuit schools, ranging from large comprehensive institutions such as Georgetown, Fordham and Boston College to small liberal arts colleges like Massachusetts' College of the Holy Cross and Alabama's Spring Hill.

Steady refinement of the university's distinctive core curriculum has been an ongoing process; adjustments were made to the core at several points in the university's

history, so that John Carroll's students continue today to receive the elements of a classical liberal education, even as they gain the specialized training essential for professional career paths. The core curriculum, which supports students in a quest to think critically, communicate effectively and act ethically, is at the heart of a John Carroll education. The university embraces the intention of educating the whole person and giving young women and men the tools needed for the challenges and opportunities encountered in careers, civic pursuits and relationships. An indispensable aspect of that preparation is training in understanding and appreciating the complexities of the student's own heart and soul.

A university's graduates are the best testament to its quality, and John Carroll is proud of the men and women who have carried the institution's diploma into the world. Alumni such as Tim Russert of "Meet the Press"; Don Shula of the NFL Hall of Fame; the late Anthony Celebrezze, Cleveland mayor and secretary of the U.S. Department of Health Education and Welfare; Cleveland's Bishop Anthony Pilla; astronaut Carl Walz; Kate O'Neill, Federal Reserve vice president; Sherwin Williams CEO Jack Breen; Cablevision CEO Charles Dolan; John Boler, CEO of the Boler Company; and Mary Ann Corrigan-Davis, senior vice president of American Greetings Corporation are only a few examples of the host of American leaders who were formed at the university in University Heights.

Rev. Edward Glynn, SJ, John Carroll's president as the university moves into the 21st century, is fond of saying that, "Institutions shape society and individuals shape institutions." Cleveland's Jesuit university has long been committed to shaping skilled, engaged and ethical women and men who graduate and go on to have a positive impact on every dimension of our society.

At the turn of the millennium, the members of the John Carroll community are gratified that the university has been experiencing its highest enrollments in recent years; that endowment has been rising steadily; and that JCU has successfully completed major construction projects and technological upgrades over the past decade. Recently established university components such as the Edward M. Muldoon Center for Entrepreneurship and the Institute for Catholic Studies are extending the range of John Carroll's scholarship in new directions. The university will soon begin construction of the $60 million Dolan Center for Science and Technology, which will advance John Carroll's leadership in undergraduate research and pre-professional education. That center, which will also be the locus of new efforts to improve science and mathematics education in northern Ohio's elementary and secondary schools, will be the clearest testimony yet of John Carroll's resolve to continue being one of the region's premier universities and a higher education model of service to the community.

Cleveland Public Library

On February 17th, 1869, the Cleveland Public Library opened in a small room on the 3rd floor of a building on Superior Avenue, near where the parking garage of the Renaissance Cleveland Hotel now stands.

Though it was hugely popular with the public — during its first year citizens checked out the library's 5,800 books more than 65,000 times — the library's fate was uncertain. It moved 3 times during its first 15 years, and due to the micromanagement of the businessmen appointed to oversee it by the board of education, its first two directors resigned.

The library finally gained the autonomy and leadership it needed to fulfill its destiny in 1884. It was in that year that John G. White, the library's greatest benefactor, joined the board. In May 1884, under White's leadership, the board made a historic decision when it hired William Howard Brett to direct the library. During his 34 years as librarian, Brett instituted revolutionary changes at the library, and he also shaped the library profession through the school of library science he helped found in 1904 at what is now Case Western Reserve University.

In 1890 Brett's groundbreaking "open shelf" policy turned standard library wisdom on its head. Books locked away behind glass doors was the norm in the nation's libraries. Trust patrons to choose their own books, he said, and they will honor your trust.

In the early 1890s he began growing branches. Some were stations in neighborhood schools or fire stations or factories; others, including Carnegie West, the system's oldest and largest branch, were stand-alone facilities built with money donated by steel magnate Andrew Carnegie. In 1898 he opened the library's first separate reading room exclusively for children, a novel concept for the time. By 1918, when Brett was struck by a car and killed, the library had the highest circulation of any metropolitan library in the nation, and it served patrons through 648 community agencies. Brett had realized his vision of the library as "The People's University" and was lauded as a great educator in memorial tributes.

Linda Eastman, Brett's successor, piled on more milestones. As assistant director, Eastman had initiated many new programs and services, including service to the blind and physically handicapped in 1903. As director she oversaw the construction and opening in 1925 of the magnificent beaux arts Main Library. Then, with little money, she navigated the library safely through the darkest days of the Great Depression, when library use reached record highs. To improve service to children, she sent the "Book Caravan" — a specially outfitted truck filled with books and materials for children — out into Cleveland's neighborhoods on a regular basis. This mobile outreach program grew to include scheduled visits to hospitals, nursing homes, shut-ins and jails.

Due to many factors, including decreasing funding and the migration out of Cleveland that took place following World War II, the system was essentially at a standstill by 1974 when Ervin J. Gaines became director. A pragmatist, he eliminated many programs that were not cost-efficient and began a levy-financed capital-improvements program that built new branches and/or renovated and modernized old ones throughout the city. Gaines brought the library squarely into the world of computers, automating the extensive card catalog and in 1982 founding CLEVNET, the visionary electronic consortium that now contains the

Personal computers in children's areas feature an exciting array of age-appropriate educational software.
©1999 Photo by Eric Hanson Cleveland Public Library Archives

holdings of more than two dozen library systems throughout Northern Ohio.

When Marilyn Gell Mason became director in 1988, she built on the foundation of community goodwill Gaines had laid. She instituted groundbreaking technological changes that made the Cleveland Public Library among the first in the nation to offer its patrons free dial-up access to the library's online catalog and electronic databases. Mason's greatest contribution to Cleveland was the modernization of Main Library by completely renovating the Main Building and constructing the architecturally inspired Louis Stokes Wing. Under her leadership, the library also constructed the Lake Shore Facility, and the Langston Hughes and Memorial-Nottingham branches. Today, the Cleveland Public Library has more branches for its population size than any urban library in the nation.

When Andrew A. Venable, Jr., became director in 1999, he inherited a system with a $56 million annual budget and state-of-the-art main and branch libraries. Its collections — everything from rare books to computer software — make the library one of the best and largest public research libraries in the United States. It has a two-fold mission: "To reinvigorate community use of the branch libraries — especially use by children — while at the same time maintaining our competitive edge both locally and nationally."

To do both, the system has expanded to 15 branches the Family Learning Connection Program, whose parent-child workshops, programs and story hours enable parents and children to connect with books and each other. It has increased the number of computers available at the Main Library and branches and redesigned the system's Internet site to make access easier. It has extended services for the blind from the Memorial-Nottingham Branch to five other branches. It has partnered with the Cuyahoga County Public Library to create the Greater Access Card, a dual-system library card, and works with local institutions with similar goals — especially the city's school system — to increase library use. "Our library card sign-up program with the school district has introduced more than 25,000 youth to the system since 1999," says Venable.

Under Venable's watch, the library has increased its visibility in the national news media, published a quarterly community newsletter, *Speaking Volumes*, and brought together a neighborhood library services advisory panel.

Venable has also increased the library's presence as a repository for and preserver of the city's history and directed a Holiday Staff Chorus. By opening up the library system's meeting rooms to community groups, he has positioned the library to be the city's civic forum. "We are a neutral place," says Venable, " where people can come to read and hear all sides of an issue."

And as it did over half-a-century ago, the library has rolled out of its buildings and into Cleveland's neighborhoods with a brightly colored library-on-wheels bus. "It has everything a branch has — librarians, 2,000 to 3,000 books, computers and Internet access," says Venable, "but it's meeting people where they are in the community, not where our branches are."

From a one-room library with all its books behind locked glass doors to an open-access, electronic system with a block-long main library, 28 state-of-the-art branches and over 10 million items, the Cleveland Public Library is truly "The People's University."

Cleveland State University

Both in physical presence and in educational and economic impact, Cleveland State is Cleveland's university. It provides a high-quality education to students of diverse backgrounds, an education that is broad-based and adaptable to the continually unfolding demands of a global marketplace, an education that equips a student with the knowledge and experience to move from one specialized career to another during a working lifetime.

Cleveland State University is tied closely to the city in a manner that is mutually advantageous. Approximately 85 percent of alumni remain in the metropolitan area to work, raise their families and contribute to the overall economy. The university is sensitive and responsive to the urban community's needs and continues to produce the professional work force that is part of the industrial mainstay of Northeastern Ohio business. Many of the university's programs are tailored to this goal.

An acclaimed example is the Advanced Manufacturing Center of the Fenn College of Engineering. The center benefits both local manufacturers and students who, in conjunction with faculty and staff engineers, have the opportunity to use their classroom theoretical learning to solve specific challenges found in industrial situations.

Located in downtown Cleveland, Cleveland State University is convenient for working and commuting students.

In recognition of its successful strategy for teaching within a community partnership, the AMC was awarded a National Science Foundation grant to help other universities devise comparable facilities.

In its expressed desire to be a leader and catalyst for positive change in Northeast Ohio, Cleveland State University has extended its resources beyond the campus and formed collaborative relationships with local businesses, educational and social service agencies, metropolitan development groups, and international institutions. The university has more than 100 partnerships through which to channel its expertise in the identification, examination and resolution of issues benefiting the community. One of the most eminent is the Cooperative Education Program, one of the largest in the country. Each year more than 300 employers are involved in Co-op and more than 2,200 students learn to apply their newly acquired knowledge to tangible concerns outside the academic environment and earn money while doing so.

Utilizing sophisticated technology, Cleveland State is extending its academic expertise through distance learning. Several years ago, the university undertook a $17 million upgrade of its technological capabilities in order to develop new instructional delivery systems where none existed before so that more Clevelanders could avail themselves of educational advances. The Council on Social Work Education has granted accreditation to a joint program between the Cleveland State College of Arts and Sciences and the University of Akron that offers a Master of Social Work degree. This is the first of its kind in the country that is both totally available through distance learning and also fully accredited.

Continuing the legacy of Fenn College, Cleveland State University is affordable and accessible to the majority of prospective students from the community. Photograph by Hastings-Willinger & Associates. University Archives

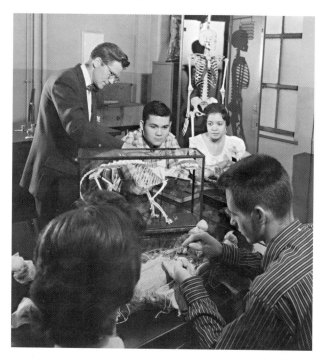

The Maxine Goodman Levin College of Urban Affairs ranks among the top 10 in the country. Its city management/urban policy specialization, which trains people for positions in city planning, government, and public service, has been rated second in the nation by *U.S. News and World Report*.

The Cleveland-Marshall College of Law boasts an expansive new library that is a top-quality resource for the legal and judicial sector of the area. By combining law with other specific disciplines, Cleveland-Marshall offers students unique programs coupled with field experience that prepare them to eventually serve as public defenders, prosecutors and judges, and other leadership positions.

Not only does Cleveland State excel in academic innovation and learning partnerships, it also engages the community in other, more cultural, endeavors. One is the Cleveland Chamber Symphony Orchestra, known for being a showcase for new works by contemporary American classical composers. For nearly 40 years, the Cleveland State University Poetry Center has spread awareness of and support for contemporary poetry through workshops and the publication of poetry collections, more than 130 of which have been in national distribution.

The ability to evolve its educational mission is part of Cleveland State's history, which can be traced to the 1870s when the YMCA began offering adult education classes in the downtown neighborhood where the university is currently located. Increased programming led to the formation in 1923 of Fenn College, a nonprofit institution of higher education. By 1964 Fenn encompassed three buildings on a 4.5-acre campus, which was the infrastructure that became Cleveland State University when it received its state charter.

At this time, the university had three undergraduate colleges — Arts and Sciences, Business Administration and Engineering, which adopted the historically significant name Fenn College of Engineering. Soon other colleges were added: Education, Graduate Studies and Urban Affairs. Cleveland-Marshall School of Law merged with Cleveland State in 1969. Today, these seven colleges serve a student body of 16,300; undergraduate, master's and doctoral-level degrees number 117. The campus has grown to include 40 buildings on 82 acres in the center of Cleveland.

As a testimonial to its leadership status, Cleveland State University has a major role in the city's Mid-Town Corridor project, a revitalization initiative stretching from downtown east along Euclid Avenue to University Circle, home of several museums, health care facilities, and other educational institutions. The keystone structure connecting the campus to the Playhouse Square district and the center of downtown is the new College of Urban Affairs building, which features a tree- and shrub-landscaped courtyard as a prominent gateway into the campus. In keeping with the university's objective of urban support, the building houses a Civic Forum for public debate on significant community issues.

Cleveland State University continues to make itself a vital and eminent part of Northeast Ohio because it has applied its distinguished academic instruction and research capabilities to authentic community and business needs. It succeeds notably in graduating well-trained, job-ready professionals who are dedicated to the region and become constructive participants in the community, helping to stimulate economic activity and contributing their talents and consciousness to addressing societal concerns.

Corporations throughout Northeast Ohio look to Cleveland State University for their professional work force.

Cleveland State University attracts students of all ages and backgrounds.

Cuyahoga County Public Library

Information. Education. Inspiration. Enrichment. Entertainment. Service. These six words sum up the mission of Cuyahoga County Public Library. It's a mission that has made the 28-branch library one of the premier library systems in Ohio and the eighth-busiest library in the United States. It circulates around 12 million items each year to the 600,000-plus residents in 47 Cuyahoga County communities. It's a mission that has also elevated the system, which has a $49.8 million budget and the highest per-capita circulation of any of the nation's top 10 libraries.

Established in the fall of 1922 by a countywide vote of residents who were not already served by an established library, the Cuyahoga County Public Library opened in 1923. Soon it was serving book-starved communities — Chagrin Falls, Brecksville, Berea and Bedford joined the system immediately — out of basement offices it rented from the very supportive Cleveland Public Library. Despite the fact that it was run from center-city Cleveland; circulated most of its materials from "book cars" or at "stations" set up in school classrooms, town hall meeting rooms or local stores; and saw its funding shrink dramatically due to the Depression, the county library experienced steady growth during its early years. In 1942 it outgrew its basement

In 1991 Cuyahoga County Public Library moved its administrative offices to Parma. This central location makes it efficient to deliver materials to its 28 branches six days a week.
Photo by George Shuba, Shuba & Associates Photography

quarters at the Cleveland Public Library and moved to the first of two buildings — still in Cleveland — that it occupied before finally moving into its current 101,000-square-foot administrative office building in Parma, the largest community it serves, in 1991.

From the early-50s through the late-70s, Cuyahoga County Public Library experienced such explosive growth — 20 new branches were added to the system — that it became the third-largest library system in the state. During this period — when the system served an all-time high of 54 communities — it developed the policy now used to grow branches. "If a community wants a library today, it has to commit to providing a building. Then we will come in and staff it, stock it and maintain it," explains librarian John Lonsak, the system's current executive director.

Since the early 80s, with its building boom behind it and with good state funding and excellent local support — county voters have approved every operating levy put before them every five years since 1974 — the county library has been operating as a mature system. Maturity has allowed the system to focus on collections, especially its non-print media and foreign-language collections, and to broaden and strengthen the research collections at the system's four regional libraries. Today, 18 percent of the county library system's budget is devoted to this task.

Maturity has also allowed the system to focus on staff development — the library actively recruits and retains enthusiastic, creative, customer service-oriented people — and to increase its services and programs. Serving the needs of children and young adults has always been a Cuyahoga County Public Library priority, so branches have historically had large and specially staffed children's sections, story hours and summer reading programs. To these have been added a toy library, a groundbreaking parent-child program that promotes child safety on the Internet, programs that help parents select age-appropriate reading materials for their children and Project LEAP, a reading-readiness program for day-care providers.

In addition to these library-based programs, the library promotes its Young Adult resources with librarians who constantly update "how-to" guides on everything from researching term papers to surviving being a teen-ager (or a teen-ager's parent). Recognizing the need for a service that could help overworked school librarians, concerned teachers and home schoolers evaluate and select reading and instructional materials, the system also provides a monthly "best of" new books and materials program. This unique service is open to all public and school librarians.

Adults and seniors have always enjoyed one-on-one service; timely interlibrary transfers; book discussion programs; a wide array of services for people with special visual or hearing needs or those who are home- or hospital-bound; and free use of the system's meeting rooms for civic, educational, and cultural programs and activities. These services have been augmented with nationally recognized programs such as InfoPLACE, which offers career counseling and adult education information; DIAL-LAW, which offers free dial-up legal information to the public; and hands-on computer orientation programs that put even the most computer-shy patron on the electronic superhighway in record time. Recently initiated collaborative programs with local institutions with similar cultural or educational goals such as The Cleveland Play House, The Cleveland Museum of Art and the Cleveland Museum of Natural History have led to programs and activities, both inside and outside the system, that extend the library's impact and mission far beyond the boundaries of Cuyahoga County.

Few of these services and programs would be possible without the library's commitment — over 12 percent of its budget — to state-of-the-art technology. Administrative operations and customer services are faster, more efficient and less costly due to the 1,050 computers Cuyahoga County Library has installed to do everything from track book transfers to provide customers access to the Internet and the system's many online catalogs, electronic subscription databases and indexes. The colorful dual-system library card developed with The Cleveland Public Library has made access to both systems' resources faster.

The maturity Cuyahoga County Public Library is enjoying hasn't just positioned the system to meet customer and community needs, it has positioned the library to strategically plan for them, too. Based on demographic trends and economic forecasts, plans to increase funding for senior services and electronic/digital media are moving forward. Plans have also been set in motion to grow community and customer involvement with systemwide planned-giving programs and ownership programs focused on the Friends of the Library groups. Capital expansion plans — for several branches and the administrative complex — are being critically examined.

Current library leadership is also laying groundwork for the library system of the future: "Someday," predicts Executive Director Lonsak, "we will be wireless and everything will be hand-held."

On that not-too-distant day, the Cuyahoga County Public Library will still be walking the path county residents set it upon in 1922 when they overwhelmingly voted to: "...provide our communities free and open access to information giving every person the opportunity for enrichment, inspiration, and entertainment."

The new Fairview Park Regional Library opened in 1997. A state-of-the-art facility, it features specialized collections and services in the areas of history, genealogy, travel and biography. *Photo by George Shuba, Shuba & Associates Photography*

Computers play a role in every facet of library operation. Internet access and online databases are available to the public. Here, two youngsters sit at a CD-ROM workstation to listen and learn.

Ursuline College

To a first-time visitor, Ursuline College is a lovely surprise. Situated on 115 rolling acres, the college campus is tucked away in a peaceful, pastoral setting — yet it is just minutes from a major interstate, bustling shopping district and upscale residential area.

Ursuline College is a Catholic liberal arts college located 13 miles east of Cleveland in picturesque Pepper Pike. Most of its 1,300 students are from the Cleveland area. Indeed, most of them commute. Although it is primarily a women's college, about 6 percent of Ursuline students are men. Nearly 20 percent of its students are minorities. Almost half of the students are over age 22, and within that group the median age is about 37.

Ursuline offers more than 30 undergraduate majors and five graduate programs. Education, nursing and business attract the largest number of students, with many enrolled in Ursuline's Saturday School Program and the recently established Ursuline College Accelerated Program (UCAP). UCAP graduates earn a business management degree after successfully completing a series of evening courses over nine consecutive five-week terms.

Ursuline College's beautiful 115-acre campus, located just 20 minutes from downtown Cleveland, attracts students, alumnae and friends to make up a vibrant learning community. The Grace Residence Hall is in the background.

A student-to-faculty ratio of 14-to-1 means Ursuline classes are small and students are known as individuals, rather than names and numbers. Ursuline students are taught by more than 70 full-time faculty and several adjunct instructors whose real-world experiences provide students with valuable industry contacts and opportunities outside the traditional classroom.

The history of Ursuline College has its roots in the history of the Diocese of Cleveland. In 1850 Amadeus Rappe, first bishop of the then recently created Catholic Diocese of Cleveland, sent an urgent request to friends in his native France. Bishop Rappe desperately needed volunteers from the Ursuline Sisters at Boulogne-sur-Mer to start a school for the children of immigrants settling in the diocese. Four Ursuline Sisters and a laywoman packed their bags and set sail for Cleveland: Sisters Mary Beaumont, Victoire Boudalier, Sylvia Picquet, Theresa Young and Arabella Seymour, who later became an Ursuline nun. Three weeks after their arrival, the volunteers welcomed about 300 girls at their newly established Ursuline Academy.

The academy and surrounding community grew rapidly. The Ursulines subsequently established several more parochial grade schools and high schools for girls. In 1871, recognizing the need for higher education for women, Mother Mary of the Annunciation Beaumont (Mary Beaumont) founded Ursuline College. It is the first chartered college for women in Ohio and one of the oldest Catholic women's colleges in the country.

The school has known five locations since it was founded: at East 6th and Euclid Avenue in the first convent for Ursuline Sisters; at the corner of Willson (now East 55th) and Scovill Avenues; in University Circle, next to Severance Hall, in a building that later became Hitchcock Hall at Case Western Reserve University; at the top of Cedar Hill on Overlook Road in two mansions; and its current suburban campus, which opened in 1966 to accommodate Ursuline's steadily increasing enrollment.

By 1970 that increasing enrollment included more nontraditional students. Ursuline saw the need for, and became, the first college in the Cleveland area to establish a continuing education program. Similarly, in 1974 Ursuline was the first college in northern Ohio to establish

off-campus credit accumulation options toward a baccalaureate degree.

Perhaps one of Ursuline's biggest milestones was its 1975 merger with the St. John College nursing program. Ursuline's decision salvaged the only Catholic Bachelor of Science in Nursing (BSN) program in the area, as St. John was closing its doors. Within a few years, Ursuline stretched its wings even more when it developed an RN-BSN track in the nursing program with the same curriculum. This was in direct response to requests from area registered nurses — male and female alike.

Educating future educators is another Ursuline specialty. This strength was underscored in 1981 when Ursuline College was accredited to offer its first graduate program with a specialty in non-public school administration. Since then Ursuline has added graduate programs in nursing, ministry, education and art therapy.

At the root of all Ursuline programs is a strong foundation in the liberal arts. The school's own mission truly says it best: "In the liberal arts tradition, an Ursuline education emphasizes critical thinking; clear and graceful expression; free, mature judgment and choice; and commitment to continued learning ... Acknowledging that the liberal arts are life arts, we help students search for wisdom within the context of theology and philosophy, the fine arts and humanities, the natural and physical sciences."

In the early 1990s Ursuline launched a new core curriculum called the Ursuline Studies Program. Based on research about models of women's learning, it remains the only curriculum of its kind in the country.

The Ursuline Studies Program is composed of five semester-long seminars and 10 courses from various departments, distributed over a student's college career. Teaching methods encourage students to relate what they learn in class to life beyond campus and to make connections between their personal experiences and those of their classmates. Students work in small collaborative groups where they feel free to speak; professors serve more as facilitators and less as authority figures. Ultimately, the curriculum seeks to help Ursuline students find their voice, make decisions based on values and take responsibility for society.

In the bigger picture, Ursuline is widely acclaimed as a valued community resource. The school opens many of its programs and facilities — including lectures, fitness facilities, an art gallery, library and chapel — to the public, often at little or no cost. But Ursuline's greatest resource is its graduates. Ninety percent of nursing graduates and more than 80 percent of all graduates remain to heal, teach and work in the Cleveland area.

Ursuline has distinguished itself in many ways over the years. The new century promises many more firsts. A new sports program includes Ursuline's entry into the National Association of Intercollegiate Athletics Division II volleyball, basketball and golf. New construction includes a student learning center and major campuswide renovation. Goals include increasing the geographic diversity of students, increasing the use of distance learning via the Internet and other technologies, and to increase collaborative efforts with other area colleges and organizations.

Throughout its history, Ursuline has remained true to its founding premise: leadership in the higher education of women. As it looks to the future, Ursuline will strive to remain at the forefront of women's education.

Ursuline College is student-focused, preparing its graduates to be leaders in their families, community and professions.

Ursuline College is well positioned to remain at the forefront of technology with a fully wired campus, computer labs throughout the college and a commitment to ensuring that every student is prepared for the high-tech world that awaits.

Cuyahoga Community College

Cuyahoga Community College (CCC) opened its doors to over 3,000 students on September 23, 1963, the largest first-day enrollment of any two-year college in the nation. The school serves as a vital resource to the economic health and stability of the Northeastern Ohio region and has established education and training partnerships with the community's public and private sectors. The publicly supported institution serves over 55,000 students each year, and over 500,000 Cuyahoga county residents have passed through CCC's doors. One of the top 10 community colleges in the nation, the college offers certificate programs, the associate's degree and the first two years of the baccalaureate degree. The curriculum includes nearly 900 credit courses in 70 career and technical programs and the liberal arts at its three campuses, through television and the Internet, and at more than 50 off-campus sites.

When classes began in the old Brownell Junior High School building, the school offered a curriculum of traditional university parallel programs along with business, vocational and technical programs. During its second year, CCC created 16 associate's degree programs in engineering, health sciences, industrial supervision and law enforcement. Enthusiastically supported by local tax levies, the school continued to expand as enrollment quickly grew, and by spring 1966, the opening of a second westside campus in Parma, on the site of the old Crile Veterans Hospital, was announced.

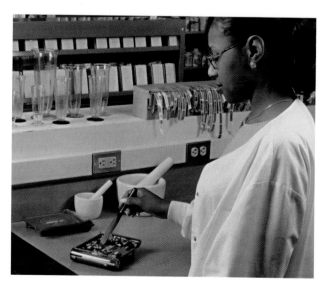

Responding to the need for more space, CCC moved to its permanent, 40-acre Metropolitan Campus in 1968. On October 13, 1971, the brand-new Eastern Campus opened its doors to students in Highland Heights. Two years later came the opening of the school's new administrative offices on Carnegie Avenue, and in 1975 the rebuilt and expanded Western Campus facility opened its doors. That year also brought administrative changes as CCC moved toward a more unified and comprehensive college structure. In 1979, as an offshoot of its new Cultural Arts program, CCC held the first of its now nationally renowned jazz festivals, the Tri-C Jazz Fest.

The college was in the forefront of the movement to retrain the country's work force during the hard economic times of the late 1970s and 1980s. This involvement led directly to the establishment of the Unified Technologies Center on the Metropolitan Campus and to a major technological upgrade of the school's computer system across all three campuses. In 1999 CCC dedicated its new classrooms, theater and conference center at the Eastern Campus, located in the heart of the Chagrin Highlands Project, a world-class corporate community. The new facility is uniquely positioned to provide training, education and conference facilities for the area's growing business population.

Through the years, CCC has taken the lead in work force training for northeastern Ohio, making it a national model. Cutting-edge programming using information technology like television and the Internet, non-credit professional development classes and independent learning are just some of the reasons why CCC truly is the place "where futures begin."

East Cleveland Public Library

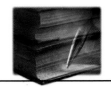

Amidst the high-tech businesses, family-owned storefronts and restaurants along Euclid Avenue stands the East Cleveland Public Library, a fortress built in the classic Dutch Renaissance Carnegie style, a beacon to enlightenment, a bridge to countless possibilities. For the past 84 years the library has met the community's educational and cultural needs.

Built in 1916, the East Cleveland Public Library helped immigrants learn English and generations of school children discover the joy of reading. Today, the library has broadened its resources to include CD-ROMs and videos.

Over the past 10 years, East Cleveland has had little community-based support. The library has filled the gap, offering adult literacy education, a math and science enrichment center, one-on-one tutoring, computer classes, educational social awareness and self-improvement programs for young adults. The library also hosts preschool story hours, summer reading programs for younger children, outreach programs at adult day care centers, book deliveries to shut-ins, and job and career resources. All of these services are free.

Much of the East Cleveland Public Library's success can be attributed to visionary and supportive board members, a dedicated staff and its director, Gregory L. Reese, an innovative planner committed to preserving its tradition as well as meeting the community's growing needs. Named director in 1988, Reese revitalized the library with innovative programming such as its Sunday Jazz series and its popular "Write On, Cleveland!" seminars, drawing visitors from all over Northeast Ohio and Pennsylvania. Guest authors host the weekly filled-to-capacity seminars, sharing secrets of the trade with eager listeners.

"We respond to the informational needs of the community for education as well as entertainment," Reese says. "We've done such a great job for so long, we've run out of space."

In 1991 the main library underwent a $1.4 million renovation. In 2000 the library launched a $4 million fund-raising drive to build a 20,000-square-foot addition to the west wing to include a reading gallery, a 250-seat auditorium, a black heritage room, a media center, a math and science center, a computer lab and a children's center.

The Regional Transit Authority gave the East Cleveland Public Library the chance to grow by donating land adjacent to the library. Unlike similar projects in other cities, the board of trustees decided not to overburden the citizens of East Cleveland with another levy.

Instead, the library board contacted Greater Cleveland foundations and corporations for donations. The George Gund Foundation kicked off the private donations with an offer of a $250,000 grant to underwrite the cost of a fund-raising consultant and additional campaign expenses.

The East Cleveland
Public Library
©1992 Peter Renerts Studio

Recognizing the importance of the East Cleveland Public Library to the broader community, the Cleveland Foundation stepped up to the plate with $1 million for the expansion. Turner Construction Co., The Cleveland Clinic and other foundations also contributed to its success.

"We couldn't have done this without the support of our board of trustees," Reese says.

Reese, the East Cleveland Public Library board of trustees and the 50-member staff were gratified by the support from the foundations and public sector and look forward to a grand opening in Fall 2001.

Hiram College

When a youthful James A. Garfield, later the country's 20th president, first glimpsed the school that would become Hiram College in the fall of 1851, he was eager to continue his education. But he could not have been impressed with the campus that comprised, according to one observer, no more than a "cornfield with a solid plain brick building in the centre of it."

The Western Reserve Eclectic Institute opened November 27, 1850, a year after a group of men, Disciples of Christ churchmen, had responded to the crying need for schools and teachers in the growing settlements in what were at the time the Western states. When the doors opened, the school was not prepared for the crush of students who enrolled. By 1852, 529 students enrolled, a number not exceeded until after World War II. Most came from Ohio. But Disciple families from as far away as Georgia, Vermont, Wisconsin and Canada all wanted their children to have a proper education.

The influx of students strained the rural community's ability to house several hundred who did not live at home. Eventually, all found adequate, if crowded, accommodations, some paying an exorbitant $1.50 a week for room and board. While any school would be proud simply to have a U.S. president among its alumni, Garfield returned to Hiram as a teacher in 1857. A year

Gerstacker Science Hall is the newest addition to Hiram College's campus. The $6.2 million building offers state-of-the-art facilities to students studying the sciences.
Photo by Ken Love

Old Main, the original Hinsdale Hall, was once home to the Hiram College administration and students alike. Hiram Principal and later U.S. President James A. Garfield once had offices in this building.
Hiram College Archives

later he became the Eclectic's president and his ideals still shape the college's mission.

During his tenure, Garfield expanded the horizons of students, adding, for example, a series of lectures on the then-unheard-of subject of American history. The school, which took the name Hiram College in 1867 to better reflect its nature, continues Garfield's tradition of innovative curriculum. In the 1930s Hiram adopted the revolutionary single-course study plan and now offers the Hiram Plan, a schedule of study that divides each 15-week semester into a traditional 12-week term and a three-week, single-course session. Later, the college was one of the first schools to adopt the four-quarter academic year and, in 1977, was the first in Ohio and second in the country to offer a Weekend College program for working adults.

Hiram College now attracts 900 students to a picturesque campus in Portage County, southeast of Cleveland. It includes dozens of buildings, including a new $7.1 million library that houses archival collections highlighting the careers of Garfield and poet Vachel Lindsay, another Hiram alumnus. They are attracted by Hiram's reputation as a respected liberal arts college offering unique opportunities. Ninety-five percent of the faculty members hold doctoral degrees, and the college grants bachelor of arts degrees in majors ranging from classical studies and history to physics and psychobiology. In addition, because of its 12-3 calendar, it offers special opportunities for students at the college's Northwoods Field Station in Michigan's Upper Peninsula; a Washington, D.C., semester; and other short-term courses on campus and around the world.

Rocky River Public Library

Rocky River residents have always loved books. As far back as 1877, when it was a mere hamlet, Rocky River had a subscription lending library. Dissolved in 1902, a year before Rocky River became a village, its memory lived on.

Which is why, when the Cuyahoga County Library System was created in 1922, Riverites voted to have their village join the new system. When their branch library opened in 1924 in a second-floor classroom at the high school, residents quickly realized that a one-room library was woefully inadequate.

In 1926, at the urging of the Rocky River Library Association, which had been lobbying for "our own" library since December 1924, the Board of Education placed a $60,000 library bond issue on the November ballot. It passed 513 to 342. In February 1927, Emily and Thomas Macbeth, members of the Library Association, donated $25,000 for the purchase of land for the building. In November 1928, under the direction of Head Librarian Katherine E. Wilder, who would direct the library until 1967, the red-brick, Georgian-style Rocky River Public Library opened to the public. A year later, to "assure good service and proper maintenance of the library," Riverites approved a local library tax.

With Rocky River growing — becoming a city in 1930 and surging past 10,000 residents in the late 1940s — the library expanded in 1956 with a $100,000 bequest from Sophia Schlather to add the Leonard Schlather Wing. The wing nearly doubled the library's size and gave it a much-needed auditorium.

In 1974, with a bond issue wholeheartedly supported by the community, the library expanded again. The new addition again doubled the library's space, which allowed it to concentrate on developing the outstanding adult fiction and children's collections it is known for today. In 1978 a bequest from Maude W. Michael allowed the library to purchase an outstanding collection of Art Deco-era Cowan pottery and create the nationally recognized Cowan Pottery Museum.

In the early 1990s the library made the physical, structural and electronic updates necessary to fully automate access to the library's collections — which today feature over 150,000 print and electronic media items — and allow it to enter the computer age with "full vigor." In 1998 the library opened a technology training center that offers a variety of public computer classes. Entering the computer age merely enhanced the library's ability to provide the quality individual and personal service for which Rocky River Public Library has always been known.

With a $3.2 million budget and a dedicated and creative staff of 70-plus, Rocky River Public Library serves its community 70 hours a week and circulates over 700,000 items annually to over 26,000 cardholders. It sponsors over 650 in-house programs and activities — everything from "lap sit" story hours for infants and moms to arts and crafts for youth to medical information programs for adults, attracting almost 20,000 participants. And with the help of the library's outreach department, it provides a full spectrum of library services to almost 100 homebound community residents.

Katherine Wilder, the library's first director, summed it up best when she said, "For a little library...we do a lot."

Rocky River Public Library's original 1928 building

The Children's Room in 1950 — a long tradition of service

The University of Akron

When Akron industrialist John R. Buchtel founded a small liberal arts college in his hometown in 1870, he gave the school a motto both concise and powerful: *Fiat Lux*, a Latin phrase meaning "Let there be light." The words also proved prophetic.

The 19th-century Buchtel College, which housed 46 students and seven faculty members in a single building, has grown into The University of Akron, northern Ohio's leading public university.

Buchtel Hall, named for the university's founder, is located in the center of The University of Akron campus.

Spanning 170 acres in the heart of Summit County, The University of Akron also has a vigorous regional campus in Wayne County and delivers lessons via state-of-the-art distance learning classrooms in three counties. More than 23,000 students from around the world attend classes at The University of Akron, which offers more than 200 undergraduate majors and areas of study, 100 master's degree programs, 17 doctoral programs and four law degree programs.

National recognition has been awarded to University of Akron programs in polymer science and engineering, international business, dance, law, sales and marketing, industrial and organizational psychology, and engineering.

This success is due to the university's responsiveness to the region's educational needs and the institution's pioneering research. It is a combination that was developed early in the school's history.

In 1913 Buchtel College trustees transferred its assets to the city of Akron. For the next 50 years, The Municipal University of Akron, supported by city tax funds, brought a college education within the reach of many more young people. During those years, enrollment swelled to about 10,000 students.

The university's growth paralleled the remarkable expansion of Akron. People were drawn to the city — already a major manufacturing center — by the promise of jobs. Companies such as Goodyear, Firestone and Goodrich were headquartered there, so it was only natural that the world's first courses in rubber chemistry would be offered at the university, beginning in 1909. When World War II erupted in 1939, University of Akron researchers and students were well prepared to help fill a critical need by contributing to the development of synthetic rubber.

A long era of expansion followed the war. Overseeing much of this growth was the university's 10th president, Dr. Norman P. Auburn. Under Auburn's leadership, the institution made the transition in 1967 from a municipal to a state university.

In 1988 the university established the world's first College of Polymer Science and Polymer Engineering, which is now the largest academic program of its kind in the world. Led today by its 15th president, Dr. Luis M. Proenza, the university has embarked on an ambitious $200 million campaign to create a "New Landscape for Learning."

Construction of six new buildings, renovation of 14 other structures and the addition of 30 acres of green space are under way. New degrees and certificates are offered in such areas as computer engineering, intellectual property law, e-commerce and international business. And research into biomaterials, nanotechnology and other emerging sciences offers hope for astounding medical and technological breakthroughs.

The 21st century finds The University of Akron still lighting new paths of opportunity and growth for itself, its students and the city for which it is named.

Fiat Lux.

The Weatherhead School of Management at Case Western Reserve University

Graduates of the Weatherhead School of Management at Case Western Reserve University possess far more than a degree from one of the top management schools in the world. They have benefited from the Weatherhead School's strategic emphasis on competency-based education, action learning, entrepreneurship, international perspective and community service.

Weatherhead School graduates may be found in the upper echelons of virtually every type of organization, across the country and worldwide. In northeast Ohio, Weatherhead graduates lead major banking, financial service, manufacturing, consulting, technology and health care organizations, as well as scores of entrepreneurial firms.

The Weatherhead School traces its roots to the 1920s, when MBA courses were first offered at Cleveland College of Western Reserve University. With the federation of Western Reserve University and Case Institute of Technology in 1967, the CWRU School of Management was established. In 1980 the school was dedicated as the Weatherhead School of Management in honor of one of Cleveland's most respected entrepreneurial families. Since then the School has seen dynamic growth in the size of its student, faculty and alumni bodies and the range of its program offerings, including a wide variety of international study opportunities.

To accommodate its growth, the Weatherhead School built Enterprise Hall in 1988 and the George S. Dively Building in 1994. In 1999 ground was broken for the Peter B. Lewis Building, named in honor of the chairman, CEO and president of Progressive Corporation. Designed by world-renowned architect Frank O. Gehry, the Lewis Building reflects the innovative, entrepreneurial spirit of the Weatherhead School and is certain to become a national landmark.

The Weatherhead School's commitment to the Cleveland community is expressed in many ways. For students, community service is an integral part of the Weatherhead experience, from orientation to graduation.

Students participate in service projects such as construction of Habitat for Humanity housing and community gardens, and providing career development counseling to local high school students. At graduation, students' contributions are acknowledged with Community Service Recognition Awards.

Promoting the growth and development of the regional economy is another expression of the Weatherhead

School's commitment. Through research and education, the school's Center for Regional Economic Issues fosters understanding and promotes dialogue on issues vital to the future of the northeast Ohio economy. Programs of the Health Systems Management Center strengthen the health care community in Cleveland and beyond. The Mandel Center for Nonprofit Organizations adds value to the increasingly important nonprofit sector. Enterprise Development Inc. assists entrepreneurs in launching new businesses as well as strengthening growing enterprises. Among Weatherhead's highly respected entrepreneurial recognition programs are the Weatherhead 100, which recognizes northeast Ohio's fastest-growing companies, and the Weatherhead Family Business Hall of Fame.

Today, the Weatherhead School of Management is one of the world's foremost creative learning communities. Recognition of Weatherhead's enduring achievements will continue to grow in the future; its contributions to management education and practice, as well as to the Cleveland community, are an inspiration for schools everywhere.

Scheduled for completion in 2002, the Peter B. Lewis Building will anchor the Weatherhead School of Management's Peter B. Lewis Campus — which includes the George S. Dively Building — at the intersection of Ford Drive and Bellflower Road in the heart of Cleveland's University Circle.

MANUFACTURING
& DISTRIBUTION

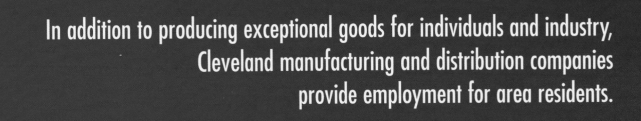

In addition to producing exceptional goods for individuals and industry, Cleveland manufacturing and distribution companies provide employment for area residents.

TRW Inc.

Five years after the first sale of an American motor car (a Cleveland-made Winton) and two years before the Wright Brothers' flight at Kitty Hawk, a Cleveland company was formed that would have a dramatic impact on both the automotive and aerospace industries.

Automobiles and airplanes were far from the minds of the five Clevelanders who pooled $2,500 in 1901 to start the Cleveland Cap Screw Company. Its first products were bicycle bolts and cap screws.

The 29 employees working at the first plant have grown to more than 100,000 employees in 35 countries around the world.

The company's first several years were comparatively successful, but it was not until 1904 that the basis for real success was created. A company welder, Charles Thompson, had the idea of changing the way automobile valve stems were made. His plan — welding the heads to the stems rather than shaving down a rod of metal that was the diameter of the valve head — impressed Cleveland automaker Alexander Winton. It impressed him so much, in fact, that he not only bought the idea, but he also bought the company and named Thompson general manager. In 1908 Cleveland Cap Screw became the Electric Welding Products Company and in 1915, when Winton relinquished the reins to Thompson, the firm was renamed once again, to Steel Products Company.

That same year the company produced the first valve for aircraft applications. During World War I its valves were used in the French Spad fighter plane and in American aircraft engines. Those early aviation applications were overshadowed in 1927 when the renamed Thompson Products provided valves for the *Spirit of St. Louis,* flown by Charles Lindbergh in his pioneering solo flight across the Atlantic.

The growing interest in aviation led the company to establish the Thompson Trophy Race in 1929. This 50-mile speed race on a circular course at Cleveland Airport (now Cleveland Hopkins International Airport) focused the nation's attention not only on the heavens, but also on the company's aircraft products.

It also proved to be a race to the Great Depression, and when Charles Thompson died in 1933 the company was in poor financial shape.

The new president, Fred Crawford, was a Harvard graduate who began working for Thompson as a millwright's helper in 1916. As president and chairman, he would lead the company for the next 25 years into new ventures on the ground and adventures in space.

Fortune magazine described Crawford as "the only human being around Thompson Products that runs faster than a turbine wheel, hotter than a valve head, and noisier than a drop forge."

Crawford managed to keep the company in good financial health during the Depression, diversifying the firm — especially in the growing field of aviation. At a time of employee unrest around the country, Crawford instituted "one-in-five" meetings. Every week, one of every five workers was invited, on a random basis, to sit down with top managers and discuss ideas for improvements or air grievances in an open forum.

In anticipation of World War II, the company, with government funding, built Cleveland's TAPCO plant in 1941 to increase its production of aircraft engines. During the war the plant operated 24 hours a day, seven days a week.

Just about all of the firm's peacetime products were adapted to wartime use. Conversely, after the war, many products created for the war effort found new uses in America's peacetime economy.

But on the horizon — actually, above the horizon — was a new market and a new direction: aerospace. But Thompson Products would not go it alone.

Its new partner was the Ramo-Wooldridge Corporation, founded by two young aerospace engineers, Simon Ramo and Dean Wooldridge. The two had helped develop a missile and electronic firing control system for the air force while working at Hughes Aircraft in California. Orders for the system during the Korean War helped make Hughes a very successful defense contractor.

By 1953 the two men wanted more of a challenge and, with the support of Thompson Products, started their own company.

In 1958 Ramo-Wooldridge formally merged with Thompson Products to form Thompson-Ramo-Wooldridge. That same year, the company became the first to build a spacecraft when it created Pioneer 1.

The 1960s began a period of accelerated diversification for the company, both through internal growth and acquisition. It was during this decade, in 1965, that Thompson-Ramo-Wooldridge became TRW Inc. That same year TRW supplied the Lunar Module Descent Engine for the Apollo moon landing mission and, in 1967, pioneered the development of automotive rack and pinion steering in England, introducing it in the United States five years later.

In the following decades additional growth was achieved through aggressive global expansion. The company's pioneering efforts in the automotive and aerospace industries during that time read like a textbook on advanced technology.

Some of TRW's achievements during the 1970s and 1980s included building the Viking Biology Instrument package that searched for life on Mars; creating Pioneer 10, which was launched in 1972 and in 1983 became the first manmade object to leave the solar system; with the acquisition of a German company, becoming one of the first to aggressively move into vehicle occupant restraints; and producing the first functional Very High Speed Integrated Circuit (VHSIC) chip.

In the mid-1980s TRW moved its world headquarters to a 180-acre site in Lyndhurst, the former estate of the Bolton family, long-time Cleveland benefactors and politicians. From this eastern Cleveland suburb, TRW continued to expand its global operations and the frontiers of achievement.

Checking complete auto restraint system — sensors, diagnostics, air bags and seat belts

In the late 1980s the company developed the first original-equipment remote keyless entry system, delivered the first complete frontal air bag and sensor system and produced the VHSIC SuperChip, the world's first self-repairing electronic device.

Through internal expansion and external acquisitions, the company's growth and diversification continued. In 1997 it bought BDM for $1 billion, adding to its already extensive information system technology capability. In early 1999 the company acquired LucasVarity of Great Britain for $7 billion, further enlarging its global leadership position in automotive and aerospace markets.

As TRW headed toward its 2001 centennial, it intended to continue its growth as a leader in high-technology products and services for automotive, aerospace and information systems customers worldwide.

Anchor Tool & Die Company

"In this business you take a calculated risk. If you succeed, you're a hero. If you don't, you're not here to tell about it," says a smiling Ed Pfaff, chairman of Anchor Tool & Die Co. Pfaff's talent for successful risk-taking, combined with his characteristic humor and straightforward style have been major factors in the success of this family-owned-and-operated business. The company supplies just-in-time delivery of custom stampings, assemblies and metal processing to the "Big Three" auto manufacturers, their first-tier suppliers and general industrial customers. Anchor, whose annual sales top the $70 million mark, was one of the first companies in the state of Ohio to receive QS 9000 certification in all areas of its manufacturing operations in 1996.

Originally from Austria, Pfaff came to the United States with his parents at age 18 and soon after volunteered to serve in Korea. Granted citizenship during his tour of duty, he returned from overseas to work part time as a tool and die maker, attending college at night. Motivated by the prospect of sending his three adolescent sons to college, the journeyman tool and die maker decided to go out on his own in 1970. The Anchor Tool & Die Company was founded in May of that year by Pfaff and two investors who were later bought out. The first facility was located in a two-car garage on the westside of Cleveland with a small paneled office, a lathe and a milling machine. First-year sales were a mere $20,000, but Pfaff was undaunted. "I was so motivated that money had no bearing on it," he recalls. "I would have worked for a penny an hour."

"I had a plan; I had a vision," says Pfaff. "Knowing that everything is cyclical and that sometimes machining would be a big item, sometimes fabricating, sometimes stamping. The secret to staying in business is staying busy at all times. And, obviously, provide jobs for the people and in the process make profit." In an effort to diversify his product line, Pfaff bought two punch presses in 1975. It was a risk because until that time he had been a tool supplier to stamping concerns and was now, basically, in competition with his former customers. Nevertheless, sales increased steadily year by year until the company outgrew its original space. In 1980 Pfaff bought a building located on Brookpark Road. The move represented a substantial increase in space for the business, going from 18,000 square feet to 100,000 square feet. Employing 30 people at the time, diversification caused the business to really take off. The Anchor Metal Processing division added precision machining and powder coating to the company's capabilities in 1992. The company purchased an adjacent building, expanding to 350,000 square feet in 1994.

But it is Anchor's more than 350 employees that have truly made the company successful. "The investment in each and every one of our employees in so substantial that

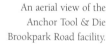

An aerial view of the Anchor Tool & Die Brookpark Road facility.

it is in our interests to train them well and retain them," says Pfaff. "Subsequently our turnover is very low." From the beginning, Pfaff has made it a personal policy to get to know each and every employee and really listen to what they have to say. In 1993 the company instituted a policy of making each worker the final inspector of his or her own product, which included training and a pay increase. As a result, the quality level of Anchor products increased by a factor of five over the next two years.

Getting to know the people and the jobs they do is a practice Pfaff encouraged in his sons. As youngsters, each of them worked on the factory floor to get an appreciation for the process and to get to know the people. Middle son Frederick came into the business in 1985 with a degree in engineering and an MBA from Cornell University. Originally his job was quality assurance, and he wrote the company quality manual. He performed a statistical analysis that resulted in an equipment purchase of $10 million, which paid for itself in two years. That contribution resulted in his promotion to vice president. Now president and CEO, he puts his own spin on the company philosophy. "We try to find out not just what our customers want right now but what they might want months, years from now,"

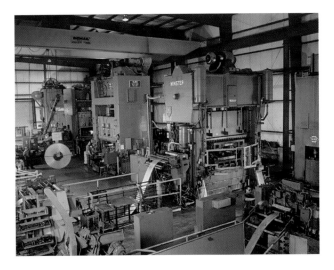

he remarks. "Then put those items into place so that when they come ask for them, they're already there. We stay a step ahead that way."

Youngest son Jeffrey came on board in 1989. With an engineering degree from Case Western Reserve University, he naturally began in the engineering group. Two years later he took over responsibility for the family's other business concern, Condor Tool & Die. Condor, a separate corporate entity, fabricates the custom stamping dies that Anchor uses to create its custom parts and assemblies. This division of responsibility enables Anchor to meet customer requirements more swiftly. After taking the helm at Condor, Jeffrey also took over responsibility for the engineering group and operations at Anchor in 1993 — a logical step, since that department designs specifications for much of the tooling Condor manufactures. Eldest son Robert took a different path, joining the firm as legal counsel in 1986 with a law degree from Ohio State University .

Modest to a fault, Ed Pfaff gives a great deal of credit for the company's rapid growth to his star salesman, Gene Hickerson, a former Cleveland Browns football player who became affiliated with the firm in 1980. He also acknowledges the support he has received over the years from the city of Cleveland through expediting building permits, enabling the company to meet increasing customer demand.

Having enjoyed real prosperity in Cleveland and proud of their people and their products, the Pfaff family has a simple and sincere commitment to the city, now and in the future. As Ed Pfaff puts it, "We just want to be part of something good for Cleveland."

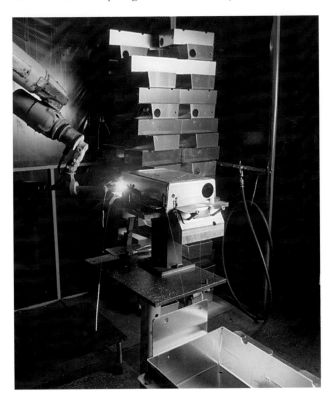

Argo-Tech Corporation

Computer and telecommunications businesses captivated the world's imagination in the last decades of the 20th century. But that doesn't mean that new manufacturing companies are not thriving and innovating. Take Euclid-based Argo-Tech Corp., for example.

A child of the leveraged-buyout trend of the 1980s, Argo-Tech is today a leading supplier of critical parts to the aircraft industry. It designs, engineers and manufactures sophisticated fuel pumps and related components used in the jet engines of commercial airliners and military aircraft. The company also provides spare parts and repair-and-over-haul services to more than 200 airline and other customers.

Argo-Tech was created in 1986 to buy and operate the power-accessories division of TRW Inc. The division made aircraft fuel pumps, torpedo-propulsion systems and structural components for the U.S. Navy's nuclear reactors. Included in the deal was the so-called TAPCO plant that had been built during World War II on 180 acres on Euclid Avenue in the Cleveland suburb of Euclid.

The acquired businesses employed 1,250 workers, over 1,200 of which were in northeastern Ohio.

Argo-Tech's new owners included members of the TRW division's management team, with financial support from Prudential Insurance Co. The company embarked on a capital improvements plan that included a transformation of

the TAPCO plant, which has 1.8 million square feet of floor space. The plant has been turned into an industrial park called Heritage Business Park, with Argo-Tech sharing space with 25 other companies, including other former TRW units.

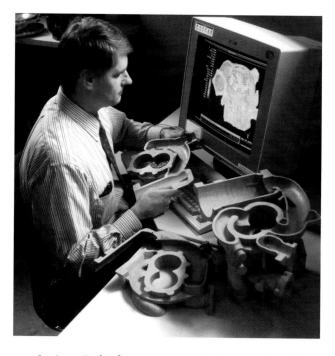

In Argo-Tech's first years annual sales rose from $160 million to more than $250 million.

In 1988 the company acquired the assets of Indiana Gear Works, which manufactured trans-missions and other parts for military helicopters. The business was moved to Cleveland and renamed International Gear Corp.

The early 90s was a period of readjustment for the whole aviation-supply industry as first defense spending was curtailed and then commercial aircraft building sagged. In response, Argo-Tech restruc-tured in the early 1990s, deciding to retain only the fuel-pump business and the TAPCO facility. The torpedo and propulsion-system businesses, as well as International Gear, were purchased by Technautics Corp., a new company formed by the managers of those units. Technautics kept its head-quarters and operations in Euclid. It later was restructured and renamed Marine Mechanical

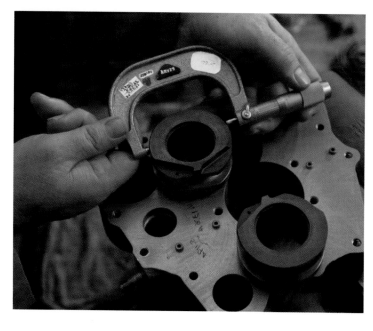

Corp. The Argo-Tech restructuring was engineered by Argo-Tech's management, with financial support from new investor Vestar Capital Partners of New York City.

In 1994, Argo-Tech, under the leadership of its president, Michael S. Lipscomb, initiated an employee stock-ownership plan. Forty company managers held ownership before the ESOP, which expanded ownership to 296 salaried employees. By early 1999 the company was 70 percent owned by managers and employees.

Argo-Tech expanded again in 1997, purchasing J. C. Carter Co. of Costa Mesa, California. Carter manufactures aircraft fuel system components as well as cryogenic pumps and aircraft ground-fueling equipment. At the time, Argo-Tech chairman Lipscomb said, "The combination of Carter's world leadership in on-ground fueling of commercial aircraft and airframe fuel components with Argo-Tech's airframe and main engine fuel pump expertise marks the first time in the aerospace industry that a single company has the ability to handle the fuel from the fueling hydrant as the plane is parked on the ground until it is delivered to the engine in flight."

The acquisition positioned the company to be more competitive, as aircraft builders, like their auto-industry counterparts, seek suppliers who can provide complete systems. It also added $50 million in sales.

Today, the company is a leading designer and manufacturer of high-performance fuel-flow products for jet aircraft. It makes high-pressure pumps that deliver fuel directly to jet engines at precise rates and low-pressure pumps that move fuel through airframes to engines. Its ground-fueling systems serve more than half of the airports around the world. It also provides mid-air refueling systems. While military purchasers use Argo-Tech pumps, 80 percent of the company's business is with commercial aviation. At the end of 1997 Argo-Tech's main-engine fuel pumps were used in 8,500 commercial aircraft. The aftermarket, including spare parts and overhaul services, plays a significant role in Argo-Tech's business since aircraft typically have a 25-year lifespan.

The company supplies more than 30 fuel delivery components for the F-16 fighter jet.

In 1999 the company was moving ahead with plans for an $11 million expansion including new machinery and equipment at its Euclid plant. It believes its future lies in expanding further into fuel-movement related businesses. A revitalized Argo-Tech now has sales of approximately $175 million and more than 900 employees in Ohio, California, Arizona, Japan and England. Looking ahead, the company is building on its expertise in pumping devices to design similar products for industrial applications, including gas turbines.

Its strength in the future, however, is likely to remain up in the sky as the aircraft industry continues a $1 trillion building program to keep up with the demand for air service.

The Argo-Tech line of fuel pumps links state-of-the-art design with advanced materials technology.

Beck Aluminum Corp.

Smart men recognize a need and brave men decide to do something about it. Paul C. Beck was both smart and brave when he quit his job as chief metallurgist for Alcoa's Casting Division in Cleveland at the end of World War II in 1947 to become an independent consultant for producers of high-quality aluminum alloy castings. By 1950 he had recognized a need for higher-quality raw materials and subsequently built and ran an aluminum smelter in Mentor, Ohio, to fulfill that need.

Paul Beck's nationwide reputation in the industry as an expert in metals combined with the prominence given to the use of aluminum over steel after World War II helped the business to grow. But by 1955 he had decided to stop producing the product and instead concentrate solely on distribution. His son, Gerald R. Beck, joined him in the business in 1956 and together they achieved the goal of matching the best ingot with each customer, at a competitive price, when they needed it.

The mixture of hard work and an increasing demand for aluminum by the automotive and trucking industries helped father and son to build a large customer base, and the company flourished. Paul Beck retired in 1973, but his grandson Scott W. Beck, current company president, joined Gerald in 1978 after he completed training as a metallurgical technician at National Aluminum's NSA smelter, one of the company's primary producers. With Scott's help, Beck Aluminum's territory expanded to include Ohio, Michigan and Canada.

In 1985 Gerald's second son, Bryan C. Beck, current company executive vice president, also joined the family business after he too completed training in metallurgy at National Aluminum's NSA smelter. Again the company territory grew, this time to include regions in the Midwest and Great Lakes.

Throughout the 1990s Beck Aluminum continued to prosper by responding to changes in the aluminum market. The automotive industry began utilizing more recycled scrap and secondary ingot as the need for lighter, more economical cars with better mileage increased. The company reacted by aligning with producers who could fulfill the growing demand. Recycled and secondary business currently represents

Paul C. Beck founded Beck Aluminum Corporation in 1950.

50 percent of the company's sales and is forecasted to represent approximately 75 percent by the year 2005.

Beck Aluminum's tremendous growth led to a move of its corporate headquarters in 1999 from a location on Euclid Avenue in downtown Cleveland, where it had been for 48 years, to Landerhaven Corporate Center in Mayfield Heights, Ohio. To better serve its customers throughout the United States and Canada, it also maintains sales offices in Fort Wayne, Indiana; Roanoke, Virginia; and in Pittsburgh and Lancaster, Pennsylvania, in addition to five warehouses in the Midwest and Ontario, Canada. With its large concentration of foundries — there are over 30 in the area and over 100 in the Great Lakes region — Cleveland will always be the company's home.

Beck Aluminum's commitment to great customer service has helped it to become the leading distributor of aluminum ingot products in the United States. Few companies in the aluminum industry supply the same wide range of products. It handles over 300 foundry accounts that serve automotive, trucking, aircraft and electrical manufacturers. But whether the customer is large or small or the order is for one or 1,000 tons, Beck Aluminum is there to meet the need, making it a competitor with every other company in the industry.

The company also uniquely serves its clients by providing not just distribution services, but commodity services as well — managing supply and risk, pricing futures and recommending the best value for their money. As the trend of merging big producers of aluminum products continues, Beck Aluminum's individualized service as a family-owned, independent company has become a welcomed rarity in the industry, especially to smaller foundries that might otherwise not be able to remain competitive in today's economic climate.

Another way Beck Aluminum supports its customers is through its membership in several professional organizations, including the Non-Ferrous Foundry Society (NFFS), the Society of Die Cast and Engineers (SDCE), the Institute for Scrap Recycling Industry (ISRI) and the American

(Left to right) Executive Vice President Bryan C. Beck, Chairman Gerald R. Beck, and President Scott W. Beck

Foundry Society (AFS), of which it has been a member for over 40 years. By being active in these organizations, the company promotes the use of aluminum and works with the Environmental Protection Agency (EPA) and the Occupational Safety and Health Administration (OSHA) to develop industry standards. The company is also proud of the ISO 9002 certification it earned in October 1999. The quality standard is internationally recognized in the industry.

Beck Aluminum has nobly grown from a small family business to an industry leader. Its future plans include an eventual assumption of leadership by a fourth generation of Becks. It also plans to remain an independent family business and to expand its distribution to regions in the southern and western United States.

With the demand for aluminum products predicted to increase for at least the next 10 to 20 years, hard-working, innovative Beck Aluminum should have no problem growing along with the increase for another 50 years or more — smartly and bravely exceeding its customer's expectations.

Bonne Bell Cosmetics

When J.G. Bell was deciding where to locate his newly founded cosmetics company, he remembered that one of the best salesman he knew was from Cleveland. He looked up Cleveland in the library and learned that it was within 500 miles of half of the population of the United States — the best location in the nation. So though he'd never been further east than St. Louis, he moved his wife and three children from Kansas City, Missouri, to Cleveland with dreams of making it big. Seventy-three years later, Bell's company is one of the top 10 cosmetics companies in the United States, a family-owned private cosmetics company and one of Cleveland's greatest success stories.

It was 1927 when J.G. Bell began operating the cosmetics company, which was then called Virginia Allen, out of the basement of his home on Lee Road in Cleveland Heights. He had previously worked in Kansas City as a sales manager for Luzier Cosmetics and had become enthralled by the cosmetics industry. He sold his products door to door, asking his customers, "What do you want — the package or the product?" since he couldn't afford both.

The company grew slowly and Bell opened an office in downtown Cleveland. In June 1930 it was incorporated as Bonne Bell Cosmetics. It was named after Bell's daughter Bonne, who herself was named for a character in a short story that appeared in the April 8, 1916 issue of the *Saturday Evening Post* called "The Man Next Door." In 1933 Bell bought a building in Lakewood, Ohio, where the company headquarters still remains today.

Bonne Bell's first products were popular cosmetics of the day, such as vanishing cream and face powder, and they were mainly sold in beauty shops. But in 1936 Bell was at a restaurant that was selling a dermatologist-created skin care product called RX1006. It was being marketed to people with acne and other skin problems, but Bell knew he could sell it to the general public. He bought the formula from the dermatologist and greatly believed in its benefits.

J.G. Bell worked the rest of his life selling "ten-o-six" and the many other quality Bonne Bell products. Though he had little formal education, he was a self-educated, hard-working man with a vision and a strong desire to see that vision come to life. He worked every day until he passed away at the age of 80 from Parkinson's disease.

J.G. Bell's son, Jess A. Bell, took over as company president in 1959. He, along with his sister Bonne, had worked at Bonne Bell almost all their lives. Around the same time, the company made an important move when it decided to specialize in products for teenagers, with ten-o-six as its lead product. Bonne Bell continues to focus on teens and pre-teens today, with 6 to 16 year olds as its main consumers.

In 1967 Bonne Bell became associated with sports when it signed on as the first corporate sponsor of the U.S. Ski Team, resulting in the company becoming widely known during the 1968 Olympics. When jogging became popular in the early 1970s, Bonne Bell again aligned with fitness by becoming the first company in the United States to sponsor a series of races for women.

Fitness is still a priority at Bonne Bell. Jess Bell started running in 1972 and credits the everyday habit for changing his life. When the company built a manufacturing plant in Westlake,

(Left to right) The three generations of Bells that have managed the successful cosmetics company: Jess A. Bell Jr. ("Buddy Bell"), a portrait of company founder J.G. Bell and Jess Bell Sr.

Ohio, in 1976 it included a 2-mile running track on the property that is still frequently used by both employees and the public.

Bonne Bell's over 500 employees in Cleveland not only have rewarding jobs in an environment that is friendly and fair, they also enjoy a fully equipped company exercise room and exercise classes during the lunch hour. It's just one of the many reasons Bonne Bell has a long list of employees with over 25 years with the company. Jess Bell is especially proud of the company's Senior Program. Started in 1997, the inspiring program employs over 100 senior citizens part time for light manufacturing and assembling. Seniors work with and are supervised only by other seniors and age is not a factor. The oldest worker is 90 years old.

One of Bonne Bell's most innovative and successful products is its Lip Smackers flavored lip glosses. Created in 1973, Lip Smackers were the first flavored lip product on the market. Today, Lip Smackers are the No. 1 selling flavored lip gloss in the world.

Bonne Bell's corporate headquarters in Lakewood, Ohio, was built to resemble a row of houses at Georgetown University in Washington, D.C., and has become a Cleveland landmark.

The third generation of Bells is firmly entrenched at Bonne Bell. Jess Bell Jr. (Buddy) took over marketing and sales in 1995. The business has tripled in five years. A complete line of products under the Smacker label has been introduced nationwide, as well as in Canada, Australia and many countries in Europe.

Buddy Bell was named CEO and chairman in August 1999. The entire senior management represents the third generation. Jess Bell Sr. has successfully passed on the baton and fulfilled a dream he shared with his father. Julie Bell, who has worked for the company for over 40 years, joins her husband in semi-retirement.

In addition to remaining a private family business, Bonne Bell's future plans include remaining in Cleveland and supporting the community that helped make it a success. It plans to continue expanding its line of fun, functional products and hopes to soon be one of the country's top five cosmetics companies. It is a momentous goal, but one the company is likely to achieve.

Bonne Bell's manufacturing plant in Westlake, Ohio, on Crocker Road

Ferro Corporation

As the leading global producer of performance materials for manufacturers, Ferro's presence in Cleveland enhances the city's reputation as a location vital to the way the world lives and works in the modern age. Ferro's downtown offices serve as world headquarters for its sites around the world, which provide a variety of specialty coatings, colors, ceramics, electronic materials, specialty plastics and specialty chemicals.

From the high-performance enamel coating that adorns ranges to the decorative surface of a tile and even the coating on the wheel trim of an automobile, Ferro has a hand in improving the performance and appearance of all these products and many more. Its key end-use markets, including building and renovation, major appliances, household furnishings, transportation, industrial products and a host of other products, easily illustrate that this is a company that matters to thousands of other businesses and people throughout the world.

The beginning of Ferro was humble enough. Two men, Harry D. Cushman and Robert A. Weaver, each had an interest in the future of porcelain enameling. Cushman worked as a salesman for the American Rolling Mill Co. and sold enameling iron to the appliance industry in the early 1900s, an industry about to surge with the introduction of modern-day household appliances. In 1919, with a total investment of $1,000, he incorporated the Ferro Enameling Company and produced enamel frit — a complex glass that is a core ingredient in porcelain enamel — in a plant on East 56th Street.

Weaver had held sales and advertising positions with porcelain companies, but his ultimate ambition was to create his own sales agency in the industry he had come to learn so well. He approached Cushman, whose Ferro Enameling Company was already a well-established name for excellence and quality. The two men founded Ferro Enamel & Supply Co. in 1920 to sell frit and service products made by Cushman's company. His first offices were in the Bulkley Building in downtown Cleveland about six miles from Ferro Enameling. A third person, Henry C. Luebbert, was persuaded to join them. Luebbert was an enameling superintendent at The American Stove Company and held a similar position with the new company. In 1921 Cushman adopted the check-in-circle insignia, still the company's trademark, representing the quality of products they sold.

Since that humble beginning, Ferro has managed itself with an incredible combination of inventiveness and expertise. Whether it has been the bold scientific pursuit in shaping an entire industry, or facing a challenge such as the scarcity of fuel and raw material during World War II, the company has continually emerged successfully with one customer solution after another. One example of this ingenuity was demonstrated by Ferro France in 1941, when the company created an innovative electric smelting method for producing frit to deal with wartime limitations. Its other wartime efforts were focused on the many defense contracts the government awarded Ferro, resulting in five Army/Navy "E" Awards for Excellence.

Throughout the postwar years Ferro met the challenges of a booming population and growing world economy. To sustain growth, Ferro continually diversified its product

Ferro's world headquarters in downtown Cleveland is home base for operations in 20 countries around the world.

The world's largest porcelain enamel on steel mural was commissioned by Ferro for the 1939 World's Fair to promote the use of porcelain enamel. The mural now resides in the Reinberger Gallery at the Western Reserve Historical Society.

offering. It produced ceramic glaze in the late 1920s and colors in the late 1930s. That diversification was most evident after World War II as it expanded geographically, too. With plants already located in Canada, France, Brazil and Argentina, following Word War II and into the 1950s Ferro moved into South Africa, Mexico, West Germany, Hong Kong and Italy. The 1960s proved as productive, as the company established itself as a major force in the glass-color business and continued its expansion to Spain and India. By 1964 Ferro Holland served over 50 countries in Europe, the Middle East, the Far East, Africa and Asia.

It was a 1969 Ferro development that gave the average homemaker the best reason for celebration. As more and more women began to enter the work force outside of the home, Ferro created a specialized porcelain enamel coating that continuously cleaned household ovens. In the 1970s Ferro began in powder coatings and saw the beginnings of a successful business in plastics and chemicals. In 1980 Ferro acquired Thick Film Systems, Inc., a high-tech producer of specialty materials for the electronics industry. In 1988 Ferro reached the $1 billion worldwide sales mark and the following year moved into its current headquarters on Lakeside Avenue in downtown Cleveland.

Today, Ferro is the largest world producer of ceramic glaze and porcelain enamels. It also holds leading market positions in colors, plastic compounds, powder coatings, polymer additives and electronic materials. One of its lesser-known accomplishments is its technological applications to the auto-motive markets, particularly to the suppliers of automotive glass. In the late 1960s and 1970s, automotive glass assembly started to move toward gluing the glass to the car body. An early discovery indicated that the adhesives needed protection from UV light degradation, and ceramic printing enamels were found to be an ideal solution to the problem.

As automotive technology has advanced, Ferro has remained ahead, especially in heeding environmental concerns by developing lead-free and cadmium-free technologies. Along with continuous improvements that allow the production of complex bend back lights and side windows for the automotive designs of today and the future, Ferro has demonstrated that the best solutions are those that combine scientific know-how with a compassionate under-standing of the people their products will be helping.

Ferro has shown its commitment to the automotive industry by providing desirable, less costly, olefin-based polypropylenes for components that are more durable, lighter weight and designed for ease-of-assembly. In fact, Ferro received the "Keep America Beautiful" Award from the Ford Motor Company for its accomplishments as one of only two suppliers in the industry (and only four globally in the plastics industry) that attained the 25 percent post-consumer polypropylene recycling goal set by Ford. Today, Ferro supplies the automotive markets with polymer additives, powder coatings and electronic materials as well as plastic compounds and colorants.

Although now a company with over 7,000 employees worldwide, including the establishment of operations in China in 1998, Ferro still has its heart in Cleveland. At the core of its many community-minded activities is a long-term partnership with the Charles W. Elliot Middle School in the inner city. The program matches Ferro's research and development team and other staff volunteers with students as they explore together the scientific advances that will be shaping their future as well as the future of the city itself. This example of how business can join forces with education to offer the best opportunities for the hope of a child's future role in society speaks to the commitment to the quality of life that Ferro values.

Ferro is increasingly focused on building its electronic materials business, which enjoys rapid growth in supplying products that are used in a variety of electronic applications such as cell phones.

Ferro supplies the automotive industry with a variety of materials, including plastic colorants and compounds, powder coatings, polymer additives, electronic materials and glass enamels.

LTV Steel Company

Since its earliest days the steel industry has played an essential role in America's social and economic evolution from an agrarian society. From the Industrial Revolution to our contemporary high-tech, service-oriented culture, steel has been a constant component in the growth of the country, and in particular it has been the centerpiece of Cleveland's manufacturing economy.

With locations throughout the Midwest, LTV Steel Company is the third-largest integrated steel maker in America and the leading producer of value-added carbon electrical steel sheets, electrolytically galvanized sheets and ultra-low carbon steel that can be formed into more complex shapes than other grades of steel. LTV's steel is used by the automotive, appliance, construction and electrical-equipment industries.

The largest flat-rolled steel complex in North America is LTV Steel Cleveland Works, which each year produces about 5 million tons of flat-rolled steel — commonly known as sheet metal. The mill operates 24 hours a day, 365 days a year and employs about 4,300 people. Located just two miles south of Public Square, Cleveland Works stretches over 1,200 acres with the Cuyahoga River — in the past a dividing line between two separately owned mills — running through the middle.

LTV Steel is an integrated steel company, which means raw materials are brought to the plant and converted into finished steel. Iron ore pellets from Minnesota and Michigan, limestone from Michigan and coke — a form of pure carbon refined from coal — are joined in the blast furnace, a large reactor that turns these

materials into molten iron. This iron is further processed in a basic oxygen furnace to remove the carbon and refine it into liquid steel. This is poured into the oscillating mold of the continuous caster, which transforms the liquid metal into a solid slab of steel about 10 inches thick and up to 73 inches wide. At the hot-strip mill the steel is transformed into flat sheets of one-half inch or less in thickness. From this basic process, the hot-rolled steel can be sent to other LTV facilities for further processing: it can be made thinner, shinier, coated with zinc to resist corrosion or pre-painted for refrigerators and stoves, among other products essential to modern life.

The lineage of LTV Steel is complex; the name derives from the legendary deal maker James Ling, who in 1947 formed Ling Electric Company, an engineering and contracting firm based in Dallas, with an initial investment of $2,000, and went on to build the first conglomerate, focusing primarily on the electronics and aerospace industries.

Ling moved into the steel business in 1968 when he obtained a controlling interest in Pittsburgh's Jones & Laughlin Steel, a company founded in 1853 by Benjamin Franklin Jones and James Laughlin. The Cleveland Works facilities on the west bank of the Cuyahoga River were purchased by J&L from Otis Steel Company in 1942. LTV's steel business grew in 1978 with the consolidation of the Youngstown Sheet and Tube Company, acquired in LTV's merger with the Lykes Corporation.

Republic Iron and Steel Company was established in 1899 when more than 30 small iron companies were banded together in Youngstown. In the late 1920s legendary investment

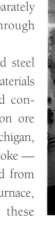

All of LTV Steel's high-quality steel is produced in state-of-the-art continuous slab casters.

The continuous anneal line at LTV Steel's Cleveland Works is designed to produce a new generation of flat-rolled steels. Continuously annealed steel has superior mechanical properties and provides manufacturers with design and production advantages.
Photo by Score Photographers

banker Cyrus Eaton and a group of investors purchased a major interest in Republic; despite the 1929 crash, the company expanded and rapidly became the third-largest steel producer in the United States. In 1935 Republic Steel Corp., as it was now named, bought the Corrigan McKinney steel plant on the east bank of the Cuyahoga and the next year moved its headquarters to Cleveland.

LTV Corporation, with its subsidiary, Jones & Laughlin, merged with Republic in 1984 to create LTV Steel Company, with the plan of becoming a more effective competitor in the increasingly difficult global business of steel production. American steel makers lost over 30 percent of the domestic steel market to unfairly traded imported steel. The industry was driven into crisis by an overvalued dollar relative to other world currencies and lax enforcement of long-standing trade laws.

In 1986, as a result of the steel-trade crisis, LTV and its 65 principal subsidiaries were forced into an extensive reorganization. For the next seven years, the company sold its aerospace and defense business and other non-steel divisions. The company then modernized and upgraded its integrated steel facilities and achieved world-class levels of quality and productivity. It also developed a strategy for long-term profitable growth and shareholder value enhancement. In 1995 it formed a joint venture with Sumitomo Metal Industries and British Steel to build a flat-rolled steel minimill to serve the southeast U.S. market. In 1997 LTV expanded its role in metal fabrication by purchasing VP Buildings, the second-largest producer of pre-engineered metal buildings, a new construction technology that is thriving.

Expansion continued in 1999 with LTV's purchase of two steel-tubing manufacturers which, when joined with its existing division, became LTV Copperweld, the largest producer of structural and mechanical tubing in North America. LTV teamed with iron-ore producer Cleveland Cliffs; they built a plant that utilizes the latest technology to make reduced iron, which is sold to minimills for mixing with their scrap to improve its quality. While frequently thought of as a mature industry, steel making today is one of the most rapidly changing, technology-driven industries in the country, so much so that almost half of today's products did not even exist five years ago.

Given its lengthy history in Cleveland, a city that understands and values manufacturing, LTV Steel has provided jobs for generations of Clevelanders and remains the largest industrial employer within the city limits. LTV is a very significant economic engine for the region and continues to offer well-paid, family-supporting jobs.

The company contributes to the well-being of the community in other ways as well. During Cleveland's bicentennial in 1996, LTV provided steel framing for the construction of 40 new houses, a project undertaken with Habitat for Humanity, with volunteered assistance from LTV employees. To help high school students learn what they might do with their aptitude in science and math, the company created the LTV Steel Institute of Science and Technology, a summer program taught by Case Western professors and LTV technical experts that has been quite popular. Many other programs are sponsored, such as the adoption of South High School near the mill, and several scholarship opportunities provided, exemplifying the company's commitment to its employees and its community.

LTV Steel Company's strategy for the future is to do the very best job possible in its integrated steel business, while growing profitably in steel-related businesses to create value for its shareholders.

Modern, computer-based technologies enable LTV Steel's Cleveland Works to continuously improve the performance and quality of its flat-rolled steel.
Photo by Score Photographers

LTV Steel's Cleveland Works produces over 5-million tons annually of high-quality, flat-rolled steel for automotive, appliance and other demanding industries.
Photo by Score Photographers

Miceli Dairy Products

When grocery shoppers all over the country pick up a package of one of Miceli Dairy Products' fine Italian cheeses, they may not realize the humble beginnings and hard work that led to the product being on the shelf. They only know that they are purchasing a fresh and all-natural cheese that will make their recipe come alive with flavor. But if it weren't for the tenacity of a young John Miceli, the Miceli cheese business would have curdled over 70 years ago.

Miceli Dairy began in 1923 as an attempt to use up surplus milk from the Newbury dairy farm of John Miceli's father, Anthony Miceli. Instead of discarding the extra milk, the Micelis made cheese, curdling by hand. A 15-year-old John Miceli sold the cheese in Cleveland, 20 miles east of Newbury, from his Model-T pickup, which was loaded with ice slabs covered with sawdust to keep the cheese fresh.

Scamorza, the forerunner of mozzarella, and ricotta were the first cheeses the Micelis produced. Because they were made with the ingredients and the technique John

Miceli had learned from his father, who grew up in Sicily, the "old-world" cheeses quickly became popular among the shopkeepers of Cleveland's East Side Italian neighborhood. Christmas, Easter and Thanksgiving were especially busy times for the small cheese business. When cheese products became popular among other nationalities, Miceli started to sell throughout the year.

The business slowed during World War II, when John Miceli worked long hours in a defense plant. But after the war, Miceli turned to making cheese full time. The business took off as independently owned grocery stores throughout Cleveland requested the excellent ricotta and mozzarella that they could only get from the newly founded Miceli Dairy Products Company. In 1949, to keep up with the demand, Miceli moved his company from the Newbury farm to E. 90th Street in Cleveland, the same location the company inhabits today.

During the following 51 years, Miceli Dairy has seen tremendous expansion with fast-growing product lines and markets. All four of Miceli's children — Rosemarie, John Jr., Carol and Joe — became active in the day-to-day operations of the company and continued their father's legacy of consistently high-quality products and service to the customer. Recently a third generation has become involved, with several of Miceli's grandchildren joining the business. The charismatic John Miceli never retired, devoting every day to his cheeses and his employees until he passed away at 91 years of age.

Miceli Dairy is now a leader in the fresh Italian cheese market, with a wide variety of products, including specialty cheese and shredded lines, sold in 50 states to grocery stores, restaurants and other food manufacturers. There are several different varieties of most of the cheeses produced, including low-fat versions and premium products. What was once just one style of ricotta cheese

Family owned since 1923, Miceli Dairy Products has earned a reputation for fresh, high-quality cheeses.

being an integral part of the growing Cleveland community

Since the beginning, Miceli Dairy has sustained a good relationship with its loyal customers. A priority at the company is educating customers about how to use its products in recipes, particularly products that are a part of its specialty line. This particular line includes a variety of gourmet cheeses such as asiago, bocconcini and the pepperoni roll, which many customers have never heard of before. Company technicians create recipes and often focus on nutritional recipes using part-skim and "lite" products. Miceli Dairy's Web site includes a plethora of information on its various cheese products, including nutritional data, and many exciting cheese recipes.

Miceli Dairy's future includes many exciting plans, but a definite future plan is to remain family owned and operated. The Miceli family will go to great lengths to continue to supply customers with high-quality products that are fresh and all natural — every one a tribute to the life's work of John Miceli Sr.

is now many different ricotta products. Key to the authenticity of the products is their freshness and the packaging techniques that keep the products fresh without preservatives. To accomplish this, technicians work 24 hours a day in the Miceli Dairy laboratories.

Miceli Dairy Products revolutionized ricotta cheese by developing a 15-ounce sealed container for the product that extended its shelf life to 90 days without using preservatives. Previously, ricotta had to be bought the day it was produced and used within seven days. Miceli Dairy was also one of the first Italian cheese companies to get Kosher certification on its ricotta and one of the first to volunteer for USDA approval.

Miceli Dairy has also stayed successful by taking advantage of modern technology to keep up with the demand for its products and to help the business grow. Its plant utilizes state-of-the-art equipment manned by over 100 talented employees. But cheese making is still considered an art by the Micelis, who brought cheese makers from Italy to ensure they are producing cheese the traditional way and are maintaining the original taste and quality. Miceli Dairy's "old-world values" can also be seen in the pride the company takes in

MTD Products Inc

MTD Products Inc is a privately held company with three major business units, over 10 American manufacturing plants and products in use throughout the world. Yet it remains a humble family business seen by its owners as a gift from God.

Theo Moll in 1932, the year he founded the Modern Tool & Die Co. along with Emil Jochum and Erwin Gerhard. The company would later be known as MTD Products Inc.

The story of MTD begins with three German immigrants — Theo Moll, Emil Jochum and Erwin Gerhard. Moll arrived in Cleveland during Christmas week of 1923 and with the assistance of his cousin, Ruth Moll, began to establish himself in the American workplace. In February of 1928 he was joined by his cousin Jochum and the two quickly found work as tool and die makers in the Cleveland area. While in fellowship meetings at the Cleveland YMCA, Jochum met Gerhard, another German immigrant. It quickly became apparent that the three men shared a common heritage as devout Christians and an interest and expertise in machine tools.

Sixty years after they founded MTD Products Inc, Theo Moll and Emil Jochum were still active in the company's day-to-day business.

In 1932 they founded the Modern Tool & Die Company on the fourth floor of the Whitney Power Block in Cleveland and began making metal stampings, tools and dies. Despite the Depression, the company prospered through hard work and modern ideas. Automotive

parts manufacturers, including Eaton Corp., were its first customers. MTD Automotive remains one of the company's core divisions today, manufacturing chassis, bumpers, heat management systems and structural body systems.

The company steadily grew through reinvestment of profits. In 1938 the company was able to purchase a facility on W. 130th Street in Cleveland. During World War II the company's business shifted from automotive work to supporting the war effort. Although MTD did not have any prime contracts, it produced wing fixtures for airplanes, mess kits and trigger housings. After the war, diversification became necessary.

MTD opened a second plant in Willard, Ohio, in 1953, which at first manufactured toy wagons and tricycles. But those products only sold well during the holiday season, so in 1954 it entered the field that would become its hallmark — lawn and garden equipment — with a line of wheelbarrows. By 1958 the line of products had grown to include garden, landscape and recreational equipment.

The lawn and garden business had phenomenal growth and by 1960, the Modern Line Products Co. was built in Indianola, Mississippi to better serve the southern markets of the United States. In 1962 MTD entered the Canadian market when it purchased Sehl Engineering in Kitchener, Ontario and increased its product line to include snow throwers.

The Consumer Products group continued to grow throughout the 1960s and 70s, while the Automotive group remained steady. Modern Tool & Die Co. officially changed its name to MTD Products Inc in 1968 to reflect its ever-increasing line of products. With the passing of Erwin Gerhard in 1954, the company continued to be driven by the visions of Theo Moll and Emil Jochum and in 1970, it began to develop plans for a research and development center. A working farm in Valley City,

Ohio, that Moll had purchased in the late 1940s was chosen as the site. In 1979 the corporate headquarters was also moved there. An integral feature of this site is a 350-400-year-old white oak tree. The tree, with its deep roots and strong sheltering branches, has come to symbolize the company's protective commitment to its employees and communities.

In 1975 MTD purchased the first of what would become one of its five core brand lines, the Yard-Man Co., from Montgomery Ward. In 1981 MTD acquired two additional brand lines, Cub Cadet from International Harvester and White Outdoor from White Consolidated Industries.

The consumer products business grew rapidly through the 1980s, but a majority of the product was private labeled. Dramatic changes in the retail industry and the growth of discount and home center stores, such as Lowe's, The Home Depot and Wal-Mart placed a greater emphasis on brand name products. MTD committed its resources in the early 1990s to building its own brand portfolio. National advertising and sport sponsorship programs were developed to support the individual brand lines.

MTD now has five brands designed to provide a wide variety of outdoor power equipment: Cub Cadet, White Outdoor, Yard-Man, Yard Machines and MTD Pro. The premium lines, Cub Cadet and White Outdoor, are distributed through independent retailer/dealers. The value lines of Yard-Man and Yard Machines are sold at discount retailers, hardware stores and home centers. MTD Pro, which was introduced in 1997, is available through independent retailers/dealers for the commercial landscaper.

In 1994 MTD expanded to include another business group. The Mechanical Systems group began when the company built Modern Transmission Development Co. in Leitchfield, Kentucky. The plant manufactures leading technology transmissions for washing machines, personal mobility vehicles, tractors and self-propelled mowers.

Continuing to expand upon the goal of becoming a global supplier, MTD acquired Gutbrod, a German lawn and garden manufacturer, in 1995. This led to a larger presence in the European marketplace and the world.

In the early 1960s, MTD salesmen gathered to discuss the company's growing line of lawn and garden equipment.

Today, MTD products are sold around the globe, including North and South America, Europe, Asia and Australia.

Though its customer base continues to grow and diversify, MTD has remained as modest and caring a company as it was in the 1930s. It remains privately held and continues to honor the tradition of a strong work ethic and Christian values, rewarding its employees with genuine caring. At the age of 95, Emil Jochum continues to lend his years of experience and knowledge to the company, arriving at the West 130th plant nearly every day. Theo Moll passed away in 1996 at the age of 91 without ever having seen a day of retirement.

Moll and Jochum's generosity lives on; not only through the blessings they shared with their families, friends and employees, but also through the contributions to charities in the communities where they worked. A few of the Cleveland area institutions that have benefited from the success of MTD include The City Mission, Baldwin-Wallace College, Lutheran Hospital, C.A.M.P. and United Way. Yet Moll and Jochum never asked for recognition or tributes. It is said that they were good at everything but fame.

MTD's goals for the future include continuing to lead the industry in manufacturing capabilities, marketing and customer support programs. Though it's one of the world's leading manufacturers of outdoor power equipment, it will never forget the importance of supporting its employees, its customers and its communities.

MTD now offers a wide variety of outdoor power equipment, including the Cub Cadet, White Outdoor, Yard-Man, Yard Machines and MTD Pro product lines.

Reiter Dairy Inc.

Ralph Reiter started his business life as a baker, but he soon figured out where his bread was buttered.

So after World War I he moved from Rochester, Pennsylvania, and began Miller-Maid Creamery to churn and sell butter from a plant on Forge Street in Akron. As home refrigeration became more widespread, American households began to use more milk.

So in 1933 he transformed his business into Reiter Dairy, selling fluid milk produced by nearby dairy farmers for 8 cents a quart. The business grew and Reiter expanded as rapidly as he could, with financial help from friends and suppliers. At the time the business was almost entirely the door-to-door delivery of milk in reusable glass quart jars by horse-drawn cart. The dairy had a horse barn on Union Street and the company's animals became so accustomed to the trip from the dairy to the barn that they could make the trip unsupervised at the end of the day.

Reiter was an innovator in the milk business, the first to use plyofilm, a product of Akron's Goodyear Tire and Rubber Co. similar to cellophane, to cap milk bottles. Reiter also invented a machine to secure the caps with rubber bands. By the 1940s the company was selling "Mello-Milk," the first homogenized milk in the Akron area.

In 1946 Reiter Dairy began making ice cream and in 1954 merged with Belle Isle Dairy Farms, which was a large ice cream maker. Belle Isle was owned by former Ohio State Senator Fred S. Harter, and the company was renamed Reiter & Harter Dairy Inc. The industry was consolidating and Reiter decided he wanted to be a buyer rather than a seller. Over the next few years, the company acquired 20 smaller dairies. "We were aggressive in acquiring companies," Rollin Reiter recalled to a reporter a few years ago. Among the dairies it purchased in the Akron area were Kesserling, Chestnut Ridge, Parker and Frederick.

Ralph Reiter ran the company until 1959 when his son, Harold, succeeded him. Rollin Reiter took the reins when his father retired in 1966. The company name was changed to Reiter Foods Inc. in 1969, reflecting the company's expansion into refrigerated and frozen food products and the addition of a convenience store operation. "We owned a frozen food institutional supply company in Ashland, then we developed some convenience stores called Stop and Go," Rollin Reiter recalled to a reporter. "We later sold the convenience stores to concentrate on the dairy."

The name was changed again in 1978, this time to Reiter Dairy Inc., and the company continued to expand through acquisition. In 1982 it acquired a milk plant and distribution center in Springfield, Ohio, from Lawson's. In short order it added Oak Farm Dairy in Findlay, Ohio, and a frozen food distribution center in nearby Tallmadge.

By the mid-1980s the company had grown to 550 employees and $100 million in sales annually by being an acquirer. But now Rollin Reiter began to ponder his business' future. His two sons were interested in other professional careers.

"There were no more family members interested in staying in the business and we were facing major capital requirements, as do most dairies if they grow," says Rollin Reiter. He knew that "to go further constantly requires an infusion of new capital for new equipment and expanded facilities."

So he looked around for a bigger partner. He found Dean Foods in 1986.

Dean Foods and Reiter Dairy could have been twins separated at birth. Like Reiter, Dean grew up after World War I. In 1925 Sam Dean created Dean Evaporated Milk Co. in Pecatonica, Illinois, 100 miles west of Chicago. Like Reiter, Dean moved into fluid milk production in the 1930s and began making ice cream in 1947. Soon after, it began acquiring smaller dairies.

Unlike Reiter, though, Dean diversified into the pickle busi-ness and became a public company in the early 1960s. In 1970, Howard Dean, Sam's grand-son, became president and continued

the growth-by-acquisition strategy. By the time it acquired Reiter, Dean had reached $3 billion-plus in sales. "Dean Foods was the strongest and best-managed company in the industry, with the highest ethics," Rollins told *Small Business News* of Akron. "They started out as we did, as a small family company that grew and expanded by buying other independent dairies. It was just a bigger version of what we were."

Today, Dean is the country's second-largest fluid milk processor, with $2.3 billion in wholesale sales in 1999, according to *Dairy Foods* magazine. That is 10 percent of the total U.S. milk market.

Reiter fit well into the Dean family of companies. Dean always sought to acquire well-managed, prof-itable businesses with strong management in place so they can run autonomously. The Dean acquisition strategy was well timed. Its important customers, the supermarket chains, were also growing. Expansion allowed Dean to remain a valuable supplier.

Rollin Reiter stayed in Akron to run the dairy, which

continued to sell milk under the Reiter name, for four years before a promotion took him to Dean's headquarters in Franklin Park, Illinois. He served as vice president for milk and ice cream sales and marketing for Dean Foods' 22 dairies until he retired in 1993.

Today, Reiter's is the largest Dean Foods operation in its northeast division, producing fluid milk, fruit drinks and, in particular, ice cream. The Reiter plants in Akron and Springfield distribute ice cream for Dean customers in seven states.

Reiter and Dean continue to work to improve their positions in the marketplace through creative sales and marketing techniques. The latest addition to the groups' product line is the "Chug," a single-serving plastic milk container that is sold in 8-, 12- and 32-ounce sizes. Its attractive package — it fits into vehicle beverage holders, unlike the traditional, square paper milk carton — proved a shot in the arm for fluid milk sales. The product, imitated by competitors, was named one of *Dairy Foods* magazine's "Products of the Decade," along with Starbucks Frappuccino and Ben & Jerry's Chocolate Chip Cookie Dough Ice Cream.

RPM, Inc.

Medina-based RPM's name is derived from its forerunner, Republic Powdered Metals, which was founded by Frank C. Sullivan in 1947. At that time, it had one product, Alumanation, a heavy-duty aluminum coating still sold by RPM today. First year sales were $90,000.

Today, RPM is the home to more than 100 leading brand names, with sales around $2 billion. The company's products are manufactured by about 8,000 employees in 39 subsidiaries at 68 plant locations in 17 countries and sold in more than 130 countries.

From the Statue of Liberty to the Kennedy Space Center at Cape Canaveral, from the Sydney Opera House to the Tokyo Industrial Forum, the firm's products protect some of the world's most famous structures — and a great deal more of the nation's do-it-your-selfers' favorite projects.

In Cleveland, RPM products protect landmarks such as Jacobs Field, Cleveland Browns Stadium and Severance Hall, as well as local institutions such as The Cleveland Clinic and University Hospitals.

The company has become a world leader in the consumer and industrial coatings and sealants markets by following the philosophy espoused by Frank Sullivan — "Hire the best people you can find, create an atmosphere that will keep them and let them do their jobs."

Frank Sullivan began his venture on a 1-acre site on Cleveland's west side, but by 1962 the firm needed more space, initially for research and development. The company purchased 100 acres south of Cleveland, in Medina County, and put up an R&D center. In 1967 the Cleveland location was sold, and everything and everyone moved to Medina.

In 1969 Republic Powdered Metals had its first national public stock offering, with 300,000 shares being sold. Sales at the time were $7 million.

With the unexpected death of Frank in 1971, the second generation of Sullivans — Thomas C. — took over. A third generation — Frank C. — after a dozen years in various company locations and in various positions, was named president in 1999 as part of a succession plan.

In 1971, the same year the company's founder passed away, RPM, Inc. was formed as a holding company, with Republic Powdered Metals becoming one operating company under the corporate umbrella. Meanwhile, RPM, Inc. developed an aggressive acquisition program in a rapidly consolidating painting and coatings industry.

"Letting them do their jobs" remains integral to the company's success. Industry observers have said RPM could be the only coatings company that acts as a holding company, with the presidents of its operating groups given a good deal of autonomy. Once it buys a company, RPM keeps hands off. Each company becomes a wholly owned subsidiary and management is given a great deal of leeway. Each company is encouraged to continue enhancing its own products' names, not RPM's, in the marketplace. As a result, decentralization gives the company an entrepreneurial outlook in spite of its size.

The company's business has grown through both acquisitions and internal expansion and by concentrating on market niches, with its more than 100 products divided between industrial and consumer markets.

Among the firm's industrial products are Tremco roofing systems; Alumanation coatings; Vulkem and DYmeric sealants; Dryvit exterior insulation-finishing systems;

Thomas C. Sullivan, RPM chairman and CEO, shown in a 1970s photo in front of a portrait of his father, Frank C. Sullivan, founder of RPM's predecessor company, Republic Powdered Metals

RPM headquarters in Medina is decorated and protected by its own products.

corrosion-protection coatings sold under the brand names of Carboline, Plasite and Mathys; Day-Glo fluorescent colorants and pigments; Euco concrete and masonry specialty products; Stonhard and Duracon industrial and commercial floor coatings; and Wolman industrial lumber treatments and specialty coatings, including Westfield and TCI.

The better-known consumer products, which make up nearly half of RPM's business, target do-it-yourselfers and hobbyists in North America. Consumer brand names include Rust-Oleum, the market leader in consumer rust-preventive coatings; DAP caulks and sealants; Zinsser, a leading maker of primers, sealers and wall covering preparation and removal products; Wolman wood deck coatings; Bondex household patch and repair products; Bondo automotive specialty repair products; Testor hobby products; Flecto wood finishes and finishing equipment; and Plastic Wood patch and repair products.

Several of the companies making these products, including Day-Glo Color Corp., Tremco, Mameco and Euclid Chemical, had well-established reputations in the Greater Cleveland area before joining RPM.

Early in the 21st century RPM announced a plan for the future that would help it maintain its well-earned reputation as "The World's Leader in Specialty Coatings and Sealants." Plans included an aggressive new product development program, a major commitment to e-commerce and creation of a unified consumer distribution and warehousing system to better address the changing needs of retailers.

Product innovation to meet market needs is another cornerstone to RPM's success. The company's Zinsser unit, for example, which pioneered bleached shellac in the United States in the mid-1800s, is a constant innovator. Recent new products from the unit include Perma-White mildew-proof bathroom paint, and Gardz, a wallcovering preparation product that creates a smooth surface on damaged drywall. Day-Glo, which introduced fluorescent pigments more than a half century ago, has recently begun

marketing computer ink jet printer cartridges featuring fluorescent-enhanced inks. And Rust-Oleum has built on its leadership in small package rust-preventative coatings to extend its market by offering decorative coatings and general-purpose coatings in small aerosol and can packages.

It is this willingness not only to meet change, but to anticipate it, that has enabled RPM to rank high in the estimation of investors. More than 300 institutional investors own company stock, and RPM typically ranks in the top 10 of all publicly held companies in the number of shares held by the National Association of Investment Clubs. About 95,000 shareholdes own the stock, which is traded on The New York Stock Exchange. For more than a quarter century, the company has increased its cash dividend on common stock every year.

As long as wind, rain and sun break things down, customers have to buy protective coatings from someone. Those customers may not recognize the RPM name, but they recognize the quality of the products they are buying — the same way they have recognized it since 1947.

Consumer brand Rust-Oleum is North America's largest producer of rust-preventative coatings.

Zinsser, another consumer brand, is a market leader in primers, sealers, shellac-based coatings and wallpaper-removal products.

The Sherwin-Williams Company

In 1860 Cleveland was a city on the grow. The population had more than doubled in a decade, to almost 44,000. Although lumber and clothing were the city's primary businesses, dramatic changes in the city's industrial makeup would take effect during the decade.

It was to this thriving community that 17-year-old Vermont native Henry Sherwin came in 1859. Over the next half-dozen years, he worked in a dry goods store and then in a wholesale grocery operation. In 1866, after saving $2,000, he became a partner in a wholesale paint company.

His partners saw the company's future in linseed oil; he saw it in paint. As a result, the partnership lasted only three years. Shortly after it dissolved, Edward Williams and Alanson Osborn each invested $15,000 for equal shares of a new partnership with Sherwin. The new firm, Sherwin, Williams & Co., opened a retail store and had amazing — for the time — first year sales of more than $422,000.

In 1871 the company began manufacturing its own coatings. At the time, there was no such thing as ready-mix paint. Professional painters mixed paint on-site, combining a base of oil or varnish with pigments, thinners and other ingredients as needed.

In the mid-1870s, Henry Sherwin developed a new type of grinding mill that led to the development of the first quality, ready-mix exterior coating in 1880. To overcome customer resistance to something new, Sherwin offered a money-back guarantee. Sherwin-Williams Paint (or SWP) quickly became the country's best-selling exterior house paint. Needing something other than buckets in which to sell its paint, the company created the industry's first paint can, the same shape used today.

In 1884 the company incorporated and changed its name to The Sherwin-Williams Company. Henry Sherwin designed the firm's new logo, a chameleon curled around the edge of an artist's palette. The company also hired a chemist to ensure the quality of the its products, apparently the first chemist ever employed by an American paint manufacturer.

With the success of its exterior paint, Sherwin-Williams began an acquisition and growth program that is still underway.

In 1888 the company bought controlling interest in the Calumet Paint Co. from the Pullman Standard Car Company, makers of the famed sleeping coaches. Calumet made coatings for rail cars, carriages and buggies, manufacturing equipment, ships and marine equipment, and commercial buildings.

In 1897 Sherwin-Williams entered into its first foreign venture, a joint investment in a Montreal plant. According to corporate histories, the company's vision was to decorate and protect the world by covering the earth with Sherwin-Williams paint. This concept became the new cover-the-earth corporate logo that was adopted in 1905 and still is in use.

In 1911, 20 female employees met to exchange skills and ideas and formed the Brighten-Up Girls' Club (B.U.G. Club), named after the popular Sherwin-Williams paint called Brighten-Up Finishes. Soon after, these women pursued money-making projects and used the proceeds for charity. Seventy-three years later the club's name was updated to The Sherwin-Williams Women's Club, but its commitment remained the same — helping those who are less fortunate.

During the first couple of decades of the 20th century, company revenues rose from $2.3 million to $57.1 million as it opened new paint and varnish factories, its first retail stores and in 1917 acquired the Martin-Senour Company, a well-known maker of premium-quality paints.

By the end of World War I, the company was supplying coatings and chemicals from plants throughout the United States, Canada and England. Sherwin-Williams and its affiliates and subsidiaries owned and operated 36 manufacturing plants, 90 warehouses and 30 retail stores.

In 1920 the company purchased Acme Quality Paints of Detroit, a multimillion-dollar business specializing in coatings for the carriage and automobile industries.

In spite of the depressed economy of the 1930s, the company expanded into Mexico, Cuba, Argentina and Brazil, an expansion that helped the company recover rapidly from the decade's economic doldrums.

During World War II, two Sherwin-Williams innovations not only changed its business, but changed the industry as well. Because of the war-related shortage of pig bristles from China used for paint brushes, a company engineer invented the jute and wood Roller-Koater™. It helped the company roll on to even greater growth. The company also developed a product called Kem-Tone®, a "modern miracle wall finish." It was the industry's first water-based, fast-drying paint. The two items not only changed the coatings market — they changed the way the American consumer purchased and used paint at home, spurring the development of do-it-yourself painting.

To make painting at home even easier for postwar Americans, the company developed the Kem Colormeter Mixing Machine, which enabled customers to choose from more than 2,000 colors mixed to their specifications and dispensed in the store. Previously, all paint was premixed and prepackaged at the factory.

While the sale of Sherwin-Williams branded products exclusively through more than 2,400 company-owned stores constitutes a majority of the company's sales, many consumers choose to shop at other retail outlets. Sherwin-Williams reaches these important consumers through businesses it has acquired with such well-known brands as Dutch Boy®, Dupli-Color®, Krylon®, Pratt & Lambert®, Thompson's® and Minwax® among others. Its acquisition of Desoto made it the leading supplier of private label paints sold through mass merchants.

In 1995 it extended its South American business, begun in the 1930s, with nine acquisitions of well-known local coatings businesses, making it a leading coatings company in the area.

Sherwin-Williams and The Sherwin-Williams Women's Club share a long history of supporting a variety of philanthropic endeavors. The company is committed to investing in the communities it serves, and in keeping with the nature of its own business, has supported many historical building rehabilitation programs in Cleveland and other cities.

Just as the company has not moved far from its original headquarters, it has not moved far from its original purpose. In 1866 Henry Sherwin established exemplary product quality and customer services as his company's

business objectives. Today's marketplace is not the marketplace of the 19th century, but Sherwin-Williams' continued success is a result of not only anticipating and changing with the market, but also remaining committed to the principles of its founder.

Dedication to these principles has resulted in only two years of financial losses to its shareholders (1921 and 1977) in its history and a company with more than $5 billion in sales as it entered the 21st century.

State Industrial Products

To truly understand the rich history and bright future of State Industrial Products, one need look no further than the five generations of successful leadership provided by the Zucker and Uhrman families. A single premise has been the foundation of the company's growth and success generation after generation — solving customers' maintenance problems with high-quality products and personal service.

Since opening its doors in 1911, strong family leadership has guided the company through nine decades of challenges and opportunities. Jay Zucker, who began the company with a $75 investment and one product — a green floor-sweeping compound made by hand — would be astounded by the size, technological capabilities and scope of State's marketplace. What hasn't changed is the drive and sound business practices that would remind him of the company he started. When Jay's son, Malcolm (Mac) Zucker took over in 1973, the company philosophy didn't change. Nor did it change in 1989 when son-in-law Hal Uhrman was named president.

In a constantly changing world, many organizations often react slowly — if at all — to new challenges. State Industrial Products'

approach is aggressive and proactive. New ideas are valued, cultivated and implemented with a sense of urgency. This commitment to continual improvements has allowed the company to set industry standards in product development, service and innovation.

State Industrial Products' world headquarters remains in Cleveland, just east of downtown. Corporate employment is rapidly approaching 2,000. However, with the company's current strategic growth and expansion plans, worldwide employment will grow accordingly.

In addition to the Cleveland facility, State Industrial Products operates state-of-the-art, strategically located manufacturing and distribution facilities around the world. For instance, the Tulsa, Oklahoma, manufacturing plant is equipped with cutting-edge technology. Designed for expansion to meet the company's growth, it is one of many locations that exemplifies State's commitment to excellence and its focus on the future.

State Industrial Products operates three divisions in the maintenance, repair and operation (MRO) industry — State Chemical Manufacturing Company, UZ Engineered Products and Neutron Industries.

State Chemical is a worldwide leader in the manufacturing and distribution of specialty maintenance products. Its product line, designed to promote a cleaner environment through technology, is virtually limitless, given the continuous introduction of new products. State Chemical products are used around the world in

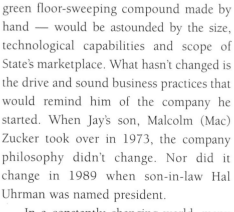

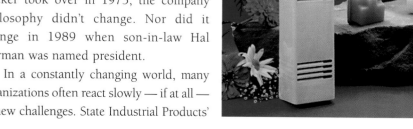

manufacturing plants, water treatment facilities, schools, hotels and hospitals. Whether it's supplying lubricants for multimillion-dollar machinery or finish for a gym floor, State Chemical provides solutions to maintenance problems.

In both industrial and institutional organizations, maintaining production equipment, fleets and physical plants is demanding and vital. Having the right part at the right time can be the difference between success and failure. UZ Engineered Products provides its customers with the products and services necessary to keep equipment running and downtime at a minimum.

UZ offers a comprehensive line of fasteners, anchors, welding products, electrical supplies, drill bits, abrasives, cutting tools, battery terminals and thousands of additional specialty items.

Neutron Industries, twice ranked among the nation's fastest-growing companies by *Inc.* magazine, is a premier telemarketer of maintenance supplies for schools, hospitals, offices and retail locations. Using sophisticated software, Neutron is able to meet, and often anticipate, the needs of its expanding customer base. Neutron markets its products throughout North America from its main office in Phoenix, Arizona.

State Industrial Products has created a growth strategy that plans to grow the company beyond the $200 million sales level. However, President Hal Uhrman already is focused on the next plateau.

Uhrman emphasizes his goal is to be the largest privately held organization in the MRO industry, and that the company's quality products, service and commitment to growth will enable State to achieve that goal. To reach that

level, the company continues to invest in education, training and recognition programs for its worldwide team of sales professionals, with millions of dollars annually allocated to attract and train quality sales associates.

The same diligence is applied to product development, as the company continually strives to meet the challenge of improving its products in conjunction with increasing regulatory and service demands. Creatively using new technologies, the company can provide solutions that work and have an overall positive impact on its customers' operations.

The commitment to the latest advances in technology is evidenced by its recent investment of installing the world's best manufacturing and distribution software program. The increased speed, capacity and information available through this program translate into superior customer service.

While its business strategy now spans the globe, State Industrial Products remains an active participant in local community affairs. More than 400 employees work at the Cleveland headquarters, and the company and its employees traditionally participate in the United Way, Cleveland Corporate Challenge, Harvest for Hunger and other charitable organizations and fund drives.

The multinational company remains focused on the three basic principles on which it built its long-standing tradition: Get it right the first time; be easy to do business with; lower the customer's total cost of doing business.

Keeping those principles in mind, State Industrial Products has seen its influence reach from its humble beginnings to worldwide stature.

Neutron Industries' consultants provide professional cleaning and maintenance solutions, such as NI-712, to customers throughout North America and Europe.

UZ Engineered Products distributes more than 20,000 products, including fasteners, cutting tools, specialty welding rods, electrical components, lubricants, adhesives and fleet-related products.

A-ROO

"Plastics!" That word whispered into the ear of a new college graduate (played by Dustin Hoffman) in the 1967 film classic, *The Graduate*, was designed to point him toward a rapidly growing and exciting career.

Robert Gilbert not only anticipated the movie, he envisioned plastics as a growth market before the movie, turning his vision into a highly successful plastics-oriented business, A-ROO. Today, that company is the largest manufacturer of conical shaped packaging materials in the Western Hemisphere.

In 1965, Gilbert and a friend, tired of the constant travel necessitated by their corporate positions, formed a partnership to sell plastic packaging to the perishable food industry. Wanting a corporate identity, they chose the kangaroo. The marsupial with a baby in the pouch proved to be the ideal image for a packaging firm.

When the partnership dissolved, Gilbert needed a new name for his new company. At the time, the Yellow Pages was a primary advertising medium, and AROO was created to lead off the packaging listings. It didn't! A disappointed Gilbert changed the name to A-ROO, and its been a leader ever since.

For years, the company remained solely a distributor of packaging products on a comparatively regional basis. Selling during the day and ordering from manufacturers at night to fill those orders became a way of life.

In the early 1970s Gilbert realized buying from manufacturers in quantity and selling from a warehouse made a great deal more economic sense. Warehousing was the only change, as the company continued to sell, but not manufacture, labels, bags and other plastic packaging to supermarkets and other users.

Then, as company President Scott Gilbert points out, in the mid-70s there was an evolution in the supermarket industry. Meat departments added deli sections and produce departments started selling flowers.

Just as Robert Gilbert chose the right field in 1965, the company chose the right direction in the 1970s, selecting flower growers as its primary market.

But A-ROO remained solely a distributor until 1991, a couple of years after it moved into a 50,000-square-foot facility in Strongsville.

Company growth is visually depicted behind A-ROO founder Robert Gilbert.

The rest is history.

The company's Strongsville plant manufactures 160 million plant and flower sleeves a year and distributes an additional 200 million a year to nurseries and greenhouses. The firm has sales and distribution offices in Texas and Miami (where 95 percent of the flowers sold in the United States enter the country from Central and South America). It has its own in-house creative department that uses the latest CAD applications to design packages, including special shapes for special needs.

In spite of its blossoming success in the floral industry, Scott Gilbert realized there were other markets that had a need for shaped or conical plastic bags.

As a result, A-ROO has become the world's largest manufacturer of disposable cake decorating bags. It also has developed cone-shaped packages for such candy companies as Hershey's, Smuckers and Jelly Belly.

The company, which had 12 employees when it came to Strongsville, has 75 employees there, and an additional 12 employees in Texas and six in Florida.

With that kind of growth, one has to wonder what would have happened to Dustin Hoffman's character if he had heeded that 1967 advice.

Acme Spirally Wound Paper Products

It was not an auspicious way to take over a business. In fact, there almost wasn't a business to take over. When Christina Kobak-More and Donald Kobak Jr. wanted to carry on the family's business, Acme Paper Tube Co., Inc., in 1982, a fire left them little more than ashes.

It didn't look promising for the business started by their grandfather, Henry Kobak, in 1951 and nurtured by their father, Donald Kobak Sr. But accepting the fire as a challenge, not a disaster, the siblings determined to rebuild Acme. They successfully met their own challenge.

The company, renamed Acme Spirally Wound Paper Products, Inc., has moved two times and undergone seven growth expansions since the two took over. Their success has been recognized by Cleveland Mayor Michael White, who not only congratulated the company for its revitalization but also for its investment in the city and commitment to remaining there.

Acme's "customer first" attitude is a primary reason for the company's continued growth and success. That success has been recognized by *Inside Business* magazine, which twice has selected the firm as a Manny Award finalist from among 12,700 manufacturing firms in northeast Ohio. Finalists are determined by a panel of judges that looks for firms that combine a flair for innovation with a focus on excellence.

Although not one of the judge's criteria, Acme also is extremely sensitive to the environment. All of its products are recyclable and are made mostly from previously recycled materials. Those paper tubes and cores are distributed throughout the United States and Canada. Internet access is expanding the company's markets as requests for information have started coming in from all over the world.

Acme's products range from decorative wound paper tubes that support point-of-sale displays to mailing tubes for calendars, artwork and posters. Its diverse consumer product line also can be used on umbrellas, golf clubs and ballpoint pens. The company's products also serve the automotive, electrical, printing, mailing and packaging industries.

To meet the needs of these markets, Acme's 50 employees work 50 hours a week. Among those employees are several other family members, including brother David; and Hilliary Moore, Christina's husband, who is sales manager. Christina is responsible for operations and human resources and Don Jr. manages production.

In 1997 Christina had the idea to open a new retail division, The Tube Shop, specializing in stock mailing tubes. The division, which initially occupied the company's former lunchroom, gets overruns or leftover sizes from the manufacturing side. Customers can walk into the shop, inspect the tubes and purchase what they need on the spot. It's another flair for innovation that has helped keep the company's 36,000-square-foot facility continuously busy.

With several competitors within 50 miles, it's innovations such as The Tube Shop, and a fourth generation — both Christina's and Donald's young children are getting an early start — that will keep Acme Spirally Wound Paper Products growing.

Christina Kobak-Moore and Donald Kobak Jr. proudly display some of their diverse line of products.
Photo by Herbert Ascherman Jr.

American Spring Wire Corp.

It was a year of burning down in Cleveland and across the nation. But 1968 was a year of building up for Larry Selhorst, who opened the doors of the new American Spring Wire Corp. (ASW) that year.

A veteran of the wire-making industry, Selhorst began the firm with two fellow entrepreneurs, $210,000 borrowed from family and friends and two business tenets: Build a better place to work and bring something new to the spring wire marketplace. The original corporate concept, "Innovators, not Imitators," remains a constant in the 21st century.

At the time the company was founded, valve springs were a relatively unsophisticated automobile component, frequently failing and occasionally causing total engine breakdown. As automotive companies began insisting on a better product at a better price, spring makers began looking for more consistent raw materials in economical packages.

It was a great opportunity for the new company, but it needed access to the best available supply of raw materials. Traditional supply channels already were committed to other manufacturers, so ASW turned to Japan. Japan

Company founder Lawrence O. Selhorst (left) is CEO and chairman of the board. Timothy W. Selhorst serves as executive vice president and chief operating officer.

turned away. That country's steel producers couldn't be bothered with such a small company.

But Larry Selhorst was nothing if not tenacious. He worked hard to get himself included on a foreign trade trip to Japan sponsored by the Ohio Department of Development. Proving he was more than an able salesman, within three months of the trade visit the Japanese began shipping steel rod that was twice the quality of steel previously available to ASW.

The company further capitalized on its relationship with the Ohio Department of Development by obtaining a $1 million loan to purchase its current headquarters/plant in Bedford Heights.

Fulfilling its "innovation" philosophy, the firm introduced the industry's first 3,000 pound coil in 1972, replacing the old 500-600 pound coils and significantly increasing the productivity of spring makers by reducing down-time. Recent innovations include the firm's improvement on eddy current testing and its proprietary paint system that identifies defects on all valve quality wire.

To take advantage of the innovations it introduced to the industry, ASW opened a second manufacturing plant in Kankakee, Illinois, in 1980 to meet growing demand for its products, which no longer are found only in auto engine valve springs. The company also manufactures wire for door and window springs, counterbalances for trunks and hoods, picker tines for agricultural equipment, overhead garage door springs and other basic parts required primarily by the automotive, construction, appliance and electrical industries.

ASW is one of the largest producers of PC strand in the country. Manufactured primarily in the Houston, Texas, facility, it is used extensively in prestressed and post-tensioned concrete structures, including bridges, parking decks and industrial and commercial buildings.

American Spring Wire is now under the direction of Larry's son, Tim. It has grown from 35 employees its first year to more than 550 employees in five facilities, and from $35,000 in net sales to almost $120 million in annual sales.

Through innovation, ASW has taken quite a spring forward to become a world leader in spring wire manufacturing.

Calvin Klein, Liz Claiborne, Chanel, Ferragamo and Saks Fifth Avenue. The client roster for Artemus Lighting reads more like a "who's who" at an haute couture fashion show. Add several churches — including Cleveland's landmark Old Stone Church, shopping malls, government buildings, hotels and stadiums to the mix and you have the recipe for a successful business.

Artemus Lighting specializes in the design, manufacture and renovation of custom lighting fixtures, including chandeliers of all shapes and sizes, sconces, display lamps, dome lights, uplights and lanterns. Examples of Artemus craftsmanship can be found both domestically and abroad — spotlighting artwork at the trendy SoHo Grand Hotel in New York, casting a glow in churches and restaurants, and illuminating Gucci displays in Hong Kong, the United Kingdom and Singapore.

In 1999 Artemus Lighting celebrated its fifth year in business. But collectively the three principals have more than 120 years of experience in the custom and specialty lighting industry. Arthur Klein, Bernard Klein, David Babin and many of the 15 employees at Artemus Lighting gained their experience at the NL Corporation, founded in Cleveland nearly 100 years ago by an earlier generation of Kleins and widely known for its work in church and custom lighting.

Both Kleins (father Bernard and son Arthur) and Babin learned their craft during years of on-the-job training and became savvy in the key areas of design, manufacturing and marketing. When the younger Klein decided to strike out on his own and establish Artemus Lighting, he was armed with years of hands-on experience and business contacts and able to hit the ground running. His father decided 50 years was enough time at the previous firm and retired to start a second career with Artemus. Babin followed suit soon after.

All design, engineering, electrical and finishing work is handled at the Artemus plant near Collinwood High School on Cleveland's East Side. Part of the metal processing is jobbed out, including work in bronze, stainless steel, aluminum, copper, and galvanized steel, then returned to Artemus for finishing. Other materials used include glass, acrylic, alabaster and fabric shades, which come from a host of suppliers as far away as Germany, Italy and Spain.

The Artemus artisans are part of a small industry —with only 6 or 7 competitors in the United States — where "everyone knows everyone else." Many of their projects are referrals from architects, design firms and lighting consultants in New York, Chicago, Dallas, Los Angeles and San Francisco. Artemus also works with select agents across the nation who promote the company.

"The secret to our success is the custom work we do," notes the senior Klein. "We don't sacrifice quality to deliver projects faster. It's all handwork and takes a definite amount of time."

While very satisfied with the company's progress in the first five years, Arthur Klein would like to continue growing his market beyond retail and shopping malls.

What's his advice to others contemplating a dive into the small business pool? Know your limitations. Don't over promise and under produce. Grow slowly. "There's nothing like a good foundation."

Bronze carriage lantern created for the trendy SoHo Grand Hotel in New York

Artemus Lighting fixtures cast a glow in many churches, including St. Joseph/St. Thomas Church, Staten Island, New York.

Brennan Industries

Brennan Industries, an international supplier of hydraulic fittings and adapters, is a natural outgrowth of Ohio's industrial history and its role as a vital manufacturing center.

Before Ford Motor Company and General Motors established themselves in Detroit, a lot of automobiles were built in Ohio. One of the earliest practical uses of hydraulics was in the braking systems of cars, systems that allowed for more precise control of movement.

With the outbreak of World War II, the hydraulics industry as we know it today started to blossom as the country looked for ways to deal with the sudden and substantial loss of manpower — men going off to war left huge gaps in the industrial workplace. Where once a group of people would physically carry a large, heavy stack of material, now it was moved by the hydraulically operated forklift. The 1940s also spawned a huge war machine of ships, tanks, airplanes and submarines — all engines of movement and requiring ever-increasing levels of control.

During the war Michael Brennan, a native Ohioan, worked for several companies in Ohio and Michigan learning the hydraulics business from the inside. In the period of prosperity and optimism sweeping the country after the end of wartime hostilities, the spirit of entrepreneurship caught the 46-year-old Brennan and he struck out on his own in 1953 to form Brennan Incorporated, selling tube fittings and adaptors to some of his former employers. Mike Brennan had the foresight to start his company when the hydraulics industry was in its youth, at a time when there were only about 300 different connectors being manufactured. Today, there are over 10,000.

Brennan Industries Inc. was created in 1960 when Michael's son, Dennis Brennan, and his son-in-law, David D. Carr, joined the operation. Today, it is still owned and operated by these two families. From the beginning the company's specialty has been in the marketing aspect of the business and in the expert service it provides its customers by purchasing products from fabricators, maintaining a large inventory and promptly filling customer orders.

In 1985 Brennan bought the warehouses and inventory of a major manufacturer, expanding its customer base throughout the United States. With five fully stocked warehouses — in Cleveland, Atlanta, Dallas, Los Angeles and Seattle — that are strategically located across the country, Brennan Industries is able to offer its customers shorter-distance freight costs and even same-day delivery service. This expansion also led Brennan to begin manufacturing some of its high-demand products, and it now produces 60 to 65 percent of what it sells.

With over 4,000 customers, Brennan is the largest independent supplier of hydraulic connectors in the United States, and its business is rapidly moving into other areas around the world: Australia, Canada, Europe, Mexico, the Middle East, New Zealand, Philippines and South America.

During a time of buyouts and corporate mergers, Brennan Industries has remained steadfast in its commitment to be a family-owned and family-controlled enterprise. The company has proved that independent individuals can not only successfully compete and hold their own against large multinational corporations, but they can thrive and grow in their endeavors.

Cleveland-Cliffs, with over 150 years of experience, is a leader in the iron ore mining industry.

Cleveland-Cliffs had its beginning in 1847, when vast amounts of iron were discovered in Michigan's Upper Peninsula. Cleveland businessman Samuel L. Mather partnered with a few other area business leaders and formed the Cleveland Iron Company, which later became The Cleveland-Cliffs Iron Company following its merger with Iron Cliffs Company.

Under the leadership of Mather, and later his son, William G., Cleveland-Cliffs became the largest independent producer of iron ore in the United States.

The firm contributed to the strength of the iron ore industry in Cleveland, which by the early 20th century was one of the largest industries in the area. Though Cleveland-Cliffs was once one of four iron ore companies, it remains the only one headquartered in the city today.

The Mather name has left Cleveland-Cliffs, but its legacy remains with the firm, which is now headed by John S. Brinzo, chairman and CEO, and Thomas J. O'Neil, president and chief operating officer.

Throughout its long history, Cleveland-Cliffs has diversified its product line and its areas of expertise, at one point owning more than 300,000 acres of forest land in Upper Michigan and even drilling for gas and oil in Texas and Louisiana. It also operated two different mines in Australia but has since returned to its core business, which is mining and producing iron ore for the steel industry.

Cleveland-Cliffs now has full or partial ownership of six different mines in North America. The company shares ownership in the mines with the major players in the steel industry, including LTV Steel of Cleveland. Currently, Cleveland-Cliffs manages three mines in Minnesota, two in Michigan and one in eastern Canada and produces about 40 million tons of iron ore pellets each year. Though its employs just 160 people in its Cleveland headquarters, there are about 5,800 employees in Cliff's various managed properties.

As it looks to the future, Cleveland-Cliffs has established a three-pronged strategy.

Most importantly, it will continue nurturing and improving the competitiveness of its established iron ore operations in its six mines.

Secondly, it plans to become a significant player in the area of ferrous metals. Though most of the work the firm does now is in pellets, it plans to expand its operations to include a very-high grade of iron — nearly 95-percent-pure iron — that is produced for mini-mills, which is a growing segment of the steel industry. These mini-mills produce steel in electric furnaces rather than blast furnaces.

The final leg of Cleveland-Cliffs' strategy is to expand its international operations. With its expertise in low-grade ores and its movement into high-grade iron development, the company is ready to take on the world.

Computers play an important role in today's modern iron ore mines. Cleveland-Cliffs recently spent $25 million and two years upgrading its computer systems.

Larger mining equipment has significantly improved productivity at the iron ore mines managed by Cleveland-Cliffs. Shovels with up to 38-yard dippers and trucks up to 240 tons are common in modern mining operations.

Decker Steel & Supply Inc.

Decker Steel & Supply Inc.'s evolution over the last 70 years demonstrates the crucial role between manufacturers and finished products and the value to the economy of well-run, nimble family businesses.

The business began when three employees of J.M. & L.A. Osborn Co., a steel-warehousing firm that could trace its roots to 1859, broke away to form a new business, Decker-Reichert Steel Co., in 1929. The three were John F. Reichert Sr. and brothers Arthur J. and John A. Decker. They also took with them telephone operator Madge Pierce Decker, who had married John Decker in 1919.

The trio took an office on the third floor of Terminal Tower as the final touches were still being completed at the top of the building. Reichert, who was nearing retirement age, never took a salary from the new company, but had made a gentleman's agreement with the Deckers that his two sons, John Jr. and James, would have jobs at the Decker-Reichert when they graduated from college.

Decker-Reichert was a steel brokerage. Unlike a warehouse, it didn't take physical possession of the steel products it sold. Instead, it was primarily a sales organization, linking producers with users.

Soon, however, the company bought a steel warehouse below the Brooklyn-Brighton Bridge on the West Side to expand its services. By 1936 the company moved all of its operations into a new warehouse, its current home, on Train Avenue on Walworth Run. Though now under one roof and one name, Decker-Reichert was two businesses. One was a warehouse that supplied galvanized sheet steel, copper for roofing, downspouts and gutters and later, stainless steel pipe, valves and fittings. The other was a steel service center that manufactured galvanized pipe and elbows for heating, ventilating and air conditioning systems.

After World War II, the business lines that supplied homebuilders boomed and the company eventually began selling complete furnace and air conditioning systems.

Through this evolution, members of the Decker family led the company. In addition, Reichert family members also contributed to the growth, especially in the pipe, valves and fitting division of the business. So did other families. The current vice president and treasurer, Kenneth S. Ross, for example, is the second generation of his family employed at Decker. Another employee, Dan Paul, a warehouseman, is the third generation of his family working at the West Side firm.

"This is a well-oiled operation with good employees," says John W. Decker, grandson of founder John A., who retired in 1982 at age 88. John W. joined the company in 1978, after a career as a teacher. His father, James W., was CEO at the time.

John W. Decker says his company's products can be found in many area buildings, including Jacobs Field, the BP Building and the new federal courthouse at Tower City. Decker sees his firm as closely tied with the growth of Northeastern Ohio. "Our future is in watching Cleveland grow and being a part of that growth," he says.

The Decker-Reichert Steel Co.'s 25th anniversary, May 1, 1954

For more than 50 years, the family-owned-and-operated Earnest Machine Products Company has been successfully supplying quality fasteners from nearly every U.S. fastener manufacturer to industrial aftermarkets and heavy-equipment manufacturers throughout the world. Brothers Paul, Phil and Victor Zehnder established the Zehnder Engineering and Machine Co. in 1947, which manufactured and sold license-plate holders, spring spreaders and thread gauges. After Victor left in 1948, Paul, who was in charge of sales, came across an opportunity to purchase a train carload of army-surplus track-shoe bolts used to secure cleats on tanks and heavy construction equipment. As post-World War II construction on highways and projects began, track-shoe bolts became scarce and heavy-equipment contractors were desperate for replacements. A hastily convened dinner meeting resulted in an $1,800 order from Ohio Machinery Company, a major Caterpillar tractor distributor. The company quickly contacted other Caterpillar distributors around the country and was soon on its way to being one of the nation's leading distributors of industrial fasteners.

Zehnder instituted same-day delivery to Cleveland customers, extended its warehouse space and installed a second telephone line to accept collect calls. By 1950 the company was becoming a recognized distributor of replacement fasteners and moved to Triskett Road, relocating down the block a year later. In 1951 the company name was changed to use Paul's middle name, "Ernest," modified to "Earnest," an Old German word meaning "something of value given by a buyer to a seller to bind a bargain."

The company introduced NU-MA-SHEEN, high-quality industrial enamel paints for heavy equipment, in 1958. Later Earnest explored other products, but fasteners still dominated the product mix and hex-head cap screws, socket-head, button-head and slotted cap screws joined the line along with structural bolts, machine bolts, saddle bolts, elevator bolts, nuts and washers. Enjoying sustained growth, the company established its first branch sales-and-distribution office in Tampa, Florida, in 1968. By this time manufacturers of everything from automobile steering and undersea pipe-repair kits to hydraulic pumps and riding lawnmowers looked to Earnest for on-time delivery and product integrity. The company aggressively pursued industrial hardware distributors across the nation until by 1977, Earnest supplied customers in all 50 states and was establishing contacts in Puerto Rico, Canada and the world. 1984 saw the company establish its Midwest distribution center in Davenport, Iowa.

An innovator in integrated supply, Earnest established early partnerships with its customers through Earnest Express, controlling the delivery of the fastener portion of a manufacturer's production line, delivering fasteners and related products on an as-needed basis. The company's in-house testing lab, established in 1963, became accredited by the American Association of Laboratory Accreditation in 1998. Today, a second generation of Zehnders, James P. and John, oversees the operations as alternating CEOs. Through hard work and continuing to build customer loyalty, Earnest Machine Products looks forward to another half century of family-run success.

Paul E. Zehnder c. 1938

Jim Zehnder, chairman (standing), and brother John Zehnder president and CEO pose with the company's vintage 1937 Ford pickup.

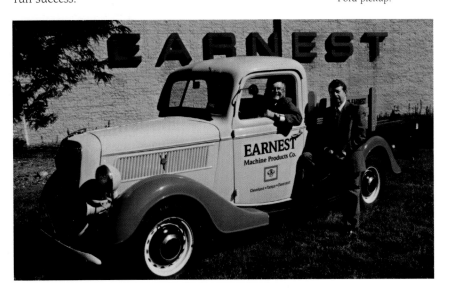

Fay Industries Inc.

Fay Industries Inc. is more than a business. It's a family. The Strongsville firm, which operates as a full-line steel service center, has built itself and its business around family values and leadership.

Fay Industries had its beginning in Brooklyn. The business was known as Fay Machine Products in 1974 when Jack Notarianni and his brother-in-law, Dick Schnaterbeck, decided to buy the firm. Both men had a strong background in steel, so it was not long before they began to work heavily as a steel service center, and less and less as a machine shop. In 1989 they changed the name of the business to Fay Industries, phased the machine shop out of the business, sold it and then began to concentrate solely on steel.

As a steel service center, Fay Industries buys large quantities of steel from the steel mills, and then supplies it in smaller amounts to its customers. Although some of its 1,600 customers in Northeast Ohio purchase the steel from Fay Industries without having the firm do anything to it, many of its customers seek value-added services when they purchase the bar or plate steel from Fay Industries. Thus, the company now has 12 saws in its shop to cut according to customer specifications. Using these saws they are able to take any shape or size of steel, including tubing, angles, channels and flat bars, and turn it into something useful for a variety of industries, ranging from the automotive to the toy industry and original equipment manufacturers to medical equipment manufacturers.

(Left to right) Conley Schnaterbeck, vice president of credit and human resources; Dick Schnaterbeck, president and treasurer; Jack Notarianni, vice president and secretary; Craig Notarianni, salesman; John Notarianni II, vice president and controller; and Brad Notarianni, material manager, have built up a strong, family-owned-and-operated business.

Fay Industries' new state of the art facility in Strongsville

What Schnaterbeck, president and treasurer, and Notarianni, vice president and secretary, have created is nothing unusual in the Greater Cleveland area. They compete within a large industry. But the family-oriented firm has been able to provide close, personal attention to customers. It was not long before both men's sons joined the firm. Today, R. Conley Schnaterbeck is vice president of credit and human services. Jack's sons, John II, vice

president and controller; Craig, salesman; and Brad, material manager, have also come on board to help Fay Industries continue its growth. Together with their fathers, they manage about 50 employees, 26 of whom belong to 10 families that also work at the firm.

Both Notarianni and Schnaterbeck have always had an intimate knowledge of the steel industry and what it entails and admit that they have known many of their customers since day one. This has allowed them to not only serve customers better, but to grow as they grew. This continual growth was the reason behind the firm's move from Brooklyn to Strongsville. It left Brooklyn in 1986 but was forced once again to expand in June of 1999. This led Notarianni and Schnaterbeck to Strongsville's Foltz Industrial Park, where they built a state-of-the-art facility on five acres of land with the option to buy five more acres — which they anticipate will be needed within five years, as more customers and businesses realize who they are and what they do. And what Fay Industries does is provide quality service in a personal manner.

Fosbel, Inc.

Since 1980 the Fosbel group of companies has forged its way with advanced repair and treatment for furnaces throughout the international marketplace. Initially a joint venture of two of the most respected companies in the metallurgical and glass technology fields, Foseco and Glaverbel, Fosbel has been a member of the Burmah Castrol group of companies since 1990. Fosbel delivers innovation in service with its ceramic welding technology, which repairs damaged refractories without the need for furnace shutdown. Its customers include the glass, coke, aluminum, cement, power generation, petrochemical and refining industries.

For decades Cleveland projected the image of a heavy industrialized sprawl along the shores of Lake Erie, a city covered in a smokescreen telling the world that this was where America worked. Blast furnaces and smoke-stacks were visible everywhere. By the end of the 1970s, when steel production slowed down, an aging industry gave Cleveland the more apt title as capital of the "rust belt." What mills remained were bearing the wear of time. Fosbel chose to headquarter itself in Cleveland due not only to the market potential here, but because it was ideally located between East Coast and Midwestern centers.

An ISO 9001-certified company since 1994, Fosbel has sought excellence in the design and supply of refractory repair and maintenance services. When the group acquired two Hotwork businesses, operating since 1963, Fosbel was able to expand service to include a range of furnace heat and cool down operations, including refractory dry out, controlled furnace heat-up and cool-down operations, tie-rod adjustment, cullett filling, furnace draining and sulphate burnout. In 2000 a new method implemented by the Hotwork group recycles the hot water during a furnace drain. This process eliminates the environmental concern caused by the previous method using cold water, which had the potential for carrying contaminants and hot water from the drain into streams, rivers and municipal water systems.

Its joint venture, Cetek, enabled Fosbel to provide thin film, high-temperature ceramic coatings for use on both refractories and metal components in the chemical and petrochemical industries. The key to Fosbel's success is the comprehensive service it is able to offer. Its diversity allows it to handle up to 40 projects simultaneously. As a member of the Burmah Castrol global group of businesses, Fosbel and its components draw the support to continually enhance the capabilities of their services.

Fosbel, Inc.
Berea facility

In 1996 Fosbel was given the BAC Craft Award of "Best Project" from the International Union of Bricklayers and Allied Craftworkers in recognition of their Gulf States Steel coke oven rebuild in Gadsen, Alabama, with Fosbel maximizing the availability of the plant, thus improving production. The company has also been recognized by SRI, Quality System Registrar, Inc.

Locally, Fosbel continues an annual commitment to numerous local charities and charitable events, including the Northeast Ohio "Race for the Cure" in the fight against breast cancer; Berea's Spring Fling for Leukemia; and the Ohio Kidney Foundation Annual Chili Cook Off.

Ceramic welding
of coke oven wall

Gent Machine Co.

A penchant for innovation and reliability has made the Gent Machine Co. a significant player in the automatic screw machine industry.

Founded in 1929 by Arthur and Richard Gent Sr., this father-and-son team descended from a line of inventors and innovators. Among them were Arthur's brother, William, who established the William Gent Machine Company in Rockford, Illinois, in 1880 to make machinery used to manufacture barbed wire. In the 1920s, Arthur's nephew, William, invented the penny arcade machines that were so popular at Euclid Beach Park.

The Gents launched their new business at the intersection of Highland and Richmond roads in Highland Heights. Housed in a barn that had a machine shop on one side and a house on the other, the company began manufacturing screw machine parts for a variety of industries. Even though the country was in the throes of the Great Depression, the Gents established a reputation for success.

The engine for this success was Richard, a mechanical and business genius who routinely worked 18 hours a day, seven days a week to keep the company healthy and thriving. In 1940 he was instrumental in landing an enormous Army-Navy contract to produce shells for the war effort. This contract gave the company the financial boost it needed to fund a move in 1941 to a sorely needed larger facility on South Green Road in South Euclid, a move that came after the family homestead attached to the shop burned to the ground.

Arthur had a strong work ethic that he wanted reflected in the work environment. As the structure for the new building was erected, he had time-honored sayings printed on the I-beams of the factory — sayings such as "Order is heaven's first law and it should be obeyed"; "There is a place for everything and everything in its place"; and "Cleanliness is next to godliness." It was his way of reminding employees that an honest day's work was something to be admired.

When Arthur died in 1954, the company continued in the hands of Richard and his siblings. A decade later, Richard Jr. joined the business while working on an engineering degree from John Carroll University. When his father retired in 1977, Richard Jr. became the sole owner. In 2000 the company became a fouth-generation business when his son, Richard IV, joined the company.

The Gent Machine Co. produces a vast array of automatic screw machine parts in a wide variety of metals, including cold rolled and stainless steel, aluminum, brass and alloys. These parts are used in applications ranging from control cables for tractors and boats, to strip wheels in air conditioners, valve seats for tractor hydraulic pumps and bleed-off valves for automobile manifolds. The company's Davenport 5-spindle automatic machines provide the drilling, tapping, reaming and broaching processes needed to produce around 20 million parts per year for use in a variety of industries.

One asset that sets The Gent Machine Co. apart from its competition is its focus on personalized service. Not only do companies deal directly with the owner, they also can count on Richard Gent himself to make a site inspection should a question about quality control arise. It's attention to detail like this that has made the company successful and will contribute to its longevity in the years to come.

Richard Gent Sr. is a proud onlooker during a ceremony to award an Army-Navy work contract to his father, Arthur (fourth from left on dais).

The power of innovation to reshape the way we live and work is widely recognized as a form of creativity. At HI TecMetal Group (HTG), entrepreneurs associate innovation and creativity with technological breakthroughs. HTG has received attention from the media because of its ability to create and implement new technology initiatives.

Several years ago, HTG's sales and marketing group visualized and created an innovative trade show display featuring an animated Old World blacksmith. "Historically, the thermal processing industry has been viewed as a dirty, low-tech field," said Terry Profughi, chief executive officer at HTG. "Our goal in the creation of this animated display was to paint a new picture of our industry, by changing the stereotypical image of smoke, fire and oil to what it actually is — an engineering- and technology-driven field."

HTG has no blacksmiths among its 800 employees. Instead it has engineers, technicians and managers who use the art and science of engineering in a family of more than two dozen businesses that braze, weld, coat and heat-treat metals.

Between 1984 and 1999, HTG either acquired or started more than 39 businesses and now offers over 100 different metal services to its customers. The company also manufactures dozens of proprietary engineered products. Sales have increased from $1.6 million to more than $55 million annually. Half the revenue growth has come from added sales, the other half through acquisitions.

HTG owns a portfolio of companies located in five states serving diverse markets from aerospace to automotive. The company is deeply entrenched in the heart of the metal industry, with more than 17 facilities located in Ohio and Michigan.

In 1999 HTG made its first venture into the plastics industry with the purchase of Custom PlasTech, Ltd., a northeastern-Ohio manufacturer of blow-molded plastic products for customers in industries such as materials handling, waste management, building and construction, hospitality, packaging, signage and displays. Profughi said his customers now use both metals and plastics in their products. "We saw an opportunity to broaden our services," he says.

Despite the firm's technical achievements, Profughi believes HI TecMetal Group's real strength is its commitment to customer service. HTG considers itself not a supplier but a technological partner. It offers overnight service on some processes and has even purchased a trucking company to offer transportation and warehousing services to customers.

To Profughi, his co-workers are as important as his customers. This is demonstrated by the fact that over the years, HI TecMetal Group has won many prestigious awards for growth and management excellence. In 1999 HTG won the Northcoast 99 award, recognizing it as one of the 99 best companies to work for in Northeast Ohio by the Employers Resource Council and Enterprise Development, Inc., a business-development arm of Case Western Reserve University.

HTG is committed to painting a new picture of its industry by changing the stereotypical image of smoke, fire and oil to what it actually is — an engineering- and technology-driven field.

HI TecMetal Group member companies offer over 100 different metal services and manufacture dozens of proprietary engineered products.

Husqvarna Viking Sewing Machines

The secluded Cleveland suburb of Westlake houses the U.S. headquarters for international sewing machine giant Husqvarna Viking. Its line of products, like the Husqvarna Viking Designer I and the White Superlock 1934 D, represents a revolution in engineering design to match the evolution of sewing from a necessity to a hobby. As the technology and profit leader in the sewing machine industry, selling 1.5 million units in 1999, the history of

Husqvarna Viking Sewing Machines (formerly known as Viking and White Sewing Machine Companies) is the history of the industrial revolution and its impact on the daily lives of people on both sides of the Atlantic.

In 1866 Thomas H. White moved his Massachusetts machine shop to Cleveland to be closer to his suppliers when sales of his small, hand-operated, single-thread sewing

machine began to grow. At 6-inches high, 9-inches long and designed to fit in the palm of the hand, this little marvel sold for $10. In 1876 White incorporated the concern into the White Sewing Machine Company and began a tradition of innovation that made it one of the best-known names in sewing machines. But White made other products, including bicycles, roller skates, phonographs, kerosene

lamps, automatic lathes and screw machines, and in 1901 it introduced the White Steam Car. The balance of the 20th century saw the growth of White into an international conglomerate bringing innovations like portable sewing machines, electric motors and the open-arm design to the sewing machine industry. In the 1980s White introduced the first overlock machine or serger for home use, and in 1986 the company was bought out by the Swedish household-products firm, Electrolux AB.

Meanwhile, on the other side of the Atlantic, another sewing machine giant was coming into its own, paralleling White in both its product line and reputation for excellence. Husqvarna was founded as a Swedish royal arms factory in 1689 and was transferred into private hands in 1757. The factory began making sewing machines in 1872 and branched into household products in 1874. Husqvarna manufactured its first bicycle in 1896 and its first motorcycle in 1908. The company made its first electric cooker in 1934, its first free-arm sewing machine in 1947 and its first chain saw in 1959. The company merged with Electrolux AB In 1978.

Today, thanks to the 1986 joining of these industry legends, a sewing hobbyist can log on to the Internet and download an embroidery design onto a floppy disk. The disk can then be placed in the built-in disk drive of a computerized sewing machine, which will then sew the pattern while the sewer walks away. The Cleveland-based operation is the North American headquarters for both training and product distribution and is referred to as a "virtual factory." From its environs emerge a wealth of sewing

products, including software for the PC to cater to sewers of the new age. The company even has a public television show called "America Sews with Sue Hausmann," which has taped over 200 broadcasts. Still, the company maintains a firm commitment to the Cleveland area and its skilled workforce and looks forward to another millennium of sewing evolution.

Kraft Fluid Systems

Kraft Fluid Systems specializes in the selection and application of hydraulic and power-transmission products for manufacturers of construction, mining, material handling and industrial machinery. Solutions involve standard and custom-design components, packaged assemblies or the development of a complete system.

Ever since Bob and Marie Kraft founded Kraft Fluid Systems in 1972, the company's mission has been to provide customers with increased value through superior application and technical assistance, quality products and responsive service. Bob adds, "Customers are the focus of everything we do, and we value long-term customers as our greatest asset. Our goal is to learn and satisfy customer needs by helping them utilize the latest technology."

The company's first office was the second floor of a small machine shop in Strongsville. In 1975 they moved to larger space and added their first employees. They occupied larger leased space as the business grew, and moved to their current building in 1986, now totaling over 30,000 square feet. The facility includes "state of technology" test stands and assembly equipment for hydraulic pumps, motors, valves and gear reducers. Sales offices are located in Columbus, Ohio; Pittsburgh and Philadelphia, Pennsylvania; Covington, Kentucky, and Lafayette, Indiana.

Executive Vice President Diane Baker captures the Company's culture and long-term employee tenure by quoting from the company's value statement. "Our employee-owners are our greatest resource and we value their suggestions for improvement. We respect individual and family needs and encourage personal and professional growth. The positive attitudes of our employee family are responsible for our continued growth. We believe that respected and rewarded employees lead to satisfied long-term customers." Kraft Fluid Systems became an ESOP employee-owned company in 1998.

Kraft Fluid Systems, Inc. is a corporate member of the Fluid Power Distributor Association, the Cleveland Industrial Distributor Association, the Fluid Power Society, the Strongsville Chamber of Commerce, the Strongsville Historical Society, the ESOP Association and the Greater Cleveland Growth Association (COSE).

Bob and Marie Kraft encourage corporate and individual volunteer activities. The company is an annual corporate supporter of the Fluid Power Education Foundation, the Strongsville Education Foundation, Strongsville High School Athletics, City of Strongsville Recreation Program, the Optimist Club of Strongsville, the March of Dimes, the Strongsville Food Bank and the Southwest General Health Foundation. It was a corporate supporter of the Southwest General Health Foundation's 1993 Capital Campaign. For Christmas of 1999, the employee-owners adopted two families through the Berea Children's Home and the St. Vincent De Paul Society, and they are planning to make this an annual charitable project.

President Harry Schoenfeld closes with Kraft's vision for the future. "We will be the leading value-added supplier of hydraulic, power transmission and motion control technologies for mobile original equipment manufacturers."

Leader Electric Supply Co.

You could say that Harry and Rose Strauss are the perfect example of a couple who fulfilled the American Dream.

Harry and Rose, co-founders of Leader Electric Supply Co., founded the company in 1961 with just $20,000 — $10,000 of their own savings and $10,000 from a partner who later left the firm. Though those first few years at E. 34th and Superior were difficult, Harry and Rose managed to build strong relationships with the leaders of the electric supply business and create a family-owned business to be proud of.

Leader Electric has about 17,000 items in inventory, including wire, pipe, lighting fixtures and lamps. The company now calls home a 45,000-square-foot building just 10 blocks down from its original facility. The electric supply store served mostly "mom-and-pop" contractors in its early days but now relies mostly on larger property owners and companies as its customer base.

Harry, who has since passed away, was a first-generation American with not even a high school education behind him. Rose was born in Europe and came to Cleveland as a child. Despite these hardships, the couple survived tough times.

Leader Electric Supply continues to thrive as a small, family-owned business because of its continued focus on one-on-one, personal relationships with customers. It was not unusual to see their son, Archie (Arthur), and daughters, Susan and Terri, working in the warehouse after school when they were growing up. Archie and

The Leader Electric Supply Co. has a vast inventory in its 45,000-square-foot facility.

Susan have continued to strengthen and build the business for the past 15 years.

After the third partner left the business in 1964, Rose and Harry worked both night and day to prove themselves and maintain quality relationships. Rose worked the counter, while Harry would make deliveries in the early

morning and on his way home from the shop because they had few employees. Today, Leader Electric employs 30 people.

During the early years, Harry convinced manufacturers to sell to Leader Electric, and the company was proud to call Oster Electric and Elo Electric two of its biggest customers.

Although the firm has not grown dramatically in its 39 years of business, Rose believes her and Harry's philosophy of integrity and loyalty was the reason behind the gradual success of the supply store. Customers and dealers became friends, and it was not unusual for Harry and Rose to attend customers' weddings and bar mitzvahs. And if a customer needed to borrow on credit, then Leader Electric would do what it could to help that customer out.

"Those were the days when you could count on people's loyalty," Rose says. "Our reputation, honesty and integrity are the main things that we feel are different from our competitors."

Though this philosophy has hurt the business on one or two occasions, Rose believes it is this that would make Harry so proud.

Harry and Rose Strauss, founders of Leader Electric Supply Co.

In 1937 a college student named Al Moen, who was working in a garage to earn tuition money, stopped at the end of the day to wash his hands. When the hot water from the conventional two-handle faucet gushed out too quickly and startled him, he was struck by a sudden idea.

A single-handle mixing faucet would be better, he realized, because it would give people exactly the temperature of water they wanted every time.

That sudden inspiration turned out to be a concept that would not only revolutionize the faucet industry, but set into motion a steady stream of innovation and technological firsts that would help to make Moen the No. 1 brand of faucets in North America.

It took Al Moen a decade to perfect his invention and persuade the company he worked for, later renamed Stanadyne, to manufacture the faucet in the early 50s. By 1959 the Moen single-handle faucet was in hundreds of thousands of American homes.

Since that time Moen Inc. has been the driving force behind countless technological innovations that have improved the operation of faucets and plumbing accessories. Equally important, Moen has earned unparalleled success by ensuring these innovations could be shared by the majority of consumers by making them more durable, user-friendly and affordable.

Much of Moen's success, in fact, can be traced to its ability to give its customers what they want. Case in point is the one-piece filter cartridge, which replaced the washers in a faucet with a one-piece, easy-install cartridge that made it much easier to maintain.

Another example is the LifeShine finish. While faucets have been available in a variety of finishes for years, the only really durable substance was polished chrome. The LifeShine innovation maintains the beauty of a delicate finish like brass, but adds exceptional durability for a best-of-both-worlds solution.

Moen is also responsible for popularizing the kitchen pull-out faucet, a design idea that originated in Europe and came to the United States with a cost that was prohibitive to most consumers. Moen redesigned and restyled the pull-out faucet and then priced it right, making it accessible to most people — and still one of the most popular faucets in homes today.

Most recently has come the new Pure Touch Filtering Faucet System, the first-ever faucet to incorporate a water purification filter right in the faucet wand. So revolutionary is this concept that the faucet has to date been awarded nine design and product-of-the-year awards from publications like *Popular Science* and *Home*.

Owned by Fortune Brands Inc., Moen maintains a beautiful corporate headquarters in North Olmsted, a building actually designed by a residential architect using soft, pleasing colors, multiple windows and large open spaces to create a home-like environment, conducive to teamwork and inspiration.

Al Moen amassed a total of 75 patents in his lifetime — most not related to the plumbing industry. But his spirit of invention remains alive and well at Moen and promises to keep the innovative spirit flowing for years to come.

Moen's beautiful North Olmsted headquarters building was designed to provide a comfortable, home-like atmosphere for employees.

Moen's revolutionary Pure Touch Filtering Faucet, which incorporates a water purification filter in the faucet wand, exemplifies the company's ongoing commitment to product and design innovation.

North American Wire Products Corp.

It started out in 1976 as the quandary of a master's thesis — how to find the right manufacturing plant, even one that's idle; successfully borrow against the value of the real estate; and with only a pocketful of cash, create a successful business.

Now, it is North American Wire Products Corp., a thriving Solon company manufacturing and selling high-quality, precision steel wire. Bradley K. Martin was an MBA student at Long Island University in the mid-1970s. He was running Martin Enterprises, a steel service center and brokerage started by his father. For his thesis he described how an entrepreneur with the right idea and energy could on a shoestring create what Martin, now president of North American Wire, has described as "the most advanced wire mill in the country." He's well on his way to achieving that goal.

The plant Martin found was in Solon. In 1983 he purchased the closed GHA Lock Joint Inc. pipe-wire

manufacturing plant. At first, the new company concentrated on supplying wire for reinforced concrete high-pressure water pipe. Soon, the plant was manufacturing upholstery and mechanical spring wire. The company quickly realized that it needed to shift its production from supplying common wire products to producing the higher-quality specialty-steel products.

The company targeted music spring wire, which is used by the automotive and other industries but which, until North American entered the fray, was supplied primarily from steel firms abroad. Martin also realized he had an opportunity to sell this precision steel to companies that made fiber optic cable since they use wire to strengthen and armor the cable, which carries telephone and Internet communications." Steel is 80 percent of the weight of fiber-optic cable, Martin realized. "The Silicon Valley couldn't survive without Ohio steel."

To make that move, the company needed sophisticated equipment capable of drawing the wire to demanding tolerances. A late 1990s $3.5 million modernization added computer-controlled machines that draw wire at up to 5,000 feet per minute and to tolerances of plus or minus 1 ten-thousandth of an inch. This upgrading has allowed the company to compete for the business of customers who need high-quality, high-carbon steel wire. North American Wire also began to prepare a new electro-galvanizing line to move into the galvanized wire market.

All of these moves were expected to enable North American Wire to double tonnage and triple revenue.

During the early years, Martin remained in New York. Starting a steel wire business in New York would have been more convenient personally, but Martin believed it was the wrong place for the new business. "We had to be in Cleveland," he says, adding that it was the best place to find skilled workers and was a focal point for steel distribution. "If you want to be an actor, you go to Hollywood," Martin observed. "If you want to be in the steel business, you come to Cleveland."

Finally, Martin took his own advice. In 1992 he merged Martin Enterprises into North American Wire, closed his Long Island depot and bought a home in Cleveland's eastern suburbs.

Ohio Machinery Co.

Long before there was an Ohio Machinery Co., the Taylor Tractor Company met the needs of Ohio's Caterpillar and Deere equipment users from its central Ohio location in Columbus. Ironically, it wasn't any of today's owning Taylor family members who were associated with the original Taylor Tractor Company.

In 1945 the company was reorganized as Ohio Machinery Co. and moved its headquarters to Cleveland. It wasn't until 1961 that a Cleveland-area Taylor — Thomas H. Taylor Sr. — took over as president. Tom Sr., a long-time successful Taylor Tractor salesman, had become the company's vice president of sales. After taking control of Ohio Machinery, Tom Sr. and his son, Tom Jr., initiated an expansion program to satisfy the constantly changing market for its Caterpillar earthmoving equipment and engines. Prior to the Taylors' succession, Ohio Machinery had expanded into Toledo and Youngstown.

The first expansion after the Taylors took over was to Zanesville in 1962, where an office was opened in the front of a feed store. The location was chosen to meet the needs of Ohio's very active coal mining industry. As interstate highway construction boomed, the company enlarged its operations in 1971 with a new headquarters in Broadview Heights.

In 1975 Ohio Machinery opened a new location in Cadiz, which also focused on the coal mining industry. In 1980 the company opened an additional Broadview Heights facility to support the growth of its truck and commercial engine sales, rental, parts and service business — a division now called Ohio Engine Power.

Since that time the company has opened new, or improved, facilities in Canton, Painesville and Youngstown. Its relatively new Hydraulics Division in Bolivar repairs and remanufactures Caterpillar and non-Cat hydraulic components. The firm's Con/Agg Division in Cincinnati sells and supports such equipment as crushers, screening plants, Gradall excavators, small pavers and other equipment used in general construction and aggregate processing.

For the most part, the company's equipment and engines still are sold and rented to contractors, industrial concerns, mine operators and governmental entities. But "rented" and "retail" are among the biggest changes in the industry following a trend very popular in Europe and Japan. Since many contractors don't wish to pay for expensive equipment they may need only occasionally or seasonally, and many homeowners want a "do-it-yourself" capability, the firm's rental business has grown dramatically. To meet this expanding need, the company's Miller Tool Rental subsidiary specializes in renting contractor's tools, light- to medium-sized Cat equipment and a full line of industrial lifts on a short- to medium-term basis. Miller Tool Rental is growing and conducts its business through four Greater Cleveland and Youngstown retail outlets.

Under Ken Taylor, the third generation of Cleveland Taylors to run the company, Ohio Machinery has shown the ability to diversify and anticipate changing customer needs. The company has changed its product lines, services and capabilities in recent years enabling it to provide the equipment "to move mountains" and pave highways. Its more than 500 employees in eastern Ohio continually sharpen their focus on providing exceptional, personalized customer service.

As a result, Ohio Machinery has moved to the forefront of the industry and is paving its way to success.

Ohio Machinery's corporate headquarters in Broadview Heights

Plastic Safety Systems, Inc.

Motorists caught in a construction zone traffic jam may not be very happy, but if it's a work zone outfitted with temporary traffic control devices from Plastic Safety Systems, Inc. (PSS), at least they are safe.

Safety is the number one concern at PSS, a family-owned company. Products that are innovative, environmentally friendly and give a superior performance are also high on the list. PSS products are used by construction companies throughout the United States, Canada and Puerto Rico and include channelizers, delineators and reflective safety fencing.

Founder David A. Cowan started PSS in the early 1980s as a subsidiary of Electro-General Plastics Corp., a company with roots dating back to 1962. Electro-General custom made both light-gauge and heavy-gauge vacuum-formed plastic products. Then in the late 1970s, one of its researchers designed a temporary traffic light. The idea was ahead of its time, but it led to the company's entry into the traffic control industry.

Plastic Safety Systems, Inc. patented the innovative Lifegard® orange construction barrel in use today on roadways across North America.

Electro-General then designed its own one-piece orange construction barrel, a relatively new invention at the time that was quickly replacing dangerous steel drums. The company took a few hundred prototypes of its barrel to a construction contractor. The contractor tested the barrels in a storm and they held up beautifully. In fact, the barrels were such a hit that Electro-General decided to form a separate company devoted solely to the product. An employee from the contractor that tested the barrels was hired, and PSS began as a one-product, one-person company in September 1982.

The late 1980s saw a change in the safety standards set by the Federal Highway Administration. The rectangular barrel sold by PSS would soon not be up to regulation. The company responded by designing a round barrel that not only fit the new dimension requirements, but also featured a base made out of recycled truck tire sidewalls, eliminating the need for sandbags. Construction companies could save significant amounts of money and hassle with the new barrel, and motorists would be safer in work zones with barrels that didn't move or slip. PSS patented the new barrel, called the Lifegard, in 1991. It was the first sandless barrel on the market and the archetype for the modern barrels being used today.

PSS continued to grow, even outlasting its parent company when Electro-General was sold in 1990. The company remained in the Cleveland Office that had been occupied by Electro-General since 1968, and grew into the space within a few years.

In addition to barrels, PSS offers a complete line of complementary products such as delineators, fencing, vertical panels, speed bumps and barricades. Though it recently began taking orders over the Internet, most of its products are still sold the same way they were back in the 1960s — with a handshake.

The number of government safety tests continues to grow and federal regulations continue to change. Plastic is increasingly accepted as a safe and durable material, which is good news for the future of PSS. The company plans to expand to keep up with the high demand for its products and will continue to stay one step ahead of the federal mandates.

Royal Appliance Manufacturing Company

Creating unique and state-of-the-art cleaning products is nothing new for Royal Appliance Manufacturing Company. The Highland Heights maker of Dirt Devil® floor-care products has been recognized for years for its highly acclaimed consumer products, including the much-imitated Dirt Devil Hand Vac and the revolutionary Broom Vac®.

Not immediately apparent is how deeply this spirit of innovation is ingrained into the heart of the company. Royal's roots can be traced all the way back to the development of the very first metal vacuum cleaner, produced in 1905 in P.A. Geier's garage in Cleveland.

To manage the almost immediate success of the new product, P.A. Geier Company moved to a four-story building on East 105th Street, where it produced vacuum cleaners along with a host of other appliances, like mixers, hair dryers and washing machines. But vacuum cleaners remained the key product, and dedication to developing improvements to this flagship product was at the forefront of the company.

In 1937 the company developed the first hand-held vacuum, the Royal Prince, which buoyed its success for many years. In 1953 the Walter E. Schott organization, which owns the Cincinnati Reds baseball team, bought the company and renamed it the Royal Appliance Manufacturing Company.

The company's most significant innovation came in 1984 with the introduction of the Dirt Devil Hand Vac, which to this day remains its signature product and the largest-selling hand-held vacuum in the United States. Since its debut more than 23 million units have been sold, opening the door for many new product innovations under the Dirt Devil brand name.

In fact, new product development is so much a part of its foundation, the company has vowed to produce at least one new upright vacuum cleaner each and every year, along with another unique, first-to-market floor-care product. This aggressive commitment to research and development has resulted in a number of highly successful products. These include the 1996 introduction of the revolutionary Broom Vac®, a new-to-the world product that sweeps and vacuums in one simple step, making the dustpan virtually obsolete; and the recent introduction of its Swivel Glide® line of upright vacuums, which most notably includes the Dirt Devil Vision®, the company's first bagless upright vacuum cleaner and one of the best-selling upright vacuums at retail.

The success of the Vision ignited the growth of the bagless vacuum category in the floor care industry and laid the groundwork for Royal's development of new and innovative bagless vacuums such as the Vision® with Sensor, the first Dirt Devil-branded upright to be priced above $200.

But Royal's new product development doesn't stop there. With the introduction of the Dirt Devil Easy Steamer™, the company has also recently entered another rapidly growing segment of the industry — the carpet shampooer category.

The company applies the same aggressive spirit to its marketing, evidenced by a host of memorable television ads, including the much-touted campaign featuring classic movie clips that paired Fred Astaire with several Dirt Devil "dance partners," including the Broom Vac. Thanks to such creative advertising campaigns, Dirt Devil enjoys brand name awareness with more than 98 percent of the U.S. population.

Innovation yesterday. Innovation today. Royal is one example in which "more of the same" will make for an even brighter tomorrow.

Michael Merriman, Royal Appliance president and CEO, with the Dirt Devil Vision with Sensor, the company's first upright to be priced above $200

Due to its continued growth, Royal Appliance is moving to a larger facility on Cochran Road in the city of Glenwillow at the end of 2000.

Samsel Supply Co.

Frank J. Samsel, founder of Samsel Supply Company, worked most of his life on the Great Lakes, first as a deckhand then as a salesman for Upson Walton Company. Along the banks of The Flats, lake vessels

Frank Samsel oversees the delivery of marine supplies at Edgewater Park in 1969.

.TOMMY B..
CLEVELAND

loaded and unloaded cargo up and down the Cuyahoga River. Businesses along the river sold maritime supplies and equipment catering to the visiting marine commerce. It was there that Samsel decided to throw in his hat as a merchant. Samsel started with cutting and selling wire rope and cordage in April 1958. He then purchased the Upson-Walton Marine Division in 1961.

With the purchase of the Upson Walton Company, Samsel continued a more than 100-year tradition of marine service on the Cuyahoga River from the building

on Old River Road. The company sold wire rope, chains, block fittings, load binders, canvas products, tarps and cordage. In 1977 the company again moved north to its current location on Old River Road.

Delivering supplies to the big freighters, Frank Samsel saw firsthand the affects of pollution on the Cuyahoga River. His company was one of the first to begin cleanup activities, long before the infamous fire of 1969. As a direct result of this involvement, the company expanded into safety supplies. "In those days, when they were out on an oil spill, there was no special clothing, no EPA regulations," says company president Kathleen Petrick. "The need to protect our employees was evident. Before OSHA mandated safety rules and personal protective equipment, we were using the equipment." The need for safety equipment grew with the new regulations and Samsel was there to provide education and equipment. The company also expanded into supplies for construction and industry.

In 1978 Samsel became a second-generation company when son Michael came to work there, followed by Christopher in 1988 and daughter Kathleen in 1993. In 1981 the company was renamed Samsel Supply Company to reflect the changing customer base.

Today, Samsel Supply Company has over 30,000 different items to outfit a construction, marine, or industrial job site, including clothing, tools and equipment. There is a canvas shop where tarpaulins for wintering building sites

Firestone Professional Softball Stadium in Akron, Ohio; winter enclosure by Samsel Supply Co.

are fabricated. Samsel also provides inspection of life rafts for lake carriers. The Old River Road showroom also caters to the regular hardware consumer with a landscaping or improvement project. Frank Samsel set the bar on what keeps the company successful. "It's because of the firm foundation our father gave us that we have been able to grow the business and move forward into the future," says Petrick. "Our goal is to provide service and education to our customers, allowing them to perform their jobs with the proper tools and knowledge."

Standard Signs, Inc.

Now a third-generation business, Standard Signs Inc. has been characterized by a tradition of quality and pride since 1936. The corporation was founded as Cleveland Porcelain Enameling Co. by 35-year-old Vern E. Messner after the porcelain-coating plant where he worked closed during the Depression. Relying on his knowledge of ceramics and metallurgy, he set up shop in a garage and offered porcelain-enameling services primarily for stove parts, as well as enameled signs in copper, cast iron and steel. Within six months he had the financial backing he needed to relocate the business to the Cleveland neighborhood on East 65th Street known as Slavic Village, where the Polish and Czech immigrants who lived in the friendly enclave provided a pool of steady labor for the fledgling company.

Recognizing that further diversification would ensure future success, Messner expanded his product line in 1941 to include porcelain-enameled industrial safety signs that he marketed through a new subsidiary he named Standard Signs Inc. He also supported the war effort at this time by heat-treating aircraft parts.

More than a decade later, Messner seized another opportunity to grow his business when the Federal Aviation Administration (FAA) developed an airfield guide for regional airports that had strict requirements for signage and other safety equipment. Aided by his sons, Andrew and Stephen, who joined the company in 1955 and 1960, respectively, Messner developed a line of lighted taxiway-guidance signs in 1955 that met the FAA's exacting specifications and took the company into a new phase of operation.

When Messner retired in 1970, Standard Signs was still one of the few companies in the country to make FAA-approved airport signage. But by the late 70s Andrew and Stephen realized that improvements to the signs were necessary to remain competitive.

Thus in 1982 they began to market Lumacurve taxiway and runway signs. These retro-reflective, internally lit signs had a flexible, modular design capable of withstanding both jet blasts of up to 200 miles per hour and unforgiving weather conditions. Today, an updated version of these signs are Standard Signs' signature product and mark airfield ground traffic routes at more than 1,000 airports around the world.

In the early 1990s Standard Signs stopped stocking the porcelain safety signs it had manufactured for decades in favor of custom orders, an efficiency that paid off by allowing the company to produce higher-volume products instead. Another significant milestone also occurred around that time, when management of the company was passed down to a third generation of Messners: Andrew's sons, John and Neil; and Stephen's children, Mark and Marianne. But although a new generation is now at the helm, the commitment to quality and customer satisfaction fostered first by their grandfather and then by their respective fathers has continued unabated. Standard Signs seems destined to stand the test of time thanks to its history of innovation and solid dependability.

Founder Vern E. Messner

A Standard Signs employee inspects Lumacurve signs at busy Ontario International Airport in California.

Tesar Industrial Contractors

What began as a local trucking company in 1919 has grown to become one of Cleveland's complete industrial contractors, offering such services as plant relocation, on-site machinery moves, plant maintenance, rigging, steel fabrication and equipment installation.

Tesar Industrial Contractors started as The James Tesar Motor Trucking Company in 1919.

James Tesar founded what was then called Tesar Trucking Company over 81 years ago as a young man in his early 20s. Located in a small office on Central Avenue in downtown Cleveland, it was primarily a local cartage company when most long-distance transportation was done through rail service. The company grew slowly, adding other services based on client need. By the mid-1970s it had moved to its present location on Jennings Road.

When James Tesar died in 1978, James Tesar Jr. took ownership of the thriving business. His wife Sharon joined him in 1993 as co-owner. Together they diversified the company's services even further and reflected the changes with a new name — Tesar Industrial Contractors. They also added a second office and warehouse on Granger Road and increased the staff to over 60 employees.

In 1980 Tesar was awarded a contract with the Department of Energy to install equipment for the Gas Centrifuge Manufacturing Program at the National Aeronautics and Space Administration's (NASA) Plumbrook facility in Sandusky, Ohio. In 1990 it won a five-year contract with NASA, which helped stimulate its growth and solidify its reputation as a millwright contractor. Tesar's millwright crews are experts at installing specialized machinery and equipment using precision optical alignment equipment. Some of the jobs it has performed for NASA include installation of a research compressor for jet

Tesar Industrial Contractors provides a wide variety of transport and lifting services for heavy equipment such as this 2,500 ton erie press.

engines, as well as the installation of solar panels for charging the batteries that supply power to the space station.

Tesar's rigging and erecting services safely and accurately transport and lift a variety of heavy equipment. An adaptable gantry system is used to transfer, erect and position equipment up to 500 tons. Mobile cranes, lift trucks, hydraulic jacking and skidding equipment are also utilized and operated by one of four unions who combine to form the Tesar team. Its crews include certified lift truck and crane operators who are trained in federal safety standards and regulations.

Many manufacturing industries such as chemical, power, plastic, steel and food processing have called upon Tesar for a wide range of custom services. Skilled ironworkers fabricate and erect structural steel for the construction of industrial manufacturers, such as LTV Steel.

Of course Tesar still maintains its trucking service with a high-quality fleet of tractors and trailers for both local and out-of-state moves. Special equipment for loading and unloading all sizes of equipment and machinery are available to take jobs from start to finish. Temperature-controlled warehousing services are also available.

Tesar's hard work, diversification and dedication to the customer has helped it to generate a long list of clients from Ohio and surrounding states, including Continental Airlines, The Cleveland Clinic, Alcoa and MTD Products, among others.

Future plans include the addition of machinery rebuilding and repairing services, and a hope to keep the company in the family with a succeeding generation of Tesars. Given the company's record of commitment and diligence, it hopes to progress many years into the millennium.

The family-run Varbros Corporation is a leading QS 9000 and ISO 9002 manufacturer of high-production stamping, tapping and welded assemblies for heavy-truck oil filter manufacturers like Fleetguard and Dana and for consumer-oriented companies like General Motors, Goodyear and Bose. Its affiliated company, Trimline Die Corporation, makes progressive dies and high-production stampings. The companies have maintained a reputation for innovation since the beginning.

July 13, 1951 was the day the Vargo brothers first embarked on their great adventure. Both die makers with local manufacturers, the two bought used equipment and set up shop on the near westside. Starting with about 700 square feet and eight tool room machines, they began making metal stamping dies. Elder brother Louis E. handled production while younger brother Richard (Dick) handled sales. One of their first customers was Dick's former employer, Boehm Pressed Steel. "They were kind enough to give us a couple of projects to help us get over the initial shock of no income," he recalls with a chuckle.

With help from their father, the brothers moved the fledgling firm to Associate Avenue in Brooklyn, Ohio, six months later and bought a small punch press. Fate took a hand when the brothers were referred to a stamping company in need of a temporary contractor for rotor lamination stampings. But instead of being temporary, the orders kept coming until Varbros was able to hire its first part-time employee in 1952. Later, the order expanded and Varbros bought a punch press to run motor laminations in coil form. Sarting in 1957 the company made three additions to their building and bought their first automatic stamping press.

In 1958 sales representative James T. Millican brought the firm a lead to a manufacturer with a new product, a disposable, spin-on oil filter. It marked a revolution in auto and truck design and maintenance — and in Varbros Corporation's fortunes. The business began by making rotors, went on to threading oil filter tapping plates and then began shipping welded assemblies to customers. Orders grew until the need for more room forced another move to the present location on Brookpark Road in 1974. The company focus then turned to more automation. Because of increasing customer quality requirements, Varbros decided to retool and purchased it first new punch press in 1979.

Dick's son, Richard (Rick) Vargo Jr., began working at the plant in 1975, directly out of high school. He graduated from Cleveland State University with a degree in business administration. In 1985 both Louis and the plant manager retired and in 1991 so did Millican. This left Rick to wear two hats until the company hired a new plant manager in 1991. Now company president, Rick is primarily concerned with administration and sales. According to him, the company found its niche in making filter plates for heavy-duty trucks because of its ability to meet the more stringent quality demands of the industry. "Trucking industry plates are more complex, with higher strength requirements and better thread quality," says Rick, "and that's something we're very good at."

(Left to right) Dick Vargo and Rick Vargo, with the present Brookpark facility as a backdrop

A view of the interior of Varbros Corporation's first facility in Brooklyn, Ohio.

Voss Industries, Inc.

Like the sailing yachts he raced years ago, William J. Voss captained Voss Industries to become one of the world's leading suppliers of V-retainer couplings, T-bolt band clamps, strap assemblies and other specialty products to aerospace, food and chemical processing, medical, telecommunications, transportation and other industries.

Voss was born in Cleveland and graduated from the Case School of Applied Science with a degree in mechanical engineering. He worked as a researcher for the National Advisory Committee for Aeronautics (now known as NASA), and as a manufacturer's representative; but in 1951 he began to design and manufacture his own band clamps part time. By 1957 he formed Voss Engineering Co. and he and his wife, Marianne, devoted themselves full-time to the business. He held several U.S. and foreign patents on band clamps, couplings and flange designs and safety features.

By 1961 Voss Industries was incorporated. To better serve the various markets, Voss created several divisions — Clamp Technology, Finned Tubed Products, Aerospace and Heat Exchange Applied Technology. The finned tube and heat exchanger product lines were eventually sold so that Voss could concentrate on its clamp and coupling markets, especially the company's aerospace business.

Voss' aerospace business got off the ground in the early 1980s when it solved an emergency problem on Boeing 747s. Since then Boeing has become one of Voss' biggest customers. Other major companies that utilize Voss products include Lockheed Martin, Honeywell, Northrop Grumman and General Electric.

Bill Voss proudly displays one of his original Rauch & Lang electric cars in front of the building that houses Voss Industries, once the factory where the cars were built.

In the early 1960s, when Voss Industries was first beginning, the company moved into a building in Cleveland's historic Ohio City District. When he learned that it had housed the original Rauch & Lang Electric Automobile factory in the early 1900s, Mr. Voss became fascinated with the history of electric cars.

In 1996, after a few years of searching, Voss purchased a Rauch & Lang Electric. He later purchased a second car, as well as a period carriage. Mrs. Voss also had a connection to the cars since her father had worked in the building in the fender department. Mr. and Mrs. Voss intended to build a museum dedicated to the electric cars of Cleveland. Unfortunately, the project was put on temporary hold with the deaths of Bill Voss in 1997 and Marianne Voss in 1998.

Seventy-six years old at the time of his death, Voss had never seen a day of retirement. Voss Industries had been his life's work and his greatest joy. A dominant force within the company, he was reserved in public, which belied his heart of gold. He and Mrs. Voss took great care of their employees. They often helped them out financially and Mrs. Voss shopped year-round for very personalized Christmas gifts. Their giving overflowed into the community as they supported several local charities, especially during the holiday seasons.

Though greatly missed, the legend left by Bill and Marianne Voss through their dedication to their company and to the Cleveland community will remain as strong as the north winds of Lake Erie that carried their yachts to victory.

Bill and Marianne Voss (far right) were honored by NASA for Voss Aerospace's contribution to the space shuttle program at Kennedy Space Center in March 1996.

MARKETPLACE

Cleveland retail establishments and service industries offer an impressive variety of choices for Cleveland residents and visitors.

Gamekeeper's Taverne

The transformation of Crane's Canary Cottage to a ladies' tea room to the Artist's Palate to Gamekeeper's Taverne is the half-century history of a facility that northeastern Ohio diners have voted as one of the area's best outdoor restaurants.

The Inn of Chagrin Falls, established in 1927 as Crane's Canary Cottage

It began in 1927 when Arthur Crane, the candymaker who developed LifeSavers (and father of noted early 20th century poet Hart Crane), purchased two Chagrin Falls cottages and joined them with a 10,000-square-foot addition. The newly created building became famous as Crane's Canary Cottage, a restaurant that drew such luminaries of the time as Duncan Hines, Will Rogers, Charles Lindbergh and Cleveland industrialists, the Rockefellers.

After Arthur Crane's death in 1932, Mrs. Crane remarried and her new husband began to collect antiques from around the world. Part of that collection can be seen in the restaurant and the adjacent Inn of Chagrin Falls, which closed at the beginning of World War II because of gas rationing.

Over the years other retail businesses, including a ladies' tea room, were started in the space. Although the tea room wasn't a success, part of the building did house a successful retail establishment. Tom Lutz, a Kent State University business school graduate, heard about the tea room's availability from the retailer and immediately contacted his former KSU business school roommate, Erik Heatwole, who was working in a Ft. Lauderdale restaurant.

Although neither had envisioned becoming hospitality entrepreneurs so early in their careers, it was an opportunity Lutz compared to finding an antique car in someone's garage, dirty and covered with weeds, which turns out be a real gem.

Using the acumen they had gained in business school to obtain this tarnished gem, Heatwole and Lutz negotiated the asking price down to a song and purchased the business in September 1976.

When they opened, the restaurant was only an outdoor facility, and cooking was done exclusively *al fresco* on a grill. Everything was handled by Heatwole, Lutz and one waitress. Usually this trio could handle the crowd, but one evening when Heatwole was out of town and the waitress called in sick, Lutz literally became chief cook and bottle washer as he greeted, seated and waited on guests and bussed tables.

Exclusively outdoor dining, cooking and a small staff lasted only for a couple of years as the partners put their efforts into renovating the inside of the restaurant. Heatwole and Lutz did all the work themselves, refinishing tables, paneling and decorating so they were able to complete the restaurant for under $10,000. The result was the Artist's Palate, a restaurant in which local artists displayed their work and made them available for sale. After a year the partners were not satisfied with the concept and began to rethink the restaurant.

Then the idea for Gamekeeper's Taverne, featuring game on the menu, was born. The name was not created through a computer search or by hiring a team of research specialists. While walking through a local store, Lutz noticed a department called Gamekeeper's that sold outdoor clothing.

The partners had envisioned a restaurant more in keeping with their tastes, something outdoorsy, yet sophisticated and warm. Since the name connoted the exact environment they were trying to create, their vision was a step closer to reality.

Although low-fat, high-protein game such as venison, elk and ostrich are featured at all Gamekeeper locations, the menu can best be described as American traditional, with innovative, creative twists reflecting changing food trends.

The success of this approach can be attested to by the fact there now are five Gamekeeper's restaurants — and two inns — in northeastern Ohio.

In 1988 Lutz and Heatwole took over operation of Chardon's Bass Lake Taverne & Inn, then opened Gamekeeper's Lodge in Rocky River in 1994 and Gamekeeper's Taverne in Fairlawn in 1997. Each restaurant is independently operated by talented individuals who share common goals, food styles and entrepreneurial spirit. Each features wood paneling and fireplaces for the fall and winter months, and courtyards and decks for the spring and summer.

The story came full circle in 1989 when the partners teamed up with general partners Carl and Beverly Vessele, took over the one-time Crane's Canary Cottage and created The Inn of Chagrin Falls, which is adjacent to Gamekeeper's Taverne.

The inn, "Victorian charm amid Western Reserve tradition," was described in a national magazine as being "reminiscent of an English Hunt Club," with 15 lovely rooms decorated and appointed to reflect the grace and charm of Victorian elegance. Each room bears a name that honors the history and geography of the Chagrin Valley. The inn's fountains have been restored and its gardens carefully nurtured.

Chagrin Falls has a vibrant business and retail community, surrounded by charming architecture, scenery and history. This has lured a diverse group of professionals, artists and corporate executives to the valley both as a

home and a destination. The inn has been a home away from home for business leaders visiting their fellow executives in the area. Travelers and vacationers choose the inn as a restful stop. Couples enjoy the privacy for a getaway or a honeymoon. Whatever the occasion, the facility's comfortable Gathering Room can accommodate up to 35 people for meetings or events and provides complete A/V equipment to enhance business gatherings.

After half a century, its name may have changed, but the facility still exudes the same feeling of warmth and hospitality that brought Rockefeller, Lindbergh and Rogers there 50 years earlier.

Another thing that has changed since Lutz and Heatwole began is the size of the staff working under the Gamekeeper's aegis. The one-waitress staff has grown to 250 people, including the general manager, who started with the company as a dishwasher when he was 14 years old.

The restaurant's capacity also has expanded, with room for 125 diners inside and another 250 outdoors, in season.

Lutz and Heatwole describe their mission as being to exceed customers' expectations by purchasing and preparing quality food; providing service by customer-responsive people; creating casually sophisticated, entertaining atmospheres; and adapting the menu and surroundings to the season.

More than 20 years after two young men took a chance in a risky business venture, Gamekeeper's continues to thrive and expand. A fifth restaurant, Timberfire, opened in Bainbridge in spring 2000. Designed by former Browns quarterback Brian Sipe, and in partnership with the Dolan family, owners of the Cleveland Indians, Timberfire is carrying the warmth of Lutz and Heatwole's vision into the 21st century.

Relaxing fireside dining is a winter favorite.

The original Gamekeeper's Taverne in Chagrin Falls

Cuffs

When 20 years ago Rodger and Patty Kowall decided to combine their love of fashion, design and fine wine into an upscale men's clothing shop, neither imagined that Cuffs would not only attract fashion-conscious executives, doctors, lawyers, athletes and celebrities — it would also become one of the top men's stores in the nation.

Cuffs' charming men's fashion boutique, located on the scenic Chagrin Falls River, attracts customers from all over Northeastern Ohio and beyond.

Cuffs not only carries Kiton, Brioni, Attolini, Oxxford, Luciano Barbera and Polo, but Loro Piana, Agnona, Borelli and Charvet. In 1993 Cuffs' quaint Chagrin Falls store became the first privately owned Hermes boutique in the United States, featuring its signature ties and scarves as well as Hermes jewelry, watches, fragrance, leather, ready-to-wear, porcelain, shoes and even a leather saddle.

Cuffs' well-appointed rooms resemble an exclusive men's club. Customers are immediately attracted to a billiard table draped with top-shelf ties from Kiton, Brioni, Hermes, Charvet, Barbera, Venanzi and Hilton. Bottles of French and California wines, scented soaps, cigars, olive oils from Provence and Italy, teas and mustards from French restaurateur Roger Verge and fruit jams from Provence are displayed amidst the world's finest clothing collections.

Kowall recently launched wine-tasting parties in a renovated carriage house adjacent to Cuffs. Kowall's collection includes more than 5,000 bottles of French and California wines, naturally insulated in Cuffs' cellar. Built from stones taken from the banks of the Chagrin River, the cellar is perfect for wine storage. Cuffs recently hosted an invitation-only wine tasting party featuring Chateau Mouton Rothschild vintages from 1959 to 1997.

Kowall knew at an early age that he wanted to work in the men's fashion industry. He first worked as a stock boy for a clothing store while attending Cathedral Latin. Then, as a student at John Carroll University, Kowall landed a job in a menswear shop located near the campus.

"Back then kids bought clothes," he says. "And I was hooked."

But after graduation in 1968, Kowall received his greetings from Uncle Sam and soon found himself wearing camouflage attire and combat boots in Southeast Asia. Back on American soil following his tour of duty, Kowall landed a sales position at the prestigious Bunce Brothers in Shaker Heights. Under the tutelage of mentor John Munro, Kowall learned about the fashion industry from the ground up.

After 15 years of moving up through the ranks, Kowall realized he had gone as far as he could in the family-owned Bunce Brothers. That's when Rodger and Patty Kowall began talking earnestly about their dream to own their own business. It was 1979 or 1980 and the couple was at Nighttown enjoying a meal and good wine. Kowall has forgotten who came up with the name but remembers that Patty drew the Cuffs logo on a napkin.

To come up with the necessary seed money, Kowall borrowed $200,000 from investors in the Greater Cleveland area. From the start, he sought to create a store showcasing the top designer labels but without the air of stuffiness and snobbery found in other elite men's shops.

Anybody can feel comfortable coming into the store. Someone could spend $5,000 for an ensemble or $7.99 for a decent bottle of Chardonnay, have it gift-wrapped and feel like they got something special, Kowall says.

Once, a group of Hell's Angels rumbled up on their motorcycles and walked into Cuffs to buy cigars. The bikers stood outside in front of the Cuffs sign smoking them, then got back on their bikes and rode away.

A well-known celebrity recently strolled into Cuffs wearing shorts, T-shirt and baseball cap. He needed something to wear at a wedding in Chagrin Falls that night. He was asked to sign the guestbook or no one would believe he had been in the store. The customer signed: "David Letterman. N.Y.C."

Although Cuffs customers are used to seeing the top designers displayed, the jackets looked great and every one was quickly sold.

While the trend over the last decade, even among executives and professionals in the workplace, has been to replace the three-piece business suit with "corporate casual," the fashion industry has seen a return in some circles to more traditional attire. The trendy, casual, corporate dress code has resulted in a lack of professionalism in the workplace and the pendulum is starting to swing back. When the investment firm of Morgan Stanley Dean Witter recently opted for a less-formal dress code, its Boston office overruled corporate's decision and went with the more traditional business attire instead.

For young men graduating from college into the workplace, a nice suit was a rite of passage. That trend seems to be returning. Over the past year or two, interest in better suits is overwhelmingly apparent at Cuffs. The sales staff remembers when men would buy two or three suits at a time. Now customers come to Cuffs for their best suits, favorite suits or hand-made Italian suits using the highest-quality fabrics.

Despite market trends, Cuffs has remained at the top in its field in formal and casual menswear.

The competent Cuffs staff travels to New York four or five times a year and France, Italy and England twice a year on shopping sprees for the next season, searching for high-quality items.

Cuffs likes to stick with familiar labels, but recently, on the advice of an assistant, it bought sports jackets made of a fabric called "tencel." They sold for just $195, but 24 jackets were purchased and placed in the store.

Ichiban Salon & Day Spa

With its pristine white walls, spacious treatment areas and innovative beauty services, Ichiban Salon & Day Spa has distinguished itself as an oasis of pampering and relaxation right in the heart of the bustling Cleveland metroplex.

Established in 1989, this full-service beauty center offers all forms of hair and body care for women, men and children. The salon's highly trained, proficient staff provides a full range of hair care services, from hair styling and permanent wave or straightening, to color services like corrective color, balayage (hand weaving), silver coloring, highlighting and lowlighting, and mustache and beard blending. It also offers nail services that include deep penetrating treatments for both the hands and feet as well as artificial overlays and natural nail cultivation, all in an atmosphere of calm and serenity. There's even a private men's area, where clients can receive haircuts and chemical processes in complete comfort.

But nowhere is this sense of serenity more apparent than in Ichiban's lower level spa. Here, trained estheticians and massotherapists work their magic on every part of the body in private treatment rooms that are softly lit and tastefully decorated. Clients can receive soothing body treatments like mud facials, mud wraps and Vichy showers, all of which foster deep physical relaxation while increasing circulation and rejuvenating the skin. They can benefit from the latest anti-aging treatments for the face and body, such as paraffin body treatments and seaweed body therapy, as well as artistic eyebrow arching and eyelash dying. They can experience intensive hand treatments that exfoliate the skin and stimulate nail growth. Or they can feel their stress ebb away with a Swedish or chair massage, aromatherapy or foot reflexology treatment.

Ichiban is the creation of Renee Sucre, Nakanishi Strauss and Kathleen Caito, three friends who are all natives of greater Cleveland. Sucre and Strauss attended beauty school together and later met Caito when the three landed jobs at a suburban beauty salon. They worked at that salon for nine years, then decided it was time to strike out on their own and formed a partnership based on friendship and a strong desire to succeed.

After buying a 1,500-square-foot fixer-upper house in Rocky River for $105,000, the partners spent another $115,000 gutting and renovating it to create a cozy salon complete with 11 hairstylist stations and one manicurist station. They named the salon Ichiban, which means "No. 1" in Japanese, because they wanted a one-word name with a catchy sound that reflected the customer focus they envisioned. When they finally opened the new salon in March 1989, they had just $100 in the cash drawer, one employee, and a lot of hope and determination in their hearts.

Ichiban was an immediate success. The partners were fully booked the first

Ichiban founders (left to right) Renee Sucre, Nakanishi Strauss and Kathleen Caito

day and for two months afterwards — far in advance of the grand opening — thanks to the loyalty of the many clients who followed them to their new shop for services like hair styling and coloring, and manicuring. But there were some rough spots. Over Memorial Day weekend the first year, for instance, the basement flooded when an old sewer line backed up, resulting in a $40,000 plumbing bill at a time when money was already rather tight.

It wasn't long after they moved in that the partners got a strong feeling they weren't alone in the salon. They often heard tapping on the walls in the upstairs rooms or a voice playfully calling out from the basement when no one was there. A client (who was also a psychic and medium) confirmed that there was a spirit present. Her name was Mrs. Peterson, and she had lived with her family in the house for more than 50 years. According to the client, Mrs. Peterson's spirit had moved on because the "energies" in the house had changed with the renovation. But because she liked what the partners had done, she often visited, bringing with her a feeling of warmth and maternal kindness the partners and their staff said they could feel. They also noticed that good things happened to them or the business whenever Mrs. Peterson's spirit was present.

By October 1997, however, the partners knew they had outgrown their comfortable surroundings. With a staff of 18 people, a burgeoning client base and just 10 parking spaces outside to accommodate the steady stream of patrons, it became obvious that an expansion was necessary. So the women set their sights on the Turning Point office complex in Westlake, where they built a 6,200-square-foot luxury day salon. The new space allowed them to install 20 hair styling stations, four private men's stations, and four manicure and three pedicure stations. To fulfill a long-time dream, they also added a day spa that would allow them to offer the ultimate in luxurious skin and body treatments.

One of the things the partners did before opening their new salon was to have a Feng Shui reading to ensure that the building would be a mecca of relaxation and harmony. Adhering to the tenets of this ancient Chinese art of placement, the partners hung wind chimes in what is thought of as the "finance area" of the building to counteract the space's odd shape. In addition, they chose to erect a chic black awning over the entrance on the north side of the building because Feng Shui maintains that black is the color of the north, and the awning would enhance the flow of "chi," or positive energy, into the salon.

The technique must have worked, because Ichiban continues to enjoy great success in its Westlake location. An average of 150-200 people a day come through the salon's wide front doors and leave feeling better about themselves, as well as pleased with the level of personal service they have received. This feeling of satisfaction also extends to the staff, many of whom wear a diamond-studded, platinum-and-18 karat gold band ring that's bestowed on them after five years of valued service. It's a small gesture that sets Ichiban apart from its competition and is the embodiment of the close bond Sucre, Strauss and Caito have always felt between them, both as business partners and friends.

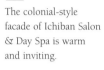

The colonial-style facade of Ichiban Salon & Day Spa is warm and inviting.

Red brick and cobblestone-like pavers characterize Ichiban's main entrance.

Beachwood Place

The world-class shopping experience at Beachwood Place is big news everywhere in Northeast Ohio. Indeed, Beachwood Place is the upscale shopping mecca for Greater Cleveland. Boasting the state of Ohio's first Nordstrom store and anchored by Saks Fifth Avenue and Dillard's department stores, Beachwood Place offers a first-class shopping experience.

Located in the center of Cleveland's most affluent neighborhoods and sitting conveniently near the junction of Cedar and Richmond Roads just off Interstate 271, Beachwood Place opened a new era of retail shopping in Greater Cleveland in 1978. With its two levels and five indoor courts, the key word here is "ambience." Owned by The Rouse Company and designed by RTKL Associates, Inc., the 918,000-square-foot facility incorporates a "jewel box" design with meandering, intimate courts that give an inviting feel to an otherwise huge space. The French limestone floor and contemporary furniture groupings create a homelike atmosphere for shoppers needing a rest, while a series of fountains features backlit glass platforms that double as runways. Mannequins perch on sofas and stand frozen in the midst of spontaneous fashion shows on the catwalks, displaying some of the latest fashions on sale in the stores.

Center Court at Beachwood Place

One of the mall's intimate conversation areas

Beachwood Place received a major makeover in 1997, with a carefully assembled array of unique national and local boutiques such as The Coach Store, BCBG Max Azria, Georgiou, Mann Jewelers, Sunny Choi, Swarovski and Weiss Furs. Nordstrom, the most recent addition to the mall's anchor stores, brought its incomparable brand of elegance along with its quality merchandise and amenities like complimentary wardrobing and shopping service, and personal shoppers for cosmetics.

The Dallas-based retailer Neiman Marcus made its entrance into Northeast Ohio in November 1998, when it introduced The Galleries of Neiman Marcus at Beachwood Place. The company chose the region because of Cleveland's rebirth as a destination of choice. Another unique mall boutique, Sephora, specializes in women's cosmetics, offering 275 shades of lipstick along with scores of perfumes and nail polishes. Mario's International Spas pampers customers with specialized treatments and total health and beauty care.

Another of the mall's unique features is the Premier Shopper Club program. Through the Rouse Company's centralized advertising/marketing plan, extensive research with mall patrons identified service as the key point of differentiation between shopping destinations. The resulting marketing campaign was designed to increase shopping center traffic and sales, promote stores and service, and build lifetime value for customers. Premier Shopper Club members receive special customized value offers, exclusive gift-with-purchase offers by mail and free gift certificates. Free services for members include gift wrap, shopping bags, coat and package check, stroller and wheelchair checkout, and local telephone calls. Members can search for gifts by categories via the Premier Shopper Club Web site. The Web site also creates an online shopping list with the locations of stores that carry the specified merchandise along with the best place to park. Members can also access shopping advice, trends and tips, news and member information.

Brides by Donna

Brides by Donna, tucked away on the edge of picturesque Chagrin Falls, is no ordinary bridal shop. Proprietor Donna Pickett's penchant for beauty and romance greets her visitors immediately on entry. The foyer is decorated with a blend of soft and luxurious textiles. The gentle tier of entry steps is adorned on either side by delicate, antique bridal and trousseau finery, a simple yet elegant 19th-century bride's dress, shoes, veils and other mementos that remind a bride-to-be that this is a place where she will be taken care of in the same tender fashion afforded the items on display.

The shop itself is a series of rooms, each one filled with the enchantment of a great-grandmother's parlor and the eye-catching dresses that Donna has brought together to fulfill the dreams of brides not only in the Cleveland area, but around the world. A collection of antique boudoir caps is on display throughout the shop's many nooks and crannies, along with antique wedding photos.

Donna Pickett, the wife of a retired Lutheran pastor, devoted mother of four and grandmother of eight, ventured into business as her children grew and began leaving home. Growing up in the Detroit area, Donna relished the

The main room at Brides by Donna

influence of her immigrant Armenian grandmother, who used to spin and dye her own cloth as well as piece together exquisite works in crochet, lace and needlework. Her grandmother's award-winning textiles not only won blue ribbons at county and state fairs, they captured the heart of a granddaughter who was inspired to create some of her own magic, first in interior design. The idea for a bridal shop reached fruition in 1988 when she opened her first in Aurora, where she stayed three years. She moved the shop to Chagrin Falls in 1991.

With eight full-time employees, salespeople and seamstresses alike, Brides by Donna is not simply a place to buy a dress. The store offers a variety of wedding services and outfits bridesmaids, flower girls, ring bearers and, to a limited extent, mothers of the bride and groom. A small gift line is available as well, offering brides the option of selecting gifts for the bridal party. Still, with the breathtaking dresses by exclusive designers such as Richard Glasgow, to name only one of many well-known designers she offers her clients, the word has spread to brides-to-be as far away as Europe that Donna offers a selection unequaled anywhere.

Among its many distinctions, Brides by Donna has further enhanced its work toward creating a more beautiful world by donating gowns to the American Cancer Society, raising funds each year to provide mothers with cancer the fulfillment of a wish they can share with their children. As an incentive for area high school students to pass the state proficiency tests, Donna has also participated in a program that offers prom dresses for girls who have gained "purchase points" through passing those exams.

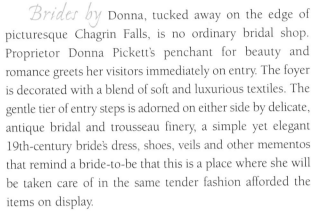

Katie and Tyler, two of Donna Pickett's grandchildren

The DiSanto Group

The DiSanto Group has a success-driven philosophy: Seek out what people really need and consistently strive to find creative ways to deliver it. Discover the need, and create an exciting solution. This strategy has taken three inventive partners from a 2,500-square-foot office front in 1993 to an impressive 16,000-square-foot production facility in Cleveland's newly remodeled Midtown Corridor.

The DiSanto Group provides what it describes as "Heroic Custom Embroidery and Stellar Silkscreening," as well as in-house creative services to companies all over the country. It has been the company's willingness to take on every project, from 1 to 10,000 pieces, that has helped The DiSanto Group secure a client list that includes Sherwin-Williams, Nestlé, Sysco Foods, Restaurant Associates in New York, Primavera Software in Philadelphia and Cleveland's own Orlando Baking Company.

From custom-printed T-shirts to terry cloth towels, leather bomber jackets, soft-sided briefcases, imprinted specialty items, sweatshirts, caps or a new corporate identity — there's nothing The DiSanto Group isn't prepared to tackle.

DiSanto takes a team approach with its customers to provide them with the freshest and most innovative ideas. The company positions itself as a cost-efficient advertising agency, only without the hefty monthly retainer that most corporations are used to paying. Service with a personal touch has earned the company a loyal following and a reputation for quality, integrity and excellence. All work is done in-house, and customers are invited behind the scenes to witness the goods being created. They even put a few chocolate mints in every package that ships out. It's small extras like these that its competitors would consider foolhardy; but The DiSanto Group sees these things as the definitive way to treat every customer.

Like most entrepreneurial ventures, The DiSanto Group sprang from the seed of an idea that grew and blossomed. In 1991 Anthony DiSanto was a one-man corporation. Along with owning and operating a successful bar/restaurant, DiSanto created a corporate sportswear/apparel business — DiSanto Activewear. As an aggressive marketer, DiSanto coordinated creative and manufacturing all from his home office. It wasn't long before he got corporate Cleveland's attention. He soon enlisted the help of his older brother and business partner, Dennis DiSanto, who was then working in the world of corporate finance. Dominic Russo, then associate creative director at a popular Cleveland advertising agency, was brought on to help bring creative services under one roof.

The home office gave way to a 2,500-square-foot storefront. In less than two years the partners were offered the opportunity to take their uncommonly popular business to another level. When a downtown Cleveland landmark property went up for sale, Anthony jumped at the chance and never looked back. Armed with only 14 days, the partners, along with a family network of investors, raised the one quarter million dollars needed to seal the deal. The DiSanto Group was born.

The company continues to grow and prosper. The DiSanto Group recently launched two unique offshoot divisions: ID18, providing golf flags and printing services to the professional golf market; and DiSanto Equestrian Supply, which lends its creative sensibilities and identity-building services to the Arabian horse market.

Anthony P. DiSanto achieves an unquestionable measure of success in everything he does. Dennis DiSanto combines an amazing work ethic with an intrinsic understanding of people. Dominic Russo is a visionary; an eccentric in a world that sometimes forgets how to have fun. Together, this trio brings a passion for their business and an irrepressible camaraderie that is evident in the quality and vitality of their work.

Executive Caterers at Landerhaven

Whether serving clients to the thunderous roar of Grand Prix race cars or to the sublime sounds of a string quartet at a wedding, Executive Caterers at Landerhaven has established itself over four decades as one of the Midwest's top-quality caterers.

But in 1960, the furthest thing from company President Harlan Diamond's mind was an 80,000-square-foot facility on 10 acres of land that serves almost half a million meals annually, on and off the premises.

That year, the 20-something Diamond took over operation of the Executive Club on Chagrin Boulevard in Woodmere. It was a health club of the times, with a steam room, swimming pool and squash courts on the first floor, and a dining room, restaurant, banquet facilities and a couple of small meeting rooms on the second floor.

Its success was impetus enough for Diamond to take over the Landerhaven Country Club in 1985. A couple of years later, the building was expanded and Executive Caterers at Landerhaven became a reality.

Executive Caterers at Landerhaven is almost a misnomer. Even though the facility has seven party rooms, a grand ballroom with twin floating staircases, patios for outdoor entertaining, and acres of landscaped gardens and picturesque waterfalls, Executive Caterers has the ability to go anywhere and serve quality meals.

The roaring Grand Prix cars serve as background to three races (Cleveland, Michigan and Pennsylvania) where tent/chalets are home for several days to corporate sponsors who are served gourmet meals from Executive Caterers' complete mobile kitchen.

Executive Caterers also provides exclusive food service at The Rock and Roll Hall of Fame and Museum Café, at the English Oak Room in Tower City Center and at the University Circle Arabica coffeehouse. The company has served meals on airport runways and for oil sheiks waiting to leave Cleveland for home.

Although Executive has handled functions for as many as 6,000 people, it provides the same service and quality when it hosts as few as five or 10 people.

The organization recently opened a Kosher kitchen, the result of increasing requests by many potential patrons who found it difficult to find a facility that combined ambiance with Rabbinical supervision.

Executive Caterers has its own in-house floral, decorating, linen, laundry, landscaping and engineering departments. Its in-house bakery creates 95 percent of all pastries and desserts and 70 percent of all breads and other baked goods it serves. In addition to the innovative and creative party planners who are an integral part of any catering establishment, Executive Caterers has an in-house decorator who works directly with clients to create the desired atmosphere.

As the company gets ready to begin its fifth decade, plans are underway to further develop in-house audio-visual services, expand valet service, take advantage of 21st-century technology — including a new state-of-the-art conference center — and incorporate skylights and windows to increase natural lighting in the Grand Ballroom.

As Executive Caterers' ads state, "we cater parties seven days a week...wherever your imagination can take you."

The exterior of Executive Caterers at Landerhaven creates an image that is fulfilled inside.
Photo by Michael Spear

Fish Furniture

For three quarters of a century, superior products, exceptional value and outstanding customer service have made Fish Furniture the first choice for fine home furnishings throughout greater Cleveland.

The thriving retailer had its genesis in 1925, when Seymour and Esther Fischgrund opened a small store on Euclid Avenue in downtown Cleveland. That store specialized in dinette and dining room furniture, and Mr. Fischgrund would stain or paint the furniture to order. Then Mrs. Fish, as she was affectionately known in the trade, would decorate it or stripe the seat backs and legs to match a color in their customer's wallpaper.

During the Depression customers asked if they could buy the furniture unfinished so they could save money. So the store began stocking "raw" furniture, thus becoming the first retailer in the United States to specialize in this type of furniture.

After Mr. Fischgrund died in 1955, Al Geller, a young man who had been a salesman at the store until Uncle Sam called him to active Army duty during the Korean War, took over the reins of the company, which had just three employees. He made the decision to decrease the store's inventory of unfinished furniture while significantly increasing its inventory of solid-wood, finished furniture.

In 1960, when industry developments made finished "knock-down," or disassembled, furniture less expensive than unfinished-wood products, Geller discontinued the unfinished furniture department altogether and concentrated instead on selling the finest solid-wood home furnishings.

The strategy proved to be extremely successful, and in 1963, Geller bought the company from Mrs. Fish. In 1971 he opened a 3,000-square-foot second location in North Olmsted. Ten years later he relocated the downtown store to Mayfield Heights. After an expansion of that store in 1989, Fish Furniture had more than 100,000 square feet of showroom and warehouse space and employed 70 people.

Known for its quality, value, selection and service, Fish Furniture carries the finest traditional, country, mission and contemporary furniture at unbeatable prices. Among its specialties are youth furniture (Fish Furniture has the largest selection in the state) and its leather, entertainment, home office and mattress galleries from well-known manufacturers like Durham, Flexsteel, Moosehead, Clayton Marcus, Stanley, Serta, Sealy, and Stearns and Foster. It also has an extensive clock gallery that includes timepieces by Howard Miller and Sligh, as well as many other premium accent pieces like classic Quoizel lamps. In addition, the store offers an interior design service for discriminating customers who wish to turn their houses into warm and inviting places they love to come home to.

Today, Geller remains at the helm of Fish Furniture, and has been joined in the business by his son, Daniel, who was named one of 20 outstanding professionals by the Sales and Marketing Executives of Cleveland in 2000. Like his father, the younger Geller is a firm believer that a fine-quality product and superior customer service are the keys to success for Fish Furniture. And if nearly eight decades of sales and service are any indication, it's a strategy that will continue to serve Fish Furniture well into the future.

The blooming success of Gale's in Westlake actually has its roots in Akron in the early 1950s when Sam "Salvatore" Donzelli returned from naval service after the Korean War. Sam wanted to make a better life for himself, deciding to open a business on some of his father's hard-earned investment property.

Sam's initial idea was to start a restaurant, but area residents did not want the traffic of such an establishment, and contested it legally. In a final debate, Sam proposed this question, "What kind of business would they not object to?" After some discussion, the residents responded with "a beautiful one, a flower business." So in 1953 Belle Rose Florist was born.

But customers wanted more than just cut flowers and corsages. They wanted vibrant, fragrant and living flowers, and so Belle Rose Florist evolved and grew into Donzell's Flower and Garden Center as we know it today.

Shortly after opening his Akron location, Sam and his wife, Bonnie, met Bill Gale, an established Cleveland-area nurseryman. Sam and Bill became partners in the Gale's Willoughby Hills location, while Sam continued to own the Akron site.

In February 1966 Sam and Bill continued their expansion with the Gale's Westlake location, which is now owned by the Donzelli family. Keeping their father's vision alive are daughters Pam Donzelli, currently located at the Gale's Westlake store, and Julie Donzelli DiFeo, currently located at the Akron location. The two grew up playing in the peat moss and watering petunias while other children were playing in sandboxes.

Today, there are five store locations — four in the Greater Cleveland area operating under the Gale's Garden Center name, and the Donzell's location in Akron. Although there are some interrelationships, they are joined together primarily for purchasing and advertising power. The five stores rank in the top 10 in sales nationally among independent retail garden centers, and currently are 33rd nationally among all garden centers.

To maintain this level of achievement, the company's buyers regularly attend gift and nursery trade shows across the country to keep current with the best-selling merchandise. They also regularly visit nurseries to find the best plants and attend national management clinics to study trends in the industry. The company also owns and operates Bonnie Oaks Farm, a 63-acre facility in Canal Fulton where they grow their own chrysanthemums, roses, perennials and some nursery stock.

Gale's Westlake has grown from a small florist shop into a full-service garden center.

The seasonal nature of the garden center business in northern Ohio is limiting to most in the greens industry. The company considered this a challenge and utilized what is now the booming fall and holiday season market. Currently, Gale's and Donzell's have a thriving year-'round enterprise.

The five stores have not only managed to continue to grow financially but they have also transformed themselves into centers for family entertainment and tradition. Even as it continues to evolve and grow and change right before one's eyes, it still remains a business of beautiful flowers.

Sam Donzelli's original Akron Belle Florist has evolved into today's Donzell's Flower and Garden Center.

Herbert Ascherman, Jr., Photographer

Herb Ascherman considers himself a photographer and a businessperson who has made an avocation a lifetime vocation. But in his coveted role as the official portrait photographer of the world-renowned Cleveland Orchestra since 1986, Ascherman brings his keen eye to brilliantly capture the musicians in breathtaking clarity. As a working studio photographer, his regimen runs the gamut between nationally known political figures and elegant coverage of social affairs. He has the ability to transform mundane annual reports or a publicity brochure into a work of art. With his work on museum and gallery walls in London, Paris and Tokyo, Ascherman has established an international reputation for portraiture and photographic artwork. Numerous museums and galleries in cities across America and throughout the world are graced with his photographic art. And yet, one visit to his suburban Cleveland studio reveals him to be far too modest. Ascherman is as much of a poet and historian as he is photographer, businessman and artist.

His office is filled with family portraits that range from his son's bar mitzvah portrait to the beautiful images of his two elderly grandfathers, in addition to images that encompass the history of photography by many well-known masters. Ascherman chronicles history, enriching it by his vision of the faces that shape it. With annual sittings, he weaves stories of families sometimes using such unusual portrait settings as a family excursion to the grocery store and transforms the ordinary into something unique and poetic. Ascherman manages to bring to life the delicate movement of people's lives that have brought them to the moment he snaps their pictures. He lets his audience know where his subjects have been and where they are going. In his work as a political photographer, he has photographed three presidents and has been on site for nearly every major political event throughout the region. Ascherman brings a personal touch to the ordinary publicity photo.

Ascherman quickly realized that his love of the English language put him more comfortably into the world of words. After two master's degrees, however much he found himself engaged otherwise, his longtime love of photography, an art he taught to himself, lingered as his most desirable career option. This is a pursuit that he had since childhood and has been fortunate enough to turn into a lifetime opportunity. In the mid-1970s Ascherman decided to start his own photography business. Over 25 years later, working with 4 full-time staff members at his tightly run, independent studio, Ascherman's entrepreneurial spirit thrives.

Ascherman's work in black-and-white photography has garnered particular attention, given the wide resurgence of interest in the medium. His darkroom assistant for black-and-white photography, a craftsman in his own right, processes about 10,000 black-and-white frames a year and does all of the printing. Another assistant processes close to 25,000 color negatives a year. In fact, the quality of his business places it in the top one-half of one percent of family-owned studios in the country.

Herb Ascherman is a professional problem-solver. More than that, he is a man who takes some of the best pictures of Cleveland, pictures that encompass the vitality of both the people and the city.

"Self-portrait with Poodle"
©2000 by
Herbert Ascherman, Jr.,
Photographer

Hot Sauce Williams

Great food is a family tradition at Hot Sauce Williams, Cleveland's premier soul-food restaurant and catering chain. The family-owned-and-operated business has won numerous awards for its unique, mouth-watering barbecue from numerous county and state fairs and cookoffs in 10 states. With four stores in the city, the credit for the restaurant's success goes primarily to Lemaud Williams, who, along with his brothers Alonzo, Bill, James and Herbert, started the firm way back in February 1962.

When the restaurant chain for which he was assistant manager passed him over for advanced management training, Williams, who hails originally from Tougaloo, Mississippi, purchased an existing business for $500 and opened up shop on Hough Avenue. In 1966 another store

James "Pops" Williams, longtime employee Emma Barnett, and brothers Lamaud, Willie and Herbert enjoy a well-deserved break at the Buckeye location.

was opened at East 75 Street and Euclid Avenue, while a sales decline following the Hough riots forced the closing of the original location. In 1968 a third restaurant was opened on Hayden Avenue and in 1971 a fourth location opened on Lee Road. Yet a fifth store opened on Buckeye Road in the mid-1970s.

Through the mid-1970s, the business expanded to include full-service catering for anything from birthdays and special events to weddings and formal receptions. Williams also purchased a mobile unit for fairs, cookoffs and fund-raising events. Hot Sauce Williams has participated in Cleveland's world-famous Rib Cook-Off since its very first event. In 1980 the company opened the Q-Five Party Center, a popular night spot, and closed its Euclid store. October 1989 brought the opening of another

location on Superior. The newest location on East 79 Street and Carnegie Avenue opened in April 1994 as Hot Sauce Williams' Family Restaurant, featuring soul food and barbecue.

Hot Sauce Williams Corporation has built a reputation for providing great food and entertainment and continues this tradition with the Inner Circle entertainment complex. The huge complex has a party center, a restaurant, a cocktail lounge, a game room and houses a bottling and food-processing plant and bakery. The company plans for a dinner theater and concert hall and has room to house other small businesses. The family commitment to personalized service, fresh food and convenient locations will continue to make Hot Sauce Williams a Cleveland mainstay for years to come.

Local businessmen join Lamaud Williams (far right) and the Rev. Jesse Jackson at a reception for a local mayoral candidate in 1971.

Crowds at the 1987 Richmond, Virginia, World Invitational Rib Championship line up for that unique, mouth-watering taste.

IMG Jewelers

One Cleveland family's tradition of excellence in the art of fine jewelry began in the court of Czar Nicholas before the turn of the 20th century. When Abraham Sheremet humbly created masterpieces for the Romanovs, he might never have imagined that his true gift would be the legacy he passed on. A hundred years later, his great grandson, Steve Greenberg, continues to transform that gift in a fourth-generation business that has been a trusted member of the Cleveland-area community since 1949.

vide their customers with an intimate setting that allows comfort and convenience. But while the sleek building might be a masterpiece in itself, the real work showcased is the designer jewelry, quietly surrounding the customer in simple yet exquisite cases and illuminated by expertly placed front windows and lighting design. The works of in-house designers rest comfortably beside those of such names as Versace and Cyma; the key designer is Steve's wife, Hannah, who is more commonly known under her artist's name, Hanchu.

IMG Jewelers

IMG is the largest importer of loose diamonds in Ohio and is known around the world for the quality of its designs. One of the many awards bestowed on IMG was the 1973 American Design Award from *DeBeers Diamonds Today*, perhaps the most prestigious. IMG's original designs are created even today by beginning with a wax carving before proceeding on to the precious metal that will become the final product. One step away from the showroom and downstairs on the premises, the diamond setters and artists are busy at work on the jewelry. Whether it is a custom design or one of the several presented for sale in the showroom, the care of their customers is visible. In a day of mass-market production, IMG presents a window to the past with its tradition of honoring the desires of all who comes through the front door. From the young couple starting out to the husband buying something special for his wife of 25 years — to celebrate their marriage and their success — IMG customers come away with more than jewelry.

IMG represents the initials of Steve Greenberg's father, Isadore Moses Greenberg. He brought the skills he learned from his grandfather in diamond setting from his boyhood home in Pittsburgh and established himself in downtown Cleveland only a few years after the end of World War II. His family had already survived a revolution and another world war and emerged at mid-century with some of the finest work in the Cleveland area. Isadore's mother (Sheremet's daughter) a skilled watchmaker as well, was a living example for her son to provide people with only the best they could offer.

At its current location on Mayfield Road in Lyndhurst since 1986, IMG is tucked into a beautifully designed modern building commissioned by the Greenbergs to pro-

IMG also extends the value of family concern to the community at large, sponsoring innumerable charities, including muscular dystrophy, cancer and Jewish charitable organizations.

Joseph Scafidi Inc.

Fine tailoring and an unerring sense of style have made Joseph Scafidi Inc., custom tailors and shirtmakers, a Cleveland institution since 1984.

The elegantly appointed men's clothier, located in the arcade of the Huntington Building, offers a wide array of men's suits, sport coats, shirts and furnishings in the finest fabrics. Wardrobe items are custom-made for an individual fit that flatters the figure, while the classic designs ensure stylish wearability for many years to come.

The shop itself has the feel of an exclusive men's club, with an oak-paneled exterior, exquisite mahogany cabinetry and understated Oriental rugs. Framed art prints accentuate the smooth marble walls and are subtly enhanced by the light of a distinctive Chapman chandelier.

Along the wall in the private fitting studio hang hundreds of lengths of choice suit fabrics — from luxury Italian woolens to conservative English cashmeres — suitable for impeccably tailored corporate wear or tuxedos. Customers who don't immediately find what they're looking for among the handsome goods on display can instead browse through thousands of swatches representing the finest fabrics available the world over. They'll also find a wide array of premium fabric samples for casual-day sport coats as well as hundreds of dress and casual-shirt fabrics ranging from pure Swiss cottons to imported broadcloths.

The shop's two tailors transform these one-dimensional swaths of cloth into wearable pieces of art by working closely with each customer to achieve optimal fit. Each client's measurements are painstakingly taken and recorded, then are periodically rechecked to ensure an accurate,

comfortable fit. Fittings and alternations also are handled with the same kind of efficiency and eye to detail.

The shop was founded by master tailor Jospeh Scafidi, who began to learn his craft at the age of 9 in his native Sicily. After serving as an apprentice to the master tailor his own father patronized, Scafidi worked as a tailor in Milan for a year. He emigrated to the United States in 1967 and settled in Cleveland, where he first worked as a tailor cutting suits at Richard Bennett Tailors. Then in 1973, he teamed

Joseph Scafidi Inc.'s oak-paneled exterior is understated and inviting.

up with a partner to buy the store, which was highly successful under their tutelage. But after 10 years, the partnership was dissolved, and in 1984 Scafidi opened the shop that bears his name.

Since then, Joseph Scafidi Inc. has become a favorite of corporate presidents and CEOs, lawyers, doctors and other professionals who have discriminating taste — and often, little time to indulge it. For that reason, personal service has always been a mainstay of the business. The shop's tailors personally serve their valued clients right in their own offices or homes several times a year, which allows them to update or augment their wardrobes in a minimum amount of time and with the least amount of effort. Customers also can choose from an impressive selection of silk neckwear, belts and other accessories to add panache to their personal look.

This is the kind of personal service not often seen these days. Yet it is the mainstay of this oasis of European craftsmanship in the heart of Cleveland that sets Joseph Scafidi Inc. apart from its competition.

Master tailor Joseph Scafidi, shown shortly after the opening of his well-appointed Huntington arcade shop

La Fiesta Mexican Restaurant

It's primarily a restaurant, not a bar. There are, however, patrons unwinding with favorite beverages while conversing with friends. But mostly they are savoring the aromas and tastes of spicy Mexican dishes in a festively decorated dining room. Yet there is the ring of familiarity between staff and patrons that one finds in a neighborhood pub. Patrons are greeted by their first names when they enter.

"It's a place where everybody knows everybody's name," Hortencia "Toni" Valle, owner of La Fiesta, says unapologetically. About three-quarters of the patrons are repeat customers, many of them from the days when Valle's mother operated the restaurant. "If I'm not here to greet them, customers will say 'where's Toni?' They are accustomed to seeing other customers that they know. It's very comfortable here."

Some of that comfort is provided by the presence of familiar, traditional Mexican fare, some with a North American twist, that has been served there for half a century. Staples include enchiladas, tostadas, burritos, soups, and beans and rice. There is also a Mexican steak with hot sauce, chicken mole and Mexican stuffed peppers. More vegetables and seafoods have been added in recent years to accommodate expanding tastes. But ultimately, the more traditional dishes are the more popular items. They and the familiar faces that prepare and serve them have helped the restaurant thrive.

That familial feel can be traced to Valle's mother, Antonia Valle, who started the restaurant in 1952 at age 59

Hortencia Valle, between her son and daughter, Jim and Renee Boges, is now owner of La Fiesta, which has been revamped and relocated.

on the near west side of Cleveland. The matriarch had not worked in a restaurant before, nor had she cooked for a group much larger than her own family. In fact, she was a hotel laundry worker. Antonia Valle had emigrated to the Cleveland area in the early 1920s from Michoacan,

Mexico, where she had been a school teacher. Yet she decided to start her own business. "She was bright, organized and way ahead of her time," Valle says admiringly of her mother.

Hortencia Valle, who resumed her maiden name, and her former husband bought the restaurant from her mother in 1976, closed it, then reopened it in 1977 in suburban Richmond Heights. It has been at its present site since 1992. Hortencia Valle's own work background had been in office sales, personnel and purchasing. Her restaurant experience had come as a result of periodically helping her mother. The family legacy now is being carried on by two of Hortencia Valle's four children. Her son, Jim Boges, is a bartender who is known for his margaritas. Her daughter, Renee Boges, is the main cook; her specialties are the soups, sauces and all the main entrees.

Managing a restaurant is time-consuming, Valle says. The restaurant, which seats 105, is open six days a week. She says she could hire someone to take over some of her duties — greeting customers or shopping for supplies. But Valle says one of the rewards of being at La Fiesta is hearing the familiar greetings from familial customers. The most important reward, she says, is being able to carry on the legacy of the restaurant's beloved founder, Antonia Valle.

Salvador and Antonia Valle and their daughter, Hortencia, are seen in the La Fiesta restaurant started by Antonia Valle on the west side of Cleveland.

Becoming the largest and most successful document imaging company in Northeast Ohio is no easy task. But Paul Hanna, president and CEO of Meritech Blue, says that dedication to quality products backed by superior service has made the move up steady.

Meritech Blue, which bills itself as a document imaging company rather than simply an office equipment supplier, has become one of the largest firms of its kind in Northeast Ohio in just five years, notching numerous awards and honors along the way.

Office Dealer Magazine, a national industry magazine, named Meritech Blue "Elite Dealer of the Year" in 1997, 1998, 1999 and 2000, making it one of the top office technology providers in the United States. Another prestigious honor was bestowed by Konica Business Technologies, which named it "Top Producing Digital Dealer of the Year" in North America for 1997, 1998 and 1999. Meritech Blue also was awarded the North Coast '99 Award by the Employers Resource Council and Enterprise Development as one of the top 99 companies to work for in Northeast Ohio. However, a huge accomplishment was when Hanna was named "Entrepreneur of the Year" for the business services category by Ernst & Young in 2000. These outstanding awards are further complemented with the following official designation: "Official Document Management & Document Hardware Provider of the Cleveland Browns."

Although the Cleveland-headquartered firm provides customers with digital printers and copiers, fax equipment, hardware and other document imaging systems, it is Meritech Blue's "Commitment to Excellence," a five-point pledge of reliability, accountability and total customer satisfaction that has made it the first pick for Northeast Ohio. The "Commitment to Excellence" performance guarantee is a way of life at Meritech Blue and is instilled in the entire staff. In fact, as people enter the front door they see its corporate mission statement, "a disciplined, well-trained, highly motivated work force."

Hanna founded Meritech Blue in 1995 after leaving a similar company. Today, Meritech Blue's owner/management team includes Keith Stump, vice president of sales; Bill Nelson, general sales manager; David Morrill, Akron/Canton branch manager; and Jim Loparich, sales manager, and has since increased the size of its staff to 122 employees.

Meritech Blue began strictly as an authorized Konica dealer and then expanded to the most recognized names in document imaging products, including Minolta, Panasonic, Metafile, Compaq, Kodak and HP.

"Because of our 'Commitment to Excellence,' all of our products are the highest-rated products in the industry," Hanna says. "This philosophy has transformed Meritech Blue into a solutions provider, which we support with world-class service."

Meritech Blue's management team (left to right): Jim Loparich, sales manager; Keith Stump, vice president of sales; Paul Hanna, CEO; Bill Nelson, general sales manager; David Morrill, Akron/Canton branch manager

This five-point service system includes a commitment to each stage of the customer's relationship with Meritech Blue. These five points include "Product Performance Commitment," "Service Commitment," "Supply Commitment," "Easy Acquisition Commitment" and finally, "Complete Satisfaction Commitment." Guided by this mission statement, Meritech Blue ensures that every customer is well looked after from the very first handshake and throughout the long-term relationship.

The company's customer base can surely attest to this. Meritech Blue serves customers from Ashtabula County to Lorain County and down to Tuscarawas County, serving a 10-county area of the state.

Meritech Blue's "Commitment to Excellence" is continually stimulated through its steady growth plan. An office in Canton helps the firm garner new clients south of Cleveland, and Hanna says he anticipates doubling in size every couple of years through growth in market share and strategic acquisitions.

Nighttown

Since its humble beginnings in February 1965, Nighttown has been attracting loyal customers who consider the place an extension of their living rooms. With its eclectic menu and atmosphere, it is a rarity in the restaurant business in more ways than one.

Top-quality certified angus beef, milk-fed veal and fresh fish and chicken are served in four distinctly different dining rooms and two lively bars decorated with leaded, etched and stained glass, mixed with a clutter of memorabilia. Customers come for the food and stay for the live jazz, performed seven nights a week by local and national musicians.

Nighttown's business has doubled in recent years — not bad for a place begun on $3,000 by a high-school dropout and self-proclaimed "bum." John Barr never dreamed when he started the business, chiefly as a hangout for his friends, that it would grow to become one of Northern Ohio's most successful restaurants.

Previous to 1965, the space at the top of Cedar Hill in Cleveland Heights was occupied by a saloon called the Silhouette Lounge. Barr was a regular there, and according to legend, his bar bill was so high that rather than paying it he decided to buy the place instead. He borrowed $1,500 on his mother's insurance policy; a silent partner fronted another $1,500 and Nighttown was born, named after the Dublin red-light district in Barr's favorite novel, *Ulysses,* by James Joyce.

In June 1967 Barr began to turn Nighttown from a bar and poolroom into a restaurant. There were just five items on the menu — lobster and steaks. The menu was expanded from 1970 to 1974. By the late 70s Nighttown's menu included veal, free-range chicken and seafood.

Since the beginning, Nighttown's crowd has been like a family. Though it is very much open to the outside world, some 30 to 70 regulars from all walks of life can be commonly seen at the bar discussing the world's social injustices. It is a network of genuine caring and social consciousness, reflective of the life of John Barr. It is such an unpretentious place that one has to look twice to find the sign outside, discretely placed on a black awning.

Brendan Ring joined Barr as managing partner in 1996. One change he made was making the restaurant more accessible. It is now open from 11 a.m. to midnight, seven days a week, 364 days a year, with live jazz performed all seven nights. It only closes on Christmas day, and, offering customers a break, bans Christmas music and decorations during the holiday season. Menu prices, too, are accessible to all, with dinners ranging from $7.95 to $28.95, and the varied wine list includes the latest labels.

Nighttown takes care of the neighborhood that has brought it success by giving generously to Cleveland Heights charities and by being active in the Cedar-Fairmount Business Association. It recently bought the building it has grown up in and plans renovations — including an elegant outdoor patio — that will make it the "eyepiece" of Cleveland Heights.

Nighttown sits discretely at the top of Cedar Hill in Cleveland Heights.

Parker's Restaurant

To owner and Executive Chef Parker Bosley, Parker's isn't just a restaurant; it is an art form he considers an extension of himself and a reflection of his unorthodox beliefs. One of Cleveland's foremost culinary figures, Bosley doesn't just preach the gospel of using locally grown, seasonal ingredients, he lives it everyday in the dishes he creates and in the message he spreads.

Perhaps it's because Bosley grew up on a farm himself that "farm to table" is his life's motto. After studying music and art in college and working as an elementary school teacher, Bosley turned his cooking hobby into a profession. He soon earned a reputation for creating fine food using only regional ingredients. This led to him catering events for some of Cleveland's most prominent food and wine groups, including the Cleveland Wine and Food Society, Les Amis de Vine, Commanderie de Bordeaux and Chevalier de Taste de Vin.

In 1987 he opened Parker's on Cleveland's Near East Side, and his following grew as word spread throughout the food community. Customers enjoyed the formal atmosphere, respectful treatment and regionally reliant menu. Five years after it opened, fire destroyed the original Parker's. Bosley partnered with Jeff Jaskiel and moved the restaurant to its current location in the charming neighborhood of Ohio City, just west of downtown. The long dining room of the 60-seat restaurant is beautifully decorated in creams, charcoals and reds, and is reminiscent of a classic European restaurant complete with wafting aromas.

Bosley strongly believes that the perfect model for good food is not contemporary culture, but rather the season and the region. Parker's dishes are created using only fresh food grown by local farmers. In order to do this, Bosley had to create an infrastructure to support his mission. He cultivated a network of northeast Ohio artisan farmers to grow the high-quality specialty foods he required and, in the process, helped create a new industry. Many of his suppliers are part of the North Union Farmers Market, where they sell the same high-quality products to the general public.

Parker's has perfected the art of cooking. The menu changes frequently but always includes fresh soups and creams; veal, beef and poultry dishes; desserts laden with flavor, not sugar; and an interesting wine list. Dishes are always connected to the area. For example, the duck leg plate conjures up Cleveland's rich eastern-European legacy. The restaurant gained national recognition in June 2000 when it was praised by *Gourmet Magazine*.

Several of Cleveland's most phenomenal chefs have been attracted by Parker's unique method of cooking. This has allowed Bosley to devote more time to sharing his philosophies by traveling and speaking to farmers and restaurant industry groups all over the country.

As one of the best restaurants in the United States actively connecting the urban and rural communities through food, Parker's hopes it is spearheading a movement and inspiring the country's younger chefs. It's a quest Bosley plans to continue for many years to come. It only takes one bite of one his palatable dishes to know why.

Owner and Executive Chef Parker Bosley is one of Cleveland's foremost culinary figures.
©2000 Photo by Lisa DeCesare

The dining room at Parker's offers a comfortable setting for the presentation of the food.
©2000 Photo by Lisa DeCesare

Peter Danford, Inc.

No advertising. No credit card sales. No computers. No Internet access.

It may seem like a retailing throwback, but it's proven to be successful for Peter Danford, owner of Peter Danford, Inc., specialists in fine jewelry and gifts.

Danford is proud to point out that his is a business built on a handshake, not on technology. A handshake gave him his start when he opened the firm in 1973, and it established a precedent that remains an integral part of Danford's commitment to his customers.

Danford spent 13 years working for his father at a very well-known, well-respected Cleveland firm, Danford-Lowell, where he learned the business. Although he studied with the Gemological Institute of America (GIA), Peter Danford admits the practical experience was of more benefit than the classroom experience.

In spite of his 13 years of experience with his father, his reputation didn't precede him when he decided to go on his own. He admits he started with nothing and owed everybody in sight.

Things turned around when the head of Tiffany's silver department, a gentleman Danford had not dealt with and did not know, introduced him to the famed company's biggest jewelry supplier at the time. An agreement providing Danford with a large quantity of jewelry on consignment was sealed with a handshake. It opened the doors to a quality supplier and enabled Peter Danford to open his own doors at his first location in the LaPlace shopping center in Beachwood.

That first handshake established the philosophy that Danford still follows. Customers have gone home with an expensive piece of jewelry to determine if they want to keep it or not. No obligation. No collateral. No commitment.

That's one reason Peter Danford looks upon his customers as his friends. And it's why he has established his own niche market with classic, tailored, wearable, very fine jewelry at economical prices.

He also has remained true to New York suppliers, not only because of that first positive experience, but because he has found people in the Big Apple with whom he is comfortable and who make what he likes. And he knows what his customers like. Four times a year he travels to New York not only to learn what is available, but to renew acquaintances with those on whom he relies and has relied on for years.

The Danford shop, in Shaker Heights since 1987, reflects Peter Danford's approach to business. It provides a relaxed atmosphere in which to shop, or just to browse or select a gift from the bridal registry. The two full-time and four part-time knowledgeable employees work with customers not only to meet their very specific, very personal gift and jewelry wishes, but also to make them feel comfortable while making their purchases.

Danford's discerning clientele, who come from throughout Greater Cleveland, doesn't need advertising, e-mail access or promotions to appreciate what Peter Danford has to offer. It has learned about the firm by word of mouth — word of mouth provided by hundreds of satisfied customers.

Peter Danford's favorite model, his granddaughter, shows off a lively diamond bracelet.

"Flowers and plants can really brighten a person's day," says Angelo Petitti. "I think our business brings a lot of happiness into people's lives. Sometimes people just need a little time to themselves, so we try to help them make a special place in their yard so they can enjoy the moment." Imagine being able to bring beauty into the lives of thousands and to make a successful business out of it.

That's exactly what happened for Angelo Petitti, president of Petitti Garden Centers. Immigrating to the United States from Italy at age 16, this son of a farmer and nephew of an avid gardener used his innate sense of the land as a means of financial support while studying at Kent State University. But political science soon gave way to horticultural science as the part-time job became a full-time passion.

In 1969 Petitti and his brother, Domenico, started Petitti Brothers Landscape Contractors. Over time, the brothers had to leave much of the plant material in front of Petitti's garage. Neighbors and passersby began to stop, and the brothers soon found themselves in the retail garden center business. On the site of the old garage in Oakwood Village, Ohio, the company constructed its first official garden center in 1971. By the year 2000, Petitti owned four independent garden centers and three in area Sears stores.

Petitti's started growing its own plants in the late 1980s. By 2000 the company owned a 29-acre facility of glass and poly greenhouses known as Casa Verde Growers in Columbia Station, Ohio. Trees and shrubs are grown at Petitti's 130-acre nursery in Madison.

In 2001 Petitti's will open its supercenter location in Strongsville. This 14-acre garden center is a Victorian conservatory and is the largest and first of its kind in the United States. The supercenter was designed by English garden center designer, Malcolm Scott, and houses a restaurant and a seminar room to be used by local garden

clubs. Display gardens fill the acres of land for customers to enjoy and items are for sale from all over the world including pottery, statuary and unique garden accents.

Being involved in the community is a very important part of the Petitti Garden Center philosophy. Along with participation in area schools' gardening programs, Petitti's hosts many events for avid gardeners such as free seminars, family fun festivals and an annual charity benefit for St. Malachi Center. A favorite charity of Petitti, St. Malachi Center is a homeless center in the near-West side of Cleveland that offers the homeless a second chance at life by providing food, shelter and self-improvement programs.

Angelo Petitti, his wife, Maria, and their three children, Angelo, Andria and Lisa, manage Petitti Garden Centers' seven facilities and 300 employees. Petitti feels the most important thing he can do is reward those who have made Petitti's a success. "It's important to give back to the community and become part of it through education and support," Petitti states. "It's the community and the employees that have made this company a success and helped it grow."

Back row (left to right) Andria, Angelo. Front row (left to right) Lisa, Maria and Angelo Sr.

The garage where Angelo and his brother first began selling product to neighbors and passersby, c. 1970

Tomorrows, A Hair Salon

Seventeen years ago, Anci Brennan, the manager of a Northeast Ohio hair salon, left a thriving partnership to start her own business, an elegant hair salon tucked into the trendy Beachcliff in Rocky River. Since Tomorrows opened, Brennan hasn't looked back.

Tomorrows' decor evokes a feeling of pampered elegance. Immaculate white upholstery and fixtures combined with stark black lines lend a professional,

no-nonsense look, while a perking coffee pot and soft drink machine give the salon a friendly and homey dimension. Brennan's 15 hair stylists and four manicurists also exude a friendly but professional attitude.

The secret to Tomorrows' success is its commitment to serving and satisfying each customer. "We create an environment where our clients feel very comfortable," says Brennan. "We have a strong feeling about our clients and it's important how we treat them."

Brennan's philosophy has obviously worked. Since opening its doors in 1983, Tomorrows has tripled its gross sales in beauty salon appointments and the sale of top-of-the-line hair care products. With a client base of 3,400 and more than 32,000 appointments in 1999, the staff at Tomorrows has a keen sense of what the woman of the new millennium wants.

One of the biggest differences in styles today compared to 10, 20 and 30 years ago is there is no single hair style that is the "in" thing or current rage. "At one time you had to wear a skirt a certain length," Brennan says. "Today, anything goes. The same with hairstyles. It depends on your lifestyle." Also, Tomorrows' stylists hear fewer requests for light, bright blonde hair than 10 years ago, she says. Most women today ask for more natural color tones.

Unlike most beauty salon operators and owners, Brennan never went to cosmetology school nor does she do hair or nails. Emigrating to Cleveland from Hungary in 1968, the 13-year-old Anci had to work hard to learn English and fit in with her new American school chums in a new land.

More introspective than other young women, she pursued and received a bachelor of arts degree in psychology from Cleveland State University. But rather than pursue a master's degree toward a career as a psychologist, Brennan accepted a job as a front desk receptionist with Holiday Inn.

She enjoyed solving a myriad of problems in an often fast-paced environment and remaining calm under pressure, an essential skill in running a beauty parlor. Brennan then switched to sales, selling advanced training programs to hair salons in Northeast Ohio. But soon she was running the front desk at Today's Headlines salon. A few years later, she became a partner in the company. "After five years we parted ways and formed Tomorrows," says Brennan, the sole owner.

Brennan hasn't forgotten about the surrounding community. Each year Tomorrows donates money to the Rocky River school system and provides gift certificates to many worthy causes such as the American Cancer Society and the Malachi House, a homeless shelter and soup kitchen on Cleveland's near west side.

"I love my job," says Brennan. "The only plan I have for the future is to make sure our clients are well taken care of and our employees are well-educated."

"Our mission is to serve highway travelers in the finest full-service facilities on the interstate," says Ed Kuhn, president and chief executive officer of TravelCenters of America (TA). The company is the largest network of travel centers in the United States, covering the nation with 162 locations. Although an industry giant boasting 13,500 employees in 40 states, TA is headquartered in the quiet Cleveland suburb of Westlake.

One of the first truck stop chains in the country, TravelCenters of America was founded by industry innovator E. Philip Saunders. Along with his partners, Earl Saunders and Nelson Mason, Saunders founded Truckstops Corporation and opened the first facility in Rochester, New York, back in 1958. The second facility was opened in 1965 just outside of Ashland, Virginia, along Interstate 95. The next year Saunders bought out his partners and the company became known as Truckstops of America. The following year the company opened yet another location in Roanoke, Virginia. By the time Truckstops of America opened its first franchise operation in Dayton, Ohio, in 1971, the company had grown to seven locations in five states.

This rapid growth made the firm a prime target for acquisition and in 1972, Ryder Systems (known best for truck rentals) bought out Truckstops of America. Saunders stayed on and became a member of Ryder's board of directors. In 1984 Ryder sold TA to the Standard Oil Company of Ohio (Sohio). Sohio was in turn completely purchased by international oil conglomerate British Petroleum (BP) in 1987. In 1993, as part of its divestiture of U.S. holdings, BP sold the truck stop chain to the New York-based Clipper Group, TA management and other investors.

Growth had truly become the operative strategy, and in 1997 the chain combined with NATIONAL Auto/Truckstops (formerly the Union 76 chain) to create the largest travel center network in the nation, with 125 locations in 28 states. The name was then changed to TravelCenters of America. In 1998 the chain acquired 16 Burns Bros. Travel Stops in the Northwest and in 1999 merged with TravelPorts of America (TPOA) in the Northeast. The addition of the 16 TPOA sites, headed by TA's original founder, E. Philip Saunders, makes TA the largest of only five large chains in an industry comprising approximately 1,000 companies, most of which are small regional concerns.

TA's customer focus widened to include highway motorists in addition to professional truck drivers. The shift from a truck stop to a travel center concept affected everything, including facility design, product mix and employee training. TA's signature facility design includes travel stores with a light-filled atrium, name-brand gasolines, designated RV parking, 24-hour restaurants and well-known fast-food chains. Professional driver amenities include state-of the-art showers and restrooms, truck service, laundry facilities and 24-hour roadside service. Embracing the new millennium, the parking lots are equipped with cable television, telephone and Internet service that drivers can access from within their truck cabs.

The privately held company's focus is customer satisfaction, according to Kuhn. "We know what's important to our customers," he says. He adds with a smile, "For truck drivers it's the shower facilities. We give over 5 million showers a year. That's a lot of clean truck drivers."

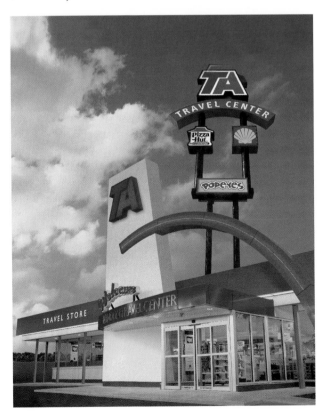

TravelCenters of America's redesigned London, Ohio, signature facility

Western Reserve Wines

Nearly 20 years ago Mario Vitale agreed to work for his family's retail wine business but only until he found his true calling. He didn't have to go far. As the owner of Western Reserve Wines on Chagrin Boulevard in Moreland Hills, Vitale is known for his vast wine selection and is sought for his extensive knowledge of Europe's vineyards

"There is nothing about the wine business I don't like," Vitale says.

and the finer points of wine tasting. But what keeps people coming back is Vitale's uncanny ability to match each customer with just the right bottle of wine for any occasion.

"The job I took in my stepfather's store was supposed to be temporary, just until I found the thing I really wanted to do," Vitale says. "But I simply fell in love with the

Mario Vitale presides over Western Reserve Wines' vast selection of premium wines from all over the world. Vitale helps wine aficionados, we well as novices, select the perfect wine for the perfect occasion.
©Photo by
Herbert Ascherman Jr.

industry, and the more I learned, the more intrigued I became. I soon realized the wine industry is a lifestyle filled with travel and intriguing people. And there was no turning back."

Vitale's big break came 10 years ago when mentor Jack Schindler gave him the chance to take over the lease to the Western Reserve Wines building, nestled in a wooded area in the upscale Cleveland suburb. Schindler liked Vitale's enthusiasm for the wine industry, his thirst for knowledge and ability to connect with customers from all walks of life.

More than 2,000 different wines grace Vitale's shelves, representing major wine-growing regions of the world from France, Italy, Spain, Portugal, Germany and the United States as well as vintages from Australia, New Zealand and South Africa.

Vitale has a low-key approach to sales, recently advising one customer to serve sparkling wine from the Alsace region instead of the more pricey champagne.

"Tuscany is my favorite place in the world," Vitale remarks. "The scenery is stunning — its gently rolling hills are dotted with walled towns, cypress trees, olive groves and of course, vineyards. Tuscany is home to Chianti and Brunello di Montalcino, two of Italy's greatest red wines, some of the greatest wine I've tasted."

Vitale reveals his most perfect wine-drinking experience was tasting wine alongside grower Christian Serafin out of barrels from his Burgundy cellar. Another high point was dining with winemaker Bruno Giacosa, whose vineyards in Barolo and Barbaresco make for some of the most intensely flavored wines in the world.

Like fine wine that improves with age, Vitale believes business will only get better. His next trip abroad is in April 2001 for the annual Vinitaly show in Verona, where winemakers from every region in Italy display their wares. Vitale also looks forward to traveling to the next frontier of fine wines, the lush vineyards of South Africa.

Future plans call for more travel, expanding his retail space and offering more wine-tasting classes.

"There is nothing about the wine business I don't like," Vitale says. "I love travel, good food and wine and I've made friends all over the world. My job often involves 18-hour days, but half the time I forget I'm working."

Photo by Robert A. Eplett

NETWORKS

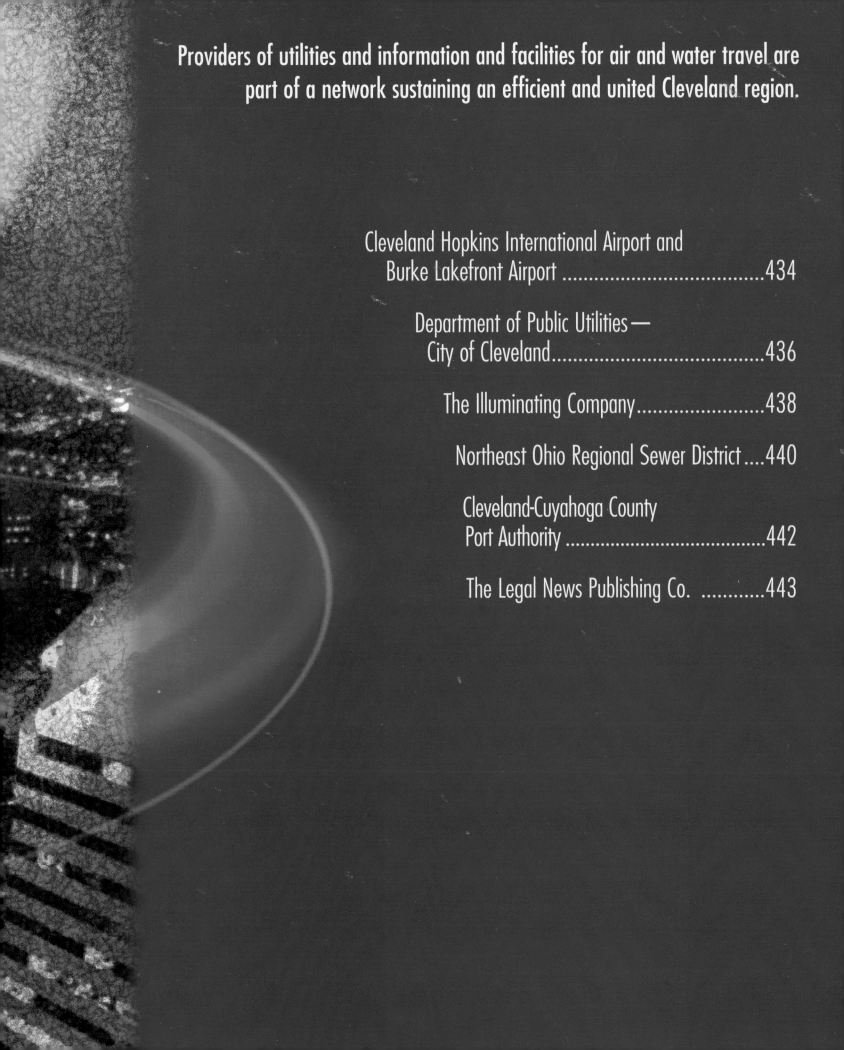

Providers of utilities and information and facilities for air and water travel are part of a network sustaining an efficient and united Cleveland region.

Cleveland Hopkins International Airport and Burke Lakefront Airport

Cleveland is on the move and so are improvements at the two city-owned airport facilities, which long have been on the cutting edge of air transportation. Cleveland Hopkins International and Burke Lakefront are key to Cleveland's status as a major city anchoring a dynamic regional economy. Increasingly, both of these airports will make it possible for Greater Cleveland to interact with worldwide markets in a timely and lucrative fashion.

Cleveland Hopkins International Airport

Founded as Cleveland Municipal Airport in 1925, Cleveland Hopkins is the oldest municipally owned airport in the country, and at one time served as a model for the development of other airports around the world. Cleveland Hopkins can stake claim to possessing the first scheduled passenger service in the United States (1926), the country's first passenger terminal building (1927), the country's first system to aid night aircraft landings (1930) and installation of the first airport control tower.

Cleveland Hopkins contributes more than $2.2 billion to the regional economy. More than 19,000 people are employed as a result of the airport and its activities. Upon completion of the airport's current expansion project — slated for 2016 — Cleveland Hopkins' annual economic impact is projected to grow to $5.2 billion, while the 6,000 jobs it creates are expected to nearly triple.

Tellingly, passenger traffic has increased more than 50 percent in the past decade, to 13 million in 1999. A driving force in this development is the rapid growth of Cleveland Hopkins' largest carrier, Continental Airlines. The Continental hub is the site of over 300 daily departures in and out of Cleveland Hopkins. In 1999 Continental opened a new $141 million concourse for commuter routes and began several daily nonstop, direct flights to London. Continental also invested more than $60 million to renovate and expand the Cleveland Hopkins baggage claim and ticketing areas to handle the increase in passengers. In addition, freight and mail are expected to increase from 135,000 tons in 1999 to 331,000 tons at the conclusion of the expansion.

In order to secure future planning options for the airport, Cleveland purchased the International Exposition Center (I-X Center) in January 1999 for $66.5 million. As part of the expansion, a new 3,800-space parking garage was completed in 1999. Construction of a new 9,000-foot parallel runway is scheduled to begin in 2000 and will be designed to increase the peak-period capacity of the airport. Extension of the other parallel runway will allow for more direct flights to other international destinatins.

Another noteworthy addition to Hopkins was a new consolidated rental car facility that has attracted the attention of airport managers from the likes of Baltimore and New Mexico. Such was their curiosity that these managers have flown into town in order to observe how the car rental facility adds yet another innovative feature to the airport

New Concourse D at Cleveland Hopkins International Airport provides a multicolored sensory experience.
Photo by Donn R. Nottage

Burke Lakefront Airport

Burke is a full-service general aviation airport located in the heart of downtown Cleveland on the shores of Lake Erie. The airport plays a much-needed role by alleviating some of the airfield pressure on Cleveland Hopkins. In 1999, for example, Burke handled 90,677 operations compared to 321,420 at Cleveland Hopkins. About 22 percent of Cleveland's air traffic is generated at Burke.

Burke was opened in 1947, and thereafter airfield and passenger terminal facilities were built to accommodate steadily increasing demand. The current terminal was last expanded in 1968, but has been updated several times over the years.

The bulk of aviation activity at Burke is comprised of corporate air operations. Consequently, Burke is a strong selling point for Cleveland in its efforts to attract new businesses while encouraging existing businesses to expand locally. The convenience of downtown and access to local interstate highways make Burke the primary corporate aviation gateway to Greater Cleveland. Crucially, most major commercial markets in the United States lie within a one-hour flight of Cleveland, making Burke a convenient and dependable hub for business travelers.

The importance of Burke likewise has steadily grown with the development of several high-profile downtown attractions like the Rock and Roll Hall of Fame and Museum, the Great Lakes Science Center and two new professional sports stadiums — including a new 72,000-seat football stadium and a multipurpose indoor sports arena — both of which are located just minutes away. In the final analysis, the importance of Burke has grown directly in proportion to the extraordinary renaissance taking place in downtown Cleveland.

Burke is home to two Fixed Base Operators (FBOs) that provide hangar space, fuel, aircraft maintenance, aircraft leasing and rental cars for private aircraft. Burke also annually hosts the Cleveland Grand Prix, a major IndyCar competition held on the airfield each summer, and the Cleveland National Air Show, which traditionally is held on Labor Day weekend.

To keep pace with the growing demands placed on Burke, the city of Cleveland installed a new Instrument Landing System (ILS) in 1999, which increases runway safety and allows the airport to remain open during inclement weather conditions. River dredging is being deposited in Lake Erie to build a surface that will hold an additional runway for Burke in the future.

Cleveland Owned and Operated

Both Cleveland Hopkins and Burke are owned and operated by the city of Cleveland. The city's Department of Port Control manages both facilities, oversees the budget, and along with Mayor Michael R. White defines short- and long-term airport policy. But because both airports are

Not a spaceship, rather the new pedestrian walkway at Cleveland Hopkins International Airport
Photo by Donn R. Nottage

self-supporting, neither of their operations or expansion projects requires funding from Cleveland's general fund.

Because the airports are located within city limits, both strive to be good neighbors in their respective communities. At Hopkins, there is an active sound-mitigation program that has resulted in the purchase of 792 homes, and the insulation of 1,369 other residences as well as three schools through 1999. Demand for this program, which is free to homeowners, remains strong. To date, the city has spent more than $100 million on the Cleveland Hopkins acquisition and residential sound-insulation programs.

"Cleveland is fortunate to have two strong airports — a large, rapidly growing international airport in Cleveland Hopkins, and a perfectly located business jetport in Burke, right in the center of Cleveland's downtown excitement," says Cleveland Mayor Michael R. White. "I'm proud of the accomplishments of our staff to provide safe, efficient and customer-friendly service to the vast traveling public."

The airport lobby at Cleveland Hopkins International — a clean, well-lighted place in which to chat with fellow travelers
Photo by Donn R. Nottage

Department of Public Utilities — City of Cleveland

Cleveland Division of Water

For nearly 150 years, the Cleveland Division of Water has supplied safe drinking water both to city residents and residents of outlying communities. Today, the division is one of the 10 largest public water supply agencies in the country, serving 1.5 million customers in a 640-square-mile area. Relying upon one the largest fresh water supplies in the world — Lake Erie, one of North America's famous Great Lakes — the Division of Water benefits from an abundant 127-trillion-gallon reserve not likely to run dry in the near future.

Cleveland Public Power lights up a new cultural institution on the city's North Coast.
Photo by Donn R. Nottage

Safe Water Makes Good Economic Sense

Several advancements have served to steadily increase water purity over the past several decades, spurred mainly by the federal Clean Water Act of 1972. Such has been the improvement in the quality of Lake Erie water that today the Division of Water needs only a tenth of the chlorine to purify untreated water compared to 30 years ago. In 1996 the division strongly supported the Safe Drinking Water Act amendments, which required public water systems to annually report on the quality of drinking water. And in 1999, when the first results of the Consumer Confidence Report were released, Cleveland's water far exceeded all state and federal regulatory guidelines.

In order to improve customer service, two major capital improvement projects have been recently completed. The Crown Waterworks plant was expanded, doubling its production capacity and enhancing both safety and security. And Harvard Yards Distribution Maintenance Facility was significantly rebuilt, with the objective being increased technological efficiency and capacity. "With investments like these, the Division of Water will most certainly increase quality, maintain reliability, and continue to meet or exceed every standard set by the Environmental Protection Agency," states Public Utilities Director Michael G. Konicek.

The degree of prominence attained by the Division of Water was not an overnight achievement. Rather, it is a result of rigorous adherence to standards of quality and safety that far exceed the minimum. Several quality-control steps are followed in order to assure delivery of only the purest water.

Advances in Automation Lead to Better Customer Service

Other advances in automation also have been implemented in order to improve efficiency and quality of service delivery. Meter-reading crews can now obtain readings from remote locations in a fraction of the time required by traditional methods. Also in place are 65 new hand-held and 51 laptop computers being used to streamline the meter-reading cycle and generate more-accurate billings for customers.

As a result of a significant expansion of service hours and the continuing education and training of representatives, the rate of customer complaints has dropped significantly in recent years — by over 50 percent. Key to the division's advances in customer service quality has been expansion of the service lobby located in the renovated Carl B. Stokes Public Utilities Building. In addition to fielding phone calls, customer service staff routinely conduct plant tours and fulfill public speaking engagements to various community groups.

Whether providing the highest-quality product and service delivery to customers, responding to customer concerns, or serving as one of Cleveland's most significant ambassadors for city services, the Division of Water remains committed to serving Northeast Ohio for decades to come. As Mayor Michael R. White frequently observes, "Our municipal water system is one of the core foundations upon which we continue to grow our businesses and indeed our entire community."

Cleveland Public Power

At the beginning of the 20th century, Cleveland's famous reform mayor, Tom L. Johnson, was determined to establish a public electric utility so that the city could "give to the people in their homes and places of business the benefit of electric light and power at the minimum of cost." Such has been the mission of CPP since its inception until today.

Today, CPP no longer generates its own power, but rather purchases electricity wholesale from a national grid — freeing CPP to exclusively focus on efficient and relatively inexpensive service delivery. Tom L. Johnson's initial vision to provide power "at the minimum of cost" thus lives on even in today's modernized incarnation of his company.

The Vision is Sustained and Grows Brighter

This philosophy has won many converts over to CPP. From 1988 to 1999 an additional 30,000 customers have switched to Cleveland Public Power, bringing total residential and commercial accounts to an all-time high of nearly 80,000. As a result, the utility is financially and operationally stronger than ever, an enviable position that did not occur by happenstance but rather from aggressive marketing and outreach. 1999 was a pivotal year, moreover, with over 250 new commercial meters and over 3,000 residential accounts established.

Unlike many electric utilities —- whether publicly or privately owned — CPP has been buying power on the open market for years. Deregulation will serve to enhance CPP's role as a power "broker" that brings customers together with the best possible rates, while maintaining a laser-like focus on quality service delivery. Thus, management expects the transition to proceed smoothly and with no noticeable discomfort to existing customers.

Bridges aglow over the Cuyahoga River. The Cleveland city skyline is in the background. *Photo by Donn R. Nottage*

In Advance of Deregulation, Focus on Even Better Customer Service

Like the Division of Water, Cleveland Public Power is doing more than talking customer service, it's investing in new systems that demonstrate a long-term commitment to customer satisfaction and streamlined service delivery. In 2000 CPP will unveil a computer system designed to enhance the information customers can access on their bills, and reduce the likelihood of billing errors.

In 1999 48 new trucks were added to CPP's fleet in order to provide crews with 24-hour, 7-day blanket coverage of all service areas. And in another customer service-related decision, Cleveland Public Power began to utilize Doppler radar in order to track severe storms in the region and dispatch crews in advance to potential trouble spots. With this and other kinds of far-sighted innovations, CPP is significantly reducing chances of prolonged power outages.

As Cleveland Mayor Michael R. White observes, "One of Cleveland Public Power's strengths is its ability to stay flexible, responding to changes in ways that benefit customers, and constantly improving its electrical distribution system." Given the challenges posed by a deregulated market, it is a given, the mayor concludes, that those utilities that expect to thrive in the new environment will find ways to set themselves apart. "With one of the most technologically competent and respected work forces in the entire industry, CPP is uniquely positioned to challenge the status quo, and to carve out a new legacy for publicly owned utilities in the new century," claims Cleveland's path-breaking mayor.

The Illuminating Company

When the industrial revolution spread to this country, Cleveland ultimately became a leader, but it wasn't until the advent of electric service in the late 1800s that industrial growth here really shifted into high gear. And from the beginning, The Cleveland Electric Illuminating Company made electricity for lighting the city streets and powering the factories and businesses that drove the revolution and the economy.

In 1878 Cleveland engineer Charles Brush patented an arc lamp that ran on electric current. Within a year, he collaborated with the Cleveland Telegraph Supply Company to build a demonstration project to light Public Square. By 1884 Brush's inventiveness led to the creation of the world's first streetcar on Central Avenue. The Cleveland General Electric Company bought Brush's electric company in 1892, along with several others in the city, and two years later changed the name to The Cleveland Electric Illuminating Company.

Now, as part of the FirstEnergy family of companies, The Illuminating Company is in a stronger position than ever to serve homes, power factories and businesses, and help fuel the economy of northeast Ohio.

FirstEnergy Corp. is a diversified energy services company that produces nearly $6 billion in annual revenues and owns more than $18 billion in assets. Along with FirstEnergy's other electric utility operating companies — Ohio Edison, Pennsylvania Power and Toledo Edison — The Illuminating Company is part of the nation's 10th-largest investor-owned electric utility system, serving 2.2 million customers in Ohio and Pennsylvania.

"Looking to the future, our vision is to become the leading regional retail energy and related services supplier," says FirstEnergy President and CEO H. Peter Burg. "We have the capability of providing all forms of energy for our customers, not just electricity. And, we will offer an array of related services that make us our customer's preferred supplier of their energy needs.

"As we enter a new century," he says, "The Illuminating Company will continue to play a pivotal role in Cleveland and surrounding areas as both an energy supplier and corporate citizen."

The Illuminating Company serves 750,000 customers in northeast Ohio. Its former parent company, Centerior Energy Corporation, merged with Ohio Edison Company in 1997 to form FirstEnergy Corp., headquartered south of Cleveland in Akron.

As part of a larger company, The Illuminating Company has improved its competitive position in the rapidly changing energy marketplace. Among the most significant challenges — and greatest opportunities — facing the electric company is Ohio's new law that opens its electric utility industry to competition.

In preparation for competition, The Illuminating Company initiated a freeze of its base electricity rates in 1998, coupled with interim reductions through 2005. This price-reduction program, amounting to as much as 8 percent a month for some customers, already has saved them millions of dollars.

Another aspect of the company's competitive strategy includes expanding

Since 1894 The Illuminating Company has been part of Cleveland's landscape. Today the company serves 750,000 electric customers in the greater Cleveland area.

its portfolio of energy and energy-related products and services to better meet the needs of new and existing customers. Through acquisitions and alliances, FirstEnergy has added an array of new products and services including natural gas, heating, ventilation, air conditioning, refrigeration, roofing construction, plumbing and process piping.

As the marketplace evolves, FirstEnergy and its subsidiaries are strengthening their partnerships with the customers and communities they serve. Becoming part of FirstEnergy was a critical step in that process for The Illuminating Company.

Those efforts are paying off. FirstEnergy's economic development efforts, including incentive rates and other business support programs, have encouraged expansions and the attraction of new companies representing billions of dollars in investments in the areas served by The Illuminating Company and its affiliated companies.

In addition, schools are benefiting as FirstEnergy and The Illuminating Company focus on enhancing their relationships with the communities they serve. More than 90 school districts are enrolled in the Energy for Education Program, which has reduced base electricity prices for participating public and private schools that sign long-term supply contracts.

"The Illuminating Company and our other operating electric utilities have been providing customers with safe, reliable and economical electricity for more

than 100 years," says Burg. "By combining a century of lessons with the strength and resources of a larger, more competitive enterprise, The Illuminating Company will be as integral to Cleveland's future as it was to the city's past."

Fabricating galvanized piping for duct work is one of many products and services provided by Roth Bros., Inc., one of 11 FirstEnergy subsidiary companies that together form the largest network of mechanical contractors in the region.

FirstEnergy Corp., the parent company of The Illuminating Company, has an extensive transmission system covering more than 6,500 miles in Ohio and Pennsylvania, and has 35 interconnections with eight electric systems.

Northeast Ohio Regional Sewer District

The Cuyahoga River is "an open sewer through the center of the city," according to Mayor Rensselaer Herrick. The year was 1882.

It took almost a century for change to occur, and that change didn't take place until a few years after the Cuyahoga caught on fire on June 22, 1969. Although it burned for "only" 20 minutes, flames rose as high as five stories and required units from three fire battalions and a fireboat to bring it under control. In addition to making Cleveland an international joke, the fire drew attention to the river's pollution problem and the lack of a comprehensive pollution-abatement program.

In reaction to nationwide water quality problems, Congress enacted the 1972 amendments to the Federal Water Pollution Control Act, later called the Clean Water Act.

Rowers prepare for competition on a clean Cuyahoga River.

Relief sewers on Fairmount Boulevard in Cleveland Heights

But even with that and other federal legislation, problems with northeastern Ohio's polluted water persisted. Many Cleveland suburbs refused to finance their share of improvements unless the city of Cleveland gave up its exclusive authority over sewage treatment, including rate setting. In spite of court action by the suburbs and the Ohio Water Pollution Control Board against the city, the litigants could not agree on a solution to city-suburban problems.

Consequently, Judge George McMonagle created a new regional agency in 1972 to protect the area's water resources. The agency, originally the Cleveland Regional Sewer District, became the Northeast Ohio Regional Sewer District (NEORSD) in 1979. NEORSD was divided into two subdistricts. Subdistrict I covers the city of Cleveland and Subdistrict II represents suburban communities.

To satisfy the suburban communities' need for more representation in the newly created sewer district's decision-making process, the District's seven-member board of trustees included representatives from both the city of Cleveland and the suburbs.

NEORSD had three initial charges. The first was to assume operation and management of wastewater collection, treatment and disposal facilities serving the Cleveland metropolitan area. The second was to build new and improved facilities, and the third was to prepare a regional plan for sewerage and drainage.

These were difficult tasks. At the time of NEORSD's creation, the Cuyahoga River was filled with industrial waste, oil slicks and raw sewage. As a result, Lake Erie's abundant fish species disappeared, beaches closed and swimming was prohibited.

The new organization inherited three wastewater-treatment plants from the city of Cleveland, the newest of which was 44 years old. All three plants needed upgrading to meet the requirements of the Clean Water Act. The District also inherited a system of interceptor sewers that frequently overflowed into the environment and needed rehabilitation and improvement. Shortly after its creation in 1972, NEORSD undertook a capital-improvement program of more than $1 billion to address those pollution-abatement requirements.

The District's first priority was to upgrade the plants. Those upgraded plants now stand as a symbol of NEORSD's success, since all have received national awards for meeting permit limits established under the National Pollutant Discharge System.

With treatment-plant improvements well under way, the District turned its attention toward improving its interceptor sewers, which collect sanitary and combined sewage from suburban communities.

One of the District's biggest challenges while serving more than 1 million customers in 54 communities is addressing the water pollution caused by overflows from the older combined sewer systems in Cleveland and inner-ring suburbs. These sewers were built to convey both sanitary and storm waters to waterways during heavy rainfall. Although designed to overflow during heavy rain under the theory that the excess water would dilute the pollutants and reduce their impact on the environment, the resultant discharges of debris, pollutants and bacteria still threatened the ecosystem and public health.

To address the problem of old and overburdened sewers, the District spent millions rehabilitating and constructing the Cuyahoga Valley, Northwest, Southwest and Heights/Hilltop interceptors.

Additionally, the District controls overflows as much as possible with fixed regulators and newer, computer-controlled autoregulators. After heavy rainfall, wastewater overflows are routed to the nearest plant for treatment.

Having largely completed improvements to the interceptors (the Heights/Hilltop interceptors are almost complete), the District is completing facilities-planning studies leading to long-range improvements to the combined sewer system.

However, many Northeast Ohio homeowners still experience flooding. These incidents are due to inadequacies in the community-owned separate storm-sewer systems, especially if the homeowners live in a flood zone.

Fortunately, NEORSD has begun to address those storm-water drainage and flooding issues. The District has completed Phase 1 of the Regional Plan for Sewerage and Drainage (RPSD) Study. This study of storm-water issues will help the District develop an understanding of the regional storm-drainage network; pinpoint community storm-drainage problems; and identify legal, regulatory and institutional issues related to storm-water management.

A solution must be found. But because the District's jurisdiction crosses so many communities, the study raises almost as many questions as it resolves. For example, who will be responsible for intercommunity drainage? And what are the roles of the District and participating communities?

Some of the answers may come from a detailed study, the Regional Intercommunity Drainage Evaluation (RIDE), which is seeking to find the best solution for everyone. But until the solutions are found, the District continues to educate the public about its role as an environmental agency.

In addition to wastewater treatment, the District works to maintain water quality by monitoring and regulating various industries to ensure they are not dumping toxins and various other pollutants into the sewers. The District, in cooperation with a consortium of state, regional and local health agencies, also monitors the water of area beaches to make sure it is safe for public recreation and tracks aquatic life populations, which are a strong indicator of water quality.

NEORSD's improvements to the treatment plants and their associated combined and separate interceptor sewer systems have helped revitalize area waterways. The river and lakefront have become popular and economically viable recreation areas. And as technology changes and evolving legislation and compliance create more challenges, NEORSD will continue to provide answers to the problems troubling northeastern Ohio's waterways.

Southerly wastewater-treatment plant, one of three such plants upgraded by NEORSD

Cleveland-Cuyahoga County Port Authority

The Port of Cleveland plays host to hundreds of massive vessels that deliver over 17 million tons of cargo to the shores of Cleveland each year. Over 1.18 million tons of international cargo crossed the Port Authority's docks in 1998 — an all-time record. Shipments of steel, iron ore, cement, limestone and other bulk materials from other Great Lakes ports and from countries such as Russia, the Netherlands and other European countries are received, then transported to the region's large manufacturing base. More than 4,800 jobs and over $440 million in spending are linked to Cleveland's maritime industry.

Massive vessels deliver over 17 million tons of cargo to Cleveland docks each year.

Lesser known but equally important to Cleveland's growing economy is the Port Authority's Development Finance Group, which has partnered in several projects that resulted in some of the city's most visible and important land developments, as well as job growth and even tourism.

Authorized under Ohio law to provide for a variety of bond financing programs, the Port Authority entered the development finance arena in 1993. As a key partner on the Rock and Roll Hall of Fame and Museum project, the Port Authority issued $39 million of revenue bonds to help build the $92 million museum.

The Port Authority has also used its financing capabilities to issue $18 million of revenue bonds for the construction of Applied Industrial Technologies' $37 million headquarters in

Through its Development Finance Group, the Port Authority issued revenue bonds to help finance the construction of Applied Industrial Technologies' headquarters.

MidTown Cleveland. More recently, the Port Authority financed the construction of a $20 million worldwide back-office facility for OfficeMax.

The Port Authority has also developed a Bond Fund Program that provides long-term, fixed rate financing of $1 million to $6 million to creditworthy businesses for owner-occupied industrial and commercial projects.

With its development finance efforts in full swing, the Port Authority continues to make improvements to its traditional maritime operations. The Maritime Facilities Master Plan, developed in 1998, addresses critical issues of capacity, cargo diversification and public access. The plan provides a map for maritime facilities capital improvements to support the regional economy through the year 2025, by which time it is estimated that the port's international tonnage will have nearly tripled.

The Port Authority began capital improvements under the Master Plan with the development of Dock 22 East. This $9.5 million project is one of the largest in the port's history and will accommodate the growing need for cargo handling and storage space along the waterfront.

Through its recognized maritime operations and its equally important development finance programs, the Port Authority has become a part of the backbone of Cleveland's continued economic growth. With its two-pronged mission in force, the Port Authority has done more than most people know in helping to keep Cleveland's renaissance afloat.

The Legal News Publishing Co.

The Legal News Publishing Co. has been serving the city of Cleveland and Cuyahoga County legal, business and governmental communities for more than a century. Since 1897, the company has been owned and operated by a branch of the Karlovec family, making it one of Cleveland's oldest family-owned businesses.

The creation of a court stenographer and a *Plain Dealer* courthouse reporter, *The Daily Court Record*, as it first was called, made its debut on Saturday, November 28, 1885, as a four-page publication about the size of a church bulletin. Two years later, the paper had another publisher and another name — *Daily Legal News* — and was housed in a book-bindery and printing shop on a winding lane off Public Square. From 1925 until 1965, the company was located on Ontario Street near the Cuyahoga County courthouse, a convenient location for lawyers, judges, bailiffs, reporters and trial buffs to visit. When the entire block was demolished to provide space for the Justice Center, Legal News Publishing moved to its current location on Prospect Avenue in the Midtown Corridor.

The company has the distinction of never having missed publishing an edition of the *Daily Legal News* in its entire history, of being the first legal newspaper in Ohio and of being the only daily legal paper published in Cuyahoga County today. The *Daily Legal News* is the designated newspaper of record for the Cuyahoga County court system, as well as the county's official law journal. Available in all public office buildings and libraries in Cuyahoga County, the newspaper is circulated primarily through paid subscriptions.

When Ralph C. Karlovec purchased the paper from his brother-in-law in 1919, he launched a family-owned business that continues to this day under the direction of his grandson, Lucien B. ("Luke") Karlovec Jr., whose two sons Jeff and John are in training for the next generation of leadership. Ralph Karlovec and his son Lucien ("Lu") were savvy businessmen. They not only expanded the company's publications list, but also in 1928 established a commercial printing shop, the Cadillac Press, which today offers complete commercial printing services on Web offset and offset machines. The company also has printed since the 1920s *The City Record*, a weekly transcript of all proceedings of the Cleveland City Council.

In the mid-1930s the Karlovecs acquired more than a dozen suburban newspapers that were discontinued during World War II due to labor and paper shortages. As with most commercial enterprises, Legal News Publishing has adapted to the technological innovations of its time. Linotype machines, type galleys and the huge ink-laden letterpress printing presses have been displaced by computerized typesetters and offset presses.

In its early days, the *Daily Legal News* shared many of the attributes of other papers — news stories, features, book and theater reviews and interviews with sports figures. After a period in which the newspaper focused primarily on court docket listings, the *Daily Legal News* reinstated front-page news stories and features of particular interest to its readership. From its beginning as a four-page leaflet to its current editions of 24 to 36 pages, the *Daily Legal News* consistently has provided the factual information needed by the Cleveland-area legal, business and governmental communities.

PROFESSIONAL
SERVICES

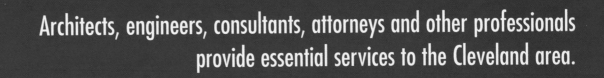

Architects, engineers, consultants, attorneys and other professionals provide essential services to the Cleveland area.

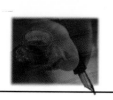

Climaco, Lefkowitz, Peca, Wilcox & Garofoli Co., L.P.A.

It was the early 1990s and Clevelanders were thrilled that the city had been chosen as the site for the national Rock and Roll Hall of Fame and Museum. Yet almost five years had passed since the awarding of the coveted hall, and still no one had found the funds needed to build it. The situation looked hopeless.

The financing for the Gateway complex was handled by CLPW&G.
Photo by Scott Pease

As bond counsel to the Cleveland-Cuyahoga County Port Authority, CLPW&G was instrumental in securing the financing for the headquarters of Applied Industrial Technologies, Inc.

Fortunately, problem solving is routine at the law firm of Climaco, Lefkowitz, Peca, Wilcox & Garofoli Co., L.P.A. (CLPW&G). It was Principal Anthony J. Garofoli who thought to utilize the Cleveland-Cuyahoga County Port Authority as the developer for the Rock Hall. This allowed the issuance of tax-free bonds and a financing package that turned the Rock and Roll Hall of Fame and Museum from a dream into a reality, opening its doors in September 1995.

The realization of the Rock Hall is just one of the many turning points in Cleveland's history driven by the expertise of CLPW&G. In fact, since its founding in 1969 by John R. Climaco, the firm has helped lay the groundwork for most of Cleveland's major projects and has played a key role in the city's recent revitalization.

The firm first gained national attention in 1978 by representing the Cleveland City Council during the dark days of the Cleveland default hearings. CLPW&G's continuing relationship with the city of Cleveland, along with a variety of other municipal and government agencies, led to its involvement in a number of city developments, including the establishment of cable television and the Northeast Ohio Regional Sewer District.

As general counsel for the Gateway Economic Development Corporation, the Port Authority and the Ohio Turnpike Commission, CLPW&G has also helped bring to life Jacobs Field, Gund Arena, the Great Lakes Science Center, the new world headquarters of Applied Industrial Technologies, Inc. and expansions to the Ohio Turnpike.

Respected throughout the Greater Cleveland community for more than 30 years, the key to the success of CLPW&G is simple common sense and client commitment. This is reflected in the firm's credo: "We work hard to solve our client's problems efficiently, not to create more work." Though the firm is well known for its zealous litigation, it is the claims that never get filed — because of preventive counseling and strategic advice — that give CLPW&G attorneys the greatest amount of satisfaction.

CLPW&G's commitment to creative strategy development is what helped the city of Brook Park and Ford Motor Company come to an agreement on the construction of a municipally owned power plant. As a direct result of the advice of CLPW&G, the residents of Brook Park received $1.5 million per year for five years and Ford Motor received substantial savings in energy costs. The far-reaching effect was a significant expansion of the Brook Park Ford plant, which continues to generate additional dollars for the community.

CLPW&G's contributions to the Greater Cleveland community don't end there. The firm feels it has an obligation to share its success and therefore is extremely active in community service and charity support. Not only does it give generous financial donations to a wide variety of charities, but the firm also takes great pride in donating the time and talents of its professional staff to worthwhile causes.

One of CLPW&G's most unique and popular fundraising events began quite accidentally one day. Managing Principal John A. Peca wanted to share his culinary talents with his fellow attorneys, so he cooked them lunch. The next week, the lunch grew to include a few clients as well. Within a few months, lunches were being served to groups of 10 to 12 people. Word spread quickly and soon Mr. Peca and his staff were cooking monthly lunches for up to 40 friends and clients. To accommodate the growing guest list, CLPW&G expanded its dining space to fit 150 guests and built a full institutional kitchen in its offices.

A charity asked to hold a raffle at one of these well-attended lunches, and before long the gatherings had evolved into CLPW&G's Gourmet Charity Events. Now at least four times a year, the firm's principals plan and prepare extravagant meals and the professional staff provides service for lunches and dinners of up to 150 guests. All proceeds benefit local organizations in need, such as The Center for Mental Retardation, Coats for Kids, the Parents Volunteer Association, the Holy Rosary Montessori School and a host of others. It's estimated that these festive get-togethers have raised over half a million dollars in the last 10 years.

Unique in its commitment to its clients and its community, CLPW&G is also unique in its fundamental belief in staying in the background. Whether the client is a small-business owner or a national politician, CLPW&G lets them shine, handling the client's tough issues quickly and favorably.

CLPW&G is not a specialty firm. Its attorneys each have different areas of expertise, and they combine to form a dedicated group of generalists. The firm has extensive experience in all types of law, including litigation, corporate and business law, environmental law, municipal and public law, public finance, intellectual property, employment law, white collar criminal law, real estate law, and health and

Founding Principal John R. Climaco being actively involved in a reverse raffle for a local charity

insurance law. Individuals, corporations, entrepreneurs, CEOs, councilmen, mayors, governors and even presidential candidates have all asked CLPW&G to solve their problems. Remarkably, the firm has always exceeded their expectations.

As far as the future is concerned, CLPW&G doesn't have any plans for major change. And why should it? Its practice of solving client's problems efficiently is what CLPW&G does best, and by doing so, the firm will continue to gain respect from its clients and its community.

Fortunately for the Greater Cleveland community, innovative ideas from CLPW&G are often followed by Cleveland milestones, and continued success for the firm means continued growth for the city.

Extravagant dishes are prepared and served by CLPW&G staff at one of their many Gourmet Charity Events.

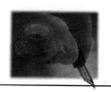

Computer Sciences Corporation

They have seen change before. Executives at Computer Sciences Corporation (CSC) say they not only have seen it, but they manage it everyday. The rapid changes taking place in Information Technology today are behind such assertions; so are the opportunities presented daily to CSC to use that technology to design innovative business solutions.

The global corporation, which operates a management consulting and systems integration office in Cleveland, creates, develops and implements business strategies for Fortune 500 companies, new and established businesses and government agencies. Strategies are devised to help

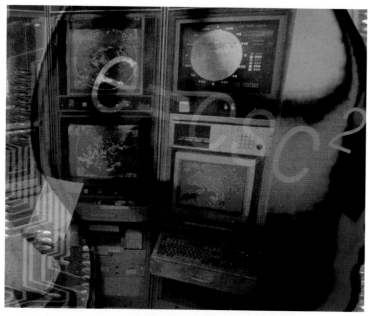

clients achieve internal management, production, marketing and distribution goals by combining the consulting and marketing expertise of the CSC professional staff with the opportunities presented by the Internet and other communications technology.

CSC thrives on the ability to anticipate rapid changes in that technology. That ability allows the company to present the most sophisticated and most comprehensive "end-to-end" business operations strategies to clients to help them maintain a competitive edge. It also allows CSC to maintain an edge over its own competitors in the management consulting industry. The company is a pioneer

in the design and implementation of business solutions that go beyond the use of technology.

The company is part of the new economy that is blending new ideas with new technology and helping to revolutionize traditional business practices. One CSC executive refers to the pace of change brought about by the Industrial Revolution as a basis for comparison. That revolution began in England in the mid-1700s and extended into the 19th century for some countries. It transformed many rural, agricultural communities into town-centered manufacturing sites with the new machinery and emerging technology of that era.

"If you go back to the Industrial Revolution and the length of time it took for that to occur, the same phenomenon is taking place right now at a rapid pace, in a condensed time period, and we're right in the middle of it," says Stephen J. Keener, a Cleveland-based senior partner in the CSC Consulting Group. "We're at the forefront in helping companies make changes in the middle of this big change revolution."

The company, which has corporate offices in El Segundo, California, was founded in 1959 by programmers Fletcher Jones and Roy Nutt. Jones and Nutt, both deceased, pooled $100 to start the business. A couple of years later, the new company began a long-standing business relationship with the federal government by first providing computer systems data support services to NASA to track data from unmanned space probes. The strength of that relationship is still evident. A CSC astronaut flew on the Space Shuttle during the 1990s as a payload specialist. In 1968 CSC became the first information sciences company to be listed on the New York Stock Exchange.

The company's client base has broadened dramatically in the last several years into the commercial arena, as it has acquired smaller firms and expanded its services. The multibillion-dollar firm today provides services in several major categories. Its Technology Outsourcing component assumes certain technology management, or other business processes for a client, which allows that client to focus on its core business. The Systems Integration component designs, builds and links the hardware, software and communications systems needed to support business operations. Various e-Business services components develop strategies and solutions to leverage the power of the Internet. CSC's Management and IT consulting component helps businesses find new strategies to gain a competitive edge and remain at the forefront of emerging business and technology trends.

Teams and networks are culled from these components to provide clients with technical and management expertise needed for projects. The clients are from a broad range of industries, including financial services; energy; health care; information, communications and entertainment; consumer and industrial products, retail services and public sector. The consulting and technical needs of these clients are backed and supported by a corporate giant that has some 800 offices and some 60,000 employees worldwide.

Management consulting and systems integration services are the focus of the CSC Consulting Group office in Cleveland. The local presence was established with the 1989 acquisition of Cleveland Consulting Associates (CCA), a logistics and supply-chain consulting firm. CCA,

which was founded in 1974, worked with manufacturers and retailers to develop more cost-efficient strategies to get products from the manufacturing site to the distributor or retailer. Co-founder Roger W. Kallock has since gone on to become an assistant undersecretary with the U.S. Department of Defense. An award is given annually to the local CSC consultant who most exemplifies the company's core values of partnership, respect, excellence and innovation in serving clients.

The acquisition of CCA and other small consulting firms helped CSC move more aggressively into the commercial consulting business, which now exceeds the government consulting business in revenue generated. The local CSC Consulting Group office, which is one of 15 in the U.S., creates and implements business solutions that are tailored to achieve internal and external goals of businesses from throughout North America. Those goals could involve the way a food or appliance manufacturer gets its product from the factory floor to the distributor or consumer. Another client may want to improve its corporate culture — how its executives and staff interact with each other or with customers, or how staff members perform their jobs.

CSC resolves the problem in either scenario by designing, developing and implementing a business strategy tailored for that company. That strategy could mean clarifying customer relations with a new customer-interface strategy. It could mean developing an internal strategy to energize and mobilize the client's work force. The latest technology and business strategies are used to provide these solutions. "We have worked hard as a team to create solutions that reflect sound business and operational strategies with leading-edge technologies," says William F. Read, a Cleveland-based vice president for CSC Consulting Group. "In today's business world there are very few enterprises that develop a strategy without incorporating technology as a key enabler."

The company's own strategy for assisting clients includes maintaining personal contact with them and demonstrating its trademark flexibility in designing strategies. Unlike other major consulting firms, CSC doesn't own a software product line that it would be obligated to promote. The company, therefore, has been able to establish partnerships with various software developers. This allows it to tailor a strategy to suit the needs of a particular client. The

Roger W. Kallock co-founded Cleveland Consulting Associates, which was acquired by CSC and helped that corporation establish its presence in the community.

William F. Read, a Cleveland-based vice president for CSC Consulting Group

Michael R. Klaus, a Cleveland-based vice president for CSC Consulting Group

boutique firms that specialized in specific, stand-alone services. The shift to providing "end-to-end" services began several years ago. Many major manufacturers started to downsize to become leaner operations. They began contracting out some services that were cut or eliminated. The manufacturers also wanted contractors or consultants that could handle a number of responsibilities simultaneously, rather than hire several contractors to assume different duties. In some cases, Klaus says, a consulting firm would be retained to develop a marketing strategy for a manufacturer's product and would indicate a certain cost that would be incurred to implement that strategy. A second consulting firm might be hired to actually implement that strategy but might disagree with the cost estimates or determine that the technology does not exist to implement the strategy. Manufacturers began to demand more comprehensive services from consultants.

CSC is part of the revolution of consulting firms establishing longer-term, more comprehensive business relationships with these large businesses. As a result, CSC now keeps clients for years rather than months. It doesn't cede consulting, management or information technology services to another consulting firm on a strategy it has developed for a client. And CSC not only helps create the business strategy, it stays around to make sure key staff are educated on the strategy and ensures that it is properly implemented.

In addition to creating and seeing that a strategy is implemented, CSC in some cases may assume the responsibility the strategy was designed to address. Manufacturing and service firms hire CSC to assume responsibilities that may take time and resources away from providing their core services. An insurance firm, a company that sells sneakers or a paint manufacturer may want to focus its resources on what it excels at rather than auxiliary business operations. Outsourcing such tasks as payroll, debt collection or other operations allows the client company to focus on its core business. In these instances CSC Consulting would provide the strategy to outsource these responsibilities, while a sister CSC division might assume the actual responsibilities.

The CSC Consulting Group is expected to become more involved with creating business strategies as a result of new and emerging business trends. One such trend is

company's flexibility on behalf of clients is evident in other areas. CSC, more than any other major consulting firm, also embraces partnerships with competing consulting firms to serve clients.

That ability and willingness to explore nontraditional options to develop business solutions helps CSC keep pace with the changes in communications technology and management trends. The company's flexibility extends to decisions about where its consultants report for work. On any given day, nearly three-quarters of the local office's 100 employees are away from home base. There was a time when employees would have been expected to work full-time out of the office site. Now, employees frequently work at a client's work site. The only real concern for the CSC consultant is whether an airport is nearby. "We're testing the bounds of a virtual company," explains Michael R. Klaus, another Cleveland-based vice president for CSC Consulting Group. Being flexible about work sites is important because competition among consulting firms is as stiff as it is among manufacturers. Consultants must be accessible to clients as well as knowledgeable about new services if they want to survive in the industry, he says.

CSC is helping set the standard among management consulting firms as to how they can respond to the needs of clients in this arena. In the past, consulting firms were business-to-business commerce, involving industry-related firms engaged in producing a product. Automobile manufacturers, for instance, already have business relationships with other manufacturers to supply parts and accessories that will be added to their vehicles. The next level for that relationship, CSC executives note, is to implement collaborative production scheduling and inventory management capabilities across supply chain partners.

Suppliers of automobile parts would have access to information about inventories from dealers, so placing an order would not be necessary. The relationship would save time for the dealer and give the supplier more advanced notice about the types of products to keep stocked and the kinds of sales that can be anticipated. Financial, logistics, sales and confidentiality issues need to be addressed and resolved in these cases for the exchange of information to take place smoothly.

This is also the era of the "Web-enabling" large manufacturers, says Bruce M. Ferraro, another Cleveland-based partner for CSC Consulting Group. The benefits of the Internet are being realized and incorporated into the business practices of major manufacturers. New Internet-based companies have effectively used the Internet to conduct business or provide avenues for other companies to give speedy service to consumers. Large manufacturing firms have relied upon the more traditional means to advertise and sell their goods. But those firms want to explore similar opportunities provided by the Internet. Management consultants will play a major role in helping these large firms develop strategies to use the Internet to reach marketing and sales goals.

Large manufacturing companies already have the advantage of having an established operation and products to market and distribute. Some startups, on the other hand, may only be a liaison and cannot guarantee a product after an order has been placed, Ferraro says.

CSC also is anticipating the future needs of manufacturers and service providers. Beyond providing high-tech management solutions for existing problems, CSC also is providing clients with data they can use to determine steps they want to take for growth and expansion. Information about consumers — their purchasing habits for instance — can be provided to help clients market their goods to specific consumer groups. Keeping pace with new technology and continually anticipating the needs of clients has helped CSC become one of the world's largest management consulting firms. Says Klaus, "We're always on the edge, anticipating the next level of change."

CSC astronaut Ron Parise flew on the shuttle as a payload specialist.

Computer Sciences Corporation was founded in 1959 by programmers Fletcher Jones (standing) and Roy Nutt (seated, center).

Calfee, Halter & Griswold LLP

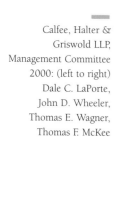

Calfee, Halter &
Griswold LLP,
Management Committee
2000: (left to right)
Dale C. LaPorte,
John D. Wheeler,
Thomas E. Wagner,
Thomas F. McKee

Calfee, Halter & Griswold LLP is a full-service corporate law firm headquartered in the heart of downtown Cleveland with a government relations and litigation practice in Columbus, Ohio.

The firm was founded in 1903, making it one of Cleveland's oldest law firms. Robert M. Calfee, a graduate of George Washington University Law School, received his master of law degree from National University in 1902. While working as a clerk in Washington, D.C., Calfee heard about a job opportunity with Cleveland attorney Alton A. Bemis. Within a few months, Calfee moved to Cleveland and joined Bemis, Zigelman & Calfee, which was simply Bemis & Calfee a year later.

In 1908 Calfee decided to hang out his own shingle in the venerable Williamson Building on Public Square. He was joined a year later by Joseph G. Fogg, a no-nonsense, cigar-chomping football fanatic, who became a prominent member of the community and true leader of the firm from 1917 until his death in 1946. "Joe laid the foundation for the corporate business of our firm," recalls John D. Wheeler, managing partner of the firm from 1992 through 1999. Fogg is credited with forging the firm's initial ties with regional investment firm McDonald & Company, a flagship client for many years; for serving as a trustee in the 15-year Van Sweringen bankruptcy case during the 1930s and 1940s; and for representing several public and private companies that remain clients to this day.

Calfee and Fogg maintained a successful partnership for many years. By 1916 Calfee chose to spend most of his time in Washington, D.C., working exclusively on a project for the U.S. War Department with Col. Isaac N. Lewis. Calfee was hired to fight a patent infringement on a machine gun invented by Lewis. Lewis, in turn, marketed the gun to the U.S. military, but to no avail. The British, ultimately, were quite interested in Lewis' invention and used it in World War I.

In 1929 Calfee and Fogg were joined by a recent Western Reserve Law School graduate, Edwin Halter. Five years later, the firm moved to the Union Commerce Building. Halter was the driving force for the firm from 1946 until his retirement. He was managing partner from 1956 to 1967. Halter was a highly regarded corporate attorney and is reputed to have prepared one of the first-ever corporate stock registration statements — for Cleveland-based Carling Brewing Company — shortly after the Securities and Exchange Act of 1933 was adopted.

By the early-to mid-40s Calfee & Fogg had gained national recognition for its work in securities law. The firm remained strong during World War II because many of its clients were manufacturing firms that ramped up their businesses to meet wartime needs. Brilliant attorneys, including one legendary Addison Brennan, continued to join the firm. But in 1946 Calfee and Fogg lost one of its original luminaries: Joe Fogg died in December of complications from a stroke. On the same day, Ed Halter, John McChord and Ken Ressiger of the firm formed a new partnership. Halter and McChord were co-managing partners, but Halter was "really running the firm," according to Griswold. The firm was renamed Calfee, Fogg, McChord and Halter — a name it kept until the late 60s. R. M. Calfee's son, Jack, an associate at the time,

recalled years later, "There were a lot of people around town who thought the firm would fold up, betting on who would go where."

How wrong they were. The firm not only survived, it prospered and grew during the 1950s. Bruce Griswold, hired in 1950, contributed significantly to that success. A former math teacher at University School, Griswold was stricken with polio in 1940. He left teaching for law school at Western Reserve University and, after graduation, served as a law clerk for U.S. Supreme Court Justice Harold H. Burton. Griswold was quite charismatic and well known in social circles on Cleveland's East Side.

In 1953 the firm employed 12 lawyers. But by the end of that decade, three of the firm's leaders died of sudden heart attacks — McChord in 1956, Ressiger in 1958 and hard-living, fun-loving Brennan in 1959. Once again, people around town wondered if the firm could survive. But Halter stood firm. Al Sommer joined the firm in 1951 and headed up securities law at the firm during the 60s and early 70s until his appointment as an SEC Commissioner in 1972. In 1965 Chuck Emrick joined the firm and, for the next 35 years, successfully led the firm's strong growth in representing the private corporate sector. In 1969 the firm moved to the Central National Bank Building at the corner of East 9th and Superior, and has remained there since.

The firm was renamed Calfee, Halter, Griswold & Sommer in 1967 and finally renamed Calfee, Halter &

Griswold in 1986. Several managing partners followed Halter, including Jack Calfee, Griswold and Sommer. But it was Halter's protégé, Dan Ekelman, who was the key management figure during the 70s and 80s and was managing partner from 1978 to 1985. Rush McKnight, a highly regarded labor attorney, was managing partner for the balance of the 80s.

Today the firm's 175 attorneys serve over 3,500 clients ranging from smaller, privately held entrepreneurial ventures to some of the area's largest publicly held corporations to healthcare organizations, public agencies and utilities. Practice areas include all facets of litigation and corporate law, from antitrust and trade regulations to information technology and, of course, securities law. The firm's depth in intellectual property (25 attorneys) has made it a leader in representing today's technology-transfer initiatives.

Industry pundits speculate that law firms may consolidate over the next decade or so. But senior partners at Calfee, Halter & Griswold say they plan to stay the course with limited modifications designed to meet changing times. As John Wheeler notes, "While our attorneys are engaged worldwide, we have always concentrated on northern Ohio businesses and that strategy has been very successful for us. The challenge for us is how to export our expertise while remaining true to our corporate base here at home."

Calfee, Fogg, McChord & Halter, 1946

Cannon Advertising Specialties

Nestled amidst the tree-lined neighborhood along East 40 Street, the venerable, red-brick St. Paul's parish school is the unlikely home to Cannon Advertising Specialties, a savvy, multimillion-dollar business aimed at providing creative ideas for promotional products to business, industry and government.

On some days Cannon's think tank can hear the strings of a tamburica playing traditional music for the Klezmer dance students in the basement of the school, which was built in 1906 to educate the children of Croatian immigrants.

Cannon CEO Ross Salupo has leased the building from the Catholic Diocese of Cleveland since 1989, defying a popular belief that a creative advertising business needs to locate in the heart of the downtown business district to ensure its success.

But Cannon's location is one of its main strengths. Retaining the character of the schoolhouse, seven classrooms and the old cloakroom are filled with thousands of advertising items and gimmicks such as a tiny basketball hoop and ball to promote the recent MAC basketball tournament. Dazzling sports showcases display pro, college and high school team sportswear, trophies and paraphernalia, and one entire room is devoted to creative golf ideas.

Salupo, 53, cut his advertising and marketing teeth at *The Plain Dealer* in the early 1970s. He started the Ross Salupo Advertising Agency in 1978 at the trendy downtown

Reserve Square location where he wrote ads for print and broadcast and designed layout and graphics. Salupo soon noticed how his clients wanted "promotional stuff" such as calendars, pens, posters and mugs to use as giveaways and perceived the specialties market as a potential gold mine.

Salupo was becoming burned out with the ad agency and realized he enjoyed the challenge of coming up with creative promotional items. So in 1989 he leased St. Paul's school and opened its doors to Cannon Advertising Specialties. "Now, I have more fun just coming to work every day," Salupo says. "It's like a dream come true."

Over the past 10 years, Cannon's growth has paralleled the growth of the multibillion-dollar advertising specialty industry, building its business and reputation through service and technology. Cannon's creative dream team is currently providing product ideas for more than 1,000 clients, including the Convention & Visitors Bureau of Greater Cleveland, Eaton Corporation, the Cleveland Growth Association, Ernst & Young, the U.S. Postal Service, Cleveland Clinic and major shopping malls.

Through the use of custom imprinted messages on various products from penny matchbooks to $10,000 watches, Cannon is able to assist other businesses create consumer awareness, increase sales, motivate employees, promote plant safety, recognize achievement, commemorate special occasions and celebrate family reunions.

The key to Cannon's extraordinary success has been its ability to combine the latest technology with imaginative and creative ideas to launch campaigns that capture the attention of the target audience and communicate a message forcefully and effectively, Salupo says.

Every Wednesday manufacturers' reps from all over the United States sit around Cannon's conference table in the school principal's office to pitch products and brainstorm ideas. The informal atmosphere is more relaxing than a corporate boardroom and gets the creative juices flowing, Salupo says. Plus, what other multimillion-dollar agency has 250 parking spaces right outside its door?

Much of Cannon's rise to success can be attributed to its technology. On its state-of-the-art computer system, Cannon has access to 711,000 different products such as balloons, pens, mouse pads and even Waterford Crystal,

Cannon Advertising is located in a charming old schoolhouse built in 1906. The school has been converted into a fantasyland of promotional products and the home of a thriving, successful business.

customized with corporate logos and messages for events ranging from a business opening or retirement party to a political rally to a charity event.

It used to take the Cannon team days to find a particular item to promote an event or product. Now, thanks to technology, most any item is only a mouse click away. Cannon's dedicated staff can usually get product samples within the day.

"Because we are among the top 5 percent of all distributors in the country, our manufacturers go above and beyond to meet our clients' requests," Salupo says. "We have a lot of friends all over the world coming through for us every day."

Thanks to Cannon's technological expertise, its sales have grown in volume from 17 to 20 percent each of the last three years. Salupo's goal is to increase sales 100 percent over the next two years while continuing to upgrade its resources.

Much of Cannon's success hinges on its ability to communicate with its customers. Cannon's staff asks its clients three questions: What is your objective, what is your target market and what is your budget? The answers have enabled Cannon to come up with countless creative solutions for accounts with client budgets ranging from $12 for a family reunion to hundreds of thousands to promote brand awareness.

Cannon launched one of its most successful campaigns in 1996, promoting the U.S. Conference of Mayors, held in Cleveland. Considering this was a summer event in a secondary market, the event was figured to draw a couple of hundred visitors. Working closely with the Convention

& Visitors Bureau and the mayor's committee for the event, Cannon was able to tie into the national exposure of the new Rock and Roll Hall of Fame.

Cannon's creative staff put their heads together and pulled out all the stops trying to capture the attention of mayors' secretaries across the United States. "Our intention was to dazzle, to excite people," Salupo says.

Rather than send promotional Rock Hall t-shirts to mayors' offices, Cannon's staffers sent the t-shirts inside canisters decorated with a colorful Cleveland logo. Peeling open the lid, the first thing to fall out was a personalized invitation to the U.S. Conference of Mayors from Mayor Michael White.

A week later Cannon sent each mayor what appeared to be a CD, but turned out to be a desk calendar with each day leading to the event depicting different Cleveland attractions such as the Rock Hall, the Museum of Natural History and the Cleveland Museum of Art.

"Not only were we giving away a product, but creating a postcard memory," Salupo says. "The conference was extremely successful, drawing nearly four times the number of mayors and guests who would usually attend the conference in the summer."

It's not tough promoting Cleveland, says Salupo, a former Collinwood High School and John Carroll University student. Cannon believes in the city. And anything good for the city is good for Cannon, he says.

As far as Salupo is concerned, Cannon Advertising Specialties has no competition. Cannon is in a league of its own.

The "Main Classroom" of Cannon Advertising displays just a fraction of the over 700,000 products that are available for advertising promotion. In addition to the main classroom there are several other distinctive display areas in the "olde schoolhouse."

The addition of computers, motion-activated lighting, dazzling showcases and thousands of advertising promotional items makes Cannon Advertising a truly exciting place to visit.

The third-floor "principal's office" has been converted into a presentation room and houses an array of Cannon's most successful advertising programs. Numerous creative ideas have been initiated in this tower of the old schoolhouse.

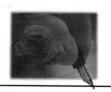

Donald Martens & Sons Ambulance Service

Achieving recognition in MetroHealth Medical Center's *Metro Life Flight* publication is not the raison d'être for Donald Martens & Sons Ambulance Service — being the first on the scene of an accident and treating the critically injured, is. A firsthand account of the accident and subsequent medical treatment by a Life Flight surgeon gave appropriate credit to the Martens' ambulance staff.

Providing ambulance service or becoming a funeral director may not have been the furthest thing from Don Martens' mind when he began college, but it certainly wasn't in the forefront. He had all good intentions of becoming a dentist, but decided against it, deciding he could do more good for more people as a funeral director.

In 1953, four years after graduating from high school, Martens became the youngest person in Ohio at the time to become a licensed undertaker and embalmer. Since his brothers had funeral homes on Cleveland's West Side, he went to work for them part time.

Deciding that he wished to open his own establishment, Martens was able to buy an existing funeral home on Cleveland's West Side in 1959. Five years later he established the Donald Martens & Sons Ambulance Service. The service's first vehicle was a new 1964 Oldsmobile Vista Cruiser station wagon converted into an ambulance by the manufacturer. At the time, converted station wagons were used by all safety forces and rescue squads as ambulances.

Funeral homes historically had ambulances, using them primarily to transport people between home and hospital, and back. It was a public relations gesture, even though there was just enough of a fee to cover expenses.

Using his one ambulance, Martens provided nighttime assistance at a nursing home. Because of the service he provided and the positive attitudes of his employees, the nursing home owner asked him to provide ambulance service for his entire chain of nursing homes.

In order to meet the needs of the chain, Martens expanded his fleet, buying several Cadillac ambulances. It was the start of what was to become Ohio's largest family-owned ambulance service.

At the beginning of the 21st century, the firm had 74 units strategically located at five sites throughout Cleveland and its eastern and western suburbs.

Change has not only been evident in the number of the firm's vehicles but in the services available on those units. A far cry from that initial Vista Cruiser, recent additions to the Martens' fleet are two mobile intensive care units, each staffed by a registered nurse, an intern and two paramedics. The units contain defibrillators, heart monitors and just about everything that an emergency room provides.

In addition, because of the quality of care provided in Cleveland hospitals, Martens' ambulances have been dispatched to locations as far away as the states of California and Washington to bring critically ill patients to Cleveland. Although returning them by air may be faster, an airplane's pressurized cabin may not be conducive to patients' well-being.

As a Shriner, Martens has made his ambulances free of charge to take burned and crippled youngsters to hospitals in Buffalo and Cincinnati for treatment.

The service also has vehicles available at Jacobs Field for Cleveland Indians baseball games, where sometimes as many as five fans may require transportation to a hospital.

Responsible for the organization's success are (left to right) Don Martens Jr., Don Martens Sr. and Dean Martens.

Each of Martens' two mobile intensive care units are staffed by a nurse, an intern and two paramedics.

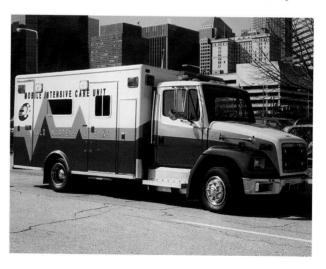

Donald Martens & Sons Funeral Home

Martens has served on the governor's licensing board for ambulance service since its creation in 1990 and is vice president of the Ohio Ambulance Association. He and his sons, Donald Martens Jr., who joined the firm in 1975; and Dean, who joined in 1980, also are active in the

stress and emotion of a family death. One of the most popular aspects of preplanning is that it protects the individual from rising funeral costs and inflation with payments for a future funeral at today's prices.

Members of the Martens family have found other ways to maintain the personal touch at such a trying time by determining what the bereaved family wants and what it can afford, and then meeting those requirements. They work with the family and work out ways to maintain dignity while reducing costs, if that is what is required.

One example is Martens' use of its own minihearse instead of renting a costly full-sized hearse if the family wishes. Martens and his sons also have recommended elimination of limousines in favor of the family using its own cars, pointing out there is nothing that requires the use of a fancy vehicle. And, Martens emphasizes, there is nothing wrong with adhering to a budget.

Martens' decision to make a career change in 1959 is providing employment for 130 people. For them, his decision has become a way of life.

Exterior of Donald Martens & Sons Funeral Home

Cuyahoga County Embalmers Association, Ohio Funeral Directors Association and National Funeral Association, as well as in a variety of civic and fraternal organizations.

Just as the ambulance service has grown, so, too, has Donald Martens & Sons Funeral Home.

Martens Sr. emphasizes the funeral home's success has been the result of the personal touch he, his sons and all employees provide to those families seeking assistance. He also is quick to point out that many of those seeking assistance are not necessarily grieving families.

One of the fastest-growing aspects of the funeral home industry is the preplanning of funerals, which provides peace of mind to families before they are caught up in the

The tasteful interior of Martens' funeral home

KA, Inc. Architecture

After four decades of award-winning architectural design and client-oriented service, KA, Inc. has achieved a national reputation for its standard of excellence and for creating structures that fulfill its clients' goals.

The firm began as a one-person operation in 1960 when Keeva J. Kekst received his first commission — to design a 13-story, 254-suite apartment building in Cleveland. Kekst made his first foray into retail design two years later with a shopping center in Richmond Heights. Nearly 40 years later, the firm was asked to update this mall, now named Richmond Town Square. Both of these early commissions set the tone for the firm as it grew to become one of Cleveland's top five architectural firms, ranked by number of registered architects. The consistent goal has been a high standard of design and a commitment to client satisfaction.

"We are an organization that designs projects to meet our client's expectations and not our goals for what we think the client should have," explains President James Heller. "We want to design buildings that have residual value to the client and provide them flexibility for what their business may be in the future." KA's client roster is long, prestigious and national in scope, with 75 to 85 percent of its projects being outside its home state.

The firm operates as three studios that target primary client segments:

The Site Planning and Landscape Architecture Studio offers complete site analysis, often before a client acquires or assembles the property, to determine the suitability of

Courthouse Towers, Cleveland, Ohio, mixed-use/hotel

The Promenade, Temecula, California, retail/regional shopping mall

the land to the client's needs. Code restrictions, zoning issues and site conditions are investigated to assess the financial feasibility of the overall project. Land planners maximize a site's potential, considering the issues of parking, environmental concerns, wildlife habitats and native vegetation. KA provides expertise in the planning stage by understanding the client's end product and uncovering hidden site development costs. On behalf of its client the firm deals with city officials, community groups and neighborhoods and has extensive experience making presentations to architectural review boards and planning commissions.

The Interior Architecture Studio designs owner-occupied buildings and provides a complete line of services: planning the physical facilities to match the corporate clients' goals; planning interior spaces; assessing current and future needs; and performing ongoing facility management. KA goes beyond good design to help create a work environment in keeping with the corporate culture dynamics of the client.

The Commercial Real Estate Developer Studio works with professional developers who create investment properties, including shopping centers; department stores; large-scale, mixed-use complexes; multifamily residential buildings; speculative office buildings; and hospitality buildings. KA is registered in 44 states and has designed projects in many of them, attesting to its leadership role in the industry.

As a measure of its national reputation for large-scale retail design, KA, Inc. designed and opened six regional malls for six different developers in 1999: Arbor Place Mall (Georgia), Jersey Gardens (New Jersey), Rivertown Crossings (Michigan), The Promenade in Temecula (California), Plaza del Sol (Puerto Rico), and the expansion and complete renovation of Richmond Town Square (Ohio).

To accomplish such a monumental feat requires a combination of experience, major resources and an operating philosophy structured for maximum client service and satisfaction. For commissions in any of the three studios, KA selects a project manager and a team of architects, designers, technical support staff and consultants in mechanical, electrical, plumbing, structural engineering and whatever other service is required to meet the goal of delivering a product of high quality that meets or exceeds the client's expectations. Throughout the ebb and flow of the process, the project manager functions as the client's personal architect, ensuring that the client's needs are being addressed.

KA, Inc. has integrated new technologies into its organization and turned them into invaluable tools. Computer-aided design programs allow for speed and accuracy in developing concepts to present to a client and in incorporating any changes or variations requested. When designs are rendered in 3-D animation, the client can virtually walk through the structure and make modifications before ground is broken on site. Clients better understand their projects, are more involved in the design process and help further the objective of eliminating guesswork and minimizing surprise elements.

About this intensive client involvement, Darrell Pattison, director of design, says: "The way we get most of our work is from clients who say 'You gave me exactly what you said you would, you did it in a short period of time for a reasonable fee and my next project is coming to you because I like this working relationship'." KA has cultivated longstanding client relationships spanning many decades. At any given time, 80 to 85 percent of KA's project list is from repeat clients.

With e-commerce and the exponential growth of technology, the business of KA is changing. "There's a trend toward redeveloping older, outdated properties and making them more compatible to today's uses," says Noel Cupkovic, senior vice president. "We'll be doing more master planning and architectural redevelopment of urban areas and more adaptive work in office buildings located near fiber optic networks." Even with e-commerce expansion there is still a demand for bricks-and-mortar retail venues, although the industry, according to Cupkovic, is experiencing a shift away from huge regional malls to smaller "main street" retail villages or lifestyle centers.

(Left to right)
Noel L. Cupkovic, architect/senior vice president;
James B. Heller, president;
David H. Bader, director of site planning/landscape architecture;
Darrell K. Pattison, director of design;
Thomas M. Milanich, COO

Whatever direction the industry takes, it is clear that KA, Inc. will continue to honor its mission statement: "to provide full architectural services in a manner to balance each client's creative and economic goals; to create state-of-the-art, imaginative architecture within the framework of a responsible business organization that will be the pride of our clients and members of our firm."

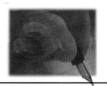

Professional Travel, Inc.

In 1963 two enterprising young men combined their considerable talents to form Professional Travel, Inc., a travel service company specializing in group and business travel. They were Ron Howard, a cruise specialist with Cunard Lines, and Bob Sturm, an account executive for Pan-American Airways. Their first office was located in Fairview Park, Ohio, and concentrated on escorted trips, cruises, customized golf programs and tours with local radio and television celebrities.

By 1982 Professional Travel was able to expand its horizons, largely the result of an upswing in business travel. Companies conducting business on a regional, national or global level realized the importance of travel to their own growth and turned to professionals in that field to provide guidance. Professional Travel's expertise in business travel management made it a natural choice for these businesses.

Also in 1982, Professional Travel opened a second office in downtown Cleveland's historic Statler Office Building. This enabled it to service downtown accounts

Robert A. Sturm, president and CEO

with ease and flexibility while establishing a presence in the city. They quickly outgrew the Statler office and for the past 10 years have occupied spacious offices in the Halle Building.

The management and employees of Professional Travel have made it their personal goal to become one of the top 25 travel mangement companies in the country.

As businesses became more aware of the need to control travel costs, Professional Travel was establishing a wealth of resources to step in and provide that service. It has grown to include an expansive headquarters located in North Olmsted, Ohio, with branch offices in Solon, Ashtabula, Hudson, Strongsville, Medina and Wooster, Ohio, as well as locations in Chicago and Detroit.

Today, Professional Travel ranks 42nd out of 33,000 travel-management companies in the United States. The company is a founding member and owner of Woodside Travel Trust, the world's largest travel management organization, comprised of 125 independently owned market dominant agencies representing 6,600 worldwide locations in 80 countries. Woodside Travel Trust will soon be known as Radius, the global travel company.

Professional Travel is also the largest independently owned travel management company in the region. Clients include such industry leaders as Forest City Enterprises, The Kirby Company, Cleveland-Cliffs Inc., Cooper Tire, Pioneer Standard Electronics Inc., MTD Products Inc., Royal Appliance (Dirt Devil) and Shiloh Industries, to name a few.

In 1998, when Ron Howard tragically passed away, Mr. Sturm accepted the responsibilities of president and CEO of the company and, together along with Rob Turk, executive vice president, operates the business from its North Olmsted corporate headquarters. They both sit on the national advisory board of Continental Airlines and Mr. Sturm also sits on the national advisory boards of TWA and Northwest Airlines, giving the company added leverage when negotiating discounts and service benefits for clients.

Today, Professional Travel is a benchmark in the travel industry for integrity, service and a high caliber of employee skills that deliver measurable results for its growing list of clients. The company has received honors and recognition from its peers in the business travel world and enjoys a leadership position in the field of innovative travel solutions.

New technology has played an integral part in Professional Travel's development. The past few decades have seen a myriad of changes in the travel industry, with the beginning of the computerized age, making access to information easier for both agents and consumers.

Professional Travel has remained at the forefront of the technology revolution, with its consistent growth and size enabling it to implement new products as soon as they become available. It maintains an Information Technology Department to provide accurate and timely reports and data analysis to clients, and has recently been instrumental in developing the company's Web site.

Professional Travel's management believes in giving back to the community that has enabled it to become an industry leader. Consequently, they are visible contributors to many vital charities. Almost every charitable organization in the Greater Cleveland area has at one time or another received financial or volunteer support from Professional Travel. Its list of contributions include those made to the Boy Scouts, Youth for Christ, United Way, The Lupus Foundation of America, The March of Dimes, The Cystic Fibrosis Foundation and the Fellowship of Christian Athletes, to name a few.

Bob Sturm, while enjoying the success his company has achieved, credits his employees with continually providing the service levels clients have come to expect and value. He has cultivated and maintained a family atmosphere in a workplace with over 170 highly skilled employees. A variety of company sponsored events are held each year, such as picnics and Christmas parties, and incentives are provided for perfect attendance and outstanding performance. Mr. Sturm expects all employees to deliver the highest standard of dedication to client service, which he has emphasized as the company's Golden Rule for over 30 years.

The management and employees of Professional Travel have made it their personal goal to become one of the top 25 travel management companies in the country. Additional expansion is planned, and the company intends to continue its commitment to being the best travel management company in the industry for the benefit of its clients and employees alike.

Whether it is an important client meeting overseas or the adventure of a lifetime, Professional Travel exceeds expectations by serving clients worldwide with first-class total travel management.

Rob Turk,
executive vice president

Vorys, Sater, Seymour and Pease LLP

In 1909 four attorneys came together to create a different kind of law firm, dedicated to a spirit of teamwork, integrity and the highest level of ethical service to its clients. They founded their firm on a handshake. Vorys, Sater, Seymour and Pease LLP continues to flourish today under the same honorable principles — and the same handshake. Operating without a formal partnership agreement, the firm is governed by traditions of teamwork, collegiality and a commitment to excellence.

Headquartered in Columbus, Ohio, with offices in Cleveland, Cincinnati, Washington, D.C., and Alexandria, Virginia, Vorys, Sater, Seymour and Pease LLP is the largest full-service law firm in Columbus, and one of the top 100 firms in the country. With more than 90 years of growth, the firm is composed of approximately 780 employees, more than 340 of whom are attorneys, all dedicated to ethical, cutting-edge representation of their clients.

Much of the firm's growth has come within the past 20 years, with the Cleveland office representing a significant portion of that growth. Opened in 1982 with a single full-time attorney, the office has grown to 24 lawyers, three paralegals and a support staff of more than 20.

Vorys, Sater, Seymour and Pease LLP serves more than 13,000 clients, ranging from conglomerates such as The Limited, Inc., Honda of America Manufacturing, Inc., and Wendy's International, Inc., to small businesses and individuals. The firm's areas of practice include commercial and corporate transactions, creditors' rights and bankruptcy, banking and finance, securities, litigation, labor and employment law, workers' compensation, antitrust and unfair trade competition, intellectual property, international trade, real estate and insurance.

The firm attributes its ongoing success to the level of dedication, integrity and loyalty its partners and attorneys provide to their clients. This, the firm contends, is nurtured through a sense of pride employees take in their performance and their workplace.

The firm is dedicated to providing a work environment in which all attorneys have continuing opportunities to learn, give and receive support, and thrive personally and professionally. The firm supports a unique "First Year Associate Program" that enables young attorneys to practice in a number of different areas of law, allowing them to focus on the area in which they have the greatest interest.

The firm devotes a considerable amount of time to the development of its young lawyers. All associates have mentors within the firm that rotate on an annual basis. The mentor program is just one example of Vorys' commitment to the personal and professional development of its young attorneys.

Greetings at the entrance of Vorys, Sater, Seymour and Pease LLP. (Left to right) Attorneys Margaret Everett, Jerome Webbs and Kenneth Stump

(Left to right) Attorneys Lisa Forbes, Bruce Batista and Marcel Duhamel discuss case materials.

Vorys operates under the concept that employees who are satisfied with the firm's commitment to them will, in turn, enhance their commitment to servicing their clients. The firm encourages its partners and associates to be dedicated first and foremost to their families, and at the same time promotes participation in civic, bar association and charitable activities, as well.

The firm recruits top law students from the best schools in Ohio and throughout the country. Its summer clerkship program has been highly rated by law clerks in surveys by several legal publications.

Another unique benefit for attorneys with Vorys is the "Seymour Plan." This trust, established by James O. Seymour, son of the founding partner, subsidizes travel to Europe for attorneys and staff members each year to provide them with valuable experiences of other cultures and continents.

The Vorys law firm believes in the strength of diversity in the workplace and is committed to actively recruiting female and minority law students through on-campus activities and job fairs. Vorys was the first central Ohio law firm to hire a female attorney and promote her to partner. Partners Sandra J. Anderson and Carl Smallwood were the first female and African-American presidents, respectively, of the Columbus Bar Association.

The firm has been an active participant in the American Bar Association's Minority Partners Conference. Vorys partner Reginald Jackson is a past chairman of the conference. Partner Cory Amron served as chair of the American Bar Association's Commission on Women in the Profession and has been an active member since its inception.

In addition to law-related activities, Vorys, Sater, Seymour and Pease LLP encourages its employees to participate in civic and charitable events and sponsors several important fund-raising activities throughout the year. Of particular importance have been sponsorships of the Juvenile Diabetes Foundation, the Cleveland Speech and Hearing Center, the Cleveland Food Bank, the Salvation Army's Adopt-a-Family holiday program and the Cleveland Zoological Society. In fact, Vorys has been the primary sponsor of Zoolights at the Cleveland Metroparks Zoo, an annual holiday tradition visited by tens of thousands of Greater Cleveland families.

With a commitment to maintaining a family of motivated, dedicated and ethical attorneys, Vorys' growth has been ongoing. In response to its clients' globalization, the firm has added international law and immigration to its expanding portfolio of expertise. Additionally, its computer law and electronic commerce experience continues to evolve, keeping pace with the needs of dot-com companies regarding initial public offerings, venture capital and intellectual property issues.

The firm's success has resulted from its flexibility and its responsiveness to clients' ever-changing business climates. Vorys has been able to balance change and business evolution while still maintaining its fundamental course charted in 1909. The firm expects the best from its organization and its lawyers, underscores it with the highest level of support and delivers it to its clients with integrity, honesty and sincerity. And what's more, they're willing to shake on it.

Cleveland Partners (standing, left to right) Daniel Balmert, Anthony O'Malley, (seated, left to right) John Read, Drew Parobek, John Saganich and David Tocco

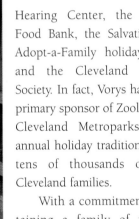
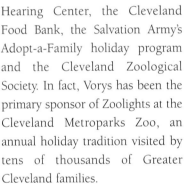

Wendy Rice-Isaacs and Drew Parobek with Zoolights mascot "Olivia"

Alex N. Sill Company

It was nearly 8:00 p.m. on a frigid Saturday night and 100 wedding guests at the venerable Chagrin Valley Hunt Club in Gates Mills were sitting down to a sumptuous banquet. Suddenly somebody shouted, "Fire!" Coats, hats and purses were left behind as guests fled into the subzero night, shivering in horror as the 85-year-old, clapboard-sided clubhouse went up in flames.

"The main clubhouse and contents were totally destroyed," says Senior Vice President John Woodward of the Alex N. Sill Adjustment Company, headquartered in Independence.

Within days of the January 1994 tragedy, Woodward and his team of loss appraisers sifted through the ashes documenting any remaining physical evidence.

"Part of the difficulty was in reconstructing all that was destroyed, including the building and equipment, furniture, fireplaces, antiques, artwork, trophies and memorabilia," Woodward says. After compiling a detailed claim presentation for the building, contents and other coverages, Woodward expedited and negotiated a very favorable settlement of $4.2 million for the Chagrin Valley Hunt Club.

Since 1928, Sill Company's loss consultants and appraisers have built an international reputation on responsive and skillful assistance to policyholders in commercial and industrial insurance claim settlements in the aftermath of fires and other natural disasters. Today, Sill Company prides itself on being the nation's leading authority in adjusting claims exclusively for the insured.

The key to the company's success is specialization.

"Unlike other firms in our industry, we have in-house adjusters, building appraisers, contents and equipment appraisers, inventory specialists, engineers and certified public accountants who can be mobilized within hours to begin on-site damage and loss assessment," says Sill

(Left to right) President and Director Jack H. Kunz, Chairman of the Board and CEO Robert L. Sill, Senior Vice President and Director John Woodward

Company President Jack H. Kunz. "We can document and estimate the damage in a clear, concise format acceptable to the insurance industry. Although we are an advocate for the insured, we have maintained a very credible reputation with the insurance industry, which is very important in this business."

Today, Sill Company prides itself on being the nation's leading authority in adjusting claims exclusively for the insured.

Company founder Alex N. Sill was in the real estate business before going into the building and remodeling business, often repairing fire-damaged properties.

"When things got bad during the Depression, Cleveland banks would call on my father for a damage appraisal if there was a fire or flood," says Chief Executive Officer Robert L. Sill. "He would then meet with the insurance companies and try to make the best settlement. He was known to be trustworthy and also a good negotiator.

"I never thought of doing anything else but working at my father's business," says Sill, who joined the firm in 1954. His first large settlement was for $1 million after a fire gutted the old Westlake Hotel in Rocky River.

One of the firm's recent settlements was $40 million to client Maho Beach Hotel and Casino in St. Maarten in the aftermath of Hurricane Lenny, a late-season storm that rocked the Caribbean.

With offices in Atlanta, Denver, Indianapolis, Los Angeles, New York, Orlando, Pittsburgh and Toronto, Ontario, Alex N. Sill Company is clearly a leader in the loss consultants industry.

Buckingham, Doolittle & Burroughs, LLP

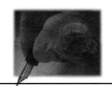

Buckingham, Doolittle & Burroughs, LLP is a full-service law firm with four Ohio and two Florida offices. It assumed its present name in 1940, having grown by mergers with firms established in 1913 and 1922. The Cleveland office opened in 1990 and is located on East 9th Street. Buckingham, Doolittle & Burroughs, LLP represents clients in 47 states, from sole proprietors to multinational corporations, tax-exempt organizations, governmental bodies, charities, foundations and public organizations. Practice groups include Business, Creditors' Rights and Bankruptcy, Employment Law, Environmental Law, Family Law, Finance and Public Law, Health Law, Intellectual Property, Litigation, Medical Malpractice, Mergers and Acquisitions, Real Estate and Construction Law, School Law, Tax and Employee Benefits, Trusts and Estates, Venture Capital and Emerging Companies, and Workers' Compensation.

The character and values of the Firm were established by its co-founder, Lisle Buckingham. Totally dedicated to the welfare of the client, he demonstrated by example that integrity, courage and forthrightness are indispensable to a successful law practice. Believing that success carries with it both social and economic responsibilities, Mr. Buckingham urged his partners and associates to become involved in community affairs. The Firm continues to maintain this tradition.

The Business Practice

The Firm's Business Law practice encompasses business organization and operation, including start-up joint ventures, agreements among shareholders, corporate reorganization and business contracts. Attorneys, certified public accountants, registered engineers and legal assistants serve the Firm's clients in the areas of computer and technology law; copyrights and trademarks; corporate matters; environmental compliance; finance and public law; franchise, distribution and licensing; and taxation and employee benefits.

The Firm's clients are representative of virtually every industry and trade, including transportation, food production, chemical manufacturing and distribution, rubber and tire manufacturing, technology, automotive, steel, agriculture and horticulture, financial and banking, insurance and medical, accounting and other professional practices. Buckingham attorneys have expertise in establishing businesses and counseling their owners to encourage prosperity. The Firm advises clients concerning mergers and acquisitions, intellectual property, succession planning and related areas of significance to rapidly expanding businesses.

The Litigation Practice

The Litigation practice of Buckingham has steadily grown to meet clients' complex legal demands. Areas of focus include appellate, commercial law and litigation, construction, domestic relations, employment, school law, medical malpractice and workers' compensation. The Firm is committed to finding innovative solutions to clients' legal problems. The breadth of Buckingham's practice in all forums often enables the Firm to avoid disputes by providing legal guidance before problems arise.

(Left to right) Mr. Gillum H. Doolittle, Mr. Lisle M. Buckingham and Mr. Edmund Burroughs

Buckingham represents clients in complex litigation and arbitration matters before courts, administrative agencies and arbitration panels. The Firm's attorneys focus on meeting client objectives, optimizing recovery and containing litigation costs.

The Future

The Firm's goals for the future are centered around maintaining the trusting relationships developed by putting its clients first and working as a team to serve their evolving needs. The Firm will continue to develop its solid foundation in Cleveland by following Mr. Buckingham's model for success: honesty, forthrightness, a focus on client welfare and giving back to the community.

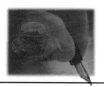

Garrett & Associates, Inc.

For these surveyors, the most challenging assignments can often be the most exhilarating. Confirming the basic dimensions of a plot of land is not to be taken lightly, but having these technicians do the same for a project that encompasses indoor and outdoor sporting arenas and a parking garage on the same site brings even more excitement to this quiet profession.

And then there is the precision needed to substantiate the dimensions of prime downtown property, where miscalculations involving inches can push wronged parties into the arms of lawyers. This world of exact measures is occupied by Garrett & Associates, Inc. of Cleveland. The company provides topographical maps that are primarily used for large industrial and institutional building projects.

The firm is the descendent of the one founded by George M. Garrett around 1890. Garrett once worked in the City of Cleveland's engineering department. When he was replaced during an administrative change, he started his own civil engineering and land surveying company. Years later, one of his most enthusiastic apprentices was his grandson, Richard T. Garrett, who has guided Garrett & Associates since 1948. He had worked alongside his grandfather during his high school years in the early 1940s and later attended engineering school. Garrett says his grandfather performed surveying services for most of the major utility plants in the

region; neighborhood parks; and military barracks and camps in Virginia during World War I.

Surveyors verify property lines and corners by researching public and private documents about the property. Those lines are confirmed by measuring tools, such as electronic distance measuring instruments. The most extensive topographical service also would include documenting everything above and below the ground surface, including other utility lines, sidewalks, curbs and ground elevation. A map of all findings is crucial to help developers build on precisely identified properties and identify available utility services.

"Every job has its own challenges," says Garrett, adding that the Gateway sporting complex was among his firm's most challenging and gratifying projects. His company employs 12, half of whom are engineers and surveyors. Frank Cirnski, former chief surveyor for Cleveland, now oversees daily operations. "We have to provide precise measurements, determine the right positions for property lines. We tell the developers how much land they have to work with."

During the past 50 years, the company has provided field personnel for many major building projects in the region, including local utility and nuclear power companies, office complexes, government buildings, and medical and education facilities. Company engineers make weekly trips to the nearby Perry Nuclear Power Plant to monitor erosion along the Lake Erie shore near the plant and observe plant conditions.

The monitoring provided there is an ongoing service being offered by the company, which has adopted many changes to keep up with the times. In the last few years it began moving away from producing hand-drafted topographical maps to providing computer-generated drawings. These computer-generated versions allow for quicker revisions. This willingness to meet changing demands of the marketplace has helped the company maintain its status as a leader among civil engineering and land surveying firms for well over a century.

Headquarters for Garrett & Associates, Inc.

Work crew on a building site

Maria Heckaman & Associates

At 8 feet high and still growing, the schefflera plant that grazes the ceiling of Maria Heckaman & Associates' conference room is more than just a beautiful fixture. This decades-old office-warming gift is a living testimony to the success and longevity of this job specialist organization, both of which have flourished since the company's founding in 1979.

President and founder Maria K. Heckaman was a volunteer and community leader in the early 1970s when an acquaintance recruited her to work as a consultant in an employment services firm. She soon learned she had a knack for successfully matching job seekers with the positions best suited to their talents and abilities, and as her experience grew she became a placement specialist in the arts, medical and professional services fields.

After gaining further experience with two other employment agencies, Heckaman decided to try her hand at running her own firm. Although she was apprehensive at first about signing a lease bigger than the average home mortgage, she trusted her instincts and made the commitment to move into her first office in Beachwood.

Heckaman's first placement was a general office position with Fabric Centers of America (now Jo-Ann Fabrics), which made her confident that her business could be a success. And successful it has been. Today, Maria Heckaman & Associates has a staff of five and places thousands of permanent and temporary employees every year, ranging from front-line employees to middle managers in fields like advertising, nonprofit, manufacturing, public accounting, banking and distribution. Because the firm serves only the northeast Ohio area, the staff knows both the local marketplace and its competitive salaries well. That increases the likelihood of a successful placement and a harmonious relationship between the company and its new employee. It also induces client companies to return to the agency again and again for their personnel needs.

A quality that sets the firm apart from other employment specialists is the staff's attention to the human side of job placement. Heckaman — who is a certified personnel consultant — and her staff pride themselves on their personal touch in the placement process, which includes getting to know applicants well and thoroughly understanding their goals, capabilities and work ethic. It's a personalized process that places the candidate at ease in what can be a stressful and challenging situation.

Other services the company offers job seekers include resume preparation and critiquing, computer tutorials and a referral bonus program for applicants who refer other potential employment candidates. By the same token, the firm offers employers a unique slate of additional services, including background checks, drug screening, employee testing and payroll management.

Heckaman & Associates has undergone a number of changes over the years to ensure its viability. When technology led to the demise of jobs in fields like PBX and key punch operation, the firm moved quickly to learn new technology as a way to reinvent itself and stay in step with the times. Eventually, several physical moves also were needed to keep up with the growth of the company; first to Tower East, then to Science Park and eventually to the current location in Commerce Park Square.

Twenty years and tens of thousands of placements later, Heckaman & Associates continues to make a distinctive mark on the Cleveland employment market. One only has to look at the schefflera plant in the conference room for a visual reminder of just how far this company has come.

President and founder
Maria K. Heckaman

Staff members
(left to right) Cindy
Zubek, Linda Raulinaitis,
Donna Van Oosten and
Laurie Tieber

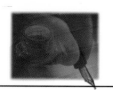

Mark Freeman Advertising

With its soaring ceilings, hardwood floors, trendy artwork and wide-open spaces, the offices of Mark Freeman Advertising (MFA) may look more like an art gallery than a communications think tank. But in this rarefied creative atmosphere, words are art, especially when coupled with provocative images that have the power to compel, convince or persuade those who look upon them.

Conceiving those words and pictures is the *raison d'etre* of MFA, a business-to-business marketing and communications agency with hundreds of prestigious industry awards under its belt and countless innovative concepts simmering in its creative kitchen. The agency has become renowned for its hard-hitting collateral and Internet work, rendered for clients primarily in the electronics, telecommunications and medical industries.

But the agency's expertise goes beyond mere words and pictures. The firm also serves as a comprehensive, integrated marketing communications expert that combines today's technologies with the appropriate print and electronic media to ensure that each client's message is seen, heard and remembered.

The agency was founded in 1983 by Mark Freeman, a former creative director and copywriter, who worked out of a makeshift office in his laundry room. He teamed up with Allen Lottes, an art director right out of art school, and set up shop in a 1,000-square-foot space in the Brush Building. They were so committed to making the business work that it wasn't unusual for them to work seven days a week, 15 hours a day in the early years to meet the demands of their business.

The partners' first client was an engineering company for whom they produced trade advertising, collateral materials and direct mail. This client relationship, which still exists today, was so successful that the pair quickly gained a solid reputation for creating effective marketing communications plans and integrated campaigns, as well as providing insightful business development advice and counsel.

By 1989, MFA had entered the computer age, having acquired its first PC three years before. This made an enormous difference in the way the company handled its client work. Art production processes like typesetting and film making that once had to be sent to outside vendors could be done right in house, saving considerable time and money.

Just six years after its founding, MFA had a staff of 26 people that included art directors, writers, media, production and traffic personnel. To accommodate the team more comfortably, the agency moved into a 6,000-square-foot Victorian mansion on Prospect. Yet another move was made in 2000 to an even larger building on Carnagie that had previously served as a sculptor's studio and art gallery.

Today, MFA is well-known for a diverse menu of services, ranging from international marketing, database management and advertising to multimedia presentations, media relations, public relations, trade show implementation and Internet development. It's also renowned for the meticulous research it conducts to find out what makes each client tick and how it can best represent that client's interests.

Mark Freeman Advertising strives to bring insight and innovation to every client it serves, and it's this winning combination that has made the company a major player in the field of marketing communications.

(Left to right) Mark Freeman; Karen Phillips, vice president of operations; and Allen Lottes, vice president and executive art director, enjoy their unique office environment.

Osborn Architects-Engineers

Design for the future has been the motivation of Osborn Architects-Engineers for over 100 years. Founder Frank Osborn's initial idea set the tone for a brilliantly diverse operation that is ongoing. At the beginning of its second century, the company motto, "Designing Tomorrow since 1892," is apt as America moves into the 21st century. It serves as a reminder that Osborn's long-standing tradition of excellence in building design and engineering for industry has allowed it to not only keep pace with technological advancements and their accompanying social and environmental changes, it has been one step ahead. Evidence of this tradition of excellence is embodied in New York's timeless Yankee Stadium.

Osborn was present to help mold the Cleveland of the 20th century with innovations in the use of concrete, designs for structures and structural systems. Later, Osborn again stood at the forefront in redesigning the city in its nationally acclaimed renaissance of the 1990s. Projects during this period ranged from the historic Society Bank Building's renovation on Cleveland's Public Square to the design of the structural systems for the acclaimed Jacobs Field and the new Cleveland Browns Stadium.

Beyond the local, state, regional, national and international directions it has taken, Osborn has taken steps to expand the frontiers of space. Osborn designed the NASA-Glenn Space Center Power Systems Facility, a 26,000-square-foot research facility designed to develop and test the electrical systems for use in the first permanent International Space Station. The building's 9,500-square-foot, "class 100,000" clean room boasts being one of the largest in existence in which electrical power systems are investigated. That project was followed with nearly 2,000 other projects during the years that followed. Osborn continues its fine partnership with NASA in the new millennium.

Frank Osborn was a civil engineer who started his own firm at the age of 35. His book, *Osborn's Tables of Moments of Inertia*, published in 1886, served as a standard for the use of structural steel in civil engineering until 1924. The key to Frank Osborn's success — offering as wide a range of quality services as possible — remains the cornerstone of the company's philosophy today.

The elegant plaza adjacent to Key Center warmly welcomes visitors and residents to this place of remembrance.

Osborn's goal is to maintain long-term, quality relationships with industry-leading clients such as Goodyear Tire and Rubber Company, Lubrizol Corporation and General Motors, and to enhance its experience with local, state and federal projects. A staff of 120 professionals, technicians and support personnel keep Osborn well-positioned to assist clients requiring specialists for all aspects of a design project, enjoying their role of providing corporate clients with personal service that satisfies their unique requirements.

The end of the century was a hallmark for Osborn. Not only did it achieve recognition for its commitment to quality by acquiring the prestigious ISO-9001 quality certification, the firm was designated as one of *Engineering News Record's* Top 500 architectural/engineering firms in the country — out of more than 82,000 firms.

In Cleveland and in locations throughout the world, Osborn creates tangible, sound evidence of skill and vision, planning continually for the future.

Lubrizol Corporation's World Headquarters Building is gracefully integrated into, and enhances its business campus setting.

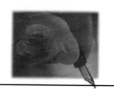

Pinkney-Perry Insurance Agency, Inc.

Arnold R. Pinkney was a struggling law student back in 1958 when he took a summer job with the Great Lakes Life Insurance Company (GLLIC). Little did he know that job would change the course of his life and the course of history in Cleveland. Today, Pinkney-Perry Insurance Agency, Inc. is the oldest existing African-American-owned, full-service insurance brokerage in the state of Ohio. The company handles the gamut of insurance products including commercial, life, group, health, and surety and fidelity. The highly regarded firm has a list of clients that includes Cleveland Browns Stadium, Rock and Roll Hall of Fame, TRW, Warner-Lambert Corporation, National City Bank, Cuyahoga County, Polytech, Greater Cleveland Regional Transit Authority (GCRTA), Operation Push and University Hospital Systems, to name a few. Its owners, Arnold R. Pinkney and Charles B. Perry, were business pioneers during the most momentous years of the Civil Rights Era.

With GLLIC, Pinkney went on to become a manager, then went out as an independent broker for many insurance carriers, including Prudential. While at the Cleveland Municipal Court building for a wedding, and ever on the lookout for new clientele, Pinkney met Deputy Clerk Charles B. Perry. The two found they had much in common, including selling insurance. Together they approached and worked for a life insurance broker and in June 1961 decided to combine their talents for their own profit.

In those days there were no major African-American insurance brokers that carried property and casualty insurance, so the savvy partners hired a public relations firm to intercede with Royal Globe Indemnity on their behalf. The strategy worked and other companies soon began signing on, including Aetna, Travelers and Jefferson. They also wrote homeowners', auto and life insurance policies for companies like Michigan Life and Summit. As African-Americans, they often encountered hesitancy from property and casualty carriers, even though the firm was consistently profitable. But despite these roadblocks the company kept growing, representing over 20 companies by the close of the 1960s.

As African-American business began to prosper in the 1970s, Pinkney-Perry began to offer commercial insurance, fighting to get coverage for these smaller, black-owned concerns. In 1976 the firm turned to corporate America. "I made cold calls to the CEOs," says Pinkney, who through his widespread civic and political involvement including the Greater Cleveland Growth Association, had connections in the right places. "Where I would have gotten a 'no' from the risk managers and human resources people, the CEO would call them in and we would talk together."

Perry also had his share of contacts from his tireless efforts on the behalf of minority business interests, including the Ohio Fair Plan Underwriting Association, National Minority Suppliers Development Council and Northern Ohio Minority Business Council.

As the company looks toward the future, it is preparing for the next generation to take the helm, says Perry. "When we first began, we hoped the business would last 100 years. I don't know of any businesses besides funeral homes in our community that have lasted for over 100 years. We hope in June 2061 that there will still be a Pinkney-Perry Insurance."

Arnold R. Pinkney, chairman and CEO of Pinkney-Perry Insurance Agency, Inc.

Charles B. Perry, president and COO of Pinkney-Perry Insurance Agency, Inc.

Richard Fleischman Architects, Inc.

Richard Fleischman Architects, Inc., founded in 1961, is a multifaceted design firm of innovative professionals committed to excellence in architecture. The firm is organized to provide broad design and planning services, including research and programming, program management, feasibility/threshold studies, land use analysis, facilities evaluation, master planning, graphic and interior design. RFA's services also include cost estimating, value engineering, scheduling, competitive bidding and contract negotiation, coordination and observation of construction activities, and financial management.

Eighteen architects at Richard Fleischman Architects (RFA) have put their special mark on a great deal of recognizable work in the Eastern Region of the country. Their designs have been identified as timeless: a creative blend of technology and imagination. They incorporate spaces that reflect their clients' expectations. Building designs as early as the 1970s have maintained their design integrity during the past three decades. RFA believes that economic, political and technological factors all have an impact on the creative process and the perception of the built environment.

Project types for the public and private sector include urban planning, transportation centers, library and educational facilities, religious centers, recreation centers and performing and visual arts centers.

Their professional services have been performed throughout the United States and Europe.

Richard Fleischman Architects, Inc. consistently employs architectural principles as well as urban design criteria, and has initiated innovative planning concepts that produce solutions while maintaining the developed character of the city. Unquestionably, it is the concentration

Ohio Aerospace Institute, Brookpark, Ohio

Polymer Science Building, Akron, Ohio

of great buildings and people that gives cities their dynamic quality. It is the further definition of architecture of space and people with energy and ambition that provides a critical combination of urbanism and special concepts. Unique to this mosaic is the invention of walls, windows, doors and public spaces that resolve existing ambiguities in the form of architecture and space.

Richard Fleischman Architects, Inc. has refused to yield to the temptation of form as pure image or technology as pure language. Its architecture from the very start introduces each separate architectural project as an experience in itself and the embodiment of significant abstract design theory. The firm has remained faithful to the notion of architecture as incessant research in which innovation is counterbalanced by powerful bonds with the physical, historical and anthropological environment.

SKW Americas, Inc.

Societies find security in tradition. Governments and peoples find comfort in the sure footing provided by past achievements, the assured sturdiness of buildings only a few stories high, the coarse feel of long-lasting fabrics, and the familiar tastes and textures of favorite foods. Tamper with those successes and somebody's got a lot of explaining to do.

SKW provided concrete admixtures and other construction chemicals that were used in building materials for the Denver Airport.

But change is inevitable. Fast-moving technology and advances in chemical research encompassing the life sciences guarantees it. Helping explain why product change is good falls to companies like SKW Americas, Inc. The young, Cleveland-based holding company has as one of its tasks assuring government officials and potential clients that buildings that seem to reach the clouds are quite sturdy if concrete is reinforced with the proper chemicals; and that with the right food enhancers, new twists on standard fare are waiting to tantalize our senses even more.

SKW Americas was established in 1997 and became a legal entity two years later as an extension of the corporate arm of its parent company, SKW Trostberg AG, an international chemical company. The American arm provides centralized support services to SKW affiliates from Canada through South America that deliver specialized chemicals to manufacturers. These chemicals are added to products in the construction, food, fabric care, health and other life sciences industries. The chemicals improve concrete, enhance the flavor and lengthen the shelf life of foods, improve the performance of cosmetics and help deliver internal medicines directly to infected sites.

A staff of 23 at SKW Americas, on the site of SKW affiliate Master Builders, Inc., provides specialized services

Cultures, enzymes and other nature products supplied by SKW are added to foods and beverages to improve flavor, texture, shelf life and other properties

to a growing network of chemical manufacturing subsidiaries serving disparate industries. The company plays no role in the operation of those affiliates. Staff members lend their expertise to assist affiliates in complying with local operation laws, understanding tax obligations, resolving financial difficulties and in centralizing internal operations. They also provide information technology, internal communications, and public and government relations support.

"We support each company in its area of operation and expertise," explains John Logan, vice president of public affairs at SKW Americas. "We provide those services that would be more efficient to have centralized than have each affiliate provide for themselves." Additionally, SKW Americas helps identify potential acquisitions for the parent group. SKW employs more than 40,000 worldwide. Sales for U.S. affiliates alone now top $1 billion annually.

Located in the southern Bavarian town of Trostberg, Germany, SKW is a major player on the world scene in the manufacture of specialty chemicals. The parent company, launched in 1908, has experienced tremendous growth in recent years, significantly through acquisitions. Affiliates globally fall into one of five core divisions: Construction Chemicals, Nature Products, Specialty Chemicals, Performance Chemicals and the Developmental Unit. SKW needed a base across the Atlantic to look after and help expand its growing interests in the Americas.

"Explaining our different product services to government and elected officials and regulatory agencies in all of these industries is quite a broad task," says Logan of the challenge facing his team.

van Dijk Pace Westlake Architects

van Dijk Pace Westlake Architects has been one of the most influential forces in renovating, restoring and revitalizing Cleveland's celebrated downtown area. Among the oldest continuing premiere architectural practices in the country, van Dijk Pace Westlake has achieved national recognition for its restorative work on some of Cleveland's most recognizable cultural and historical landmarks.

The impact this prestigious firm has made on Cleveland is easily visible from the windows of its 19th-floor Huntington Bank Building offices, from the beautifully restored Federal Reserve Bank to MK Ferguson Plaza, Society Bank, the Warehouse District's Hoyt Block and the exquisitely renovated Huntington Bank building.

But most notable, perhaps, is Playhouse Square. The dramatic restoration of the Ohio, State and Palace theatres in the early 1970s has been credited with helping to spark the renaissance of the entire city and has served as a model to other cities as a premiere example of urban revitalization through cultural arts.

The growth of the firm has been inextricably linked to the growth of Cleveland. As Cleveland has been recognized as a model of cultural and community revitalization, van Dijk Pace Westlake has been equally recognized as a partner in that leadership. This has led to the firm being asked to export its services to a wide range of other U.S. cities looking to mirror Cleveland's success.

The firm has since completed the restoration of a dozen historic movie palaces across the country, all of which have been instrumental in paving the way to the economic and cultural revitalization of their host cities. For example, the firm designed the Orpheum Theatre in Phoenix, the jewel in that city's crown, a project that led the firm to open its second office, in Phoenix, to handle its burgeoning business in the western region.

Founded in 1905, van Dijk Pace Westlake has been the recipient of over 100 significant design awards in the past 25 years and has earned international acclaim for the integrity of its design in four areas of specialization: performing and cultural arts; restoration and adaptive reuse; healthcare; and workplace environments.

In the area of performing and cultural arts, its Blossom Music Center has been acclaimed as the world's finest outdoor concert pavilion and has led to projects including the design of the 2,800-seat Temple Hoyne Buell Theatre at the Denver Center for Performing Arts.

Within the health care industry, the firm assumes a partnership role in helping to accommodate medical innovations. The firm has worked on hundreds of projects for the Cleveland Clinic, including the world's first facility for cardiac catheterization, and planned and designed the world's first dialysis facility, as well as the largest.

This attention to the quality of the environment has made the firm important, too, in the specialized design of workplace environments and office interiors. In Cleveland, the firm has completed a number of high-profile corporate headquarters, including Invacare in Elyria, BF Goodrich, Parker Hannafin and the Ohio Motorists Asssociation.

Through its design innovation and commitment to urban revitalization, van Dijk Pace Westlake has had a dramatic impact on the city of Cleveland. As its national recognition and practice grows, it will continue to share Cleveland's success story with other communities across the country.

van Dijk Pace Westlake's Blossom Music Center has been acclaimed as the world's finest outdoor concert pavilion.

QUALITY OF LIFE

Medical and religious institutions, as well as civic services and community organizations, contribute to the quality of life enjoyed by Cleveland area residents and visitors.

Sisters of Charity of St. Augustine Health System

In 1851 four courageous Augustinian Sisters self-lessly agreed to journey from Boulogne-sur-Mer, France, to a dangerous new frontier — Cleveland, Ohio. The Sisters were prepared for the worst, expecting to do battle with Indians and wild animals as they served in their mission as public health nurses.

Upon their arrival, they were gratefully welcomed by the Most Reverend Amadeus Rappe, first Bishop of Cleveland. Much to their surprise, the Sisters found Cleveland to be a burgeoning city, teeming with residents and growing businesses. They were equally surprised to

Sisters caring for babies at Saint Ann Hospital and Infant Home in 1911

find that their health care services were in even greater demand than they had expected, due in part to large numbers of abandoned children and immigrants suffering from "ship fever."

Because of their white habits and caring natures, the Sisters were frequently referred to as "angels" as they carried out their mission with extraordinary dedication. Propelled by the urgency of their mission and charism, they expressed their Christian concern for the sick and suffering, manifesting love, truth and justice for the people they served. They sought out people in need, particularly those who were spiritually, socially, psychologically, physically or materially neglected and implemented unexpectedly

aggressive solutions, regardless of how impossible the task may have seemed.

The first example of such dedication came in 1852, just a year after their arrival, when the Sisters opened St. Joseph's Hospital in Ohio City. By 1856 a number of considerations forced the closing of St. Joseph and the facility was used as an orphanage until the Sisters opened St. Vincent Orphanage in 1859. As their involvement in caring for the poor continued to expand, the Sisters, at the request of Bishop Rappe and Dr. Gustove Weber, a retired army surgeon, opened St. Vincent Charity Hospital at its current location in downtown Cleveland in 1865.

Throughout their long history, the Sisters of Charity of St. Augustine have been responsible for numerous groundbreaking achievements in health and human services, particularly in the Cleveland area. In 1873 the Sisters opened Saint Ann Hospital and Infant Home to care for unwed mothers and neglected children, a highly controversial move for a Catholic charity that caused significant repercussions at the time. Undaunted, the Sisters worked tirelessly to meet any and all human needs they were able to address, despite public pressures.

The Sisters founded Cleveland's first school of nursing at St. Vincent Charity Hospital in 1898. Responding to regional needs and a request from the Canton community, in 1908 they opened Mercy Hospital in Canton, soon followed by Mercy Hospital School of Nursing. Throughout this period, the Sisters' support for orphans and children continued. In 1925 they opened St. Augustine Academy in Lakewood, and over the next 10 years they staffed parochial schools across northeast Ohio. Also in 1925, Catholic Charities of the Cleveland Diocese relocated the orphans cared for by the Sisters to 180 acres of land outside the city. Today, this facility is known as Parmadale, the nation's first cottage-plan home for dependent children.

In 1951 a new Saint Ann Hospital for women was built on Cleveland's East Side, but the infant home remained on Woodland Avenue and was then called

DePaul Infant Home. Upon the sale of Saint Ann Hospital in 1973, the Sisters used the proceeds of the sale to create the Saint Ann Foundation and donated the De Paul Infant Home facility to the Diocese of Cleveland. The Foundation's support of health, human services and educational programs for women, children and youths is ongoing today.

A Long Tradition of Caring

For 150 years, the Sisters of Charity of St. Augustine have been involved in both sponsored and individual ministries that are far-reaching and expansive. Sponsored ministries revolve around their mission of meeting the needs of the underserved as directed by the Congregation, including hospitals, schools, foundations and other programs. In 1982 the Sisters of Charity of St. Augustine incorporated the Sisters of Charity of St. Augustine (CSA) Health System to guide and manage these health and human service-sponsored ministries.

While many Sisters have dedicated their lives and careers in sponsored ministries, some have chosen to pursue individual ministry in the community, which is embraced by the Congregation, all of whom fulfill the charism of the Congregation, "charity and love for all people." Individual ministries carried out by the Sisters have also resulted in some extraordinary contributions — not only to the local community, but to the world. In the mid-1940s, for example, Sister Ignatia Gavin, CSA, was one of the first individuals to focus on the as-yet-unrecognized disease of alcoholism. Despite considerable risk, Sr. Ignatia found creative ways to admit alcoholics into St. Thomas Hospital, Akron, Ohio. Through the efforts of Sr. Ignatia and Dr. Bob Smith, the co-founder of Alcoholics Anonymous, St. Thomas Hospital became the first general hospital in the country to treat persons with the disease of alcoholism as inpatients.

In response to the needs of the time as well as unmet needs in the community, individual ministries of the Sisters of Charity of St. Augustine address a broad and diverse range of issues every day, including parish work, homecare, wellness and the environment. In 1965, Sr. Henrietta Gorris, CSA, drew attention to Cleveland's riot-torn Hough area as she worked to provide neighborhood residents with education for self-reliance along with food, clothing, housing and jobs.

More recently, Sr. Marian Durkin, CSA, and a colleague established "The Open House" in Cleveland Heights, developing services to counsel people impacted by HIV and AIDS, including those infected with the virus, as well as their family and friends. Innovative, highly personal programs started by Sr. Marian include massage therapies, specialized support groups and "AIDS Buddy," the pairing of each client with a special friend in the group who prays for them.

Concerned with the fate of homeless people following hospital discharge, in 1999 a group of Sisters of Charity of St. Augustine and CSA Associates approached Sr. Joan

A kindergarten class in the 1950s at Parmadale shows off its May baskets.

Gallagher, CSA, to oversee the establishment of Joseph's Home, a renovated building that serves as a transitional home for homeless people recovering from medical illness. Joseph's Home also offers its residents a variety of social services, such as educational support, counseling and substance abuse counseling in order to help them attain employment and homes of their own.

The Tradition Continues

Keenly aware that the nature of health care has changed dramatically over the years, the Sisters of Charity of St. Augustine have been very progressive in adapting to the shifting needs and pressures of their health care ministries. Prior to the 1970s their hospitals were largely staffed by Sisters and others belonging to the religious order. After the Second Vatican Council the role of the laity as co-ministers in the church grew. The Sisters of Charity of St. Augustine rely on the talents of the laity, which are critical in the ever-changing health care environment.

In the mid-1990s, the Congregation examined its activities and recommitted itself to a primary focus on the original institutional health care ministries that have continued to play a large part of its core values. In recognition of the increasingly competitive nature of health care, the CSA Health System acknowledged that to achieve more growth and strengthen the delivery of Catholic health care it would be necessary to identify a strong partner in the provision of services.

The result was a highly publicized and extremely controversial 1995 pairing with Columbia/HCA Healthcare Corporation, an international for-profit corporation. Despite legal provisions requiring the new partnerships to maintain and strengthen the hospitals' Catholic mission and identity, the move was widely criticized by many religious organizations.

In time, the joint venture was recognized as having been the driving force in creating much of the CSA Health

System's newly created expansion of its mission. Columbia/HCA's 50-percent investment in each hospital enabled the facilities to pay off debt with the aspirations of developing communitywide integrated delivery networks.

The funding allowed the CSA Health System to establish three new foundations in Canton and Cleveland, Ohio; and Columbia, South Carolina, each with a distinct vision to address the needs of the poor and underserved in each community. And following the Sisters' decision and example, many other Catholic health organizations began to look at new relationships and alliances to facilitate the preservation of Catholic health care.

Due to the recognition by the Sisters of Charity of St. Augustine and Columbia/HCA that the future success of partnerships would require a local health care partner, a mutual decision by both partners was made to restructure. In June 1999 the CSA Health System restructured its Ohio partnerships, linking with University Hospitals Health System (UHHS), a nationally recognized leader in health care and medical research. This alliance also includes unyielding provisions for the commitment to the mission of Catholic values in all facets of the hospitals' operations.

Today, the CSA Health System is a thriving and growing organization, with more than $400 million in assets, including hospitals, foundations and outreach organizations. The organization's health care ministries include joint ventures with UHHS in Canton and Cleveland, Ohio, composed of Mercy Medical Center in Canton; St. John West Shore Hospital in Westlake; St. Vincent Charity Hospital/Saint Luke's Medical Center; Cuyahoga Physician Network; Professional Medical Equipment; and Ohio Health Choice, a statewide Preferred Provider Organization (PPO) in Cleveland. Providence Hospital/Providence Heart Institute and Providence Hospital Northeast in Columbia, South Carolina, are part of the remaining joint venture with Columbia/HCA.

The Foundation for Care

The Sisters of Charity Foundations of Canton, Cleveland and South Carolina, along with the Saint Ann Foundation, implement "strategic grantmaking," a process designed to address root causes of poverty, nurture the growth of healthy communities and families, and measure the outcomes of these efforts.

St. Vincent Charity Hospital first opened its doors in 1865 and continues its legacy of serving the needs of Cleveland and supporting communities.

Each Foundation has approached solutions to poverty from a different perspective. After conducting extensive research with low-income children, daycare providers, educators and other experts, the Sisters of Charity Foundation of Canton chose to focus on childcare, specifically early childhood development in their Quality Childcare Initiative. Although the most significant emotional and educational development occurs in children under age 3, the Foundation's staff discovered a lack of formal qualifications, licensing or education for area childcare workers. This Foundation has funded the opening of the Early Childhood Resource Center, an educational center for caregivers that it hopes to leverage as a career path for participants by offering transferable credits to colleges and universities. International child-care researchers have visited the Foundation to review and praise its groundbreaking work. This program represents a new service and a new ministry to the residents of Stark County.

In Cleveland, the Sisters of Charity Foundation of Cleveland has targeted the community's need for affordable housing for the working poor and other special-needs populations. The Foundation launched the Affordable Housing Initiative to focus not only on the bricks and mortar of low-cost housing for single-parent families, adult men and the elderly, but also on the related issues of first-time home ownership. Through its grantmaking in support of established organizations, the Sisters of Charity Foundation of Cleveland helps to spotlight this important issue while working toward the development of a sustained model of successful housing programs.

The Sisters of Charity Foundation of South Carolina selected its direction in response to research indicating that the absence of a father in the home too often results not only in poverty but also in children's mental health deficiencies, higher rates of juvenile crime, teen pregnancies and subsequent child abuse. This Foundation has received statewide recognition for its work in the community to support men in meeting the emotional, spiritual and material needs of their children through its Fatherhood Initiative. In support of this initiative, the Foundation has recently launched the Fatherhood Policy Project, which will focus on addressing public-policy issues regarding fathers' engagement with their children. The Foundation's staff are currently developing a blue-ribbon task force to lead the

A group of Sisters of Charity at the first planning conference for the CSA Foundations in 1996

Foundation's efforts in impacting public policies through researching key issues, and developing and supporting the implementation of their recommendations.

A Bright Future

Through its sponsored ministries, the Sisters of Charity of St. Augustine Health System is poised for a long future of sustained growth and service to the communities it serves. Its health care organizations are positioned to continue the provision of state-of-the-art medical services combined with the exceptional emotional and spiritual support associated with Catholic health care. Outreach programs operated through these organizations will respond to the needs of the poor and the sick for many years to come.

In addition, the broad contributions to the community made by the Sisters of Charity of St. Augustine through their individual ministries will also continue, as will the ongoing efforts by the Sisters' Foundations to reduce generational poverty. New outreach programs are envisioned to continue to respond to gaps and newly emerging needs in the communities served by the Sisters.

Since the day they arrived in Cleveland in 1851, the Sisters of Charity of St. Augustine have made a difference in the well being of the people whose lives they touch, and that impact has not ceased. With their founding philosophy and charism etched indelibly on every facet of their lives, these formidable women have led the development of superior health and human service organizations that have helped more people than they ever dreamed possible, and promise to touch the lives of many, many more.

The MetroHealth System

What started more than 160 years ago as Cleveland's first hospital has evolved into one of the region's most outstanding comprehensive health care systems. Currently a leader in patient care, research, medical education and community service, The MetroHealth System has always been a place that treats people the way they want and deserve to be treated.

In 1837, just a year after the city of Cleveland was incorporated, City Hospital was created to provide quality health care to all of Cleveland's citizens. By 1889 a growing population led to the building of a modern facility and City Hospital began its transformation from a "poorhouse" to a modern health care institution. Quality health care remained a priority, regardless of a patient's ability to pay. To ensure its physicians were trained in the latest medical advances, the hospital became affiliated with (Case) Western Reserve University's (CWRU) School of Medicine in 1914, a relationship that continues today with all staff physicians holding CWRU faculty appointments.

Unsanitary housing and a lack of food and clothing during The Great Depression contributed to an outbreak of tuberculosis (TB), a chronic infection that filled City Hospital's beds for over 15 years. The hospital responded by building Lowman Pavilion in 1933 and by conducting the nation's first research and treatment of bone and joint TB. It worked in conjunction with Sunny Acres Tuberculosis Hospital, which was set on 850 acres in Warrensville Township and served as a sanatorium for recovering TB patients.

The 1940s and 50s saw the outbreak of another fatal epidemic — polio. City Hospital again responded aggressively and gained national attention for its research and treatment of the disease. In 1952, Dr. Frederick C. Robbins,

The MetroHealth System began serving the Cleveland community in 1837 when it was founded as City Hospital. Pictured is one of its first modes of patient transportation from 1898.

By 1929, ambulance service had moved from horse-drawn to motorized at City Hospital.

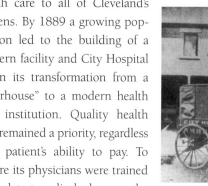

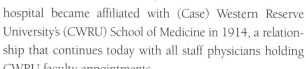

recipient of the Nobel Prize for Medicine in 1954, joined the staff as director of pediatrics and contagious diseases and continued his quest for new advancements in treating polio.

By the 1960s management of the hospital had been transferred to Cuyahoga County and City Hospital became Cleveland Metropolitan General Hospital (Metro). The hospital's consolidation efforts allowed it to build the Twin Towers in 1972 on Cleveland's near West Side and expand its outpatient clinics. Today, the Henry E. Manning Towers are recognized throughout Greater Cleveland as the defining symbol of MetroHealth Medical Center, one of the nation's most successful publicly owned hospitals. Augmenting the hospital are outpatient clinics across the city where quality medical care is made conveniently available to patients of all income levels. Some of the clinics, such as the Clement Center for Family Care, which opened in 1976, are located in Cleveland's poorest neighborhoods and are often the only medical facilities in these areas. MetroHealth is Ohio's leading provider of medical service to the impoverished and underinsured.

MetroHealth Medical Center presently offers an integrated program of services that provides a lifetime of quality medical care for more than 25,000 inpatients and 600,000 outpatients a year. These services include comprehensive primary care, dentistry, dermatology, emergency medicine, family practice, intensive care, internal medicine, obstetrics and gynecology, orthopedics, pediatrics, physical medicine and rehabilitation, psychiatry, radiology, and medical and surgical specialties.

MetroHealth is nationally known for its trauma care and is the region's leader in responding to life-threatening emergencies. Its Emergency Department averages some

70,000 visits a year and annually admits more adult and pediatric trauma patients than any Ohio trauma center. Familiar to many are the yellow and blue Metro Life Flight helicopters, a critical care transport service that has provided essential care on-site and in transit to residents in northeast Ohio and beyond since its inception in 1982. As one of the nation's busiest services, Metro Life Flight transports more than 3,000 patients a year.

A compassionate staff combined with quality facilities, treatment, prevention and research programs make MetroHealth's Burn Center one of the best in the nation. Established in 1970, the center is widely recognized for treating severely burned patients and for restoring both physical and emotional health.

MetroHealth's Women's and Children's Services include a full spectrum of services aimed at preventing and treating medical conditions affecting women, babies, children and adolescents. Delivering an average of 3,600 newborns a year, MetroHealth excels in its care of high-risk obstetrical and newborn care. Its Neonatal Intensive Care Unit provides the highest level of care to premature and critically ill newborns and in the Cleveland area.

MetroHealth is also a leader in caring for persons with cancer through comprehensive services in medical, pediatric, surgical, gynecologic and radiation oncology. Its Cancer Care Center was established in 1973 and has since grown into a key regional referral center, with more than 90 percent of patients referred from physicians and hospitals throughout northeastern Ohio and surrounding states. Patients receive optimal comfort, compassion and convenience along with state-of-the-art facilities and the latest treatment options.

With its long-standing reputation for high-caliber research and education, MetroHealth has always attracted the country's best physicians. Its affiliation with CWRU's School of Medicine has allowed MetroHealth to provide clinical settings for undergraduate medical school programs and graduate residency programs. It also allows for breakthrough research, such as the Functional Electrical Stimulation Program, which allows spinal cord injury

patients to regain use of a paralyzed hand. MetroHealth is the leading research center in the world for this technology.

MetroHealth also offers its superior staff of some 400 physicians and 1,000 registered nurses the unique opportunity to partner with management on patient care decisions. Policies are determined by a Medical Management Council, composed of physicians, nurses and administrators. Physicians are given the time and resources necessary to develop a unique doctor/patient relationship — the feel of a community hospital backed by the facilities and expertise of

Today, Metro Life Flight, based at MetroHealth Medical Center, is one of the nation's largest and busiest critical care transport services.

a large academic medical center. The MetroHealth System board of trustees, a group of 10 committed to public service, along with senior administrative leadership, are devoted to the continuation of this important aspect of MetroHealth's mission.

The board and administration also keep a keen eye on the future in this ever-changing health care environment. Plans include expanding and repositioning outpatient sites throughout Greater Cleveland and the recent opening of a new skilled nursing facility and outpatient surgery center on Cleveland's West Side.

MetroHealth will continue its physician-driven leadership in quality patient care for all, its superior education and research programs and its unwavering commitment to fulfilling community needs. With a rich heritage and over 160 years of experience, The MetroHealth System faces tomorrow's challenges with confidence.

Judson Retirement Community

Cleveland is home to many unique and exceptional communities. One of its most vibrant, active and diverse is Judson Retirement Community. With its front door facing Cleveland's skyline and its back door facing the quiet suburbs, location is only one of the many elements to Judson's appeal. The community's impressive environment, numerous activities and interactive programming make it so much more than a typical retirement home.

Currently located on two campuses in University Circle, Judson has been a part of Cleveland for over 90 years. Its history began on January 9, 1906, when a group of women from area Baptist churches established the Baptist Home of Northern Ohio. The home used residences on Prospect Avenue and Cedar Road before it purchased the 7-acre estate and mansion of prosperous Cleveland contractor Warren G. Bicknell in Cleveland Heights in 1939. The mansion underwent many changes and was expanded in 1973 with the construction of the 10-story Jordan Gardner Tower Apartments. In 1974, the apartment complex, on a steep hillside, was dedicated Judson Park in honor of the respected Baptist missionary Adoniram Judson.

In 1983 Judson's growing need for space led to its interest in expanding its mission through the acquisition of the famed Wade Park Manor hotel, which was remodeled and renamed Judson Manor. Together they formed what is known today as Judson Retirement Community. In 1991 the Bruening Health Center opened and provides both campuses with a home-like environment for long-term skilled nursing care, short-term rehabilitation therapy, medical offices, and a beautiful therapeutic pool and hot tub.

Judson's latest milestone came in 1998 with the transformation of the Bicknell mansion into The Mansion Courts — seven independent-living suites directly adjacent to Judson Park. The Mansion Courts provide its residents customized suites with complete access to all of the amenities and services offered at Judson Park and Judson Manor. The renovation earned an award from the prestigious Cleveland Restoration Society. The suites were also featured in the 1999 Cleveland Heights Heritage Home Tour.

Always a pioneer in the field of senior care and enrichment, Judson recently adopted an innovative approach to care. The Eden Alternative™, a philosophy developed by Dr. William H. Thomas, eliminates loneliness, helplessness and boredom by making pets, plants and children the center of attention in daily life. Judson is proud to have been the first in Northeast Ohio to provide this new concept of care.

Judson has earned and maintained a national reputation for excellence. Its variety of lifestyle options makes it an ideal choice for any retired senior and supports changing needs with little disruption. They include independent living, independent living with services, assisted living, licensed nursing care and a separate unit for persons with Alzheimer's disease. A contractual agreement assures that residents receive ongoing care for life — no matter how their physical needs or financial situation may change.

Judson's Health and Wellness Programs are at the core of its offerings and are an integral part of the healthy energy that pervades the community. The focus is on preventative maintenance, wellness and independence above all. Much of the activity is self-directed through the Resident Health Promotion Committee. Innovative classes that address the connection between the mind, body and spirit such as water aerobics, massage therapy, strength training, yoga and tai chi are held regularly. Individualized programs for pre- and post-operative conditioning, rehabilitation and pain management are also offered. Weekend Family Swims give residents and their families an opportunity for fun times together. Nonresidents are invited in for pool programs and use of

The beautiful grounds of Judson Park look over the Cleveland skyline and up into the treetops of Cleveland Heights.

the exercise rooms. In addition, Judson reaches out to nonresidents with activities that include respite care, adult daycare and a speaker's bureau.

Judson is defined as an accredited, not-for-profit, interdenominational Continuing Care Retirement Community. Its continuing success can be attributed to "the not-for-profit difference." Since the community's goal is to enrich the lives of those it serves, all revenue is used for enhancing its services. Its governing body is a board of trustees — a dedicated team of visionary leaders whose goal is not only to change the options available to seniors, but also to change the very notion about what it means to age. Judson has been named one of the best Continuing Care Retirement Communities in the nation for six consecutive years by *New Choices* magazine, a *Reader's Digest* publication.

Forty-five cultural, educational, medical and philanthropic institutions are within easy access to both campuses, including the Cleveland Museum of Art, Cleveland Orchestra concerts at Severance Hall, theater at The Cleveland Play House and educational programs at Case Western Reserve University. Residents often choose Judson because they are from the University Circle area and enjoy the extraordinary location, full of activity. The community has formed many partnerships with these surrounding institutions to keep residents active and involved.

The more than 500 residents of Judson are a diverse group of older adults with a wide range of interests. Walk into Judson on any given day and one might find student groups engaged in projects with the residents, arts and crafts classes, one-on-one weight-training sessions, music appreciation and computer classes, trips to University

Judson Manor is located in the heart of University Circle and provides easy access to Cleveland's finest museums, concerts, educational institutions and health care facilities.

Circle's museums and many other interesting activities. Other residents may simply be spending quiet time reading or seeking each other out for some pleasant conversation.

Residents include parents of board members, children of past and current residents and even administrators from other retirement homes. Many have enjoyed successful and often remarkable personal and professional achievements. They include former teachers, social workers, nurses, artists, engineers, lawyers and parents — people who have spent a lifetime creating who they are today. Many of Judson's residents are still connected to their professional lives in varying degrees. Others have become so involved in volunteer opportunities that it has become their second or third career choice. They are individuals who approach their later years with anything but a retiring outlook on life. They continue to engage themselves in their lifelong passions and hobbies, often carving out time for new pursuits. Their interests take them traveling, exploring new places, learning new things and meeting new people. They are constantly expanding their horizons and have learned that life forever changes. By embracing these changes and taking charge of their lives, Judson's residents continue to live vibrant lives, adding to the rich personal histories they have already created.

Judson's future plans include remaining a model of excellence for Senior Services throughout the country. Its unwavering commitment to its mission of offering older adults quality services and facilities that afford individual choice and meet individual needs will endure for many years to come. The residents of tomorrow will benefit from Judson's vision today.

Judson Retirement Community's latest edition — the beautiful Mansion Courts — consists of seven independent living suites and was formerly the home of Cleveland businessman Warren G. Bicknell.

The Federation for Community Planning

During the 19th century, Cleveland grew into one of the nation's great cities. Yet as the city's population grew, human problems — poverty, child neglect, sickness, unemployment — grew with it. A broad array of charitable organizations sprang up to address these needs, relying on the generosity of citizens for financial support. But by the early 1910s, lack of coordination hampered the effectiveness of their services and fund-raising efforts.

The Federation for Charity and Philanthropy was founded in 1913 by a group of community leaders whose goal was to better organize and coordinate the efforts of these charities. They developed one of the first modern Community Chests in the United States — the Community Fund — and led its first campaign in June 1913. This first Community Fund drive raised $127,000, which the Federation distributed to 55 social service and charitable member organizations. The first president of the organization was Martin A. Marks. Other founders included such prominent community members as Samuel Mather, Mr. and Mrs. Newton D. Baker, Homer Johnson, Judge Alexander Hadden, Mrs. Frederick Goff, Chester Bolton and Rev. James DeLong Williamson. They named Whiting Williams to be the organization's first director.

Many minority families immigrating to Cleveland after World War I found housing shortages, unemployment and poverty rather than golden opportunities.

The establishment of this new organization was big news across the country. On April 6, 1913, *The New York Times* told the story under the headline, "Unique Attempt To Solve Philanthropy's Big Problem," and the subhead, "Cleveland has Organized a Federation for Charity and Philanthropy Which Will Make a Concerted Appeal for All Charities and a Gift to It Will Make the Donor Immune from Separate Gifts to Institutions." Early acceptance of the concept of "federated fundraising" was expressed by John D. Rockefeller Sr., who sent a pledge larger than all his previous gifts to the separate charities. "I believe in the spirit of combination and cooperation...and that this principle will eventually prevail in the art of giving," he wrote.

In addition to raising and distributing funds, the Federation educated the public about health and social issues and programs. To build knowledge of and support for local services, the organization developed a weekly poster series, articles in the local newspaper, *The Social Bulletin* newsletter, "magic lantern" shows, and annual reports in 1913 and 1916.

The new organization took on the cutting-edge issues of its time. Its first major projects included the Conference on Illegitimacy, a survey of people with disabilities, "baby week" in Cleveland and the closure of substandard tenement nurseries.

In 1917, to improve the planning and provision of social services, civic leader Belle Sherwin helped bring about the merger of the Federation with the Welfare Council, which had been formed three years earlier to assist the city welfare department and serve as a clearinghouse for surveys and other social-service activities. Through the new Welfare Federation of Cleveland, social workers joined philanthropists and civic leaders on the board of trustees, and the Federation's role in, and capacity for, social and health planning became an example to communities across the country.

During the years following World War I, Cleveland was an industrial beacon for African-American families looking for better jobs and housing opportunities. Like other population groups who moved to the city, many instead found housing shortages, unemployment and a separation from their families. Between 1919 and 1920

Cleveland's African-American population increased 325 percent from just over 8,000 to more than 34,000. Sherman Kingsley, board secretary and future executive director, brought this matter to the attention of the Federation, beginning the discussion that would lead to the organization of the Negro Welfare Association, which today is a chapter of The Urban League.

In 1921, on the leading edge of professional social work practice, the Federation encouraged "group work" as a method comparable to "case work," making Cleveland one of the first cities to employ this approach. At the same time, the Service Information Bureau was formed to help people locate specific human services.

The Great Depression caused unprecedented suffering and greater demands on the limited resources of the community's human services agencies. In response, the Federation advocated a welfare levy, which was placed on the ballot and approved by Cuyahoga County's voters in 1932. This became one of two general-purpose human-services levies that continue to support services today.

During World War II, while thousands of men were away from home, the Federation administered child day-care centers to permit women to take war-related jobs, assisted the Civilian Defense agency in recruiting and training 50,000 volunteers, recruited foster "war homes" for 400 children and supported the community's efforts to combat the increasing problem of juvenile delinquency. In 1943 the Federation held its first annual Health and Welfare Institute (now known as the Human Services Institute), an all-day conference on critical community problems and issues for professionals and volunteers. Toward the end of the 1940s, the Federation's Committee on Older Persons became involved in the creation of social and recreational activities for seniors, leading to the founding of the first Golden Age Center in 1955. Today, a number of Golden Age Centers provide services for thousands of Greater Cleveland's seniors, and the Federation's Council on Older Persons still serves as a catalyst for improving services to older adults.

Also during the 1950s, a number of community information and referral services were consolidated into the Federation's Community Information Services. Thirty years later, the Federation's information and volunteer services merged with similar community services into an independent organization. In 1988, First Call for Help

became a part of United Way Services, where it continues to assist thousands of people with information and referral each week.

In 1961, a monumental project — the Health Goals Project — was begun under the leadership of William C. Treuhaft. Over the next five years the project prepared a "healthy community" model. The next two decades witnessed developments inspired by this landmark project's recommendations, including the county's move toward comprehensive health care services through the county hospital system, the establishment of neighborhood health centers, the inception of comprehensive health services in city centers, improvements in access to dental-health services, development of family-planning services for the poor and the creation of a health "campus" where hospital services link with community social services.

As the Welfare Federation celebrated a half-century of work in 1963, it underwent a significant reorganization. A new central planning board worked with an augmented planning and research staff. The Welfare Federation maintained five major councils supported by the work of staff and hundreds of volunteers. This period of renewal contributed to its capacity to mobilize for a statewide campaign to create a community mental health services system overseen by local mental health boards.

The 1970s brought new initiatives to the community and the Federation. In 1971, the Federation facilitated the merger of five of its member agencies into one organization providing comprehensive services for families and children. That organization continues to serve thousands of Greater Clevelanders today as the Center for Families and Children. In 1972, an internal reorganization resulted in a new name, Federation for Community Planning, and a new focus on planning, research, community education and advocacy. The role of fund raising and allocation was taken on by United Way Services.

In 1973, the new Federation gave serious attention to the problem of abused and neglected children, developing a comprehensive, communitywide plan to control the problem. Over the next several years, implementation of the plan led to a wide range of programs, including a 24-hour hotline, a self-help organization and educational programs to help professionals identify child abuse. Those services evolved into another new organization — Bellflower Center for the Prevention of Child Abuse. Continuing its work on children's issues during the late 1970s, the Federation worked with local human service agencies to help them address the implications of court-ordered busing to racially desegregate Cleveland's public schools.

During the 1980s, several major Federation initiatives addressed the needs of specific population groups. One project worked to increase accessible facilities and services for people with physical disabilities, another looked at the various systems involved with juveniles who commit violent crimes or repeated serious offenses and a major study focused on the use of community mental health aftercare services by discharged psychiatric patients.

Two human needs reached alarming proportions during the 1980s: homelessness and HIV/Acquired Immune Deficiency Syndrome (AIDS). To address the unmet health care needs of the homeless, the Federation established clinics at two homeless shelters where, in addition to acute health services, patients were connected with social-service resources. After several years under the Federation's umbrella, this project evolved into an independent organization — Care Alliance — that continues to provide for the multiple needs of homeless people. Concurrently, HIV/AIDS had reached epidemic proportions. The Federation formed the AIDS Commission of Greater Cleveland, which administered state-funded programs for community-based research, education and outreach. As other organizations developed to address this public-health problem, the commission released a major report and community plan for addressing future needs related to HIV/AIDS before disbanding itself in the early 1990s.

During the 1990s, the Federation continued serving as a catalyst for improving health and social services on such

The Health Goals Project of the 1960s produced a model of a "healthy community" that led to significant improvement in illness prevention and health care services.

The 21st Century

As it has since 1913, the Federation for Community Planning continues to tackle the tough issues of the day. Today, it seeks to serve as a catalyst for change through its core competencies of applied research, policy analysis and advocacy, and community organizing. Behind the leadership of a diverse board of trustees, new targeted initiatives in the areas of youth social development, public health and behavioral health continue the Federation's long and successful history of "helping people who help people."

What makes the Federation unique is that it positively impacts the community but does not provide direct services. Rather, the Federation works quietly behind the scenes, helping those who do provide services. It brings together the people, the organizations and the systems that must work together to address the community's problems. It encourages and takes the lead in building and strengthening partnerships that work. It facilitates discussion, turns research data into useable information, recommends courses of action, develops and nurtures pilot projects, evaluates the impact of programs, and builds the community's knowledge of issues and services.

As new challenges emerge, or as opportunities for addressing old problems present themselves, the Federation for Community Planning will organize effective responses by the Greater Cleveland community, fulfilling the promise of its motto, "Teamwork for a Greater Cleveland."

Advocacy on behalf of human services is a core competency of the Federation. Activities include preparing and delivering testimony, organizing bus trips to the state capitol and educating other nonprofit organizations about being effective advocates.

matters as child immunization. In 1998, the Federation developed a community immunization registry to help ensure that all children receive preventive health care. It was implemented by the Cuyahoga County Board of Health.

The latter half of the 1990s saw the Federation focus its work on targeted issues of welfare-reform implementation and linkages between local health and social-service organizations and Cleveland's public schools. The Federation took the lead in both areas by building formal and informal partnerships among public and private organizations and systems, with the goal of better serving Greater Cleveland residents. Those partnerships have become models for other communities.

From its beginning, the Federation recognized the importance of engaging public officials at the local, state and national levels in social welfare issues. One of its first projects involved encouraging the city council to enact an ordinance banning overcrowded "mushroom nurseries" that kept children in unsafe environments. Throughout its history the Federation has been active in legislative advocacy, often taking the lead in efforts to change or create legislation to improve the lives of Ohioans. The Federation's legislative agenda has included such issues as welfare reform, nursing-home standards, child- and elder-abuse reporting, patients' rights, group-home zoning and health care for seniors. Significant ongoing attention is focused on government funding of human services.

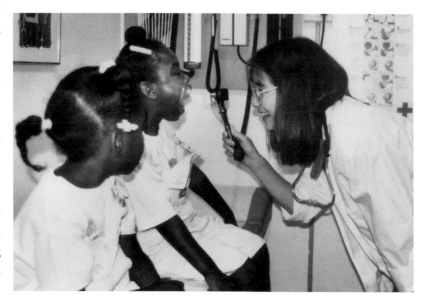

Child health and welfare is always a Federation priority. The 1990s saw the development of an immunization registry to help ensure that preventive health care is provided to Greater Cleveland's children.

The Cleveland Clinic Foundation

The world-renowned Cleveland Clinic Foundation opened in February 1921 with just one building and 13 professional staff members. Founded by four established physicians who were highly regarded in the medical community, the Cleveland Clinic was created to conduct medical research, provide medical education and deliver complete patient care.

When they served as soldiers in World War I, Cleveland Clinic founders Frank E. Bunts, M.D., George W. Crile, M.D., William E. Lower, M.D. and John Phillips, M.D. were quite impressed with the teamwork approach of military medicine. Bunts and Crile, in particular, are credited with formulating plans for the clinic while stationed in

The Crile Building at the Cleveland Clinic Foundation and the sculpture "Three in One," symbolizing the clinic's three-part mission of patient care, research and education
Photo by Tom Merce

France. In 1919 Bunts, Crile and Lower returned to Cleveland to rebuild their surgical practices in offices they had shared before the war. Realizing the need to broaden their medical services, the three surgeons recruited John Phillips, M.D., an internist and pediatrician. Phillips had also worked in military hospitals during the war and shared the others' opinion that patients could benefit most if served by a group of specialists trained in various branches of medicine.

The clinic was initially built as an outpatient medical facility, largely funded by the founders, at the corner of East 93rd Street and Euclid Avenue. The clinic building was four stories tall and included everything from examining rooms to a pharmacy and research laboratories. The clinic was so well received when it opened that the founders soon realized they needed more space. Nearby houses were purchased and converted into hospitals and other

treatment facilities. A 175-bed hospital opened in 1924. By 1928 an eight-story research building was added. Sadly, in that same year, Bunts died suddenly of a heart attack. Fortunately, he had hand-picked a young associate and former student, Thomas E. Jones, M.D., to take over his practice one day. Jones stepped in and grew to become a widely acclaimed surgeon.

Overall, the 20s were a period of rapid growth for the clinic. Professional staff and new departments were added to keep up with the demand for outpatient and inpatient services. The future was bright. But that all changed May 15, 1929, when at least two explosions rocked the clinic building. Toxic fumes killed 123 people, including Phillips, and sickened another 50. A leak in a high-pressure steam pipe had triggered the incomplete combustion of old x-ray films, generating huge quantities of poisonous gases. The disaster nearly closed the clinic forever. In its wake, safety codes for storing x-ray films were revised worldwide and safety film (nonexplodable) was used thereafter.

With its separate hospital building still intact, and temporary quarters provided across Euclid Avenue by the Laurel School, the clinic was able to carry on. Although structurally sound, The clinic building was closed for a time and later remodeled. The two surviving founders, Crile and Lower decided to risk all, despite lawsuits from the disaster and the stock market crash, and add another building. The new facility opened in 1931.

The clinic survived the Depression largely because it was a nonprofit organization. All staff, including physicians, were paid fixed salaries, yet many were actually earning much more than their salaries. The excess went directly to the Cleveland Clinic Foundation and enabled it to continue.

The 40s and early 50s have been described as a period of "turbulent success." The number of surgeries and new patient registrations were never greater, yet World War II reduced staff and residents considerably. The remaining staff were too busy to even think about administrative needs. But the founders were aging, and no replacements had been tapped. In 1955 professional staff unanimously agreed that major administrative decisions for the clinic could best be handled by a board of governors composed of physicians. Professional staff appointments, promotions and terminations were among their chief responsibilities. Reviewing and handling patient criticisms was another. The creation of physician governance is considered an administrative milestone for the clinic, which has had physicians in top managerial positions ever since.

Many of the clinic's pioneers were medical pioneers, as well. Crile was known worldwide for his work in thyroid surgery and for developing patient-to-patient blood transfusions. Irvine H. Page, M.D., was instrumental in the discovery of serotonin, which mediates impulses in the brain and elsewhere, and angiotensin, a hormone used to control blood pressure. Willem J. Kolff, M.D,. invented kidney dialysis. Ralph A. Straffon, M.D., chief of staff from 1987 through 1999, helped pioneer kidney transplantation. F. Mason Sones Jr., M.D., invented coronary artery angiography, which enables physicians to use X-rays in diagnosing coronary artery disease. Sones' invention, in turn, enabled Rene G. Favaloro, M.D., to develop coronary bypass surgery while he was a fellow at the clinic in the late 1960s. Bernadine Healy, M.D., later to head the National Institutes of Health and the American Red Cross, was instrumental in developing the Lerner Research Institute, a world-class facility. Floyd D. Loop, M.D., chairman of the clinic's board of governors and CEO since 1989, is a well-known cardiac surgeon, who also is credited with putting the clinic on sound financial footing in the late 1980s.

By the end of the 20th century, the clinic was a nationally and internationally acclaimed leader in many fields of medicine and research. The Cleveland Clinic Heart Center was the recognized world leader in diagnosing and treating cardiovascular disease. The world-record 109th heart transplant in a single year was performed there in 1998. In 1999 *U.S. News & World Report* recognized the Heart Center as the best in the nation for the fifth year in a row and ranked The Cleveland Clinic, overall, as one of the top 10 hospitals in the nation — a distinction it has held since the beginning of these rankings.

More than 10,000 personnel work on the clinic's main campus, which includes more than 30 buildings on 140 acres. But beyond that, the clinic has grown into the 11-hospital Cleveland Clinic Health System, which includes hospitals in nearby communities. Moreover, Cleveland Clinic Florida, which opened in 1988, was expanded in 1998, and plans additional facilities by 2001.

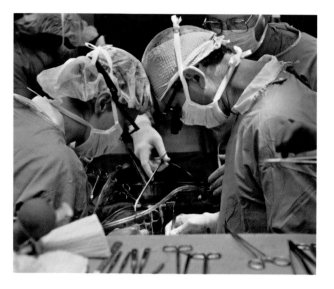

The Cleveland Clinic is America's leading heart center, year after year, in *U.S. News & World Report* magazine's annual "Best Hospitals in America" survey.
Photo by Tom Merce

A $225-million, five-year philanthropic campaign, "Securing the 21st Century," was well underway with more than $140 million raised in the campaign's first two years. The funds were earmarked for several projects, including the Lerner Research Institute, the Cole Eye Institute and the Cleveland Clinic Taussig Cancer Center.

As the 1990s came to a close, hospitals nationwide wrestled with regulatory restrictions and strained budgets. The Cleveland Clinic was no exception. Still, the very quotable CEO Loop remained optimistic and said: "Through good times and bad times, fits and starts, tragedies and triumphs, the Cleveland Clinic model of medicine has persevered... " and " ...those who think our best years are behind us are looking in the wrong direction!"

The original Cleveland Clinic building in 1921
Cleveland Clinic Archives

Cleveland Today

In the late 1970s, perceptions of Cleveland locally and nationally were at an all-time low, shaped in part by such disparaging events as the city defaulting on its debt obligations and the mayor accidentally setting his hair on fire. A group of community leaders reasoned that they would have to proactively speak out about the city's positive points if they hoped to break the cycle of negative perceptions.

In 1978, these leaders joined together to form The New Cleveland Campaign, a program dedicated to raising awareness of the area's real and emerging strengths and to restoring local and national confidence in the Greater Cleveland area.

Chief among its founders was Thomas Vail, then publisher of *The Plain Dealer.* Vail became the Campaign's first chairman; in no other city had such a high-profile media figure stepped forward to create and head this type of marketing and communications effort. The Campaign became the first and only independent, nonprofit marketing communications program for Greater Cleveland.

The Campaign was formed, and continues to exist under the name of Cleveland Today, through the volunteer commitment of community organizations, businesses and citizens. Its efforts are guided by a board of trustees of high-level business and civic leaders representing a cross section of the community, and its funding is derived from the financial and service contributions of a broad array of companies, foundations and organizations.

Early Communications Strategies

Cleveland's need for positive local communications was reinforced by two surveys commissioned by the Campaign in 1978 and 1981 that showed dismal opinions about the city by residents. Throughout its first decade, the Campaign relied almost exclusively on local communications — advertising in particular — aimed at boosting appreciation of Greater Cleveland among Greater Clevelanders. At that time, advertising was a necessity — purchased space was the only viable way to talk about Cleveland's attributes, as editorial coverage inevitably played on negative perceptions. This approach supported the strategy that local audiences, if encouraged to focus on the positive, could in turn begin acting as Cleveland "ambassadors" to outside audiences.

In addition to its local efforts, the Campaign began providing needed support to the direct marketing initiatives of the Greater Cleveland Growth Association, the Convention & Visitors Bureau of Greater Cleveland and others. Working together, the three organizations saw their effectiveness enhanced by the city's steady progress throughout the 1980s.

Acting On McKinsey's Recommendations

In 1987, the Campaign, the Growth Association and the Convention Bureau, together with Cleveland Tomorrow and the Greater Cleveland Roundtable, commissioned McKinsey & Company, Inc., to develop a comprehensive economic development marketing study of Greater Cleveland.

As a result of the McKinsey study, Dix & Eaton Inc. was asked to develop a communications action plan with specific strategies to support each of the recommendations for retaining and increasing jobs, attracting tourists and conventions, marketing

Cleveland to Clevelanders and others. Dix & Eaton was retained as the Campaign's public relations counsel, and soon afterwards as its advertising counsel as well.

In 1989 the Campaign commissioned a follow-up study of local and national perceptions to help gauge its progress and guide its future communications efforts. The study, conducted by the national pollster Louis Harris and Associates, showed a dramatic increase in confidence locally. Yet, despite substantial inroads in awareness of the city's strengths nationally, significant perception gaps remained.

Focusing on National Media Relations

To help close the gap and take maximum advantage of Cleveland's positive momentum and economic advances, the Campaign shifted its focus to national communications and its strategy to media relations, a highly credible and cost-effective tool to reach opinion leaders and decision makers nationwide. The Campaign's expanded efforts to document and promote the story of Cleveland's turn-around played to increasingly receptive national media, and Cleveland became widely known through media coverage as the Comeback City.

In 1991, James M. Biggar, CEO and chairman of Glencairn Corp. and former chairman of Nestlé USA, Inc., succeeded Vail as chairman of the Campaign. During Biggar's term the Campaign enjoyed considerable success in obtaining positive coverage of Cleveland in influential regional, national and international media.

In early 1996, Thomas M. O'Donnell, then CEO and chairman of McDonald & Company, succeeded Biggar as chairman of the Campaign. Throughout 1996 the Campaign used the city's bicentennial celebration to position Cleveland nationally and internationally as "The New American City".

Similarly, throughout 1997, the Campaign, with the assistance of Dix & Eaton, capitalized on a series of major sports and other special events held in Cleveland, leveraging the spotlight of the national and international media to tell the full story of Cleveland's renaissance and relevant strengths. Such events included the all-star games of both Major League Baseball and the National Basketball Association, the annual induction ceremony of the Rock and Roll Hall of Fame and the Cleveland Indians' appearance in the World Series.

In 1998 the Campaign chose to change its name to Cleveland Today, but its mission continues. Cleveland Today remains the only organization focused on Cleveland's broad image and responsible for communicating the strengths and progress of Cleveland to regional, national and international audiences.

Recent accomplishments include partnering with local PBS affiliate WVIZ to help bring the "Wall $treet Week with Louis Rukeyser" and "Nightly Business Report" shows to Cleveland for live broadcasts; developing a program with *Continental* magazine (Continental Airlines' in-flight publication) to produce three special Cleveland editorial sections each year; creating a new Web site for media use; being designated one of six International Press Centers in the country by the U.S. State Department and hosting a tour of foreign press; creating an advertorial series on *Forbes* titled "Voices of Cleveland"; and talking with dozens of national reporters about the economic development, quality of life and tourism attributes of the Greater Cleveland area.

Congregation of Saint Joseph

"To love another person is to see the face of God." So goes a line from the play *Les Miserables*, a line that sums up the concept at the heart of the Congregation of Saint Joseph (CSJ), a Catholic religious order that has served the people of Cleveland for more than 125 years.

From their motherhouse and gathering center on the city's west side, the Sisters of Saint Joseph have devoted their lives to serving those who are physically and spiritually in need. Their benevolent mission has led them to create a community of people, united in the Gospel of Jesus Christ, who gather in love and prayer and share compassion, seek justice and take action to improve the world in which they live.

The community that became the Cleveland CSJ can trace its roots back to 1650, when six women in Le Puy, France, with the support of Jesuit priest Jean Pierre Medaille, joined together to combine their calling to a profound spiritual life with their equally profound desire to help humankind.

Built in 1929, Saint Joseph Academy provides quality education for young women of diverse backgrounds.

In an effort to expand their good works, six Sisters of Saint Joseph came to the United States in 1836 to establish a motherhouse in St. Louis, Missouri. The Sisters soon began to spread through the United States and Canada, and in 1872 the congregation was founded in Painesville, Ohio, under the direction of Mother St. George Bradley.

Life was simple for the Sisters. In addition to giving piano lessons, they earned some income by embroidering shrouds for a local undertaker as well as by teaching at St. Mary's School. These funds allowed the Sisters to live a life of prayer and service to their neighbors while spreading the message of the Gospel.

In 1875 three of the Sisters came to Cleveland, where they ran a small boarding house for girls and gave private lessons in French, art and music. The Sisters eventually purchased property on Starkweather Avenue on the south side of Cleveland, where in 1890 they erected a three-story stone motherhouse and established Saint Joseph Academy for Girls.

Three years later they purchased 52 acres of farmland and woodland in Rockport Hamlet on Cleveland's far west side. By that time, there were 85 members in the congregation, so a small frame house already on the property was enlarged to serve as the Sisters' residence. The building also housed the academy, which was moved to the site to function as a school and boarding house for both boys and girls in grades one through 12. A large four-story convent and school was completed in 1907 at a cost of $115,000, most of which was borrowed by the Sisters at a time when each earned just $20 a month.

By 1909 the Sisters were teaching at the academy and at 13 elementary schools in Ohio. The need for parochial education was so great that in 1929 a new Saint Joseph Academy building was completed and dedicated on the Rockport property. With accommodations for both day and boarding students, classrooms, residential quarters for the Sisters and a gymnasium that also served as a 500-seat auditorium, it provided a much-needed, valuable Catholic secondary school for girls on the west side of Cleveland.

In the years following their arrival in Cleveland, the Sisters continued their teaching duties while serving as champions of those in need. For instance, in the years just preceding the 1920s, they responded to the sick when influenza ravaged the city. During the 1940s they offered support to those serving in the armed forces during World War II by selling war bonds, rolling bandages and encouraging academy students to participate in Red Cross projects.

By 1950 the community's 350 sisters staffed Saint Joseph Academy and 25 elementary schools in the dioceses of Cleveland, Youngstown and Los Angeles. They also established Nazareth Academy in 1957 in Parma Heights as a secondary school for girls.

Beginning in the late 1960s the Cleveland CSJs underwent a metamorphosis like no other in their history. In response to the new direction of the Second Vatican Council in the Catholic church (1962-65), the Sisters made significant changes in their manner of life, dress and relationships with the laity as well as in the scope of their service to others.

Since then, the Sisters have been prominent in the fields of pastoral ministry and have served in hospitals and inner-city neighborhoods; engaged in justice advocacy activities; worked with deaf and mentally challenged adults; staffed telephone prayer lines; opened drop-in centers, shelters for women and crisis nurseries; and served as companions and support for the sick and the dying. There was virtually no work that the Sisters could not incorporate into their own expression of care and Gospel response.

In 1978 the Sisters invited lay women and men to join their mission as co-members. They also established new ministries to enhance the healing, health and wholeness of the individuals and families of Cleveland. Among

those ministries are the Saint Joseph Wellness Center, founded in 1990, and Seeds of Literacy, an adult literacy program founded in 1997 on the occasion of the congregation's 125th anniversary of coming to the Cleveland diocese.

The motherhouse itself has undergone a major transformation since its construction in 1927. Now called Saint Joseph Center, it is home to the St. Joseph Conference and Learning Center. Situated on tranquil, verdant grounds at the edge of Rocky River Reservation, the conference center provides a unique setting for seminars, conferences, training sessions and retreats. The property is also home to Saint Joseph Wellness Center, whose mission is to provide holistic services and programs to heal the mind, body and spirit.

Spirituality. Service to their neighbors. Work on behalf of justice. Health and wellness. These continue to be the imperatives of the Cleveland Congregation of the Sisters of Saint Joseph because now, as in the congregation's earliest days, the Sisters still see the face of God in every person they meet.

Mother St. George Bradley, founder of the first Northeastern Ohio CSJ in Painesville *Painting by Sr. Mary Magdalen Prochaska, 1981*

Saint Joseph Center overlooks Cleveland MetroParks.

Council for Economic Opportunities in Greater Cleveland

"*Words whether* spoken or written are inadequate to properly tell the story of what has taken place during the past year in Cleveland in the 'War on Poverty.' ... We are sure that thousands of lives have been touched for good. ... Willing hands of every walk of life have joined together to fight the causes of poverty which feeds on the economic and spiritual growth of the Greater Cleveland community." So wrote Ralph W. Findley, the first Executive Director of the Cleveland Council on Economic Opportunities in Greater Cleveland (CEOGC), in the council's 1967 Annual Report. And his words still ring true today. His work helped to build CEOGC, laying the foundation for what is today Ohio's largest community action agency.

CEOGC was established in 1964 to develop, administer and coordinate President Lyndon B. Johnson's War on Poverty in Cleveland. Mandated by the 1964 Economic Opportunity Act, CEOGC and sister agencies across the country fight the good fight against poverty with the over-riding goal of counseling, supporting and carrying people towards economic self-sufficiency.

The agency first opened its doors in 1966, and during an open house tour of CEOGC's programs, visitors and trustees were treated to a glimpse of what the *Call & Post* newspaper called the "innovative and motivating techniques" used by CEOGC. The tour covered CEOGC-established Neighborhood Opportunity Centers in the Central, Kinsman, Hough and Glenville neighborhoods and on the Near West Side. Both board members and agency representatives were impressed with the sheer scope of the undertaking.

In the latter half of 1967, funding increased from $6 million to $15 million. CEOGC expanded its planning department, which provided technical assistance to neighborhood-based programs. The expansion led directly to the establishment of programs such as AIM-JOBS, Youth Employment and the Mayor's Youth Opportunities program. CEOGC's research department conducted extensive studies and tracked each implemented program, along the way developing advanced long-range evaluation procedures to monitor the success of these programs in the community as a whole.

One of those programs was the Hough Parent and Child Care Center. The services provided through this program enabled families to function independently and

CEOGC's first Executive Director, Ralph W. Findley

(Far right) A classroom awaits its young charges at the Carl B. Stokes Head Start Center on Torbenson Avenue in Cleveland.

The Kinsman Opportunity Center was one of the first such centers established by CEOGC.

ensured the full development of young children. These services included part-time employment and in-service training for mothers and family interest groups, counseling, home instruction for infant care, child care for infants and small children, and family-night activities that encouraged parents to serve the community.

Today, Head Start, Neighborhood Opportunity Centers (Hough, Glenville, Central and Tremont), the Emergency Home Energy Assistance Program (EHEAP), and the Workforce Development and Family Development Programs are but a few of the programs and services housed under CEOGC's umbrella.

CEOGC's largest and most renowned program is Head Start. Head Start was created to increase the educational and social preparedness of low-income, school-aged children through an extensive, holistic learning curriculum before they enter kindergarten. The program involves parents in the planning stages through meetings of policy groups. These groups help govern the program at the center, delegate and grantee levels, making Head Start a true partnership for all its participants. Health examinations and health care referrals are provided. In 1967, 2,466 children and more than 2,000 adults were involved in the program. The current enrollment for CEOGC's Head Start program is approximately 8,000 students, making it the largest in the state of Ohio and one of the largest in the country.

CEOGC has developed and implemented innovative programming as the community's needs have changed. One of these programs is the Family Development Unit, created to help low-income families resolve problems that prevent self-sufficiency. The unit receives referrals for residents facing eviction with inadequately supported medical problems and the chemically dependent. It also assists with mental and emotional problems, family relationship issues, parents needing support and training, those finding themselves in emergency situations and even grandparents who are guardians for their grandchildren. The comprehensive program seeks to develop and enhance skills that lead to better economic opportunities and personal growth.

Cleveland Mayor Michael R. White receives a gift from the children at the Carl B. Stokes Head Start Center.

The Workforce Development Program promotes economic self-sufficiency through economic development, education and human services programs. These include Office Management Technologies Training classes to prepare students for clerical or secretarial jobs. General Education Development (GED) classes help to prepare students for their high school equivalency diplomas and Job Readiness Services help students develop personal and social skills needed to get and retain productive employment. Job Retention and Placement Services provides job referrals and serves as a liaison between client and employer.

CEOGC Executive Director Jacqueline A. Middleton says, "We are empowering families through increased interactive social services, with dignity and respect. We are diligently assessing the needs of the impoverished community so we can plan and direct our services appropriately."

In 1997, the Louis Stokes Head Start Center opened its doors to children in the Lee-Harvard area.

Jewish Community Federation of Cleveland

Tikkun olam (making the world a better place), *tzedakah* (righteousness) and *chesed* (kindness) are ancient values that have sustained Jews around the world for thousands of years. These values, providing tremendous sources of spiritual strength and inspiration, are the foundation upon which the Jewish Community Federation of Cleveland was established in 1903. They remain at its core as the Federation has grown into one of Northeast Ohio's premier fund-raising, grantmaking and community-planning agencies, improving lives in Cleveland and worldwide.

Cleveland's first Jews arrived from Germany in the 1840s and 1850s. By the late 1870s they had settled in, created congregations and supported agencies to care for the orphaned, infirm and aged. In the 1880s this small community was swamped by a wave of *landsman schaften* ("old country" newcomers) who continued seeking asylum in America until the 1920s. Driven from their Russian and Eastern European homelands by war, famine and bloody oppression, the newcomers looked to the Jewish community's welfare agencies, synagogues and trade associations to survive and build new lives in America.

These organizations were all funded by a handful of generous individuals and social-civic groups. Donors were overwhelmed by competing and often contentious fund-raising efforts. In 1902 the largest charities proposed a solution: pool resources and time to form an umbrella organization — a federation — of charities. Then, let this federation coordinate fund raising and allocations for member charities with a once-a-year campaign. One gift, these visionaries said, will touch many lives.

On November 20, 1903, eight charities — the Jewish Orphan Asylum (later known as Bellefaire Jewish Children's Bureau), Montefiore Home for the Aged, Denver Hospital for Consumptives, Council Educational Alliance (later the Jewish Community Center), Infant Orphan's Mothers Society, Council of Jewish Women, Mount Sinai Hospital and the Hebrew Relief Association (later Jewish Family Service Association) — united to form the Federation of Jewish Charities. Its first campaign, in 1904, raised $41,350; some 96 years later, the campaign raised $28,650,513 to fund 16 local beneficiaries, national organizations, and international relief and resettlement programs.

The Federation's original mandate was to raise and distribute funds. But founders soon added budgetary oversight and coordination of programs to meet community needs in the most effective and efficient way. In 1926 the addition of new agencies brought a name change — Jewish Welfare Federation.

In the mid-1930s, alarmed at anti-Semitic developments in the United States and abroad, especially in Germany, the Federation created an advocacy agency, the Jewish Community Council. It broadened relations with national and overseas agencies, and started to build strong relations with non-Jewish organizations in Greater Cleveland. In 1951 the Jewish Welfare Federation and the Jewish Community Council merged to create the Jewish Community Federation of Cleveland. Today, the Federation's community relations activities address critical domestic and international issues and foster informed civic participation in collaboration with diverse cultural, social and political groups and individuals, as well as help bring together Jews of all backgrounds.

From the late-1940s through the late-1970s, the Federation took firm steps to ensure the growth of Cleveland's Jewish community, absorbed thousands of Jewish survivors of World War II, and played a pivotal role in the birth and survival of the state of Israel. It took on a community planning role for social services, guiding the Jewish community through the biggest capital-expansion

The Federation's founders were among Cleveland's top civic leaders in philanthropy, business and religion.

FIRST BOARD OF TRUSTEES
The Federation of Jewish Charities
CLEVELAND, O., 1904

program it has experienced, including the construction of several synagogues and agencies such as the Jewish Community Center in Cleveland Heights. During this time, the Federation began to significantly strengthen its endowment and foundations program, sensing that increased philanthropy was the best guarantee for future vitality. Today, endowment and foundation grants support innovative services, and the grantmaking program is engaging succeeding generations in philanthropic activities that benefit the Jewish and general communities.

In the 1980s, a hundred years after the first Russian Jews began arriving in Cleveland, the Federation, spurred on by local activists, took a prominent role in bringing the plight of Soviet Jews to the nation's notice. It assisted their aliyah (immigration) to Israel and helped resettle thousands of Soviet Jews in Cleveland.

On the home front, the Federation made a bold decision to develop and dramatically increase funding for formal and informal Jewish education programs. Today, its ambitious agenda for Jewish continuity is strengthening the Jewish identity of thousands of youth and adults each year. It also began a working partnership with local synagogues that Federation President Stephen H. Hoffman calls the finest Federation-synagogue relationship in the nation.

The Federation's strength lies with countless dedicated volunteers who set policy and oversee its work through dozens of committees. Today, this partnership of lay leadership and professional staff has created a consensus-building process that makes the best use of human and financial resources to identify and solve problems and plan for the future. Volunteer participation keeps fund-raising costs low and enables the Federation to allocate about 93 cents of every annual campaign dollar it collects directly to help people in need — ranking it among the most efficient fund raisers in the country.

Throughout the last half of the 20th century, the Federation looked inward to focus its resources on meeting the needs of a growing and changing community (today there are 81,000 Jews in Cleveland). Increasingly, the Federation has been reaching outward and encouraging the Jewish population to engage in volunteerism throughout Greater Cleveland. "The Federation is a central gathering place for Jews of all beliefs and self-identifications. We are the common meeting ground. As a result we can work

The Federation, working with local activists and community members, played a significant role in helping free Soviet Jews during the 1970s and 1980s.

things out on behalf of the greater community and the Jewish community in a way that can't be accomplished in any other setting," Hoffman says. Recent programs have matched volunteers to a growing number of Cleveland organizations, such as the United Way, the Cleveland Municipal School District and Habitat for Humanity.

The Federation also has become an international leader in redefining relations between the North American Jewish community and Jewish communities around the world. It is building bridges between Cleveland's Jews and those overseas through hands-on programming that brings people together and has direct impact on their lives.

As the Jewish Community Federation of Cleveland heads into the 21st century, it continues to reach out — across time, across the community, across borders — to carry out the mission its founders envisioned almost a hundred years ago: to help Jews connect to Jewish life and make the world a better place.

Recently, the Federation's hands-on programming has connected Jewish community members as volunteers with Cleveland's public schools and other groups in the general community.

Lutheran Home

Lutheran Home has made its home in suburban Cleveland since 1935. Located on its original site of nearly 20 acres in Westlake, Ohio, Lutheran Home is a nonprofit facility dedicated to providing a Christian residence for seniors in need of long-term care.

Planning for the home began in the fall of 1926, when a Lutheran minister attending a meeting of fellow clergy in Northern Indiana declared a need for an "Old People's Home" for the Central District of the Lutheran Church-Missouri Synod. The Central District excluded certain congregations in Ohio, Indiana, northern Kentucky and West Virginia. Rumor had it that Fort Wayne would be the site of the new facility.

Several Cleveland delegates at the meeting decided Fort Wayne was too far from home to drum up interest among church members in Cleveland. Planning for a separate facility to serve this region began in the late 1920s, and incorporation papers were filed in 1932. In 1935, after considering several dozen locations around Greater Cleveland, Lutheran Home Association selected a farm on Dover Center Road owned by Henry Kluever. As part of the purchase agreement, Kluever stipulated that he would donate his property, farmhouse and barn if the new facility would take care of him for the rest of his life. Indeed, he was the first resident of Lutheran Home, occupying the frame house on the property with five other residents.

The original Kluever home where Lutheran Home started in 1936

Groundbreaking for a larger Lutheran Home was on May 21, 1939. Five months later, the three-story brick facility — looking very much like a college dormitory of that era — was dedicated and opened its doors to the home's first 28 residents.

Within five years, plans were unveiled for an addition. By 1951 a wing was added that included 16 resident rooms, a chapel room, a solarium and an elevator. In 1959 a second addition was dedicated, providing 39 more resident rooms, nurse's stations with audio-visual nurse's call, a doctor's examining room, a physical therapy room, a large recreational and all-purpose room, an enlarged kitchen, new dining hall and more. The new wing set the stage for expanded care and service. Modern nursing and health equipment were added over the years to ensure high standards of health care. In 1961 the first of three cottages was built to provide independent living opportunities at Lutheran Home. In 1964 a part-time medical director was added to the staff and the home entered into an affiliation agreement with Fairview General Hospital. In 1971 Lutheran Home Association opened a facility in Mayfield Heights in Cleveland's eastern suburbs. Luther House, an independent living HUD facility, serves nearly 150 residents.

By 1979 several hundred people were on a waiting list for Lutheran Home. A 152-bed expansion was completed in 1983 to accommodate them.

As of fall 2000 Lutheran Home is planning a $30 million expansion to replace 94 skilled nursing beds and add 90 assisted-living units, as well as independent living units. Renovation of the 1979 addition and replacement of the original buildings from the 30s and 50s will create a more homelike environment and allow the home to better care for residents with increased health care needs. Additional services under consideration are adult day care, home care and outpatient therapy.

The home is closely linked to the local community and the Lutheran community, in particular, through its 90 volunteers and the many community groups who take part in programs to enhance the lives of Lutheran Home residents. Thanks to a dedicated staff and volunteers, Lutheran Home was named one of the best nursing homes

Life at Lutheran Home in 1959

in Ohio in *The Inside Guide to America's Nursing Homes* and was awarded a five-star rating.

Lutheran Home also works in cooperation with local colleges and universities, offering hands-on experience for students in nursing, dietetics, physical and occupational therapy and nursing home administration. Participating schools include Baldwin Wallace College, Case Western Reserve University, Cuyahoga Community College, Lorain County Community College and the University of Akron.

As more Americans live longer, fuller lives, technology has played an increasingly important role at Lutheran Home. Sophisticated physical, occupational and speech therapy programs permit the home to return stroke or fracture patients to previous levels of activity and mobility. Diagnostic equipment available at the home and by providers affiliated with the home permits an improved quality of care for residents.

Many individuals are credited in Lutheran Home's "roll call" of key players over the years. Four gentlemen are especially noteworthy.

Henry Vogel Sr., first superintendent of the home, is known as "The Father of the Home." Vogel, who served from 1928 until 1953, was part of the core group who dedicated themselves to establishing the home.

Under the leadership of Pastor Rolland Bosse, executive director from 1953 to 1971, Lutheran Home became the first nursing home in Cleveland to affiliate with a hospital, to establish a physical and occupational therapy program, and to provide independent living cottages. Pastor Bosse was also instrumental in the development of Luther House.

In 1964 Carlos A. Maldonado, M.D. became medical director of Lutheran Home. Maldonado's services originally were secured through a three-year pilot project grant from The Cleveland Foundation in which Lutheran Home became one of the first nursing homes in the country to employ a medical director. As medical director, Maldonado oversees health, medical and ancillary services provided to Lutheran Home residents.

Since 1971 Richard E. Stilgenbauer has been executive director of the home. During his tenure Lutheran Home was one of a handful of nursing homes to maintain Joint Commission Accreditation. Stilgenbauer also managed the home's 152-bed expansion that was completed in 1983 and is working on current development plans for the home.

Today, nearly 300 employees and 100 volunteers serve residents at Lutheran Home. The facility includes a greenhouse, beautifully landscaped grounds, enclosed courtyards and a beauty salon/barber shop. Activities include concerts, bingo parties, grandparenting groups, pet visits, movies, a resident council and more. Lutheran Home is governed by a 24-member board of trustees selected by the 74 Lutheran congregations that sponsor Lutheran Home. While Lutheran Home is a ministry of Lutheran congregations in Ohio, it welcomes men and women of all races, creeds and nationalities.

One of four courtyards added in the 1983 Lutheran Home expansion

Olivet Institutional Baptist Church

The church has been more than a place of worship and Christian fellowship in the African-American community. It has nurtured leaders who have championed civil rights and equality for minorities and the poor, and especially the issues of poverty, health care, employment, education and human rights.

By this measure, Olivet Institutional Baptist Church in Cleveland is on the cutting edge of service and relevance. It has melded the spiritual needs of worshippers with their more practical day-to-day concerns. Olivet and its leaders have been at the forefront of the civil rights struggle locally and nationally and played host to some prominent national leaders of this era. Its ministry has extended to the opening of a medical center that bridges medical treatment and prayer and spirituality in the treatment of patients.

The result for Olivet today has been a membership that continues to grow. The opinions of its leaders on social policy are sought by political, civic and other religious organizations. All the while, the church provides an expansive mix of community initiatives to teach, feed and comfort whoever walks through the church doors. The church, as an advocate for social justice as well as spiritual renewal, is uniquely qualified to help residents

The sanctuary at Olivet Institutional Baptist Church

in all aspects of their lives, says the Rev. Dr. Otis Moss Jr., pastor of Olivet since 1975.

"The role of the church is salvation, liberation and reconciliation," Moss says. "The three cannot be separated. Salvation through faith in Jesus Christ is fundamental. But salvation without liberation is not salvation at all. It is a feel-good religion that does not impact a person's economic, social, political and civic standing. You cannot preach the gospel without getting involved with social policy. The church has the ability and responsibility to be the conscience of a community."

Olivet's course was charted in 1931; it was called New Light Baptist Church. It began with 40 members, but that number grew to 150 over the next two years. By the end of the decade, membership reached 500 and the church moved to its present East Side location. The name Olivet Institutional Baptist Church ultimately was adopted in the early 1950s during the stewardship of the late Dr. Odie M. Hoover Jr.

It was during Hoover's pastorate that Olivet expanded the church's ministry to more aggressively embrace civil rights causes. Olivet was the Cleveland headquarters for the late Dr. Martin Luther King Jr. when he visited the region. Hoover was a friend and supporter of Dr. King and the Southern Christian Leadership Conference, which Dr. King helped found.

That leadership and tradition of involvement in the civil rights movement was continued by Moss, who also was active with SCLC and later, the Rev. Jesse Jackson's Operation PUSH. Moss also has maintained friendship with the King family. He was four years behind Dr. King at Morehouse College in Atlanta. The strong foundation in the civil rights movement at Olivet continues to manifest itself in the programs and services church leaders support and provide to the community.

"The church has always been a spirit-filled congregation, and for the last half-century has combined salvation, liberation and reconciliation," Moss says. "We often narrowly view politics as something that should be left to other people, that we as religious people shouldn't be 'tainted' by it. But we get our Social Security cards and Medicare cards through the political process. We are all affected by public policy issues and governmental institutions. Dr. King recognized that we could participate in public policy issues and be true to the ministry of Jesus Christ; the two are not divorced but inextricably tied together."

The community ministry at Olivet included the 1997 opening of the Otis Moss Jr.-University Hospitals Medical Center across the street from the church. The full-service, private practice facility was opened in partnership with University Hospitals of Cleveland. The concept was introduced by Moss in 1982. Over the years the church acquired property and planned the facility, which was constructed for $2 million. The goal was to provide inner-city residents with more accessible, quality outpatient care. Physicians affiliated with the hospital system staff the center, which provides internal medical, pediatric, obstetric-gynecological and rheumatological care.

The Olivet Health and Education Institute is housed there with a full-time staff. The Institute helps the church and Medical Center explore and incorporate faith and prayer into health, healing and wholeness. Some medical professionals have only recently concluded what religious leaders have known all along, that prayer and spirituality impact a person's health, Moss says. A weekly prayer service is held at the Medical Center. Staff members also may pray with patients, who additionally enter and leave the facility facing a beautiful and inviting chapel.

The Medical Center is a tangible manifestation of community outreach initiatives at Olivet. The church's walls are bulging from the number of programs being run out of church offices and meeting rooms. The church sponsors the Odie M. Hoover Education Fund to help youths

with financial assistance to attend college and identify other funding sources for their education.

An emergency food pantry and clothing program are housed there, as well as a weekly catalogue of job opportunities and fellowship programs for members. A prison ministry helps incarcerated persons and family members learn to live productive, creative and Christ-centered lives. Alcoholics Anonymous operates a weekly program there called "Free At Last."

More space is needed to house these programs and the growing church membership. The sanctuary seats 1,400, but almost twice that number worship at Olivet. Two Sunday services are held to accommodate the overflow.

A new home is on the horizon. The proposed complex would accommodate a larger worship center; a family life center to house the Christian education programs; and a community center to house community education and recreation activities, and retail space for selected commercial enterprises.

The complex is another challenge Olivet is prepared to meet. "God gives us a vision. It's up to us to embrace it," Moss says. "Twenty years ago some people could not see the Medical Center, but here it is by the grace of God."

And it does not yet appear what we shall be through faith and vision. Olivet's Mission is to preach, teach and practice the unconditional love of Jesus Christ.

University Club

According to one account in a dusty, leather-bound journal in the University Club's wood-paneled library, in June 1898 Charles Harris, Samuel Platner and Abraham Lincoln Fuller hashed out the details that founded the 102-year-old club over a meal in the Faculty and Trustee Dining Room at Adelbert College (now part of Case Western Reserve University).

The club's only requirement for membership was a degree — from an accredited college or military school — notes the Articles of Incorporation, which were signed in December 1898 by 140 Cleveland businessmen and professors. Its main purpose was to "promote literature and art," and the club's scrapbooks are full of dance, theatrical and lecture programs from the 20s through the 50s announcing dinner dances, plays and "educational" lectures by the likes of Charles Laughton, Rafael Sabatini, Cornelia Otis Skinner and Frank Buck.

But the University Club, which moved into the elegant Beckwith Mansion on fabled Euclid Avenue in 1913, was incorporated for "other kindred purposes," too.

Kindred purposes? That's what is called networking today. With its athletic facilities — including, from the very beginning, some of downtown Cleveland's best squash courts — spacious and elegantly appointed sitting rooms, cozy members' dining room and relaxing bar, the University Club has always been networking central. And

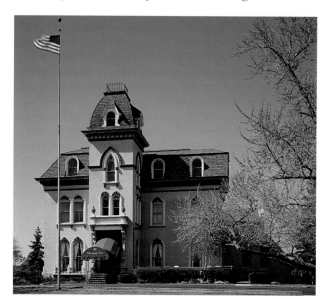

The stately Beckwith Mansion is home to the University Club of Cleveland.

Cleveland's movers and shakers — among whom numbered industrialist and philanthropist Charles W. Bingham, the club's first president; iron-ore magnate William G. Mather; Cleveland banking wizard and philanthropist George Gund; and Warner and Swazey Company President Walter K. Bailey — have been networking there for 87 years. "When I joined the club [at 26]," says longtime member and attorney Wilson A. Leece, "many of the members had been here together socially for 50 years. It was an education," he adds with just a tinge of awe in his voice, "to sit at the table in the dining room and listen to them talk."

Ups and Downs

Membership had its ups and downs during the first half of the 20th century. When World War I started, almost half the club's membership sailed to Europe. The 1929 stock market crash thinned out membership; so did World War II, though it rebounded immediately when the war ended. The University Club grew, both membershipwise and physically. The club, whose club "house" is now listed on the National Register of Historic Places, even added members' sleeping rooms.

"For all of us living there — bankers, judges, doctors, businessmen, professors — it was like a frat house, yet totally convenient to where we worked," says 84-year-old John F. Ellis, a retired stockbroker who moved into the University Club right after he was discharged from the army. "I lived at the club," he adds with a chuckle, "until they kicked me out...in the mid-60s. I still do most of my entertaining there."

The mid-60s — especially July 1966, when Cleveland's east side erupted in a week of mayhem that has come to be called the Hough Riots — began a period of decline for the in-town club that culminated in the late 70s with a membership of 63.

The purchase of the club in 1980 by a group of local investors ended the club's history as a member-owned-and-managed club, but it also ensured that the club would not become history. In a groundbreaking move, that investor group opened the club membership to women and minorities: "That's standard in clubs today," notes Randall Conradt, the club's general manager, "but then it was a revolutionary idea." It was an idea that paid off handsomely. As the club lost its exclusionary reputation, it became the business-dense Mid-Town Corridor's community center. Membership grew to almost 1,100.

But things took a turn for the worse in late 80s. U.S. tax law changed club dues and entertainment deductions, and the club began losing members and member-generated revenue in the dining room and other areas.

A New Beginning

The gracious and historic old club's slide into "banquet hall-dom" distressed club member William A. Hite III so much that the business and human resource consultant approached the owners to buy it.

"This is a window onto Cleveland's past. It's the only remaining 19th-century mansion that's still on Euclid Avenue, and it's one of the few continuously occupied Civil War-era buildings in the whole city," says Hite. "It needed a champion, someone who would have compassion for what needs doing and the passion needed to do it. I couldn't not buy it."

Realizing that he was buying in for the long haul, Hite bought the University Club in December 1998 for $1.55 million. He immediately pumped over a million dollars into the club for mechanical upgrades; the opening of several of the old sleeping rooms; touching up the exterior, whose stately colors hark back to the 1860s when the mansion was built; and to make much-needed roof and gutter repairs. "You can't see it from the ground," Hite says, "but the new gutters are copper. They are going to last forever."

Hite revamped the dining room's menu, upgraded the fitness amenities and brought in a new management team. He then rethought how the club's non-member spaces should be allotted to maximize the historic mansion's potential as a meeting center and reopened several of the member sleeping rooms to create a "members B&B." He also reaffirmed the club's standing in the 190-plus university club network to which the University Club belongs. "If you are a member here, you have club privileges with many other clubs in the U.S and around the world," Hite explains.

Now he is rebuilding the club's membership based on its prime assets: its free parking and prime location in the heart of the Mid-Town Corridor near all major Interstate and Shoreway exits; its excellent dining, small meeting and banquet facilities; its expanding athletic facilities; its there-to-serve staff; and its member-only services, which will soon include high-speed Internet access in all the sleeping rooms and a business center equipped to serve every member's needs.

But those are changes that will move the University Club into the future. Hite's plans for the University Club include going back in time, too. The Club will become a member-owned-and-run club like it was in the beginning.

The University Club ballroom, set for one of the many weddings held there each year.

And it will become the social setting that it was in the first half of the 20th century, where relationships can be built, and where the kinds of activities that distinguished the club — the plays, the dinner dances, the speakers, the programs — will again take center stage.

"Today, the University Club is a common professional and personal meeting ground — for the recent college grad, for the working woman, for the small-business owner as well as the corporate executive," says Hite, "much like it was 100 years ago."

University Hospitals Health System

University Hospitals of Cleveland and University Hospitals Health System have succeeded because of their commitment to excellence in patient care, emerging technologies and serving the health care needs of northern Ohio and the nation.

In a forward-looking response to the changes in the national health care market, UHHS in 1993 devised a strategy to deliver comprehensive services to patients throughout northeast Ohio. The challenge was to maintain quality care, improve patient outcomes and find ways to reduce costs. UHHS instituted an ongoing process called clinical integration, which uses systemwide standards to secure a uniform level of patient care, the best clinical practices and management of costs. This plan converted University Hospitals of Cleveland from a traditional, single-site, academic medical center into a regional, tightly integrated, health care delivery system that encompasses more than 120 locations in northern Ohio.

At the hub of University Hospitals Health System is University Hospitals of Cleveland, whose mission has been and continues to be "to heal, to teach, to discover." Healing occurs through the most advanced, superior-quality care available. The teaching component is achieved by educating the next generation of health care providers and by keeping current caregivers apprised of breakthroughs in medicine. The discovery goal is met through groundbreaking research that helps keep American medicine the world leader.

The lineage of UHHS began as a response to the needs of people displaced by the Civil War with the founding of the Cleveland City Hospital Society in May 1866, which eventually led to the formation of Lakeside Hospital. The affiliation with Western Reserve University Medical School began in 1895 and gave students valuable hospital experience. Separately, in other parts of the city, Rainbow Cottage, for convalescing children, and Maternity Hospital, one of the earliest to offer specialized care for women, were formed in 1891; the Infants' Clinic, later named Babies and Children's Hospital, was established in 1906.

By 1925 Lakeside, Maternity, and Babies and Children's hospitals had merged to create University Hospitals of Cleveland, with the distinction of being the first multi-hospital system in the region. Rainbow joined the complex the following year. In that same decade new buildings were opened at University Circle, where the medical complex continues to expand. Today, University Hospitals of Cleveland and its academic partner, Case

Western Reserve University, form the largest center for biomedical research in Ohio and the 13th-highest recipient of funding from the National Institutes of Health.

Instituted in 1988, University Hospitals Health System today includes primary, speciality and academic physicians; outpatient centers, community and specialty hospitals; wellness programs; skilled nursing; elder health care; rehabilitation and home care services; and managed care and insurance. The success of UHHS has been achieved through the development of a tightly integrated delivery plan that resembles a pyramid in its function.

Primary and community-based care, the foundation of the pyramid system, is emphasized because that is the care that people need most often, and UHHS has assembled a network of more than 325 primary-care physicians. Strategically located ambulatory and urgent care centers are the next step up the pyramid, providing specialty and diagnostic services such as radiology and laparoscopy. These centers also offer limited outpatient surgery, biopsies and laser surgery. On the next tier of health care are community hospitals for inpatient needs. At the top of the delivery system is the University Hospitals of Cleveland campus, for the most complex medical conditions. With this structure the system provides convenient access for patients while offering the very best in advanced technology and research.

Among the facilities at the UHC campus is the Rainbow Babies & Children's Hospital, providing the most advanced pediatric care available in the country. A leader in research, it ranks second in National Institutes of Health funding. Because studies have shown that family support has a positive impact on the healing process, Rainbow developed family-centered training programs to involve parents in this process. Rainbow is the only hospital in Cleveland dedicated entirely to the comprehensive care of children.

Adjoining Rainbow is MacDonald Women's Hospital, ranked among the top 10 maternity hospitals in America and a model for women's health care in obstetrics, gynecology, midlife health, breast health and infertility. It is the only women's hospital in Ohio.

University Hospitals Ireland Cancer Center, created by University Hospitals of Cleveland in 1985 in partnership with Case Western Reserve University, met the standards of excellence established by the National Cancer Institute and in 1998 received the nation's highest designation from the NCI as a Comprehensive Cancer Center, the only center in northern Ohio to win this recognition and one of only 37 in the country. Of primary focus at Ireland is research and the technology to discover why and how cancer begins and how it can be treated and even prevented. The most investigational therapies are translated into innovative and effective treatment.

As a continuance of its mission to heal, teach and discover, UHC founded in early 1999 the Research Institute of University Hospitals of Cleveland, a nonprofit entity forming an infrastructure through which to expand clinical and sponsored-research capabilities. In collaboration with pharmaceutical, biotechnology and medical-device industries, the Research Institute is better able to bring the results of laboratory research to the bedside of the patient.

With the creation in 1997 of the University Hospitals Regional Network, an affiliation of northern-Ohio health care systems, UHHS expanded its service area. Network members collaborate on developing programs to improve clinical quality, measure outcomes and enhance patient services. Keeping health care services as local as possible so patients can be close to their families during treatment is a goal shared by network members.

With its more than 15,000 physicians and employees, UHHS is the second-largest private-sector employer in Cuyahoga County. University Hospitals Health System continues to deliver superior health care and to engage in significant medical research that benefits not only the residents of northeast Ohio but also the nation and the world.

At Rainbow Babies & Children's Hospital, staff sees to it that young patients have time for fun and stimulating developmental activities as well as nationally recognized advanced pediatric care.
©Joe Glick Photography

West Side Ecumenical Ministry

"Truly I say to you, to the extent that you did it to one of the least of these my brothers, you did it to me." — Matthew 25:40

This passage from the New Testament truly expresses the inspiration of the West Side Ecumenical Ministry (WSEM). WSEM was conceived and founded in 1966 by the leaders of five churches: Bethany Presbyterian, Calvary Reformed, Franklin Circle Christian, St. Luke's Episcopal and St. Paul's Community Church. Created against the backdrop of the War on Poverty, the organization faced issues of urban blight, hunger, and inadequate jobs and housing in an area of shifting populations, a declining job base and changing ethnicities. These once tightly woven neighborhoods were now facing the challenges of pervasive poverty, juvenile delinquency and family disenfranchisement.

WSEM's five founding churches came together to respond to the community's needs. Although each church leader came from a different denomination, they all shared a dedication to Judeo-Christian values and a commitment to the betterment of their fellow man. "They were visionaries," says Elving Otero, the organization's sixth executive director (now President/CEO) and the first layperson in that capacity. "They had a tremendous vision of bringing together an organization that was independent of national organizations and other institutions that would encumber their ability to provide missions. That is one of the unique factors that makes WSEM one of the most productive human-care service organizations in the city."

WSEM's Head Start program makes a big splash with its children.

The founding director was the Rev. Byron "Bud" White, whose six years of service helped shape the organization's vision into reality. In the early years, the churches opened their doors to provide hot meals for immediate survival needs and assist individuals and families in crisis. Today, through various programs of education, empowerment and enrichment, WSEM offers multi-service programming to meet the needs of children, teens and adults and help families attain self-sufficiency and independence. These core programs, located at 69 sites, include Food and Outreach Services, Child and Youth Programming, Hot Meals and Senior Nutrition, Family Enrichment, and Education and Cultural Arts Programming. "The church community has really provided the bricks and mortar for these programs to survive. The church is the cornerstone of the neighborhood," observes Otero.

WSEM'S Family of Programs

In the 1970s, WSEM linked with the Council on Economic Opportunities in Greater Cleveland (CEOGC) to create its own Head Start program. "The child care program that was then in existence," remarks Otero, "became part of the Head Start program and expanded the number of children. Now, there are more than 700 children registered at any time in the program."

WSEM's Head Start program is offered at 13 sites throughout the west side of Cleveland. The program includes both half- and full-day sessions. There is also a unique Home Base program that includes weekly home visits by a teacher and weekly group socialization activities to accommodate families with transportation difficulties. As a measure of the program's effectiveness, WSEM Parent Involvement Coordinator Kathleen Sullivan was awarded the honor of an appointment to the fifth class of the prestigious National Head Start Fellowship held in Washington, D.C., from September 2000 to August 2001.

Feeding the hungry is the focus of Brookside Center, Community Corner, and the Near West Food and Family Service Center, the three food and outreach centers operated by WSEM. The Hunger Network of Greater Cleveland provides in-kind food supplies to help these centers serve the Cleveland community. Clients can receive a three-day supply of food for a family of four 12 times a year. Additionally, adult education classes, children's enrichment activities, employment services, health services, gardening activities and community diversity and educational workshops are offered by these programs. WSEM's Senior Nutrition Program also assists those in need, specifically the elderly who otherwise might not be able to prepare food for themselves or participate in community resources to meet their vital socialization needs.

Another unique program is the Cleveland Youth Theatre, which opened the doors to its first all-arts teen center in February 2000. The Reinberger Auditorium, which houses the Cleveland Youth Theatre, provides a safe space where youths express themselves through music, theater, dance, creative writing and the visual arts. WSEM has expanded the Cleveland Youth Theatre's services to the east side by forming partnerships with the Cleveland Public Schools.

In conjunction with WSEM's Teen Center Program, which is funded through Ohio's AmeriCorps Project, WSEM operates 13 centers for 12 to 18 year olds — eight centers on the west side and five on the east side. These safe havens give over 2,500 inner-city youths a place to build self esteem, enhance academic performance, exercise life skills and become — through hands-on experience — agents of positive change.

Three relatively new programs have become an integral part of WSEM's family of programs: Counseling Solutions, Workers' Network, and The Early Learning Center. Counseling Solutions provides support services to address the mental health, emotional and developmental needs of clients throughout WSEM's family of programs. With its recent certification from the Ohio Department of Mental Health, Counseling Solutions continues to grow and evolve into an even more professional community resource.

Workers' Network is WSEM's response to the Welfare-to-Work initiative, providing job-readiness training, basic computer workshops, GED classes and instruction in budgeting, parenting, nutrition and other useful skills for individuals who are challenged in their efforts to join the work force. The Early Learning Center provides full day-care services to working families with infants and toddlers so that they can continue working with the understanding that their children are being cared for in a safe and educational environment.

Today, WSEM serves over 51,000 unduplicated individuals through its family of programs and has the capacity to touch the lives of all residents who are in need throughout the Greater Cleveland community. No one is turned away. The organization has 301 full- and part-time employees and over 2,500 volunteers. A measure of the organization's effectiveness are these 1999 statistics: hundreds of teens stayed in school and avoided crime, arrest and vandalism; more than 1,500 3 to 5 year olds received immunizations, hot meals and went to school properly prepared; more than 39,000 individuals received emergency food supplies; over 1,500 individuals received clothing; and a total of 152 adults earned their GEDs, many of whom received employment placements that removed them from their welfare roles.

WSEM is endorsed by seven religious denominations: American Baptist, Catholic, Disciples of Christ, Episcopal, Presbyterian, United Church of Christ and United Methodist. Together, they are placing an emphasis on the needs of youth in the years ahead. Leading these efforts is Otero, who has 35 years of experience working with youth in a social service environment. He uses as his guiding principle the words of Henry Drummond: "You will find, as you look back upon your life, that the moments that stand out are the moments when you have done things for others."

WSEM's Administrative Headquarters: then (1966-1998) and now (1998-present).

The Western Reserve Historical Society

The Hay-McKinney Mansion — part of The Western Reserve Historical Society History Museum

At The Western Reserve Historical Society, visitors discover history that lives, laughs, loves and moves them. Its seven historical sites in northeast Ohio allow people to take a grand tour of a grand mansion; zoom, loop and soar with vintage autos and aircraft; see fashions and fads through the years; and discover family trees that bloom and grow. But why is it called the The *Western Reserve* Historical Society instead of the Northeast Ohio Historical Society?

It all goes back to 1786, when the state of Connecticut ceded its claims to Western lands of the United States, except for a portion of northeastern Ohio known as the Connecticut Western Reserve. Later, the land was sold to the Connecticut Land Company, which surveyed and settled the region. As time went by, "Connecticut" was dropped, and the area became known as simply "the Western Reserve." The Western Reserve Historical Society was founded in 1867 to preserve for future generations the records and artifacts of Cleveland and northeast Ohio.

The Society's headquarters in University Circle includes a library and two museums. The History Museum features a mansion built in 1911 that reflects the lifestyles of the rich and famous, and of the servants whose lives differed dramatically from the main house glamour. Also featured are garments from the late 1700s to the present in the Chisholm Halle Costume Wing, and stories of Cleveland's development from settlement to a booming industrial force. In the Crawford Auto-Aviation Museum, more than 100 antique, vintage, and classic automobiles, ranging from Model Ts to modern-day Jaguars, tell about Cleveland's early leadership in the auto and aviation industries. In both museums, rotating special exhibitions focus on many of the different chapters of life in the Western Reserve.

The library is the principal repository for histories, records and papers relating to the growth and development of Cleveland and the Western Reserve. Important archival collections include urban, African-American, ethnic, Jewish and labor histories. The library houses more than 5 million books, rolls of microfilm, photographs and manuscripts. It also includes one of the best genealogical collections in the nation.

The Society operates historical and architectural landmarks in outlying areas. Visitors can travel a few miles and 152 years away to Hale Farm & Village in Bath, Ohio, where they can explore life in Ohio's Western Reserve region just as it was when it was being settled and the population was starting to boom. In Hale Farm's village area, the gardens and the characters are firmly planted in the year 1848. One can meet settlers like Jacob and Hannah Meredith, a prosperous dairy farmer and his wife, who are quick to say that their house is a little more "substantial" than most of the other homes around. Ephraim Tibbals, a founder of the village, and his wife, Sebra, regale visitors with stories about the "old" times and how much the village has grown and changed. And widow Sophronia Hadley is a wealth of gossip about all of her neighbors. While visiting with the residents of the village, guests can pitch in to help make bricks or to weed a kitchen garden. Skilled artisans demonstrate glassblowing, blacksmithing and pottery making, as well as domestic crafts such as spinning and weaving, candlemaking and basketmaking. And what farm would be complete without horses and sheep and cows?

The James A. Garfield National Historic Site in Mentor, Ohio, home of the 20th U.S. president, was recently restored to the period 1880-1904, during which Garfield campaigned for president. Two major additions were made to the home. The 1880 addition was overseen by James Garfield, and the 1885 addition was overseen by Lucretia, his wife, and includes the Presidential Memorial Library. The Visitor Center is housed in an 1893 carriage house on the grounds of the 20th president's home. It features scenes from Garfield's career as a politician, including his inauguration, his nomination at the Republican Convention and his death after an assassin shot him. Also featured are documents, clothing and funeral memorabilia. An 18-minute video describes President Garfield's life and career. The grounds feature wayside exhibits describing the buildings and historical events.

The first Harpers built Shandy Hall in Unionville, Ohio, which was considered a mansion in 1815, and three generations of Harpers after them preserved written records, furnishings, tools and traditions. Modest in appearance on the exterior, there are 17 rooms inside, including the original cellar kitchen with cooking fireplace, bake oven and buttery; a formal parlor furnished with American Empire furniture; and a splendid banquet room with coved ceiling and 1815 scenic French wallpaper. On the grounds, original shrubs and trees shade flower and herb gardens.

Loghurst in Canfield, Ohio, is one of the oldest log houses in the Reserve. It was built in 1805 by Conrad Naff from Berks County, Pennsylvania. The structure was built as a farmhouse and inn on the Pittsburgh Road, now Route 224. It is a three-story log home, built to be a permanent structure, not a temporary cabin. It is constructed of local hardwood — mostly poplar and walnut — foot-square logs. It is believed to be the oldest log dwelling in the Western Reserve, and is definitely the oldest log dwelling of this size in the Western Reserve. In 1826, Loghurst was purchased by Jacob and Nancy Barnes, who used it as a farm and inn as well. Barnes was an ardent abolitionist, and there is some evidence that he aided runaway slaves. The house and farm were purchased in 1902 by Arthur and Ina Kyle. Their daughter, Josephine, left Loghurst to The Western Reserve Historical Society.

The programming and purpose of the Society's facilities adhere to its mission statement, to "...help build an informed and enduring community by preserving and providing direct access to the history and heritage of all of the people of Northeast Ohio."

1938 Mercedes-Benz at the Crawford Auto-Aviation Museum
Photo by Studio Martone

Applewood Centers, Inc.

The mission of Applewood Centers, Inc., one of the largest social services and behavioral health care agencies in Northeast Ohio, is to work with children, youth and families to manage life's challenges. It meets its goals by providing outpatient counseling, psychological testing, psychiatric services, residential shelter care, adoption, foster care, family child care and other services.

One of Applewood's unique programs is its Center for Research, Quality Improvement & Training. Directed by Ph.D. psychologists, the center conducts research to develop new interventions in children's behavioral health. Over the years, the center's commitment to this applied research has led to the development of innovative programs in the areas of parenting and youth-violence prevention.

Built in 1903, the Jones Home, now called the Carlos and Mary Jones Center after its founders, is a part of Applewood Centers Campus.

The Eleanor Gerson School serves students who, because of emotional or behavioral difficulties, cannot adapt to conventional school life and find educational and personal accomplishments beyond their reach. This alternative high school is committed to having its students succeed through the development of their self-confidence and the enhancement of strong relationships with caring adults.

With a skilled and compassionate staff, Applewood Centers arranges for child care within private homes and promotes an environment that is not only safe but also stimulating for the child's development. Applewood actively recruits and trains foster parents to care for children and adolescents whose parents are temporarily unable to care for them. For children with emotional or medical needs, there is specialized foster care. When needed, adoption services facilitate the complex process of placing children in permanent homes.

The base of operations for these foster care and adoption programs is found at Applewood Centers Campus, a state of the art facility that also makes available 24-hour, 7-day shelter care for teens involved with the juvenile justice system. Applewood is developing staff-supervised living arrangements for young people aged 16 to 21 to help prepare them for an independent adult life. Programs and facilities will encompass education, housing, mentoring, job coaching, behavioral health care, tutoring and recreation.

This tradition of caring goes back to 1886 with the founding of the Jones School and Home for Friendless Children, an orphanage that later teamed with the Cleveland Humane Society, an institution that was finding foster homes for abandoned children. By 1966 the two had merged and become Children's Services.

In a parallel development, Demonstration Child Guidance Clinics were founded in cities throughout America in the 1920s to provide psychiatric services for children. Cleveland's Demonstration Clinic, established in 1924, was the sixth of 10 such projects and eventually became the Cleveland Guidance Center, offering training and research in addition to diagnostic and treatment services. For its high-quality mental health services, The Guidance Centers was named "Outstanding Agency of 1988" by the American Association of Psychiatric Services for Children.

In January 1997 The Guidance Centers merged with Children's Services, Inc. to form Applewood Centers, Inc., which serves about 10,000 children a year in its various locations throughout the greater Cleveland area. Each day Applewood's staff of psychiatrists, nurses, social workers, psychologists, licensed counselors, teachers and other professionals helps children, youth and families cope with the difficult circumstances of their lives.

Center for Families and Children

Family Matters. Children Matter. You Matter. This is the message the Center for Families and Children (CFC) sends every day — to children who are often eating their only hot meal of the day; to youth who are trying hard to cope in families plagued by substance abuse; to adults who are challenged by mental illness and are in desperate need of support; and to families who are frightened of what welfare reform means to them and are wondering how they will feed their children.

One of the largest and most comprehensive human service providers in Ohio, CFC was founded in 1970 as the Center for Human Services as a result of a merger of five nonprofit organizations including The Day Nursery Association, Traveler's Aid Society, Cleveland Homemaker Service Association, Youth Service, and Family Service Association, whose origins date back to 1830. CFC is committed to providing human services to families and individuals, preparing them to achieve hope, dignity and purpose in their lives. CFC fulfills its mission and vision by offering programs that meet the needs of more than 20,000 individuals and families annually from 20 locations.

CFC's programs are unique in the depth and breadth of their diversity. Its Behavioral/Mental Health Programs, for example, provide therapeutic individual and group services that assist individuals and families coping with severe mental illness, as well as marital, family, child/parent, personal loss/grief and alcohol/drug counseling services

from eight locations across Cuyahoga County. Bilingual and bicultural counseling services are available to assist Hispanic individuals and persons who are hearing-impaired. All services are provided by licensed clinical and medical staff.

CFC directs many of its resources toward nurturing and assisting children and families as a way of helping them become self-sufficient. For instance, the agency offers quality child care through five fully accredited child care

A father and daughter enjoying quality time together

centers and six Head Start and Early Head Start programs that integrate education with health activities such as nutrition screenings, parent involvement and social services. CFC also initiated the innovative curriculum-based Father and Families Together (FAFT) Program in 1996 as a way to strengthen the father-child bond and to help urban fathers assume greater parenting responsibilities while enhancing their self-sufficiency. CFC also offers programs like Safety Net, a service that reaches out to families impacted by welfare reform and works to re-engage them in a productive search for employment.

All of these and other critically needed programs and services would not be possible without the many dedicated volunteers, staff, board of trustees and funders who ensure that the individuals and families in Greater Cleveland who need a hand up will always find it extended to them in their time of need.

CFC staff member Cyndee Long works with a child in the RapArt program.

City of Shaker Heights

Called "The Valley of God's Pleasure" by its early settlers, the city of Shaker Heights is one of America's most unique and beautiful cities, with a national reputation for historic architecture, excellent schools and cultural diversity.

The land bordering Cleveland's East Side was first settled in 1822 by the United Society of Believers in Christ's Second Appearing, better known as the "Shakers"

The city of Shaker Heights is an area rich with beautiful residences and landscapes.

because of the members' physical displays of religious zeal. They were a society that dreamed of a utopian community, and they prospered until the late 1880s when the booming industry in Cleveland caused a declining membership. In 1889 the remaining 27 Shakers sold the land to a Buffalo land syndicate and relocated.

Shaker Heights City Hall was built in 1929 under the influence of the Van Sweringens.

The land remained empty until 1905 when two enterprising real estate businessmen, brothers Oris P. and Mantis J. Van Sweringen, became interested in building a wealthy residential community. They eventually bought more than 4,000 acres from the land syndicate and began selling lots in what they planned would be an extraordinary community designed under the principles of the English "Garden City" movement.

The brothers made several improvements to Shaker Village, as it was called until 1931 when it officially became the city of Shaker

Heights. They added Green and Marshall Lakes to the two lakes built previously by the Shakers, and built a high-speed commuter train line to and from downtown Cleveland. Completed in 1920, the rapid transit system, as it is known today, is still a major draw for new residents.

The development of Shaker Heights, an early suburb of Cleveland, was carefully controlled to attract buyers from among wealthy Euclid Avenue families, where growing industry was taking over neighborhoods. Uniform lot sizes were subdivided among large areas of green space and each neighborhood had its own elementary school, nine in all. Public and private schools and churches were attracted to the area by offers of low-cost land.

To assure homes met their principles of good taste, the Van Sweringens set strict architectural standards and outlined them in a booklet to prospective buyers. Whether a stately mansion or a charming two-family home, only leading architects were allowed to design them in one of three approved styles — English, French and Colonial. The meticulous planning worked. From 1911 to 1930 the population soared from 200 to almost 18,000 and the magnificent houses and parks still attract awestruck visitors to this day.

Another "Van" that greatly influenced Shaker was William J. Van Aken, the city's mayor from 1916 to 1950. His 35-year leadership carried forward the Van Sweringens' vision and transformed a small village into a world-famous community. Among his accomplishments was the establishment of a high-quality public-services department. Van Aken died in office in 1950 and currently has a shopping center and boulevard named in his honor.

Today, the unique community of 31,000 continues to attract diverse, accomplished and community-minded residents with its outstanding schools, homes, city services and conveniences. Shaker Heights continues to combine heritage and tradition with a commitment to progress and a vision for the future.

"*Pride in* our past, faith in our future," is the way Strongsville Mayor Walter Ehrnfelt describes his city.

The pride is manifested in the city's Historical Village, a re-created village representing almost 100 years of change in the community, from 1822 to 1904. Faith in the future is evidenced by the new $18 million, 157,000-square-foot Strongsville Recreation and Senior Complex, which opened in 1998.

When Vermont's John Stoughton Strong came to Ohio in 1816, he already had made arrangements to purchase a portion of Township No. 5 in the 14th range from the Oliver Ellsworth family. Ellsworth, a native of Hartford, Connecticut, had purchased the land from the Connecticut Land Company. (The company had been authorized by the state of Connecticut to purchase and resell a majority of the lands of the Western Reserve. It obtained the right to the Western Reserve by exchanging claims to other western lands with the U.S. government.)

By 1818 the area achieved township status and was named in honor of Strong. It took almost 100 years, until 1923, for Strongsville to become incorporated as a village and less than 40 more, until 1961, to become a city.

Outside of the city of Cleveland, Strongsville is the largest city in Cuyahoga County, encompassing almost 25 square miles.

As early as the 1960s — long before most suburban cities — Strongsville was preparing for the future by using professional planners to develop a comfortable separation of residential, industrial and retail areas. Within the community are more than a dozen planned housing developments, and each developer is required to keep 20 per cent of the area open, either for a recreation complex, playgrounds or just plain green space.

Apartment living is at a premium, but not because people don't want to live in them. A 1970s referendum voted to limit apartment suites to 15 for every 100 single-family homes. The people of Strongsville felt strongly that apartment living created a transient neighborhood. They wanted Strongsville to be a stable community — and still do.

The small group of settlers that Strong brought from Connecticut has grown to a population of 45,000, with a peak of 65,000 possible, according to the mayor.

And those 45,000 have become accustomed to a very pleasant community lifestyle that successfully blends the neighborliness of a small town with the amenities of a large suburban community.

In June there's a rib burn-off on the commons sponsored by Strongsville City Club. Each July 40,000 residents and former residents are drawn "back home" for the annual Chamber of Commerce-sponsored Homecoming Festival.

The community also celebrates an annual Breakfast on the Bridge, a Sunday get-together on a covered bridge in the Big Creek Reservation of the Cleveland Metroparks, a couple of thousand acres of which are in Strongsville itself.

A few years ago, a new shopping center, one of the largest in the county, opened in Strongsville. It has meant more local jobs and more tax revenue. But it hasn't changed the values the city has cherished for 185 years. In fact, it has further validated the city's pride in its past; its faith in the future.

Strongsville's clock tower in the center of town reflects the strong sense of community.

Cleveland Metroparks, with more than 2,000 acres in Strongsville, provides tranquility amid the hustle of the 21st century.

Cleveland District of the United Methodist Church

John Wesley, an English Anglican cleric, believed everyone was a child of God; salvation came by faith in Jesus Christ; and the church should reach out to people with personal holiness, social justice and contemporary worship. He sent Bishop Francis Asbury to the American frontier to ride on horseback for much of the

The diverse district of Anglo, African-American, Hispanic and Korean congregations enjoy getting together for worship, study, inspiration and mission.

18th century, starting communities of faith called Methodist societies. Today, the Cleveland District of the United Methodist Church continues to share the good news of God's love through worship, study and service.

Many of Cleveland's early settlers were Methodists, and the city's first Methodist church, Brooklyn Memorial, was formed in 1818. Its eight original members met in a log town hall at the corner of what is now Denison Avenue and West 25th Street. By 1840 the Cleveland area had five Methodist churches — Brooklyn, First, Euclid Avenue, Miles Park and Franklin Avenue — that formed the North Ohio Conference. In 1848 the Cleveland District of the Erie Conference was formed. The late 1800s and early 1900s were a time of growth for both the city of Cleveland and the Methodist church, with over 30 new churches created. Today, the Cleveland District consists of 50 churches with over 21,000 members.

The district functions to encourage, equip, connect and support its local churches so that they may faithfully serve their communities. It accomplishes this through a wide variety of programs and initiatives. In the year 2000 over $450,000 will be spent on programs aimed at low-income neighborhoods. The district recently joined "The Church in the City," an interfaith movement to combat urban decay, and is the largest builder of Habitat for Humanity homes in Cleveland, completing its 10th home in 2000.

Each district congregation excels at offering a variety of worship, study, mission and fellowship opportunities. Their youth groups, choirs and music programs are some of the best in Cleveland. Similar to John Wesley's use of the newly invented printing press to print and distribute literature, the churches needed to strengthen their strong community presence by taking advantage of current technology. The district secured funding so that every church has an answering machine, fax machine with a dedicated line and e-mail. The district also improved communication with its members and the public when it launched its Web site in April 2000. The site features detailed information about the churches and their activities, with links to individual church Web sites where available. The district's purchase of a digital camera allowed Web site visitors to view daily photos of summer 2000 mission trips by local church members to North Carolina and Africa.

The district also unites with its churches to train and inspire people to share their faith. Its Lay Speaker Training Program consecrated 110 speakers in 2000, the largest group in its history. When the churches celebrated Pentecost, traditionally called the birthday of the church, in June 2000, the celebrations included posters, ads and radio spots inviting the public to join. The district's annual Leadership Academy provides leadership development.

There are many other district initiatives, too numerous to mention, and a plan for the future that ensures the fulfillment of Wesley's vision throughout Cleveland for many centuries to come.

Cuyahoga County Board of Mental Retardation and Developmental Disabilities

"Imbecile," "mentally deficient" and "feeble-minded" were not eliminated from the Ohio Revised Code until 1969, two years after the state's legislature created county boards of mental retardation in each of Ohio's 88 counties.

There are those who say mental retardation "came out of the closet" in the early 1960s when President John F. Kennedy didn't hide the fact that he had a sister with retardation. Whatever the catalyst, it triggered reaction across the country, not only in Ohio.

When the Cuyahoga County Board of Mental Retardation and Developmental Disabilities (CCBMR/DD) became reality in October, 1967, as a result of the lobbying efforts of parents, it assumed responsibility for 51 school classes previously under public operation. As early as 1936 the Cleveland Board of Education had initiated pilot classes for children with mild mental retardation, but had passed that function to the Division of Child Welfare.

Although the idea behind establishing county boards had been to provide a full range of services to children, they found themselves quickly getting into the adult side of things as the children got older.

As they grew older, individuals had different needs. One year after creation of the CCBMR/DD, the first attempts were made to create a sheltered adult workshop. Even though clients had to be least 16 years old, there were no senior participants. Now, individuals over 50 account for a large percentage of the adults enrolled.

Today, the CCBMR/DD, successfully funded on a regular basis by voter approval of a property tax levy, serves more than 7,000 individuals of all ages with a staff of 1,500 well-trained professionals.

The board's early childhood program provides intervention services at six sites to very young children with significant developmental delays. The CCBMR/DD operates three schools for children and young adults, ages 5 through 21, who are eligible for multi-handicapped programs determined by the Ohio Department of Education.

A comparatively recent "inclusion" program allows youngsters to attend classes taught by CCBMR/DD teachers in 10 school districts across the county. They take ancillary classes such as gym, music and art, and enjoy lunch, recess and other activities with students from the school.

Another changing program is the CCBMR/DD's community employment activity. The board has eight adult training centers, but an increasing number of adults want to work outside the centers in the community. And an increasing number of employers want to hire them.

The CCBMR/DD also has community homes in more than three dozen cities throughout the county, giving adults with mental retardation or developmental disabilities the opportunity to live and work on their own, with supervision.

The CCBMR/DD is not content to live on yesterday's success. It recently instituted "person-centered planning," a process that enables people with mental retardation and other developmental disabilities and their families to communicate their wants and needs to the organization, so it can help them get the supports needed for a better place in life in the community.

"We as a nation have long neglected the mentally ill and the mentally retarded. This neglect must end if our nation is to live up to its standards of compassion and dignity," President Kennedy stated. Since its inception, the CCBMR/DD has been quietly, but effectively, responding.

One of the earliest classes conducted by the CCBMR/DD in 1967, after the legislature created county boards of mental retardation

Cuyahoga County Community Mental Health Board

Adults and children in Cuyahoga County with a mental illness or emotional disturbance have depended on the quality services and programs developed by the Cuyahoga County Community Mental Health Board for over 30 years.

Created in October 1967 by the Ohio Legislature, the board was first known as the Cuyahoga County Mental Health and Retardation Board. It was a result of the efforts of President John F. Kennedy, who in 1963 in a report to Congress had addressed the need for community-based, government-funded services for the mentally ill and retarded.

By 1968 the board was formally incorporated and charged with the responsibility of developing services for residents within the county. In 1990 it was one of only seven county mental health boards in Ohio that chose to separate from its county's drug and alcohol board.

The board functions as a nonprofit planning, funding and policy-making body. Its $90 million annual budget is provided by federal, state and county public funds and is disbursed and monitored by an 18-member board of governors. It accomplishes its mission by contracting with over 36 agencies in Cuyahoga County that directly provide mental health services for adults, children and seniors of all income levels. The board is mandated to plan, review and evaluate the services and facilities to ensure they are of high quality and are tailored to individuals. Services are required to help individuals better control their illness, achieve their personal goals, and develop skills and supports that will lead to their living the most constructive and satisfying lives possible in the least restrictive setting available.

Whether a client is just looking for a means of prevention or is severely affected by a mental illness, the services provided by the agencies fulfill a wide range of needs. They include mental health assessment, psychiatric counseling, medication, 24-hour crisis and case management, partial hospitalization and support groups for both clients and their family members. The many services for children and adolescents with emotional and developmental problems may begin with children in day care and in school programs. Also available is career help from employment agencies and a variety of opportunities for housing. All services are provided on a sliding-scale fee and no one is turned away.

In addition the board facilitates advocacy programs and educates the public on mental health issues, often involving clients and family members. Other unique programs include its Consumer Operated Services Program, which encourages the operation of neighborhood "drop-in" centers. It also works with local hospitals on training programs for psychiatrists and with local universities on research projects.

Thanks in part to a 1999 Report to the Surgeon General on Mental Health, which verified that mental disorders are a real health condition and that services such as those the board provides are essential to the nation's health, it can expand its services even more in the future. Its plans include further funding of research projects, advocating treatment coverage to insurance carriers, assistance with recovery, and expansion of its children's services and crisis systems.

By managing its funds and resources efficiently and working hard at building a system of caring, the Cuyahoga County Community Mental Health Board will continue to get closer to its goal of a healthy mind for every Cuyahoga County citizen.

The board supplies greatly needed funds to over 36 agencies in Cuyahoga County that directly provide mental health services to residents of all income levels.

The Holden Arboretum

The Holden Arboretum — one of the country's largest — is testimony to the diligence and dedication of the Holden family almost a century ago.

Albert Fairchild Holden was born in 1867 to Liberty E. Holden, founder of *The Cleveland Plain Dealer.* Though he achieved great wealth in his career as a mining engineer, his life was marred by tragedies. His wife died just six years after their marriage, his daughter Elizabeth Davis died at the age of 12, and he died abruptly of cancer at the age of 46.

Mr. Holden had always enjoyed studying trees, plants and minerals. He frequented the Arnold Arboretum at Harvard University, where he had attended school, and considered leaving his estate to the institution. But his sister, Roberta Holden Bole, convinced him that Cleveland deserved an arboretum. After Mr. Holden's daughter Elizabeth died and he faced his own impending death, he established the Elizabeth Davis Holden Memorial trust in 1912 to fund an arboretum in her memory and provide for his two surviving daughters.

Though the trust was not accessible until after the deaths of the daughters, Mrs. Bole was determined to move the arboretum project forward. The final location in Kirtland, Ohio, about 25 miles east of downtown, was chosen for its unique land formations.

It was 1931 when work on the arboretum began on 100 acres donated by Mrs. Bole and her husband. An arboretum is a long-term project and it wasn't until 1937 that Holden first opened to the public for a single day. In 1947 it opened for the month of May. In its early years various boards from the Cleveland Museum of Natural

History managed the arboretum, but in 1952 it was incorporated as an independent, nonprofit institution.

The colorful Arlene and Arthur S. Holden Jr. Butterfly Garden is radiant from July through September.

Early contributors of both time and money were Mr. Holden's daughters, Mrs. Emery Norweb and Mrs. Katharine Thayer; and Warren H. Corning, a prominent Cleveland banker, and his family.

Mr. Holden had envisioned an arboretum dedicated to higher education in botanical sciences and horticulture. The present day arboretum fulfills this wish with over 350 educational classes and hikes yearly.

The Holden Arboretum is also dedicated to collecting and researching the woody plants with ornamental and scientific merit for northeast Ohio. Several trips have been made to countries such as Korea, China and Russia to collect seeds and plants. Like any museum specimen, every plant is labeled and mapped by a new computerized record keeping system. Holden's Corning Library houses over 8,000 horticulture and landscaping books.

Today, Holden encompasses over 3,400 varied acres, with display gardens, including a butterfly garden; horticultural collections; natural woodlands; Little Mountain; ponds, fields and ravines. Hikes range from easy to rugged, and fishing and cross-country skiing are popular with the thousands of families enrolled as members.

Memberships, private contributions, public admission fees, gift shop revenues and the trust fund started by Mr. Holden over 88 years ago ensure Holden's thriving future. Expanded gardens, nature classes and new horticultural buildings are all being planned to continue to entice visitors from the Cleveland area to explore, learn or just enjoy nature.

Autumn's vibrant colors can be seen throughout Holden.

Jennings Hall Center for Older Adults

Laughter coming from the Early Childhood Enrichment Center and the twittering of colorful parakeets in the Jennings Hall Goudreau Pavilion make visitors think they've walked into the sunlit lobby of a neighborhood community center. In a sense, they have.

Community, respect, hospitality, discovery of potential and celebration of life are the values upon which the first Jennings home was built in 1942 with a bequest from Monsignor Gilbert P. Jennings. As pastor of St. Agnes Parish at E. 79th Street and Euclid Avenue for 49 years, he knew that without a suitable home, members of his parish and others who were "deserving aged persons with inadequate income" would end their days in poverty and despair. Monsignor Jennings firmly established the Catholic roots and ministry of Jesus that continues at Jennings Hall today.

Jennings Hall Center for Older Adults. *Collins, Gordon, Bostwick Architects*

Sister Patricia Raelene assists resident Ruth Zaniewski after a stroke.

The "hall" that gave Jennings its name was a grand hotel-style building. It was constructed in 1942 on 3.5 acres of land in Garfield Heights donated by the Sisters of the Holy Spirit. At the request of the Catholic Diocese of Cleveland, the Sisters staffed and ran the home and presently continue their ministry in both direct care and leadership roles. The building burned down, with a loss of 14 lives four years later, but by 1949 a 106-bed "rest home" had risen in its place. Over the next 40 years, with guidance from Monsignor Michael B. Ivanko, head of the Diocesan Division of Care for the Aged, and others, Jennings Hall established one of the first on-site rehabilitation centers in the Greater Cleveland area and became a catalyst for raising nursing home standards on a local and national level.

In 1995 Jennings Hall surpassed existing nursing home standards and built a 150-bed, state-of-the-art nursing facility. Light and spacious, with private quarters for each resident, it wraps around a rose garden and provides long-term nursing care, short-term rehabilitation services and innovative dementia care for older adults. Quality of life and personal dignity are achieved through intergenerational programs, art and horticultural therapies, pet care programs, religious activities and an emphasis on individual choice. Jennings' progressive reputation has made it a training site for local nursing students and visitors from abroad.

As Jennings Hall moves into the 21st century, it is expanding its mission and leadership in Catholic health care and supportive services for older adults. In 1998 Jennings partnered with the Department of Housing and Urban Development to build Jennings Manor, a 60-unit senior apartment building. The Sisters of the Holy Spirit initiated the Holy Spirit Villa in 1999, a planned development of independent housing options at Jennings.

Today, plans are in place to build low- to moderate-income senior apartments, additional market-rate apartments, assisted living, an adult day center and community-based services.

If Monsignor Jennings could walk the Jennings Hall campus today, he would be proud of what his vision has brought forth.

Kendal at Oberlin

Cultural events in a serene setting, educational opportunities to exercise the mind, first-class health care and predictable fees — Kendal at Oberlin truly is a premier retirement community. Located 35 miles west of Cleveland in Oberlin, Ohio, Kendal at Oberlin is part of a larger family of retirement communities in the United States affiliated with The Kendal Corporation. The Quaker-directed, nonprofit organization has more than 25 years of experience providing communities and services for older people. Every Kendal community reflects the Quaker values of respect for the individual, excellence in service, social responsibility and fiscal integrity.

Kendal at Oberlin opened in 1993 and by 1996 was recognized by *New Choices*, a *Reader's Digest* publication, as one of the top 20 continuing care communities in the country. It also is one of the youngest continuing care communities in the nation accredited by the Continuing Care Accreditation Commission.

Kendal residents choose from independent living in cottages and apartments to varying levels of assisted living and skilled nursing care. The facility is situated on 92 acres, including wetlands and ponds, and serves about 300 residents from 26 states. Approximately 40 percent of Kendal's residents have previous affiliations with Oberlin College as former students, faculty or staff. More than 20 percent of Kendal's residents are from Oberlin. Many selected Kendal because of its homelike atmosphere, including tastefully furnished seating areas, dining rooms with linen tablecloths, a library with more than 6,000 books and periodicals, and cozy courtyards for outdoor retreats.

Health care at Kendal focuses on continuing wellness, physical fitness and maintaining each individual's highest level of independence. Facilities include a state-of-the-art fitness center, lap pool, therapeutic pool, tennis courts and a paved, mile-long outdoor path. Kendal also offers nursing care, assisted living and a comprehensive rehabilitation program to the greater community. In 1999 42 percent of nursing care residents and 34 percent of assisted living residents came from the community at large. In addition, in long-term care, Kendal is nationally recognized for its efforts to eliminate the use of physical restraints.

More than 70 activity groups, including art, music, photography, horticulture and computers, are resident-directed. "Kendal attracts people who want to be active," says a Kendal administrator. "They tend to be 'doers' who have been leaders throughout their lives. They don't stop leading just because they retired."

Activities available at Oberlin College include concerts, lectures, films, sports events, drama and dance performances. Many residents attend college classes or "Living and Learning" classes — an affiliate of the Elderhostel Institute Network — at Kendal.

Community service is important to many "Kendalites." In 1999, residents, staff and board members volunteered more than 38,000 hours at more than 80 community organizations. Kendal also welcomes area residents to its art gallery talks, lectures, and drama and music performances. Water aerobics and arthritis water exercise classes at Kendal's pools are open to the community, as is an on-site child day care center.

The long-term goal of Kendal at Oberlin is to ensure that older adults — residents and neighbors alike — lead fulfilling lives in ways that are meaningful to them. As one trustee notes, Kendal is not really a retirement community, "it's a place where people come to live the rest of their lives."

Kendal at Oberlin — one of the top 20 continuing care communities in the country

The names inscribed in granite read like a "Who's Who" of Cleveland business and industry, law, politics, medicine and science, and civic endeavors. Industrialist John D. Rockefeller, *Call & Post* publisher William O. Walker, Cleveland Orchestra founder Adella Prentiss Hughes, Prohibition-era crime fighter Eliot Ness, Dr. George F. Crile, 22 former Cleveland mayors and U.S. President James A. Garfield are just a few of those memorialized at Lake View Cemetery.

Founded in 1869 as a nonprofit "rural" garden cemetery, the 285-acre site, spanning Cleveland, East Cleveland and Cleveland Heights, was chosen for its lush grounds and scenic view of Lake Erie. One of the most impressive garden spots in the Cleveland area, the cemetery maintains an arboretum of hundreds of varieties of flowers, plants and trees such as rare Japanese Maples, Ginkgos, Dawn Redwoods and Sargent's Weeping Hemlocks.

Visitors not only place flowers at gravesites but participate in Lake View's architectural, horticultural, and historical walking and driving tours. A favorite landmark among schoolchildren is a black granite monument with bronze relief engraved with the names of 172 students and two teachers who perished in a fire at Lake View Elementary School in Collinwood, March 4, 1908.

"We still maintain a garden cemetery, but we see ourselves more as guardians of history," says Mary Krohmer, director of community relations. "Lake View's primary purpose is to serve each new generation with dignity and respect while preserving and honoring our past generations."

A popular site is a granite memorial in honor of Cleveland Indians shortstop Raymond Chapman (1891-1920), killed by a fastball thrown by New York Yankees pitcher Carl Mays at the Polo Grounds. As a tribute, fans often leave behind baseballs, bats and Indians memorabilia.

This 70-foot-tall obelisk, an architectural form used by ancient Egyptians to memorialize their rulers, was built in honor of John Davison Rockefeller (1839-1937), a financier, philanthropist and founder of Standard Oil Co. in Cleveland.

A world-renowned architectural jewel is the Jeptha Wade Memorial Chapel, built in 1901 to honor the founder of Western Union and first president of Lake View. Bronze doors open to a gold and glass mosaic depicting Old and New Testament scenes and a priceless Tiffany window.

A Carrara marble statue of President James A. Garfield stands in the center of his monument, a circular tower of sandstone surrounded by stained-glass windows and walls of mosaic. A frieze along the exterior depicts the life of Garfield, and the caskets of both the president and his wife, Lucretia, are on display in the lower crypt.

The Rockefeller Monument is a 70-foot tall granite obelisk, an architectural form used by ancient Egyptians to memorialize their rulers. John Davison Rockefeller (1839-1937) was a financier and philanthropist who started his career as a store clerk and later founded the Standard Oil Co. in Cleveland. His benefactions totaled $550 million.

A sculpture of the archangel Michael hovers over the burial site of John Hay (1838-1905), a poet, journalist, historian and statesman. Hay was Abraham Lincoln's private secretary for four years, ambassador to Great Britain in 1897, and as President McKinley's secretary of state, proposed the Open Door policy with China in 1899.

In 1985 the Lake View Cemetery Foundation was created as a 501(c)(3) recipient organization to assist the cemetery association in funding educational programs and the maintenance of its historic landmarks. According to James Goodwin, vice president of development, the foundation offers a unique opportunity through tax-deductible gifts for friends and families to perpetuate the beauty and celebrate the lives of those entrusted to Lake View.

New Avenues to Independence has spent nearly a half century helping people with mental retardation or other developmental disabilities find services to help them live independent, productive lives. The nonprofit organization has also been an advocate for its constituents.

"We're always pushing the envelope for social policy change," says New Avenues Executive Director Thomas Lewins. "We've been a true civil rights leader as it pertains to disabilities."

The organization's staff and volunteers help many children and adults with services ranging from occupational and recreational therapies; medical, nursing and psychological services; and housing and living services.

New Avenues was founded in 1952 as Parents' Volunteer Association for Retarded Children & Adults Inc. by a group of parents who were seeking to improve the services available to their children with mental retardation. It quickly became an advocate for better care for children with disabilities.

The movement to keep children with special needs in home surroundings was just taking root at this time and New Avenues was a part of that effort. By 1959 the group was raising money to lobby the state of Ohio to build a home for children with mental retardation in northeastern Ohio. About the same time, the group opened a nursery school that would help prepare children with disabilities for school or other training classes.

In 1961, Ernest Zeve, a volunteer, was named the organization's first executive director. Zeve's business office had been the organization's de facto headquarters for nearly five years.

By the late 1960s the organization began to shift its focus to residential services. The group bought its first group home for adults with mental retardation in 1970 on Overlook Road in Cleveland Heights. At this time the organization joined with the Circle Workshop to establish a network of group homes. The Circle Workshop, which had been created in 1962, offered job training and employment in a sheltered workshop environment.

The goal of its own residential center was achieved in 1974 when the organization bought a former Catholic Youth Organization building on Euclid Avenue. The site was renamed the Community Living and Skills Center, and two cottages were added in 1980, expanding services to 50 residents.

Today, New Avenues continues its traditional mission with an expanded array of services. Its nine group homes

The Edgerton Home

in Lake and Cuyahoga counties provide facilities-based residential services. It also offers visiting, supported-living services at 60 sites in Cuyahoga, Lake and Ashtabula counties. Sheltered workshops provide job coaching and temporary employment, and a summer camp in Lake County helps 75 special-needs children. In addition, it has plans to expand its services to more adults and children with developmental difficulties. According to Lewins, "The agency has developed skills and is working to offer its services to whoever needs them."

Rotary Club of Cleveland

The distinctive wheel emblem of Rotary International is a familiar sight in 23,700 cities around the world, but Rotary Club of Cleveland has the distinction of being among the first clubs to be founded under its aegis.

Chartered as a service organization of leading business professionals, Rotary Club of Cleveland was established in 1910, just five years after Paul Harris instituted Rotary International's first club in Chicago in 1905. Four businessmen were instrumental in bringing Rotary to Cleveland: William Downie, Herman Eisele, Herman Moss and Ed Sloan. Their first meeting place was in a now-unknown private dining room, but by 1917 the club had moved into a wing of what was then the Statler Hotel. The rooms club members used there had typical hotel amenities, including working bathrooms, and shelving space was created by covering the bathtubs with sheets of plywood.

Founded on principles of service and fellowship, Rotary Club of Cleveland has supported major community projects since 1920, when it began making substantial contributions to the Society of Crippled Children (now the Achievement Centers for Children). In 1941, under the direction of President R.J. Schmunk, Cleveland Rotary Foundation was formed to contribute to and support local community, youth and vocational efforts. Over the years the foundation has provided funds and services to a wide array of charitable organizations, including the Cleveland Foodbank Inc., Vocational Guidance Services, Greater Cleveland Chapter of the American Red Cross, Cleveland Scholarship Programs, Inc. and Old Stone Foundation. It introduced the Character Education program into the school system to benefit thousands of junior and high school students. It also awards scholarships to local students for international study and helps to fund Polio Plus, Rotary International's humanitarian project to immunize all children around the world.

Until 1987, all of this good work was carried out by the men of Rotary, because Rotary International had no provision for women to join. But since then, women in business have joined Rotary Club of Cleveland in increasing numbers, bringing their unique perspective and dedication to the community to the already thriving organization.

Rotary members meet weekly over lunch to hear speakers, exchange ideas and network. Part of the focus of these meetings is to develop friendships with other business executives and professionals while encouraging high ethical standards in business.

Membership in Rotary Club of Cleveland is by invitation. Existing members may propose and sponsor new members, who must be persons of good character and reputation and actively employed in an executive capacity in the Greater Cleveland area. Those who join are expected to support worthy Foundation projects as well as serve on at least one committee. Active committees include the community, international, vocational and youth service committees. There also is an extensive number of additional committees that serve a wide variety of community needs.

Located in the University Club since 1995, Rotary Club of Cleveland increased its community visibility with the 1999 dedication of Rotary Plaza, a little urban oasis across from the Rock and Roll Hall of Fame and Museum. Inlaid in the ground near the plaza's benches is the Rotary wheel, which now serves as a constant reminder of the club's good works and longevity in the Cleveland community.

A memorial to Arch C. Klumph, fourth president of the Rotary Club of Cleveland and father of the Rotary International Foundation, graces Rotary Plaza.

Cleveland's ethnic-European neighborhoods were beginning to transform the city by the summer of 1914 when a group of Italian immigrants first celebrated the Feast of St. Rocco. The natives of Noicattaro, in the province of Bari, had gathered for the celebration for years. Led by Francesco DiDonna, they collected money to defray the expenses for their hometown's annual celebration of Our Lady of Mt. Carmel. The memory of their country stayed close to their hearts, and they participated with the gift of their money now that an ocean separated them. In 1913 DiDonna had the idea to seek a $5 contribution from all of his friends for their new community so they could enjoy a religious celebration of their own.

Because the July feast of our Lady of Mt. Carmel had already passed, the group decided to honor St. Rocco, the next feast on the calendar. Because it was a religious observance, and because they had no church, they raised a tent for the celebration on Trent Avenue in their West Side neighborhood. The procession through the streets was accompanied with band music and a portrait of St. Rocco.

St. Rocco, born in France in 1293, became a beloved patron, especially to Italy. He was known for his miracles during the dark years of the Plague, and later during the 19th-century cholera epidemic. St. Rocco's miracles lived on in the tradition of these immigrant Clevelanders. In 1915 the religious festival was held with the statue of St. Rocco, which they had bought to honor him. For the two years until 1917 when the first church was built on Trent Avenue, Blessed Sacrament first stored the statue in a coal shack until Mrs. Victoria Lioce moved it into her house.

In 1924, at the invitation of Bishop Joseph Schrembs, the Fathers of the Order of Our Lady of Mercy (O. de M.), an order founded in Spain in 1218, arrived at the parish. Those first priests, Fr. Sante Gattuso and Fr. Martin Campagna, saw the little church grow into a vital parish, complete with a school opening in 1927 served by the Sisters of the Most Holy Trinity. Both orders continue to serve St. Rocco's. Pastor since 1972, Fr. Michael Contardi, O. de M., and associate, Fr. Paschal Rosca, O. de M., celebrate the parish's five weekend Masses, including one in Italian, every Sunday morning; daily weekday Masses; and the Wednesday-evening devotion of the Perpetual Novena to Our Lady of Mercy. Brother Martin Joseph, O. de M., also serves the parish along with the school principal, Sr. M. Judith, O. SS. T., who oversees the school, which thrives with an enrollment of over 200 children.

The present church, located on Fulton Road, was dedicated in 1952 after three years of the dedicated labor and contributions of parishioners, and in 1988 the parish dedicated a newly remodeled social hall. The active parish boasts its own Web site and several social and religious organizations, including a Parent-Teacher Union founded in 1932. Its Good Friday procession and annual Italian Festival, held over Labor Day weekend, highlight the spirituality and the spirit of a culture that continues to enhance the city's rich ethnic history.

Statue of St. Rocco

The Benjamin Rose Institute

The first act of kindness was directed toward a friend — someone who had fallen on hard times financially and needed assistance — but thousands have gone on to benefit from that act. They are individuals Benjamin Rose would never meet, but wanted to help.

Mr. Rose, a native of England, came to this country in 1848. After locating in Cleveland, he formed the Cleveland Provision Company, which eventually became one of the largest in the country. His wife, Julia, and his two children tragically preceded him in death.

Mr. Rose was deeply committed to his adopted community, and remembered it at his death in 1908. The bulk of Rose's $3 million estate was used to create The Benjamin Rose Institute, an organization to care for elderly persons in need. The institute pioneered in providing a safety net system for the poor, a concept later adopted by the federal government.

Initially, the agency provided monthly $17 stipends to the elderly. Often the money meant the difference between death and survival. The board of trustees, 15 prominent women hand-picked by Mr. Rose, visited recipients to evaluate the effectiveness of the assistance. "The practice set quality-of-life measures for the board to gauge the impact of the program," explains Alice Kethley, Ph.D., executive director of the institute.

The nature of that assistance changed after the passage of the 1935 Social Security Act. The agency purchased group homes and began caring for the elderly in homes provided for them. The homes served residents with the philosophy of addressing what people needed and what they wanted.

The 1960s brought new directions for the institute. The Margaret Blenkner Research Center attained national status as a leader in applied gerontology research. Other changes included the first use of home aides. Margaret Wagner House, a 111-bed skilled nursing facility, was constructed. It replaced the group homes.

Today, the institute continues its benefactor's mission. The institute is the city's seventh-largest nonprofit organization, with an annual budget of $24 million and employing 580 full- and part-time workers. Its Community Services Division serves 6,000 senior citizens annually through home health programs, telephone information and referral, senior companion and adult day programs. Kethley House at Benjamin Rose Place opened in 1997. The 184-bed skilled nursing facility houses residents who once lived at Margaret Wagner House.

The institute is involved in partnerships to further enhance care of the elderly. In 1986 Fairhill Center for Aging, a comprehensive campus of social, health, educational and enrichment services, was initiated with University Hospitals. In 1996 HealthRays Alliance, a coalition of 28 nonprofit, long-term care providers for joint planning, group purchasing and setting high standards for residential services, was started. Concordia Care, housed at Margaret Wagner House, resulted from a partnership with MetroHealth Systems. Concordia Care is a replication of a national PACE model, which serves very frail older persons who remain in their homes because of an enriched set of health and social services.

Mr. Rose set the example by helping his friend. The Benjamin Rose Institute continues to fulfill his mission by annually helping thousands of Clevelanders. Mr. Rose would be pleased.

"How can I help elderly men and women maintain their dignity, security and self-respect in their final years?"

This question tormented Sophia McCrosky, sister-in-law of Ambrose Morrison McGregor.

One day, as she glanced out the window at the idle farm across from her East Cleveland home, she had the answer: "Build a gracious, loving home for them on that unused land."

The land Sophia envisioned for her dream belonged to Ambrose and her sister, Tootie. It stood idle because Ambrose, an executive with John D. Rockefeller's Standard Oil Company, had moved the family to New York City in the 1880s.

When Ambrose died, Sophia shared her vision with Tootie. In 1904, as a memorial to her husband, Tootie donated land and money for the A. M. McGregor Home. Following standards of the day, it was incorporated as a non-denominational life-care facility.

In 1908 the stately A. M. McGregor Home opened at the northeast corner of Lee and Terrace Roads in East Cleveland. With Sophia heading its board of directors and strong support from the community — which it still enjoys — McGregor was soon sheltering a family of 25 residents.

Tootie died in 1912, leaving McGregor $100,000 and a substantial trust fund. Both were soon used to expand the facility's mission: quality care for the elderly. In 1916 the original building was enlarged to care for an additional 20 residents. In 1922 the purchase of two nearby farmhouses enabled the home to increase family membership to 65.

By the late 1930s all the buildings were showing their age. So in 1940 ground was broken for the country manor building that now graces the crest overlooking Lake Erie and Forest Hill Park. A year later the McGregor residents moved into their new home. In 1961, without disturbing the pastoral feel of the 32-acre campus surrounding the home, two wings were added that enabled the facility to increase the number of residents to 100.

The last 20 years have been a time of steady change for McGregor. While a number of life care residents still reside at McGregor, other choices, including Assisted Living, Respite, Convalescent and Hospice Care, have been offered since the early-1980s.

In 1987, due to the similarities in their missions, the A. M. McGregor Home and Amasa Stone House, founded in 1877, merged to form The McGregor Retirement Community. In 1992 the facility opened The Meadow, a safe and secure environment for persons with memory impairment.

Throughout the years, McGregor has partnered with the Benjamin Rose Institute and Eliza Bryant Center in the development of care services that reach a broader spectrum of elderly in the Greater Cleveland area. Today, McGregor prides itself on specializing in "high touch" rather than "high-tech" care to all of its residents.

As McGregor envisions a future of growth and expansion of services, it continues the mission of two sisters who, almost a hundred years ago, dreamed the dream of a gracious, serene and nurturing community for its residents.

The A.M. McGregor Home

Visiting Nurse Association of Cleveland

"Home health care makes health sense, family sense and economic sense," says Mary Lou Stricklin, president and CEO of the Visiting Nurse Association of Cleveland (VNA). "We at the Visiting Nurse Association are proud to care for Greater Clevelanders in their homes, delivering innovative, high-quality, cost-effective community health services to all." The VNA provides in-home health services including specialized nursing services, home care aides, rehabilitation services, health promotion and disease prevention. From its beginnings in Cleveland's neighborhoods, the VNA has expanded its services to a nine-county area covering most of the northeastern quarter of Ohio.

Founded in 1902, the VNA pioneered high-quality home health care for patients with limited access to hospital care, for communicable disease treatment and chronic health problems. When sophisticated procedures and technologies made hospitals the preferred sites for treatment, VNA initiated a system of follow-up care. Today, VNA maintains its mission of delivering care that promotes health, independence and dignity as the home regains its place in the health delivery system.

Working with United Way Services, VNA funds charitable care and teaches people to care for themselves and each other, while maintaining a tradition of health care innovation and the development of community-based programs. In 1903 the VNA's vanguard district nursing services (which stationed nurses at community locations)

exposed a significant rise in tuberculosis, leading to the foundation of the Anti-Tuberculosis League. Industrial nursing began when the VNA first assigned a nurse to the Cleveland Hardware Company in 1907. The next year a nurse was assigned to the Cleveland Board of Education, heralding the birth of modern school nursing. The VNA was among the first agencies to establish a fee-for-service policy under which families were charged according to their income. The VNA also pioneered in maternity and pediatric health care when, in 1908, it assigned nurses to the newly opened Western Reserve University Medical School Maternity Dispensary for prenatal and postpartum visits to in-home delivery patients.

Through the years, the agency established a wide array of services for the elderly, children, the terminally ill and other underserved people of the community. Today, VNA professional nursing services include pediatric and maternal care, behavioral health services, hospice care, older adult services, diabetic management and instruction, cardiac rehabilitation, infusion, chemo- and enterostomal therapies. Home care aides provide personal care, light housekeeping, meal planning and preparation, and companionship. Rehabilitation services include physical and occupational therapy, speech-language pathology, medical and behavioral social services and nutrition. Together, VNA and the Cleveland State University Division of Nursing founded "Vision on 22nd Street," an innovative educational practice partnership. VNA also serves as a living laboratory for students in all health professions.

The VNA anticipates continued success due to the increasing importance of home health care, which is more cost-effective and more comfortable for patients, and because sophisticated technology facilitates administration of complex procedures in the home. Additionally, VNA nurses can enhance care delivery through direct, online communication with physicians. "The most important effect of information technology will be its ability to transform the delivery of home care to a flexible network of people and services where needed," says Stricklin. "The VNA is prepared for and pursuing the information age's impact on home care, all the while sustaining the personal touch of a century of caring."

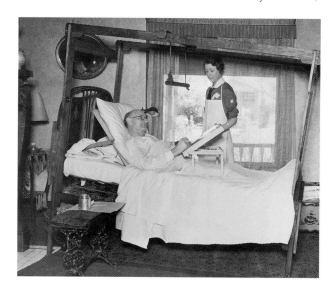

The Visiting Nurse Association has provided in-home health services since 1902.

City of Cleveland Heights

The city of Cleveland Heights preserves the distinct aspects of both a cosmopolitan suburb and a small town with a luxuriant green natural environment. Located on the eastern edge of Cleveland about 20 minutes from its downtown, Cleveland Heights is only minutes away from University Circle, which boasts more than 200 cultural, educational and medical facilities. Within its 8.14 square miles, Cleveland Heights designates 135 acres for parkland with recreational activities, including two outdoor swimming pools; tennis and basketball courts; and a community center with a year-round, Olympic-sized ice rink, indoor track, gymnasium, and child care and senior centers. Numerous programs, activities and special events are offered for residents of all ages.

A notable feature is Cain Park, a historic summer arts complex that presents two self-produced musicals; concerts headlining nationally prominent performers; an intimate cabaret series; an art gallery; and the Cain Park Arts Festival, which is rated as one of the top 10 festivals in the country. In addition to year-round cultural and recreation programs, Cleveland Heights contains unique neighborhood shopping districts, award-winning restaurants and the largest suburban public library system in Cuyahoga County.

In the 1800s, the area was a flourishing farm community with vineyards, orchards and a dairy. In the early 1890s, Patrick Calhoun, a cotton and railroad tycoon from the south, visited Cleveland on business. He recognized the potential of this naturally beautiful landscape on top of a bluff as an elite garden suburb for wealthy Clevelanders. With loans — including a substantial one from John D. Rockefeller, Sr. — Calhoun's subdivision, then known as Euclid Heights, was developed, using gently curved streets and English-derived street names. In 1903, with a population of 1,500, the village of Cleveland Heights was created and for a time conducted governmental business in the Superior Schoolhouse, now home to the Cleveland Heights Historical Center. Cleveland Heights was incorporated as a city in 1921.

Being at the top of a steep hill, Cleveland Heights could be difficult to access when the dirt roads became muddy, and the town's successful growth depended largely on the concurrent development of the electric streetcar. The first rail line entered the suburb around 1891, and the population expansion in the first three decades of the 20th century necessitated additional streetcar routes that continued to serve Cleveland Heights until 1949. Access to public transportation was important for people of all means. New streetcar lines and energetic developers rapidly transformed Cleveland Heights into a thriving suburb.

Historical development has created a city with eclectic building styles, including Colonial Revival, Tudor Revival, Craftsman and Bungalow, with some earlier Queen-Anne-style homes. Seven Cleveland Heights properties are listed on the National Register of Historic Places, as is Forest Hill Park. Four National Register Districts are located within the city's borders: Fairhill (partially), Fairmount Boulevard, Forest Hill (partially) and Overlook Road (Carriage House District).

Today, Cleveland Heights is a vibrant, thriving and diverse city of more than 54,000 interesting and talented residents with a strong sense of community.

Cleveland Heights has homes in every style imaginable, including gracious Colonials, stately Tudors, Arts and Crafts bungalows or contemporary ranches.

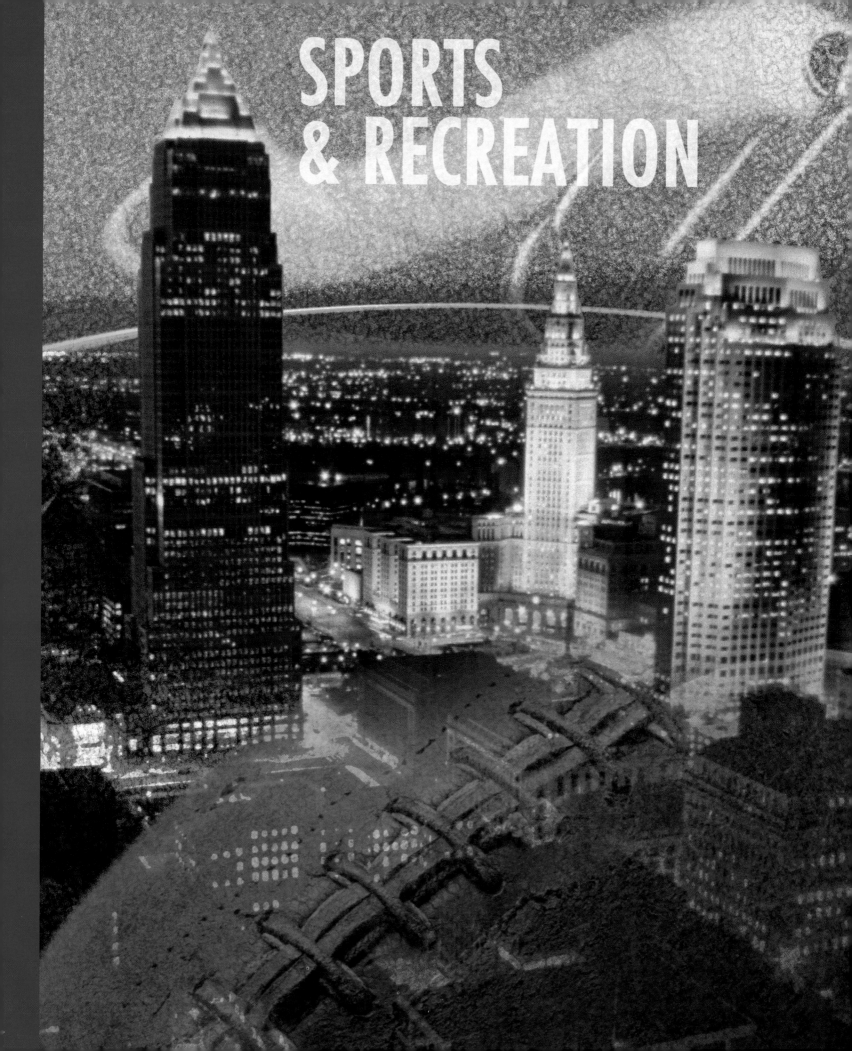

SPORTS & RECREATION

As a center for spectator sports and a variety of parks and recreation areas, Cleveland offers a myriad of leisure activities to its residents and visitors.

Cleveland Browns

World War II entered a new phase with the invasion of Europe by Allied forces on June 6, 1944. Cleveland professional football also tried to enter a new phase that year when a new Cleveland team tried to invade the previously sacrosanct National Football League. Arthur "Mickey" McBride, a Cleveland taxicab company owner, was rebuffed in 1944 when he attempted to purchase the existing Cleveland Rams.

Hall of Famer Jim Brown rushes for some of his team record 12,312 yards, set between 1957-65.
Post Gazette Photo by Morris Berman

At the urging of *Chicago Tribune* Sports Editor Arch Ward, who created baseball's All-Star Game, McBride and several other wealthy men formed a new professional football league in 1944. The All-America Football Conference (AAFC) was to start in 1946.

Although the Rams won the 1945 league championship, it was not drawing the fans its owners felt it should. As a result, in January 1946, the team became the first sports franchise to move to the West Coast. The newly renamed Los Angeles Rams left the local pro football field open to McBride's as-yet-nameless Cleveland franchise.

McBride liked football, but was not a "football man." At the recommendation of a Cleveland sports writer, he met with a young man named Paul Brown. Brown, who had

Otto Graham, Paul Brown's first quarterback, who led the team to AAFC championships and back-to-back championships in the NFL in 1954-55

coached at Ohio high school powerhouse Massillon Washington and at Ohio State (where his team was 1942 national champion), was coaching at the Great Lakes Naval Station near Chicago during the war.

Brown agreed to coach the new team in the new league, and brought in a variety of new methods and ideas. Those methods and procedures were so successful that the Browns (named for their coach after a McBride-sponsored contest) had a 47-4-3 record, winning the conference championship all four years of the league's existence.

One of Brown's new ideas was hiring black football players. (The relocated Los Angeles Rams helped break the color barrier that same year, a year before Jackie Robinson played his first major league baseball game.) The two players, Bill Willis of Ohio State and Marion Motley of the University of Nevada, went on to gain entrance into the Football Hall of Fame as did Brown, Otto Graham, Dante Lavelli, Lou Groza and Frank Gatski of that inaugural team.

The Browns' dominance and such economic facts of life as the cost of talent and dwindling attendance led to the demise of the AAFC and an approach by the NFL about a semi-merger in which only three AAFC teams were invited in.

In spite of the Browns' dominance in their league, NFL stalwarts looked askance at these upstarts. On September 16, 1950, the AAFC Browns met the Philadelphia Eagles, 1949 NFL champions, in Philadelphia's Shibe Park. To the consternation of the locals, the Browns scored in every quarter and rolled to a 35-10 victory.

It was the first of many victories and NFL championships. During the rest of the 50s, the Browns played in seven NFL title games, six straight, and won three. (The Super Bowl did not begin until 1967.)

In 1953 McBride sold his interest in the Browns to a group of local businessmen for $600,000. In 1961, Art Modell, a New York television advertising executive, purchased the team for $3.925 million. Two years later Modell fired long-time coach Brown in a still-controversial decision.

The change seemed positive in 1964 when the Browns defeated the Baltimore Colts 27-0 to win the NFL title. During the rest of the decade, the Browns won four divisional titles, but no championships.

Not winning championships almost seemed a "positive" during the 1970s when the Browns just about played .500 football and had only five winning seasons. That was one more season than coaches, as four came and went during the period.

In Cleveland one only has to mention the Kardiac Kids to recall the exciting Browns of the 80s. The appellation was the result of five 1980 games won in the last few minutes. The Browns had enough victories to make the playoffs seven times during the decade, but were 3-7 in the playoffs. Five of the losses were by five or less points.

After the semi-successes of the 1980s, the 1990 season's 3-13 record — worst in the team's history — seemed a dire omen of things to come. And not just on the playing field.

In November 1995 Modell announced he was going to move the Browns franchise to Baltimore. The last game at the Depression-era-built Cleveland Stadium was on December 17, 1995. Die-hard fans, many of whom had tear-streaked faces, walked out with stadium seats and any other memorabilia they could carry.

But rather than the beginning of the end, it became the end of the beginning.

Cleveland civic leaders and thousands of fans inundated NFL headquarters with calls, faxes and letters seeking return of a pro football team to Cleveland. In February 1996 the NFL agreed to put another team in Cleveland.

But fans didn't want just any team. They wanted the Browns. No expansion team! No new colors! No new logo! No records expunged! They wanted the Browns!

And in an unprecedented move, they got 'em. But it didn't come cheap.

Several groups and individuals expressed interest in taking over the "new" Browns, and the team that Modell bought for less than $4 million went for more than $500 million. The new owner was Al Lerner, founder of MBNA,

the nation's largest credit card company. The team not only had a new owner, it had a new $280 million stadium, erected on the site of its former glories.

On August 9, 1999, the "millennium" Browns took the field for their first exhibition game, part of the NFL's weekend Hall of Fame induction ceremonies and program. It was fitting that Ozzie Newsome, tight end for the "old" Browns, was inducted into the Hall of Fame. In addition to those previously mentioned, he joined Jim Brown, Len Ford, Bobby Mitchell, Paul Warfield, Mike McCormack and Leroy Kelly.

In 1950 Mickey McBride stormed out of an NFL meeting, saying, "They made a deal and now they don't want to go through with it."

Almost half a century later, the NFL went through with its deal. The future will be played out on the field.

Brian Sipe, quarterback of the Kardiac Kids, holds the team record for passing yards (23,713) and passing touchdowns (154).

Quarterback Tim Couch, from the University of Kentucky, first player drafted by the "new" Browns
© John Reid III

Cleveland Metroparks

The scenic wonders, beauty and vastness of the lands that make up Cleveland Metroparks owe their preservation to a young, self-taught engineer who had the courage and the perseverance to lobby for his vision. In his 1905 annual report, William A. Stinchcomb, the city's chief engineer of parks, wrote:

"Through the valleys of Rocky River on the west, and Chagrin River on the east, lie some of the finest stretches of natural park lands to be found in the northern part of Ohio. While all this is now entirely outside of the city, it will be but a short time before they will be inside or very near the limits of a 'Greater Cleveland' and it seems to me that such fine stretches of natural parkway should be secured for the benefit of the entire public before private enterprise or commercial industry places them beyond reach."

Like-minded West Side businessmen, wanting to preserve the Rocky River Valley, helped establish in 1912 a Board of Park Commissioners of Cuyahoga County; the board offered the position of engineer to Stinchcomb with the stipulation that he work without pay until the board could receive funding. Engaging the services of Frederick Law Olmsted of Massachusetts as landscape architect and consulting engineer, Stinchcomb laid out an extensive system consisting of large rural parks connected by scenic boulevards, all encircling the city of Cleveland. This plan created what is known as the "Emerald Necklace" which exists today in nearly the same configuration as was originally laid out in 1916. The Ohio legislature, in a bill passed on March 6, 1917, provided for "the conservation of natural resources by the creation, development and improvement of park districts." Stinchcomb, appointed the first director of the Cleveland Metropolitan Park District in 1921, continued to serve the people of northeast Ohio until his retirement in 1957 by guiding the development of the Park District and by acquiring additional lands for it.

Starting with a $195 purchase of less than four acres along the walls of the Rocky River Valley, the Park District has grown to encompass over 20,000 acres within 14 reservations. In the early days the priority was to obtain, through gifts whenever possible, as much land as could be had before urban expansion devoured natural habitats and drove up real estate prices. With the Great Depression came, ironically, an opportunity to pursue the improvement phase. Employing thousands of jobless citizens through President Franklin D. Roosevelt's work relief projects, the Park District was able to forge ahead with opening up the acquired wilderness to the public. The Civilian Conservation Corps (CCC), Works Projects Administration (WPA), Public Works Administration (PWA) and the Federal Employment Relief Agency (FERA) provided more than 5,000 men who laid water mains; built roads, retaining walls, trails, culverts, shelterhouses, water fountains and toilets; cleared and graded picnic grounds and parking areas; and transplanted thousands of trees and shrubs. By 1939 the "Emerald Necklace" could tally 55 miles of roads suitable for automobiles, 53 miles of foot trails, 10 shelterhouses, 33 picnic grounds and many other amenities to make it undeniably a visitor-friendly environment.

From the beginning, the reservations of Cleveland Metroparks have been connected to one another; the ability to travel from one natural area to another through a trail linkage affords atypical opportunities for recreation. This concept of interconnection within a park system is best exemplified by the Ohio & Erie Canal Reservation, the newest park, whose 7.2 miles of trails connect to the existing 20-mile Towpath Trail of the Cuyahoga Valley National Recreation Area (CVNRA). Portions of both trails are incorporated into the 87-mile National Heritage Corridor, which follows the route of the Ohio & Erie Canal built in the early 1800s.

As early as 1930 the Park District had a naturalist, Arthur B. Williams, who interpreted the unique habitats of the Cleveland area to visitors, instilling in them as he put it, "a friendly and sympathetic attitude toward wildlife." In July 1931 the Park District opened its first trailside museum in the North Chagrin Reservation.

This unique connection among individual parks is also beneficial for wildlife because it, too, can move about the "Emerald Necklace" within natural habitats vs. isolated green spaces surrounded by houses and industry. This concern for wildlife made the annexing of the city's zoo in 1975 by the Park District an appropriate move. Cleveland Metroparks Zoo, the seventh oldest in the country, was founded in 1882 when Jeptha H. Wade donated to Cleveland 14 white-tailed deer and 73 acres of land on the eastern edge of the city. When it was determined that the Cleveland Museum of Art was to be built nearby, it was also decided to relocate the growing zoo to the west side of Cleveland to accommodate further expansion. The main building at the new Brookside Park, Wade Hall, was completed in 1909 and currently houses a gift shop and ice cream parlor.

Having been managed by the city of Cleveland, the Cleveland Museum of Natural History and the Cleveland Zoological Society, the Cleveland Metroparks Zoo is now under the management of the Park District. It is a modern, world-class facility benefiting from the investment of over $60 million in the last 25 years. With a new master plan intact, the Zoo began to restructure its 168 acres into regions based on the bioclimatic life zones — or biomes — found throughout the world. This method of presentation shows the inherent intermingling among plants, animals and humans of each biome. Covering more than two acres, The RainForest, which opened in 1992, depicts the complexity of life within this rapidly disappearing jungle ecosystem that generates about 20 percent of the oxygen supply for the entire planet.

Wolf Wilderness presents the environment and its wildlife of a northern temperate forest, while Australian Adventure, the most recent and the largest biological habitat exhibit, focuses on teaching young children about Australian wildlife and acquainting them with the role of animals on a working ranch. Education is one of the missions of the Zoo — to combine recreation with learning and to turn this educational experience into a commitment to preserve the world's diminishing wildlife.

It is the Zoo's goal of preservation that joins it to Cleveland Metroparks with its mission of conserving natural resources and providing a pleasant environment in which to appreciate and learn about nature while also enjoying it.

The RainForest, completed in 1992, showcases 10,000 plants and 600 animals from the jungles of Africa, Asia, and the Americas. This unique two-acre, two-level exhibit is one of the largest of its kind in the country.

Squire's Castle was built at the turn of the century and was to serve as the gatehouse to the large country estate of F.B. Squire, an oil magnate. The remainder of the estate never materialized and the castle is now part of North Chagrin Reservation.

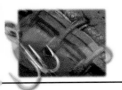

Cedar Point®

Listing the awards, honors and firsts Cedar Point has accumulated can be as dizzying as riding one of its amazing roller coasters.

With 68 rides over 364 acres, the Sandusky park has three times been voted the Best Amusement Park in the World by readers of *Amusement Today*, an industry publication. Cedar Point has also received the Applause Award from the International Association of Amusement Parks and Attractions, the industry's most prestigious honor.

Cedar Point's Millennium Force™ is the world's first giga-coaster. America's tallest and fastest roller coaster was introduced in 2000.
Photo by Dan Feicht

Cedar Point has 14 coasters in all, according to the *Guinness Book of World Records Millennium Edition*, including Millennium Force™, at 310 feet tall the world's first coaster to break the 300-foot barrier, with speeds of 93 miles per hour.

Cedar Point's history began in 1867, when *The Sandusky Register* discussed interest in bathhouse facilities on the breezy peninsula. In 1870 an enterprising businessman built a bathhouse at Cedar Point and ferried bathers across Sandusky Bay. By 1880 the first amusement ride appeared — a water trapeze that whirled riders above Lake Erie. The first roller coaster debuted in 1892.

Visionary businessman George A. Boeckling took control of the resort in 1897. His leadership brought amazing growth that continued for 30 years. Entertainment and amusement park rides became fixtures. In 1905 Boeckling opened the grand Hotel Breakers. Nearly 100 years later, its magnificent chandeliers and Tiffany windows still enchant visitors.

Daily excursion trains and steamship service from nearby cities, including Cleveland, sparked the love affair Clevelanders have had with Cedar Point ever since.

With the Depression and Boeckling's death in 1931, the resort's growth stalled for more than 25 years. In the 1930s and 1940s visitors were entertained by big bands in the Coliseum ballroom, but their numbers were dwindling.

A real estate syndicate headed by George Roose of Toledo and Emile Legros of Cleveland bought the park in 1956. Their initial plans were to turn Cedar Point into a housing development, but inspired by the success of Disneyland, they decided to give it a try as an amusement park. Their $16 million investment in 1960 heralded the rebirth of the historic park as a modern family theme park.

Today, Cedar Point operates under the management of Cedar Fair L.P., a publicly traded master limited partnership. Since the late 1980s President and CEO Richard Kinzel has crafted continual surprises as the park continues to break records in everything from its world-famous coasters to its cutting-edge business management and creativity.

During the past decade, the park has made major improvements that have changed Cedar Point's skyline forever. Five world record-breaking roller coasters amazed thrillseekers. Camp Snoopy, populated by the delightful PEANUTS™ characters, charmed families. On the resort side, Sandcastle Suites, the 10-story Breakers Tower, Breakers Express and Soak City® water park encouraged overnight visits.

Even though much has changed since 1870, one thing has not: the smiles that guests have been sharing since the first ferry crossed Sandusky Bay. The same smiles are sure to be echoed at Cedar Point in the future, as Lake Erie's summertime tradition continues with the very best in family fun and excitement.

Cleveland Crunch

The Crunch is an appropriate name for a team that has done just that to its opponents since the Cleveland team joined the indoor Major Soccer League (MSL) in 1989. Although the MSL folded its nets in July 1992, the Crunch joined the National Professional Soccer League (NPSL) the following month, where it continued to defeat its rivals on a regular basis.

In the first decade of its existence, the team won three league championships and seven conference championships. When the Crunch won the 1993-94 NPSL championship, it was Cleveland's first sports championship since the football Browns won a title in 1964, before the Super Bowl.

As one measure of its potency, beginning in 1993 a Crunch team member was named league MVP in seven out of eight years. Hector Marinaro has won it an unprecedented six times and teammate Zoran Karic once.

When the Crunch joined the NPSL in 1992, it also shifted its home venue from the Richfield Coliseum to the downtown Cleveland State Convocation Center. With a season that overlaps those of Cleveland's other major sports teams, the Crunch manages a very respectable average attendance of 8,000 in the Convocation Center.

The growing popularity of indoor soccer is the result of a high-scoring game with rapid ball movement. In fact, indoor soccer is more comparable in many ways to hockey than it is to its outdoor counterpart. Like hockey, there are penalties assessed, with the guilty party sent to a penalty box. There are no yellow cards, no red cards and resulting disqualification. The ball can be played off the dasher boards that surround the field and scoring is predicated upon from where on the field the shot is made.

In late 1999 North Coast Professional Sports, LLC purchased the team. Under the direction of President and General Manager Paul Garofolo, the Crunch has expanded its marketing program and increased its commitment to, and expanded its presence in, the community.

During the summer of 2000 the Cleveland Crunch teamed up with the Cuyahoga County Public Library to promote the Young Adult Summer Reading Program. A poster featuring three Crunch players surrounding a stack of library books was available to all reading-program participants.

The team's summer soccer camps, which in 1999 drew 600 campers to 13 sites, attracted 3,000 campers to more than 50 sites in 2000. The camps offer a variety of programs for players of varying skills between the ages of 4-18. In 2000 the Crunch introduced a girls' team program staffed exclusively by young women.

Before the start of the 2000-2001 season, the NPSL expansion Toronto Thunder Hawks contacted the Crunch for advice and recommendations, indicating its management had been told the Cleveland Crunch was the league's prototypical team and it should be the team on which to model itself.

The recommendation proves that regardless of what league the team plays in or on which home field it plays its games, the Cleveland Crunch players have learned that they can get their kicks from soccer.

Perennial all-star and league MVP Hector Marinaro
Photo by Bill Barrett Photography

Celebrating after winning the 1998-99 NPSL championship

The Convention & Visitors Bureau
of Greater Cleveland

The Convention & Visitors Bureau of Greater Cleveland is an independent, non-profit organization responsible for promoting Greater Cleveland as the destination of choice. Its efforts have increased travel to nearly 8 million visitors annually. The economic impact is even greater, travel and tourism is generating more the $2.3 billion for the local economy each year, making the hospitality business one of the largest industries for the Cleveland area.

In 1934, when the CVB was established, it was hard to imagine Greater Cleveland becoming the gem it is today. The city and surrounding area have blossomed into one of the nation's most interesting cities, and naturally travel and tourism have flourished.

In promoting the renaissance, the CVB addresses specific travel and tourism markets to ensure maximum success.

The Convention Sales and Marketing Department is responsible for the development of convention, meeting and trade show business to national, regional, state, local and corporate organizations. These markets are reached through aggressive direct sales, advertising, communications, special events and direct marketing. A program called Team Cleveland targets those in the Cleveland area as well. This grass-roots effort asks residents and local businesses to look only to their backyards when their groups and associations need to schedule meetings.

Working hand in hand with Convention Sales and meeting planners to ensure a successful event is the Convention Services Department. The department serves as a liaison between the customer and the members of the CVB. The main goal is for each visitor and convention delegate to have an enjoyable and memorable experience during their stay, resulting in many return visits to Greater Cleveland.

The Travel and Tourism Department works to position Greater Cleveland and Northeast Ohio as the "destination of choice" for leisure, group and international travelers. Using marketing, sales, promotion and public relations initiatives, the department provides opportunities for members to generate additional business by increasing their exposure to target markets.

The Business Development Department advances the mission of the CVB to impact economic vitality and quality of life for Northeast Ohio and member businesses by serving the membership base. The CVB offers valuable networking, educational and marketing opportunities to engage members in the development of the area's travel and tourism industry and to develop opportunities for members to increase sales. The benefits of membership include access to CVB resources such as video footage of Cleveland, providing materials to enhance recruitment efforts, still images for corporate publications, resource referral for meetings, corporate events, and entertaining and hosting out-of-town clients. In addition, the CVB offers a seminar in customer service that can be tailored to specific businesses.

The Community Affairs and Special Projects Department develops projects and relationships that enhance the recognition of the tourism industry as a stable economic generator. One such program, the Spirit of Hospitality, provides career training to individuals on public assistance. The training is in the hospitality industry and once completed, job placement is done within the hospitality community.

Hospitality is a leading industry in the Cleveland area, and an industry in which the corporate community has a stake.

Photo by Louie Anderson

In the early-1950s long-time Lake Countians began talking about preserving the county's dwindling natural areas, but it wasn't until 1958, when Lake County's commissioners published the results of a land-use study, that talk turned into action. The far-sighted study, citing the county's explosive population growth and evaporating green space, recommended the creation of "a system of large open space reservations and park lands." That fall, county residents voted to create the Lake Metroparks.

In 1959, Bill Wyman — whose roots reached deep into the county's past — donated 30 acres of land along the Grand River to the new park system in memory of his mother, Helen Hazen Wyman. With Wyman's donation, Lake Metroparks began its mission of preserving, maintaining and protecting Lake County's unique natural areas. Today, with a budget of approximately $10 million and 26 parks encompassing over 6,000 acres, Lake Metroparks serves the recreational and educational needs of nearly two million visitors a year. A dedicated staff is supported by over 2,000 volunteers who assist in virtually all areas of park system programming, including environmental and recreational pursuits, animal care and the planning and implementation of some 60 special events annually.

The park system grew slowly. The first naturalist came on board in 1964; the first executive director was hired in 1972. Parks were acquired or land was added to already existing parks through donations, carefully planned purchases, management agreements or long-term leases. By 1980 the park system had grown to 19 properties — including the geologically unique Penitentiary Glen Reservation, secluded Hidden Valley Park, beachside Lakeshore Reservation, rugged Chapin Forest Reservation and the well-groomed Erie Shores Golf Course. But at 3,500 green acres, it was still only a little over half the size of today's park system.

The Lake Metroparks' major growth, in terms of land acquisition, staffing, programs and services came with the passage of the first major parks levy in 1986. The levy, renewed in 1996, gave Lake Metroparks the funds needed to dramatically increase purchases of natural areas. It also allowed the park system to increase its commitment to "green" education with the purchase of the 235-acre Lake Farmpark (designated the nation's best new theme park by the National Association of County Park & Recreation Organizations when it opened in 1990), and the expansion and renovation of Penitentiary Glen Nature Center. Farmpark, a working farm where visitors can learn about all aspects of agriculture, educates almost 200,000 visitors a year. The Nature Center at Penitentiary Glen welcomes over 150,000 visitors and its Wildlife Center receives nearly 2,000 animals for rehabilitation annually.

The last few years have brought challenges that Lake Metroparks' leaders see as a way to further fulfill its mission, such as to create the consensus needed to lay a north-south bike trail from the Geauga County Line to the mouth of the Grand River, and to expand mutually beneficial partnerships with the private sector. Lake Metroparks works collaboratively with like-minded organizations such as the Ohio Parks and Recreation Association, Grand River Partners, Cleveland Museum of Natural History and the Lake County Historical Society. Lake Metroparks is teaching the three environmental "Rs": reverence, respect and responsibility for the land, while preserving and maintaining Lake County's green jewels — now, and for the generations to come.

Lake Farmpark welcomes 200,000 visitors a year.

TECHNOLOGY

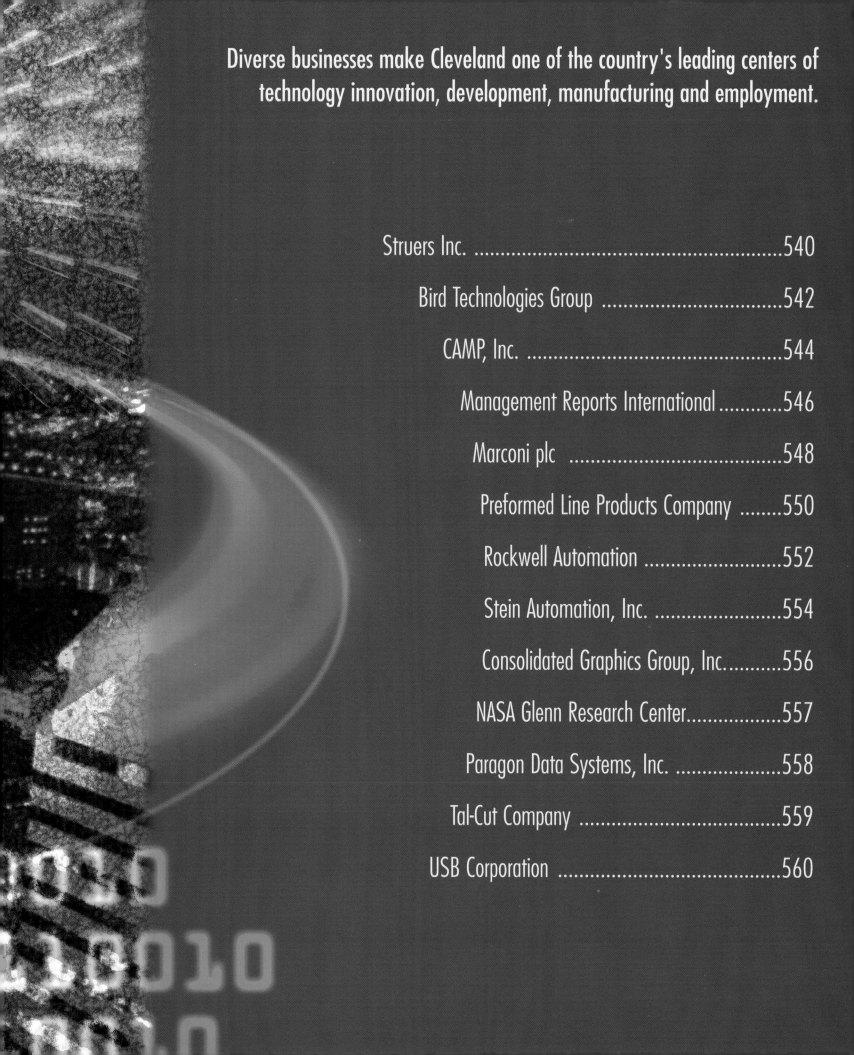

Diverse businesses make Cleveland one of the country's leading centers of technology innovation, development, manufacturing and employment.

Struers Inc.

When a manufacturing company wants to improve the quality of its products or detect a possible cause for failure, it often turns to Struers for help. By designing, manufacturing, selling and supporting the world's leading equipment and consumables for materialographic surface preparation, Struers helps thousands of companies around the world with an increasingly vital phase in modern industry — the preparation of solid materials for examination under a microscope. A nearly limitless list of materials used in many manufacturing processes are typically cut, mounted, ground and polished to ultimately reveal their true microstructure. Once this has been completed, a solid evaluation of the material can begin. The indispensable results can be seen in almost every form of modern technology available today, such as safer automobile airbags, more-efficient jet engines and longer-lasting materials used for artificial joint replacements.

Holger F. Struer (1846 - 1931) founded Struers in Denmark in 1875.

Struers was founded in Denmark by Holger F. Struer in 1875 and was originally a supplier of traditional laboratory equipment. In 1944, a Danish scientist, Eggert Knuth-Winterfeldt, invented a small, yet revolutionary machine for electrolytic polishing of metal samples. Soon after, Struers A/S, the European parent company to Struers Inc., began selling these and other materialographic equipment and consumables to laboratories and manufacturers throughout Europe.

In the early 1970s Struers invented a truly advanced group of products — the Abra line — that revolutionized the industry by automating much of the materialographic process and differentiating itself from the manual equipment of the day. Struers' grinding and polishing equipment — Abraplan, Abrapol and Abramin — allowed operators to prepare more specimens at a faster rate and yet return a higher-quality finished product. Remarkably, the Abra line continues to be a mainstay of the Struers product line and a strong contributor to the company's success.

The type of revolutionary thinking that invented this unique product group also formed the basis for the company's current success based on Knowledge, Quality and Process Control. Struers' unparalleled history and knowledge of the materialographic industry enables it to provide its customers with the most technologically advanced, yet cost-efficient products available. Coupling this with outstanding quality (many of the original Abra machines are still in use today) has led Struers to become the world leader in its field. By improving the science and processes involved in materialography, Struers enables its customers to produce better products, whether it is through improvements in research and development or subtle changes in production techniques.

Based on the success brought about by these three principles, Struers Inc. was formed in 1976 and began selling groundbreaking products from its headquarters based in Cleveland, chosen for its large concentration of steel and automotive industries. Even though Struers products were more of an investment than those of its competitors were, the technological advances and high-quality results made them an unbelievable success.

The range of truly unique products continued to grow rapidly throughout the late 1970s and early 1980s, encompassing everything from sophisticated cut-off machines to computerized, fully automatic preparation solutions. Most notable was the invention of the Prepamatic in the early

In the late 1800s and early 1900s Struers was a supplier of traditional laboratory equipment.

1980s. Prepamatic was the first fully automated, microprocessor-controlled machine that could prepare up to nine material specimens at once. Given that it works totally unattended, can prepare almost any material and offers an extremely high rate of reproducibility, the Prepamatic allows the operator to concentrate on other aspects of the job rather than specimen preparation.

In the early 1990s Struers once again revolutionized the industry when it invented and introduced the Modular Automatic Preparation System (MAPS). MAPS brought the concept of fully automatic specimen preparation to high-volume facilities working with large pieces. Never before could laboratory personnel automatically prepare multiple 3-inch pieces of steel or titanium and get quality results. This revolutionary product once again helped to solidify Struers' lead in the materialographic field.

Struers also takes great pride in its development of advanced consumable products such as rigid grinding disc technology (RGD), which consolidated several grinding steps into one and resulted in excellent preparation quality. Most recently, Struers stunned the materialographic world with the introduction of the MD System, a completely new line of grinding and polishing consumables that reduces costs, eliminates many preparation steps and increases the quality of the finished specimen.

Another Struers creation is The Metalog Guide. This valuable book was completed in the early 1990s and is the world's first complete guide to materialographic specimen preparation. The Metalog Guide capitalizes on the years of experience of Struers materialographers to combine thousands of different processes for preparing materials into 10 standard scientific preparation procedures. The Metalog Guide offers efficient and systematic guidelines to help metallographers do a better job in their everyday work. It is just one of the ways that Struers demonstrates its unsurpassed commitment to excellent customer service. The company also typically sends one or two staff members to train users on the operation of its equipment. And if one of its pieces of equipment happens to malfunction, Struers will travel to the customer site to service it. In addition the company has four experienced, full-time metallographers on staff to research and answer questions or problems a customer may have. Buying materialographic equipment from Struers can be a significant investment for a company,

but the quality technology and service it receives in return ensures that it is an investment worth making.

Struers A/S also has daughter companies in eight countries throughout Europe and Asia as well as a worldwide network of dealers. The list of U.S. customers served by Struers Inc. encompasses almost every major corporation that works with materials, including Boeing, Ford Motor Co., General Motors Corp., TRW Inc., General Electric, Intel Corp. and Johnson & Johnson, among many others.

Struers is proud to be able to give back to the local community through its work with Cleveland's Business Volunteerism Council. Through the council, the company's Cleveland employees can take two paid days off a year to volunteer for an activity of their choosing. Struers will remain committed to supporting the Cleveland community as it maintains its record of steady growth. Though the demand for materialographic equipment from U.S. corporations has remained steady during the past few decades, the company's sales have continued to rise, confirming the increase in demand for its advanced products over its competitors.

It only makes sense that the company that continually revolutionizes its industry by inventing, selling and supporting the most advanced technological products on the market should remain No. 1 in the future. Struers' main goal is to make its distance from No. 2 even bigger as it leads the way with even more new and exciting products that solve today's problems while paving the way for tomorrow's solutions.

Struers' Prepamatic-2 is a fully automated, microprocessor-controlled machine that prepares up to nine material specimens at once, all while completely unattended.

Bird Technologies Group

Brief History

When industry legend J. Raymond Bird earned his master's degree in electrical engineering from the Massachusetts Institute of Technology in 1932, the relatively new phenomenon of radio broadcasting was fast becoming a household necessity.

Following his education, Mr. Bird first worked as an assistant chief engineer for radio station WGAR, and later as chief engineer for Astatic Corporation, which specialized in microphones.

Legendary Model 43 Wattmeter

The many products that the Bird companies design and produce fall into the following technology groups: portable test and measurement instruments, RF sensors, dummy loads and attenuators and site peripheral products.

Industry's first fully digital portable RF power measurement instrument

In 1942 he founded the Bird Engineering Company in Cleveland, which was later incorporated as the Bird Electronic Corporation. During his lifetime, he was identified with over 40 patents. Many consider his most significant contribution to be a fast,

TX RX Multicoupler Subsystem

simple and accurate method of measuring radio frequency (RF) forward and reflected power in coaxial transmission lines. Until Bird devised his breakthrough technique,

taking such measurements required tedious, time-consuming procedures.

This technique, or Thruline Principle, as it came to be known, remains a trademark for the company today. It became the industry standard as well as the basic operating theory behind countless instruments used for RF power measurement. In 1952 the legendary model 43 Thruline Wattmeter was introduced and is still in use nearly 50 years later.

Bird Technologies Group

In 1995 Bird Technologies Group was created by the vision of the new board of directors, headed by David Hessler, to become the parent corporation for building the future of the three "Bird" companies. Today, Bird Technologies Group is recognized as a worldwide leader in the ever-changing market for wireless communications equipment and components based on RF technology.

The many products that the Bird companies design and produce fall into the following technology groups: portable test and measurement instruments, RF sensors, dummy loads and attenuators and site peripheral products.

Expansion into Site Peripheral Products (TX RX Systems Inc.)

With the 1995 acquisition of TX RX Systems Inc. located in Angola, New York, BTG expanded its product offerings and capabilities to include a broad range of site peripheral products.

TX RX designs and manufactures multicouplers, combiners, duplexers, signal boosters, antenna and a range of RF components for an industrially diversified customer base in the public safety, land mobile radio, wireless communication and government agency markets.

The company enjoys a distinctive reputation for engineered products of the highest quality and performance in its key markets.

The Bird name is being renewed by some of the best and brightest people the "world of RF" has to offer.

Daniel P. Kaegebein, the legendary founder of TX RX, served in the dual capacity of president and chief technologist for approximately 25 years of his distinguished career. Mr. Kaegebein remains technically active in the company, serving as president emeritus and chief technologist at the time of this publication.

Bird Component Products

Located near Tampa, Florida, Bird Component Products designs and produces a broad range of RF components. Its products are used by a broad range of customers in all segments of the expanding wireless industry.

Growing Recognition in an Expanding World

The products of the Bird companies are sold around the world to a broad base of customers in the communications, public safety, semiconductor, broadcast, medical equipment, test and measurement, and defense industries. Its product lines are expanding through internal development, joint ventures and acquisitions.

The brand recognition of each Bird company is distinguished by the indelible commitment to customer service, technical innovation, product reliability and employee empowerment.

Ideals Beyond Cutting-Edge Innovation

Each Bird company is more than a technical enterprise with cutting-edge innovations. Brilliant product solutions and applications are tempered by a devotion to a belief in long-term relationships with customers, suppliers and employees. The Bird companies have understood that creation needs an environment open to trial and error — a place where ideas are as crucial as the product solutions that ultimately reflect them. Bird Technologies Group is a growing corporation whose ideals are based on providing its best to its customers while enriching the quality of life of its employees around the globe.

In 1998 the Bird companies began their "Journey to World Class Excellence" under the leadership of Richard Hannan, the first outside president to lead the privately held corporation.

The Bird name is being renewed by some of the best and brightest people the "world of RF" has to offer. To honor its pledge to continuous improvement and employee empowerment, the Bird companies share a portion of their annual profits with all associates through a corporate-wide Gainsharing incentive program.

Each Bird company is more than a technical enterprise with cutting-edge innovations. Brilliant product solutions and applications are tempered by a devotion to a belief in long-term relationships with customers, suppliers and employees.

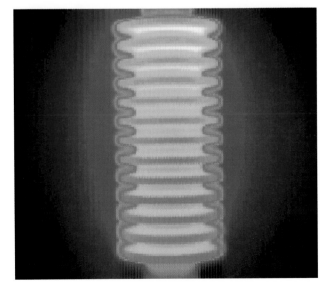

Bird engineers deploy the latest analytical and modeling tools.

CAMP, Inc.

Cleveland was built on industry. From the early days after the Civil War to the late 1970s, the city's economy thrived on the manufacturing of products such as steel and iron. However, times took a turn for the worse when the rust belt recession of 1981 hit. Companies began moving out of the area or downsizing, and the future of Cleveland's manufacturing industry looked bleak.

Cleveland Tomorrow, a group of top executives from the area's largest companies, knew something had to be done if Cleveland's economy was to survive. Pat Parker, chairman of the board for Parker Hannifin Corporation and Cleveland Tomorrow, decided that a nonprofit organization was needed to help resurrect Cleveland's manufacturing base. This organization became known as the Cleveland Advanced Manufacturing Program, or CAMP.

Robert Brown, a retired senior vice president from Eaton Corporation, was recruited to act as CAMP's president. Around the same time, the state of Ohio announced an initiative to help solve similar problems statewide called the Thomas Edison Technology Program. The small group of executives who constituted CAMP in those first few months of existence got together a proposal and, in 1984, CAMP was chosen as an Edison Center. It now had both the funding and the recognition it needed to begin its mission of motivating and helping regional manufacturers become more competitive.

CAMP remained small throughout the 1980s, with a very limited staff operating out of the back offices of Parker Hannifin. Brown saw the solution to Cleveland's economic problems in local universities, which possessed both the technology and the expertise that, if facilitated, could help Cleveland's manufacturing companies prosper. So began CAMP's relationships with Case Western Reserve University, Cleveland State University (CSU) and Cuyahoga Community College — partnerships between public and private sectors that would be vital to its future success.

CAMP's alliance with CSU is unique because the university didn't originally have any knowledge of manufacturing technologies. But it did have an empty building. So CAMP, with the help of a grant from Ameritrust, started the Advanced Manufacturing Center, a facility dedicated to strengthening the region's manufacturing base by providing the products, processes, ideas and people needed to become internationally competitive. Automation machinery design, engineering analysis and process optimization are just some of the services provided by CSU students and faculty. It's an idea that not only benefits local businesses, but is also a hands-on learning experience for the students.

Toward the end of the 1980s, a defining event changed CAMP's focus and incited its further growth. It was 1988 when CAMP was chosen by the National Institute of Standards and Technology as one of its first three federal manufacturing technology centers. This resulted in additional funding and, more importantly, a new challenge for CAMP. It now had to develop methods for helping not only large companies, but smaller to medium-size companies as well — over 3,000 manufacturers in 22 counties surrounding Cleveland.

Universities could do very little for smaller companies, so CAMP began building a permanent staff that could either directly deliver needed services or manage subcontractors. It expanded its services from development to deployment — bringing existing technologies into smaller companies so they can stay competitive, remain in Cleveland and avoid laying off employees.

Similar organizations throughout the United States that were also trying to ensure the stability of local manufacturers now saw CAMP as a model. It essentially had

Solid relationships with major area universities enable CAMP to offer customers a unique blend of state-of-the-art technical and academic expertise.

created a new type of business — a nonprofit organization utilizing the most advanced business practices available for the increased profit of local industries. Though limited by a nonprofit salary structure, CAMP is able to recruit a staff of over 180 people motivated by a challenge and a desire to help.

A recent growth period for CAMP came in 1994 when, even before the widespread public use of the Internet, it predicted the importance of electronic commerce to the survival of business. It discovered a program in the Department of Defense that was attempting to prepare defense agencies and contractors to do business electronically. CAMP competed for the bid and was soon designated as an Electronic Commerce Resource Center for the Department of Defense. Consequently, CAMP developed electronic commerce capabilities, not only for federal defense contractors, but for all of its clients.

This experience led to CAMP's newest venture, called A.C.C.E.S.S., the Ameritech CAMP Center for E-commerce Services and Solutions. At A.C.C.E.S.S. businesses can learn, develop and implement the latest information technologies to build a better company. The center includes a hands-on demonstration center, a training lab and a customer solutions center.

In addition to its own amazing growth — CAMP has quadrupled in size since 1990 — it has hundreds of success stories from businesses that have come to CAMP for answers. As a small local electronics manufacturer, Sterling Co. depended upon its contract with General Motors (GM) to survive. In 1991 that contract was in jeopardy when GM learned it could get an electrical device manually assembled much cheaper in Asia. CAMP stepped in and built a machine for Sterling that not only

allowed it to keep its GM contract, but eventually led to Sterling becoming GM's sole contractor for the device.

Carol Latham and her company, Thermagon, is another one of CAMP's success stories. When Ms. Latham introduced T-Flex, a revolutionary, thermally conductive material in 1994, it quickly became popular with manufacturers. T-Flex got a big boost in 1995 when Intel, the giant manufacturer of computer processing chips, not only used it in its Pentium® processor, but also recommended it to other manufacturers. Ms. Latham was thrilled, but concerned about keeping up with the increased demand. Fortunately, she came to CAMP's Advanced Manufacturing Center at CSU for help. The center not only developed the equipment needed to manufacture T-flex faster and better, it helped involve the local Hispanic community as employees of the growing plant.

Recognizing both a need by local manufacturers for trained employees and the lack of good job opportunities for welfare recipients, CAMP helped create one of its most significant success stories, CET, the Center for Employment Training. CET is a partnership program involving CAMP and several other organizations, including city and county agencies, that provides marketable vocational education, training and support services to low-income people. Occupations that provide good wages such as welding, machining and printing are among the courses taught at an individual pace in a real-world work environment. CET students graduate to jobs at local manufacturers that are pleased to hire people who are job-ready.

CAMP is also ready — ready for its continued growth as a parent organization, creating centers that deliver expert technical, business and training services to the regional manufacturers that are the backbone of Cleveland.

With a strong assist from Parker Hannifin, CAMP began operations at Parker's headquarters on Euclid Avenue. Today, with CEO Duane E. Collins at Parker's helm, it remains a staunch supporter of CAMP's efforts to maintain manufacturing excellence in northeast Ohio.

CAMP's Manufacturing Learning Center is molding tomorrow's manufacturing workforce, offering students experience in setting up and operating today's high-tech machinery.

Management Reports International

Since 1971, Management Reports International (MRI) has remained on the cutting edge — providing property managers, developers and owners from the office, industrial, retail and residential management industries with the latest solutions to their information and accounting needs.

As a leader in its field, MRI's clients include some of the world's largest businesses. Its clients worldwide have many choices. The MRI for Windows client/server software suites include solutions for every phase of real estate and asset management. Clients can choose to manage their own in-house solution or turn to MRI's experts for application hosting.

MRI's application hosting service, known as NetSource, utilizes the latest technologies to provide access to MRI for Windows from anywhere around the world. MRI hosts the system in Cleveland. NetSource is the latest

Committed to client service, MRI offers the most advanced equipment, the latest technologies, and extensive expertise in the real estate technology industry.

generation of MRI's three decades of experience as an application service provider, which makes MRI the oldest and largest application service provider in the real estate management industry.

All of MRI's products earn high ratings from reviewers and are recommended by national accounting firms and associations. Its software products are customizable and include a "tool kit" that helps the client tailor it to meet their specific needs, giving the client unprecedented control.

MRI prides itself on the superior quality of its client support services. Its toll-free hotline number is manned by a dedicated team of professionals and provides fast and effective support to users regardless of their location. It offers a wide variety of personalized training services performed by its own employees and conducted either on-site or at MRI's corporate training center in Cleveland. In addition, MRI will send its expert implementation group to install, execute and adapt its systems to suit the client's specific requirements.

Though MRI today inhabits almost an entire building in Beachwood, Ohio, it began in just one of the building's small offices. From the start, MRI's goal was to provide quality information services and solutions to the property and asset management industry on a national level. MRI's first computer, the IBM 360-20, produced reports that were logical and easy to use. Real estate owners and managers

The MRI solution is used on five continents and in 20 countries. Here a client in the United Kingdom uses MRI for Windows client/server software to turn property management information into intelligence.

across the country used the company's batch processing and online computer services to process rent receipts, write checks and produce financial statements and other property reports.

In 1977 MRI developed and patented a pegboard system, a one-of-a-kind solution for companies who manage remote residential properties. At its peak, over half a million managers across the country used it.

During the 1980s the market was rapidly changing as businesses starting purchasing their own computers and producing their own reports. MRI traveled the county and listened intently to clients and other large commercial management companies — an approach that the company continues today. MRI exceeded client expectations by creating complex reports with more information than had ever been seen before.

In 1984 the company was changed forever with the acquisition of Real Estate Computer Systems, a small software company in Atlanta. Suddenly, a revolution was underway as MRI became a software developer.

In the 1990s MRI grew rapidly, tripling its number of employees. It also went global — selling its innovative software products around the world. By 1997 it had opened offices in the United Kingdom, South Africa, Australia and Singapore. Today, the MRI solution is used in more than 20 countries, and MRI's worldwide client base continues to expand.

Though MRI offices are worldwide, 70 percent of its employees are based in its main office in Beachwood and the company is committed to staying in the Cleveland area. MRI supports a variety of local charities, including the Boys and Girls Clubs of Cleveland. MRI is also a long-standing member of the Northeast Ohio Software Association (NEOSA), a private, industry trade association that encourages the growth and development of area information technology-based companies to compete in a global market.

Today MRI is looking forward to an exciting future. Internet technologies will change the entire concept of information access and software delivery, and MRI will create systems that take full advantage of this evolution. It will grow its market base of clients by developing new solutions to support the entire real estate life cycle. It also plans to continue to evolve its application hosting services and to expand its client base.

MRI's client support services are unsurpassed in the industry. Here a member of the MRI training staff conducts a personalized class.

Almost 30 years after MRI started as a small, mainframe-based service bureau, it still focuses on providing information management solutions to the real estate management industry. When technology changed, the company stayed one step ahead by developing new products and services. Today MRI products are being used to manage more real estate, for a longer period of time, in more places around the world than any other solution ever.

By listening closely to clients and the industry, MRI develops easy-to-use, easy-to-learn solutions. The intuitive Residential Management system is just one example.

Marconi plc

Guglielmo Marconi's finest hour inspired a century of innovation. When Marconi sent the first wireless message over 100 years ago, he showed the world that technology empowers people to do amazing things.

Today, Marconi plc is one of the world's fastest-growing communications and IT companies, with a strong record of innovation and technological breakthroughs. Marconi is headquartered in London and has more than 45,000 employees worldwide and sales in 100 countries.

In Cleveland, Marconi is part of the business community. Marconi Communications and Marconi Medical Systems are both member companies of Marconi plc, continuing the tradition of innovation started by Marconi with leading-edge technologies.

Marconi Communications

Marconi Communications provides industry-leading solutions for communications networks. The range of network solutions includes enterprise, incumbent and competitive telephone companies, cable television and Internet service providers. These network providers and their end customers benefit from the company's research centers, development labs, electronic and software engineers,

The experience and expertise of Marconi Communications' worldwide staff provides exceptional customer support.

physicists and computer scientists exploring the latest thinking in their fields.

A global manufacturer of intelligent communications systems, Marconi Communications is ideally placed to take advantage of the explosive growth in data traffic brought about by the Internet revolution, the fasting-growing section of telecommunications. With the recent explosion in Internet use, data traffic is predicted to increase by approximately 1,000 percent a year and will soon overtake voice traffic. Marconi Communications is prepared to help its customers address these challenges with world-leading transmission technology and a strong position in the access and switching markets.

Marconi Communications' Synchronous Digital Hierarchy (SDH) technology has captured one-third of the total telecommunications market, and has provided the backbone of the world's two largest telecommunications networks in China and Australia. Other countries that have upgraded their telecommunications networks with Marconi Communications equipment include France, Holland and Belgium, as well as more than 80 percent of the operators in the United Kingdom.

In North America, Marconi Communications has a strong position in the high-growth access market, with significant deployment of innovative fiber-in-the-loop solutions. Consumers of voice, video and high-speed data services benefit from the high bandwidths. The company is also a leader in the design and manufacture of outside plant and power systems used by telecommunications companies to build their networks. And as the leading systems integrator, it also designs, installs, commissions and supports these networks.

Marconi Communications and its North American predecessors offer products and services that ensure day-to-day functioning and reliability of the existing telecommunications infrastructure. In Cleveland the company manufactures more than 800 different power products and systems that are essential for operating existing telephone, cable television and Internet services under the Lorain® brand name. The broad offering of products, experience and expertise supports service providers in their critical requirement for network reliability.

Marconi Communications is a combination of the strengths of the original London company's North American presence and the products from the acquisition of Cleveland-based RELTEC in May 1999, as well as its leadership in ATM switching from its June 1999 acquisition of FORE Systems, a Pittsburgh-based company. These and other acquisitions have positioned the company to be a leading player in the new public network and enterprise markets.

Marconi Medical Systems

Marconi Medical Systems is another premier Marconi plc business based in Cleveland. Formerly Picker International, it traces its roots back to 1915, but in 1999 took the Marconi name of its parent to reflect a new vision of information management. It shares its parent company's global leadership in communications and information technology, but the communications it helps its customers navigate is one of the world's most complicated — health care.

Marconi Medical Systems is a world leader in medical imaging, with a focus on computed tomography, magnetic resonance, nuclear medicine, X-ray technologies and supplies distribution. Its technology focuses on imaging and information systems with expanded clinical applications that help customers improve the quality and efficiency of health care delivery. The company's success lies in its quick responses to changes in the world of radiology and health care delivery, as well as its commitment to customer satisfaction. Its customer surveys consistently show that it ranks top among medical-imaging suppliers worldwide in quality, customer service, technology innovation and solutions.

Marconi Medical Systems is organized into three businesses that combine to form a comprehensive range of choices for its customers in the medical and diagnostic imaging field. Whether in the United States, the Americas, Europe, Africa, Asia or Australia, its customers can select from a wide range of products.

Picker Medical Imaging combines all of the company's medical imaging systems, services and sales operations worldwide into a single business. It designs, manufactures and markets a full line of medical-imaging systems, including computed tomography, magnetic resonance, nuclear medicine and X-ray modalities. It also oversees the company's many services that meet its customer's demands for ownership and operation of clinical equipment, including multi-vendor equipment service and support and a wide array of financing and service options.

Radiology Information Services meets the needs of its solutions-based information technology. The need for innovative, reliable medical-information technology and real-time medical-information management has dramatically increased and the business has responded by providing a full line of solutions, including teleradiology, computed radiography, centralized reading and filmless radiology departments. These products not only improve productivity and reduce costs, but also improve the clinical responsiveness of radiology organizations.

Picker Health Care Products is the leading distributor and manufacturer of supplies and accessories for the medical-imaging industry. It employs distribution centers throughout the United States and a fleet of private delivery vehicles to provide hospitals, imaging centers and other health care providers with personalized service and simplified ordering and delivery. Picker Health Care Products was among the first in health care to implement e-commerce and inventory-management programs aimed at improving supply-chain efficiency.

The future of telecommunications and health care is never certain. But with a full and complementary list of technologies, an expanding and increasingly global workforce and the accumulated wisdom of 100 years in communications, the futures of customer-focused Marconi Communications and Marconi Medical Systems will certainly continue to have a profound impact on the world.

Marconi Medical Systems' UltraZ™ CT Scanner is just one of its many high-tech medical-imaging systems.

Preformed Line Products Company

The American economy felt a surge from all directions after the end of World War II. From the baby boom to the emergence from wartime rationing, this growth resulted in the need for new power lines across the country.

In 1947 a Cleveland engineer named Thomas F. Peterson was working on an idea for the power industry — a helical rod that was to be preformed with an inside diameter smaller than the outside diameter of the conductor. He

PREFORMED™ Distribution-Grip dead-ends, installed here in the mid-1950s, are mechanical termination devices for power lines. The helical design eliminates bolts, nuts and washers, and "grips" the conductor uniformly to prevent distortion.

had figured that helically preformed rods, applied over the conductor at cable suspension points, would create a fit that was secure without the need for end clamps to "armor" and protect the conductor from wear. His PREFORMED™ Armor Rod was successful and Preformed Line Products Company (PLP) was born. A quick succession of other product developments followed, including WRAPLOCK Ties, ARMOR-GRIP® Suspension units and GUY-GRIP dead-ends. Preformed Line Products became recognized as the industry leader for setting new standards in conductor support systems.

The new company purchased its first facility in Cleveland, and shortly thereafter, its first branch plant in Palo Alto, California. During the first decade PLP expanded

beyond the United States into Canada when it licensed a hardware company there to manufacture the armor rods.

The company continued to grow along with the increasing demands of the utility companies. PLP began to develop a variety of products in various materials and sizes, including helically formed spacers, dampers, splices, insulator ties and guards. The company was also providing strand products to telephone companies at this time and had received approval in 1957 from Bell Telephone Systems for its GUY-GRIP dead-ends. Its success was due not only to the reliability of the products, but to the way PLP anticipated industry needs and provided quick and workable solutions. Under the able leadership of Jon R. Ruhlman, then vice president of research & engineering and currently chairman of the company, PLP established its own research and development lab as well as the industry's first mobile testing laboratory. With this advance, company technicians could work directly with customers in the field for training, problem identification and testing.

By 1960 PLP expanded further abroad and was manufacturing products in Australia, England and Germany, in addition to Canada. In 1964 PLP received the Presidential "E" Award signifying the company's significant contributions to the export expansion program of the United States.

In 1968 PLP acquired the Smith Company in California, a leader in the telecommunications field known for its innovative line of products designed to facilitate the underground installation of telephone systems. Smith's closures, which included the SERIVISEAL Closure and the Stainless Steel Splice Case, joined the line of successful PLP products.

A Marine Systems Division was formed in 1969 in order to accommodate the offshore gas and oil industry and the U.S. Navy. Its underwater cable terminations and support systems, design and special engineering services became another trademark of PLP quality. PLP made its way into other specialized industries at that time, too, providing expertise and products for metal buildings, cable television and vineyards.

As the company grew internationally, joint ventures in Spain and Japan as well as fully owned subsidiaries in England, Brazil and Mexico solidified PLP's standing worldwide. In 1974 PLP moved its world head-quarters to the current location in Mayfield Village on Cleveland's suburban east side. The current research and engineering facility opened in 1979 at the same location. It is there that PLP engineers and technicians test everything from tension load to the impact of wind speed, humidity and other environmental factors to determine product performance and durability.

Throughout the major expansion of the late 1970s, the company itself remained as flexible as many of the cables and wires for which it is known. PLP transformed its customer service into on-site demonstrations and training, on-site diagnostics, and advanced inventory and tracking systems. As it has been with PLP since the beginning, serving the customer first translated into a standard of excellence that benefited not only the customer but the millions of people the customer served.

During the peak years of corporate downsizing and restructuring in the 1980s, PLP evolved again into a company that solved not only the technological issues facing the industry. It demonstrated its ability as a problem solver and partner that could bring added value to the relationship. In 1993 Superior Modular Products became a part of PLP and brought with it patented Category 5 patch

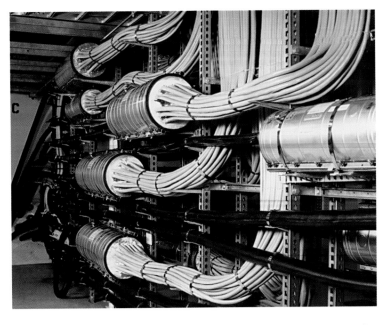

Stainless steel fire-retardant Vault Closures provide airtight enclosures for spliced cables in a telephone central office cable entrance vault.

panel designs and high-speed data cross-connect systems for communication networks. With that purchase PLP was able to expand even further in the communications market.

PLP has been recognized with ISO 9001 certification for manufacturing processes and distributes products in more than 100 countries around the world. As the leading supplier of high-quality cable anchoring and control hardware and systems, overhead and underground splice cases and related products, high-speed cross-connect devices, urethane products, extruded plastics and formed wire products, PLP is continually looking to the future while keeping the world working. What began as a small company with a good idea has become a worldwide innovator and visionary. PLP has U.S. manufacturing centers in Albemarle and Asheville, North Carolina, and Rogers, Arkansas. Its international subsidiaries are in Australia, Brazil, Canada, China, Mexico, Scotland, South Africa, Spain and the United Kingdom.

In all of its international endeavors and devotion to serving the needs of customers, PLP has shown that it does not take its loyalty to Cleveland lightly either. PLP has maintained its world headquarters here, continually enhancing the landscape that helps Cleveland keep the rest of the world at work.

Pennsylvania Electric line crew installs ARMOR-GRIP® Suspension units in the late 1950s on a rare 465,000-volt twin-bundle power conductor.

Rockwell Automation

The Industrial Age has met the Information Age, and the challenge for manufacturers is to bridge the two to give themselves the edge in today's markets. Gaining that edge is not easy, however. Manufacturers must produce ever-more sophisticated goods and services while they identify and incorporate new automation into their production processes — all more quickly and cheaply than ever.

Many turn to Rockwell Automation to provide that bridge. Rockwell Automation helps manufacturers gain and maintain their competitive edge by providing and installing state-of-the-art automation solutions for the factories of those businesses. Rockwell Automation also provides the ongoing technical support that businesses need to upgrade and optimize their manufacturing processes.

For manufacturers, a competitive edge means having the technology to create superior goods, including computer systems that can withstand the rigors of a hostile plant floor, a stamping process to produce vehicles with the most stylish and efficient body contours or producing stage gear that ensures a technically flawless Broadway production.

Rockwell Automation, with operations in several Cleveland suburbs, provides the technology, components, automation, and technical-support solutions needed to facilitate the production of such goods and services for manufacturers. The operations are part of a business unit of the multibillion-dollar Rockwell International Corp. of Milwaukee, Wisconsin. That business unit carries more than 500,000 products used by firms in more than 80

Headquarters for the Automation, Control and Information Group of Rockwell Automation in Mayfield Heights, a suburb of Cleveland

countries. Clients from around the world travel to Rockwell Automation University's Cleveland facility to learn about many of these products, including drives, controls, motors and communication networks.

Rockwell product lines can be found in virtually every factory and processing system in the region, converting manufacturers' raw materials into finished goods. Rockwell devices wind up in other machinery or processing lines at manufacturing plants that produce everything from beverages to steel to systems that gauge vehicle pollution emissions. The devices control and monitor the temperature of liquids, the flow of materials, the smooth operation of gears, and the speeds of processes and any number of functions of manufacturing or processing.

Manufacturers are running leaner operations and are more willing to hire outside experts to handle aspects of their operations, particularly the technical processes needed to create their goods. The alternative for these businesses would be to invest in personnel and training to keep employees abreast of the latest technological breakthroughs.

"Manufacturers know they can't invest fast enough in employees to keep up, because the technology changes so fast these days — so they hire someone to do it," says Cliff Whitehead, manager of marketing and business development for Information and Automation Systems at Rockwell Automation. "They want to know that when they start a manufacturing process, everything needed to facilitate that process has already been taken care of. That's where we come in. We offer broad, complete automation solutions."

Rockwell Automation is the largest business unit of Rockwell International. The other major units are Rockwell Collins, which provides in-flight entertainment systems and military communications and navigation equipment; the Electronic Commerce unit, which produces customer contact management technology for use in call centers, for example; and the Science Center, which is the research and development unit that creates new technologies.

The parent company is the result of a merger between firms that were founded in the early 1900s. Rockwell Standard Corp., which produced truck axles, and North

American Aviation, Inc., a holding company turned aircraft manufacturer, merged in 1967 to produce North American Rockwell Corp. It became Rockwell International in 1973.

The 1980s ushered in a period of diversification. Rockwell International moved into automation in 1985 with the purchase of the Milwaukee-based Allen-Bradley firm, the largest automation controls supplier in North America. With that acquisition the Rockwell Automation business unit, with its Cleveland operations, was formed. The unit became the umbrella for brand-name automation products and support services.

Other Rockwell Automation brands include Rockwell Software, which was formed in 1994 by a merger involving ICOM with the Allen-Bradley software business; Reliance Electric, a leader in industrial motor and electric drive technology, purchased in 1995; and Dodge, a leader in the mechanical power transmission market which includes adjustable speed drives, clutches and conveyor pulleys.

Such acquisitions positioned Rockwell Automation as a global leader in factory automation, especially dominant in North and South America. Providing automation solutions has meant going beyond offering just hardware. The product lines come with what division executives unabashedly call a "warm hug." With automation firms generally producing better products, Rockwell adds more value to its product lines by providing ongoing support services.

Some 3,500 employees at the Greater Cleveland operation, including sales, management, manufacturing and technical personnel, are part of a network that responds to the desires of a wide-ranging client list. They tailor their product lines to solve a client's manufacturing or production problems, monitor the effectiveness of their products and address new issues that may arise.

To create new lines and upgrade existing product lines, research and development is continuous. Rockwell is working to give a product more power, produce one that requires less space or develop a more efficient motor.

Rockwell engineers are conducting research on liquid coolants to regulate temperatures of materials and processes. The overall constants are to develop products that cost less, do more and are more effective.

The effort to provide support services extends beyond manufacturing processes. Rockwell Automation offers more than 60 courses to clients in fully equipped, high-tech classrooms at Rockwell Automation University in suburban Cleveland. Clients learn how to program, maintain and troubleshoot the brand products they use. More than 80 courses are offered to Rockwell engineers as well. In addition to having access to more formal training, clients can attend annual trade shows where product lines are showcased.

Beyond the factory floor and classroom, Rockwell Automation provides clients with data about their plant operations, which can be used to improve efficiency in the clients' use of personnel and processes. The business unit also operates a high-tech, fully equipped media production studio that produces and broadcasts promotional and training materials to Rockwell and distributor offices. The studio markets itself locally as Avid Communications, producing media for many regional businesses, education facilities, hospitals and nonprofit organizations. The "warm hug" from Rockwell Automation is evolving into a sustained embrace.

The Global Technical Training Center is located at the newly renovated Rockwell Automation University in Euclid, another suburb of Cleveland.

Rockwell Automation brings together leading brands in industrial automation, including Allen-Bradley controls, Reliance Electric power transmission products, Dodge mechanical power transmission components and Rockwell Software.

Stein Automation, Inc.

He had a well-paid, high-profile U.S. job heading a subsidiary of a Swiss Systems Integrator building production equipment for the optical recording industry, but Swiss-born Markus Leu was restless. He longed for a business of his own and was willing to risk everything he had to get it. His friends and family told him he was crazy, but a short nine years later, Leu is the sole owner of a major supplier to some of the largest manufacturing firms in the country and his sanity is no longer in question.

Pictured at his first trade show booth in 1992 is owner Markus M. Leu, who started the U.S. Stein Automation just months before.

It was 1991 when Leu incorporated a company, not knowing what it would do. Then he met Peter Stein at a trade show in Europe. Stein was the owner of Stein Automation, a German company that began in 1969 as a machine shop founded by his father, Josef Stein. In 1974 the company had designed and manufactured its first fully automated loading-and-unloading device for the machine-tool industry, and in 1984 designed the first dual-belt, non-synchronous pallet transfer system on the market.

By the early 1990s Stein had patented the revolutionary system as the first generation Workpiece Transfer System (WTS). Leu was interested in bringing this new technology to the United States. Peter Stein thought that America was too far away and had too different of a culture for his product to be successful. However, Leu was determined and asked for the U.S. licensing rights to the WTS. Stein agreed, but on the condition that Leu would financially support the effort.

So Leu took on the challenge of establishing Stein Automation in the United States. He quit his lucrative position and started the company out of a one-bedroom apartment in 1992. It wasn't easy, especially during the recession of the early 1990s. He had to convert the literature and documentation to English, market to the American culture and spend his savings, but his hard work and dedication paid off. By 1995 he was a major force behind Stein Automation's record-breaking year, which doubled its 1994 sales volume.

By 1997 Leu was able to expand the company and move from southern New Jersey to Ohio. He considered several Midwest cities, but was attracted to the Cleveland area by the large manufacturing base, the growing economy and the aggressive recruitment of the Cleveland Growth Association.

Since Stein moved to the Cleveland suburb of Solon, Ohio, it has rapidly grown from a one-man operation to a 45-employee corporation. In March of 1998 it purchased a small machine shop, and in 1999 it further enhanced its manufacturing capabilities when it acquired a medium-size machine builder. The company has also developed essential partnerships with leading robot manufacturers and Visicontrol vision inspection systems to expand its automation capabilities.

Stein not only manufactures and supplies the versatile WTS conveyor system; it also furnishes its many clients with complete manufacturing solutions. Its systems are composed of a series of modular, interfacing components that can be arranged and configured for optimal productivity. The systems offer users a high degree of flexibility and expandability. A manufacturer can easily and inexpensively add onto a line, rearrange the layout of a line or use it to manufacture an entirely different product. The systems range from one-man workstations to fully automated systems.

Although the American-based Stein Automation has not reached Fortune 500 status, it is a major player in the manufacturing industry, with an aggressive global presence. As a valued partner of the American Competitiveness

Institute, a division of the U.S. Navy, it partners with large defense contractors such as Boeing.

Stein's clients include electronics manufacturers such as Nokia, automotive manufacturers like Delphi and Visteon and home-appliance manufacturers including Eveready and Sunbeam. Sunbeam was one of the company's first clients. Leu was so determined to gain its business that he even meet with Sunbeam's representatives in Mexico City on the due date of his first born child. Luckily, he made it home in time for the birth.

Stein's future growth will take the innovative company beyond conveyors to a whole process of vertical integration that will redefine industry standards. The company's fine-tuned attention to detail is evidenced in the new pallet-conveyor system it released in late 1999.

The revolutionary, all-electrical system will feature bi-directional capabilities and will eliminate existing pitfalls. The conveyor will act as the conductor to the orchestra of interchangeable modules, helping tomorrow's manufacturers to produce specialized products in a lean way. It will also allow smaller manufacturers to have the same advantages as their larger competitors.

Stein's aggressive creation of the new system is just one way the company achieves its goal of being dictated to by the needs of its clients. It will consider the new system a success only if it performs successfully for them.

It is hard to believe that Stein is less than a decade old, yet has experienced a wealth of success and satisfaction. It shares its success not only with its clients by continually investing in product improvements, but also with its hard-working employees. They work in a unique atmosphere open to change and new ideas and are rewarded generously for their efforts.

Innovative, aggressive, different, refreshing — these are all keys to Stein's success, as well as good descriptions of

Stein Automation's Precision Pallet Transfer Systems (WTS) range from simple, manual workstations to fully automated systems such as the one shown here.

its owner. Markus Leu's young company manages to combine conventional American business practices with nontraditional European philosophies and win over a host of clients in the mix. He was not complacent back in 1992, and he is still constantly striving for improvements. He and his company are proof that the route of hard work and innovation are the way to success.

Stein's hard-working sales staff, shown here at a national trade show in 1999, is dedicated to the needs of its clients.

Consolidated Graphics Group, Inc.

The archives and files of businesses and institutions bulge with data about clients, marketing campaigns and promotional tools. Effective management of this information is as essential to the success of these establishments as the services provided. Executives are faced with the need to catalog the data and have quick access to it, or make visually compelling presentation of the information to clients.

Consolidated Graphics Group, Inc. (CGG) in Cleveland, a full-service, high-tech printing, binding and data management firm, is making both tasks easier. CGG is part of the emerging digital asset management industry that is providing businesses and agencies with "cyber libraries" to store and secure data. The company also uses the most sophisticated printing, photography and Internet technology available to enhance the quality of the materials it prints and assembles for clients.

The company's own emergence has been meteoric. It was started in 1996 by Kenneth A. Lanci, whose business acumen and work ethic were evident long before he founded CGG. An industrious high school student, Lanci once held four jobs simultaneously, one of which was as a "gofer" in his father's print shop, Offset Color & Printing.

In 1969 he took over the business. In 1978, while still overseeing the shop, he started a business consulting firm. He acquired a series of other businesses in the 1980s. Success allowed him to retire early and travel with his wife, Linda.

Lanci was lured back into business by advancements and trends in communications technology. He saw the potential in digital access management, which allows for the storage of vast amounts of data by using the Internet. CGG has created a virtual library with database "shelves." Each book on the shelves contains the art, graphics, documents and other materials for individual clients. The clients gain access to that information from anywhere in the world with a password, and the data can be updated anytime.

CGG also is benefiting from Lanci's background in printing and in other new technology for its operations. Digital prepress technology allows the company to produce sharper images for a client's promotional, marketing or other informational materials. Documents can be scanned or retouched at high-tech workstations to produce more precise images. The company's direct mail unit provides addressing, inserting and metering services to clients for

Kenneth A. Lanci started Consolidated Graphics Group, Inc. in 1996 after having started and managed other successful businesses.

mailings. Warehousing, shipping and receiving decks also are on site. In its first two years, the company went from a 25-employee business with billings of $500,000 to a 125-employee firm with $15 million in billings.

Lanci says he wants to help youths realize that they can be entrepreneurs and enjoy similar success, even if, like him, they don't attend college. He supports various programs that serve youths. But Lanci, chairman and CEO of CGG, wants to add another dimension to such efforts. He is establishing the Circle of Life Academy to provide youths with vocational skills and the mentoring they may not have received in high school. He explains, "I learned valuable life lessons from people I admired in my youth, and I want to help young people today learn those same lessons." They're not likely to find a better teacher than Lanci.

NASA Glenn Research Center

On Mars, where atmospheric conditions are vastly different from Earth's, even our most sophisticated aircraft engine would be rendered useless. Jet engines would be starved for the oxygen they need to produce thrust. Propellers would whirl so fast they would be supersonic, but still not produce the work needed to propel the airplane.

Interplanetary conditions are not typically a consideration for most engineers, but for the engineers and scientists at the NASA Glenn Research Center, they're mission critical. Interplanetary conditions are just one of the many technical barriers Glenn engineers and scientists have to overcome as they develop new propulsion systems for the small exploration craft destined to explore Mars early in this new century.

With 10-year and 25-year mission goals, Glenn engineers work light years ahead of today's technology, routinely dealing with concepts the general public still considers to be the realm of science fiction.

Although only one main campus building is visible from Brookpark Road, Glenn's Cleveland facility, Lewis Field, comprises over 100 buildings and research laboratories covering 350 acres. Its Plum Brook Station near Sandusky covers 6,400 acres and is home to some of the world's largest space-simulation facilities. More than 3,600 people staff Glenn, including civil service and contractor employees.

One of 10 NASA centers in the country, the Glenn Center's unique mission is to develop propulsion systems for both aeronautics and spacecraft. Glenn-developed aircraft engine technology is in virtually every commercial aircraft engine flying today. Its rocket technology has played a part in most space exploration projects. Most recently, Glenn engineers and staff enjoyed the success of their ion engine, which is now propelling the *Deep Space 1* spacecraft to its asteroid rendezvous.

Another of the Glenn's ongoing projects is to develop space electrical-power systems that provide electrical power for the International Space Station and other satellites, for spacecraft and for ground stations on other planets. Glenn engineers have furthered the development of solar cells, fuel cells, flywheels and greatly improved batteries.

Much of the technology developed for Glenn's aerospace missions is very effectively translated into advances in other areas through its commercial technology program. Its

NASA Glenn Research Center

microelectronic machining technology has been applied to biomedical sensors, helping doctors learn about difficult-to-access parts of the body. Its electronic transmitting tube technology made possible nationwide digital telephones and direct-to-home satellite television reception.

Students in the Mars Millennium Project

The center's education outreach program encourages students to challenge themselves by studying science and mathematics and supports teachers by introducing innovative ways to teach these subjects. Recently, the program has taken on a broader goal: Glenn is participating in the Mars Millennium Project, a national arts, science and technology initiative wherein student teams design a community of 100 people arriving on Mars in 2030. The goal of each team is to design a livable and life-sustaining community that is culturally and artistically rich.

NASA Glenn Research Center in one of the few places in the world where reaching for the stars is more than a motto. It is quite literally its mission.

Paragon Data Systems, Inc.

Paragon Data Systems, Inc. is a young company wise beyond its years. It began barely four years ago, in February 1996, as the brainchild of three enterprising young men: Larry Laurenzi, company president; David Safenovitz, executive vice president; and Giles Manias, vice president of technical services.

Laurenzi and Manias were co-workers at a bar-coding company. Happy in the industry, but bored with the company's focus on labels, they decided to break away. They joined forces with Safenovitz and began turning their dream of owning and managing a company focused on complete automated data collection into a reality.

The three men opened a small office in downtown Cleveland and began making calls and earning clients. The result was an initial investment of $12,000 growing into revenues of $350,000 in the first year. The second year, Paragon generated $1.5 million in revenues, and by year number three, it had attained a bigger office in Cleveland's midtown area, 14 employees and over $3 million in revenues.

The three partners and friends worked hard to make Paragon succeed, but they couldn't have done it alone. The company took full advantage of Cleveland's resources for emerging businesses and owes its achievements to organizations such as Provident Bank; the Howard, Wershbale, & Co. Accounting Firm; the Jones Day Legal Firm; and the local Small Business Administration. Early customers that put their trust in Paragon and helped it gain credibility include Royal Manufacturing and Hamilton Beach, which

nominated Paragon for its "Vendor of the Year" award in 1997 and 1998.

Throughout its expanding years, Paragon has maintained three key business philosophies. First is a commitment to providing high-quality products, second is a dedication to customer service and third is a pledge to make Paragon an enjoyable place to work.

Paragon's first-class products are utilized all over the United States, Canada and Mexico by consumer goods manufacturers, health care organizations, retail stores, and companies with warehouses and shipping docks. Products include radio frequency data collection devices, bar code printing systems, print and apply systems, labels and ribbons, protective enclosures and warehouse management systems. All products employ the latest technology, and they are often integrated for a total solutions system.

But Paragon doesn't just sell its products — it ensures that they'll keep working thanks to an excellent customer service department. It offers services such as technical support and repairs even during off-hours. Proof of its commitment to service is in the company's high customer retention rate and in the fact that its customers voted it an "award-winning" Zebra dealer.

Paragon also ensures its employees are pleased with good compensation packages, a casual atmosphere and flexibility. In addition, it hasn't overlooked the importance of giving back to the community. Even in its short history, the company has donated generously to local charities such as the Special Olympics, Rainbow Babies and Children's Hospital, the Jewish Community Center and the Patrolmen's Association.

Paragon will continue its growth-oriented philosophies and is preparing for the future with plans for a new, larger office, still in midtown Cleveland. It also plans to focus on the growing technologies in data collection, two-dimensional bar codes, digital imaging and e-commerce. Judging from its past success after just a few years in business, the company's future growth is both inevitable and inspirational.

Paragon Data Systems, Inc. was founded in 1996 by (left to right) Larry Laurenzi, Giles Manias and David Safenovitz.

Tal-Cut Company

Building a company from the ground up is in itself a daunting and perhaps unachievable goal for many. However, DeLois Cutter, president and owner of Tal-Cut Company, has successfully achieved this goal and is contributing to other small businesses in a significant manner — by mentoring.

The Cleveland-based company provides personnel, information management and high-technology assistance to clients. The core of Tal-Cut is small, but the company employs many technical professionals who provide various services to the government sector and private corporations. The services include, but are not limited to, information technology, engineering services, telecommunications, scientific research and experimentation, Web design and e-commerce.

Increasingly, Tal-Cut is partnering with other small companies in need of assistance in stabilizing their businesses. These companies often need support establishing internal policies and procedures and may be unaware of business opportunities available to them. Cutter believes that mentoring businesses during this initial stage is invaluable to the success of a new company. She advises entrepreneurs to join professional organizations to keep abreast of business developments in the private and public sectors. She explains that the controlled expansion of a company's services and the amassing of a network of professional alliances is practical for young companies and will ultimately lead to success. Cutter says her objective is to utilize her experience by helping startup businesses avoid mistakes commonly made. "A worthy calling indeed!" says Cutter.

Cutter has gained a wealth of knowledge, information and experience since 1982, when she and sister, Zel Talley, started Tal-Cut. Initially, Tal-Cut was a part-time endeavor. Talley and Cutter utilized their business-management and technical-consulting expertise to pursue business ventures with the federal government. Soon their own business was flourishing into a full-time company. Incorporated in Ohio in 1985, the company's first opportunities came from local and state government entities within Ohio, such as the city of Cleveland, the Cleveland Board of Education, Cuyahoga County, the Bureau of Workers' Compensation and the Ohio Lottery.

In 1989 Tal-Cut was accepted into a specialized federal Small Business Administration program. The program, which Tal-Cut participated in for nine years, exposed them to business opportunities with the government as well as large private firms. Major government contracts were secured with agencies such as the NASA Lewis Research Center and Defense Finance and Accounting Services, both in Cleveland, and the General Services Administration in New York City. In the private sector, contracts were secured with such major corporations as BP Oil, Lucent Technologies, Ameritech, Lockheed Martin, Avery, Xerox, Xpedx and Parker Hannifin. Cutter attributes her company's success to the quality of service provided by the management and technical staff of Tal-Cut to its clients.

"There are many opportunities for small businesses, including those owned by minorities and women," says Cutter, who has been sole owner of Tal-Cut since 1998. "Opportunities exist for everyone. That's where faith intercedes with the relentless passion for success. You must be prepared to take advantage of those opportunities. Persistence, determination and quality work yield rewards." Those are the messages she conveys to fellow entrepreneurs.

DeLois Cutter, president and owner of Tal-Cut, accepts a Small Business Administration Award of Excellence in 1999 for recognition of outstanding contributions and services in federal government contracting.

USB Corporation

Reagents... DNA... biochemicals... enzymes... biotech... human genome... genetic alphabet.

These are not part of the average person's everyday language, but at USB Corporation they are part of a way of life that is becoming increasingly important to science. The firm manufactures and supplies more than 4,000 different products for the life science research market.

Although a relatively new company under the USB banner, the firm — and its predecessor corporate entities — has had a long-standing reputation as a leader in science, innovation, quality and service.

R & D under way at USB

United States Biochemical was established in the early 1970s specifically to sell biochemicals to the research market. By the 1980s technology had advanced to the point that research in molecular biology, including the study of DNA and the human genome, required more high-tech reagents.

Working with Harvard scientists, United States Biochemical developed the Sequenase™ and ThermoSequenase™ products for DNA sequencing applications. The Sequenase™ enzyme allowed scientists to decode DNA more easily, more efficiently and more accurately than previous enzymes.

In addition, the Sequenase™ enzyme pioneered technology that led to development of thermostable enzymes and automated equipment for high-throughput sequencing. This in turn led to completion of what has been termed the first survey of the entire human genome in June 2000 by Celera Genomics and the Human Genome Research Institute.

In 1993 a British company, Amersham Life Science, purchased United States Biochemical. Amersham itself later merged with Swedish-owned Pharmacia Biotech Ltd., and the Warrensville Heights company became part of the newly formed Amersham Pharmacia Biotech Inc.

Late in 1998, when Amersham Pharmacia decided to close many of its facilities, including the one in Cleveland, and consolidate its North American operations in New Jersey, a group of local managers bought three of that firm's product lines as the base business of the new USB Corporation, created in the spring of 1999. The lines purchased included manual DNA sequencing kits and the biochemical and enzyme product lines used by academic, pharmaceutical and biotech scientists. Amersham Pharmacia still serves as the company's European distributor.

Mike Lachman, USB president and CEO, explains that United States Biochemical was always known as a leader in science, innovation, quality and service. The new company can once again focus on core competencies, building on a reputation to deliver quality products to its customers. USB continues to market the Sequenase™ enzyme, along with numerous other enzymes, biochemicals and reagents that fuel innovation in the biotech industry.

It may be difficult to understand the deciphering of the genetic alphabet; to be aware of what an enzyme is, what it does or how it works; or to know the difference between an agent and a reagent. It is a great deal easier to understand that USB is in the forefront of an industry that is helping to unravel the mysteries of science.

TRANSPORTATION

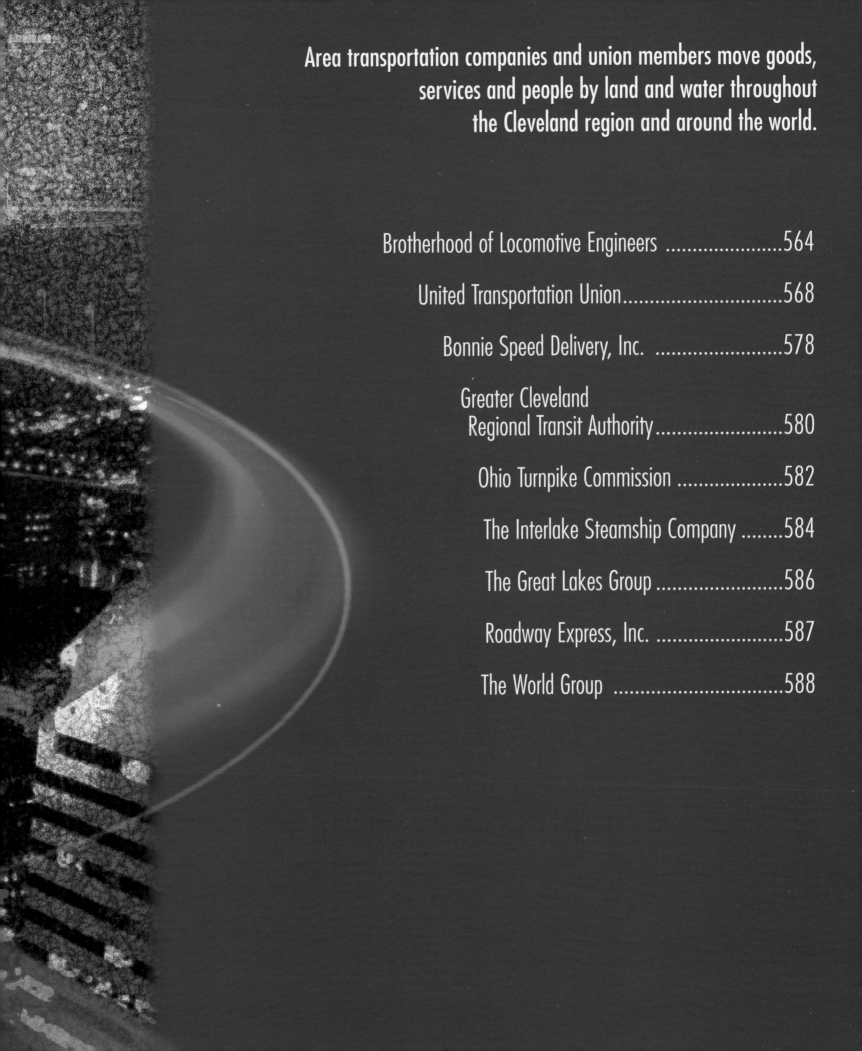

Area transportation companies and union members move goods, services and people by land and water throughout the Cleveland region and around the world.

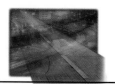

Brotherhood of Locomotive Engineers

Perhaps emboldened by President Lincoln's 1863 Emancipation Proclamation that freed the slaves, a group of locomotive engineers from the Michigan Central Railroad got together that same year to declare their own form of emancipation — a union.

The Brotherhood of the Footboard first was discussed at several of these meetings early in 1863 in Marshall, Michigan. Because of its concern about management reprisals, the group considered itself a fraternal organization and was forced to hold its meetings in secret. As a result of these meetings, organizers got together in Detroit in May of that year to draw up a constitution and bylaws. Actions taken by those locomotive engineers, employees of the Michigan Central, Michigan Southern Grand Trunk and the Detroit & Milwaukee, make the Brotherhood the oldest labor organization in the United States.

Formally founded on May 8, 1863, the Brotherhood of the Footboard changed its name one year later to the Brotherhood of Locomotive Engineers. Although it was the first successful attempt at organizing, it was not the first attempt by locomotive engineers to do so.

A decade earlier 16 Baltimore & Ohio engineers had been dismissed when they withdrew from service in a dispute over the intolerable conditions prevalent in 1854. As a result, 68 engineers from 45 different railroads in 13 states met in Baltimore in 1855 and formed the National Protective Association of the Brotherhood of Locomotive Engineers of the United States. After a couple of conventions in 1856 and 1857, the association apparently derailed itself. As important as the railroads were becoming in 1860, there were less than 31,000 miles of track extending as far "west" as Iowa, Missouri and Arkansas.

The onset of the Civil War also put a temporary stop to organizing, but by 1863 the engineers were tired of being covered with soot, being hot in the summer and cold in the drafty locomotives in the winter. They were tired of being poorly paid and of being on the road for long periods

of time. They also were tired of being required to pack pistons and valve stems, clean the headlights and lubricate moving parts — among other nonskilled tasks — while waiting to take a train on the road.

In addition, while waiting to return home on their next tour, they had to pay their own expenses. All this for $60 a month on condition they run 2,500 miles during that time. At the time, eggs cost 12 cents a dozen, butter was 13 cents a pound and ham 10 cents a pound. Because of the war, however, prices rose 100 percent while wages only went up 50 percent between 1860 and 1864.

In spite of the hardships, the specific event that brought the situation to a head was the action taken by the superintendent of machinery on the Michigan Central who had cut engineers' pay and then discharged some of the men who protested. He also dismissed firemen with top seniority and replaced them with untested workers. The engineers refused to run with them.

Warren S. Stone, BLE grand chief engineer (International President) from 1903-1924, and the man responsible for the BLE's growth in the early 20th century

Historical marker commemorating founding of BLE in Marshall, Michigan, with founders' names engraved. J.C. "Yankee" Thompson's home, where BLE was founded, is still standing (in background).

One of the earliest proponents of a union was William D. Robinson, who worked on several railroads in the east before migrating to the Midwest in 1861 and joining the Michigan Central.

As a result of his strong advocacy for a union, the engineers who gathered in Detroit in 1863 elected him First Grand Chief Engineer of the Brotherhood. Division (Local) 1 was organized at the same time and by the end of the summer of 1863, 10 divisions had been formed and a Grand National Division established.

By the time of the Brotherhood's first convention in Indianapolis in August 1864, 54 divisions sent representatives.

The rest of the decade was one of steady growth. In 1865 the Brotherhood ventured into Canada, chartering Division 70 in Toronto. A year later the growing Brotherhood established an Orphans and Widows Fund, and delegates to the annual convention authorized publication of a monthly journal that still is published today on a quarterly basis. In 1867 the Brotherhood formed the Locomotive Engineers Mutual Life and Accident Insurance Association. Independent of the Brotherhood, policy holders had to belong to the BLE.

One of the most momentous events in railroad — and 19th century American history — occurred just before the end of the decade at Promontory, Utah, when the country's first transcontinental railroad was completed. According to

one report, on hand for the Golden Spike completion ceremony were civic leaders, newspaper correspondents, immigrants, unsavory camp followers, Mormon farmers and four U.S. infantry companies with their regimental band.

Nowhere in that report does it state who brought the Central Pacific's Jupiter and the Union Pacific's N.119 together so that their cow catchers touched, symbolically completing the road. It may well have been members of the BLE.

With completion of the transcontinental line, the United States entered the decade of the 1870s with approximately 53,000 miles of track. Mileage increased to more than 93,000 during the 80s and jumped to about 160,000 by 1890.

The decade after the Civil War may have been one of growth for the railroads, but it was one of frustration for many Americans, including locomotive engineers.

During the financial panic of 1873 more than 1 million workers lost their jobs. The BLE membership called for an unsanctioned strike and when Grand Chief Engineer Wilson denounced it, the rank and file forced him to submit his resignation.

More tragic was an 1877 strike called after the Baltimore & Ohio and several other railroads cut the wages of freight train and engine crews by 10 percent. In addition, wages sometimes were held up for as long as three or four months. Adding to worker frustration was a 10 percent pay cut made during the 1873 panic that had not been restored.

Estimates are that during the bloody strike about 100 people, including women and children, were killed and several hundred injured by company strikebreakers and local militia. Among those killed were BLE members John H. Weaver and John H. Cassidy, who lost their lives in the infamous Reading Massacre. It would not be the last or the longest strike, but it was the worst. It was an unfortunate way to prove the strength of the union, but it succeeded in doing just that.

In 1887 President Grover Cleveland signed the Interstate Commerce Act, regulating a variety of organizations, including railroads, freight forwarders and other surface-transportation agencies engaged in interstate commerce.

Also in that year Division 1 of the BLE's Grand International Auxiliary was formed in Chicago. The auxiliary

BLE's 1963 centennial anniversary was celebrated by J.C. Carpenter (left), chairman of the celebration, and R.E. Davidson, grand chief engineer.

was created by engineers' wives, who were assisting the arrangements committee at the annual convention.

Another bitter strike, again with violence, began in February 1888 and lasted until January 4, 1889. Engineers on the Chicago, Burlington & Quincy went on strike to protest repeated violations of seniority agreements. A decade later, the Erdman Act, which provided arbitration machinery to settle disputes, was passed. It also forbade dismissal or discrimination because of union membership or activity on the railroads.

The new century brought additional recognition to the BLE when one of its most famous members, John Luther (Casey) Jones, not only crashed his *Cannonball* express into a freight train, but crashed into American folklore. Sheet music memorializing the dead engineer was among the country's 10 best sellers in 1903.

"Mighty Casey" may have been movin', but the BLE headquarters hadn't moved since 1870 when officials made Cleveland the union's home because of its central location. For decades the Brotherhood rented space in various buildings until it financed and built its own 13-story Engineers Building in the heart of downtown. The building was dedicated on May 14, 1910.

Ohio's governor attended the dedication of the $1.4 million facility and told the 5,000 engineers in attendance that it was the finest labor temple in the world, emphasizing it was the first of its kind built in its entirety by any branch of organized labor.

During that decade, two pieces of labor legislation that were designed to improve the lot of the locomotive engineer were passed. The 1911 Locomotive Inspection Act was aimed at preventing boiler explosions and other mechanical failures. The Adamson Act of 1916, which provided for eight-hour days on the railroads, was passed by Congress only after the BLE and three other brotherhoods threatened nationwide strikes.

The following year the government took over the railroads and ran them during World War I, standardizing wages and work rules for engineers and other crafts.

In the 1920s the BLE attempted to diversify. With 85,000 members, financial resources enabled the Brotherhood to undertake such ventures. Activities included the opening of several banks, one holding company, real estate development and operating a coal company.

The BLE National Cooperative Bank Building, (now known as the Standard Building and current home to the BLE), directly across the street from the Engineers

Building, was designed to house the Brotherhood of Locomotive Engineers Cooperative National Bank. Completed in 1925, the building was the first labor bank in the nation. Open to everyone as a commercial savings and trust company, it lent money primarily to BLE members. It prospered for several years, and then after some mergers became part of the Standard Trust Co., which was forced to liquidate early in the Depression.

Another investment during the period was made by the BLE Venice Company, which planned and developed the resort city of Venice, Florida in the 1920s during the land boom in that state. In a book about the city, one 40-page chapter is entitled, "The BLE Builds a City."

The Brotherhood maintained its activist role through the Great Depression, and on its 75th anniversary in 1938, 10,000 locomotive engineers, their wives and families came to Detroit for a week-long celebration.

Unlike the government takeover during World War I, U.S. railroads maintained their independence during World War II and carried 90 percent of all military freight and 97 percent of all military passengers.

But "the times they were a-changin'." Movement of freight by truck and of passengers by plane and on the nation's newly constructed interstate highway system was removing some of the glory from the rails.

In spite of opposition by the BLE and other rail labor unions, the Interstate Commerce Commission's approval of a merger of the New York Central and Pennsylvania railroads in 1966 was a major sign of the changing times. It was the largest, but not the only merger, that affected membership.

Passage of the 1980 Staggers Act, which deregulated the railroad industry, further affected the Brotherhood negatively. A great many of the provisions of the act set aside several of the regulatory provisions of the 1887 Interstate Commerce Act.

In 1989 the BLE was forced to sell its Engineers Building. The city of Cleveland wanted the location for a new hotel in its re-emerging downtown. Rather than fight the city in a costly eminent domain battle, the BLE moved across the street and made its offices in the Standard Building, where it still is headquartered today.

In spite of these negatives, the BLE continued to meet challenges head on. In 1993 the union initiated more than 1,300 new members and added 2,000 more when the American Train Dispatchers Association affiliated with the BLE.

Although down from its membership high of 100,000 during the heyday of North America's railroads, the BLE has more than 58,000 members, 38,000 of them active, in more than 600 divisions. This at a time when there are eight Class 1 (determined by revenues) railroads in the United States and two in Canada.

On July 31, 1999, Edward Dubroski took the reins of leadership to guide the BLE into the 21st century. He became the first International President to be elected to the union's highest office by a popular vote of the BLE membership.

Regardless of what the future holds, the principles promulgated by the group's founding fathers in 1863 remain sacrosanct — Sobriety, Truth, Justice and Morality.

Accepting a plaque on the occasion of the BLE's founding president, William D. Robinson, being inducted into Labor's International Hall of Fame in 1991 is current International President Edward Dubroski (right). Larry Sykes (left) is a member of BLE Division 1, the first division in the union's history.

International President Edward Dubroski at a United Mine Workers of America rally. Demonstrations such as this emphasize the BLE's long-time solidarity with other labor organizations.

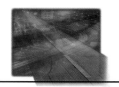

United Transportation Union

On January 1, 1969, four railroad unions, each of which had been in existence since the 19th century, joined forces to meet the challenges of America's changing railroad scene. Although each had been instrumental in raising work standards for its members, 20th century leaders realized — as had their union forefathers — that in order to serve their individual members best, strength, and perhaps survival could only be achieved through unification. It had taken more than 100 years of American railroad history to achieve that goal.

In the decade after the Civil War, America moved west on newly laid railroad tracks. U.S. Rep. James A. Garfield described the railway as the greatest centralizing force of modern times. (Ironically, Garfield would be assassinated in a railroad station.) Between 1860 and 1870, route-mile trackage almost doubled, from approximately 30,000 to nearly 53,000 miles.

As mileage increased, so too did difficulties for railroad workers. It didn't matter what job an individual held with the railroad in that era after the war. The problems for engineers, firemen, conductors and switchmen were very similar. Management imposed long hours with low wages, had minimal concerns about safety and certainly didn't provide any benefits to the surviving families of workers

killed on the job. Management's attitude didn't seem to have changed when, a century later, a railroad president emphasized, "A man ought to be willing to pay to work for a railroad."

Railroaders were not unique in their dilemma. Similar conditions existed in most American industries of the period. The country's first labor union had been formed in the late 18th century, but it was not until 1842 that labor unions were even ruled to be legal. The last 30 years of the 19th century proved a fertile time for union growth.

Even though the courts found unions legal, most initial meetings by those attempting to unite a specific group of railroad workers were clandestine. Those attempting to form such groups were not "union organizers." They were the switchmen, conductors, engineers and firemen who were facing the same daily difficulties as those they were trying to unite.

The First Postwar Brotherhood

Conductors were the first group to take action after the Civil War. These men were earning $2.10 for a trip that could be six hours or 60. Overtime pay was unknown, and OSHA was a century in the future. They were working on trains with coal stoves that could — and did — catch on fire, and riding on trains with inadequate brakes. They were being punished for accidents that were the result of long hours and fatigue.

It was all too much for 22-year-old Thomas J. Wright, an Illinois Central Gulf conductor, who had been working on the railroads since he was 15. In an effort to improve conductors' pay, working conditions and job security, the young man brought some of his fellow Illinois Central Gulf conductors together at Amboy, Illinois, early in 1868 and formed Division Number 1, Conductors' Brotherhood.

Buses operated by members of the BRT, a UTU predecessor union, for the Philadelphia Red Arrow Line

Wright's initial goal was to have members make themselves more valuable through education, sobriety and safety. That, he felt, would entitle them to higher pay and greater respect both from their associates and railroad company management. A strict moral code was an integral part of the union's program.

It didn't take long for other conductors to get the word about the Conductors' Brotherhood, and in the summer of 1868, employees of the Chicago, Burlington & Quincy started Division 2. By November there were enough divisions for the organization to hold its first U.S.-Canadian convention in Columbus, Ohio. Delegates elected officers and set up a mutual insurance service.

The union also adopted a new name, the Order of Railway Conductors of America (ORC). International headquarters were established in Cedar Rapids, Iowa, in 1884 and a women's auxiliary was created that same year. The secretary-treasurer named at the first convention was a resident of Cedar Rapids who kept the records at his home. The location was named as the permanent home of the Grand Division in 1884.

When the ORC's original concept had no impact on management, it expanded beyond its original concept and adopted a strike clause in 1885. When that didn't seem to get management's attention, it implemented a policy of fighting for the welfare of conductors in wages, hours, rules and safety. The more militant approach obviously appealed to an increasing number of conductors, with 65

percent of all conductors joining within a year of the policy change. By 1910 that number had soared to 90 percent.

Through the efforts of ORC and the other railroad brotherhoods of the time, Congress passed a 1907 law limiting the period railroaders could stay on the job to 16

At the 1969 unification of four rail unions to create the United Transportation Union are (left to right) Charles Luna, president of the Brotherhood of Railroad Trainmen; Clyde F. Lane, president of the Order of Railway Conductors and Brakemen; H.E. Gilbert, president of the Brotherhood of Locomotive Firemen and Enginemen; and Neil P. Speirs, president of the Switchmen's Union of North America.

Recognizing efforts of transportation workers throughout the United States and Canada is this monument in Hot Springs, Arkansas, dedicated in 1971.

The Committee of 40, 10-member groups from each of the four unions, worked out the 1969 Unification Agreement and UTU Constitution.

Brotherhood of Locomotive Firemen (BLF) in Port Jervis, New York. A year later, the organization, which had quickly grown to 12 lodges, created the BLF Insurance Association to provide sickness and funeral benefits for locomotive firemen.

Between 1882 and 1892, the BLF experienced such rapid growth that by the time its 16th convention was held in 1892, it had 480 lodges representing 28,000 members. It did lose at least one member that year, Eugene Debs. Debs, who later ran five unsuccessful campaigns for U.S. president on the Socialist Party ticket, had more than just a fireman's union on his mind.

Debs began his railroad career in 1870 at the age of 15, scraping paint off railroad cars for 50 cents a day. He became secretary of the Terre Haute BLF lodge in 1873 and by 1880 was elected secretary-treasurer of the National. He resigned from his office to form the American Railway Union — "one big union" — which he felt was needed to prevent railroad management from playing one labor organization against another. Within a year, the ARU had 125 locals, but after one major strike-related victory, the ARU was soundly defeated as a result of the ill-fated 1894 Pullman strike. The industrywide union concept died with it — for the time being.

The BLF, after a brief period at the end of the 19th century when it was negatively affected by a major economic depression, began a new era of growth in the 20th century.

In 1906, the Brotherhood of Locomotive Firemen expanded its membership base by adding enginemen to its roster. As a result, it became the Brotherhood of Locomotive Firemen and Enginemen. In cooperation with three other train service organizations, it began the first united wage movement in the industry.

The BLF&E continued to play a leadership role well into the century. In 1916, the union led the fight for an eight-hour day for rail workers. When the railroads refused to accede to the brotherhood's request, President Woodrow Wilson convened a joint session of Congress, urging it to pass legislation for the eight-hour day. Under the leadership of William Adamson, chairman of the House Interstate Commerce Commission — who had a reputation as a

hours in 24. The action came a little too late to help the 4,500 railroad employees who were killed and 88,000 who were injured that year in what has been termed the worst year in history for accidents among railroaders.

Early in World War II, the Order of Sleeping Car Conductors united with the ORC, and in 1954 the organization was renamed the Order of Railway Conductors and Brakemen to reflect its diverse membership.

At the time of the 1969 UTU amalgamation, the Order of Railway Conductors and Brakemen had 438 subordinate divisions in 45 states, five Canadian provinces and the Panama Canal Zone. International headquarters — the Grand Division — was located in Cedar Rapids, Iowa.

Lighting a Fire Under the Firemen

In 1873, five years after Tommie Wright brought conductors together, Joshua Leach and 10 Erie Railroad firemen did the same with their peers, creating the friend of railroad labor — the Adamson Bill, which ensured the eight-hour workday, was passed. The railroads refused to accept the law, and the unions called a strike for March 19, 1917. That morning, railroad management accepted the new law shortly before the U.S. Supreme Court, in a 5-to-4 decision, upheld the law's constitutionality that afternoon.

The BLF&E's activism and achievements, so evident in wage and safety issues, were further exemplified by the appointment of the brotherhood's president, W.S. Carter, as director of the United States Division of Labor during World War I when the government took over the railroads.

In April 1917, the BLF&E moved its headquarters to downtown Cleveland's Keith Building at East 17th and Euclid. At the time of the 1969 unification, its Grand Lodge was in Lakewood and it had 825 subordinate lodges in 49 states and 10 Canadian provinces.

No Stopping These Brakemen

Eugene Debs' name appears as a player in formation of another rail brotherhood. In 1883, eight Delaware & Hudson RR brakemen secretly met in caboose No.10 in Oneonta, New York, to organize the Brotherhood of Railroad Brakemen. Needing organizing advice, they sent for Debs for guidance. He helped them set up Lodge 1, and in gratitude, the founders named the lodge after Debs.

The first grand master was Charles Woodworth, to whom caboose No. 10 had been assigned. The caboose remains enshrined at Neahwa Park in Oneonta with a memorial plaque recognizing the 1883 achievement.

Primarily, the brakemen intended their brotherhood to be recognized "for the mental, moral and physical improvement of its members and consequently a better and more desirable class of men, who can be depended upon at all times, and into whose care and watchfulness

Historically, a full road-freight rail crew included an engineer, conductor, fireman and two brakemen.

thousands of lives and millions of dollars worth of property can be safely entrusted."

As with the other brotherhoods at the time, a primary goal was to improve safety for fellow brakemen. A major reason for the concern about safety was that one-third of the nation's railroad brakemen were killed or maimed in 1883, the year the brotherhood was founded. Members were offered insurance — death coverage to $300 — since management provided no such benefit.

Two years later the brotherhood created an insurance department, which doubled death benefits to $600. Acceptance of the brotherhood and its programs was evidenced by formation of the first Canadian lodge in 1885, while overall membership increased to 4,500.

Membership continued to grow, and by 1886 the organization's 244 lodges had 8,000 members. Increased membership and membership dues enabled the insurance department to raise benefits to $800.

In 1899, the brotherhood expanded its membership base to include railroad workers

Forging original unity plans for creation of the United Transportation Union are (left to right) W.W. Carson, Order of Railway Conductors and Brakemen; D.W. Collins, Switchmen's Union of North America; L.E. Chester, Brotherhood of Railroad Trainmen; and M.W. Hampton, Brotherhood of Locomotive Firemen and Enginemen.

The caboose in which the Brotherhood of Railroad Trainmen was founded was dedicated as an historic site in Neahwa Park in Oneonta, New York, in 1924.

in more than 14 different trade classifications. To reflect this change, the broad-based union changed its name to the Brotherhood of Railroad Trainmen (BRT).

In what may have been an omen of things to come less than a century later, the BRT joined with the Brotherhood of Locomotive Firemen in 1893 to obtain the lobbying support of L.S. Coffin, a former Iowa state railroad commissioner, to take their case for better working conditions to Washington legislators.

Apparently it didn't work, for that year 18,343 railroad workers were injured on the job and another 1,657 were killed. Nor did the BRT, or any of the other brotherhoods, have legal redress for injuries that were the result of employer negligence.

Several years later, however, all unions achieved a victory with the 1898 passage of the Erdman Act, making it a criminal offense for railroads to dismiss employees or to discriminate against prospective employees because of their union membership.

The Erdman Act was an outgrowth of Debs' 1894 strike against the Pullman Company. After that strike, general managers for the railroads used a blackball system to keep strikers from returning to work. At first, the general managers refused to issue service letters to strikers proving they had experience. Without these letters it was almost impossible for a striker to get a railroad job.

After one striker successfully sued his railroad company employer, the general managers changed direction and came up with a maneuver described as the "crane with broken neck." They wrote the service letters, but on the stationery of paper manufacturer Crane Bros., which gave them a choice of two secret watermarks, detectable only when the sheet was held up to the light. One, showing a crane with head erect, was given to non-strikers. The other, used for those who were involved in the 1894 strike, had the bird's neck hanging down. It was a warning to potential employers that the applicant had been a striker.

In spite of management's tactics, the Brotherhood of Railroad Trainmen and the other brotherhoods continued their fight for equity. Although strikes were not unknown, they increasingly used legislative means to change their work world and began to achieve success.

In 1908, the Federal Employers' Liability Act was passed. In 1910, the Accident Report Act became law, requiring formerly neglected "incidents" to be reported. It was the year the 10-hour workday became reality and standardization of pay rates and working conditions was won by the brotherhoods. In 1911, the Locomotive Inspection Act became law, and in 1916, the brotherhoods won an eight-hour day. Two years later Canada passed a similar law.

In 1928, the BRT began organizing bus companies that were subsidiaries of railroads, operating as feeder lines to reach areas not served by passenger trains. A few years later the brotherhood began organizing interstate bus operators.

At the time of the 1969 unification, the BRT, which was headquartered in Cleveland, had 1,100 subsidiary lodges in 49 states and 10 Canadian provinces.

Switching Directions

If workers on the post-Civil War railroads faced hazardous working conditions, switchmen may have faced the most hazards.

Working in the yards, these men tended to the switches and the coupling and uncoupling of cars. The couplers have been described as downright murderous. Early couplers included the infamous link-and-pin, or as it was known by the countless men who lost fingers, hands and arms, the "Lincoln pin." Since this coupler had to be set by hand, the switchman had to jump back and forth between two cars as they came together. It is reported that trainmasters interviewing prospective switchmen asked to see their hands. If the man had a few fingers missing, the trainmaster knew he had an experienced individual.

Because of such dangerous working conditions and the fact that switchmen in the Chicago area were working 12 hours a day, every day, for $50 a month, a group of switchmen formed a Switchmen's Association in Chicago in 1877. Its goal was to negotiate with the railroad owners on a variety of issues in a way individuals could not.

The association's idea caught on, and by 1886 it had become large enough to have members across the country. This national expansion caused it to also expand its name to the Switchmen's Mutual Aid Association of the United States of America. Unfortunately, six years later, as the result of a lockout on the Chicago & North Western (which ironically would be purchased by its employees in 1972) and a disastrous strike on the Chicago, Burlington & Quincy RR, the mutual aid association died in July 1894. Three months later it was reborn in Kansas City as the Switchmen's Union of North America (SUNA).

A year before the original association closed its doors, the Safety Appliance Act of 1893 outlawed link-and-pin couplers and required air brakes be installed. President Benjamin Harrison said he never had affixed his signature to anything more willingly. Even so, safety remained a cornerstone of the organization and for more than seven decades was evident in SUNA's watchword, "The injury of one is the concern of all."

In the summer of 1906, SUNA joined the American Federation of Labor (AFL), and for almost half a century was the only operating rail labor union affiliated with the AFL. According to one source, a primary reason for the unwillingness of other rail unions to join the AFL was their "aloofness." Railroad tradesmen — men in the shops,

Engineers and firemen working together in the locomotive had a natural bond, which is why they joined together to work for better wages, working conditions and benefits.

The largest of the UTU's predecessor unions, the Brotherhood of Railroad Trainmen, was founded in 1883. Created as the Brotherhood of Railroad Brakemen, it changed its name in 1889 to reflect expansion into other crafts.

yards, stations and along the tracks — did not have the same power and prestige as some of their fellow railroaders, who were described as being more like members of the lower professional class rather than the working class.

In actuality, the Switchmen's Union was organized along craft lines, and the AFL's basic premise was, and is, organization along craft and skill lines.

In 1935, SUNA affiliated with the Canadian Labour Congress and at the time of amalgamation had locals in one Canadian province. The union, headquartered in Buffalo, New York, in 1968, also had 275 locals in 35 states.

Members of all the rail unions continued to make progress in working conditions, safety and benefits, with wages gradually increasing. In 1892, engineers were receiving $3.68 a day, which increased to $4.64 by 1908. Conductors were getting $3.07 in 1892 and $3.83 in 1908; firemen went up from $2.07 to $2.76; and the brakemen's $1.89 increased to $2.64. By the turn of the century, railroad employees were making more than the average worker and were represented by 20 railroad labor unions,

compared to four in the two decades after the Civil War.

At the onset of World War I, one worker in 25 was engaged in railroad work. Industry employment peaked in 1920 when 2 million people worked for the railroads.

In spite of increased union membership and rail employment, change was inevitable. Increasing use of automobiles and the slow, but steady, growth of air travel after World War I began to affect railroad travel. And the Great Depression affected the industry even more.

Inevitability of Change

Railroaders who kept their jobs during this bleak period did comparatively well financially. In 1932, early in the Depression, conductors were making $2,729 a year. A railroad executive was making a little over $5,000, but a dentist was earning only $2,391. Since a filling cost $1, it is understandable. A new Pontiac coupe or mink coat could be purchased for $585 and a six-room house with a two-car garage in the Detroit area cost $2,800 — about a year's wages for a conductor.

The onset of World War II, with its gas rationing and limited tire availability, reversed the earlier trend of increased automobile usage. Moving freight and military personnel was the primary consideration. Passenger travel was increasingly restricted. With 350,000 railroad men called into military service (about one in five), new workers had to be trained, opening the door for women to enter the industry.

Less than a year after the war was over, President Truman, using wartime powers still in effect in 1946, took over the railroads to deal with a strike by several rail unions. Similar situations arose in 1948 and 1950. That year the government once again took over operation of the railroads as an emergency measure during the Korean War. A year later an amendment to the Railway Labor Act lifted the ban on compulsory union membership as a requisite for holding a railroad job.

With that change and the increasing consolidation of railroads in the 1950s and 1960s, the future looked bleak unless some changes could be made. Several unification movements aimed at bringing all the unions together were discussed during the period, and although they came close, each attempt failed — until January 1968.

That month, exploratory talks began among the leaders of the BRT (Charles Luna), BLF&E (H.E. "Ed" Gilbert), ORC&B (Clyde F. Lane) and SUNA (Neil P. Speirs).

Each of these men assigned their top officers to cooperate in outlining a workable merger. The merger committee met almost continuously, and an initial amalgamation document was presented to the four presidents on April 15, 1968. Each of the organizations then elected a 10-member committee to work together to write, revise and arrange an agreement that would be acceptable to all four unions.

One of the most troublesome issues the committees had to face was maintaining the autonomy of each of the crafts. The problem was resolved with a guarantee that only members of a particular craft would vote on matters affecting that craft's wages, rules and work conditions.

Unification Becomes Reality

By mid-August, the four union leaders gave their approval to the tentative agreement submitted by the 40-member group. In October, each dues-paying member of

the four unions received a ballot, the proposed constitution and the proposed unification agreement. The vote was almost 7-to-1 in favor of forming a single union, the United Transportation Union, which would represent workers in the United States and Canada. The idea of a unified railroad union had first been broached by Eugene Debs in 1893 when he formed the American Railway Union. It took more than 75 years for his basic idea to reach fruition, but at long last it did.

The UTU, with headquarters in suburban Lakewood, became reality on January 1, 1969, with the BRT's Charles Luna as first president. The former presidents of the other three unions were named assistant presidents. Luna was followed by Al H. Chesser (1972-79), Fred A. Hardin (1980-91), G. Thomas DuBose (1991-95) and Charles L. Little (1995-).

The first official UTU labor agreement covered bus operators and maintenance employees of Lockport Bus Lines in Lockport, New York, and became effective on the same day as the amalgamation, January 1, 1969.

One of the newly joined union's primary goals was to increase legislative activity at the national level. Its early efforts were successful, when in the following year the Rail Passenger Service Act, creating Amtrak, was passed in October 1970.

Formation of Amtrak was promoted by the UTU, as it became more and more evident that the United States could not rely solely upon continued massive construction of highways and airports to meet domestic travel needs. As anticipated with the advent of Amtrak, rail ridership increased, helping to stabilize the job market for many railroaders.

The UTU also took an active part in the 1976 creation of Conrail (Consolidated Rail Corporation). The idea behind the formation of Conrail was to forestall nationalization of the country's rail system, brought about by the bankruptcies of six of the nation's rail lines. The UTU's concern for its members allowed it to play a major advocacy role in Conrail's creation.

Since that time, the union's political and legislative arm, TPEL (Transportation Political Education League), has remained actively involved in helping to obtain legislation that positively impacts UTU members. Legislative offices in Washington, D.C., and Ottawa maintain liaison with

achieving significant legislative progress. Once again showing its legislative know-how, the UTU was in the forefront of the battle to win passage of the Urban Mass Transportation Act and the Intermodal Surface Transportation Efficiency Act, laws that provide billions of dollars in operating funds and capital assistance for transit systems across the country.

Another integral part of the UTU is its Auxiliary, which had its beginnings in 1886. A group of women from railroad families first organized to hold dance programs and literary group meetings. In 1892, the women petitioned the Grand Lodge of the BRT for a charter, which was granted by delegates at the 1888 BRT convention. On June 22, 1892, the first lodge was organized in Toronto. In March 1970, the Ladies Auxiliary of the UTU was chartered in recognition of its value and contributions.

elected and appointed officials to make certain they are aware of the UTU members' needs.

The UTU also sought to meet the needs of the members of other rail unions. Not content to rest on its laurels with four brotherhoods integrated into one union, the UTU instituted an open door policy to other transportation labor organizations interested in joining.

In September 1970, the International Association of Railway Employees (IARE) became the first union to accept the UTU invitation. Among those represented by the IARE were African-American conductors, trainmen, engineers, shop mechanics, porters and maintenance-of-way employees. The IARE initially had been created because of the African-American workers' exclusion from organized rail labor.

In 1985, the Railroad Yardmasters of America voted 3-to-1 to become the second union to merge with the UTU. The yardmasters had organized immediately after World War I in response to managerial abuses. The UTU's Yardmaster Department now represents 1,800 members.

A further extension of an early growth move is the UTU's 8,000-member Bus Department, which represents local, urban, over-the-road, school bus and charter bus drivers, as well as bus mechanics, dispatchers and clerical workers. Reaching out to others in the transportation industry as it did with bus drivers in 1928, the UTU's membership of 125,000 now includes airline pilots and mechanics.

The UTU has achieved substantial gains in wages, benefits and working conditions for its members, as well as

As the industry continued to change to meet the challenges of the 21st century, so did the Ladies Auxiliary, reinventing itself to embrace the increasing integration of the sexes in the transportation field. Following its Seventh International Convention in 1995, attended by more than 650 delegates from the United States and Canada, the organization dropped the word "Ladies" from its name. The "new" Auxiliary opened its doors to all family members, both men and women, who wished to become involved in the group's many good efforts.

The rail brotherhoods of the 19th century cited safety as a major reason for their creation. At the time of amalgamation, three of the four organizations had well-established benefit societies offering a wide range of benefit options to their members and families. In November 1970, the United Transportation Union Insurance Association (UTUIA) was incorporated as a fraternal benefit society, continuing the heritage established more than a century earlier.

With the 1995 election of Charles L. Little as president and Byron A. Boyd Jr. as assistant president, the UTU undertook a new dynamic, proactive approach to guarantee a strong future for the UTU.

A native Texan, Little began his rail career as a switchman in 1955 at the age of 19. He was elected to his first union position with UTU Local 1524 in Houston in 1973 and gradually rose through the local's ranks. The Marine Corps veteran was elected an international vice president in 1983, re-elected in 1987 and elected general secretary and treasurer in 1991.

A member of UTU Local 117 in Portland, Oregon, Little's assistant president, Byron Boyd, began his rail career as a brakeman in 1964 at the age of 18 on the Union Pacific Railroad. He transferred to engine service in 1968 and was promoted to locomotive engineer in 1971. Rising through the ranks of the local, he was elected vice general chairperson of a Union Pacific general committee in 1975. Three years later he became general chairperson. Elected an international vice president in 1983, he was re-elected in 1987 and 1991.

Following the team's initial election as top UTU officers, Little issued a "Blueprint for a New Beginning" including five action plans he and Boyd felt critical to the future of the UTU. Goals included 1) restructuring of the internal organization; (2) union growth; (3) craft preservation and improvement; (4) government relations; and (5) communication. Reflecting their no-nonsense approach, Little and Boyd specified that each of the topics within the action plan had to be implemented within six months.

Little pointed out that the blueprint described only the initial steps the union had to take to survive. Intermediate and long-term objectives would be refined by Little and Boyd after the immediate and urgent demands were met.

With the leadership team's victorious re-election by an overwhelming majority of the delegates' votes at the Eighth Quadrennial Convention in 1999, Little issued a "Blueprint for the 21st Century," a "plan to keep the UTU on track as North America's premier rail and transportation union." The pamphlet's foreword emphasized that the delegates had embraced the earlier blueprint and that the UTU's revitalization stood as testimony to those achievements.

While the new blueprint emphasized that the UTU and UTUIA were financially strong and secure, membership was rising and the union's political action committee was the top labor-transportation PAC, it also noted the tasks ahead.

This time around, the blueprint took aim at quality-of-life issues, enhanced education and training, expedited grievance resolution, modernization of disciplinary policies, creation of local membership initiatives, expansion of legislative activities in Washington and organizing in additional transportation industries.

An example of the enhanced approach to the legislative process has been the UTU's participation with 12 other transportation unions to form a coalition to improve the Railroad Retirement system.

But as Boyd led the union's efforts to secure a new national contract for rail workers, all was not "peaches and cream." On March 15, 2000, the UTU "disaffiliated" from the AFL-CIO for a lack of "evenhandedness." It was the second time in several years the union had withdrawn from the Federation over a major dispute. The first was for a three-year period that ended in 1989. Little pointed out that it was not a complete break, since both organizations have the same goal — to rationalize and revitalize the representation of operating employees on the nation's railroads.

Just as Thomas Wright, Charles Woodworth, Joshua Leach and other brotherhood pioneers a century earlier stood up for their beliefs and their fellow workers, so too has the administration that led the UTU into the 21st century. The withdrawal from the AFL-CIO is another case in point.

From those scattered 19th-century brotherhoods, the United Transportation Union has grown into the largest union in the rail industry. It includes more than 630 locals in North America representing railroad employees on every Class 1 railroad and on many regional and shortline railroads, as well as workers on approximately 45 bus and transit systems.

Like its predecessor organizations, the United Transportation Union continues efforts to improve safety and working conditions on the railroads and in the bus and transit industries.

Since the beginning of the 21st century, the United Transportation Union has promoted the concept of "The Power of One" union for all rail-operating employees. Those 19th-century leaders must be looking on and shaking their heads in wonderment, pleased wonderment. And Eugene Debs? He must be wondering what took so long.

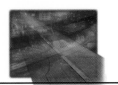

Bonnie Speed Delivery, Inc.

Bonnie Speed Delivery couriers have transported everything from circus elephants in parades to freshly coiffed dogs from the groomer; from briefcases forgotten on suburban kitchen counters to 126 pieces of luggage for a Saudi Arabian sheik who apparently had exceeded airline baggage limitations on a flight from Cleveland to New York. Still, Bonnie Speed's core business is moving envelopes and packages — about 1,200 a day — and more on Fridays.

Bonnie Speed Delivery, Inc. is a full-service transportation company founded in 1959 by M. C. Younge. After several years in military logistics, Younge settled in Cleveland and found a void in small-package delivery services in Northeast Ohio. Business owners relied on the mail carrier or even taxi drivers to expedite packages across town. Younge observed that taxi drivers seemed to move people better than packages, so he set up shop as Bonnie Speed.

Younge originally named the company Bunny Speed — he even had a logo of a rabbit racing along with a package tucked under its arm. When Younge ordered company signs and letterhead from his Scottish printer, "Bunny Speed" was interpreted as "Bonnie Speed." Younge decided it was a "bonnie" idea to stick with the new name rather than trash the printer's finished goods, and the company has been Bonnie Speed ever since.

From 1960 to 1990 the company was primarily a local messenger service with a small fleet of cars and trucks whose drivers and dispatchers communicated via CB radio.

In 1990, however, Kenneth Hardy and Darryl Stovall acquired Bonnie Speed from Younge. Hardy has an MBA in finance and a corporate finance background; Stovall brought expertise from the transportation industry and degrees in marketing and operations. The two set out to develop the company into a more diversified, full-fledged transportation business. Within two years Hardy, president, and Stovall, vice president, replaced 80 percent of the staff; built a new 10,000-square-foot facility on St. Clair Avenue near East 25th; invested in a new telecommunications system, computers, radios and alpha pagers; and instilled a new operating philosophy based on a goal-oriented work environment with budgets, departments, forecasts and accountability. Sales at the 24-hour-a-day, 7-day-a-week business have tripled since the acquisition.

Technological advances have contributed significantly to Bonnie Speed's growth. Indeed, some say the company is actually a communications business. "It's all about minimizing communication time between our customers, our dispatchers and our drivers," Hardy notes. Reduced communication time means faster deliveries and more time for additional deliveries.

These days, the company is moving faster than ever, thanks to Internet-based dispatching technology. The new equipment transacts entire deliveries online — complete with e-mail confirmations to clients. Telephone transactions are still available for customers without Internet access. "Using technology in transportation is really the only cost-effective way we can serve our clients, maintain profitability and keep costs down," Hardy says. Further, the technological advances allow employees to "work smarter and with less stress" — in short, it helps them do their jobs more easily and more effectively.

Bonnie Speed also has its own radio tower and radio frequency. The station can be accessed only by Bonnie Speed couriers, enabling company dispatchers to contact all drivers or specific drivers.

These days, the company is moving faster than ever, thanks to Internet-based dispatching technology.

But Bonnie Speed couriers are more than "drivers" — bikers and walkers are part of the delivery mix, too, particularly on downtown routes. Some companies even use Bonnie Speed couriers as dedicated mail carriers and internal package runners. One large Cleveland hospital has contracted with Bonnie Speed to deliver in-house packages throughout the medical complex each day. Additional scheduled route services include deliveries to branch offices; medical support services such as transferring records, X-rays and lab specimens between facilities; bulk mailing services; and product and parts distribution. Bonnie Speed's Route Service is pre-scheduled at daily, weekly or monthly intervals. As more companies outsource delivery requirements, Bonnie Speed plans to grow the customized and scheduled route portion of its business.

Other clients rely on Bonnie Speed for larger shipments. The company acquired a local trucking business in 1996, and about 25 percent of Bonnie Speed business is truck deliveries, including palletized materials, machinery, drums and steel. Bonnie Speed owns a late-model fleet of trucks operated by professional drivers who are experienced in handling all types of freight, including hazardous materials.

Locally, Bonnie Speed couriers also make a number of charitable deliveries, including food for Catholic Charities to the Cleveland Food Bank,

Christmas trees to area hospitals and senior citizens, and air conditioners donated for seniors during sweltering summer months.

Looking ahead, the company is working with local high schools, trade schools and two-year institutions to inform area youth about future job opportunities in the transportation industry, particularly as drivers and dispatchers at Bonnie Speed.

"We have a 40-year history of service in this community," Hardy says. "During that time the region has changed dramatically. My job is to make sure Bonnie Speed innovates and is flexible enough to make those changes to meet and exceed our customers' needs over the next 40 years. We are a niche player that tries to continually customize our service to suit our changing customer needs. We will continue to evolve as customer needs evolve."

Customer service agents ensure seamless, point-to-point service.

Dispatchers use the latest telecommunications technology.

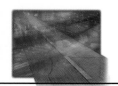

Greater Cleveland Regional Transit Authority

On the first day of service for the Greater Cleveland Regional Transit Authority, commuters swamped the bus and Rapid transit lines formerly operated by a handful of municipalities. Ridership was immediately up 10 percent, sparked by new low rates and the promise of a new future for public transit in Cuyahoga County.

RTA, as Cuyahoga County's sole transit provider, has come to be called, was created out of crisis. In the early 1970s many of the eight municipal transit systems serving Cuyahoga County were in various stages of decline, a result of the overwhelming suburban sprawl in the region and the systems' total reliance on farebox revenues to sustain them.

RTA operates 750 buses that transport more than 60 million riders annually, serving 59 communities in Greater Cleveland.

A transportation task force studying the situation recommended regionalization and the Greater Cleveland Regional Transit Authority was created December 30, 1974, by the actions of the Cuyahoga County Board of County Commissioners and Cleveland City Council. Both approved the plan for different reasons. Cleveland residents wanted access by public transportation to jobs in the suburbs and relief from the financial burden of the ailing Cleveland Transit System (CTS). The suburbs saw an opportunity for more frequent and efficient service and the ability to transfer freely between the various systems. All were eager for lower fares, including the half-priced rides for seniors, students and the handicapped that was touted by planners.

The Waterfront Line delivers 600,000 visitors a year to Cleveland entertainment attractions, including the east bank of the Flats, North Coast Harbor and the new West Third Street Station at Cleveland Browns Stadium.

The first challenge for the new RTA was to pass a 1-cent sales tax to support its consolidation and expansion plans. If passed, bus and Rapid transit fares would be reduced drastically, to 25 cents per ride for local bus lines and 35 cents for the Shaker and Cleveland Rapid lines and express buses.

The tax passed on July 22, 1975, with more than 70 percent of voters favoring the new plan. CTS general manager Leonard Ronis, who would assume the GM post with RTA until 1981, heralded "the beginning of a new era" and said the new fare structure would be in place by October 5 of that year.

RTA immediately assumed control of the Cleveland Transit System and the Shaker Rapid transit line. It purchased a private bus company serving Chagrin Falls and entered into service agreements with several suburban bus lines.

With reduced fares, which RTA had committed to for five years, passengers flocked to the system. In a news story a few weeks after RTA was created, parking lot operators complained that their business was down between 5 percent and 10 percent.

That first year, RTA added eight new routes, pushing bus service into unserved communities such as Westlake and Solon, bringing jobs in those suburbs closer to many. In total, it added 90,000 vehicle miles and 10 line extensions. RTA also created a transit police force to increase security on buses and at Rapid transit stations.

Another early achievement was the creation of the Community Responsive Transit program, which provides rides for the elderly and handicapped. Begun in 1976, it uses small vans with lifts for advanced-reservation transit to riders throughout Cuyahoga County.

The reduction in fares and the revitalization of the system pushed ridership from 81.5 million in 1975 to 121.1 million in 1980. The Middle-Eastern oil crisis in 1979 also shifted riders to public transit.

RTA stood by its pledge to retain the 25 cent and 35 cent fares while its fuel costs rose 195 percent and its labor costs were up 123 percent. Finally, facing a deficit of $3.8 million by the end of the year, the RTA board of trustees voted to increase fares 15 cents across the board, to 40 cents and 50 cents on July 1, 1980. The downtown Loop fare remained at 10 cents.

The fare increase and demographic trends robbed the system of riders over the next decade. Its foes have been a residential dispersal pattern that stretched transit resources and increased reliance on private automobiles. Cuyahoga County, RTA's service area, saw its population drop as developers carved new communities out of distant farmland along major interstate highways. The population of the city of Cleveland, the transit system's core, declined to 500,000 by 1990, after hitting a peak of 914,808 in 1950.

All the while, RTA continued to improve the system. The $100 million Shaker Rapid rejuvenation, completed in 1981, was the first using newly available federal and state transit aid. Its two tracks were renamed the Blue and Green lines. Other improvements included new bus shelters, improved maintenance facilities for buses and Rapids and new buses and new cars for the old CTS Rapid, renamed the Red Line.

In 1993, RTA began planning for the Waterfront Line, an extension of the light-rail Shaker Rapid that would carry passengers from the Tower City station to the downtown entertainment centers in the Flats and on the lakefront. Completed in time for the city's bicentennial celebration, which focused on the Flats, the Waterfront Line has more than met expectations, carrying 600,000 riders annually.

RTA continues to respond to riders' needs as the Community Circulator system proves. Community Circulators are small buses that carry passengers around a neighborhood to shopping centers, hospitals and offices.

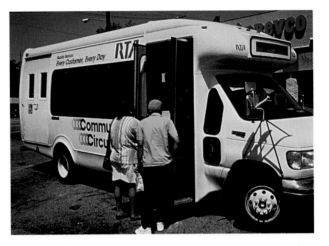

Community Circulators, small buses that help riders get around neighborhoods, proved to be a big success after their introduction in the early 1990s. The Circulators provide 850,000 rides a year.

By the end of 1999, RTA had eight Circulators. In mid-1999 RTA was awaiting 28 newly purchased Circulator buses to augment its fleet of 46. Ridership at that point was 100,000 passengers per month and continues to grow steadily.

In part because of these new additions, RTA ridership bobbed back above 60.6 million passenger trips per year after years of decline.

Looking ahead, the Authority is developing an ambitious plan for the future called Transit 2010. RTA hopes one aspect of Transit 2010 will spur economic development along the key transit corridor between downtown and University Circle on the East Side. An electric trolley bus line is planned to shuttle passengers between the two key employment and entertainment hubs. RTA, though, hopes the line does more than carry riders. The Euclid Corridor Transportation Project should give developers confidence that there are major developments taking place in the area and that the time is right to revitalize the heart of the city.

The rejuvenated Shaker Rapid line, which was overhauled early in RTA's first years, serves more than 4 million riders a year.

Ohio Turnpike Commission

The Ohio Turnpike Commission has made the trek across the northern part of the state the favored alignment for motorists. The commission manages a 241-mile toll highway extending from the Ohio-Pennsylvania to the Ohio-Indiana border. Motorists can traverse Ohio on the Ohio Turnpike without being forced to use back roads with limited lane capacity and line of sight. Travelers are assured of a safe and well-maintained thoroughfare. Additionally, 16 service plazas are destination points for refueling, food concessions, travel information and rest stops. Gino Zomparelli, executive director of the commission, says he is proud of the agency's operations and advances over the years.

The autonomous and financially independent commission recently passed the half-century mark as custodian of the Ohio Turnpike. When the commission was started in 1949, it was not expected to continue indefinitely. But state

The 1949 legislation enabling the commission was spurred by dramatic changes taking place in the travel industry and World War II era of economic recovery. The expanding role of the automobile coupled with the demand for interstate commerce dictated the need for long-distance travel. But like most states, Ohio had a spider-web connection of smaller federal and state routes that failed to accommodate the increasing number of cars and trucks. Traffic on highways was impeded by at-grade intersections and stop signs. Travel was becoming hazardous and burdensome.

In the early days of road transportation, a federal highway department existed but lacked the funds to help states build highways. States consequently were permitted to sell bonds to finance the construction of highways, and tolls were collected to pay off the bond debt. East coast states led in the construction of turnpikes, and the Pennsylvania Turnpike, opened in the early 1940s, is recognized as the first to serve motorists. The move by Pennsylvania was as much a challenge as an encouragement for Ohio to build a connecting turnpike.

The Ohio Turnpike Commission in Cleveland-Berea is headquarters for all administrative, maintenance and support services for the turnpike.

However, the idea of a toll highway did not have early widespread approval in the Buckeye State. Some Ohio public officials were opposed to the concept. A major fear was whether traffic would be sufficient enough to generate toll revenue to pay off the construction bond debt. If not, the state would be forced to assume the debt. The issues were complicated further when the ideal alignment of the turnpike was discussed. Some officials in small rural towns were concerned that it would take away travel and commerce from their communities. They could not imagine how a turnpike would look and operate. In the end, the bill creating the commission passed by a few votes. A new era and mode of transportation in Ohio was launched.

officials learned that the demand for safe and efficient travel would be ongoing. They realized that a self-supporting commission is the best vehicle to maintain the roadway. The Ohio Turnpike Commission is driven by some 800 full-time and 300 part-time employees working to serve the public. In 1999 more than $206 million — approximately $176 million from tolls — was generated for the construction, operation and maintenance of the Ohio Turnpike system.

The turnpike's budget was set at $326 million. Deciding the starting point for one end of the highway was easy given the existence of the Pennsylvania Turnpike. Some city officials, especially those in Cleveland, lobbied to have the Ohio Turnpike pass nearby to promote economic growth. After debate and review, the turnpike was constructed as a major rural highway. It cuts across thirteen counties in the northern portion of the state. Today, the turnpike connects a 2,938-mile interstate highway system from Boston to Seattle. It also is a link to another 3,204-mile road system that stretches from New York City to San Francisco.

Paving for the eastern end of the turnpike began in late 1953. The eastern-most 22-mile road project was completed in two years. Ultimately, by October 1955, the entire construction of the road, 17 toll plazas/interchanges, 16 food/fuel service plazas and eight maintenance buildings were completed in only 39 months.

As the original bond debt was near pay-off, the future of the turnpike was debated by the legislature, media, transportation organizations and, most of all, the traveling public. The debate addressed issues ranging from whether the road should remain a toll facility, be managed independently or come under the authority of the Ohio Department of Transportation.

Moreover, state officials realized that to join the federal system, the turnpike would have to undergo major renovations to meet federal standards. For instance, turnpike ramps are designed to slow motorists down to enter toll plazas — a safety feature — whereas ramps on federal highways are designed to keep traffic flowing at higher speeds. State officials and the public also raised concerns surrounding control and operation of the service plazas. The legislature in 1991 voted to indefinitely extend the life of the commission. The commission then embarked on planning the future of the turnpike.

A strategy then was developed to add interchanges, expand to a third lane, renovate toll interchanges and

Repairs and improvements are made near a toll plaza on the Ohio Turnpike to improve service to motorists.

reconstruct the service plaza restaurants, rest areas and refueling areas. The price tag will exceed $1.3 billion dollars. Like the original turnpike project, the cost will be paid without federal funds. The projects will be paid for by a combination of tolls and turnpike revenue bonds.

The new Ohio Turnpike will have a third lane on the heavily traveled 160-mile stretch between Youngstown and Toledo. Service plazas will be significantly upgraded. All toll plazas will be redesigned to add automatic ticket dispensing machines to serve transfer truck operators.

The commission is mindful of societal changes that could present other opportunities to enhance turnpike services. Agency officials are noting technological advancements that could make it possible for motorists to travel from state to state while paying the tolls electronically during their journey. The technology could then be expanded to make food and fuel purchases. Such developments are weighed by the commission to determine essential and convenient services to the millions who travel the turnpike. The Ohio Turnpike Commission has not compromised the general welfare of the state of Ohio and its citizens in terms of public transportation and public safety. The Ohio Turnpike is a road for today built and managed to be a road for tomorrow.

The Interlake Steamship Company

It is easy to spot one of The Interlake Steamship Company's nine vessels when it's "sailing" the Great Lakes from April to December. With three vessels over 1,000 feet long, a combined fleet length of 7,414 feet and a total trip capacity of 344,853 gross tons, the impressive vessels command looks of awe and amazement.

Recognized today as a premier Great Lakes transportation company, Interlake was launched over 87 years ago when it was incorporated in a consolidation that brought together all the vessels formerly managed by Pickands Mather & Company. Partners Colonel James Pickands, Samuel Mather and Jay C. Morse, who purchased a 13/20 interest in a 1,700-ton-capacity wooden steamer, the *V.H. Ketcham*, founded Pickands Mather & Company in 1883.

By the turn of the century, the demand for raw materials from the North had increased and Pickands Mather, which also had an interest in iron mines in upper Michigan, owned several fleets. In 1901 major fleet consolidations occurred in Great Lakes shipping and Pickands Mather relinquished management of two substantial fleets. Director Harry Coulby was determined to retain Pickands Mather's prominent position in Great Lakes commerce and worked hard at forming two more fleets, securing the management of other fleets and constructing new vessels. When Pickands Mather combined its separate fleets into The Interlake Steamship Company in 1913, the new fleet consisted of 39 vessels.

It was 1916 when Interlake built its first 600-foot long vessel, the *Henry G. Dalton*. It acquired 13 vessels from the Cleveland Steamship Company that same year. In 1927 the man at Interlake's helm was honored when the *Harry Coulby* was built. Larger than any other vessel on the Great Lakes at the time, it was also the first to carry more than 16,000 tons.

Over the next years, Interlake continued to modernize and expand, removing older, uneconomical vessels and adding new ones to increase capacity and diversify its fleet. In the mid-1970s Interlake converted the majority of its vessels from straight deckers to self-unloaders — a move that ensured the company's future. In 1976 Interlake launched the first 1,000-foot vessel built entirely on the Great Lakes, the *James R. Barker*.

In 1987 Interlake became a privately held, independent fleet company when it was purchased by James R. Barker, chairman of the board, and Paul R. Tregurtha, vice chairman of the board. Under their direction the company has maintained its position as an industry leader in the Great Lakes vessel community and strengthened its customer service. In 1998 Interlake built the innovative barge *Pathfinder* and the tug *Dorothy Ann*. A 600-foot barge with a tugboat at its stern, the technologically advanced tug-barge greatly increased the fleet's versatility.

Today, Interlake carries approximately 24 million tons annually for steel producers, power companies and

(Far right)
MV Paul R. Tregurtha, longest ship on the Great Lakes at 1,013.5 feet, prepares to depart the Poe Lock at Sault Ste. Marie, Michigan, and move out into Lake Superior after being raised 21 feet from the level of Lake Huron to Lake Superior.

MV James R. Barker southbound in lower Lake Huron. *MV Paul R. Tregurtha* is in the background headed north.

construction material companies. At 1,013.5 by 105 by 56 feet and with a capacity of 68,000 gross tons, its *Paul R. Tregurtha* is the largest carrier on the Great Lakes.

Interlake's success can be attributed to corporate vitality, teamwork and integrity. By blending machinery, technology and human resources it is able to provide maximum operational efficiency and service that is consistent and reliable. The many long-term partnerships it has developed with its customers are based on proven performance and individual, high-quality service. Though Interlake usually delivers taconite (iron ore) pellets, coal, stone or grain to 35 ports on Lakes Superior, Michigan, Huron and Erie, it welcomes delivery challenges and is known for the best and most personal service of any company in the industry.

Safe and efficient voyages demand cooperation and precision teamwork. The Interlake team consists of roughly 300 dedicated shipboard officers and crew, shore-side personnel and company management. Its employees are highly skilled, motivated and knowledgeable in all aspects of vessel operation. Interlake's skilled shore-side staff includes a high percentage of licensed vessel officers. The company's professional engineers, diligent marketing, traffic and operations personnel, and its skilled and caring human resources group are all governed by a cautious yet innovative upper management. Interlake provides a stimulating and rewarding environment and considers each employee a valuable resource. In addition, all employees are given the means to participate in the management and future planning of the company through open forums, winter meetings and shipboard committees.

Also key to Interlake's prosperity is its ongoing investment in improvements and new construction programs that enable it to boast a modern, competitive and well-maintained fleet. Company engineers make effective use of available technology and uphold high standards of maintenance and repair. Recent fleet modernization includes electronic charting, updated boiler automation, skewed propeller blades and the use of satellites for communication. This proactive maintenance program prevents unnecessary vessel delays while preserving a high level of readiness, efficiency and dependability.

All Interlake vessels are also equipped with modern pollution control systems and provide a dust-free and relatively noise-free workplace. In August 2000 the

Tug-barge unit *Dorothy Ann-Pathfinder* unloads stone at a dock on the Rouge River in Detroit, Michigan.

company became the first U.S. shipping company on the Great Lakes to become certified by the American Bureau of Shipping (ABS) under both the ISO 9002 standards and the International Management Code for Safe Operation of Ships and for Pollution Prevention (ISM Code). Interlake is also the first American vessel operating company, and only the second company in the world, to receive the "SQ" notation for the more stringent safety and quality standards endorsed by ABS.

Interlake's commitment to improving and expanding its partnerships with its customers and to being prepared to meet any challenge will continue well into the future — the company's immense resources culminating in a superior Great Lakes water transportation system.

SS Elton Hoyt 2nd approaches the ore dock in Huron, Ohio.

The Great Lakes Group

The Great Lakes Towing Company is the largest tugboat company operating in the Great Lakes region. Its familiar red and green tugboats bearing the squared off "G" on their stacks cover over 8,300 miles of shoreline and a water surface area of around 100,000 square-miles. The company provides services such as local harbor towing, docking and undocking, interport towing of vessels and barges, icebreaking, as well as rescue and assistance to grounded or damaged ships.

The company started its first navigating season with over 150 tugboats. Known popularly as "the towing company" for its more than 100-year history, Great Lakes Towing has been a significant marine operations link in one of the major economic lifelines of North America — the fourth seacoast and the Great Lakes Seaway System. As a part of The Great Lakes Group, Great Lakes Towing also has the capacity to move heavy lift cargo down the Mississippi to the Gulf of Mexico or off the Great Lakes to anywhere in the world.

Another affiliate of The Great Lakes Group, Soo Linehandling Services, Inc., offers linehandling assistance to vessels passing through the Soo Locks on the St. Mary's River, the only water connection between Lake Superior and the other Great Lakes. The Soo Locks are located in the St. Mary's Rapids, where the water falls about 21 feet from the level of Lake Superior to the level of the lower lakes.

Innovators in the industry, Tugz International L.L.C., another affiliate of The Great Lakes Group, was formed to design and construct a new state-of-the-art fleet of multipurpose tractor tugboats and to handle third-party and affiliate charters. In 1998 the company successfully supervised both design and construction and took delivery of its first two new "Z" class reverse tractor tugs, the *Z-One* and *Z-Two*, from Halter Shipyard, Lockport, Louisiana. These reverse tractor tugs are technically advanced towing vessels in which the conventional propeller and rudder are replaced by an integrated unit known as a "Z" drive. This innovative drive performs both propulsion and steering, allowing the tug to both push or pull in any direction.

Another affiliate, Puerto Rico Towing & Barge Company, began its operations in 1997. It provides towing services to commercial vessels and barges with a five tugboat fleet. From it base in San Juan Harbor, the company services other ports in Puerto Rico, the U.S. Virgin Islands and the islands of the Caribbean. In 1999 this affiliate was awarded a Military Sealift Command contract to provide towing services at the U.S. Naval Station, Roosevelt Roads, for a period of up to five years.

In 1999 Admiral Towing and Barge Company became yet another Great Lakes Group affiliate to be awarded a Military Sealift Command contract. This time the company is providing tugboat and harbor towing services at the U.S. Naval Station, Pearl Harbor, Hawaii, and in the waters of the Hawaiian Islands for a period of up to five years with three "Z" class tugs.

To mark the company's 100th anniversary, Cleveland Mayor Michael R. White designated July 7, 1999 as "The Great Lakes Towing Company Day". He recognized the company for its leadership in the maritime industry and its significant contributions to the economic well-being of its headquarters' city.

Tug *Delaware* assisting the *M/V Ziema Gnieznienska* into Cleveland

Tug *Z-Three* assisting a Navy ship to berth, Pearl Harbor, Hawaii

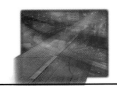

Roadway Express, Inc.

On any given day, Roadway Express delivers an incredible 59,000 shipments. The company employs over 26,000 individuals who play a critical role in moving its 10,000 tractors and 34,000 trailers throughout all of North America. These impressive statistics qualify the 70-year-old, Akron-based carrier as one of the largest shippers of its kind in the entire country, and one of the most successful.

And there's one more statistic of which Roadway is rightfully proud — its gleaming safety record. In 1998 an incredible 43 of the company's drivers achieved a record 3 million miles without an accident — even a fender bender — a feat that requires at least 26 years of professional driving. Two drivers have attained over 4 million accident-free miles; 218 drivers have achieved the 2 million milestone; while an impressive 1,364 drivers have traveled 1 million accident-free miles.

The company also takes its message of driving safety on the road with a number of community-oriented programs, including four unique trailers that feature bold No-Zone messages about driver blind spots alongside large trucks. These trailers travel the country, sharing information with the motoring public about ways to safely share the road with commercial vehicles.

Roadway moves information as much as it moves freight. This capability emerges from an extensive information system that uses bar code and laser scanner technology to capture data about thousands of shipments before, during and after they enter Roadway's vast freight network. This information helps the motor carrier gain flexibility, enhance its service and create greater efficiencies. It is also shared with Roadway customers to help them better manage their transportation needs.

This instantaneous information exchange is one of the factors that has kept Roadway at the forefront of the shipping industry. The other has been the introduction of special delivery services to accommodate the growing needs of its customers.

For Roadway Express, there's no such thing as providing its customers with too much service, or too much information. For example, if a customer needs to make a change in a shipment that's already in transit, on any given day, at any given moment, Roadway can tell the customer precisely where the shipment is — and alter the routing on the spot.

This commitment to fulfilling every possible customer demand is a deep-seated legacy in Roadway's history. Stories circulate about co-founder Galen Roush, who would frequently appear, unannounced, at Roadway terminals and load freight alongside drivers and dockworkers.

His commitment to achieving complete customer satisfaction is woven inextricably in the company's business philosophy and was one of the key factors that has made Roadway the largest LTL carrier in the country.

Today, the company operates a seamless delivery network throughout North America with unmatched destination points and unprecedented delivery services to most of Canada and Mexico. The company delivers to thousands of cities daily and provides freight transportation services to over 60 countries on six continents.

Roadway's commitment to employee and customer satisfaction, creating innovative new services and providing state-of-the-art information access has resulted in a flexible, growth-oriented organization driven to succeed.

Owner-operators in the 1930s stand proudly beside their "state-of-the-art" rig.

Roadway Express delivers to thousands of points in all 50 states, Canada, Mexico and Puerto Rico.

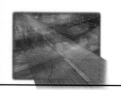

The World Group

Keeping products moving worldwide is the mission and focus of The World Group, a pioneer in intermodal services and containerization that is known around the globe.

The World Group is the umbrella organization for a group of companies dedicated to international shipping. It was founded in 1960 by Jack E. Hunger, a graduate of the U.S. Merchant Marine Academy of Kings Point, New York. The young entrepreneur had grown up in Lorain, Ohio, and began working as a port captain in Chicago when the St. Lawrence Seaway opened in 1959. Recognizing the need for a local steamship agency that could service the growing maritime interests of the Great Lakes, he launched World Shipping, Inc. from an office in Cleveland.

World Shipping, Inc. vessel operations division handles many oceangoing vessels that load and discharge cargo through the Port of Cleveland.

Hunger's timing couldn't have been better. The early 1960s ushered in the age of container shipping, which allowed huge quantities of goods to be packed into steel containers that could be transported by rail or truck to port cities, then loaded onto ocean-going vessels. Before long, World Shipping was handling containerized cargo, which led to a tremendous spurt in business for the growing company.

Hunger moved the corporate offices to Lakewood in 1971 to accommodate this rapid growth. He also established additional offices around the Midwest, as well as a secure inland container depot and rail terminal that provided equipment inspection, repair and maintenance, and cargo distribution through its bonded warehouses. Then in 1986 the services provided by these subsidiaries were combined to form ContainerPort Group, Inc., one of the largest intermodal transportation and depot companies in the Midwest.

By 1993 ContainerPort had its own subsidiary, Intermodal Container Logistics (ICL), which provided logistics services to shippers and consignees, arranged and brokered freight, and supplemented its transportation service. The World Group continued its diversification, while remaining within its competencies, by forming an international chemical logistics transport firm in 1995 named NewPort Tank Containers, Inc. NewPort focuses on the chemical industry by providing complete door-to-door, (bulk liquid) international transportation services using intermodal, 20-foot ISO tank containers.

Later that year, Hunger turned over control of the company to his sons: Frederick, who took over as president, and John, who became chief financial officer. Along with many long-time veterans of the company, they manage a multifaceted company with 425 employees in offices all around the Midwest and on the East Coast, and service clients ranging from automotive companies and their suppliers, to steel, chemical and consumer product manufacturers.

ContainerPort Group, Inc. operates the intermodal rail ramp located across from Jacobs Field.

Today, the company continues to offer specialized transport in full or consolidated loads by road, rail and ocean, as well as myriad other services so goods that must be transported internationally or into and out of the Midwest get where they're going safely and on time. It is such dedication to service, as well as its extensive strategic network, full product line and extensive resources, that have made The World Group a leader in total logistics services and intermodal transportation.

bibliography

bibliography

This is a selected bibliography of works, most of which are readily available at local libraries, relating to the topics and major themes in this book. For titles of additional works relating to Cleveland, we direct readers to the excellent annotated bibliography prepared by John Stark Bellamy II for the Cuyahoga County Public Library. The most comprehensive sources for titles relating to Cleveland are the online catalogs of the Cleveland Public Library, the Western Reserve Historical Society and the Cuyahoga County Public Library.

For detailed information on the individuals, companies and events discussed in this work, we suggest that readers consult the *Encyclopedia of Cleveland History* (available online at http://ech.cwru.edu) and the Cleveland Digital Library at Cleveland State University (http://web.ulib.csuohio.edu/SpecColl/cdl/).

Western Reserve and Early History

Butler, Margaret Manor. *A Pictorial History of the Western Reserve*. Cleveland: The Early Settlers Association of the Western Reserve, 1963.

Conlin, Mary Lou. *Simon Perkins of the Western Reserve*. Cleveland: Western Reserve Historical Society, 1968.

Ellis, William D. *Early Settlers of Cleveland*. Cleveland: Cleveland State University, 1976.

Hatcher, Harlan. *The Western Reserve: The Story of New Connecticut in Ohio*. Kent: Kent State University Press, 1991.

Knepper, George W. *Ohio and Its People*. Kent: Kent State University Press, 1989.

Post, Charles Asa. *Doans Corners: And the City Four Miles West, With a Glance at Cuyahoga County and the Western Reserve*. Cleveland: The Caxton Company, 1930.

Wheeler, Robert A. (ed). *Visions of the Western Reserve: Public and Private Documents of Northeastern Ohio, 1750-1860*. Columbus: Ohio State University Press, 2000.

Whittlesey, Charles. *Early History of Cleveland, Including Papers and other Matter relating to the Adjacent Community, with Biographical Notices of the Pioneers and Surveyors*. Cleveland: [Fairbanks, Benedict & Co.], 1867.

Wilcox, Frank Nelson. *Ohio Indian Trails*. Cleveland: The Gates Press, 1934.

Cleveland — General Histories

Campbell, Thomas F. and Miggins, Edward M. (eds). *The Birth of Modern Cleveland, 1865-1930*. Cleveland: Western Reserve Historical Society; London; Cranbury, NJ: Associated University Presses, 1988.

Chapman, Edmund. *Cleveland: Village to Metropolis: A Case Study of Problems of Urban Development*. Cleveland: Western Reserve Historical Society, 1999 (reprint).

Hatcher, Harlan. *Giant from the Wilderness: The Story of a City and Its Industries*. Cleveland: World Publishing Co., 1955.

Keating, W. Dennis, et al (eds). *Cleveland: A Metropolitan Reader*. Kent: Kent State University Press, 1995.

Miller, Carol P. and Wheeler, Robert A. *Cleveland: A Concise History*. Bloomington: Indiana University Press, 1997.

Rose, William Ganson. *Cleveland: The Making of a City*. Cleveland: World Publishing Co., 1950 (reprinted, Kent State University Press, 1990).

Van Tassel, David D. and Grabowski, John J. (eds). *The Encyclopedia of Cleveland History*. Bloomington: Indiana University Press, 1987.

Van Tassel, David D. and Grabowski, John J. (eds). *The Encyclopedia of Cleveland History*. Bloomington: Indiana University Press, 1996.

Immigration/Migration/Ethnicity

Andrica, Theodore. *Romanian Americans and Their Communities in Cleveland*. Cleveland: Cleveland State University, 1977.

Barton, Josef. *Peasants and Strangers: Italians, Rumanians and Slovaks in an American City*. Cambridge: Harvard University Press, 1975.

Bonutti, Karl B. and Prpic, George J. *Selected Ethnic Communities of Cleveland: A Socio-Economic Study*. Cleveland: Cleveland State University, 1974.

Cadzow, John. *Lithuanian Americans and Their Communities in Cleveland*. Cleveland: Cleveland State University, 1978.

Callahan, Nelson J. and Hickey, William F. *Irish Americans and Their Communities in Cleveland*. Cleveland: Cleveland State University, 1978.

Davis, Russell H. *Black Americans in Cleveland From George Peake to Carl B. Stokes*. Washington: Associated Publishers, 1972.

Fugita, Stephen, et al. *Asian Americans and Their Communities in Cleveland*. Cleveland: Cleveland State University, 1977.

Gartner, Lloyd P. *History of the Jews of Cleveland*. Cleveland: Western Reserve Historical Society, 1978.

Georgevich, Dragoslav. *Serbian Americans and Their Communities in Cleveland*. Cleveland: Cleveland State University, 1977.

Grabowski, John J. et al. *Polish Americans and Their Communities in Cleveland*. Cleveland: Cleveland State University, 1976.

Hunter, Jane Edna. *A Nickel and a Prayer*. [Cleveland]: Elli Kani Pub. Co., 1940.

Kipal, Vitaut. *Byelorussian Americans and Their Communities in Cleveland*. Cleveland: Cleveland State University, 1982.

Klemencic, Matjaz. *Slovenes of Cleveland: The Creation of a New Nation and a New World Community, Slovenia and the Slovenes of Cleveland, Ohio.* Ljubljana: Scientific Institute of the Faculty of Arts, 1995.

Kusmer, Kenneth L. *A Ghetto Takes Shape: Black Cleveland: 1870-1930.* Urbana: University of Illinois Press, 1976.

Marcron, Mary Haddad. *Arab Americans and Their Communities in Cleveland.* Cleveland: Cleveland State University, 1979.

Megles, Susi. *Slovak Americans and Their Communities in Cleveland.* Cleveland: Cleveland State University, 1978.

Mueller, Jacob. *Aus den Erinnerungen eines Achtundvierzigers. [English Memories of a Forty-Eighter: Sketches from the German-American Period of Storm and Stress in the 1850s;* translated from the German by Steven Rowan.] Cleveland: The Western Reserve Historical Society, 1996.

Papp, Susan M. *Hungarian Americans and Their Communities in Cleveland.* Cleveland: Cleveland State University, 1981.

Peskin, Allen (ed.). *North into Freedom: The Autobiography of John Malvin, Free Negro, 1795-1880.* Cleveland: Press of Western Reserve University, 1966.

Phillips, Kimberly. *AlabamaNorth: African-American Migrants, Community, and Working Class Activism in Cleveland, 1915-45.* Urbana: Univeristy of Illinois Press, 1995.

Rowan, Steven (trans). *Cleveland and Its Germans [1897-98].* Cleveland: The Western Reserve Historical Society, 1998.

Rowan, Steven (trans). *Cleveland and Its Germans [1907].* Cleveland: The Western Reserve Historical Society, 1998.

Veronesi, Gene P. *Italian Americans and Their Communities in Cleveland.* Cleveland: Cleveland State University, 1977.

Vlchek, Frank. *The Story of My Life.* English translation by Fern Long of Vlchek's published [1928] Czech language autobiography. In the Frank Vlchek Papers, The Western Reserve Historical Society.

Vincent, Sidney Z. and Rubinstein, Judah. *Merging Traditions: Jewish Life in Cleveland, A Contemporary Narrative, 1945-1975, A Pictorial Record, 1839-1975.* Cleveland: The Western Reserve Historical Society, 1978.

Neighborhoods

Cigliano, Jan. *Showplace of America: Cleveland's Euclid Avenue, 1850-1910.* Kent: Kent State University Press, 1991.

Lawrence, Ann T. and Schattinger, Joan. *Cleveland's Flats: The Incredible City Under the Hill.* Cleveland: History Associates, 1979.

Patterson, Clyde A. *Old Brooklyn: A Historic Narrative and Projection for the 1980's.* Kent: Commercial Press, 1979.

Ziats. Paul. *Tremont: Cleveland, Ohio's Southside.* [Brookpark, Ohio?]: P. Ziats, 1990.

Suburbs and Suburbanization

Bay Village Historical Society. *Bay Village: A Way of Life.* Bay Village: By the Society, 1974.

Borchert, Jim and Borchert, Susan. *Lakewood: The First Hundred Years.* Norfolk/Virginia Beach: Donning Co., 1989.

Fant, Kathleen G. *Orange Township, Orange Community: A History from 1815 to 1924.* [S.I.]: Orange Community Historical Society, 1982.

Harris, Mary E. and Robinson, Ruth Mills. *The Proud Heritage of Cleveland Heights, Ohio.* [Cleveland]: H. Allen, 1966.

Kubasek, Ernest R. *The History of Parma: A Township, A Village, A City.* [Parma, Ohio?]: Kubasek, 1976.

Molyneaux, David and Sackman, Sue (eds). *75 Years: An Informal History of Shaker Heights.* [Shaker Heights]: Shaker Heights Public Library, 1987.

Morris, Jeffrey. *Beechwood: The Book.* Beechwood, Ohio: J. Morris, [1997?].

Moving to the Corn Fields: A Reader on Urban Sprawl and the Regional Future of Northeast Ohio. Cleveland: Ecocity Cleveland Journal, 1995.

Telshaw, Helen (comp.). *History of Highland Heights.* Highland Heights: [S.N.], 1976.

Transportation, Industry and Labor

Armstrong, Arthur S. *The Persistence of Struggle: The Story of Acme-Cleveland Corporation.* New York: Newcomen Society in North America, 1976.

Boryczka, Raymond. *No Strength without Union: An Illustrated History of Ohio Workers, 1803-1980.* Columbus: Ohio Historical Society, 1982.

Bunn, Don. *White Trucks 1900 Through 1937: Photo Archive.* Hudson, WI: Iconografix Press 1998.

Chernow, Ron. *Titan: The Life of John D. Rockefeller, Sr.* New York: Random House. 1998.

Christiansen, Harry. *New Lake Shore Electric.* Cleveland: The Western Reserve Historical Society, 1978.

_____. *New Northern Ohio's Interurbans and Rapid Transit Railways.* Euclid, Ohio: Trolley Lore, 1983.

_____. *Ride the Red Devils Along Ohio's Trolley Trails.* Euclid, Ohio: Transit House, 1971.

_____. *Trolley Trails Through Greater Cleveland and Northern Ohio From the Beginning Until 1910.* Cleveland: The Western Reserve Historical Society, 1975.

Cox, Jacob D. *Building an American Industry; the Story of the Cleveland Twist Drill Company and its Founder, an Autobiography.* Cleveland: Cleveland Twist Drill Co. [1951].

Dawson, Virginia P. *Engines and Innovation: Lewis Laboratory and American Propulsion Technology.* Washington: National Aeronautics and Space Administration, 1991.

Dyer, Davis. *TRW: Pioneering Technology and Innovation Since 1900.* Boston: Harvard Business School Press, 1998.

Ehle, Jay C. *Cleveland's Harbor: The Cleveland-Cuyahoga County Port Authority.* Kent: Kent State University Press, 1996.

Eiben, Christopher J. *The Red Hand Forever: The Hugh M. O'Neill Family of Cleveland, Ohio.* Cleveland: The O'Neill Brothers Foundation, 1997.

_____. *Tori in America: The Story of Theodore Kundtz.* Novelty, Ohio: Ewald E. Kuntz, Jr. [1994?].

Ellis, William D. *The Cuyahoga.* Dayton, Ohio: Landfall Press, 1966.

Grabowski, John J. and Leedy, Walter. *The Terminal Tower, Tower City Center: A Historical Perspective.* Cleveland: The Western Reserve Historical Society, 1990.

The Great Lake Erie: A Reference Text for Educators and Communicators. Columbus: The Ohio State University Research Foundation, 1987.

Greif, Martin. *The New Industrial Landscape: The Story of the Austin Company.* Clinton: N.J.: Main Street Press, 1978.

Haberman, Ian. *The Van Sweringens of Cleveland: The Biography of an Empire.* Cleveland: Western Reserve Historical Society, 1979.

Hamerla, Richard R. *Two Centuries of Progress: A Bicentennial History of the Chemical Industry in Cleveland:* Prepared and Published by the Archives Committee of the Cleveland Section of the American Chemical Society, 1996.

Harrison, H. Stuart. *The Cleveland-Cliffs Iron Company.* New York: Newcomen Society in North America, 1974.

Hatcher, Harlan. *Lake Erie.* Indianapolis & New York: The Bobbs-Merrill Company, 1945.

Havinghurst, Walter. *Vein of Iron: The Pickands, Mather Story.* Cleveland: World Publishing, 1958.

Hays, Blaine S. *Cleveland's Dynamic Transit Heritage: Commemorating the First Ten Years of RTA.* Cleveland: Northern Ohio Railway Museum, 1985.

Hull, Robert. *September Champions: The Story of America's Air Racing Pioneers.* Harrisburg, PA: Stackpole Books, 1979.

Kraus, Henry. *Heroes of Unwritten Story: The UAW, 1934-39.* Urbana: University of Illinois Press, 1993.

Labor Day Souvenir, 1902. Cleveland: A Joint Publication of the Greater Cleveland Labor History Society, The United Labor Agency, and International Brotherhood of Electrical Workers Local Union No. 38, 1994 [reprint of the original 1902 edition].

Love, Steve and Giffels, David. *Wheels of Fortune: The Story of Rubber in Akron.* Akron: The University of Akron Press, 1999.

Phelan, Craig and Ashyk, Dan. *The Unceasing Struggle: A Chronology of Ohio Labor History, 1803-1987.* Columbus: Ohio Historical Society, 1988.

Saal, Thomas F. and Golias, Bernard J. *Famous But Forgotten: The Story of Alexander Winton, Automotive Pioneer and Industrialist.* Twinsburg, Ohio: Golias Publishing, 1997.

Scheiber, Harry N. *Ohio Canal Era: A Case Study of the Government and the Economy, 1820-1861.* Athens, Ohio: Ohio University Press, 1969.

Smithers (F.S.) & Company. *The Iron Ore Industry and the Cleveland-Cliffs Iron Company, the Hanna Mining Company [and] the M. A. Hanna Company.* New York: [1960].

Toman, Jim. *The Shaker Heights Rapid Transit.* Glendale, CA: Interurban Press, 1990.

Toman, Jim and Cook, Dan. *The Terminal Tower Complex: 1930-1980.* Cleveland: Cleveland Landmarks Press, 1980.

Toman, Jim and Hays, Blaine. *From Horse Tails to Regional Rails: The Story of Public Transit in Cleveland.* Kent: Kent State University Press, 1996.

_____. *Cleveland's Transit Vehicles: Equipment and Technology.* Kent: Kent State University Press, 1996.

Wagar, Richard. *Golden Wheels: The Story of Automobiles Made in Cleveland and Northeastern Ohio, 1892-1932.* Cleveland: John T. Zubal Publisher, 1986 (reprint).

Watson, Sara Ruth. *Bridges of Metropolitan Cleveland: Past and Present.* [Cleveland, S.N.], 1981.

Note on quotations in text

Quotations not fully identified in text are from the following sources:

Chapter I, Knepper, *Ohio*; Benjamin Franklin as quoted in Wheeler, *Visions*; Whittlesey, *Early History.*

Chapter II, Moses Cleaveland as quoted in Hatcher, *Western Reserve*, Rose, *Cleveland: the Making,* and Miller and Wheeler, *Cleveland: A Concise History*; Red Jacket as quoted in *Encyclopedia*; Gilman Bryant as quoted in Rose, *Cleveland: the Making*; Connecticut Land Company field agent, as quoted in Hatcher, *Western Reserve*; account of the Treaty of Fort Industry, Whittlesey, *Early History*; John Melish, as quoted in Wheeler, *Visions.*

Chapter III, notice requiring citizen to report for work as quoted in Chapman, *Cleveland: Village to Metropolis*; description of Cleveland as "the great mart," Henry Howe, as quoted in Hatcher, *Western Reserve*; Ara Sprague as quoted in Rose, *Cleveland: the Making; John Malvin,* in Peskin, ed., *North into Freedom.*

Chapter V, Chapman, *Cleveland: Village to Metropolis;* Vlchek, *Story*; Kniola, unpublished letter in the collections of the Western Reserve Historical Society; remaining items as quoted in to-be-published study of immigration to Cleveland, with translations by study authors Winston Chrislock, Ivan Cizmic, Julianna Puskas, and Adam Walaszek.

Chapter VI, Stapleton, "Automotive Industry," *Encyclopedia*; founding of Cleveland Automobile Club as quoted in Rose, *Cleveland: the Making;* Vlchek, *Story.*

Chapter VII, resident of Seville, as quoted in H. Roger Grant, "Interurbans," *Encyclopedia*; Hunter, *A Nickel.*

Chapter VIII, Tom Girdler, as quoted in Carol Poh Miller, "Iron and Steel Industry," *Encyclopedia.*

Western Reserve Historical Society

index

partners & web site index

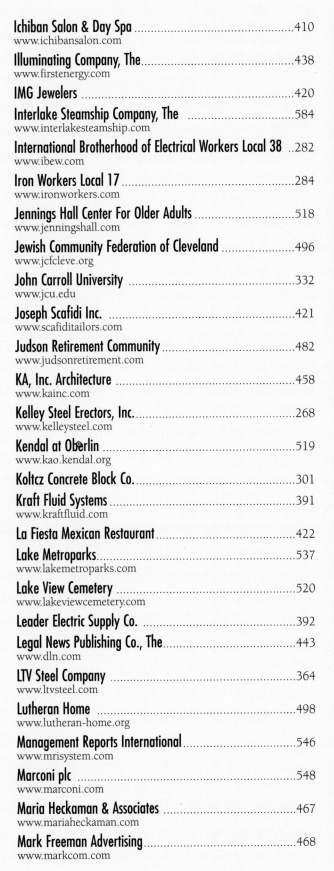

PATRONS

Autonation USA
www.AutoNation.com

City of East Cleveland, The
www.eastcleveland.org

Holcomb's Education Resource
www.holcombs.com

Ozanne Construction Company, Inc.

A worker at Thompson Products, Stella Pohorecki, created two patriotic vistas of American workers (one shown here and the other on the cover and title page) during World War II. "Thompson Products – World War II" and "Armistice Day Vision" hung in the cafeteria of Thompson Products' Clarkwood Plant. *Western Reserve Historical Society, photo by Herbert Ascherman, Jr.*